Museum of Anthropology, University of Michigan
Memoirs, Number 41

The Vijayanagara Metropolitan Survey

Volume I

by

Carla M. Sinopoli

Kathleen D. Morrison

Ann Arbor, Michigan
2007

©2007 by the Regents of the University of Michigan
The Museum of Anthropology
All rights reserved

Printed in the United States of America
ISBN 978-0-915-70365-4

Cover design by Katherine Clahassey.

The University of Michigan Museum of Anthropology currently publishes three monograph series: Anthropological Papers, Memoirs, and Technical Reports, as well as an electronic series in CD-ROM form. For a complete catalog, write to Museum of Anthropology Publications, 4009 Museums Building, Ann Arbor, MI 48109-1079.

Library of Congress Cataloging-in-Publication Data

Sinopoli, Carla M.
 The Vijayanagara Metropolitan Survey / by Carla M. Sinopoli, Kathleen D. Morrison.
    p. cm. -- (Memoirs / Museum of Anthropology, University of Michigan ; no. 41)
 Includes bibliographical references.
 ISBN 978-0-915703-65-4 (alk. paper)
 1. Vijayanagara Metropolitan Survey. 2. Vijayanagara (Extinct city) 3. Vijayanagar (Empire)--Antiquities. 4. Excavations (Archaeology)--India--Vijayanagar (Empire) I. Vijayanagara Metropolitan Survey. II. Morrison, Kathleen D. III. Title.
DS486.V56S56 2007
934--dc22
                            2007014642

The paper used in this publication meets the requirements of the ANSI Standard Z39.48-1984 (Permanence of Paper)

Contents

List of Figures, *iv*
List of Plates, *ix*
List of Tables, *xiii*
Preface, *xiv*
Acknowledgments, *xvi*

Part I. Background

Chapter 1. Background: Vijayanagara in Regional Context, *3*
    Vijayanagara: Empire and City, *3*
    A Brief History of Settlement, *4*
    Previous Research, *8*
    Goals of the Research: Understanding Urban Economies, *10*
        Production, *11*
        Layout and Infrastructure, *13*
    The Survey Area: Physiographic Setting, *13*
    Discussion: The Vijayanagara Landscape, *14*
Chapter 2. Survey Methodology, *15*
    Archaeological Survey, *15*
    The Sample Area: The Vijayanagara Metropolitan Region, *17*
        Sampling Design, *18*
        The Site Concept, *18*
        Survey Methods, *19*
    Blocks O, T, and S, *23*
        Survey Block O, *23*
        Survey Block T, *23*
        Survey Block S, *23*
    Summary, *29*

Part II. Data Presentation

Introduction to Part II, *32*
Chapter 3. Block O: Site Summaries, *33*
Chapter 4. Block T: Site Summaries, *97*
Chapter 5. Block S: Site Summaries, *147*
Chapter 6. Artifact Distributions and Analysis, *263*
    Contexts of Artifact Recovery, *263*
    Earthenware Ceramics, *264*
        Ceramic Counts and Wares, *265*
        Vessel Forms, *265*
        Vessel-Use Class Distributions, *285*
        Other Earthenware Materials, *289*
        Imported Ceramics, *291*
    Ground Stone, *291*
    Quarrying and Peg Production, *291*
    Other Chipped Stone Artifacts, *294*
    Metal Artifacts and Slag, *300*
    Other Small Finds, *301*
    Discussion, *303*
Chapter 7. End Note, *305*

Glossary of Indian Names and Architectural Terms, *325*
References Cited, *328*

Figures

1.1. The Vijayanagara empire, *5*
1.2. The study area, *6*
1.3. Vijayanagara urban core, *9*

2.1. The Vijayanagara metropolitan region, *19*
2.2. The region: intensive and extensive sampling strata, *20*
2.3. Sample transects in intensive survey area, *21*
2.4. Block O: setting, sample transects, and sites, *24*
2.5. Block T: setting, sample transects, and sites, *25*
2.6. Block S: setting, sample transects, and sites, *26*

3.1. VMS-1, plan, *33*
3.2. VMS-2, plan, *35*
3.3. VMS-2, Feature 2, *36*
3.4. VMS-9, plan, *37*
3.5. VMS-10, schematic plan, *37*
3.6. VMS-12, plan, *38*
3.7. VMS-13, plan, *38*
3.8. VMS-14, plan, *39*
3.9. VMS-15, plan, *39*
3.10. VMS-15, artifacts: iron knife blade and inscribed steatite bead, *39*
3.11. VMS-16, plan, *40*
3.12. VMS-19, plan, *41*
3.13. VMS-20, plan, *41*
3.14. VMS-21, plan, *41*
3.15. VMS-26, plan and location of collection areas, *43*
3.16. VMS-29, plan, *44*
3.17. VMS-30, plan, *44*
3.18. VMS-33, plan, *45*
3.19. VMS-34, plan, *45*
3.20. VMS-35, plan, *49*
3.21. VMS-36, plan, *50*
3.22. VMS-37, plan, *51*
3.23. VMS-38, plan, *52*
3.24. VMS-39, plan, *52*
3.25. VMS-40, plan, *53*
3.26. VMS-41, plan, *54*
3.27. VMS-42–47, VMS-50, temple complex, *55*
3.28. VMS-42, plan, *56*
3.29. VMS-43, plan, *58*
3.30. VMS-48, plan, *60*
3.31. VMS-49, plan, *60*
3.32. VMS-52, plan, *62*
3.33. VMS-59, plan, *64*
3.34. VMS-59, section, *64*
3.35. VMS-61, plan, *65*
3.36. VMS-62, plan, *65*
3.37. VMS-64, plan, *66*
3.38. VMS-65, plan, *66*
3.39. VMS-66, plan, *67*
3.40. VMS-67, plan, *67*

3.41. VMS-72, plan, *69*
3.42. VMS-73, plan, *69*
3.43. VMS-75, plan, *70*
3.44. VMS-77, plan, *71*
3.45. VMS-78, plan, *71*
3.46. VMS-79, plan, *72*
3.47. VMS-80, plan, *73*
3.48. VMS-81, plan, *74*
3.49. VMS-83 and VMS-84, plan, *75*
3.50. VMS-86, plan, *77*
3.51. VMS-88, plan, *77*
3.52. VMS-91, plan, *78*
3.53. VMS-93, plan, *79*
3.54. VMS-97, plan, *80*
3.55. VMS-99, plan, *81*
3.56. VMS-100, plan, *81*
3.57. VMS-102, plan, *83*
3.58. VMS-105, plan, *84*
3.59. VMS-107, plan, *85*
3.60. VMS-108, plan, *85*
3.61. VMS-111, plan, *86*
3.62. VMS-112, plan, *88*
3.63. VMS-113, plan, *90*
3.64. VMS-229, plan, *92*
3.65. VMS-371 and VMS-372, plan, *93*
3.66. VMS-604, plan, *95*

4.1. VMS-136, plan, *97*
4.2. VMS-292, plan, *98*
4.3. VMS-293, plan, *99*
4.4. VMS-297, plan, *101*
4.5. VMS-298, plan, *102*
4.6. VMS-299, plan, *102*
4.7. VMS-300, plan, *103*
4.8. VMS-301, plan, *104*
4.9. VMS-302, plan, *104*
4.10. VMS-303, plan, *105*
4.11. VMS-304, plan, *106*
4.12. VMS-306, plan, *107*
4.13. VMS-308, plan, *108*
4.14. VMS-309, plan, *109*
4.15. VMS-310, plan, *109*
4.16. VMS-311, plan, *110*
4.17. VMS-312, plan, *110*
4.18. VMS-313, plan, *111*
4.19. VMS-315, plan, *112*
4.20. VMS-317, plan, *114*
4.21. VMS-318, plan, *116*
4.22. VMS-319, plan, *116*
4.23. VMS-320, plan, *116*
4.24. VMS-321, plan, *117*
4.25. VMS-322, plan, *118*
4.26. VMS-323, plan, *118*
4.27. VMS-324, plan, *118*

4.28. VMS-325, plan, *119*
4.29. VMS-327, plan, *122*
4.30. VMS-328, plan, *122*
4.31. VMS-329 and VMS-328, plan, *122*
4.32. VMS-330, plan, *123*
4.33. VMS-331, plan, *124*
4.34. VMS-332, plan, *124*
4.35. VMS-335, plan, *125*
4.36. VMS-336, plan, *126*
4.37. VMS-338, plan, *126*
4.38. VMS-340, plan, *128*
4.39. VMS-341, plan, *129*
4.40. VMS-342, plan, *129*
4.41. VMS-343, plan, *130*
4.42. VMS-344, plan, *131*
4.43. VMS-346, plan, *131*
4.44. VMS-349, plan, *132*
4.45. VMS-350, plan, *133*
4.46. VMS-351, plan, *133*
4.47. VMS-353, plan, *134*
4.48. VMS-354, plan, *134*
4.49. VMS-355, plan, *135*
4.50. VMS-356, plan, *135*
4.51. VMS-357, plan, *136*
4.52. VMS-358, plan, *137*
4.53. VMS-361, plan, *139*
4.54. VMS-362, plan, *140*
4.55. VMS-364, plan, *141*
4.56. VMS-365, plan, *142*
4.57. VMS-367, plan, *144*
4.58. VMS-368, plan, *145*
4.59. VMS-369, plan, *146*

5.1. VMS-8, plan, *148*
5.2. VMS-121, plan, *149*
5.3. VMS-124, plan, *151*
5.4. VMS-125, plan, *152*
5.5. VMS-127, plan, *153*
5.6. VMS-128, plan, *153*
5.7. VMS-129, plan, *154*
5.8. VMS-130, plan, *156*
5.9. VMS-131, plan, *156*
5.10. VMS-132, plan, *157*
5.11. VMS-133, plan (VMS-226 in lower left), *159*
5.12. VMS-135, plan, *160*
5.13. VMS-137, plan, *161*
5.14. VMS-138, plan, *161*
5.15. VMS-139, plan, *162*
5.16. VMS-140, plan, *163*
5.17. VMS-142, plan, *165*
5.18. VMS-144, plan, *168*
5.19. VMS-145, plan, *169*
5.20. VMS-146, plan, *169*
5.21. VMS-148, plan, *170*

5.22. VMS-150, plan, *171*
5.23. VMS-151, plan, *172*
5.24. VMS-152, plan, *172*
5.25. VMS-153, plan and location of collection units, *173*
5.26. VMS-158, plan, *175*
5.27. VMS-159, plan, *175*
5.28. VMS-161, plan, approximate site boundaries and collection units, *176*
5.29. VMS-163, plan, *177*
5.30. VMS-164, plan, *180*
5.31. VMS-165, plan, *182*
5.32. VMS-166, plan, *182*
5.33. VMS-167, plan, *183*
5.34. VMS-168, plan, *183*
5.35. VMS-169, plan, approximate site boundaries and collection units, *184*
5.36. VMS-172, plan and location of collection units, *186*
5.37. VMS-173, plan, *188*
5.38. VMS-174, plan, *189*
5.39. VMS-176, plan and location of collection units, *190*
5.40. VMS-177, plan, *190*
5.41. VMS-179, plan, approximate site boundaries and collection units, *191*
5.42. VMS-181, plan, *192*
5.43. VMS-182, plan and location of collection units, *193*
5.44. VMS-183, plan, *195*
5.45. VMS-184, plan, *196*
5.46. VMS-186, plan and location of collection units, *197*
5.47. VMS-187, plan, *197*
5.48. VMS-189, plan, *198*
5.49. VMS-190, sluice 2, section, *199*
5.50. VMS-192, plan, *200*
5.51. VMS-193, plan, *201*
5.52. VMS-194, plan, *201*
5.53. VMS-198, plan, *203*
5.54. VMS-199, plan, *203*
5.55. VMS-200, plan, *204*
5.56. VMS-201, plan, *205*
5.57. VMS-201, Feature 1, plan, *206*
5.58. VMS-203, plan, *207*
5.59. VMS-204, plan, *207*
5.60. VMS-205, VMS-206, and VMS-207, plan, *209*
5.61. VMS-208, plan, *210*
5.62. VMS-209, plan, *211*
5.63. VMS-210, plan, *212*
5.64. VMS-211, plan, *212*
5.65. VMS-213, plan, *213*
5.66. VMS-214, plan, *214*
5.67. VMS-215, plan, *214*
5.68. VMS-216, plan, *215*
5.69. VMS-218, plan, *218*
5.70. VMS-219, plan, *219*
5.71. VMS-220, plan, *220*
5.72. VMS-225, plan, *223*
5.73. VMS-230, plan, *224*
5.74. VMS-231, Kamalapuram reservoir plan, *225*
5.75. VMS-231, western basin of Kamalapuram reservoir, *225*

5.76. VMS-237, Pattabhirama temple complex, plan, *229*
5.77. VMS-237, Pattabhirama complex, main temple, *230*
5.78. VMS-238, plan, *232*
5.79. VMS-239, plan, *233*
5.80. VMS-241, plan, including locations of sluices, *234*
5.81. VMS-244, plan, *235*
5.82. VMS-249, plan, *237*
5.83. VMS-252, plan, *238*
5.84. VMS-254, plan and location of collection units, *239*
5.85. VMS-256, VMS-257, and portions of VMS-259, plan, *242*
5.86. VMS-260, plan, *246*
5.87. VMS-274, plan, *253*
5.88. VMS-277, plan, *254*
5.89. VMS-279, plan, *255*
5.90. VMS-280, plan, *256*
5.91. VMS-281, plan, *257*
5.92. VMS-283, plan, *257*
5.93. VMS-284, plan, *258*
5.94. VMS-285, plan, *259*
5.95. VMS-286, plan, *259*
5.96. VMS-287, plan, *259*
5.97. VMS-288, plan, *260*
5.98. VMS-291, plan, *261*

6.1. Unrestricted vessels: lamps, *270*
6.2. Unrestricted vessels: shallow bowls and other bowls, *272*
6.3 Unrestricted vessels: shallow bowls, *273*
6.4. Unrestricted vessels: large shallow bowls, *274*
6.5. Unrestricted vessels: other bowls, size histogram, *277*
6.6. Restricted vessel rim forms, *277*
6.7. Round rim restricted vessels, *279*
6.8. Straight rim restricted vessels, *280*
6.9. Straight rim restricted vessels, *281*
6.10. Restricted vessels: flange rims, *282*
6.11. Restricted vessels: flange rims, *283*
6.12. Restricted vessels: flange rims, *284*
6.13. Restricted vessel categories RV1-RV6, *286*
6.14. Sculpted sherd depicting portion of a human face, VMS-372, *290*
6.15. Basalt pegs, *293*
6.16. Flaked stone artifacts, VMS-26, *298*
6.17. Flaked stone artifacts, *299*
6.18. Flaked stone artifacts, *299*
6.19. Copper bangle, VMS-35, *301*
6.20. Nandi figurine, VMS-24, *303*

7.1. Intensive survey region: all recorded sites, *306*
7.2. Block G: setting, sample transects, and sites, *319*
7.3. Block H: setting, sample transects, and sites, *320*
7.4. Block J: setting, sample transects, and sites, *321*
7.5. Block M: setting, sample transects, and sites, *322*
7.6. Block R: setting, sample transects, and sites, *323*

Plates

Cover Mandapa in Block S, VMS-220.

1.1. Temple complex in the Vijayanagara sacred center, *10*

2.1. Irrigated fields to the south of the Kamalapuram Reservoir (VMS-231), Block S, *22*
2.2.. Crew laying out surface collection unit, *22*
2.3. Block O: overview, *27*
2.4. View of Block T, looking north from southern boundary of VMS-339, *27*
2.5. Block T: overview to south, *28*
2.6. Block S: outer city wall (VMS-123) and terrain in northeast quadrant, *28*
2.7. Block S: irrigated rice fields, *29*

3.1. VMS-2, Feature 2, elephant balustrade, *36*
3.2. VMS-2, Feature 4, inscribed stone column, *36*
3.3. VMS-10, site overview showing bastion and wall, *37*
3.4. VMS-18, images carved on shelter floor, *40*
3.5. VMS-26, overview of mound and setting, *43*
3.6. VMS-35, outline of unfinished bedrock mortar, *48*
3.7. VMS-35, "horse tie" on outcrop boulder, *48*
3.8. VMS-37, structural detail, *51*
3.9. VMS-37, structural detail, path 2, *51*
3.10. VMS-40, view of stone superstructure, *53*
3.11. VMS-40, detail of ceramic water pipe, *54*
3.12. VMS-42, main temple (F1), *56*
3.13. VMS-42, mandapa (F2), *57*
3.14. VMS-42, stairway (F4) and memorial marker (F3), *57*
3.15. VMS-43, step well, *58*
3.16. VMS-50, stairs, *61*
3.17. VMS-51, stairs, *61*
3.18. VMS-59, reservoir overview, *64*
3.19. VMS-59, reservoir, sluice and embankment detail, *64*
3.20. VMS-69, column detail, *68*
3.21. VMS-79, unfinished column in situ; note flaking debris in foreground, *72*
3.22. VMS-80, view of porch and entryway into walled temple complex, *73*
3.23. VMS-80, naga stones along the south wall of complex courtyard, *73*
3.24. VMS-83, overview, *75*
3.25. VMS-84, view from south, *76*
3.26. VMS-85, fortification wall segment, *76*
3.27. VMS-91, overview, *78*
3.28. VMS-91, sluice gate, *78*
3.29. VMS-92, detail of rock surface, *79*
3.30. VMS-93, overview, *79*
3.31. VMS-101, wall segment, *82*
3.32. VMS-101, bedrock mortars, one unfinished, *82*
3.33. VMS-104, shrine, *84*
3.34. VMS-108, detail of embankment construction, *85*
3.35. VMS-111, standing column, *87*
3.36. VMS-111, inscription, *87*
3.37. VMS-111, sculpted block, *87*
3.38. VMS-112, well overview, *89*
3.39. VMS-112, columned gate, entry to well, *89*

3.40. VMS-119, temple entry, *92*
3.41. VMS-371, view of temple, *93*
3.42. VMS-604, detail of pecked cupules, *95*
3.43. VMS-607, sculpture in modern shrine, *96*
3.44. VMS-653, Ganesha shrine on boulder, *96*

4.1. VMS-292, shrine overview, *98*
4.2. VMS-292, sculpted panel depicting male and female devotees, *98*
4.3. VMS-293, temple from west, *100*
4.4. VMS-293, sculpted stone basin located northeast of the temple, *100*
4.5. VMS-295, detail of inscription; edge of lingam to left of scale, *100*
4.6. VMS-296, bedrock inscription, *100*
4.7. VMS-297, tomb overview; note rubble mound to left of structure, *101*
4.8. VMS-300, overview of terrace walls, *103*
4.9. VMS-303, overview, *105*
4.10. VMS-304, sculpted panel beneath overhang, *106*
4.11. VMS-306, rubble wall (in center of photo), *107*
4.12. VMS-309, pavement and sluice, *109*
4.13. VMS-315, sluice gate; note maintained sluice channel and standing water in rear, *112*
4.14. VMS-317, Feature 1: temple, *115*
4.15. VMS-317, Feature 4, *115*
4.16. VMS-317, Feature 3, with main temple to left, and Feature 4 in rear, *115*
4.17. VMS-325, road wall, *119*
4.18. VMS-326, overview to west, *120*
4.19. VMS-326, detail of road construction, *120*
4.20. VMS-326, game board on outcrop along route of road, *120*
4.21. VMS-330, detail of exposed sluice channel, *123*
4.22. VMS-330, close-up of eastern stone face of embankment, *123*
4.23. VMS-339, overview of wall from southern end to the northwest, *127*
4.24. VMS-339, detail of wall construction at southern end, *127*
4.25. VMS-341, view of quarried slabs, *129*
4.26. VMS-344, small structure on west edge of terrace system, *131*
4.27. VMS-359, column footing on outcrop, *138*
4.28. VMS-364, detail of embankment face, *141*
4.29. VMS-365, enclosure wall of main settlement area, *142*
4.30. VMS-365, rubble wall structure in northern area of site, *143*
4.31. VMS-365, striding Hanuman image in modern shrine, *143*
4.32. VMS-366, Ganesha and large Nandi image, smaller Nandi is to left of Ganesha, *143*
4.33. VMS-367, columned structure, *144*
4.34. VMS-368, temple shikara and sanctuary, *145*

5.1. VMS-7, overview from west, *148*
5.2. VMS-8, view to the south looking toward VMS-7, *148*
5.3. VMS-121, naga stones on platform, *149*
5.4. VMS-123, bastions southeast of Penukonda gate (VMS-217), *150*
5.5. VMS-123, wall construction detail, *150*
5.6. VMS-125, Feature 3, eastern sluice, *152*
5.7. VMS-126, concentric square game board, *152*
5.8. VMS-129, view from south, *155*
5.9. VMS-129, doorway to sanctuary with Vaishnava door guardians, *155*
5.10. VMS-132, reservoir embankment, view from south, *157*
5.11. VMS-133, terrace system, long double-faced wall in southeast of site, *158*
5.12. VMS-137, raised road bed, *161*
5.13. VMS-142, northern gopuram, *166*

5.14. VMS-142, Feature 3, sanctuary and shikara of shrine, *166*
5.15. VMS-142, Feature 4, sculptural details on northern gate to complex, *166*
5.16. VMS-142, Feature 6, grinding machine in residential area within complex, *166*
5.17. VMS-143, overview of north side, *167*
5.18. VMS-147, overview, *170*
5.19. VMS-157, inscribed sheet rock, *174*
5.20. VMS-160, alignments, *176*
5.21. VMS-162, images, *177*
5.22. VMS-163, unfinished Hanuman image, *178*
5.23. VMS-163, sculpted panel, *178*
5.24. VMS-164, Feature 1, eastern gate, *181*
5.25. VMS-164, temple (Feature 3), *181*
5.26. VMS-164, interior column in temple, early Vijayanagara, *181*
5.27. VMS-168, hero stone, *183*
5.28. VMS-170, "horse-tie," *185*
5.29. VMS-171, displaced sculptures, naga and Nandi images, *185*
5.30. VMS-172, platform detail, *186*
5.31. VMS-173, temple entry, *188*
5.32. VMS-177, Hanuman image on boulder, *190*
5.33. VMS-179, iron slag on site surface, *191*
5.34. VMS-182, road bed, *193*
5.35. VMS-182, large naga carved from natural rock formation, *193*
5.36. VMS-182, images of Virabhadra and Bhairavi, *194*
5.37. VMS-182, sculpted Nandi, lingam and inscription on slab or column fragment, *194*
5.38. VMS-183, Feature 1: temple; bastion of VMS-123 (outer city wall) on right, *195*
5.39. VMS-186, overview of platform from north, *197*
5.40. VMS-190, sluice 1, *199*
5.41. VMS-190, masonry detail from above; protruding slab with lingam carving, *199*
5.42. VMS-200, stone basin, *204*
5.43. VMS-201, Feature 1, Shaivite temple, *206*
5.44. VMS-202, naga stones, *207*
5.45. VMS-204, displaced images, *208*
5.46. VMS-208, overview of alignments from west, *210*
5.47. VMS-209, section of paved road, *211*
5.48. VMS-215, mandapa, currently in worship, *214*
5.49. VMS-217, paved roadbed to the east of the gate, *217*
5.50. VMS-217, Feature 1, *217*
5.51. VMS-217, Feature 2, *217*
5.52. VMS-217, Feature 3, *217*
5.53. VMS-219, terrace wall, *219*
5.54. VMS-220, mandapa, *220*
5.55. VMS-222, boundary column with Nandi image, *221*
5.56. VMS-223, fortification wall viewed from south, *222*
5.57. VMS-231, Kamalapuram reservoir; stone basin, *225*
5.58. VMS-231, Kamalapuram reservoir; channel of western sluice, *226*
5.59. VMS-231, Kamalapuram reservoir, view, *226*
5.60. VMS-232, northern portion of sculpture group, *227*
5.61. VMS-236, pavilion in temple tank, *228*
5.62. VMS-237, Pattabhirama temple complex; overview from south, *231*
5.63. VMS-237, Pattabhirama temple complex; view of eastern gateway from VMS-236, *231*
5.64. VMS-237, Pattabhirama temple complex, main temple, *231*
5.65. VMS-238, Hanuman image, currently in worship, *232*
5.66. VMS-239, detail of column and capital, *233*
5.67. VMS-241, sluice 3, *234*

5.68. VMS-242, reservoir embankment, cut by recent canal construction, *235*
5.69. VMS-244, road bed and boundary walls, *236*
5.70. VMS-245, soil control wall, *236*
5.71. VMS-253, shrine, *239*
5.72. VMS-254, shikara, *240*
5.73. VMS-256, Kamalapuram gate complex; double-headed goose image, *243*
5.74. VMS-256, Kamalapuram gate complex; interior passage, *243*
5.75. VMS-256, carving on Feature 1 depicting seated royal figure and supplicants, *243*
5.76. VMS-256, Kamalapuram gate complex; yali balustrade on Feature 1, *243*
5.77. VMS-257, temple overview, *244*
5.78. VMS-257, detail of partially buried elephant balustrade in courtyard, *244*
5.79. VMS-258, bastion, *245*
5.80. VMS-260, temple overview, *246*
5.81. VMS-260, temple antechamber, view toward sanctuary, *246*
5.82. VMS-261, temple, *247*
5.83. VMS-265, naga stones associated with small modern shrine, *248*
5.84. VMS-266, columns in temple antechamber, *249*
5.85. VMS-267, flooded temple, view of antechamber and sanctuary entrance, *249*
5.86. VMS-268, temple exterior, *250*
5.87. VMS-269, view of lamp column looking toward temple, *250*
5.88. VMS-271, temple complex, Feature 1, shrine, *251*
5.89. VMS-271, temple complex, Feature 2, step well, *252*
5.90. VMS-271, temple complex, detail of carving on temple basement, *252*
5.91. VMS-271, overview, *252*
5.92. VMS-273, temple overview, *253*
5.93. VMS-275, overview, *253*
5.94. VMS-281, well overview, *257*
5.95. VMS-289, standing columns, *260*
5.96. VMS-651, gate, overview from west, *261*
5.97. VMS-651, door guardian on north side of gate exterior, *262*
5.98. VMS-651, door guardian on south side of gate exterior, *262*
5.99. VMS-651, royal devotee worshipping Nandi and lingam on carved panel, *262*
5.100. VMS-651, gate interior, detail of corbelled roof slabs and supports, *262*

6.1. Basalt pegs, VMS-2, *293*
6.2. Quartz/quartzite flaked stone artifacts, VMS-145, *300*
6.3. Ceramic tuyere, VMS-7, *301*

Tables

6.1. Sherd counts by site, *266*
6.2. Sherd counts and density by site, *268*
6.3. Shallow bowls by site, *273*
6.4. Shallow bowl size classes by site, *275*
6.5. Other bowls by site, *276*
6.6. Vessel-use classes (restricted vessels), *286*
6.7. Vessel-use classes by site, *287*
6.8. Comparison of vessel-use classes between survey area and urban core, *288*
6.9a. Vessel-use classes (sites with more than 25 identifiable sherds), *290*
6.9b. Frequencies of vessel-use classes by site, *290*
6.10a Intensive quarrying and construction of structures, *292*
6.10b. Extensive quarrying (isolated quarry marks), *292*
6.10c. Peg production, *292*
6.11. Chipped stone artifacts, *295*
6.12 Edge modified flaked stone artifacts from Blocks O, S and T, *297*
6.13a. Iron working locales, *302*
6.13b. Sites containing light densities of iron slag, *302*

7.1. Vijayanagara Metropolitan Survey: sites, *307*

Preface

Although systematic regional survey has been a part of the archaeological tool kit for more than fifty years, this strategy of data collection and scale of analysis is still rare in South Asian archaeology. Nonetheless, since human activities are never constrained within a single settlement or site, many of the questions that archaeologists routinely confront—concerning ancient political formations, production, and consumption of goods and subsistence resources, and political and social relations within and between communities—are best addressed at regional scales. Regional survey provides one important method for the systematic documentation of human activities and the landscapes in which they occur.

This volume, the first of three projected volumes on our work, reports on the results of the Vijayanagara Metropolitan Survey, a ten-year regional survey project exploring the hinterland or "metropolitan region" of the fourteenth- through sixteenth-century South Indian imperial capital of Vijayanagara. As we discuss in Chapter 1, our work grew out of renewed archaeological efforts that began in the late 1970s in the monumental core of the Vijayanagara, undertaken by the Archaeological Survey of India (ASI), the government of Karnataka Directorate of Archaeology and Museums (KDAM), and the collaborative international Vijayanagara Research Project (VRP), directed by Drs. John Fritz, George Michell, and M.S. Nagaraja Rao. Both of us participated in work in the Vijayanagara urban core in the 1980s and we became interested in developing research that could situate the monumental architectural remains of the core within its larger regional socioeconomic context contexts. Specifically, we wished to bring anthropological questions to the fore, especially those concerning the economic infrastructure that supported the vast population of the capital and the lives of the non-elites who inhabited the outskirts of the imperial capital. The Vijayanagara Metropolitan Survey project was conceived in a series of conversations we held in the KDAM/VRP field camp in 1986 concerning our joint interests in political economy and production (agricultural and craft). Morrison conducted a preliminary field season in 1987, and in 1988, a full survey season was initiated with the coverage of Block O (Chapter 3, this volume). Little did we expect when we conceived the project that the survey would take ten years to complete and that this publication would take an additional ten years. Over this time, we and members of our team have (separately and together) published several books and numerous articles on the results of our research (see bibliography in Fritz, Brubaker, and Raczek 2006).

This volume differs from those more interpretive works in its emphasis on providing the raw data—standardized descriptions and illustrations of each of the sites recorded by the VMS, and of the artifacts recovered at them. These data provide the empirical foundations for all of our analyses and interpretations of the Vijayanagara metropolitan region, and are especially important given the rapid and accelerating rate of site destruction that is currently occurring here and throughout contemporary India. Expanding populations and the rapid intensification of agricultural and industrial activities in the region are resulting in the destruction of many of the region's archaeological features. Indeed, we expect that a significant portion of the sites and features presented in this report no longer exists, making the detailed documentation presented here especially valuable for future scholars.

Chapter 1 introduces the study area and the problems addressed in the research. These begin with the more specific and smaller-scale goal of understanding the nature of agricultural and craft production in the region around the precolonial city of Vijayanagara and their relation to the structure of resources, human and nonhuman. From there, we move on to an interest in the intersection of these with the political landscape of power—the forms, degrees, and spatial distributions of control over producers and consumers that were exercised by Vijayanagara's elites—and its relation to the material record. Finally, we are concerned with the construction of the empire itself and the connections between the capital city and the larger world. The research reported on here was largely carried out between 1988 and 1992, in the semi-arid hinterland of Vijayanagara, and Chapter 1 concludes with a brief discussion of the physical and natural environment of the study area.

Chapter 2 describes field methods and recording procedures used by the Vijayanagara Metropolitan Survey, including strategies of artifact recovery and analysis. Since systematic regional survey remains a relatively new and rare technique in South Asian archaeology, we begin with a discussion of the larger contributions and potentials of such an approach, before discussing the specific survey strategies adopted by the VMS. We then describe the survey region, before moving on to a more detailed discussion of our survey methods. Chapter 2 concludes with a brief overview of the three survey blocks included in this monograph—Blocks O, T, and S—each an arbitrary 4.5 km square spatial unit (20.25 km^2).

Chapters 3 through 5 present detailed site descriptions from these three blocks. Chapter 3 presents information on the 117 sites recorded in Block O, Chapter 4 on the 79 sites recorded in Block T, and Chapter 5 on the 181 sites in Block S. Information on the remaining five survey blocks will be presented in a subsequent volume. All sites are described using standard formats and terminology, with information provided on the environmental setting and land-use practices at the time of recording, as well as site form, construction technologies, artifact content, and temporal and site-use interpretations. In addition, we provide citations to other publications that discuss these sites.

Chapter 6 presents information on the artifacts recovered in the survey, both from site and off-site locations. Since ceramics were the most common remains recovered by the VMS, the bulk of the chapter is devoted to describing these materials and exploring intra- and inter-site variability in the distribution of ceramic wares and vessel forms. This is followed by a brief discussion of chipped and ground stone materials, metal artifacts and slag, and other small finds.

Finally, Chapter 7 briefly reviews some of the major patterns identified in Vijayanagara land-use and settlement in the areas surveyed. Since this volume reports only on a portion of the survey area, and a subsequent volume will follow, we do not attempt a comprehensive overview here. Nonetheless, we seek to highlight the significant results and contributions of survey in the three blocks.

Acknowledgments

A project that lasts as long and involves as many participants as the Vijayanagara Metropolitan Survey accumulates many debts. And we indeed have a very large number of people and organizations to thank for their assistance over the ten years of fieldwork and beyond. Our research in India could not have occurred without the approval of the Archaeological Survey of India, the nearly 150 year old national department that oversees much archaeological research and protection of monuments throughout India, including at Vijayanagara. We are grateful to the Director Generals who approved our projects and to the supervising archaeologists based at Vijayanagara for their support of our research.

The American Institute of Indian Studies (AIIS) has been a key sponsor and facilitator of our work, providing funding to Morrison in 1992 through an AIIS Junior Fellowship and throughout the entire period serving as an official sponsor of our project and as our main interlocutor with the Government of India. We have a tremendous debt to Dr. Pradeep Mehendiratta of the AIIS, for his wisdom and guidance, and for his tremendous efforts to secure research permits for the VMS. We extend our gratitude to the AIIS staff for assisting our work throughout.

The Karnataka Directorate of Archaeology and Museums (KDAM) has been our primary collaborator in our research in the state. Dr. M.S. Nagaraja Rao, director of the KDAM in the early 1980s, played a key role in initiating international collaborative work in the region, and has been a sage advisor and good friend ever since. He was succeeded by several able and supportive directors, who we also thank—Dr. A. Sundara, Mr. Chiranjiv Singh, Dr. D.V. Devaraj, Dr. M.L Shivashankara, and Dr. K.R. Ramakrishna. We owe particular gratitude to several other members of the KDAM. Sadly, three of these are no longer here to receive our thanks, having met untimely deaths over the last five years. Nonetheless, we wish to sincerely acknowledge both their friendship and their scholarship. Dr. C.S. Patil was an extraordinary scholar and friend; his passion and dedication for Karnataka history and archaeology remains an inspiration and we continue to learn from his many contributions to the field. Our visits to the Department's offices in Mysore are now touched by sadness at Patil's absence and we both greatly miss our lunches and lengthy conversations with Patil over recent developments in Karnataka archaeology. Dr. Balasubrahmanyam began his career at the KDAM before shifting to the new Hampi University, whose campus lies in "Block S" of the Vijayanagara Metropolitan Region. Balu passed away in fall 2005 of a heart attack. We miss his infectious laugh and warm friendship as much as his passion and dedication to Karnataka archaeology. We also acknowledge and mourn Dr. Manjunathaiah, killed in a motor vehicle accident in fall 2005, another friend as well as a vastly talented and dedicated fieldworker with encyclopedic knowledge of archaeological remains in the Vijayanagara region. Finally, we are pleased to acknowledge Mr. T. Gangadhar and Mr. H.T. Talwar, who are happily very much alive to receive our gratitude. Thanks so much for your friendship and support to both the VMS and to our current EHLTC project.

Special thanks must be extended to Dr. Mark T. Lycett, a valued collaborator throughout the VMS. From the very first season, Mark participated in all aspects of the survey—directing field crews, overseeing our major mapping efforts, and conducting analyses of all lithics recovered by the survey. Large parts of Block S, covered in this volume, were surveyed by Mark and Kathy alone through both the monsoon and hot seasons; Mark's work co-directing pollen coring operations also made possible paleoenvironmental analyses of several Vijayanagara reservoirs.

We also thank Dr. Robert Brubaker, whose dissertation work on Vijayanagara's defensive infrastructure was conducted under the auspices of the VMS. Rob developed the project's GIS and associated databases and digitized many of the site plans presented in this volume.

The fieldwork of the VMS relied on the labors of numerous student participants from American and Indian universities. We are deeply indebted to all who participated in the project over the years, and for this monograph, most especially: Shinu Abraham, S.K. Aruni, Daniel Bass, Jane Baxter, Michael Dega, J. Bailey-Goldschmidt, Rob Brubaker, Menakshi Chellam, Succhi Dayal, Lars Fogelin, Girish M., Pravin Kenkre, Jennifer Lundal, Bernard K. Means, John Norder, Rukshana Nandi, Lynn Rainville, Sonphong Rattanaphan, Tridib Sarma, Richa Thaladiyal, Nilan Thatte, Anwen Tormey, and Allison Ziff. Many volunteers from the Universities of Hawai'i, Wisconsin-Milwaukee, Michigan, Northwestern, and Chicago worked to digitize field maps and enter data.

The Vijayanagara Metropolitan Survey benefitted from the generous financial support of many funding agencies. We would like to acknowledge the National Science Foundation (Grants 9424151, 9796104, K. Morrison, principal investigator); the National Endowment for the Humanities (Grant RK-20181-95, C. Sinopoli, principal investigator); the National Geographic Society (Grants 4186-89, 4679-91, 5170-94); the Wenner Gren Foundation for Anthropological Research (Grants 5044, 5397, 5953); and the Smithsonian Institution Foreign Currency Program (Grants FR00627500, FR99B404).

In addition, Morrison acknowledges the American Institute of Indian Studies for a Junior Research Fellowship, the University of California Berkeley Association of Women Geographers Fellowship, the University of Hawai'i Research and Training Revolving Fund, the University of Hawai'i Social Science Research Institute and University of Hawai'i University Research Council, as well as the American Association of University Women, the Northwestern University Hewlett Fund, and the Adolph and Marion Lichtstern Fund of the Department of Anthropology, University of Chicago.

Additional support was provided to Sinopoli by the University of Wisconsin-Milwaukee Graduate School Research Committee, and the University of Michigan Office of the Vice President for Research and College of Literature, Science, and the Arts. To all of these individuals and institutions who made the Vijayanagara Metropolitan Survey possible, we extend our deepest gratitude.

PART I

BACKGROUND

– I –
Background: Vijayanagara in Regional Context

This monograph outlines some of the information obtained in the course of the Vijayanagara Metropolitan Survey, a systematic archaeological surface survey of the region surrounding the large precolonial city of Vijayanagara. Only the first three blocks of land surveyed are covered here, an area of approximately 60 square kilometers (see Chapter 2 for an explanation of sampling units and strategies). In this volume we focus on the presentation of data, but we also consider some of the overall patterns evident in this portion of the survey area. Given the necessarily limited coverage of this volume, such patterns are predominantly local and rather small-scale. Nevertheless, the area described in this volume encompasses a sufficient range of variability to illustrate some of the complexity and diversity of the archaeological landscape surrounding this great imperial city.

Vijayanagara: Empire and City

The dry and rocky uplands of South India's Deccan and Karnatak plateaus have seen the beginnings of several expansionist empires. Among the largest and most impressive of these was the Vijayanagara empire, a polity that expanded—or perhaps exploded—from a small regional kingdom into an empire that claimed hegemony over much of southern India from the Tungabhadra River southward (Figs. 1.1, 1.2). Areas subdued by Vijayanagara were brought into the empire at different times and were subject to varying degrees of centralized control (see Karashima 1992; Nilakanta Sastri 1966; Sinopoli and Morrison 1995; Stein 1980, 1989). It may be significant, however, that these incorporated areas included several key regions of developed craft production, high agricultural productivity, high population density, and accessibility to international ports that contrasted sharply with conditions in the Vijayanagara countryside at the time of the empire's founding.

A great deal of disagreement exists about the degree to which a centralized Vijayanagara polity existed, and about the extent to which this polity was able to direct the economic activities and exert power over areas distant from (and even near) the capital city (e.g., Stein 1989; Palat 1987; Karashima 1992). As we discuss below, this question is potentially unanswerable, conflating as it does the specifics of time, place, and interest within the empire. However, our goals here are much more modest. Rather than explicitly considering the empire as a whole, we focus instead on a small portion of what has been considered to be the "core" area of the empire (Stein 1989:58), that area immediately surrounding the capital city itself. Even in this area, there is evidence for the existence of a variety of forms and scales of production that seem to have been differentially integrated into larger patterns of political and other authority (Morrison and Sinopoli 1992; Sinopoli and Morrison 1995). This suggestion has a number of implications for the ongoing debate over the nature of the Vijayanagara polity, as we discuss in the final chapters.

In precolonial South India, scholars are often hampered by the lack of even very basic information on the times and places they wish to study. Vijayanagara is no exception to this and, in part, it was this problem that led us to undertake the Vijayanagara survey in the first place. Although India is home to a rich and productive tradition of archaeological research more than one and a half centuries old (see Chakrabarti 1988; Singh 2004), later historic periods have received comparatively little attention by archaeologists (but see Mate 1985; Deo 1985; Dhavalikar 1999; Ray and Sinopoli 2004). Perhaps ironically then, it was the recent attention given to the city of Vijayanagara by other archaeologists (see below) that has allowed us to work on situating the city in its regional context. We wish to acknowledge this connection and to extend the hope that such international and interdisciplinary research might continue.

A Brief History of Settlement

Although human settlement in what is now northern Karnataka has a long history, extending well back into the Palaeolithic, even today this dry interior region is relatively sparsely and unevenly settled. The study area described here lies within the boundaries of Bellary and Koppal Districts, state of Karnataka, India, and between 76°20-35' latitude and 15°10-20' longitude (Fig. 1.2). The political history of early states and empires in southern India is complex, a story of shifting borders, conquest, rebellion, fragmentation, and reintegration. Large urban settlements came late to the area, with the first cities established during the Iron Age (c. 1000 B.C. to 300/200 A.D.). Outside the more fertile and well-watered alluvial deltas and coastal plains (not coincidentally also the locations of important ports), urban provisioning was always problematic, and it was not until the late precolonial period that the process of urbanization accelerated.

During the period known as the Southern Neolithic (c. 2600 B.C. to 1000 B.C.; Paddayya 2002), semi-mobile villagers grew millets and other dry grains as supplements to an economy based largely on animal husbandry (Allchin 1963; Allchin and Allchin 1982; Korisettar et al. 2002; Paddayya 1973, 1993, 2002). Although nascent craft specialization in copper/bronze metallurgy and perhaps other goods was established by this time, the appearance of substantial permanent settlements dates only to the first few centuries B.C., during the Iron Age.

The South Indian Iron Age (or "Megalithic"; c. 1000 B.C. to A.D. 300/200) was a period of rapid and dramatic change, marking the advent of new technology and new forms of productive organization, and the appearance of very large, urban settlements. Rice entered the agricultural repertoire at around 1000 B.C. (Fuller 2002), and there is reason to believe that this new cultigen accompanied rather dramatic changes in the organization of agricultural production, including both the extension and intensification of food production. Changes in craft production and exchange were, if anything, even more marked across this period as southern India, never a stranger to long-distance exchange, heightened its participation in exchange networks and began to rely more heavily on the products of craft specialists (e.g., Begley 1983, 1986; Begley and de Puma 1992; Champakalakshmi 1996; Lahiri 1992; Ray 1986, 1994, 2003).

The distinction between the Iron Age proper and the Early Historic period, generally defined as the period between about 500 B.C. and A.D. 500, is less than clear-cut, based primarily on a suggestion of political conquest and socioeconomic integration of the south by the north, particularly during the Mauryan empire. The latter was one of the first expansive empires of South Asia and inscriptions or edicts of the most well known and successful Mauryan emperor, Asoka, are found as far south as the Bellary District, very close to the study area (see discussions by Thapar 1984, 1992; Parasher-Sen 1993; Kotraiah 1983; Sugandhi 2004). In the Chitradurg District, just south of Bellary District, Wheeler (1947) excavated the important sites of Brahmagiri and Chandravalli that spanned the sequence from the Neolithic to the Early Historic. An Ashokan rock edict was found at Brahmagiri; the latter has been identified with the provincial Mauryan administrative town of Isila (Thapar 1997). Certainly the extent to which northern Karnataka—an area containing several key resources, such as gold (Lahiri 1992), in demand in the Mauryans' distant Gangetic homeland—could have been incorporated into such a distant polity remains unclear. Nevertheless, this period certainly marks an important transition in the region in that large and internally differentiated settlements—towns and cities—first became established at this time and were never to completely disappear from the scene.

The so-called Early Medieval period (here, to c. A.D. 1300) saw the establishment, expansion, and dissolution of a number of small kingdoms and empires, whose complex political fortunes are beyond the scope of the brief review (see Chopra, Ravindran, and Subrahmanian 1979; Kulke and Rothermund 1986; Nilakanta Sastri 1966; Sinopoli 2003). It is important to note, however, the liminal role of the study area in the territorial definitions of many of these states. The Tungabhadra River, on whose banks the city of Vijayanagara would eventually be founded, often served as a political border, and fluctuations in the political control of the areas adjacent to it were not uncommon (e.g., Appadorai 1990 [1936]:62-63). There is some evidence for settlement in the study area during this period, including a small cluster of Chalukyan temples and a canal near the town of Hospet (Morrison 1995:34); a locus of pre-Vijayanagara temples near the village of Hampi (Michell 1991; Wagoner 1991), centered on a rocky hill known as Hemakuta Hill; and other temples in and near Anegundi, on the north bank of the Tungabhadra River. Inscriptional evidence also seems to indicate the presence of a small settlement in or near the town of Kudatini from the tenth century A.D. onward. All of these places would have been locations of small villages or towns, and, in the case of Hemakuta/Hampi, a provincial pilgrimage center (see discussion by Fritz, Michell, and Nagaraja Rao 1985).

Notably, much of the pre-Vijayanagara settlement in the survey area was clustered along the riverbank, with only Kudatini violating this locational association. Because the Tungabhadra is not navigable, except for relatively short stretches, and because it has a tendency to flood in the rainy season, a tendency ameliorated but not eliminated by the construction of a large dam near Hospet in the 1940s and 1950s, this association may be best accounted for by use of river water in agriculture. As discussed below, the survey area receives a very low and annually variable rainfall, making the irrigation of crops desirable. Overall, the degree of landscape modification prior to the fourteenth century appears to have been moderate, but there is in addition

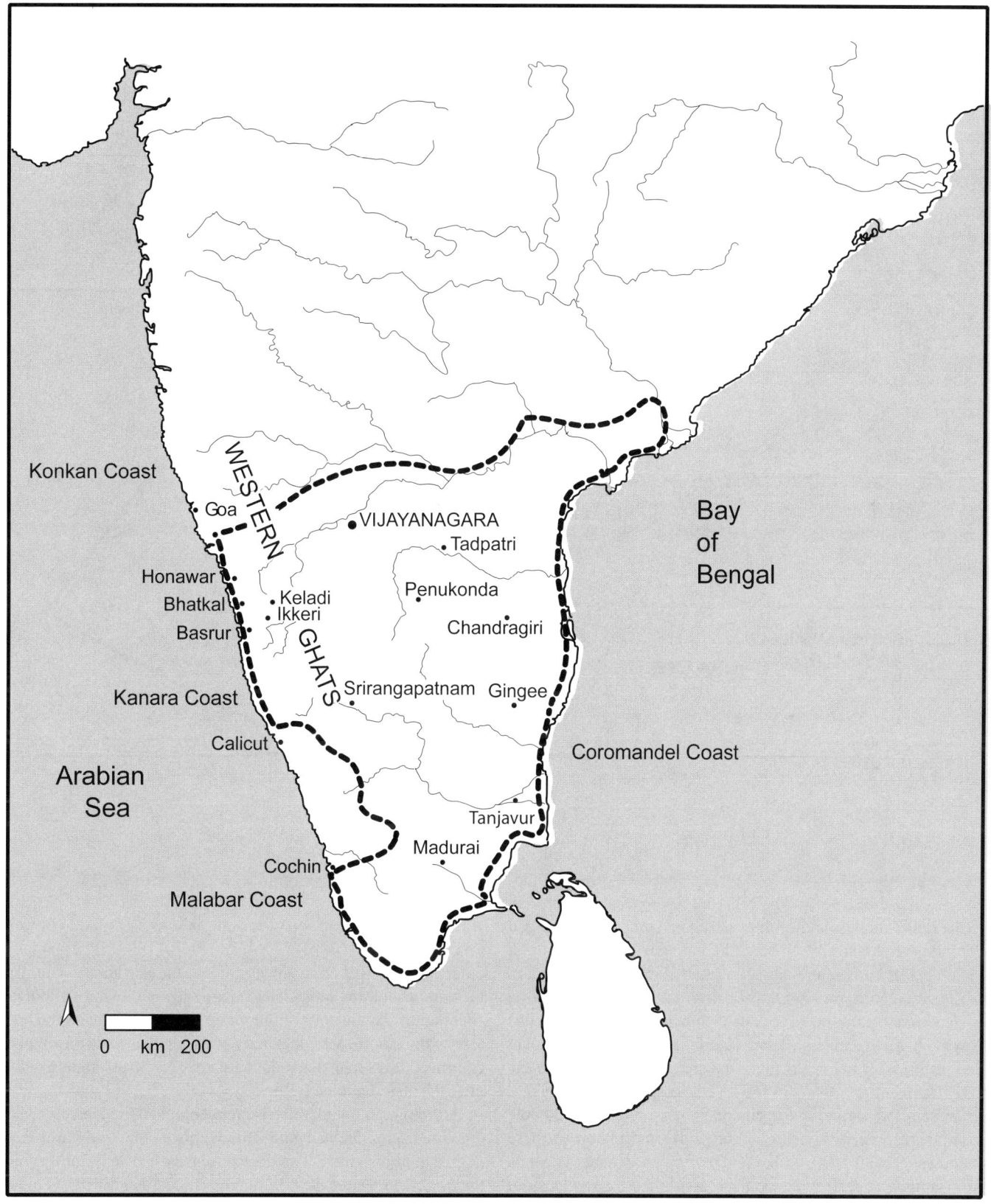

Figure 1.1. The Vijayanagara empire.

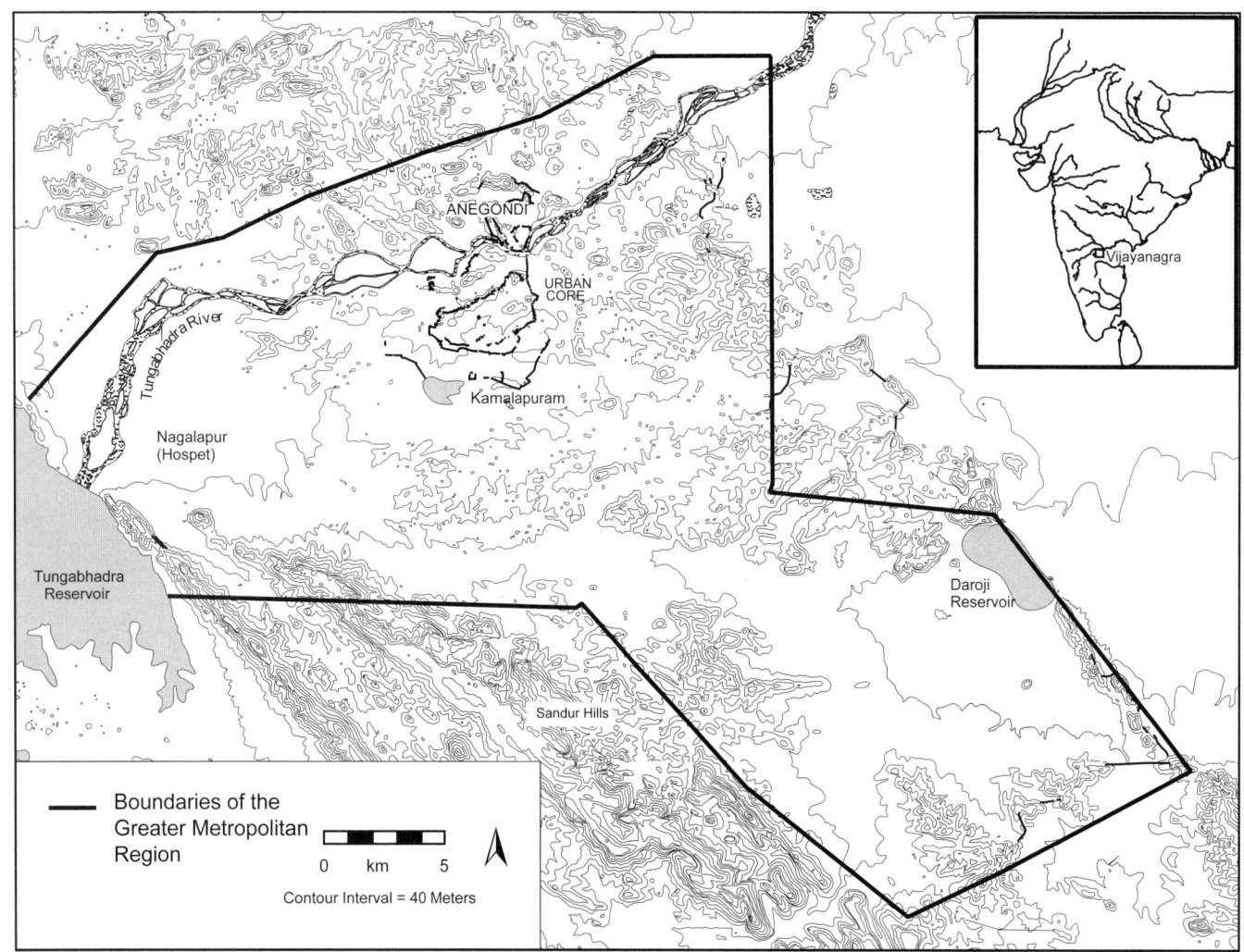

Figure 1.2. The study area.

to the rather modest archaeological record some indication that the indigenous thorn scrub forest had already been subject to a great deal of human and animal pressure prior to the founding of the city (Morrison 1995).

Traditional accounts of the establishment of the city place this "event" in A.D. 1336 (e.g., Thapar 1966:324), and archaeological and historical data concur that Vijayanagara got its start in the early fourteenth century. Several diverse origin accounts purport to explain the nature of the city and the empire; considerable disagreement exists concerning the verity and import of these accounts (Sewell 1900; Kulke 1985). Originally under Hoysala rule (although not all agree with this; see discussions by Desai et al. 1981; Kulke and Rothermund 1986; Stein 1989), the founders of the first dynasty of Vijayanagara rulers broke free of this fading power and began to expand their own reach outward. Detailed accounts of the expansion of the empire can be found in Sewell (1900), Nilakanta Sastri (1966), and Stein (1980, 1989), among others. The city of Vijayanagara lay at the northern frontier of the empire and was subjected to siege and conflict throughout its occupation. The history of the metropolitan region and the history of the empire are not exactly coterminous, since the empire continued in a somewhat reduced state for several hundred years after the abandonment of the city.

Although, as noted, there is archaeological evidence for several small pre-Vijayanagara settlements in the study area, the degree of human impact on the landscape escalated sharply with the establishment of the city of Vijayanagara and with its rapid growth as a political, religious, and commercial center. In fact, it may be fair to say that human action during the Vijayanagara period was the most significant force in shaping the regional archaeological record, vegetation, and landforms until the middle of the twentieth century.

The problem of setting chronological boundaries for analysis is less straightforward than it might seem. Although the traditional founding date for Vijayanagara is A.D. 1336, it seems clear that there was already some settlement in the area at this time and we thus begin our periodization at around A.D. 1300. The scheme is quite simple: the fourteenth century is the Early Vijayanagara period, the fifteenth the Middle, and the sixteenth the Late Vijayanagara period. This division into centuries is not as arbitrary as it might seem. It is based in part on the practical problem of recognizing internal divisions in the material record and relies on the divisions employed by architectural historians such as Michell (1991, 1992; Michell and Wagoner 2001). Further, this rough division corresponds closely to the dynastic history of Vijayanagara (see Nilakanta Sastri 1966; Sewell 1900; Stein 1989) and, not coincidentally, to the political fortunes of the empire. The Late Vijayanagara period, in particular, coincides roughly with the advent of the Tuluva dynasty and with significant attempts at political restructuring. The Early period, in contrast, covers only the initial portion of the reign of the Sangama dynasty while the Middle Vijayanagara period includes both the latter Sangamas and the short-lived Suluva dynasty. As such, only the Late period conforms closely to traditional political history. We recognize that such a division of time is only a first approximation. However, even this simple three-part distinction cannot often be reliably made and it is probably premature to propose more fine temporal divisions.

The following synopsis of occupation history in the Vijayanagara region is based on the evidence of standing architecture and archaeological remains. However, it is important to mention here an additional source of information about economic, ritual, and political activity: the inscriptional record. We do not explicitly consider inscriptions in this volume, except those recovered in the survey and those with immediate relevance to specific archaeological features in the survey area. Analyses of the regional inscriptional record do indicate several peak periods of inscriptional activity in the greater metropolitan region and in northern Karnataka (Morrison 1995; Morrison and Lycett 1994), a pattern that closely corresponds to archaeological data on construction and settlements, as described below.

During the fourteenth century or Early Vijayanagara period, the city grew rapidly and Michell (pers. comm.) has suggested that the urban core walls were constructed at this time (see also Brubaker 2004). Although the urban core need not have been densely settled, and indeed even during the later periods areas of garden and irrigated orchards were maintained in the urban core (Morrison 1995), the construction of such a massive walled enclosure suggests a growing urban population, an eye to defense and definition, and perhaps even a grand design for the future. Several of the major temple complexes of the city, including the Ramachandra temple in the heart of the royal center (Dallapiccola et al. 1992), were initially constructed during this time (Michell 1992). Although, as we discuss below, assessments of internal chronological divisions are difficult to make for many kinds of archaeological remains, there is evidence for substantial Early Vijayanagara settlement and agricultural production in the survey area (see Morrison 1995).

Imperial expansion continued during the fifteenth century, or Middle Vijayanagara period, but the volume of construction and apparently the scale of new settlement slowed considerably in the region around the city. Of the smaller settlements outlying the city, only the reservoir of the town of Mallapannagudi, and thus presumably also the town itself and its enclosure walls and gates, can be assigned with confidence to this period. There is no evidence for population loss or abandonment, but this appears not to have been a time of expansion in the metropolitan region.

The sixteenth century, or Late Vijayanagara period, left a substantial impact on the regional archaeological record, an impact that overshadows that of the previous two centuries. The pace of construction during the Late Vijayanagara period was nothing short of phenomenal and the survey data bear out the interpretation of a growing regional population and of intensification of agricultural and craft production. Inside the city, the sixteenth century saw the construction of several massive temple complexes and the elaboration of several others (Dallapiccola et al. 1992; Filliozat and Filliozat 1988; Michell 1991, 1992, 1995). This frantic pace of construction was matched in the survey area where we find, in addition to temples, new settlements or areas of settlement, gateway complexes on older fortifications (e.g., at Kamalapur), and a major expansion of cultivated fields and changes in the nature of agricultural production with the construction of reservoirs, canals, and an aqueduct.

The city was sacked and looted by a coalition army of northern polities in A.D. 1565; much of the city's population fled either immediately or within a few years. Despite sporadic reoccupations, and in spite of the continued existence of the empire, the city itself never regained its urban character after the sixteenth century. Urban abandonment and the flight of elites from the city did not signal the end of the region's settlement history, however. Instead, we see a remarkable degree of settlement continuity, with many small settlements that were established during the Vijayanagara period still inhabited today. The Vijayanagara region passed into the control of the Sultan of Bijapur after the loss of the city. By the eighteenth century, the area was counted as part of the dominion of the Nizam of Hyderabad, briefly passing into the control of Hyder Ali and Tipu Sultan of Mysore, to the south, before being regained by the Nizam (Kelsall 1872). In the nineteenth century, the part of the survey area now in Bellary District was ceded to the British, but the area north of the river, now Raichur and Koppal Districts, stayed with the Nizam. The Bellary District stayed under direct British administration as part of the Madras Presidency until Indian independence in 1943, when Raichur District was also incorporated into the newly formed Mysore State. In 1973, the former Mysore State became part of the new, linguistically-defined (Kannada speaking) state of Karnataka.

Previous Research

Until recently, archaeological work on historical periods in southern India has generally taken an art historical approach, inspired by the rich record of monumental architecture and art. This tradition has increasingly been complemented by new attempts to place historical places and peoples into sociopolitical and economic as well as artistic context. Neither approach can stand alone and the current convergence of approaches must be seen as an encouraging sign.

Michell (1985b) has reviewed the early history of archaeological work at the Vijayanagara capital, and we simply note here that active recording of the site began as early as the eighteenth century (see Nagaraja Rao 1988). In the early twentieth century, the Archaeological Survey of India began the ongoing work of stabilizing standing architecture and clearing new areas of the site (Michell 1985b:200; see Longhurst 1917). In the 1970s and 1980s, however, archaeological, epigraphical, and art historical work on the city and its monuments intensified, with the initiation of major excavation projects in the royal center and urban core by the Archaeological Survey of India (Narasimaiah 1992; Tripathi 1987) and by the Directorate of Archaeology and Museums, state of Karnataka (Nagaraja Rao 1983, 1985; Devaraj and Patil 1991a, 1991b). Work by Fritz and Michell over the last fifteen years has provided for the first time systematic documentation of both standing structures (Fritz, Michell, and Nagaraja Rao 1985; Michell 1985a, 1985b, 1990; Michell and Wagoner 2001; see Wagoner 1991) and the "archaeological" remains of collapsed structures, both monumental and modest (Fritz 1991, 1996; Fritz, Brubaker and Raczek 2006). Many other scholars worked on aspects of the city's archaeological record in these same years. This labor stands behind what we have tried to accomplish in the Vijayanagara Metropolitan Survey.

The nomenclature of Fritz, Michell, and Nagaraja Rao (1985) for different areas of the site has now become standard and we employ it in our work (Fig. 1.3). Briefly, the locus of enclosed compounds or enclosures that contains the primary concentration of elite architecture, both residential and nonresidential, has been termed by Fritz and colleagues (Fritz, Michell, and Nagaraja Rao 1985) the royal center. This defined area is surrounded by the larger but also walled urban core, an area that contained much of the city's population. The area to the immediate north of the urban core, through which the Turtha Canal runs (see below; Morrison 1995), is termed the irrigated valley and north of that, along the banks of the Tungabhadra River, lies the sacred center. The latter term refers to the high concentration of large temple complexes along the riverbanks (Plate 1.1), although it is clear that the sacred center was also an area of settlement and defense and that temples had been constructed in other parts of the city as well. The mapping system devised by Fritz and Michell also forms the basis for our maps. This system is described in the following chapter.

In their analyses, Fritz and Michell have focused largely on Block N in their map system, the approximately 20 km^2 area containing the royal and sacred centers, the irrigated valley, and the urban core. Similarly, the major excavation projects have directed their attention to the remains of the city itself, remains that have attracted substantial research in the realms of architecture (Filliozat and Filliozat 1988; Michell 1990, 1991; Wagoner 1991, 1993; Patil 1991a), art history (Pascher 1987; Dallapiccola et al. 1992; Dallapiccola and Verghese 1998; Verghese 1995, 2000), iconography (Dallapiccola and Verghese 1991), epigraphy (Filliozat 1973; Patil 1991b; Patil and Balasubramanya 1991), and surface archaeology (Davison-Jenkins 1988; Morrison 1990; Purandare 1986; Sinopoli 1985, 1986). As a result of all this research, we now have a reasonably complete record of the surface distributions of structures in the royal center (Fritz and Morrison in prep a and b) and good quality architectural drawings and descriptions and iconographic analyses of the standing structures of the royal center, urban core, and much of the sacred center (Michell and Wagoner 2001). In addition to this descriptive corpus, there exist analyses of urban form and layout (Fritz 1986), architectural development of temple and administrative architecture (Michell 1992), and fortifications (Brubaker 2004). With the notable exception of work on earthenware ceramic morphology, function, and utilization by Sinopoli (1986, 1993b), there still exists, however, no information from excavated contexts on the distribution, processing and consumption of plant and animal products or on the production, distribution, or consumption of artifact classes other than earthenwares. With a few exceptions (Morrison 1990; Sinopoli 1986), the distributional analyses from Block N have also considered only structures and not artifacts. Thus, while we acknowledge the importance and significance of previous archaeological research in the city, it remains the case that economic and organizational concerns have persisted as historical, rather than archaeological, concerns in Vijayanagara studies. Further, the focus of all previous analysis has been firmly site specific, a focus quite explicable in terms of the overwhelming size and complexity of the city of Vijayanagara. Our goal, then, has been to bring to the material record of Vijayanagara a focus on the hitherto neglected aspects of production, distribution, and (ultimately) consumption of a range of goods and to carry out this analysis in a regional context.

There exists a long tradition of historical scholarship relating to the Vijayanagara empire. Far from being "forgotten," as Sewell (1900; see also Michell 1985b) once suggested, the Vijayanagara empire has played an important role in Indian historiography (Inden 1990; Stein 1980, 1989) and has generated a sizeable historical literature. Two points regarding this literature are of note here. First, the existing historical focus is overwhelmingly on the Tamil country of the far south, an area conquered by Vijayanagara armies and incorporated into the empire. The capital and its surrounds, in northern Karnataka, are oddly missing in most historical discussions. Thus, as we discuss below, this research was designed in part to address this lack of balance and to consider the empire from the perspective of the capital rather than only from the incorporated territories of Tamil Nadu (Sinopoli and Morrison 1995).

Figure 1.3. Vijayanagara urban core.

Plate 1.1. Temple complex in the Vijayanagara sacred center.

The second point has more to do with the nature of historical scholarship itself. Much of the early treatment of Vijayanagara history stressed the political fortunes of the empire and the dynastic successions and struggles of the ruling families (e.g., Sewell 1900; Nilakanta Sastri 1966). More recently (but see Appadorai 1990 [1936]), historians have leaned toward economic history and this change in focus has provided a valuable corpus of information about the structures of Vijayanagara economic systems, and about their integration with politics (e.g., Appadurai 1978). Even the most careful economic analysis cannot, however, make up for the fact that a great deal of the Vijayanagara economy—or, more properly, some of its *economies*—are historically invisible. That is, many forms of production, distribution, and consumption do not, or only rarely, appear in texts. Only the archaeological record can inform on these activities, many of which were small-scale and/or carried out by the poor and dispossessed. The production and use of earthenware ceramics is a case in point. Although there exists a rich material record that points to the importance of these goods, only scant textual notice of pots or potters exists (Sinopoli 2003). This problem of balance, then, led us to initiate a program of regional analysis that we hoped would inform on the nature and organization of economic activities around the capital city.

Goals of the Research: Understanding Urban Economies

We began this project with the goal of understanding the operation of the Vijayanagara regional economy, particularly the organization of production of a variety of goods, in its political, social, and ecological context. As noted, previous research in the area had focused primarily on the city of Vijayanagara rather than on the region, and had considered aspects of architecture, layout, and meaning without explicitly situating the city in its economic context. As discussed below, we are not uninterested in issues of meaning, plan, and style, but we suggest that such issues cannot be fully considered without an understanding of the constitution of regional economies. The city of Vijayanagara existed within the critical context of its hinterland, an area that supplied the city with a substantial influx of human labor and its products: food, earthenware ceramics, metal objects, stone, medicines, and other items and materials. The constitution of the hinterland was never fixed, but changed with the changing population size, demands for resources, and political and social boundaries of the city and empire. Neither was this regional nexus closed. Instead, long-distance movements of people, goods, and information were always critical to the continued life of the city.

As discussed in Chapter 2, the definition of a survey area presented certain practical difficulties. Because no archaeological work on non-monumental remains had ever been undertaken outside the city and because no similar studies on other time periods or areas had been carried out in South India, we were faced with a completely unknown archaeological situation. Consequently, our Phase I survey area is both smaller than we had hoped and arbitrary in its boundaries. Nevertheless, this work represents a necessary beginning. We began to consider the configuration of the archaeological landscape in this small but important area in order to address some of the following concerns. How was the city provisioned with food, craft goods, raw materials, and people? How are nearby settlements, roads, temples, and fields structured with respect to the city and to the natural landscape? What evidence is there in this area for different forms and scales of production? How was production organized and how does this (or does this?) relate to the structure of political and other authority?

Production

We begin with the issue of production. With what materials was the city supplied, and how was this supply structured? The most ubiquitous class of archaeological materials in and around the city is earthenware. Literally millions of earthenware sherds litter the surface of the city and its hinterland, and these rather simple wheel-made ceramics were used by rich and poor alike (Sinopoli 1986, 1988, 2003). Previous research by Sinopoli on the morphology of Vijayanagara earthenware had focused on ceramics from the elite residential area known as the Noblemen's quarter and from two "neighborhoods" in the city's urban core (see Fritz, Michell, and Nagaraja Rao 1985), the East Valley and the Muslim quarter (Sinopoli 1985, 1986, 1996, 2006). Neither these studies, however, nor those of Fritz (pers. comm.) or Morrison (1990) turned up any clear evidence for ceramic production locales.

South Indian potters were among the group of *ayagars*, or village servants (Sinopoli 2003:100-102; Stein 1980:423-24), who served as specialist producers for one or a group of villages. Potters were designated as a distinct caste, a pattern that apparently predates the Vijayanagara period, even though the actual caste affiliation of potters may have been slightly more complex. In the survey area today, potters generally work in small family-run workshops (Sinopoli and Blurton 1986). Small villages may have one or more ceramic workshops while larger towns and cities often contain neighborhoods or streets where potters work and live. The partial replacement of ceramic vessels by vessels of metal and plastic makes it difficult to generalize about the pre-colonial organization of earthenware production, when demand in and around the city would have been quite high.

How, then, was Vijayanagara ceramic production structured? Village servants were "traditionally" scattered across a large area and remunerated with land or with a share of produce at the harvest, but other arrangements are not unknown (e.g., Stein 1980). For example, village-level specialization was obtained in the case of potters serving the temple of Puri in Orissa (Behura 1965); weavers also often clustered into specialist villages (Ramaswamy 1985). Were there many small workshops in the city of Vijayanagara and in outlying villages and towns? Was there a potters' neighborhood or one or more villages of potters who supplied a large part of the region? One brief inscriptional reference to an area or perhaps village of potters suggests that there may have been a ceramic production zone to the northwest of the Kamalapuram reservoir (Gopal 1985:180). Certainly, we expect there to have been relatively high levels of earthenware production, given the ubiquity of broken remains. As noted, work in the city showed no clear indication of workshops, although the practice of open firing would have left little surface indication and the degree of colluviation evident in the city (Morrison 1990) suggests that much interesting material lies deeply buried. Morphological analyses by Sinopoli (1988, 1989, 1989, 2003) do suggest that earthenwares were manufactured in multiple small workshops. Outside the city, in the study area, the problem of finding ceramic production locales is complicated by the evident reworking and reuse of domestic (and industrial?) refuse on agricultural fields. However, even given this recycling, it is expected that close consideration of the complex refuse and artifact patterns on village sites may reveal traces of ceramic production activities.

Of the many other forms of manufacturing that were important to the functioning of the city of Vijayanagara, archaeologists are most likely to recover evidence of metal and stone working. The extensive monumental and non-monumental architecture of Vijayanagara was erected very quickly, one might even say hastily. Many structures contain large numbers of granite columns that appear to have been mass produced. These columns often did not fit the structure into which they were being incorporated, so in order to use them, the tops were simply lopped off. The granite building stone used in most structures is found in large outcropping boulders throughout the study area, including the city itself. These boulders show the traces of quarrying and in general, quarrying intensity is directly related to the scale of construction. The survey data confirm the suspicion that stone working was very situational, and we have found no area of major workshops (Sinopoli 2003:213-18). Stone workers must have moved around from quarry to quarry. Only very rough cutting was done at the quarry, however; most work was carried out on construction sites themselves. If there existed some central workshop(s) for the mass-produced columns, we have not located it.

Metal working presents some similar patterns. Unlike nearby ore-rich areas now in the state of Andhra Pradesh (T. Lowe, pers. comm.), in which there is evidence for large-scale iron working, production in the survey area seems to have been relatively small-scale and mobile, perhaps organized on a seasonal schedule

(Lycett 1994; Sinopoli 2003:195-201). The Sandur Hills, just south of the survey area, contain iron and manganese ore, and the village of Kamalapuram was known in the colonial period for the production of the large iron pans used in sugar cane processing (Kelsall 1872:19). Iron working sites in the study area are almost always associated with water, but many of the water sources would have been dry in the winter season. These sites were involved in the processing of iron and perhaps crucible steel. Unfortunately, we have not yet carried out the analyses to distinguish smelting, or the processing of ores, from forging, or the shaping of metal objects. The latter would have been particularly important during the rainy season for the manufacture and repair of agricultural implements, and in context of military camps. Like potters, metal workers are often listed on the roster of village servants, but also like pottery, the demand for metal objects in the context of a large city would have been much higher than that assumed in the normative village production model. As in the case of ceramics, the existence of village specialists would not rule out the possibility of other simultaneous forms of productive organization.

In addition to ceramics, stone, and metal, there is more scattered evidence for the production of other materials, including lime, for mortar and plaster, and perhaps also precious metals such as gold or silver (see Sinopoli 1994, 2003, for a fuller discussion). Many other forms of nonfood production were certainly carried out but have not left significant surface indications.

Agriculture in the Vijayanagara region was not only the primary source of food for the city and the region, but also provided critical raw materials for weavers (cotton and dye plants) and for temple ritual (flowers, fruit, grains), among other things. Because of the dry climate and seasonal pattern of rainfall, agriculturalists in the Vijayanagara region faced significant problems of water supply in addition to those of access to arable soils, fertilizers, animal and human labor, and transportation. The organization of agricultural production was complex, geared both toward the production of food and other plant materials for the city and for subsistence. This dual pattern of production is overlain by another form of variability in production, that of wet versus dry crops. Although this distinction is not rigid—many cultigens could have been grown as either wet or dry crops—certain valued plants were only able to survive the semiarid study area with the active assistance of humans.

Dry crops were grown, at a minimum, without the aid of any special facilities and thus are quite difficult to detect archaeologically. Among the most important of these crops were the staple grains generally lumped under the category of millets: *Sorghum bicolor* (jowar or cholum), *Pennisetum typhoides* (bajra), *Eleusine corocana* (ragi), and various others (Morrison 1995). A variety of oilseeds such as castor (*Ricinus communis*) were also grown as dry crops, as apparently was cotton (*Gossypium*) (see Morrison 1995). Some dry fields were modified to preserve water, prevent evaporation, slow erosion, or mark field boundaries and these rather modest constructions can be found in parts of the survey area. In a few places, dry production was assisted by the application of manure and household waste to the fields; this practice seems to have been limited primarily to dry fields in the immediate vicinity of settlements and roads. In this study, we have been careful to document these smaller and more ephemeral agricultural features as well as the larger and more spectacular ones associated with wet agriculture, with the hope that we would learn something about the operation of this component of the agricultural economy and its integration with irrigated agriculture.

More substantial facilities designed to harvest and store the seasonal monsoon rains include reservoirs ("tanks"), hundreds of which dot the Vijayanagara landscape. Reservoirs range in size from small dams a few meters long to massive facilities stretching for kilometers (Morrison 1993). Not only the volume of water, but also the length of time it stayed in the reservoir and its reliability varied greatly, so that different reservoirs served as sources of supplemental watering for dry crops, stock tanks, domestic water supply, or even the sole source of water for irrigated crops. A few reservoirs in the survey area were fed not only seasonal rainfall and runoff, but were associated with canals originating from the Tungabhadra River. These reservoirs contained water year round and could support such water-demanding wet crops as rice, vegetables, orchards, and sugar cane.

The limited area of wet agriculture in the region surrounding the city made possible this large population concentration. The Tungabhadra River takes a wide turn just west of the city, and this turn makes possible the canal irrigation of an area more extensive than the narrow strip of river-edge land that it is otherwise possible to serve. Canals provided the water and silt that could have supported double cropping in the irrigated hinterland of the city; these canals are still in service today. The archaeological record of the zones of wet irrigation reflects their importance in agricultural production. No settlements are built right on prime irrigated land; these areas are well defended and we find abundant remains of roads and temples. Perhaps the most important wet crop was rice, a staple food of the elite and deities, and a highly storable grain (Morrison 1994a).

The structure of agricultural production cannot be dissociated from that of animal husbandry, for not only did the manure of sheep, goats, cattle, and water buffalo fertilize fields, but it seems likely that some fodder beyond that provided by field wastes and wild plants would have needed to have been grown for the flocks. Unfortunately, we have little information of animal husbandry beyond that little afforded by texts and this remains an important avenue for future archaeological research.

The issue of production, then, lies at the center of our research. As we have tried to make clear, consideration of one form of production leads inexorably to another—farmers grow crops but also use metal tools and ceramics; potters claim shares of produce or farm their own land; all pay taxes, move goods from place to place, participate in temple economies (willingly or not), resist and submit to authority. Although we begin with simple questions of production—its organizations, their structures—we come quickly to other issues. These other issues force us to examine the survey area minutely but also to move beyond it. What were the structures and paths of power and authority that existed in the Vijayanagara region, and in the empire? How was such power and authority constituted and manifest, and to what extent is its operation apparent in the material record? How were—or were?—the arenas of production just discussed integrated into changing constellations of power? As we discuss elsewhere (Morrison and Sinopoli 1992; Sinopoli and Morrison 1995; Sinopoli 2003), it is our contention that different forms of production were subject to differing degrees of elite manipulation, attempted or actual, and that the ways in which producers organized their behavior reflected both the material conditions of production and the sociopolitical contexts of that production.

Layout and Infrastructure

Allied with our concern for the organization of production is an interest in delineating the content and layout of the Vijayanagara archaeological landscape, including the disposition of settlement, areas of agriculture, roads, fortifications, markets, and sacred places. We are intent on identifying these features and placing them within their physical context—elevation, slope, soil, and substrate—as well as in their places in constructed landscapes. In general, we found two factors to have overwhelming importance in structuring the Vijayanagara hinterland, with a host of other factors of more limited significance. First, the city itself, a massive concentration of people, markets, and authority figures, exerted tremendous pressure on the entire region. Most of the major roads in the metropolitan region lead into and out of the city and some, such as those in the expansive irrigated zones of Blocks R and M (not discussed in this volume), are not associated with any settlement, but instead may have been constructed to move produce into the city. The placement of radial roadways in Blocks O, S, and T generally follows topographic constraints, with roads situated along low-lying areas or running through valleys (as in Block T), but the situation of the roads themselves seem to structure the placement of settlements more than the settlements structure the roadways. The larger temple complexes in the survey area are all situated along roads, but not all are on the major roads. The placement of sacred markers—temples, shrines, sculptures, and in some cases, inscriptions—responds to locational factors other than those of transport and population. Temples and shrines are often found on high places, in rock shelters, and near gates, doors, or openings.

The second major factor structuring land use and location in the survey area is water. Settlements required water for domestic consumption; this need was generally supplied by wells. The coincidence of towns and villages with reservoirs, however, points to both the importance of agriculture in the regional economy—a great many people were farmers—and to the multifunctional nature of reservoirs. The latter not only served agriculture, but could also be used for washing clothes, watering livestock, and fishing. Given the primary reliance of the inhabitants of this dry region on locally grown produce, it is not surprising that water availability and the disposition of arable soils strongly structured the placement of fields. Areas with developed soils and moderate slopes away from the reach of Tungabhadra River water were farmed with the help of rainfall, sometimes carefully conserved, moved, and/or gathered by terraces, walls, channels, and reservoirs. Dry farmed areas also drew livestock, needed for their manure, and we find indications of both permanent and temporary settlement even in relatively remote dry farmed areas. Even more sharply defined were irrigated wet fields, served by the extensive network of Tungabhadra channels. These channels drew river water from diversion weirs (or *anicuts*) placed in the braided river channels, and brought rich river silt and water to fields within reach of the gravity-fed canals. Where such production was possible, the landscape was almost entirely transformed. Vegetation assemblages changed; fields were leveled, ditched, built up, and walled; rocks and boulders were cleared; and, significantly, few other structures competed for space. Although settlements were located adjacent to irrigated areas, by and large villages and towns were *not* constructed on prime agricultural lands and these areas contain only occasional temples, roads, and a few artifact scatters. Where rock outcrops rear up above low-lying irrigated land, such as in the northwest corner of Block O, nonagricultural features are clustered in these dryer locations. Agricultural land use created both possibilities—the linear raised embankments of reservoirs, for example—and barriers to transportation; the muddy ground, standing water, and incised channels of canal and reservoir irrigated zones made passage by foot, cart, or horse almost impossible.

The placement of defensive features follows from both the dominance of the city and the primacy of water in structuring regional layout (see Brubaker 2004). The city itself was strongly protected by walls, bastions, and gates; several outlying settlements were also contained within strong walls. Outside the area of continuous walls, fortifications continued across such vulnerable points as passes and along roads. As noted, agricultural features created their own obstacles and opportunities; the long raised embankment of the Kamalapuram reservoir is actually built into the outer city wall and is girded with one large and one small bastion.

The Survey Area: Physiographic Setting

Elevations in the survey area range from approximately 300 to 900 m above sea level, with the Tungabhadra basin falling between 300 and 600 m and the Sandur Hills, 600 and 900 m. The region is dominated geologically by the Hampi-Daroji Hills, a series of northwest-southeast trending, low and rocky ridges. These hills are composed of granitic rocks and are shot through with occasional basaltic dikes (Krishnamurthy 1978; Naqvi and Rogers 1987). The granite hills have weathered into boulders that have the appearance of huge piles of stones rather than of coherent landforms. Interspersed with large and small granitic outcrops are expanses of granitic sheet rock, some sloping and some relatively level. To the south rise the east-west metamorphic Sandur Hills. Unlike the Hampi-Daroji Hills, the rocks of the Sandur Hills are mineral-rich, containing deposits of lead and manganese. The granite boulders of the survey area not only served as loci for construction, but also supplied the major part of the building stone used in the construction of all facilities from temples and palaces to reservoirs and roads.

The extent to which the granitic hills of the survey area once supported soil and vegetation is not clear. Today, most of these hills are stark, almost bare of soil, and support only grasses, low thorny shrubs, and stands of *Euphorbias*. That this represents the culmination of years of erosion and slope wash is suggested by the extensive colluviation of many of the narrow valleys separating the ridges. However, the degree of soil development on the rocky hills was probably never extensive and the natural vegetation never particularly luxuriant although Kelsall, writing in 1872, notes that "The slopes of these hills are well-wooded and most of the fuel consumed in Bellary is brought from them" (1872:14). The primary vegetation association in the survey area is the *Albizzia amara-Acacia* series (Gaussen et al. 1966), while the higher Sandur Hills supported more mesic forests of the *Anogeissus-Terminalia-Tectona* series (Gaussen et al. 1966) and, on their lower slopes, the *Hardwickia-Anogeissus* series. Swampy land near the river and such artificial features as reservoirs provided microenvironments for the luxuriant growth of aquatic and semiaquatic plants, particularly sedges, reeds, and grasses (Singh 1988). Cultivated plants also play a major role in the regional vegetation. Not only do fields and orchards dominate contemporary (and Vijayanagara-period, see Morrison 1995) landscapes, but many, if not most, shade trees (Neem, Banyan, Pipal, Tamarind) in and around settlements and along field borders have been deliberately planted. Trees and shrubs, even cactuslike plants such as *Euphorbias*, provide major alternative sources of fuel where manure is costly or unavailable. The Sandur Hills, in particular, must have provided Vijayanagara area residents with wood for domestic fires, for the production of charcoal for pyrotechnic crafts, and for construction.

The soils of the survey area are classified as "red" (*masab*) (Singh 1988:22) and "mixed black and red" soils, and are somewhat sandy and slightly basic, with low organic content and high permeability. Calcium carbonate (*kankar*) formation is common, and localized areas of hard pan formation can be found. Only a narrow strip of land along the banks of the Tungabhadra contains alluvial soils, although hundreds of years of canal irrigation near the river have transported river silts further inland. To the north of Tungabhadra, in the area between the Tungabhadra and Krishna Rivers known as the Raichur *doab* (land between rivers, here the Tungabhadra and the Krishna), the soils are darker, with a higher clay content and similarly low level of organic material. These soils, the celebrated *regur* (or *regada*, Kelsall 1872:1), or black cotton soils, have an excellent water-holding capacity.

Like the Raichur *doab*, the level plain to the east of the survey area, past Daroji and extending as far as Bellary, consists of black cotton soil.

The degree to which the Vijayanagara landscape allowed or encouraged planting, settlement, and movement depended a great deal on slope as well as substrate. In the south, the Sandur Hills present a formidable, but not impossible, barrier to north-south movement. These hills are not long, however, and one can easily circumvent them. The Sandur Hills, like other hills in the area, were also important as watersheds. Because almost all agricultural facilities in the region relied on the harvesting and storing of monsoon runoff, such facilities were placed carefully with respect to local configurations of slope as well as soil.

Topography structured settlement as well as agriculture. Towns and villages were generally situated along major roadways leading into and out of the city; such routes followed level ground and ran through passes in the rocky hills. Transportation was not simply a least-cost exercise, however, since fortification and defense played a major role in the locations of roads as well. It is important to note that obstacles to movement would have differed with the mode of transport. The rocky uplands in the southeast portion of the survey area would have hampered pedestrians much less than riders or wheeled vehicles. Rural settlements often, but not invariably, were situated near reservoirs, so the locations of such settlements were inevitably limited by the conditions of reservoir placement. Finally, hills proved attractive for the placement of temples and shrines and watchtowers or bastions.

The average annual rainfall of the Bellary District is just under 50 mm, based on data from collection stations at Bellary and Raichur. This figure is low, but as problematic as the low annual rainfall is its variability, which reaches thirty percent (Spate 1954; Kanitkar 1960). Most rain falls during the summer (southwest) monsoon months of June to September, but there is a minor period of rain during the so-called northeast or winter monsoon.

Discussion: The Vijayanagara Landscape

The following chapters provide information on the content and structure of the Vijayanagara archaeological landscape. This landscape is situated within the physical context outlined above, but it should be clear from even this brief discussion that this was a modified landscape, a created environment. While still subject to such apparently prosaic concerns as the locations of arable soils, the movement of runoff, and the availability of ores, fuels, clays and other raw materials for production, Vijayanagara-era residents created and confronted a landscape of cultural features. It is our goal to both document and to begin to understand this landscape and, a goal both important and difficult, to delineate how it changed through time.

– 2 –

Survey Methodology

Archaeological Survey

Regional archaeological research has a long history in South Asia, beginning in the Vijayanagara region in the early ninteenth century. Much prior work in Vijayanagara, discussed in Chapter 1, and in other regions can best be categorized as regional "exploration," known in South Asia as village-to-village survey (see Chakrabarti 2001; Shaw 2000; see also Sinopoli 2006). In such surveys, researchers start in existing villages, and rely on local informants to identify historic inscriptions, monuments (primarily temples), and other ancient sites near contemporary settlements. With more than two centuries history in South Asia, village-to-village exploration has resulted in the identification of thousands of sites and monuments across the subcontinent.

Exploration work shares with systematic archaeological survey an interest in identifying sites across a relatively expansive geographic area. It differs significantly, however, in research methodologies and the intensity of regional coverage. Systematic archaeological survey such as employed in our Vijayanagara research is, as its name implies, a systematic and highly structured technique for the discovery and documentation of archaeological remains, whether sites, features, or artifacts. Through survey, archaeologists seek to identify and understand the distribution of archaeological remains across a region, while avoiding implicit or explicit biases in where and how we look for those remains. That is, a systematic approach to site discovery helps us to avoid looking for archaeological remains only where we expect to find them (or only near contemporary settlements), and allows researchers to document both where remains are located *and* where they are absent.

Although systematic archaeological survey as practiced by the Vijayanagara Metropolitan Survey is relatively new to the South Asian context, our research builds on a long tradition of regional survey in urban landscapes as developed in Latin America (Blanton et al. 1982; Sanders, Parsons, and Santley 1979; Parsons et al. 1983; Willey 1953; Wilson 1988), the Middle East (Adams 1965, 1981; Adams and Nissen 1972; Johnson 1973; Neely and Wright 1994; Wright and Johnson 1975), and more recently in the Aegean and Classical world (Alcock and Cherry 2004; Kardulias 1994). In this chapter, we outline the procedures developed in our survey project, and provide some context on the three survey strata, or blocks, that are the focus of this monograph.

As with any archaeological project, in designing a survey, critical initial decisions must be made concerning how the survey region is to be defined, what portion of that region to explore, and how to conduct the exploration. Such decisions are inevitably then modified by actual field conditions and experience, but they nonetheless play a critical role in structuring research design. As we elaborate below, our survey was a "sample survey." That is, we quickly recognized that it would not be possible to systematically cover the entire Vijayanagara metropolitan region and designed our fieldwork to sample a representative portion of it.

Sample surveys can be contrasted with what have come to be called "full coverage" survey methodologies (e.g., Fish and Kowalewski 1990). Full coverage survey has, as its name implies, the goal of covering 100% of the defined survey region—a 100% *sampling fraction*. Criticisms of surveys that cover less than 100% of a region argue that such sampling inhibits recognition of overall archaeological distribution patterns (Kintigh 1990), increases the probability of missing significant sites (Parsons

1990), and imposes difficult statistical challenges for data analysis and interpretation (Fish and Kowalewski 1990:4). It should be noted, however, that even the staunchest advocates of full coverage survey acknowledge its limitations in areas of difficult terrain and complex logistics (e.g., Parsons 1990; Kintigh 1990; Cowgill 1990), such as the Vijayanagara metropolitan region.

Whatever the approach to survey adopted, and we discuss the reasons for our decisions below, all archaeologists must confront the awareness that numerous factors constrain our ability to completely document any site or region from surface remains, as well as from excavation (see Morrison 1995; Sundstron 1993:91; Wandsnider and Camilli 1992). A wide variety of factors, involving both surface visibility and preservation, affect our ability to recognize and document surface remains (Schiffer 1995; Lewarch and O'Brien 1981). Such factors include seasonal conditions—such as rainfall and vegetation patterns or the growing stages of agricultural crops—that influence visibility over the course of a year. Other factors affecting visibility include the impact of later construction (or destruction) activities, or other cultural or natural features or processes that affect preservation or probability of identification. Many of these factors are, of course, beyond our control; however, they still must be acknowledged and, where possible, documented.

The procedures employed during surveys also affect how thoroughly and effectively archaeological remains are documented. Thus, decisions concerning the spacing of individuals during a survey or "survey intensity" (Cowgill 1990:253) play a dramatic role in our ability to recognize and recover archaeological remains, whatever the defined sampling fraction. Such spacing critically affects the probabilities that surveyors will identify remains of particular sizes, given that the likelihood of recognizing a surface occurrence decreases dramatically as distance from it increases. If surveyors are spaced 30 meters apart, they are thus unlikely to recognize small sites or isolated features less than 5-10 meters in diameter that lie between the paths of two surveyors. The calculation of an appropriate survey intensity for any project is inevitably a compromise. High intensity or close spacing significantly increases the time it takes to cover an area, as crews are tightly packed together and can cover only a small area at a time. Lower intensity or wide spacing, on the other hand, saves time but results in the under-recording of small sites. Thus, survey intensity must be responsive to the nature and visibility of the archaeological remains in a region and the goals of the research project, as well as to logistical constraints of time and crew size. As discussed below, in our project we typically spaced members of the survey team at intervals of 20 meters.

A second issue affecting the identification of archaeological remains has been termed *sensitivity* by Cowgill (1990). Sensitivity is defined as "the probability of detecting an occurrence of evidence of ancient activity" (Cowgill 1990:253). Sensitivity is affected by a complex array of factors. These include the nature of the archaeological remains, the nature of the terrain and environment, the distance of the surveyor from surface features, the degree to which surveyors are sensitized to the presence of a particular kind of feature, and the technologies employed in detecting subsurface phenomena. In the Vijayanagara Metropolitan Survey, our awareness of and sensitivity to particular kinds of occurrences had considerable impact on site recognition. Over the course of multiple seasons of survey, we became increasingly proficient at recognizing certain kinds of features and artifacts that we did not initially anticipate as being part of the Vijayanagara region's archaeological record. In particular, the existence of a Vijayanagara period chipped stone industry was unexpected, given implicit understandings among South Asian specialists that the use of lithics effectively disappeared following the widespread adoption of iron technologies in the first millennium B.C. Our recognition of the presence of flaked stone and glass artifacts in clearly Vijayanagara period sites in the survey area thus took us by surprise. However, once this recognition occurred we became aware that crude flaked stone implements were relatively widespread across the metropolitan region and even in areas of the urban core where we had failed to identify them in previous programs of intensive surface collections. Similarly, our ability to recognize features related to transport routes, such as road boundary walls, as well as pre-Vijayanagara "megalithic" features also increased over time and such sites may have been under-recorded in the early seasons of the project.

As elaborated below, in the Vijayanagara Metropolitan Survey we chose to explicitly sample our region. Within our 250 meter wide sample transects, we adopted an intensity of 20 meter spacing between crew members, to avoid missing small sites in the surveyed areas (indeed, nearly a third of sites reported in this volume are less than or equal to 15 m in diameter). No doubt we still failed to identify some sites smaller than 20 m in diameter, but the large numbers that we recovered provide considerable information about their general nature and distribution. Further, the challenging terrain of the metropolitan region often made it necessary to zigzag across it in order to reach our sample transects, and thus covered far more area than just the sample fraction. Both our patterns of movement and our efforts to record major sites that lay outside the transects assured that large sites were not missed, even where they occurred outside the sample transects.

As noted above, all archaeological surveys involve a series of decisions—concerning the definition of the region to be surveyed, the level of sampling and coverage to be attained, whether recording will focus on the site or "non-site" (feature and artifact) level, and the structure of basic data recording and analysis. Ideally, these decisions are made to best meet specific research goals and theoretical interests; in practice, more mundane concerns such as funding levels, crew size, logistical concerns, and project duration must also be taken into account. In this chapter, we present a discussion of the decisions that guided the Vijayanagara Metropolitan Survey, through a detailed discussion of the survey region and survey methodology. As with all field projects, our methods resulted from a combination of theory-guided decisions made before fieldwork began and decisions made in the field as the result of direct experience with the nature and distribution of archaeological remains in the Vijayanagara metropolitan region.

The Sample Area: The Vijayanagara Metropolitan Region

A key issue in all archaeological research, and perhaps particularly in survey, is the definition of a meaningful project region or "sampling universe." This is a complicated process, affected both by archaeological goals and priorities and by the practical concerns of fieldwork. Our definition of the Vijayanagara metropolitan region (VMR) took into account both natural and cultural features. The region is broadly defined as the area encompassed within the outermost fortifications of the imperial capital. The metropolitan region is centered on the Vijayanagara urban core, described in Chapter 1: the densely settled and heavily fortified focus of administration and elite occupation located on the southern bank of the Tungabhadra River. In our initial definitions, we estimated that the metropolitan region encompassed roughly 350 km^2. Subsequent research on the distribution of Vijayanagara's fortifications (e.g., Brubaker 2004) and other features on the peripheries of the metropolitan region led us to extend this zone considerably, and the area, as we presently conceive it, is some 430 km^2, although even this could easily be expanded to as large as 650 km^2 if we include the Daroji Valley area to the southeast of the urban core (see Morrison in press; Sinopoli 1997). Wherever we draw the boundaries, the Vijayanagara metropolitan region encompasses a dissected territory in the rugged landscape of the southern Deccan (see Chapter 1 and Fig. 2.1). The region is bordered on the north and south by large zones of high outcropping hills; on the west by the modern Tungabhadra Reservoir; and on the southeast and east by a band of hills that separate the region from the flat open plains of the Daroji Valley and Bellary region.

To the north of the Tungabhadra River, the boundaries of the survey region are defined on the basis of topography to include the low-lying areas along the riverbank and to extend into the high outcrops to their north. The fortified town of Anegundi (Purandare 1986), lying opposite the urban core on the northern riverbank, falls within the metropolitan region and was, during the imperial period, an extension of the city core. Several other fortified settlements spread along the northern banks of the river provided an efficient system of watch posts and strategic defenses of the northern bounds of the city. Beyond the narrow alluvial band near Anegundi, the granodiorite outcrop hills that define the region's northern boundary rise sharply more than 150 m above the river plain, forming a rugged barrier to movement and settlement.

On the west, the boundaries of the survey region are defined by fortifications and on the basis of Vijayanagara period documentary sources. This area has been subject to considerable modification resulting in the destruction of archaeological features. The construction of the Tungabhadra Reservoir in the 1950s flooded an area of some 230+ km^2 and destroyed more than 200 villages. While Vijayanagara period constructions no doubt were present in the now-flooded region, sixteenth-century Vijayanagara writings concerning the construction of a suburb near modern Hospet make clear that this was considered the outer boundary of the city (see Brubaker 2004). This suburb, now a city of some 350,000 people, lies within our survey region, and was referred to by the Portuguese merchant Fernao Paes as "the principal entrance [to the capital] on the western side" (in Sewell 1900:244). A large fortification wall (VMS-1074) is located approximately three km southwest of Hospet (also illustrated in Sewell 1900, frontispiece), and effectively marks this western boundary of the metropolitan region.

To the east of the Vijayanagara urban core, the boundary of the metropolitan region is defined by Vijayanagara fortification walls and topographic features, in particular, a band of granodiorite outcrops and hills that set off the region from the more open valleys and plains to the south and east. Massive defensive walls are found at this edge of the metropolitan region, spanning gaps between hills and other passable areas of outcrops. Together these walls and hills created formidable barriers to movement into (or out of) Vijayanagara (Brubaker 2004). Large fortification walls also occur further to the east, in the Daroji Valley, an area containing a sophisticated network of Vijayanagara period reservoirs that has been documented by Morrison (in press). The Daroji region was an important focus of agricultural investment during the Vijayanagara period, particularly during the period of urban expansion in the sixteenth century. Although we have treated this region separately, and have not formally included it in our definition of the metropolitan region, by the sixteenth century it had become a critical part of an integrated defensive and productive system associated with the imperial capital. As noted above, if the Daroji region were added to the Vijayanagara metropolitan region, the total estimated area would increase to about 650 km^2.

To the south, the metropolitan region abuts the rugged metamorphic Sandur Hills, a high range of southeast-northwest trending slopes that are rich in iron and magnesium ore (see Chapter 1). These resources have been mined and transformed by humans since at least the first millennium BCE, and VMS-110 in Block W provides evidence for an iron working settlement, located at the base of the hills, dating from at least 200 BCE to 200 CE. Intensive mining continues in the area today, assisted by dynamite and railways to haul the ore, which no doubt has resulted in the destruction of many Vijayanagara and earlier remains.

As noted, Vijayanagara constructions including temples, fortifications, reservoirs, and other irrigation works are found beyond the approximately 430 km^2 region we have defined as the metropolitan region. Nonetheless, both the bands of fortifications and the distribution of other archaeological features suggest that the region described above is both significant and meaningful.

For purposes of our research, we have divided the Vijayanagara metropolitan region into arbitrary grid blocks that correspond to the mapping system developed by Fritz and Michell (1985) for documenting the urban core. This is a hierarchical mapping system with potential to extend well beyond its present limits. At the upper level, the region has been divided into a square grid of 25 square units, each 22.50 km on a side and designated by a bracketed upper case letter ([A]-[Z], excluding

[I]). The metropolitan region lies primarily within Block [N] and includes parts of Blocks [M] and [O]. These large blocks are further subdivided into a five by five grid of smaller blocks, each 4.5 km on a side, and designated with an upper case letter (A-Z, excluding I). The entire urban core is thus located in [N]N (indeed, the desire to define the urban core as a single grid unit explains the somewhat unwieldy values used in this system). Fritz and Michell have further subdivided these blocks into 25 smaller units (designated with lower case letters), although we have not employed this subdivision in the Metropolitan Survey. Figure 2.2 illustrates the locations and designations of the twenty-eight 4.5 km square blocks that comprise the metropolitan region and the sampling universe of our survey.

A 1:25,000 map series of the region has been prepared, with one 4.5 km square block to a page. The map series is derived from the 1:50,000 Survey of India maps of the region, updated in 1975 (Maps 57 A/7, 57 A/8, 57 A/11, 57 A/12). A previous edition of maps prepared in the early 1920s was obtained from the India Office Library in London; it provides information on land features and settlement prior to the construction of the Tungabhadra Reservoir. In the absence of aerial photography (not permitted in India), these maps provide the best resource for documenting both the terrain and the location of modern cultural features (including settlements and structures, roads, modern wells, power lines, and so on). The Survey of India maps also provide information on the location of some major archaeological features, such as reservoirs, forts, or temples.

Sampling Design

The preliminary survey carried out in the metropolitan region in 1987 by Morrison (1991) made clear that the density of archaeological remains was high and that the dissected terrain would make movement across the region difficult. Further, potential crew size and uncertainties in funding and permits limited our ability to consider a full coverage survey of the entire VMR. Preliminary explorations of the region suggested a significant falloff in site density and diversity with distance from the urban core. In designing the survey, we therefore chose to divide the survey region into two broad strata according to distance from the core. While it might have made sense to consider topography or additional features in defining our sampling units, given our limited prior knowledge about the nature and distribution of archaeological remains in the survey region and our desire to not bias our sample toward particular topographic or environmental settings, we decided to use the arbitrary square blocks of the Fritz and Michell grid system as our primary units of coverage (Fig. 2.2).

Thus, Stratum I consists of the eight blocks immediately surrounding Block N (Blocks G, H, J, M, O, R, S, and T). The remaining blocks constitute Stratum II. It is in the first stratum where we decided to focus our most intensive work, through surveying a 50% sample of each block. By surveying contiguous blocks that are each adjacent to the urban core, we can examine the relations between the core and its most immediate hinterland, and can examine the distribution of sites and features that crosscut these admittedly arbitrary block boundaries.

Coverage in the second stratum was less intensive, focusing on specific site categories, and primarily on large and "significant" sites (as defined by our research interests), such as large reservoirs, fortifications, major temples, or craft production locales. Before turning to a discussion of the specific context of survey in the three intensively surveyed blocks (O, S, T) that are the focus of this monograph, we briefly discuss the overall survey strategy for the eight blocks subject to intensive survey.

The Site Concept

As the above discussion suggests, our survey and recording strategy focused at the level of the archaeological site. The site concept has been criticized for imposing arbitrary boundaries on distributions (and past activities) that are essentially continuous (Dunnell and Dancey 1983:271-74; Lewarch and O'Brien 1981:320, 322), and we accept the validity of many of these criticisms. The definition of our survey region as encompassing the outermost fortified region of the Vijayanagara imperial capital implicitly acknowledges both the culturally bounded nature of the region and the coherent distribution of activities within it. There is in a significant sense no part of the metropolitan region that was *not* the location of some human activity during the Vijayanagara period. This is evidenced in the low-density sherd scatter throughout the region, a product of a range of human activities and depositional processes (see Chapter 6). Although we take note of the nature and densities of these continuous distributions in our work, it was not feasible, nor necessarily desirable, to record the location of each artifact in the metropolitan region. The distribution of archaeological features in the region clearly indicated that discrete locations of past human activities could be identified across the region and their locations and boundaries could be identified.

While some scholars have sought to come up with alternate terms to "site" to describe such locations identified in their research (e.g., "location" or "occurrence"; Cowgill 1990), this is a terminological response that does not resolve the debate about the relevance of the site concept. Rather than become involved in terminological debates, we have chosen to retain "site" to refer to the metropolitan region's archaeological remains. The site concept provides a convenient way to record the archaeological remains and a basis for making comparisons among them.

In most cases in our fieldwork, the division of the archaeological record into sites was fairly straightforward, especially where dealing with discrete architectural remains. For example, a walled temple complex, an isolated step well, structure, or reservoir embankment were each recorded as individual sites. Structures or constructions directly associated with such remains were designated as features (for example, a shrine within a temple complex, a sluice gate of a reservoir). In other cases, site boundaries were more difficult to precisely define (for example, in the case of

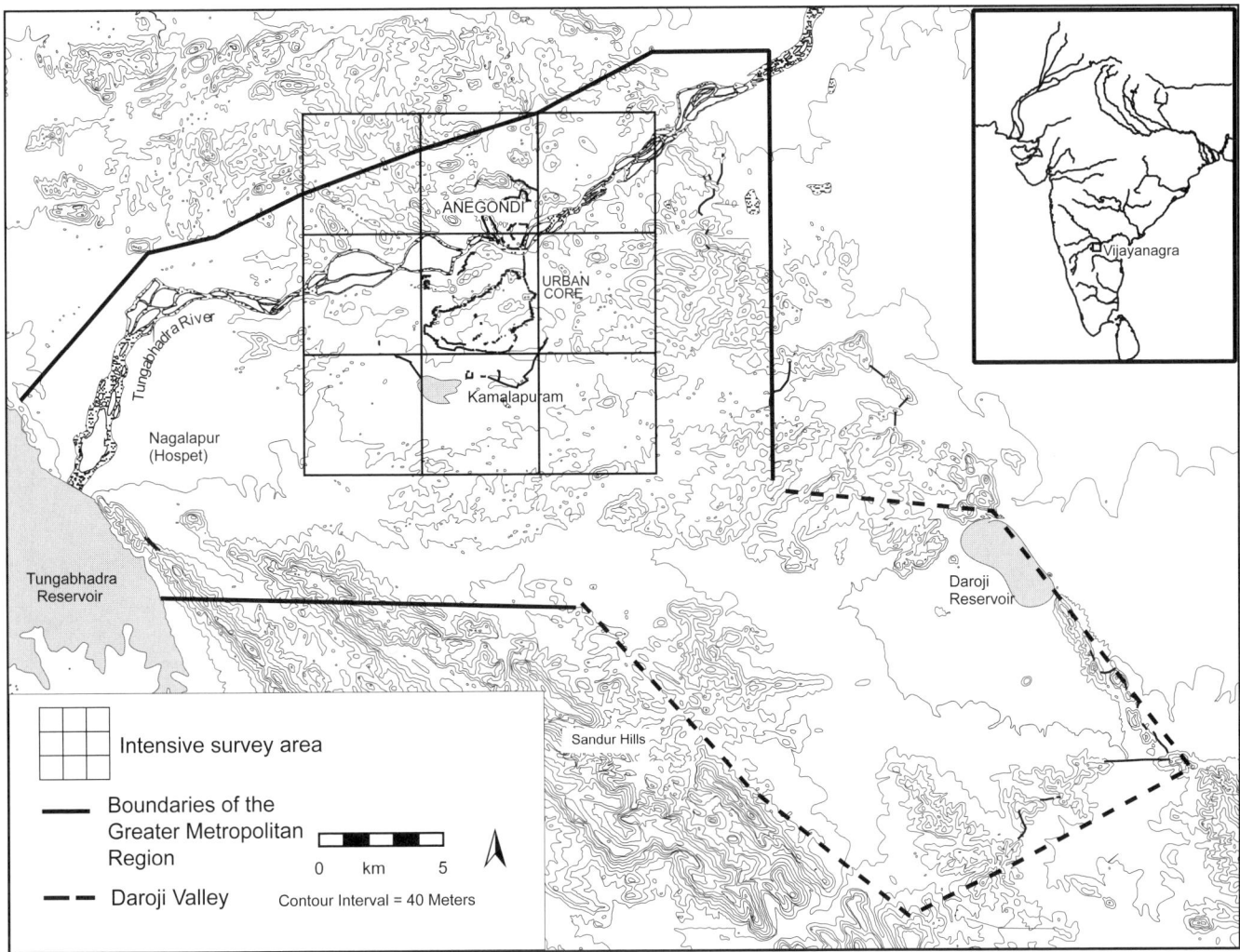

Figure 2.1. The Vijayanagara metropolitan region.

artifact scatters, or terrace systems). We did so on the basis of density falloff patterns as well as natural features (for example, terrace walls that lie within a single valley may be designated as constituting one site, while walls beyond the valley were given a different site number). Certainly in some cases remains were given separate site numbers when they easily could have been merged into a single site. Examples include long roads whose preserved segments were separated by tens or hundreds of meters. Although such segments probably were originally part of a single construction, we typically assigned discrete site numbers to each (for example, VMS-326 and VMS-360 in Block T), both for ease of recording and because contemporaneity and associations could not always be easily identified in the field.

In the development of our computerized database and Geographic Information System for analysis of the survey data, each site was subdivided into multiple features. This allows us to further parse out functional and other attributes of large complex sites (such as settlements with craft production locales, shrines, and water storage features).

Survey Methods

Each of the eight blocks of Stratum I was subdivided into eighteen north-south transects (250 m by 4.5 km). Nine transects per block were randomly selected to comprise the 50% sample (Fig. 2.3). The sample transects were overlaid on the base maps used by survey teams to locate themselves in the project area. Although higher resolution maps would have been greatly preferred, information provided on the Survey of India maps has proven remarkably accurate, and locating transect boundaries

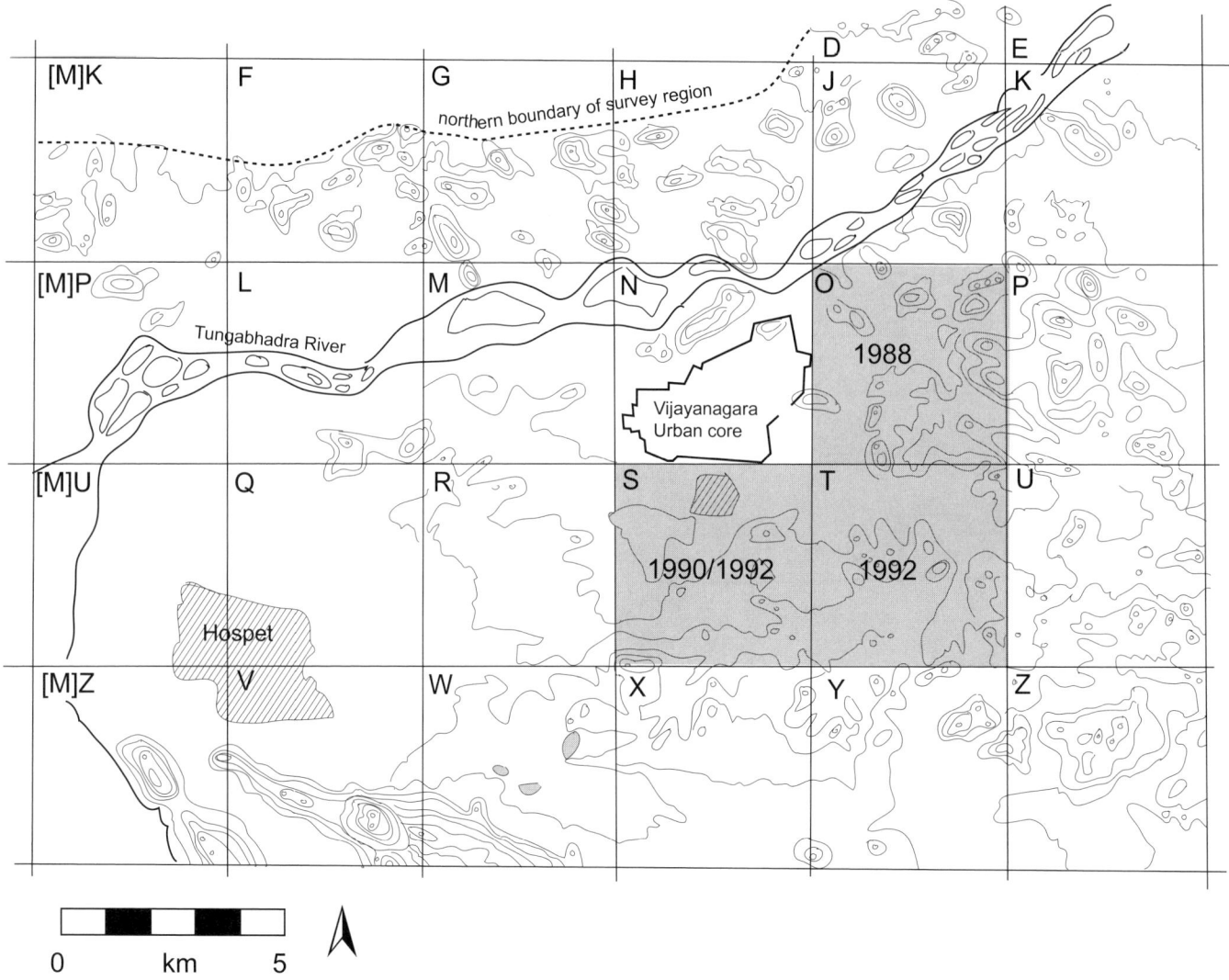

Figure 2.2. The region: intensive and extensive sampling strata.

and recording site location was relatively straightforward. These efforts were aided in later seasons of survey by the use of portable Global Positioning Systems (GPS).

Once on the transect boundary, crews consisting of three to six members walked each sample transect in a south-north or north-south direction, using compasses for orientation. As noted above, crew members were spaced at intervals of 20 m. All surveyors carried notebooks to record information about terrain, current land use, and observations of isolated artifacts or features.

The rugged terrain of the metropolitan region often posed significant challenges to straight line movement. Natural and constructed barriers had to be traversed or, where impassable, circumvented. The large stone outcrop hills presented the most formidable natural barriers to linear movement. While crews climbed small and relatively gentle outcrops, the presence of sheer rock faces in some areas required that alternate routes of movement be found. Further, on very high and rugged hills of granitic boulders and outcrops, where feasible routes of movement were limited and sites proved to be rare, we chose to cover a segment only 20% of the width of the transect (a randomly selected 50 m wide band). Since outcrops are today the focus of quarrying and herding, footpaths or roads were common among them, and most were at least partly accessible through those existing routes, even where we could not adhere to our formal transects. Many of these contemporary routes appear to have had ancient antecedents (indeed, they were often the only possible paths up the steep slopes), and features found along them were recorded whether or not they lay within a sample transect.

Along with outcrops, other zones that posed particular challenges to movement were areas of canal irrigation. The many

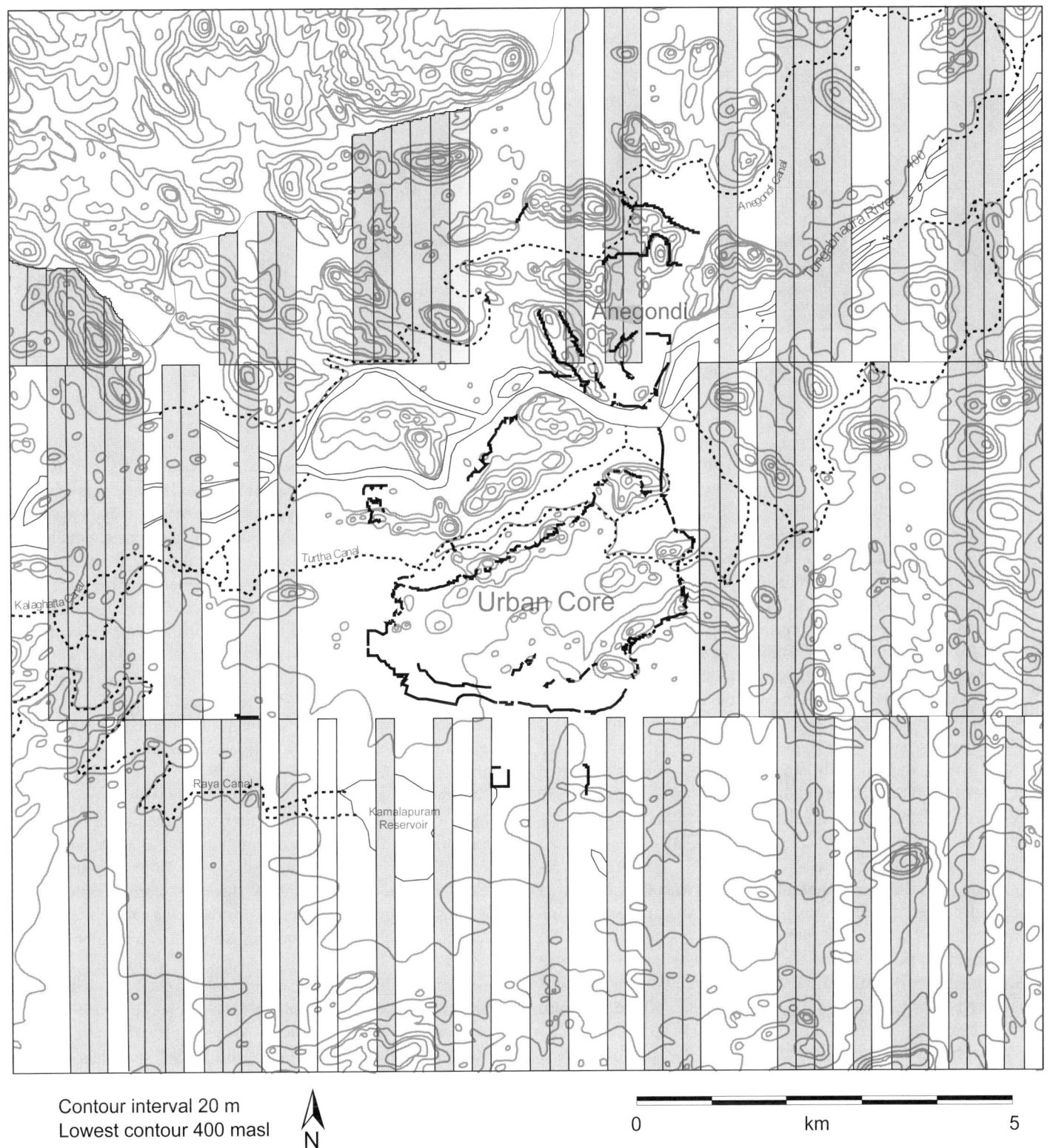

Figure 2.3. Sample transects in intensive survey area.

Plate 2.1. Irrigated fields to the south of the Kamalapuram Reservoir (VMS-231), Block S.

Plate 2.2. Crew laying out surface collection unit.

broad irrigation channels, and dispersed distribution of rice, sugar cane, and banana fields, in a range of growth stages, imposed significant difficulties on movement (Plate 2.1). Mature sugar cane and rice fields were bypassed, while crews covered other fields in as systematic a manner as possible, though they often were forced to diverge from their lines to get across canals or flooded fields. Thorn fences and the presence (or absence) of road access also affected our movement along the landscape.

Unlike North American archaeologists, one impediment to survey that we did not face was the necessity of obtaining permission from landowners to cross their property. Because of the small size and dispersed distributions of agricultural fields in India, it is not legal to deny access to individuals who may need to traverse property of other landowners to reach their own fields (though farmers certainly have the right to protect their fields from damage). The result is a network of footpaths and cat paths across the region, which greatly facilitated our movement to and from survey transects.

Any site located even partially within a sample transect was recorded, even if it mostly lay outside the transect. The archaeological record of the VMR is threatened—by population growth, expanding agricultural and construction activities, and the use of ancient quarried stones in modern construction. We therefore adopted an aggressive policy of noting and, where possible, fully recording observed sites located outside sample transects, although they cannot statistically be treated as part of the random sample. Thus, while sample areas were fully covered, areas outside the randomly selected transects were also traversed and, to some extent, documented. Total surveyed area in each block is thus significantly more than 50% and, as noted earlier, it is doubtful that many large sites were missed, even if they were not located in sample transects.

When a site was located, the entire crew participated in its documentation. Given the architectural complexity of many of the sites and the paucity of earlier documentation on most sites in the region (even major monuments), we have taken a fairly intensive approach to site documentation. Such efforts took from a half hour to several days depending on site size and complexity. Each site was assigned a unique number (VMS-1–n) and located on the base map. On standardized multipage forms, detailed information was recorded on natural setting (slope and topographic setting, vegetation, associated water or other resources); modern cultural features and/or disturbances to the site; and the presence and distribution of artifacts and artifact collection procedures. The general function of the site was also noted where possible, along with its dimensions and orientations, and a prose description of site layout, construction, function, probable date, relation to nearby sites, and so on. Where numbered features were defined in the field, information on each was recorded on separate feature forms.

Sites were mapped using Brunton compasses, tapes, and pacing for small or non-complex sites and a theodolite or total station for large or architecturally complex sites. Black and white photographs and color slides were also taken. When inscriptions were found in the course of survey, they were both recorded by us as sites or parts of sites and reported to the Department of Archaeology of the Government of Karnataka, whose personnel recorded and translated them. An account of all inscriptions known from Bellary District, in original language and English summary, has recently been published (Patil and Patil 1995).

Standardized procedures were developed for the collection and documentation of surface materials at each site (Plate 2.2). These collection strategies varied both with the size of the site and with the density of artifacts visible on the surface. Small sites or sites with extremely low surface densities were subject to 100% collection. Team members walked over the sites at intervals of approximately 2 m and collected every artifact visible on the surface. Collection areas extended 5 m beyond the defined site boundaries.

In larger sites or sites with moderate to high artifact densities, more formal collection procedures were followed. A series of 2 × 2 m collection units were laid out along evenly spaced parallel transects, oriented along cardinal axes. The precise number and spacing of units varied with the size of the site and density of materials. Transect and unit spacing was most often at intervals of 10 or 20 m, creating a grid or "checkerboard" distribution of units across sites. All surface artifacts visible in units were collected. In some cases, such as in settlements or craft production locales, a number of 2 × 2 m judgment units were also collected in areas of spatial and cultural significance, such as inside rooms or associated with specific surface features. Full coverage sweeps for the collection of diagnostic artifacts were also carried out if collection units yielded small diagnostic samples.

Artifacts from each collection unit were sorted by material type (e.g., ceramic, brick, slag, other) and weighed to the nearest 50 g using hanging scales. They were then sorted into subcategories (ceramic wares or diagnostic forms) and counted and recorded on artifact coding forms. Most nondiagnostic materials were left at the sites; diagnostics were brought back to the field camp for further analysis (see Chapter 6 for discussion of artifact analysis).

Blocks O, T, and S

Having provided a general discussion of survey methodologies that apply to the entire intensively surveyed region, we turn now to a description of the three blocks that are the particular focus of this monograph: Blocks O, T, and S. Block O, located to the east of the urban core, was surveyed in 1988. Block S, located to the south of the urban core, was surveyed in 1990 and 1992; Block T, to the southeast of the urban core, was surveyed in 1992. Together, a total of 380 sites were documented in the three blocks, with 119 sites in Block O, 77 in Block T, and 184 in Block S. As outlined below, each block differed in topographic and hydrological features, and each was characterized by significant differences in the distribution of archaeological remains.

Survey Block O

Block O contains a cross section of the topographic and environmental zones of the metropolitan region (Fig. 2.4; Sinopoli and Morrison 1991:59). The Tungabhadra River passes through the northwest corner of the block (see Fig. 2.2). South of the river, two major topographic zones characterize the block. In the northwest portion of Block O is an area of fertile alluvial and colluvial soils broken by isolated outcropping granitic hills and outcrops (Plate 2.3). The highest of these hills rise more than 150 m (to 590 m ASL) above the riverbank (at c. 440 m ASL). The large Vijayanagara period Turtha Canal (VMS-120) extends diagonally across the eastern edge of this area, creating a large region of wet or irrigated agriculture.

A transitional zone, the location of a major Vijayanagara road, separates the low-lying northwest section of the block from the much more rugged eastern and southern zone (at c. 500-560 m ASL). This latter area consists of high rocky uplands, with limited patches of colluvial deposits between rugged granitic outcrops.

The sample transects surveyed in Block O were 1, 2, 4, 5, 6, 10, 14, 15, and 18 (Fig. 2.4), providing relatively even coverage from west to east. As discussed in Chapter 3, a broad range of site types was recorded in Block O, including settlements, fortifications, sacred structures and images, reservoirs, terraces and check dams, among others. Site densities in Block O are highest in the transitional area between the low-lying northwest zone and the more rugged southeast portion of the block, and are especially high in the southwest quadrant near the urban core. This is not surprising since, as discussed in Chapter 1, habitation and nonagricultural land use were generally limited in areas of good agricultural lands, such as the irrigated regions in the northwest portion of the block.

Survey Block T

Block T is located to the southeast of Block N (the urban core) and borders Block S on its west and Block O on its north. Unlike Blocks O and S, Block T lacked perennial water sources during the Vijayanagara period, and is even today a much more desolate and empty area (Fig. 2.5, Plate 2.4). Not surprisingly, site density is significantly lower in Block T than in the other two blocks reported on in this volume.

Block T is characterized by sloping land surfaces, with terrain rising to the north and south from a relatively flat approximately one-kilometer wide band that extends in an east-west direction across the northern portion of the block. A paved road ("the Nallapur road") runs through this section of the block, roughly paralleling a major Vijayanagara period road (VMS-326, VMS-360). A post-1950s canal from the Tungabhadra Reservoir cuts through the southern part of the block, but bears no relation to any Vijayanagara features. Several very large granitic hills dominate the landscape in the southern and central part of the block (Plate 2.5).

Sample transects surveyed in Block T were 5, 6, 7, 9, 11, 12, 14, 15, and 17 (Fig. 2.5); thus, the western 22% of the block (the area closest to the urban core) was not covered in the random sample. This may also have contributed to the lower site densities recorded in this block ($n = 79$) since, as noted earlier, proximity to the urban core appears to be a significant factor affecting site location and frequency. Despite lower densities than in Blocks O or S, a wide range of site types was nonetheless present in Block T. These include several major road segments, a two-kilometer long defensive wall (VMS-339), settlements, shrines, several reservoirs, and extensive terrace systems, among others. Thus, even this relatively dry and rugged area was intensively used during the Vijayanagara period.

Survey Block S

Located due south of the Vijayanagara urban core, Block S contains extremely high site density (Fig. 2.6). Block S is an area of low relief with few granitic outcrops. The only significant upland areas of the block are in its southwest corner. In general, the southern third of the block is higher than the remainder with

24 The Vijayanagara Metropolitan Survey

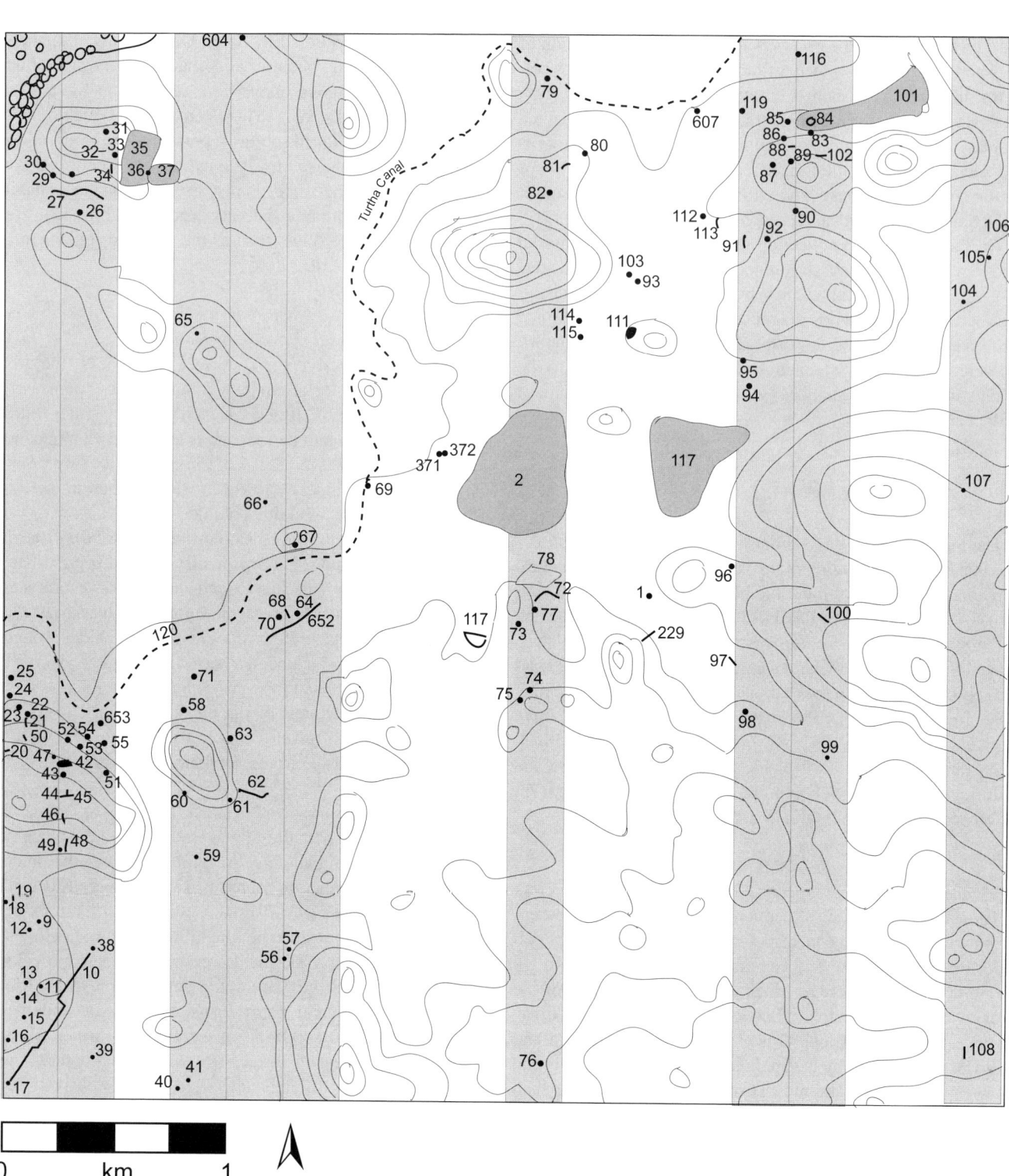

Figure 2.4. Block O: setting, sample transects, and sites.

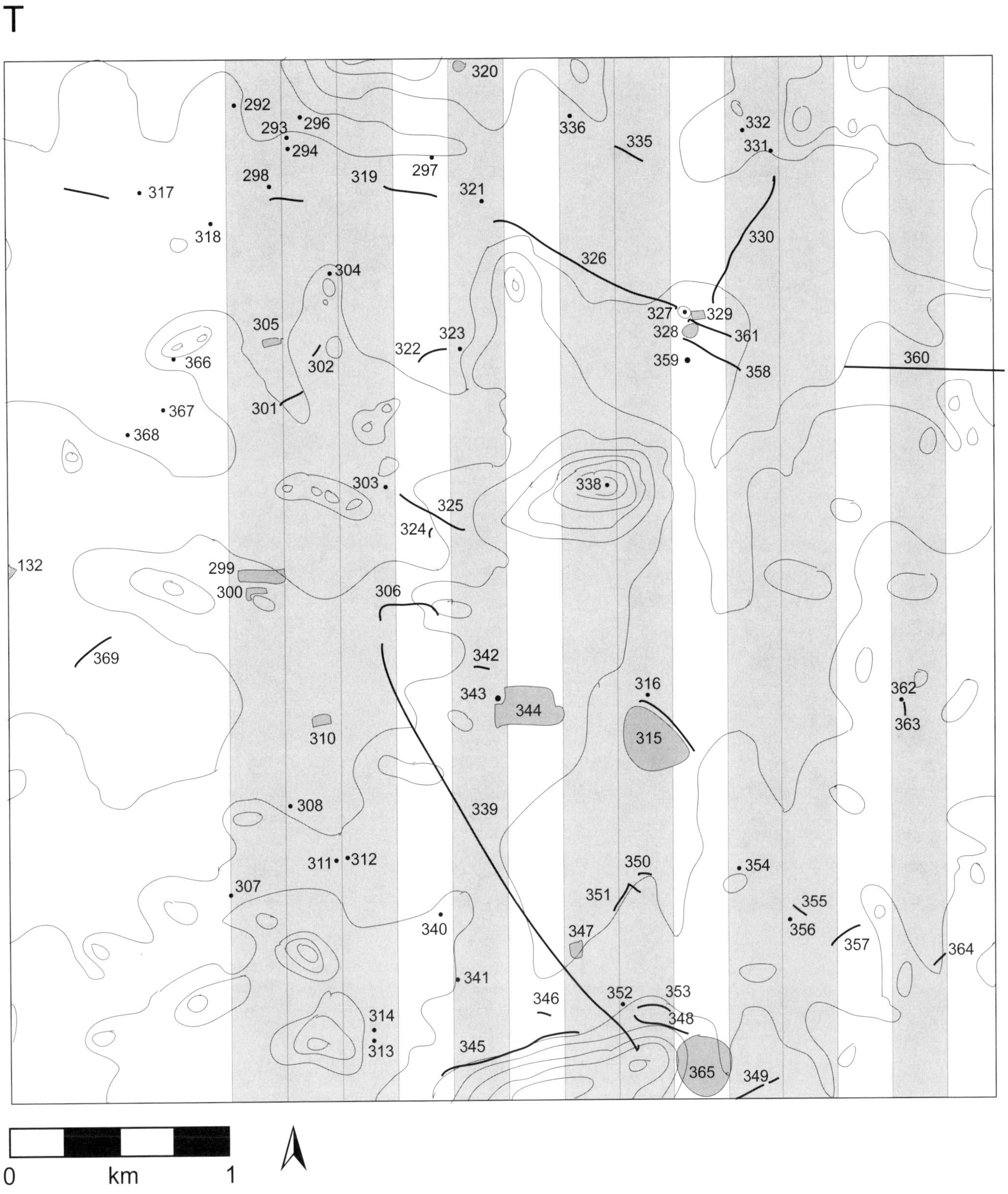

Figure 2.5. Block T: setting, sample transects, and sites.

26

S

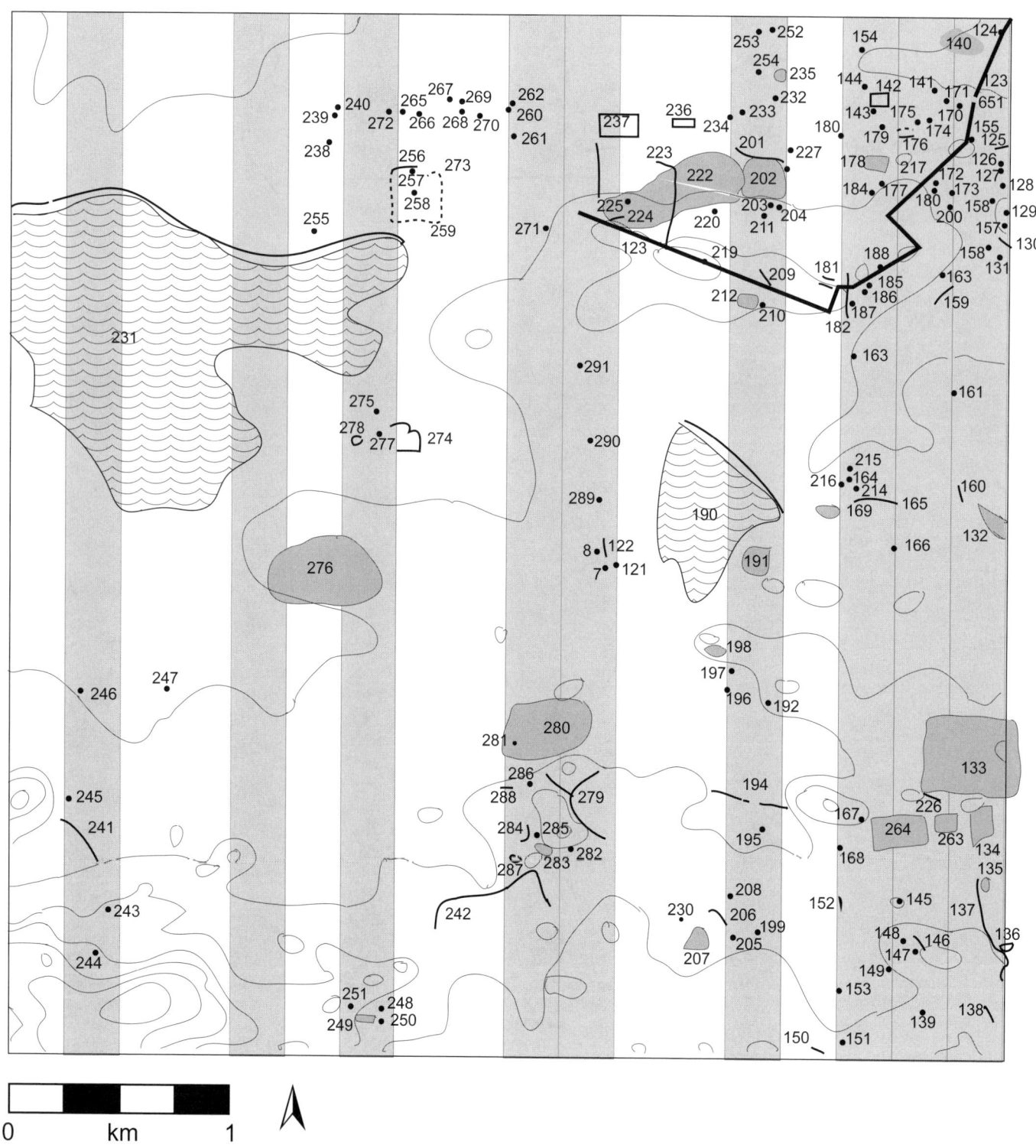

Figure 2.6. Block S: setting, sample transects, and sites.

Plate 2.3. Block O: overview.

Plate 2.4. View of Block T, looking north from southern boundary of VMS-339.

extensive evidence for dry farming activities. While topographic features play a major role in defining land use and site distribution in Block O, in Block S, two cultural features are the major determinant factors. The urban core is itself one of these factors, with site densities extremely high near the core and with a dramatic falloff as distance increases. Further, in the sixteenth century, an outer band of defensive city walls was constructed, enclosing the northern quarter of the block, and, as discussed below, site densities are especially high within these walls (Plate 2.6), which enclosed two Vijayanagara suburbs. This walled zone might, in fact, best be understood as lying within the sixteenth-century core of the city.

The second constructed feature that plays a role in determining Block S site distributions is the massive irrigation reservoir (VMS-231) that dominates the western half of the block. This reservoir, named after the nearby settlement of Kamalapuram, is a perennial canal and runoff-fed water source that appears to have been constructed quite early in the city's history (Morrison 1992:254). Its embankment extends nearly 2 km from east to west and the reservoir basin stretches about 1.5 km from north to south. The wet, low-lying areas to the north and south of the reservoir have extremely low site densities, and are even today fertile areas of wet agriculture (Plates 2.1, 2.7). A second large reservoir located in the eastern half of the block and associated with upslope (southern) terrace systems and downslope wet agriculture was another important culture feature affecting site distribution in Block S.

Sample transects in Block S were transects 2, 5, 7, 10, 11, 14, 16, 17, and 18, yielding relatively even coverage across the block. Most of the 181 sites identified were clustered in the northeast quadrant of the block, inside the outer city wall. It is in this area that site designation proved particularly complex, as this zone encompasses two Vijayanagara period settlements—Kamalapuram (which remains occupied today) and, to its east, *Varadadevi-Ammana Pattana* (or *Varada-jammana-Pattana*) (Filliozat and Filliozat 1988:13), a suburb founded in the mid-sixteenth century shortly before the abandonment of the capital. Areas encompassed by both of these communities yielded a dense distribution of archaeological remains including numerous shrines, temples, road segments, artifact scatters, wells, fortifications, and a range of other features. For analytical purposes, we chose to use individual site designations to distinguish among these features, rather than grouping the remains of either town under a single site number, each with dozens of separate feature numbers. Again, this was a practical decision, made to facilitate later analysis, and does not in any sense take away from the interrelated nature and associations of the archaeological remains in these areas.

Plate 2.5. Block T: overview to south.

Plate 2.6. Block S: outer city wall (VMS-123) and terrain in northeast quadrant.

Plate 2.7. Block S: irrigated rice fields.

Summary

The remainder of this publication contains a general gazetteer of recorded sites (Chapters 3-5) and more detailed discussions of patterns of artifact distributions in the three blocks (Chapter 6). We reserve discussion of the overall patterns of site distribution and land use for a later monograph, which will include information on the remainder of the area surveyed.

At present, it is sufficient to note that although contiguous, each of the three blocks reported here has somewhat different characteristics and posed different challenges to fieldwork. Block O, the first block surveyed, contained the most diverse range of topographic and environmental features, and movement across it was difficult. This was also the block where we did the most learning—to recognize various site types and standardize our documentation procedures. The limited nature of modern land use in parts of Block T, especially in its south, meant that road access was minimal and much effort was expended in hiking into survey locations, often two or more kilometers from the nearest drop point. In Block S, the sheer density of archaeological remains proved both exhilarating and overwhelming.

In this chapter, we have presented our survey methods as fully evolved. However, as with all multiyear research projects, our methods were refined each year, with modifications to field forms, increased standardization of procedures, and refinement of techniques or approaches that did not work. We have thus returned to some sites documented in the first season for purposes of additional documentation and, in some cases, have reinterpreted site functions and features based on later knowledge and experience. These interpretations are incorporated into the descriptions presented in the next three chapters of this volume.

PART II

DATA PRESENTATION

Introduction to Part II

Chapters 3-5 comprise the heart of this volume and contain detailed descriptions of all the sites recorded by the VMS in Blocks O (Chapter 3), T (Chapter 4), and S (Chapter 5), with illustrations of many of them. In standardizing site descriptions, we have sought to balance a desire for thoroughness with an interest in brevity. Nonetheless, we hope that the descriptions are relatively straightforward and transparent. We have retained a number of Indian architectural, religious, and art historical terms (primarily Sanskrit) (see Glossary). Artifact data from each site are briefly summarized in the site descriptions, but most of the discussion and illustrations of artifacts are presented in Chapter 6.

The site descriptions are organized in the following format:

Site: Site number, VMS-1–*n*
Block: Block O, S, or T (broad site location).
Transect: Refers to the 250 m wide survey transect(s) in which site was located; each block was divided into 18 transects, numbered 1-8 from west to east.
Primary Site Use: Sites were organized into 17 categories based on the major activities with which they were associated. Subsidiary functions were also noted, and included within the site descriptions and in our master site database. Categories include: agricultural, civic-ceremonial, hydraulic, industrial, defensive, mortuary, other, prehistoric (mortuary, rock art, settlement, unknown), recreation, religious, residential, transport, and unknown. In this report, we present the primary site use, followed by a descriptor that more narrowly describes the specific site characteristics, e.g., "residential: isolated structure" or "religious: Vaishnava temple complex."

Site Dimensions: Provides an approximate estimate of site extent.
Setting: Describes the geographic setting of the site.
GPS Location: Not available for most sites.
Present Land Use/Disturbances: Contains information on land use, surface visibility, and site disturbance at time of survey; many of the sites recorded in the late 1980s and early 1990s have undergone significant disturbance (indeed destruction) since that time, so this information primarily provides information on the limitations on our ability to describe the sites at the time, and not their current status.
Site Description: Prose description of site characteristics and interpretation.
Artifacts: Summary information on collection strategies and artifacts recovered.
Temporal Affiliation: Probable date or range of dates for the site.
References: Other published information on the site.
Illustrations: Figures and plates in the present volume.

– 3 –
Block O: Site Summaries

SITE: VMS-1   Block: O   Transect: Unknown
Primary Site Use: Industrial: lime processing site.
Site Dimensions: 45 × 20 m
Setting: Low-lying area.
Present Land Use/Disturbances: Located near modern footpath amid agricultural fields.
Site Description: Lime processing site. Three large contiguous mounded accumulations of calcium carbonate (*kankar*) in a north-south alignment. Naturally forming *kankar* deposits are processed through firing for its lime content, which is used (now and in the Vijayanagara period) for concrete and plaster. Associated with these accumulations are the remains of two furnaces: circular fired clay-lined rings (diameters 1.79 and 2.50 m) and associated piles of stone that may be the remains of furnace walls. Similar kilns remain in use in the area, making the dating of VMS-1 problematic.
Artifacts: Artifact density was low in and around the site; only three nondiagnostic sherds were collected in a judgment unit placed in a nearby plowed field.
Temporal Affiliation: Unknown.
References: Morrison 1991; Morrison 1995:61, 79.
Illustrations: Figure 3.1.

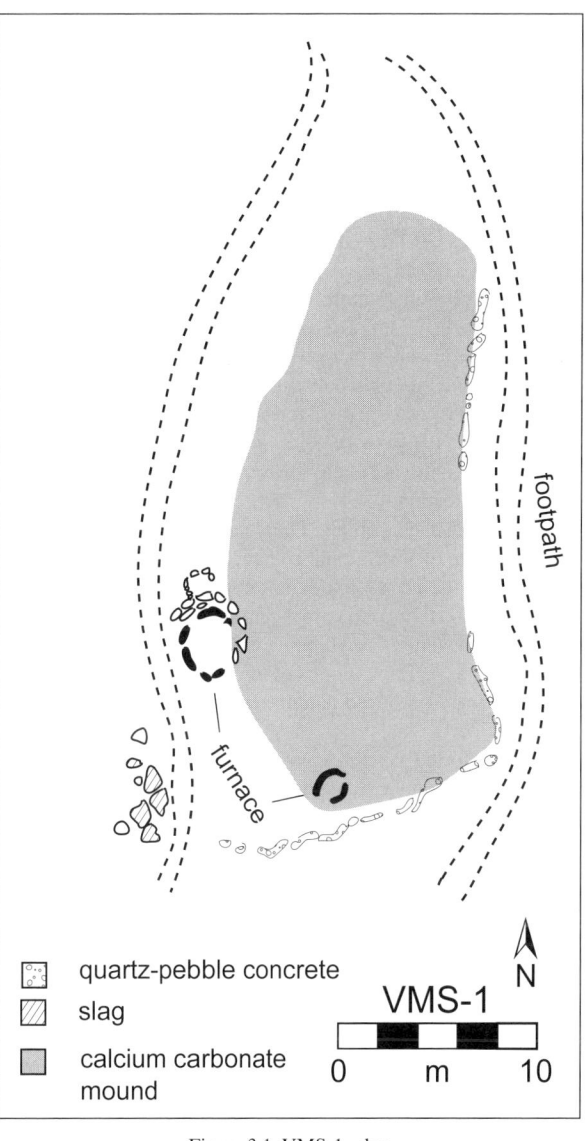

Figure 3.1. VMS-1, plan.

SITE: VMS-2 Block: O Transect: 9/10

Primary Site Use: Residential: settlement.

Site Dimensions: Preserved core is c. 100 × 390 m; estimated original site size c. 750 × 500 m.

Setting: Low-lying area on the southern edge of contemporary settlement of Venkatapuram.

Present Land Use/Disturbances: The site is heavily disturbed and partly buried under Venkatapuram. Roads cross the site from the northwest to southeast, as do several footpaths. The Tungabhadra Right Bank Canal borders the site to the south and canal construction has caused considerable disturbance. Extensive recent construction and pitting on the north edge of the site, including construction of rice paddies. The site is being used as both a quarry and dump.

Site Description: Large Vijayanagara period settlement. The site has been badly disturbed, but several features are visible. The eastern third consists of a number of rubble mounds in which partial plans of structures can be discerned, along with some wall fragments. The central area is badly disturbed, although some wall fragments and architectural elements are visible. The western area of the site is the best preserved, with many large and substantial walls visible along with a well and shrine. Several features at the site (see below) are diagnostic of the Vijayanagara period, and this appears to have been a large Vijayanagara period settlement (perhaps old Venkatapur?). The preserved site area is approximately 4 ha; however, its maximal estimated area may have been as large as 35 ha or more.

Distinctive identifiable elements have been given feature designations. These are described below and are indicated on the site plan (Fig. 3.2).

Feature 1: Large pit and associated structure (not on site plan). This pit, c. 8.5 m across, is located north of the main settlement area and is associated with a rectangular structure, c. 3 × 3.75 m, on its east edge. The sides of the pit were reinforced with walls constructed of unmodified irregularly shaped cobbles. The four-walled structure is constructed of granite blocks and slabs, with up to six courses preserved. Blocks comprising the walls are roughly dressed; no mortar or chinking is evident. The structure may postdate the depression. Two displaced rectangular slabs or columns (1 × 0.5 × 0.25 m) are located c. 3 m from the structure. This depression was likely a well, though disturbance precludes definitive identification.

Feature 2: Vaishnava temple. This south-facing temple is located on the southern edge of VMS-2 and contains two displaced elephant balustrades (Plate 3.1). The temple is now considerably below the modern ground surface and is entered via a recent stairway. The two-room structure consists of a walled 4 × 3 column antechamber and a 2 × 2 column sanctuary (Fig. 3.3). The columns of the antechamber are typical late-Vijayanagara mass-produced columns and are heavily plastered. They are square with octagonal insets. Vaishnava door guardians (*dvarapala*) flank the entry to the sanctuary and an image of Lakshmi is sculpted over the lintel. Within the sanctuary, a large Anjaneya Hanuman image is currently in worship. This was most likely not the original image in the shrine, but is also of the Vijayanagara period. A small column and several naga stones are present in front of the structure.

Feature 3: Shrine. This 2 × 2 column south-facing shrine is located in a modern enclosure on the northwest edge of the mapped area. The columns are square with inset octagons and date to the Vijayanagara period. However, the walls spanning the columns are of recent construction. Inside the sanctuary, a small image of Hanuman is in worship. A Nandi image faces the sanctuary from the paved courtyard in front of the shrine, near a large lamp column that seems out of place given the small scale of the structure. Indeed, the presence of the Shaivite Nandi, the bull vehicle of Shiva, in association with the Vaishnava Hanuman suggests that one or both images are not original to the structure. Circa 20 m to the west of the structure is a carved image base with a lingam set in it.

Feature 4: Two roughly dressed inscribed stone columns topped by sculpted images of Nandi (Plate 3.2). Both the inscriptions and columns date within the past 100 years and record temple donations made by residents of Venkatapuram.

Feature 5: Step well. This poorly-preserved well is located on the northwest edge of the mapped area. Many of the upper stone courses have been removed and the feature is surrounded by thick vegetation. The keyhole-shape well has a square basin that is accessible from a single flight of stairs on its north. Dimensions are c. 10 m east-west × 22 m north-south. The well was constructed of tightly fitted, dressed rectangular blocks, with no chinking. A fragment of a column lies nearby. There are a large number of wall fragments to the east and west of the well, many quite substantial. The well appears to have been located in a dense zone of habitation and construction.

Feature 6: Small rectangular inscribed block (c. 0.45 × 0.6 × 0.15 m) with an image of a lingam on a pedestal flanked by the sun and moon. The stone is incorporated into a modern shrine, and its date is unknown.

Feature 7: Rubble mound. This low mound on the southeast side of VMS-2 is all that remains of a very substantial structure that conforms in plan to elite residences ("palaces") within the Vijayanagara urban core. It faces east and has a U-shaped plan, with two to three stepped levels. Dimensions are c. 30 m east-west × 12.6 m north-south. The mound rises some 2 m above the surrounding ground surface. No finished architectural elements are visible, though some wall faces can be discerned. There are high densities of ceramics and basalt artifacts around the structure. Several smaller structures surround the mound, and may have been associated with it.

Artifacts: The artifact scatter is localized and highly variable in density. Along with ceramics there are a number of basalt pegs, spheres, and debris from basalt working. Basalt pegs are used to support structures built on to sheet rock; however, there is no sheet rock in the area of the site where the basalt working is evident, so it may be that basalt pegs were being manufactured for use elsewhere, either within VMS-2 or at other sites. Small quantities of iron slag were found, and a piece of worked glass. A small blue-on-white porcelain sherd was observed on the surface but not collected.

Eight 5 × 5 m judgment units were surface collected. Ceramic water pipe fragments recovered in unit 1 indicate the presence of a substantial roofed structure.

Unit 1: 1800 g ceramics; wares: 240 black plain ware, 18 red plain ware, 6 black burnished ware, 1 red burnished ware, 9 black decorated, 5 coarse ware. Diagnostics: 1 bowl, 39 jars, 11 water pipes. Other artifacts: 1 piece worked glass core, 1 iron fragment.

Unit 2: 2200 g ceramics; wares: 176 black plain ware, 11 red plain ware, 2 black burnished ware, 15 black decorated, 3 coarse ware. Diagnostics: 2 lamps, 2 bowls, 34 jars.

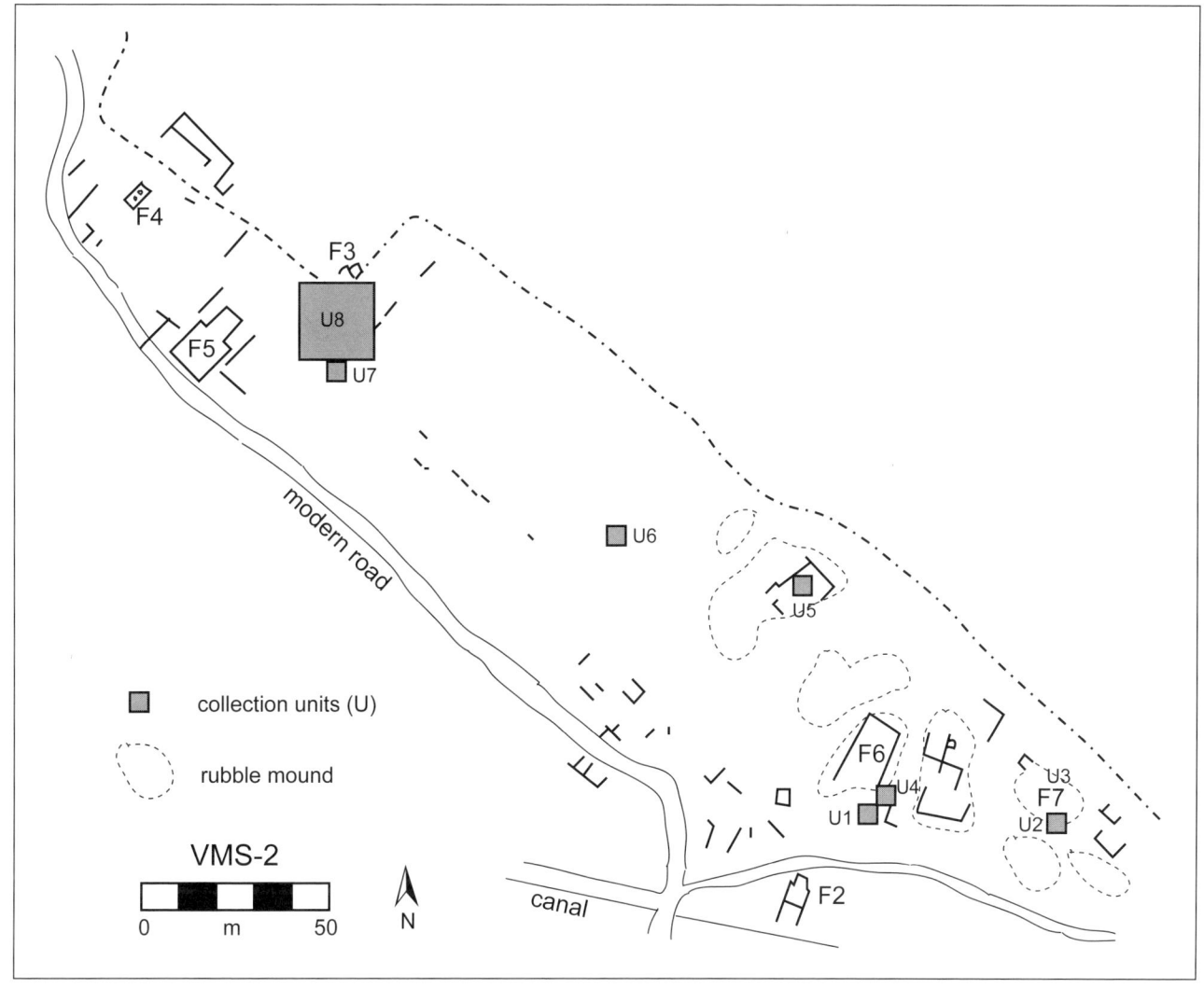

Figure 3.2. VMS-2, plan.

Unit 3: Diagnostic collections, rims and other diagnostics. Also 3 granite pegs, 1 piece slag, 1 piece worked glass.

Unit 4: 1800 g ceramics; wares: 141 black plain ware, 4 red plain ware, 1 black burnished ware, 4 black decorated, 6 coarse ware. Diagnostics: 1 lamp, 4 bowls, 28 jars.

Unit 5: 850 g ceramics; wares: 56 black plain ware, 7 red plain ware, 1 black decorated, 3 coarse ware. Diagnostics: 7 jars, 2 water pipes. Lithics: quartzite bipolar flaking debris (1).

Unit 6: 300 g ceramics; wares: 49 black plain ware, 1 coarse ware. Diagnostics: 2 jars.

Unit 7: 1550 g ceramics; wares: 53 black plain ware, 5 black decorated. Diagnostics: 3 water pipes. Lithics: 1 quartzite flake.

Unit 8: Diagnostics only; 1 quartzite core.

Other Surface Collection: Quartzite tool.

Temporal Affiliation: Vijayanagara, with later modifications.

References: Lycett 1991; Morrison 1991; Morrison 1995:63-69, 85, 89, 99; Morrison and Sinopoli 2006:427; Sinopoli and Morrison 1991:66-68; Sinopoli 1997:481; Sinopoli 2003:235-36.

Illustrations: Figures 3.2, 3.3; Plates 3.1, 3.2.

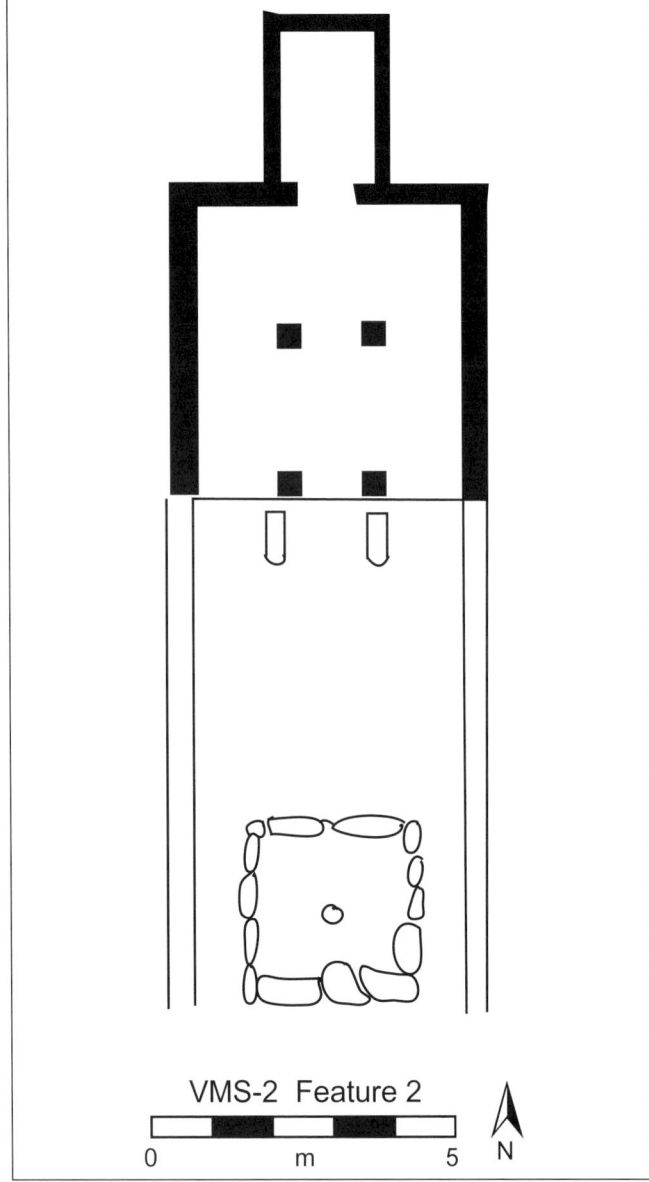

Figure 3.3. VMS-2, Feature 2.

Plate 3.1. VMS-2, Feature 2, elephant balustrade.

Plate 3.2. VMS-2, Feature 4, inscribed stone column.

SITE: VMS-9   Block: O   Transect: 1
 Primary Site Use: Residential: structure.
 Site Dimensions: 18 × 8 m
 Setting: Gentle slope on edge of area of sheet rock and small outcropping boulders.
 Present Land Use/Disturbances: Near Tungabhadra Right Bank Canal. Located in a modern dump area. Structure walls are partly disturbed.
 Site Description: Rectangular structure. This small structure consists of a north-south wall originating at the edge of sheet rock in the south and extending north for c. 18 m. The wall is constructed of small-medium unmodified stones and incorporates some larger outcropping boulders at its southern end. It is double faced in parts and 1.15 m wide. The north edge of the structure is defined by an east-west wall, 7 m long and only 0.65 m wide. A fragment of a corner and second north-south wall are preserved. A possible central wall divided the structure into two rooms, though this is poorly preserved. Traces of plaster are evident.
 Artifacts: Some recent artifacts visible on surface, light artifact scatter. 100% collection. 450 g of ceramics; wares: 53 black plain ware, 6 red plain ware. Diagnostics: 7 jars, 1 tile; modern glass, plastic tile.
 Temporal Affiliation: Unknown (possibly post-Vijayanagara).
 Illustrations: Figure 3.4.

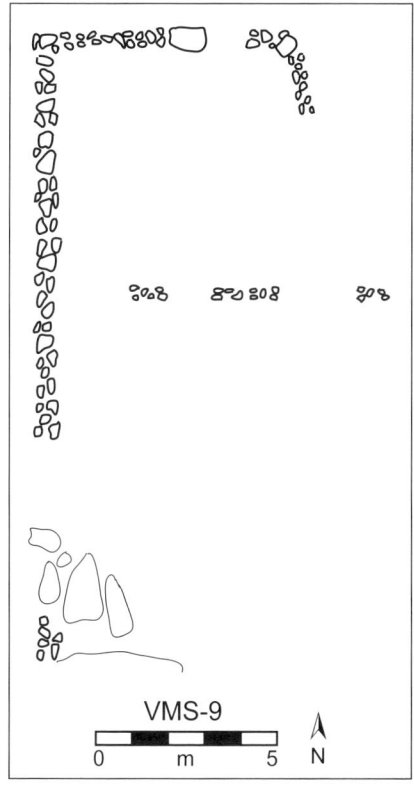

(*Left*) Figure 3.4. VMS-9, plan.
(*Above*) Plate 3.3. VMS-10, site overview showing bastion and wall.
(*Right*) Figure 3.5. VMS-10, schematic plan.

SITE: VMS-10   Block: O, S   Transect: 1-3
  Primary Site Use: Defensive: fortification wall.
  Site Dimensions: 300+ × 5-10 m
  Setting: Located in a low-lying area. The area to the east of the wall is dominated by irrigated fields; the terrain to the west is generally somewhat higher than that to the east and includes a low outcrop hill and areas of sheet rock.
  Present Land Use/Disturbances: Much of the area surrounding this site is presently under canal irrigation. Modern quarrying and roads have cut through the wall at various points.
  Site Description: Fortification wall and bastions. This is a portion of the eastern outer fortification wall of Vijayanagara; this wall extends south into Block S, where it has been designated as VMS-123. In Block O, the wall was traced for approximately 300 m, extending from the southwest corner of the block toward the northeast. It terminates abruptly in the north where portions have likely been destroyed; we expect that it originally extended further to the north and formed an outer boundary of the city core. VMS-25 on the north edge of transect 1 in Block O may be part of the northern extension of this fortification. At the south end of VMS-10 is a gate, documented separately as VMS-17.
  The wall is well preserved, with seven to eleven horizontal stone courses visible in wall and bastions. It is constructed of undressed square and rectangular medium to large trapezoidal blocks, with quarry marks sometimes visible. Some sections are very well constructed, with tightly fitted blocks and little chinking; others are more irregular with irregular coursing and abundant chinking. It is not clear if these represent separate periods of construction or if they result from different workgroups or repairs. Traces of plaster were observed in one limited area of the wall.
  Ten square bastions, c. 12 × 10 m in dimension, and filled with earth and rubble, project out (eastward) from the wall at irregular intervals. In general, bastion construction is superior to wall construction; courses are more regular, and blocks are interlocking and more neatly dressed. Typically, the bastions abut the wall and are not bonded to it. This may suggest discrete building stages, with the wall constructed first and bastions added later.
  Artifacts: No collections made.
  Temporal Affiliation: Vijayanagara period, possibly sixteenth century.
  References: Morrison 1994:63-64, 83, 99; Sinopoli and Morrison 1991:67.
  Illustrations: Figure 3.5; Plate 3.3.

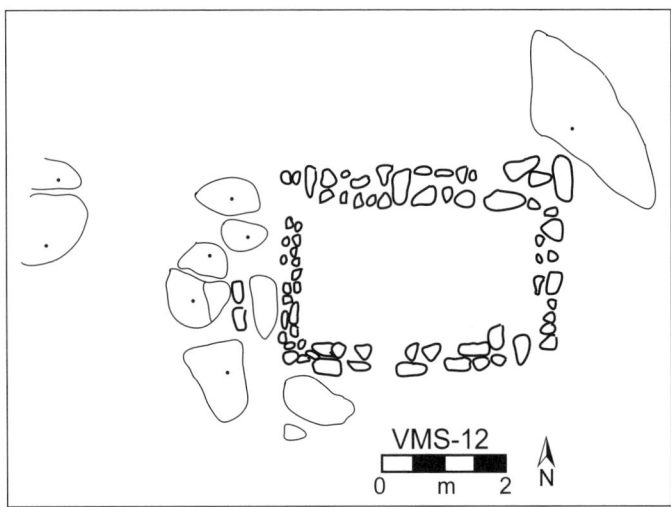

Figure 3.6. VMS-12, plan.

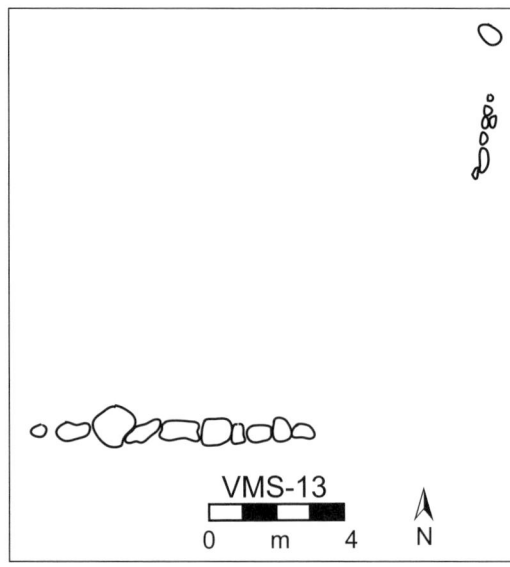

Figure 3.7. VMS-13, plan.

SITE: VMS-11   Block: O   Transect: 1
  Primary Site Use: Water storage: cistern.
  Site Dimensions: 3.23 × 2.14 m
  Setting: Located on an extensive area of exposed sheet rock, sloping terrain.
  Present Land Use/Disturbances: Recent quarrying in area.
  Site Description: Small water storage facility. This is an oval depression carved into sheet rock, 3.23 × 2.14 m. The depression is partly filled with soil, and is at least 0.42 m deep. While small depressions form naturally on softer areas of exposed sheet rock, the scale and smooth vertical walls of this feature suggest that it was modified by humans to form a water storage feature.
  Artifacts: 100% collection; no artifacts recovered.
  Temporal Affiliation: Unknown, rock is heavily weathered and water stained, not of recent date.
  References: Morrison 1995:66-67; Morrison and Sinopoli 1992:346.

SITE: VMS-12   Block: O   Transect: 1
  Primary Site Use: Residential: structure.
  Site Dimensions: 9 × 4.5 m
  Setting: On gentle slope amid outcrops. The area contains small outcropping boulders, more extensive sheet rock areas, and small patches of coarse sandy soil.
  Present Land Use/Disturbances: Some recent construction and electric power lines nearby. Paved road is located c. 12 m to the south of structure.
  Site Description: Structure and associated features. This small rectangular structure, 4 × 2.5 m in dimension, is constructed of unmodified small-medium stones. Its walls are double faced with earth infill. They range in width from c. 0.45 to 0.85 m, and may have been foundation walls for a structure of impermanent materials. To the west and northwest of the structure, seven small holes (0.03-0.05 m in diameter) have been pecked into sheet rock boulders, perhaps to set in posts.
  Artifacts: 100% collection. No ceramics, one cylindrical stone object—function unknown.
  Temporal Affiliation: Unknown.
  Illustrations: Figure 3.6.

SITE: VMS-13   Block: O   Transect: 1
  Primary Site Use: Residential: L-shaped structure.
  Site Dimensions: 15 × 13 m
  Setting: On gentle slope among thorny scrub and grasses.
  Present Land Use/Disturbances: Modern glass and metal debris, trash pit and modern road to west.
  Site Description: Wall alignments. This is a probable structure consisting of two partially preserved walls with an L-shaped plan. The east-west wall consists of a single course of unmodified large stones, 9 m long × c. 0.50 m wide. The second wall, not connected to the first, is located c. 5 m to the north of the east end of the first wall. It is oriented roughly north-south, and is preserved to a length of 6 m. It is constructed of smaller stones and rubble. A large boulder with Vijayanagara period quarry marks is located c. 7 m north of the east-west wall.
  Artifacts: Modern glass, tile, metal clustered mostly along east wall. 100% collection. 150 g ceramics; wares: 41 black plain ware, 6 red plain ware. Diagnostics: 2 jars, 1 water pipe. Modern glass, porcelain, tile.
  Temporal Affiliation: Unknown, probably recent.
  References: Morrison 1995:66-67.
  Illustrations: Figure 3.7.

SITE: VMS-14   Block: O   Transect: 1
  Primary Site Use: Residential: structure.
  Site Dimensions: 18 × 6 m
  Setting: Area of gentle slope surrounded by sheet rock and outcrops and patches of coarse sandy soil.
  Present Land Use/Disturbances: Recent quarrying on surrounding outcrops.
  Site Description: Single-room structure. VMS-14 consists of two walls of an east-west oriented structure, c. 3 × 2 m in dimension. Only the north and east walls are present; it is not clear whether they were foundation walls for a structure constructed of less permanent materials (e.g., a tent footing) or if additional walls existed but are no longer preserved. The extant walls consist of a single course of unmodified small-medium stones (0.3-0.4 m in dimension). Two bedrock mortars are found nearby—c. 3 m south of the east wall, and 15 m east of the chamber.

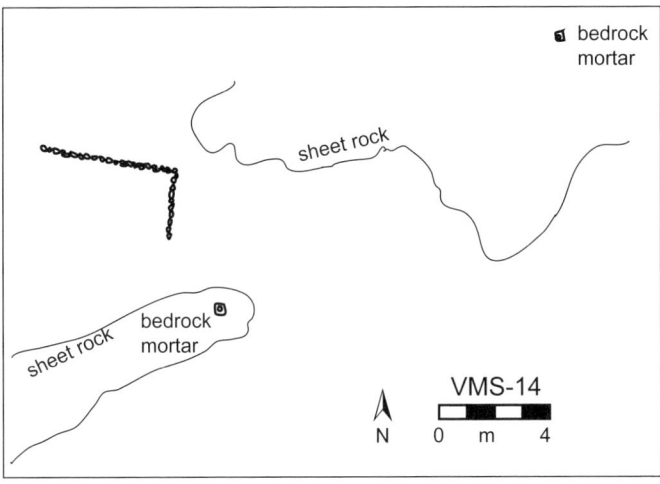

Figure 3.8. VMS-14, plan.

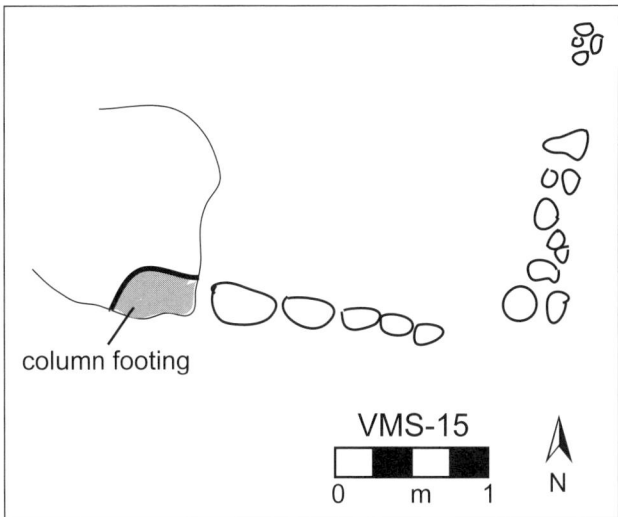

Figure 3.9. VMS-15, plan.

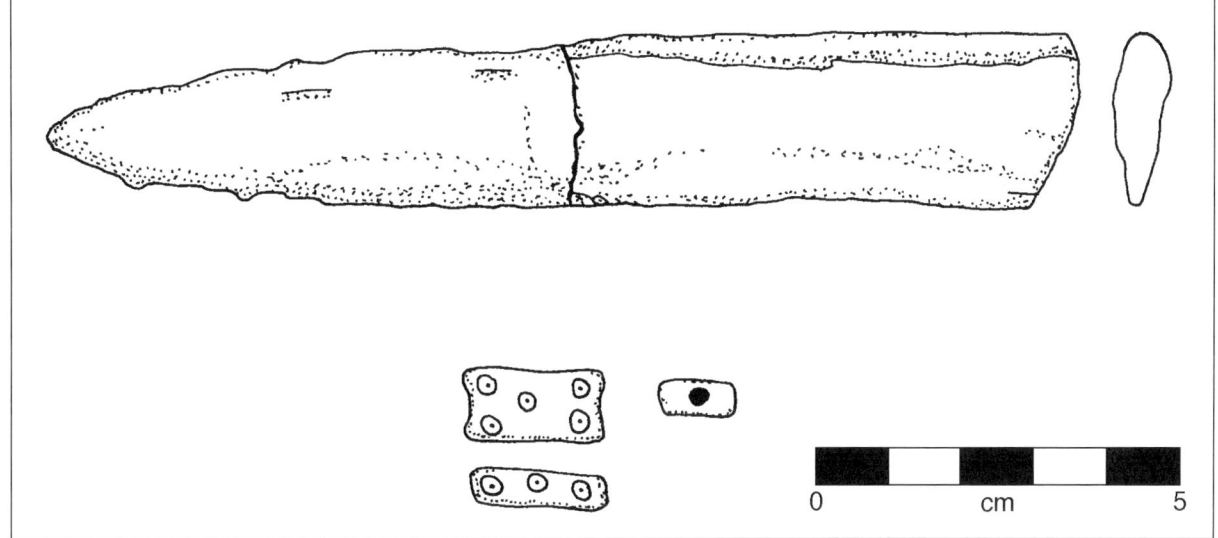

Figure 3.10. VMS-15, artifacts: iron knife blade and inscribed steatite bead.

Artifacts: Light ceramic scatter, no diagnostics, one soapstone "pencil"; rubber fragments. 100% collection. 50 g ceramics; wares: 20 black plain ware, 3 red plain ware.

Temporal Affiliation: Unknown (pencil, which is characteristic of the Vijayanagara period, suggests that at least some of the remains are pre-modern).

References: Morrison 1995:67.

Illustrations: Figure 3.8.

SITE: VMS-15   Block: O   Transect: 1
  Primary Site Use: Residential: structure.
  Site Dimensions: 2 × 2.7 m
  Setting: On extensive area of sheet rock, with shallow patches of coarse red sandy soil.
  Present Land Use/Disturbances: Modern quarrying to east of site.
  Site Description: L-shaped structure. This small structure has two visible walls. Its east edge is a 2 m long north-south oriented low rubble wall. From the south end of this wall, a 2.7 m long east-west oriented wall extends to the sheet rock on the west. A small L-shaped niche is cut into the sheet rock at the end of this wall and defines the southwest corner of the structure. Two bedrock mortars are located on sheet rock west of the structure, one at a distance of 8 m and one at a distance of 21 m.

  Artifacts: Ceramics, an inscribed steatite bead, fragments of glass bangles, iron knife blade. 100% collection. 450 g ceramics (found in crevices of sheet rock); wares: 111 black plain ware, 6 red plain ware. Diagnostics: 7 jars.

  Temporal Affiliation: Ceramics and other artifacts appear consistent with Vijayanagara period.

  References: Morrison 1995:67.

  Illustrations: Figures 3.9, 3.10.

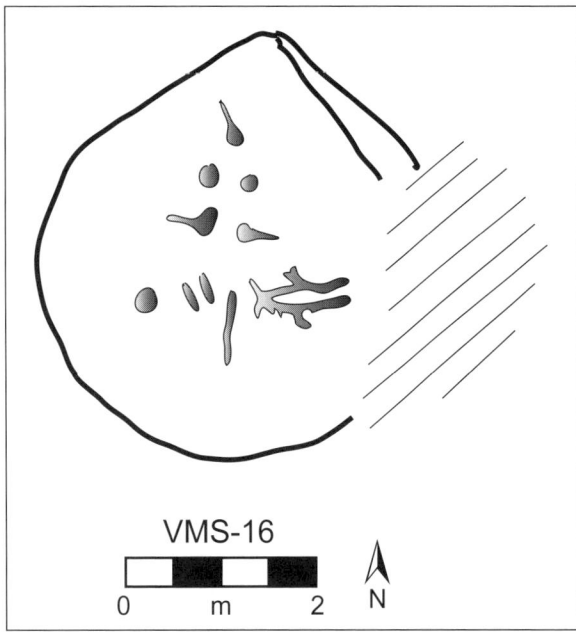

Figure 3.11. VMS-16, plan.

Plate 3.4. VMS-18, images carved on shelter floor. Lingam, devotee, and horse.

SITE: VMS-16   Block: O   Transect: 1
   Primary Site Use: Unknown: pits, pecked stone impressions.
   Site Dimensions: 51 × 26 m
   Setting: Flat area with some outcropping sheet rock and boulders.
   Present Land Use/Disturbances: Some modern artifacts on surface, extensive pitting in area.
   Site Description: Disturbed pitted area. This site consists of a large pit, 51 m east-west × 26 m north-south, containing considerable ceramic refuse (Vijayanagara period?). The pit is located in an extensive disturbed area with pitting of unknown date, likely the result of recent building activities and quarrying. The large pit is nearly 2 m deep in areas, and some stratigraphy is visible including ceramic lenses. A few wall fragments are also visible. To the south of the site, on sheet rock beneath overhang, is an area, c. 3 m in diameter, on which several images or impressions have been inscribed or pecked. These images could not be identified. The pits appear to expose an extensive area of abandoned settlement; the ceramics are consistent with the Vijayanagara period.
   Artifacts: Ceramics are abundant throughout the pitted area. Most are not recent and correspond to forms from the Vijayanagara period. Fragments of modern glass and porcelain are also present.
   Four 2 × 2 m units were collected. These were spaced at 10 m intervals along the east-west axis of the site.
   Unit 1: 100 g ceramics; wares: 44 black plain ware, 5 red plain ware. Diagnostics: 2 jars, 1 piece glass.
   Unit 2: 200 g ceramics; wares: 61 black plain ware, 3 red plain ware, 4 red burnished ware, 1 black decorated. Diagnostics: 3 jars.
   Unit 3: 650 g ceramics; wares: 46 black plain ware, 1 red plain ware, 1 coarse ware. Diagnostics: 7 jars.
   Unit 4: 100 g ceramics; wares: 19 black plain ware, 2 red plain ware. Diagnostics: 2 jars.
   Temporal Affiliation: Ceramics suggest Vijayanagara date, with later disturbance. Later pit appears to cut into Vijayanagara period refuse or settlement deposits.
   References: Morrison 1995:67.
   Illustrations: Figure 3.11.

SITE: VMS-17   Block: O   Transect: 1
   Primary Site Use: Transport: gate.
   Site Dimensions: 10 × 9 m
   Setting: Flat low-lying area, irrigated fields to east of gate.
   Present Land Use/Disturbances: Modern shrine within passage, covered drainage channel passes through the gate. Considerable rubble fall and soil deposition around the site and the southern portion of the gate has largely collapsed. Area is overgrown with thick vegetation.
   Site Description: Gate. This well-constructed gate consists of two rectilinear platforms that flank a passageway through wall VMS-10, a segment of the eastern outer fortification wall of the Vijayanagara urban core. The gate does not seem to be incorporated into the fabric of the fortification wall, but instead abuts it. The elevated north platform is 3 × 2 columns; the south platform is smaller, only 2 × 2 columns. The platforms were once roofed, as evident by lintels. No door lintel or jams are evident in the passage between platforms. A covered drainage channel constructed of quarried slabs passes through the gate; it is probably a recent addition, perhaps using Vijayanagara period slabs.
   Artifacts: Light ceramic scatter; not collected.
   Temporal Affiliation: Vijayanagara.
   References: Morrison 1995:79, 84.

SITE: VMS-18   Block: O   Transect: 1
   Primary Site Use: Residential: rock shelter, with Shaivite carvings on surface.
   Site Dimensions: 0.9 × 0.7 m
   Setting: Rock shelter in outcrops and sheet rock area.
   Present Land Use/Disturbances: Soil accumulation on floor of rock shelter; some quarrying in area.
   Site Description: Rock shelter. This small shelter is located under overhanging boulders. Several small images are carved on the shelter floor, and extend over an area of 0.9 × 0.7 m. The images include a lingam inside a square depression with a drain leading out to the east. To the southeast of the lingam, and enclosed within the semicircular drain cut, are images of a standing horse at whose feet is a prone female devotee. The horse is crudely carved, with its proportions distorted to fit the available space. The devotee has her right hand raised above her head. Traces of red pigment suggest recent worship.
   Artifacts: 100% collection. <50 g ceramics; wares: 4 black plain ware. Diagnostics: 1 bowl.
   Temporal Affiliation: The style of carving is consistent with Vijayanagara period.
   Illustrations: Plate 3.4.

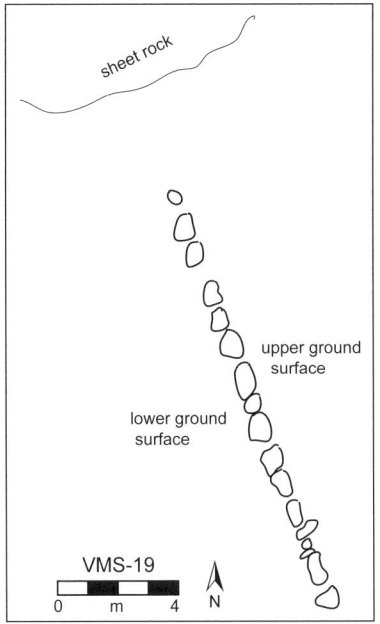

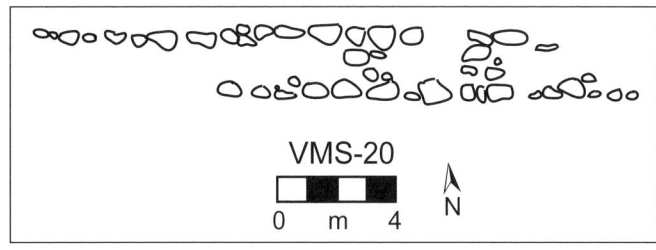

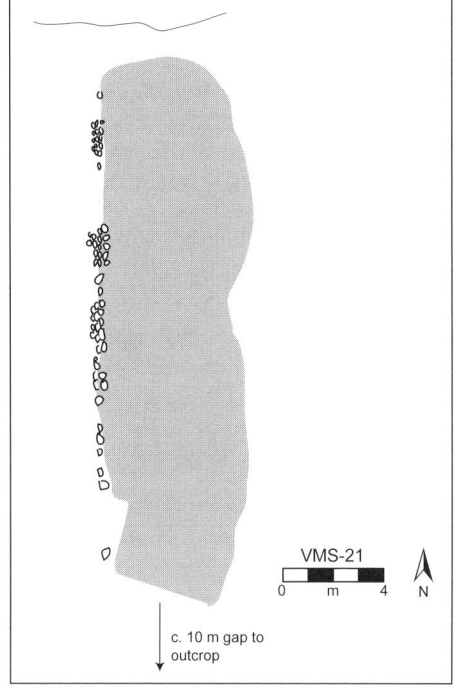

(*Left*) Figure 3.12. VMS-19, plan.

(*Upper Right*) Figure 3.13. VMS-20, plan.

(*Lower Right*) Figure 3.14. VMS-21, plan.

SITE: VMS-19   Block: O   Transect: 1
  Primary Site Use: Defensive: wall.
  Site Dimensions: 15 × 0.7 m × 0.8 m high
  Setting: Low-lying area near sheet rock slopes.
  Present Land Use/Disturbances: Soil accumulation around site probably results from decay of earthen wall above preserved foundation.
  Site Description: Wall. This single-faced north-south wall is constructed of one to two courses of large unmodified stones. The wall abuts sheet rock in the north. The extant wall appears to have been a foundation for a more substantial earthen wall as there is considerable soil accumulation around it. The wall is located in a low-lying area east of the stone fortification wall VMS-10, which it parallels. It is probable that it was associated with VMS-10 and had a defensive purpose.
  Artifacts: None.
  Temporal Affiliation: Vijayanagara?
  References: Morrison 1995:64, 80.
  Illustrations: Figure 3.12.

SITE: VMS-20   Block: N, O   Transect: 1
  Primary Site Use: Defensive: wall.
  Site Dimensions: 20 × 2.5 m
  Setting: On outcrop at break in slope of high granitic ridge, small pockets of soil accumulation.
  Present Land Use/Disturbances: Extensive modern stone quarrying in area, quarry road runs nearby.
  Site Description: 2.5 m wide wall. This 20 m long wall is constructed of one course of large unmodified stones. It is double faced with earth and rubble infill and is oriented approximately east-west. The preserved wall may have been the foundation course for an earthen wall. The wall is located in an area where the high ridge of outcrop changes from a steep to more gentle slope. It would have constrained passage across this relatively flat area of outcrop and is interpreted as having a defensive purpose.
  Artifacts: 100% collection; no artifacts recovered.
  Temporal Affiliation: Vijayanagara.
  References: Morrison 1995:64.
  Illustrations: Figure 3.13.

SITE: VMS-21   Block: O   Transect: 1
  Primary Site Use: Agricultural: reservoir embankment.
  Site Dimensions: 29 × 10 m
  Setting: Located in a flat area in a small valley (1-2 ha in area) enclosed by granitic ridges on the north, south, and east. The ground surface to the east of embankment roughly 2 m above surface levels to its west.
  Present Land Use/Disturbances: A recent road may have destroyed the north edge of the embankment, recent cuts into embankment wall.
  Site Description: Reservoir embankment. The west face of this c. 2-2.4 m high embankment is constructed of three to four stepped courses of small-medium unmodified stones. The coursing is irregular. The embankment's eastern earthen face is c. 10 m wide. No sluice gate is present, but a crude stone-lined channel on the south edge of the embankment provided an outlet for the release of water impounded by the reservoir. Vegetation is more lush to the west of embankment, suggesting that it continues to function to retain moisture.
  Artifacts: Sparse sherd scatter; 100% collection on east side of embankment. 200 g ceramics; wares: 46 black plain ware, 7 red plain ware, 1 red burnished. Diagnostics: 1 jar. Lithics: 1 green quartzite lithic tool.
  Temporal Affiliation: Vijayanagara (associated with VMS-22, Vijayanagara sculpture).
  References: Lycett 1991; Morrison 1995:85, 89, 102; Sinopoli 1991:70, 79.
  Illustrations: Figure 3.14.

SITE: VMS-22   Block: O   Transect: 1
  Primary Site Use: Religious: Shaivite shrine (rock-cut Bhairava image).
  Site Dimensions: 1.5 × 1.5 m
  Setting: Carved on south face of outcrop boulder, located due north and in alignment with VMS-21 on edge of small valley.
  Present Land Use/Disturbances: Extensive modern quarrying in region; quarrying road runs in front of site. White paint frames the image, which has been outlined with red pigment.
  Site Description: Rock-cut sculpture. This image of the Shaivite deity Bhairava is carved in the Vijayanagara style on the south face of an outcropping boulder on the south edge of an outcrop hill. No structure or displaced architectural elements are evident. The image is associated with embankment VMS-21. It is finely sculpted, depicting Bhairava in striding posture. He holds a trident in his upper right arm, a skull in his lower right arm, and a drum in the upper left; the lower left arm is folded over the chest. A dog appears at his right foot below the skull, and a naga is near the left foot.
  Artifacts: 100% collection; no artifacts recovered.
  Temporal Affiliation: Vijayanagara.

SITE: VMS-23   Block: O   Transect: 1
  Primary Site Use: Water storage: rock-cut cistern.
  Site Dimensions: 1.6 × 1.0 m
  Setting: Located on sheet rock.
  Present Land Use/Disturbances: Modern quarrying on sheet rock with quarry road to south.
  Site Description: Cistern. This is a small natural depression in sheet rock that appears to have been enlarged to form a 0.8 m deep (at least) depression with straight walls. Two rock-cut mortars in nearby outcrop (c. 8 m to the northwest × 25 m to the west) provide evidence of food processing activities. These rocky outcrop areas may have served as foci of short-term habitation.
  Artifacts: 100% collection; no artifacts recovered.
  Temporal Affiliation: Unknown.

SITE: VMS-24   Block: O   Transect: 2
  Primary Site Use: Residential: artifact scatter and associated features.
  Site Dimensions: 40 × 18 m
  Setting: Flat area on outcrop with soil accumulation, surrounded by large outcropping boulders.
  Present Land Use/Disturbances: Extensive modern quarrying throughout area.
  Site Description: Artifact scatter, wall, and mortar. Features of this site include a segment of rubble wall and a bedrock mortar. A second probable wall links two large boulders on the north side of the site. North of this is sherd scatter and some small recently excavated pits; ceramic lenses in the profiles provide evidence for past dumping activities. Other small, localized areas of high surface sherd concentrations are evident. Their localized distribution is probably largely a result of post-occupational erosion processes, with pockets of materials accumulating in areas of slope change and depressions in the outcrop.
  Artifacts: Heavy scatter of sherds concentrated in north area of site. A transect (2 × 17 m) was collected across the long axis of the site. 900 g ceramics; wares: 517 black plain ware, 47 red plain ware, 7 black decorated plain ware. Diagnostics: 1 bowl, 17 jars. Other artifacts: small stone or ceramic bull figurine (Nandi) on south side of site.
  Temporal Affiliation: Unknown.
  Illustrations: Figure 6.20.

SITE: VMS-25   Block: O/N   Transect: 1/18
  Primary Site Use: Defensive: fortification wall.
  Site Dimensions: 178 × 1.13 m
  Setting: On gentle slope.
  Present Land Use/Disturbances: Recent pitting and construction in area. Site is adjacent to Hanuman temple in current use.
  Site Description: Fortification wall. This large single-faced wall extends east-west (4° north of east) for 178 m; extending south from the wall's east end is a similarly constructed 6 m long wall segment. The main wall incorporates a small boulder outcrop near its midpoint. It is constructed of large wedge-shaped blocks (with face on north side) with Vijayanagara quarry marks and unmodified or lightly modified large stones. Only two courses are preserved. May be associated with VMS-10 and part of the outer ring of Vijayanagara's fortification walls.
  Artifacts: Disturbed area; no collections made.
  Temporal Affiliation: Vijayanagara.
  References: Morrison 1995:64.

SITE: VMS-26   Block: O   Transect: 2
  Primary Site Use: Neolithic ashmound.
  Site Dimensions: 42 × 21 m
  Setting: Set in a low-lying area amid irrigated fields in a narrow valley between two outcrop ridges. Prehistoric rock art has been reported in outcrops to south of site. The Tungabhadra River lies c. 500 m to the north.
  Present Land Use/Disturbances: Modern cultivation surrounds the mound and is cutting into it. The mound edges have been cut back by farmers, and mound surface is overgrown by thorny scrub.
  Site Description: Neolithic ashmound and associated artifact scatter. This small mound is located amid irrigated fields in a narrow valley. The mound is formed of a hard light gray burnt material (burnt cow dung) that incorporates many pebbles. It is oval in plan and rises 2.5 to 3 m above the surrounding fields. A light scatter of chipped and ground stone artifacts and ceramics is present in the fields surrounding the mound. The site is locally referred to as *Wali Ghat* and is associated with the cremation pyre of the monkey ruler of Kishkinda of the Ramayana epic. The site has been previously documented by the Karnataka Department of Archaeology and Museums.
  Artifacts: A grid (36 m north-south by 24 m east-west) was laid out in the accessible fields to the northeast of the mound site. A 100% collection was conducted in each of six contiguous 12 × 12 m units in the area. The mound surface was collected as a single unit.
  Unit 1 (0N/12E): 1 flake (volcanic stone).
  Unit 2 (12N/12E): 2 flakes (volcanic stone), 1 piece angular debris (quartzite).
  Unit 3 (0N/0E): 1 core tool (chert); gray ware everted rim jar (prehistoric), black ware everted straight rim jar (unknown date).
  Unit 4 (12N/0E): 1 piece angular debris (volcanic stone).
  Unit 5 (12S/0E): 1 flake (volcanic stone).
  Unit 6 (12S/12E): 1 core (volcanic stone), 1 piece angular debris (quartzite).
  Mound: 1 core (chert); 1 grinding stone near mound, 5 rims, 2 straight rim jars, 3 bowls (2 unmeasurable).
  Temporal Affiliation: Prehistoric: Neolithic (third to second millennia BCE).
  References: Lycett 1991; Morrison 1995:89; Sinopoli and Morrison 1991:64.
  Illustrations: Figure 3.15; Plate 3.5.

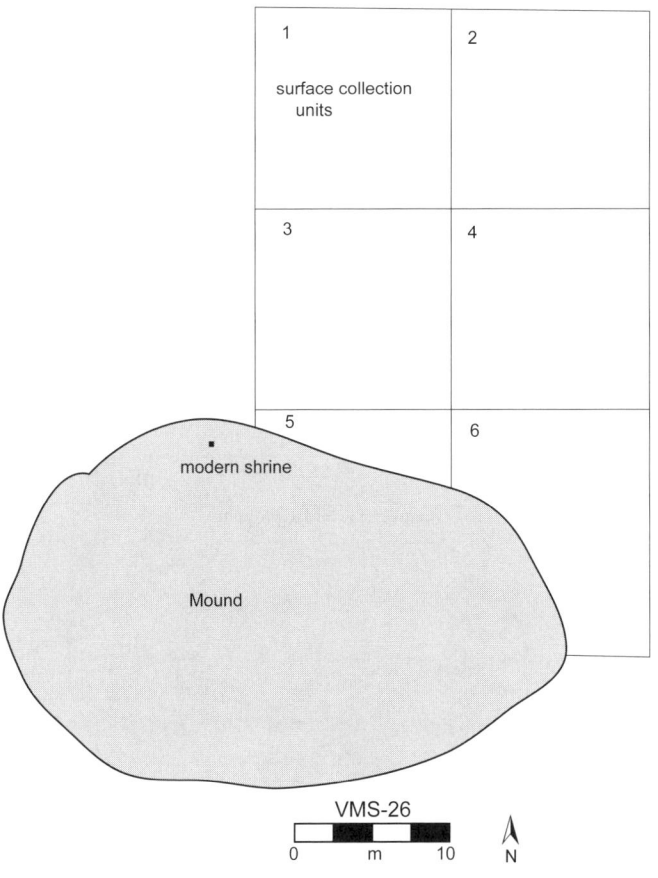

Plate 3.5. VMS-26, overview of mound and setting.

Figure 3.15. VMS-26, plan and location of collection areas.

SITE: VMS-27   Block: O   Transect: 1-2
   Primary Site Use: Transport?: wall.
   Site Dimensions: 240 × 1.5 m
   Setting: Gently sloping area near base of outcrop, located on north edge of agricultural fields and south face of outcrop, which it parallels.
   Present Land Use/Disturbances: A modern road runs to the south of the wall; brick-making workshop located nearby.
   Site Description: Wall. This single-course wall is composed of large unmodified and split stones and incorporates numerous *in situ* outcropping boulders. It is primarily oriented east-west, but is irregular as it parallels the edge of the outcrop to its north. The wall has two faces near its east end and is 1.5 m wide; otherwise it is single faced. The wall may have defined a route of movement along the south base of the outcrop and above the agricultural fields to its south. It may also have had defensive or soil control functions.
   Artifacts: 100% collection; no artifacts recovered.
   Temporal Affiliation: Vijayanagara.
   References: Morrison 1995:64.

SITE: VMS-28   Block: O   Transect: 1-2
   Primary Site Use: Unknown: lithic scatter.
   Site Dimensions: 30 × 20 m (high density area), maximal extent 57 × 50 m
   Setting: Located on outcrop area with large boulders and isolated patches of soil accumulation.
   Present Land Use/Disturbances: Thorny scrub between outcropping boulders, modern path runs along south edge of outcrop, slope wash has led to considerable erosion and redeposition of materials.
   Site Description: Lithic scatter. Dense surface scatter of probable quartzite flakes and shatter with a few possible hand stones.
   Artifacts: Collection of diagnostics over site surface yielded lithics and ground stone. Some of the debris may result from natural decomposition of quartzite lense, and/or quarrying activities; few pieces are clearly diagnostic.
   Temporal Affiliation: Unknown: c. 125 m northwest of the Neolithic ashmound, VMS-26, perhaps associated with it?
   References: Lycett 1991; Morrison 1995:89; Sinopoli and Morrison 1991:64-65.

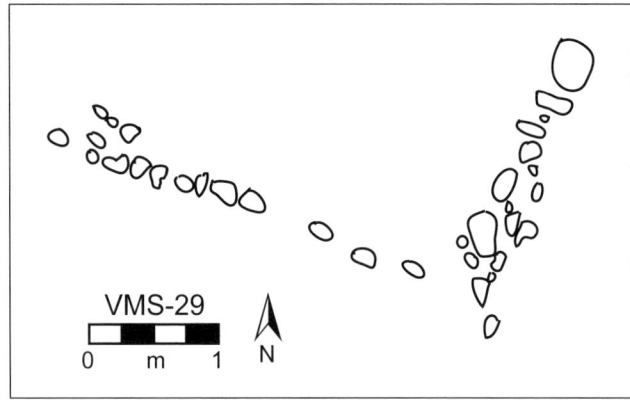

Figure 3.16. VMS-29, plan.

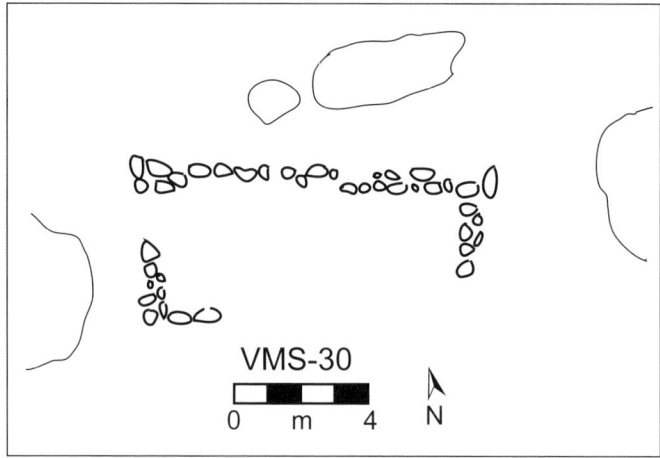

Figure 3.17. VMS-30, plan.

SITE: VMS-29   Block: O   Transect: 1
   Primary Site Use: Residential: structure.
   Site Dimensions: 3.5 × 2 m
   Setting: Flat uncultivated area near south base of large outcrop.
   Present Land Use/Disturbances: Small sugar cane processing structure c. 30 m southwest of structure; some modern agricultural debris within structure.
   Site Description: Small structure. This feature consists of two walls of a small rectangular structure, c. 3.5 × 3 m in dimension and oriented 20° south of east. Only the south and east walls are preserved, though portions of a possible north wall are also present. The walls are constructed of unmodified small-medium stones, are double faced in parts, and have only a single course preserved. They are probably foundation courses for a structure of impermanent materials.
   Artifacts: 100% collection; no artifacts recovered.
   Temporal Affiliation: Unknown, possibly recent.
   Illustrations: Figure 3.16.

SITE: VMS-30   Block: O   Transect: 1
   Primary Site Use: Residential: rectangular structure.
   Site Dimensions: 11 × 4.5 m
   Setting: Flat area near base of outcrop.
   Present Land Use/Disturbances: Sugar cane processing area nearby.
   Site Description: Rectangular single-room structure. Portions of four walls are preserved of this large (11 × 4.5 m, 10° south of east) chamber. Only one course is visible. The double-faced walls are constructed of small-medium unmodified stones. Probable foundation walls for a superstructure of less durable materials. There is no evidence that the structure was subdivided in any way.
   Artifacts: 100% collection; no artifacts recovered.
   Temporal Affiliation: Unknown, possibly recent.
   Illustrations: Figure 3.17.

SITE: VMS-31   Block: O   Transect: 2
   Primary Site Use: Residential?: artifact scatter.
   Site Dimensions: 42 × 25 m
   Setting: Flat area on outcrop amid outcropping boulders, some soil accumulation on sloping sheet rock.
   Present Land Use/Disturbances: Thorny scrub vegetation in areas of accumulated soil. Slope wash and erosion have led to redeposition of materials.
   Site Description: Surface scatter of ceramics and lithics. Sherds are all plain ware and highly fragmented. Lithics are of quartzite, with some possible chert. No quartzite vein is visible in immediate area.
   Artifacts: Judgment sample of diagnostics. Lithics: green quartzite: 2 flakes, 2 pieces angular debris. No ceramics recovered.
   Temporal Affiliation: Unknown.
   References: Sinopoli and Morrison 1991:65.

SITE: VMS-32   Block: O   Transect: 2
   Primary Site Use: Defensive?: linear rubble mound.
   Site Dimensions: 16 × 14 m
   Setting: On outcrop. Runs between the east peak of the outcrop and a rise to the west.
   Present Land Use/Disturbances: Modern footpath crosses the top of the mound.
   Site Description: Linear rubble pile, c. 16 m east-west by 14 m north-south, that extends between the east peak of a stone outcrop and a somewhat higher area to the west. This mound may have served as a barrier to movement across the outcrop.
   Artifacts: 100% collection; no artifacts recovered.
   Temporal Affiliation: Unknown.
   References: Morrison 1995:64, 67.

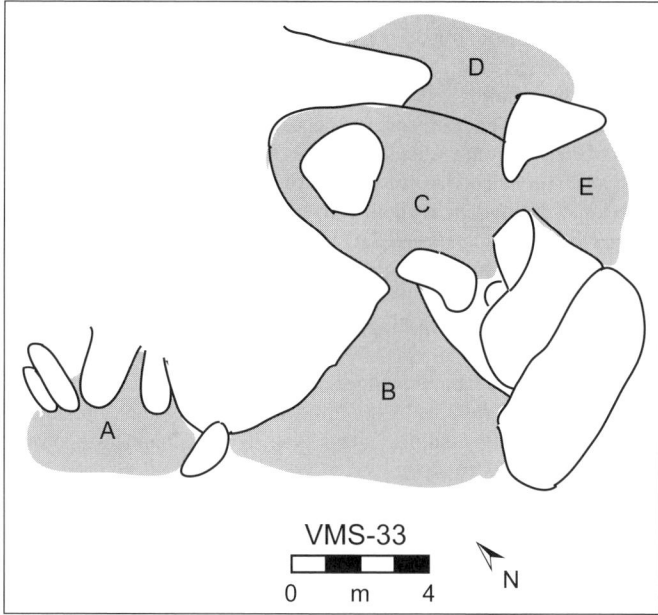

Figure 3.18. VMS-33, plan.

Figure 3.19. VMS-34, plan.

SITE: VMS-33   Block: O   Transect: 2
  Primary Site Use: Residential: rock shelter with lithic and ceramic scatter.
  Site Dimensions: 19 × 14 m, artifact scatter c. 11 m in diameter
  Setting: In small shelters formed by boulder overhang on highest point of outcrop ridge.
  Present Land Use/Disturbances: Erosion and slope wash have contributed to some redistribution of materials.
  Site Description: Rock shelters and surrounding area containing a ceramic and lithic scatter. The site can be subdivided into five discrete areas (A-E; Fig. 3.18). Area A consists of a concentration of artifacts in a small flat open area southwest of area B. The shelter contains two chambers, designated as areas B and C. Area B is a small south-facing chamber; area C lies to its north and is accessible from area B. This central chamber (area C) is c. 1 m higher than area B and is completely enclosed by boulders. A second entry to the central chamber on its northeast leads into a flat stone surface (area D) that is only partially sheltered by overhanging boulders. Area E is a small overhang to the southeast of area C. Very little soil has accumulated in this area, but there is a patchy distribution of ceramic and lithic artifacts.
  Artifacts: Each area was collected separately; 100% collection.
  Area A: <50 g ceramics; wares: 2 black plain ware. Diagnostics: 1 bowl. Lithics: quartzite, 1 flake, 5 pieces angular debris, 4 cores, 2 pieces bipolar debris.
  Area B: 250 g ceramics; wares: 67 black plain ware. Diagnostics: 2 jars. Lithics: quartzite, 3 flakes, 10 pieces angular debris, 2 cores, 2 utilized flakes.
  Area C: 100 g ceramics; wares: 4 black plain ware. Diagnostics: 2 jars.
  Area D: 650 g ceramics; wares: 281 black plain ware, 6 red plain ware. Diagnostics: 6 bowls, 18 jars. Lithics: quartzite, 8 flakes.
  Area E: <50 g ceramics; wares: 3 black plain ware, 2 red plain ware. Lithics: quartzite, 1 piece angular debris, 1 piece bipolar debris.

  Temporal Affiliation: Unknown: perhaps revisited over long time span. Ceramics are consistent with Vijayanagara period.
  References: Lycett 1991; Sinopoli and Morrison 1991:65.
  Illustrations: Figure 3.18.

SITE: VMS-34   Block: O   Transect: 2
  Primary Site Use: Defensive: fortification wall.
  Site Dimensions: 28 × 1.45 m
  Setting: On outcrop.
  Present Land Use/Disturbances: Some slope wash; no evidence for significant modern activities.
  Site Description: Large wall. This double-faced stone wall with rubble fill is c. 1.45 m wide and is located on an outcrop in an area of an abrupt break in slope (oriented 35° west of north). The wall would have served to inhibit movement to the south and was likely part of a defensive system for the village site (VMS-35-37) located immediately to its south. Up to five courses are preserved; coursing is irregular and construction is of rectangular split and unmodified medium to large stones.
  Artifacts: A light scatter of sherds and some possible lithics were observed, but not collected.
  Temporal Affiliation: Vijayanagara.
  References: Morrison 1995:67; Sinopoli and Morrison 1991:65-66; Means 1991.
  Illustrations: Figure 3.19.

SITE: VMS-35 Block: O Transect: 3
  Primary Site Use: Residential: settlement.
  Site Dimensions: 200 × 175 m
  Setting: Extends along lower slopes of large outcrop, which slopes down from west to east. The flat terrain to the south and east of the settlement is under irrigation agriculture. The settlement may have been located on the outcrop for defensive reasons and to avoid encroaching on fertile agricultural areas.
  Present Land Use/Disturbances: Modern dirt road on east and north edges (separates area of village designated as VMS-35 from VMS-36 and 37). There is intensive stone quarrying near the road. Foot trails pass through the site, much of which is overgrown by thorny scrub. Erosion and slope wash are also prevalent.
  Site Description: Village site. This 3.4 ha settlement is situated amid the boulders and slopes of an outcropping granitic hill. The terrain slopes down from west to east, with the west area of the site c. 5-8 m higher in elevation than the eastern portion. Informal paved paths or stairways link upper and lower areas of the settlement. Site layout is informal and opportunistic, with rubble wall single- and multi-room structures placed at various orientations in flat areas between boulders. The structures often incorporate outcropping boulders into their walls. Two rock shelters in the northwest corner of the site contain abundant artifacts, though little evidence for construction. In low-lying and relatively flat areas, an approximate north-south orientation of structures is evident.

The site is enclosed within "defensive" or bounding walls (including site VMS-34 to the west, and other walls to the south, east, and north). Most of these walls are formed of unmodified medium to large stones, though a wall segment (Feature 2) on the uppermost tier of the site is constructed of closely fitted modified square and rectangular blocks with Vijayanagara quarry marks.

The structures are of rubble wall construction; walls are typically single faced with only one to two courses preserved. Large numbers of bedrock mortars are found in association with the structures. Several rock-cut "horse ties" are present in upper levels, and pecked drainage channels are also evident on sloping bedrock faces. There is evidence for basalt working, most likely the production of support pegs for structures, especially near road; however, some of the accumulated fragments may be the result of more recent activities, such as the laying of the modern road bed that borders the site.

During site documentation, site remains were divided into distinctive "features"—including structures, isolated walls, bedrock mortars, and others. Thirty-four such features were identified; these are illustrated on Figure 3.20.

Feature 1: Located in the southwest area of the site, this feature consists of three bedrock mortars and a carved drain located on top of a large outcropping boulder, some 13 m north-south by 16 m east-west. Pecking surrounding two of the three mortars provides additional evidence for food processing activities. The drain slopes down to the north and is c. 3.5 m long by 10 cm wide; it appears to have been formed through pecking and grinding.

Feature 2: Wall located near the southwestern edge of the site. This L-shaped wall is oriented predominantly north-south and spans a gap between two outcropping boulders, blocking off a lower area to its east. It is constructed of up to two courses of modified rectangular blocks, with Vijayanagara-style quarry marks. The wall prevents access to the main site area from the west and likely had a defensive function.

Feature 3: Bedrock mortar located on a large outcropping boulder to the north of Feature 2; associated with food processing activities.

Feature 4: North-south wall bordering a relatively flat area to its east and a sloping area to its west. The wall is constructed of medium unmodified rounded boulders and is double faced in parts. It is not clear if this was part of a structure or was associated with erosion control or movement restriction.

Feature 5: Staircase and associated paved walkway in the southwest edge of the site. The poorly preserved stairway leads up toward the main level of the site from the south, and rises from a better preserved paved footpath. The stairway is constructed of both unquarried and quarried stones and boulders, and is bordered on its edges by low walls of stones set on edge. The footpath is c. 2 m wide and is also flanked by bordering stones. The path surface is of closely spaced small-medium rounded stones; many show evidence of polish and wear.

Feature 6: A quasi-rectangular structure located to the northwest of Feature 3. This small structure is situated between outcrops and its walls make use of natural boulders; outcrops define its southwest and northeast boundaries. Walls are constructed of rounded unmodified stones and irregular modified blocks. A small wall alignment is located to the north of the structure.

Feature 7: A long rectangular structure oriented northwest-southeast. It is bounded on the south by a wall that runs over a low outcrop. Wall construction is of unmodified medium to large unmodified stones, with only a single face and a single course preserved in most areas, although there is an internal step or ledge along the long wall that defines the western boundary of the structure.

Feature 8: Located to the east of Feature 7, this exposed area of sheet rock contains two bedrock mortars. One of these was unfinished, and only the outlines have been pecked out (Plate 3.6). There is a considerable amount of soil accumulation on the outcrop, though artifact densities are quite low.

Feature 9: Cluster of seven "horse-ties" (Plate 3.7) carved onto outcropping boulders. These are formed through carving into the boulder from two directions to create a free-standing bar or strip to which a rope could be attached. Six of the "ties" are oriented horizontally, while one is vertical.

Feature 10: A rectangular platform oriented north-south (6 m × 2.5 m). The eastern wall is a retaining wall, constructed of rounded and roughly shaped medium stones, two courses high. The top of the wall is level with the surface of the platform. On the north end of this surface is a stone slab mortar. A "horse tie" is carved into an outcropping boulder to the east of the mortar. The platform abuts outcropping boulders on the west and south. No architecture is visible on the outcrop, but there is considerable wear and polish, suggesting that this may have been a working surface of some sort. Several uncompleted quarry marks suggest construction activities were initiated in this area but never completed. There is a small rock shelter to the west of the terrace. Ceramics and lithic debris are very dense in and around Feature 10, and include prehistoric (Iron Age) as well as Vijayanagara period ceramics.

Features 11-14: (Not described; Feature 11 not illustrated.)

Feature 15: Stair and pathway leading from Feature 5 in the southwest edge of site up to the northeast through a fairly constrained route of movement. Movement across the site was constrained to restricted paths by the distribution of walls, passages, and outcropping boulders. This one consists of three fairly crudely constructed steps and pavement, composed of opportunistically placed modified and unmodified blocks that helped to smooth out the irregular terrain and ease passage up to the primary upper area of the site to the north.

Feature 16: A long northwest-southeast oriented wall that seems to define the southern boundary of an area with a high density of structures. This four-course irregularly constructed wall runs over several low outcrops and abuts a large boulder at its east end. A possible staircase is associated with the western end of the wall, which is likely associated with controlling movement and defining spaces within the settlement.

Feature 17: A short wall of large rounded uncut coarse grained stones. Only a single course is preserved. This wall may have served to block access from areas to the south.

Features 18 and 19: Two adjacent areas of dense structural remains. The boundaries between these two structures is somewhat arbitrary, and the area is discussed as a whole area. In all more than twenty walls or wall fragments appear to define the boundaries of more than a half dozen tightly-packed structures or compounds. Wall construction is of small-medium unmodified and modified stones. In most cases only a single course is preserved, and wall construction is informal and loosely fit. Many of these walls may have been foundations for larger walls of impermanent materials. This area is overgrown with cacti and other vegetation, and it is difficult to discern complete floor plans. Nonetheless, this is one of the densest structural areas of the site and likely contains the remains of multiple households. Surface artifact densities are relatively low in this area, though this may be a function of poor visibility.

Feature 20: Large curved wall to the northeast of Features 18 and 19, constructed of large modified and unmodified boulders and associated features. The wall has two faces in the southeast, but is otherwise single faced; it was probably a boundary wall. A bedrock mortar is located on an outcropping boulder to the east of the wall, as are several horse-ties. Additional fragmentary wall alignments are also present in the area. There is evidence for extensive quarrying in the surrounding boulders, with numerous Vijayanagara-style quarry marks present.

Feature 21: Located on the northern edge of the southern habitation area of the site. There is considerable soil accumulation in this area from erosion from higher areas to the north. Fragments of at least four wall fragments are visible, and appear to be the remains of one or more small rectangular structures. It is likely that other structural remains are buried. Artifact densities are extremely high in this area, with many Vijayanagara-era ceramics and a small number of possibly earlier sherds and lithics. These high densities are likely the result of the erosion and sediment accumulation from the northern part of the site.

Feature 22: Transport route or stairway leading to northern structural area of settlement. As in other areas of the site, this feature consists of elements placed opportunistically among boulders to ease accessibility and movement, and the route runs between two large boulder outcrops on the east and west. It is formed by rows of boulders and alignments that incorporate both *in situ* stones and placed modified and unmodified elements. Together these form a stepped north-south route, with the three steps sloping down to the north. A wall runs along the eastern edge of the lower step, and may serve as a retaining wall for an elevated earthen pathway and/or a path boundary. A second wall fragment is visible to the north of the stairway.

Feature 23: Rectangular chamber, 3 m east-west by 4.50 m north-south. Walls are of medium and small roughly shaped irregular stones and incorporate naturally outcropping boulders; up to two courses are preserved.

Feature 24: Structure and isolated walls. Remains of a rectangular rubble wall structure, and associated wall fragments. Walls are single course and are constructed of small to medium modified stones.

Feature 25: Boundary or defensive wall, running roughly east-west in the northwest quadrant of the site. This roughly formed c. 20 m long wall consists of modified and unmodified stones and boulders that were placed to fill in a gap between outcropping boulders and limit entry into the main settlement area from the northwest. More a low mound than a wall, this feature currently stands about 1.5 m high.

Feature 26: Located to the north of Feature 25, this wall appears to have served a similar function of defense and boundary definition. It is only c. 4 m long by 1.5 m wide, and is essentially a pile of small to medium stones that spans a narrow gap between outcropping boulders.

Feature 27: Large rectangular enclosure or structure and associated wall fragments. Located in the northern portion of the site, the walls of this feature bound a roughly rectangular enclosure, some 23 m east-west by 30 m north-south. This area has been heavily disturbed by recent pits and portions of the walls have been removed to create modern field walls. As a result, it is not possible to discern the original layout in all areas. Several wall remnants are preserved up to three courses, and have two faces with rubble infill. A bedrock mortar is presented in the center of the enclosure. This was likely a sizeable residential compound containing multiple structures.

Feature 28: Located to the north of Feature 27 and separated from it by a c. 33 m long boundary wall, Feature 20 also consists of a large structure and associated structural remains. The roughly square enclosure is approximately 17 m on a side. In the northeast corner is a walled room, containing a block mortar; two other mortars are located nearby. Parts of this feature have been damaged and obscured by recent road construction; iron slag and a dense scatter of ceramics have been exposed by this construction.

Feature 29: Boundary or defensive wall. Like Feature 26 to its west, Feature 29 is a wide wall that spans a gap between outcropping boulders. This c. 10 m long, roughly east-west wall defines the northern boundary of the settlement.

Feature 30: Located on the eastern edge of the dense architectural zone in the south of the site, Feature 30 consists of several walls, the remnants of structures that have been heavily disturbed by recent road construction. This was a dense area of habitation, and the preserved walls likely derive from at least half a dozen small rubble-walled structures.

Feature 31: Like Feature 30, this feature consists of the remains of multiple small rubble-wall structures that lie on the southeast edge of the site, adjacent to the modern road. Several wall fragments are preserved, as is a small bedrock mortar. Large piles of flaked basalt are also present in this area. These appear to be residue from industrial activities, specifically the production of basalt pegs, which were used as structural supports (see Chapter 6).

Feature 32: Walls and modern shrine containing Vijayanagara-period images. This feature constitutes the southern boundary of the settlement. At the southern end is a long (c. 30 m) east-west boundary wall constructed of medium to large unmodified and modified stones. This wall abuts large outcrops on the west; its eastern edge was disturbed by recent road construction. To the north of this wall are portions of several other walls, defining some large enclosures and, possibly, internal structures. A small recent shrine in this area incorporates Vijayanagara-era quarried triangular blocks and several sculptures—including a naga stone, seated female image (Lakshmi?) and devotee feet.

Feature 33: Located to the east of the modern road, this feature includes the remains of three small single-room residential structures, and a block mortar. Wall construction is variable; two of the structures are built of typical single-course rubble walls of small-medium modified and unmodified stones. The third, northern structure is of much larger rounded or roughly shaped blocks. This latter construction is reminiscent of late prehistoric, Iron Age construction, and given the early ceramics at the site, may be the remains of an early construction that was reused in Vijayanagara times. Several features of nearby VMS-37 are similar in construction, and likely also are reused prehistoric features.

Feature 34: On the eastern end of the site, the feature includes one small rectangular rubble wall structure, and a long north-south wall,

Plate 3.6. VMS-35, outline of unfinished bedrock mortar.

Plate 3.7. VMS-35, "horse tie" on outcrop boulder.

c. 27 m long, which forms an eastern boundary to this portion of the settlement area. The boundary wall is double faced with earth and rubble infill, and is preserved up to three courses in height.

Artifacts: The site was divided into a number of discrete features for purposes of mapping, description, and artifact collection. In some cases, features were further subdivided. Artifacts include basalt pegs, hand stones, other worked basalt fragments, and ceramics.

Feature 1: 100 g ceramics; wares: 7 black plain ware, 4 red plain ware, 1 coarse ware. Lithics: 3 pieces quartzite angular debris.

Feature 10/13: 500 g ceramics; wares: 46 black plain ware, 8 red plain ware, 1 coarse ware, 4 red burnished ware. Diagnostics: 5 jars. Lithics: quartzite lithics (200 g), 1 core, 1 piece bipolar debris, 1 piece angular debris, 1 utilized flake.

Feature 10S: 1750 g ceramics; wares: 226 black plain ware, 31 red plain ware, 13 coarse ware, 10 brown burnished ware, 18 red burnished ware. Diagnostics: 2 bowls, 21 jars. Some prehistoric black and red ware sherds, probably of the first millennium B.C. Iron Age.

Feature 14/int: 100 g ceramics; wares: 12 black plain ware, 3 red plain ware, 1 red burnished ware. Diagnostics: 1 jar.

Feature 18A: 200 g ceramics; wares: 81 black plain ware. Lithics: 2 quartzite flakes.

Feature 18B: 250 g ceramics; wares: 129 black plain ware, 14 red plain ware.

Feature 18C: 50 g ceramics; wares: 10 black plain ware.

Feature 18D: 150 g ceramics; wares: 57 black plain ware, 4 red plain ware. Diagnostics: 2 jars.

Feature 19: No ceramics. Lithics: 1 quartzite core.

Feature 21: 1200 g ceramics; wares: 275 black plain ware, 26 red plain ware, 6 coarse ware, 1 black burnished ware, 4 red burnished ware. Diagnostics: 21 jars. Lithics: 1 quartzite flake, 2 cores.

Temporal Affiliation: Vijayanagara. Ties, pegs, ceramics, quarry marks, and mortars are all consistent with the Vijayanagara period. An early Vijayanagara coin was recovered in VMS-37. Site VMS-36 contains a Vijayanagara Hanuman image. The site does not appear to have been reoccupied. There is also a small late prehistoric/early historic component at the site, evident through small numbers of black and red ware and polished red and polished black ware sherds. Prehistoric rock art has been reported in outcrops near the site (Karnataka Department of Archaeology personnel, pers. comm.).

References: Morrison 1995:63-64, 67, 71, 79, 85, 89, 99; Lycett 1991; Means 1991; Sinopoli and Morrison 1991:65-67; Sinopoli 1997:481, 484; Sinopoli 2003:235-36.

Illustrations: Figure 3.20; Plates 3.6, 3.7.

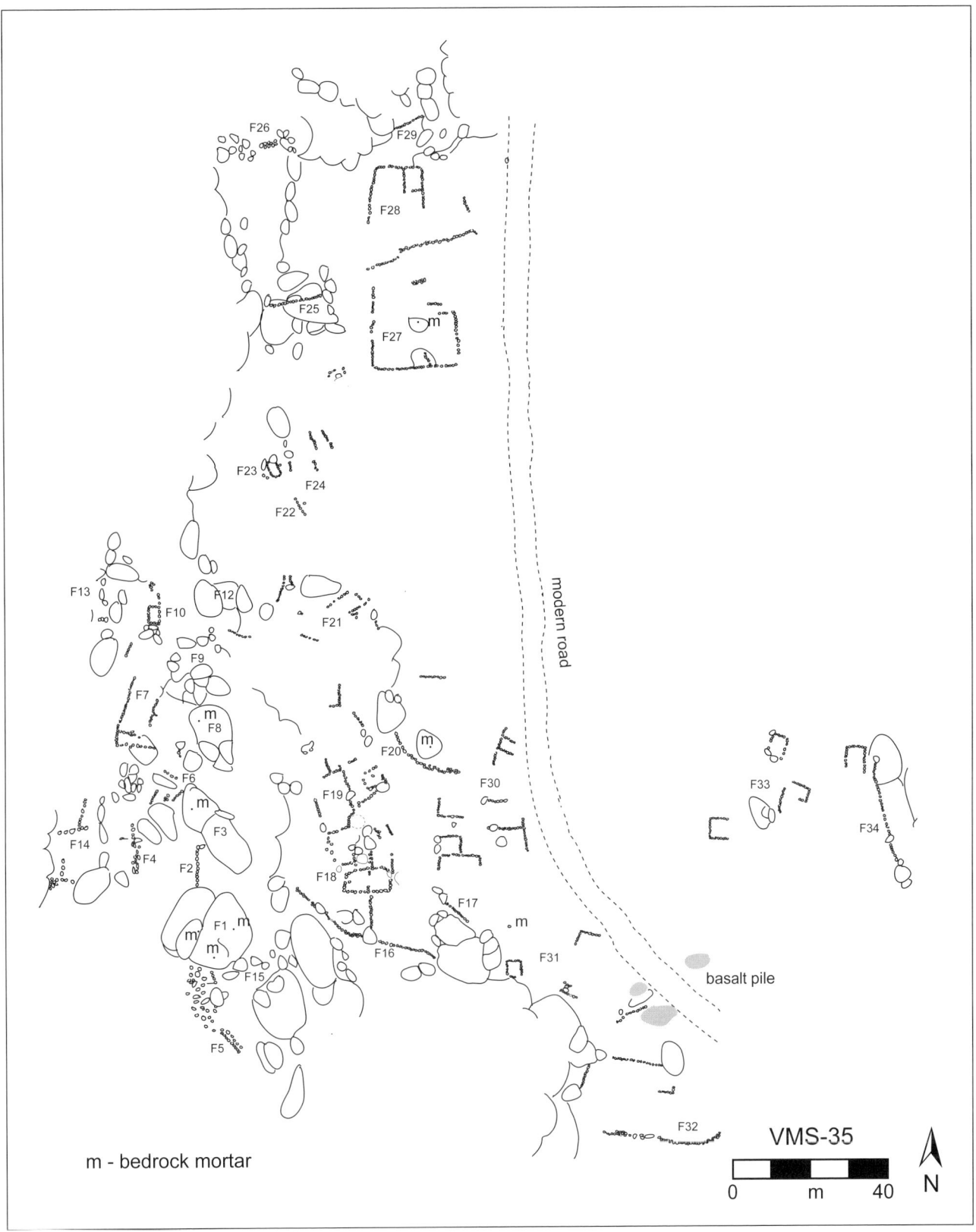

Figure 3.20. VMS-35, plan.

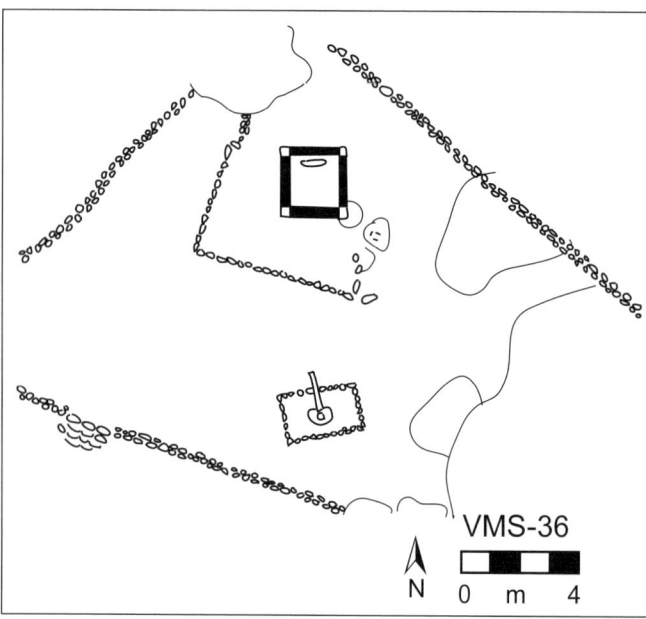

Figure 3.21. VMS-36, plan.

SITE: VMS-36   Block: O   **Transect:** 3
  Primary Site Use: Religious: Hanuman shrine complex.
  Site Dimensions: 20 × 15 m
  Setting: On flat areas of sheet rock near eastern edge of the outcrop containing settlement VMS-35.
  Present Land Use/Disturbances: A modern dirt road separates area of village designated as VMS-35 from VMS-36 and 37. There is evidence for recent worship in the shrine (paint and oil lamps) and the sanctuary has modern walls.
  Site Description: South-facing shrine. This 2 × 2 column shrine is located in a walled compound. The shrine has simple square columns, with Vijayanagara quarry marks. The columns are coarsely dressed with rectangular capitals. Modern walls span the columns. The ceiling of the sanctuary is composed of five horizontal beams, with a sixteen-petal lotus carved in the center. The central image is a large Anjaneya Hanuman of the Vijayanagara period (1.75 m tall) with a crawling demon (Apsmara) at his feet. A fallen lamp column, with insloping square base and hexagonal upper portion, lies in front of the shrine. The base of the column is sculpted with images of a conch, wheel, trident, and turtle, and corner lotus flowers. The compound is enclosed within rubble walls probably of recent construction.
  Artifacts: Some modern ceramics in shrine; no collections made.
  Temporal Affiliation: Columns, image, and lamp column are of Vijayanagara period.
  References: Means 1991; Morrison 1995:63-64, 67, 89, 99; Sinopoli and Morrison 1991:65-66; Sinopoli 1997:481, 484.
  Illustrations: Figure 3.21.

SITE: VMS-37   Block: O   **Transect:** 3
  Primary Site Use: Residential: settlement.
  Site Dimensions: 150 × 86 m
  Setting: On level area atop low sheet rock outcrop, irrigated agricultural fields to the north, south, and east. VMS-37 abuts VMS-35 and VMS-36 on the west.
  Present Land Use/Disturbances: Modern dirt road separates area of village designated as VMS-35 from VMS-36 and 37. There is evidence for recent stone quarrying and accumulation of rubble near road; modern foot trails cross the site.
  Site Description: Settlement area. This site consists of the remains of up to eighteen single- and multi-room rubble wall structures and associated features. Several walls seem to enclose the settlement and may have had defensive purposes. Construction is simple; several structures have single- and double-faced rubble walls, of small unmodified or split stones, with one to two courses preserved. Some may be part of large multi-room compounds. In other areas, construction is of much larger unmodified or flaked stone boulders, c. 0.80-1.00 m across. These form square or subrectangular enclosures, and individual gaps of 20 or more cm separate the large stones. These alignments most closely resemble pre-Vijayanagara "megalithic" alignments, and it seems likely that Vijayanagara period inhabitants of the settlement had reoccupied and utilized remains of a much earlier site, an interpretation bolstered by the presence of pre-Vijayanagara ceramics at nearby VMS-35. A possible cairn megalith was observed in the area when we first visited the site in 1988, but was no longer in existence when we revisited in the late 1990s.
  A basalt vein is visible in the outcrop where VMS-37 rests, and stone working seems to have occurred here. In contrast to VMS-35, no bedrock mortars are visible and artifact densities are low.
  Artifacts: Grass and other vegetation contributed to low visibility, and artifact density was generally low across the site. Surface collections were made within individual structures (assigned letter designations). Four 2 × 2 m judgment units were placed in areas devoid of structures. A diagnostic collection was also made across the entire site surface. Artifacts include a coin tentatively identified to the reign of Devaraya II (1426-1446 A.D.), some iron slag, a metal bracelet, lithics, and ceramics.
  Unit J: 25 g ceramics; wares: 3 black plain ware, 2 red plain ware.
  Unit K: 2 quartzite flakes, 6 pieces quartzite flaking debris.
  Unit O-2: 1 chert flake.
  Unit P: 2 pieces quartzite flaking debris.
  Unit Q: 25 g ceramics; wares: 3 black plain ware, 2 red plain ware.
  Unit Q4: 25 g ceramics; wares: 1 black plain ware.
  Unit R: 25 g ceramics; wares: 13 black plain ware, 3 red plain ware. Diagnostics: 1 jar.
  Unit T1: 25 g ceramics; wares: 6 black plain ware.
  Unit T2: 25 g ceramics; wares: 1 black plain ware.
  Judgment: 1 green-gray chert pebble tool.
  Temporal Affiliation: Vijayanagara (early?) period settlement, and Iron Age components.
  References: Means 1991; Morrison 1995:63-64, 67, 71, 89, 99; Sinopoli and Morrison 1991:65-66; Lycett 1991; Sinopoli 1997:481, 484.
  Illustrations: Figure 3.22; Plates 3.8, 3.9.

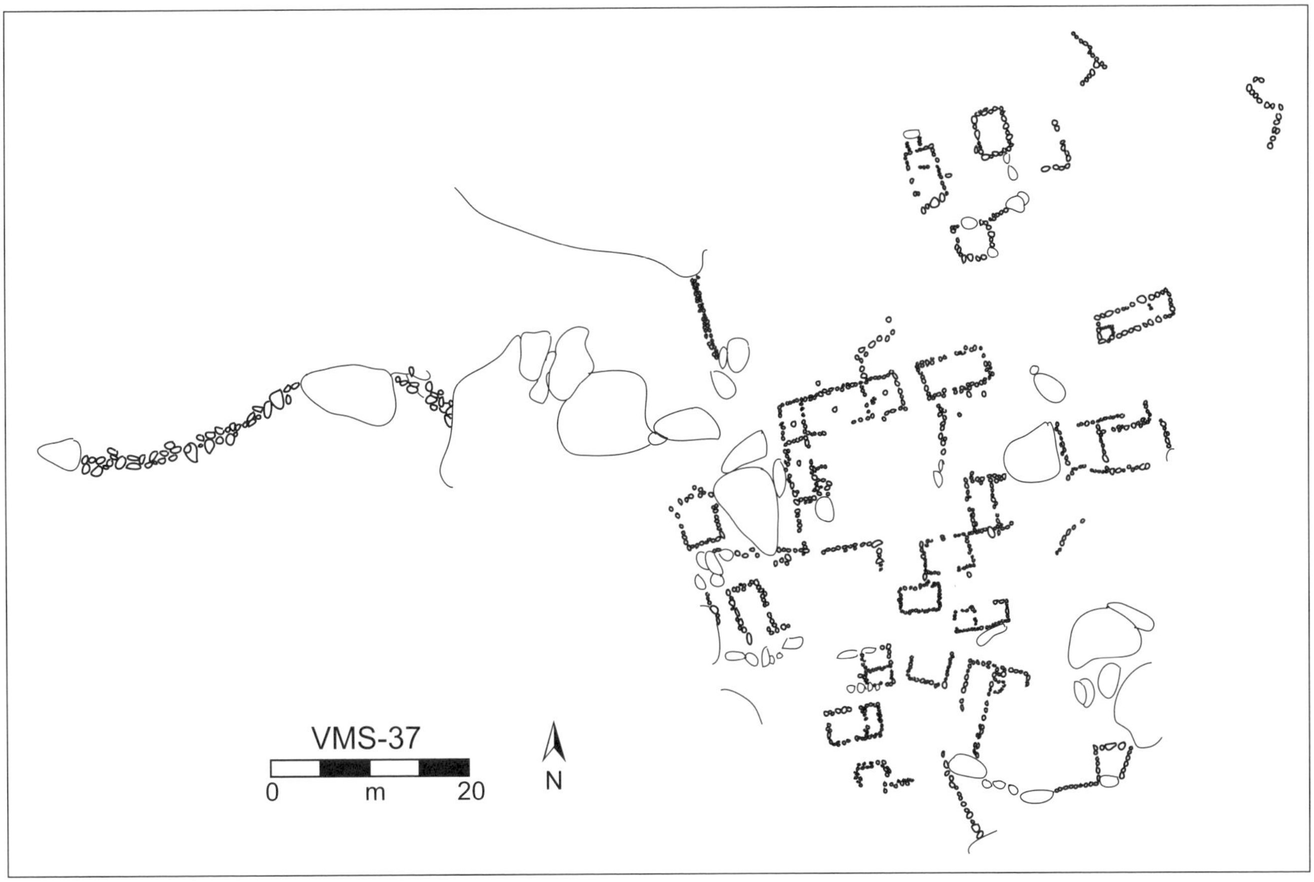

Figure 3.22. VMS-37, plan.

Plate 3.8. VMS-37, structural detail.

Plate 3.9. VMS-37, structural detail, path 2.

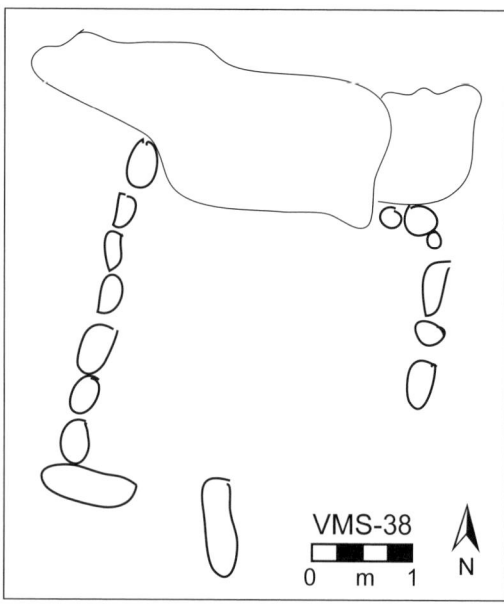

Figure 3.23. VMS-38, plan.

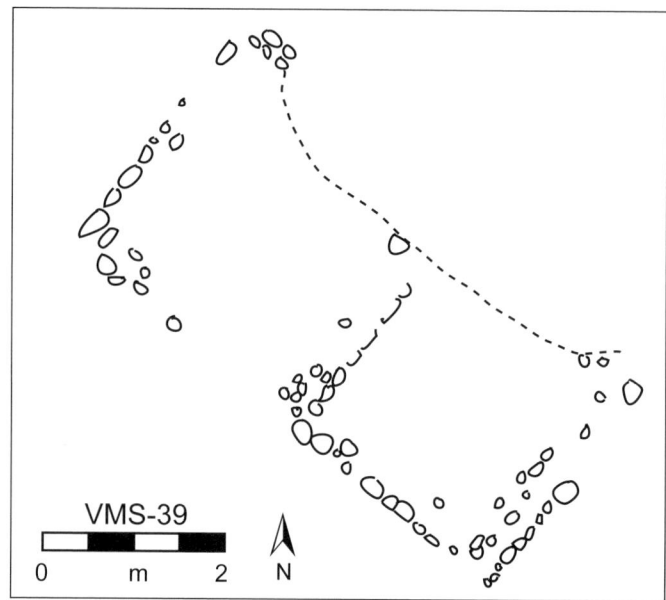

Figure 3.24. VMS-39, plan.

SITE: VMS-38   Block: O   Transect: 2
Primary Site Use: Residential/water storage?: structure.
Site Dimensions: 3.2 × 3.2 m
Setting: Flat to gently sloping low-lying area.
Resources: May be water cistern.
Present Land Use/Disturbances: Stone quarriers' road, modern canal dump to south of structure.
Site Description: Small square chamber or basin. The east and west walls are preserved, the south wall is fragmentary, and the north wall is a natural outcrop with some boulders wedged in to form a continuous face. The three visible horizontal courses of the extant walls are of medium rectangular or irregular unmodified stones. No mortar or plaster is visible. The vegetation within the structure is much lusher than in the surrounding area and the chamber interior is at a somewhat lower elevation than the exterior area. This may have been a small water storage facility.
Artifacts: Some modern ceramics in area; not collected.
Temporal Affiliation: Unknown.
Illustrations: Figure 3.23.

SITE: VMS-39   Block: O   Transect: 2
Primary Site Use: Residential: rectangular structure and associated features.
Site Dimensions: 30 × 8 m
Setting: Low-lying agricultural area.
Present Land Use/Disturbances: Piles of plaster and pebbles cleared from nearby fields are piled on the structure, as was a haystack.
Site Description: Structure and associated features. The site consists of a rectangular structure 12 × 6.5 m, oriented 38° east of north and divided into two roughly equal chambers, as well as associated features. Construction is of small, unmodified stones and rubble; up to two horizontal courses are visible. Walls are double faced and range from 0.60 to 0.70 m in width; some traces of plaster remain on the exterior surfaces. To the south of the structure is a large mound of plaster and pebbles that has been piled as a field border. The original association of this redeposited material is unknown.

Artifacts: 100% collection. 150 g ceramics; wares: 10 black plain ware. Diagnostics: 1 bowl.
Temporal Affiliation: Unknown, possibly recent.
Illustrations: Figure 3.24.

SITE: VMS-40   Block: O   Transect: 4
Primary Site Use: Agricultural: impounded spring and associated well with superstructure.
Site Dimensions: 15 × 10 m
Setting: Flat area amid cultivated dry farm fields.
Present Land Use/Disturbances: Modern fields surround the site. The impounded spring still retains water and is in use. A tomb (of a local Muslim saint) of unknown date is located at the base of the superstructure and is associated with many ritual offerings, including oil lamps and green glass bangles. Another tomb lies to the north of the site. The west face of the structure is poorly preserved.
Site Description: Well with superstructure and associated impounded spring. This is an elaborate well and associated stone platform with Islamic style arches and a complex system of pipes and chutes for distributing water.

There is a spring-fed pool of water to the east of the superstructure. The spring is bounded by a three-sided stone enclosure, mostly of recent construction. The pool is c. 18 m in diameter and a channel leads directly from it to fields to the north.

A large towered superstructure abuts the pool on the west. More than forty courses of the tower remain. This structure distributed water lifted from the well/spring through a series of pipes. The tower is preserved at least 13 m above the present water level. Water from the pool below was lifted to a platform on the tower. This was probably accomplished by bullock power, with the animals hooked to pulleys and ascending and descending the earthen ramp to the west of the structure. A smaller ramp, less well preserved, may also have extended to the south.

Stone arches are present on the platform atop the tower, with two on the east face (a larger arch to the north and a smaller one to the south) and one on the south face. The north face is not preserved but may have had a similar arch. The platform was likely roofed, as fragments of a domed

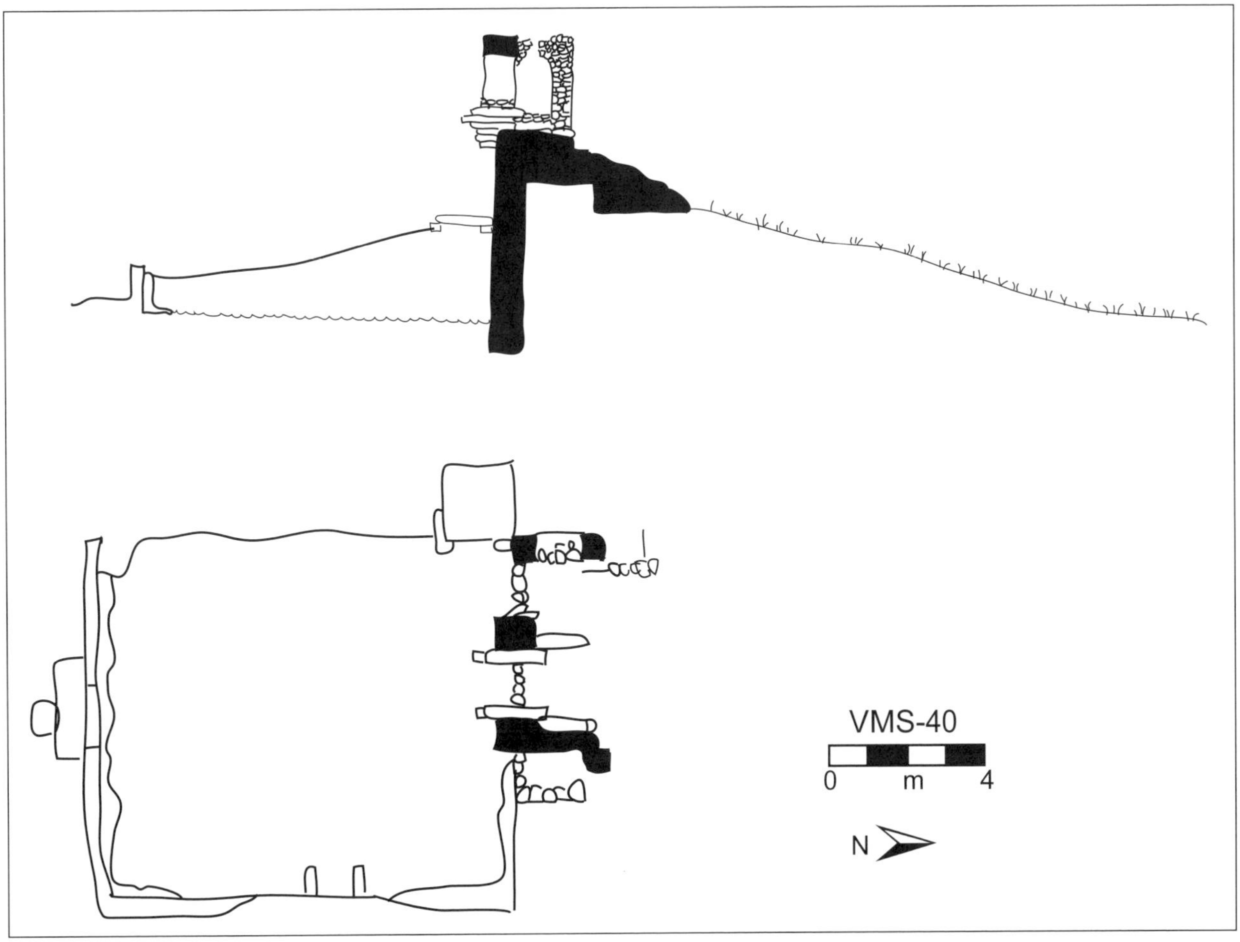

Figure 3.25. VMS-40, plan.

Plate 3.10. VMS-40, view of stone superstructure.

ceiling of plastered stone (with central lotus medallion) lie nearby. The platform may have been subdivided into two chambers.

Associated with the larger arch on the north side of the platform are the remains of an elaborate water flow system. A plastered water chute at platform level fed water down to several vertical ceramic pipes on the west side of the structure. From there, the pipes turn to the north into modern dry farmed fields. There may have been a separate chamber to the south of this flow system where those controlling the flow of water could have stood.

The well and site are currently associated with a Muslim saint (Mustafa Pir) whose grave is found here, believed by local informants to be at least 200 years old, though architecturally the structure is of Vijayanagara period.

Artifacts: Some modern pottery associated with well, sherds of unknown date in light scatter in surrounding fields. No collections made.

Temporal Affiliation: Vijayanagara, with later additions.
References: Michell 1992:27, 127; Morrison 1995:83, 89.
Illustrations: Figure 3.25; Plates 3.10, 3.11.

Plate 3.11. VMS-40, detail of ceramic water pipe.

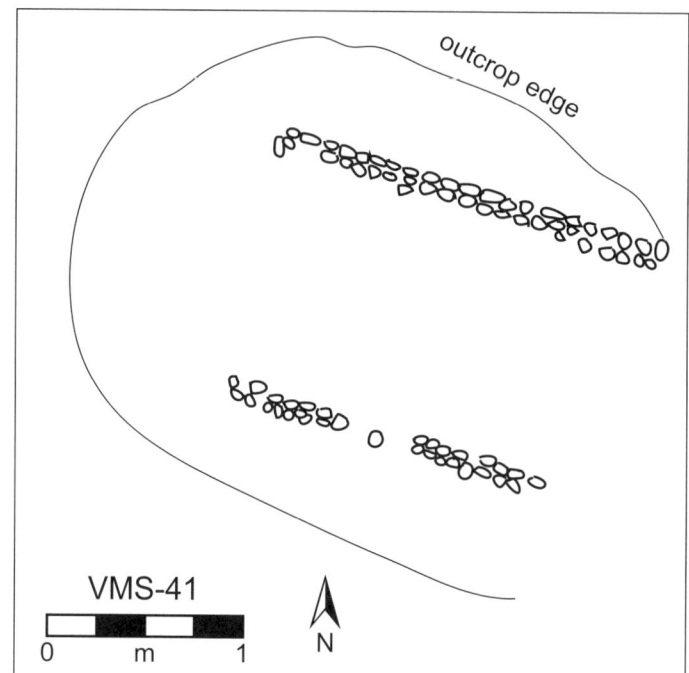

Figure 3.26. VMS-41, plan.

SITE: VMS-41   Block: O   Transect: 4
   Primary Site Use: Residential: rectangular structure.
   Site Dimensions: 3.5 × 2.2 m
   Setting: Flat area surrounded by dry farmed agricultural fields.
   Present Land Use/Disturbances: The east side of the structure is disturbed by recent agricultural activities; a recent threshing floor is located c. 8 m to the south of the structure.
   Site Description: Small structure. The north and south walls and portions of the east wall of this small rectangular structure are preserved. The walls are double faced and consist of up to four courses of unmodified small-medium stones. This is probably a recent construction.
   Artifacts: Modern porcelain, sparse scatter of earthenware. 100% collection. 250 g ceramics; wares: 21 black plain ware, 1 red plain ware. Diagnostics: 1 bowl, 1 jar.
   Temporal Affiliation: Recent?/post-Vijayanagara.
   Illustrations: Figure 3.26.

SITE: VMS-42   Block: O   Transect: 2
   Primary Site Use: Religious: Vaishnava temple complex.
   Site Dimensions: c. 40 × 25 m (walled temple compound only), associated with sites VMS-43–47, VMS-50; total dimensions c. 300 m north-south × 200 m
   Setting: Located on a flat area on the northeast slope of an outcrop hill. The outcrop slopes up to the south and east, and the south boundary of the compound is the steep face of the surrounding outcropping boulders.
   Present Land Use/Disturbances: The temple is still in worship; some enclosure walls are of recent construction.
   Site Description: Walled temple compound. The main temple (Feature 1) and associated features are found within a walled enclosure (c. 30 m east-west × 20 m north-south). The compound is entered by climbing the stairway (Feature 4) situated at its northwest corner. To the west of the stairway are two small mandapas and a water basin (Features 5-7).
   Feature 1: Temple. This two-chambered structure is oriented north-south, and opens to the east. The west and south walls of the temple abut the outcrop. To the east of the structure is a raised porch with eight unsculpted columns, paved with square blocks. The east parapet of the roof, which spans both the temple and porch, is elaborately sculpted with geese and petal-shaped lobes and miniature temple motifs. All are covered by thick plaster. Vaishnava door guardians flank the temple entry and two displaced sculptures, of Garuda and a meditating figure, are found nearby.
   The temple is entered from the east into its northern chamber. This is a 2 × 2 column antechamber (2.6 m²). The walls are of long finely dressed and well-fitted horizontal slabs and the ceiling is composed of horizontal granite slabs. The south sanctuary chamber abuts the outcrop on the south and west, and is only partly walled. The central "image" in the sanctuary is an unusual vein in the outcrop against the rear (s) wall. An arch, carved into the outcrop, surrounds this aniconic image. Two sculpted guardian figures, with peacocks above them, flank it. The sanctuary's ceiling is elaborate, of rotated square form, with a lotus medallion in the center. Yalis and anthropomorphic figures are carved around the lotus medallion. The shikara is of plaster-covered brick, and sits on top of the outcrop.

Feature 2: Mandapa. Square (3.2 m²) 2 × 2 columned mandapa, located c. 8 m to the east of the temple (F1). The structure's heavily plastered walls are constructed of rectangular blocks that span the spaces between the columns. The ceiling is of rotated squares with a central lotus medallion. A square pit for an image base is visible within the shrine and a displaced image base is present outside. The structure has a badly preserved brick shikara.

Feature 3: Platform or memorial marker. This stepped plastered platform is located c. 16 m north of the main temple (F1). It is located on top of a boulder, with a column to its east, and is probably of recent construction. A rubble wall bounds the north end of the boulder and is an extension of the north wall of the temple compound. The marker is located at the center of a small platform, 4.5 × 4.5 m in dimension. It rests on a smaller heavily plastered platform, 2.1 × 1.15 × 0.55 m, and is square in plan, 1.1 m across at the base, and stepped in three tiers. There is a small triangular niche in the center of the lowest tier and a circular niche in the middle tier. The upper tier has three protruding sculpted lotus petals or half medallions on each face. Images of the wheel, conch, trident, and parasol (?) are sculpted on the face of each petal. To the east of this marker is a column with a square base, and octagonal upper section. Near the top is a square pedestal with carved pipal leaf motif. This feature appears to postdate the Vijayanagara period. The stairway leading up to the marker consists of several stone blocks including at least one displaced Vijayanagara-style molding fragment.

Feature 4: Stairway. This feature consists of two flights of stairs extending down to the west from the walled temple complex. It provides the main point of entry into the temple complex. From the top (east end) there is a small flight of six steps oriented north-south. Below is a bedrock platform, from which the stairway continues down to the west for twenty-four steps. This lower flight of stairs is 1.5 m wide at the top and broadens to 4.5 m in width at the bottom. The stairs are constructed of rectangular blocks c. 0.60 × 0.30 × 0.15 m in dimension. At the base of the stairs is a sloping passage of smoothed sheet rock, c. 4 m wide × 24 m long (east-west). The passage is bordered by stones and large rectangular blocks to the north and south. At the western end of the passage are two low stone and rubble platforms; the south platform is 4 m east-west × 2 m north-south; the north platform is 4 m east-west × 7 m north-south.

Feature 5: Mandapa. This 2 × 2 column mandapa (c. 5 m on a side) is located c. 16 m to the west of the north platform of Feature 4 and due north of temple-tank VMS-43. The walls are of recent construction, though the columns are consistent with a Vijayanagara period date. A large Vijayanagara period Hanuman carving has been set into the structure's rear wall.

Feature 6: Square chamber or basin. This chamber (c. 2.25 m on a side) has three walls preserved to a height of 0.3 m. The interior of the structure is lined with plaster and some plaster is visible on the top of the east wall, indicating that this was most probably a basin rather than the foundation of a structure.

Feature 7: Mandapa. 2 × 2 column (3 × 3 m) mandapa located within an 8 × 12 rectangular enclosure. The mandapa's columns are roughly dressed with Vijayanagara quarry marks visible. The mandapa is partly walled with small irregular stones, though the structure does not appear to have been used for some time. The enclosure walls are of unmodified small to medium stones, with irregular coursing. While the mandapa likely dates to the Vijayanagara period, the enclosure appears to be a later addition to the complex.

Artifacts: Some modern ceramics; no collections made.
Temporal Affiliation: Vijayanagara, with later modifications.
References: Sinopoli 1993b:629; Morrison 1995:64, 73-74, 79-80.
Illustrations: Figures 3.27, 3.28; Plates 3.12-3.14.

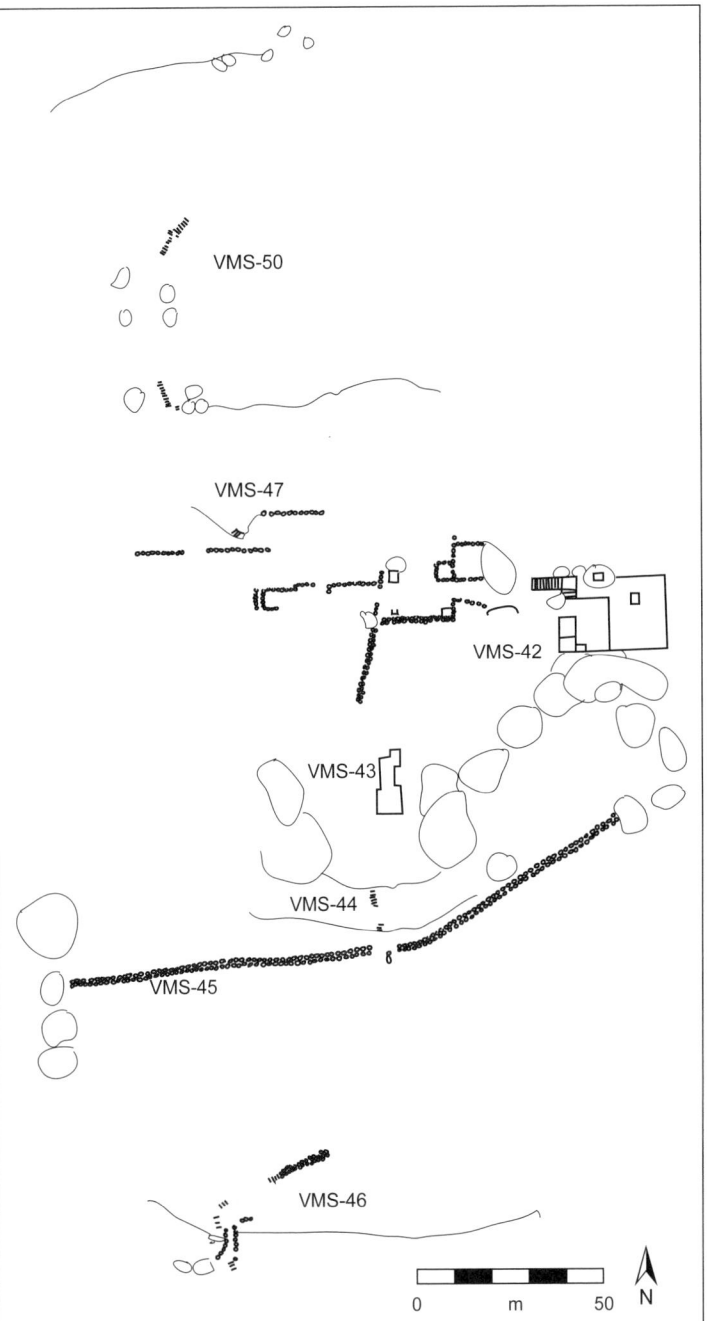

Figure 3.27. VMS-42–47, VMS-50, temple complex.

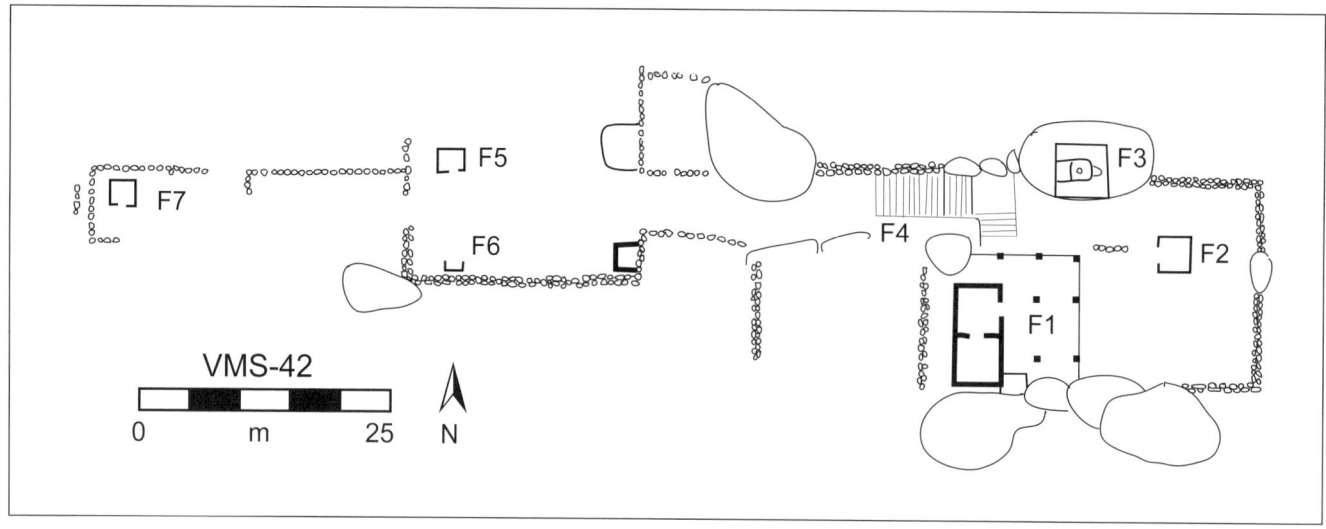

Figure 3.28. VMS-42, plan.

Plate 3.12. VMS-42, main temple (F1).

Block O: Site Summaries 57

Plate 3.13. VMS-42, mandapa (F2).

Plate 3.14. VMS-42, stairway (F4) and memorial marker (F3).

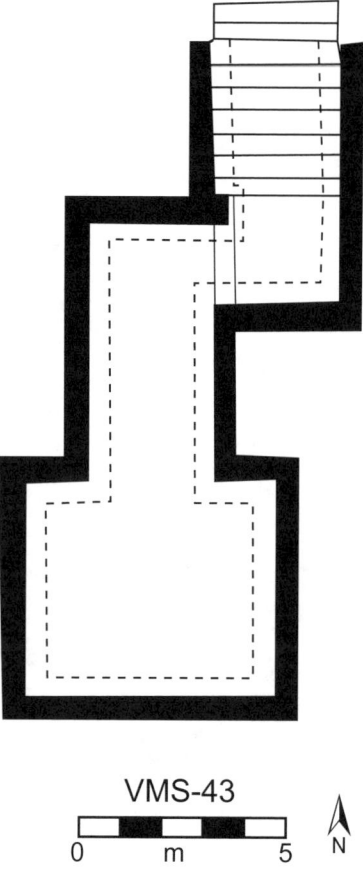

Figure 3.29. VMS-43, plan.

Plate 3.15. VMS-43, step well.

SITE: VMS-43   Block: O   Transect: 2
Primary Site Use: Water storage: temple tank.
Site Dimensions: 15 × 6 m
Setting: On outcrop above and to the south of temple VMS-42, terrain slopes down to the north.
Present Land Use/Disturbances: Modern enclosure wall around tank.
Site Description: Runoff-fed step tank. This temple tank is associated with the temple complex (VMS-42) and is located along a transportation route across the large outcrop on which it is located. It is of the Vijayanagara keyhole shape with the water basin in the south and stairway to the north. The stairway is not centered, but is offset to the east, requiring a change in direction to reach the water basin. The sides of the tank are constructed of tightly fitted rectangular slabs, c. 1.8 m long × 0.27 m high. The slabs are roughly dressed; some chinking was used. Four courses are visible above the present water level; above these is a narrow ledge that projects c. 0.10 m toward the water basin. The five courses above this are set back c. 0.35 m from the ledge edge. On the south face, an occasional square block protrudes out toward the basin. These may have served as footholds. The uppermost course of the tank protrudes slightly toward the basin interior and is constructed of much longer slabs than the courses below. Set atop this course, but set back c. 0.33 m, is a course of long undressed slabs set on edge. These form low walls surrounding the tank on the south, west, and east. The upper edges of the slab have been roughly beveled.
Artifacts: Two concentrations of artifacts are associated with this site: the largest is on the north near the top of the stairs. A smaller concentration is on the west of the tank along the traffic route. 100% collection in 5 m radius around site. 450 g ceramics; wares: 149 black plain ware, 8 red plain ware. Diagnostics: 5 jars.
Temporal Affiliation: Vijayanagara.
References: Sinopoli 1991; Morrison 1995:70, 73-74; Sinopoli and Morrison 1991:67.
Illustrations: Figures 3.27, 3.29; Plate 3.15.

SITE: VMS-44   Block: O   Transect: 2
  Primary Site Use: Transport: stairs.
  Site Dimensions: 15 × 3 m
  Setting: Near peak of outcrop hill, terrain slopes down from south to north. Site is located south of tank VMS-43 and temple VMS-42. The stairs are located at a point of change in outcrop slope, and served to facilitate movement across steeper portions of the outcrop.
  Present Land Use/Disturbances: Some thorny scrub vegetation on lower stairs.
  Site Description: Stairs. This site contains two flights of stairs extending down the outcrop slope from south to north toward temple tank VMS-43 and temple VMS-42. The flights are spaced 8 m apart, and are oriented roughly north-south. The upper southern stairway consists of six steps constructed of roughly modified large stones. They are significantly larger than the lower flight, and are c. 3.2 m wide × 0.62 m deep × 0.24 m high. The lower (northern) flight is oriented 6° west of north and consists of fourteen rock-cut steps, c. 0.55 wide × 0.24 m deep. The height of the stairs ranges from 0.03 to 0.10 m, varying with the slope of the outcrop. A low wall constructed of unmodified and split large stones extends to the east of the north end of the north stairs for 6.4 m.
  Artifacts: 100% collection; no artifacts recovered.
  Temporal Affiliation: Vijayanagara, associated with sites VMS-42 and VMS-43.
  References: Sinopoli 1991; Morrison 1995:64, 74.
  Illustrations: Figure 3.27.

SITE: VMS-45   Block: O   Transect: 2
  Primary Site Use: Transport/defensive: wall.
  Site Dimensions: 184 × 2.4 m
  Setting: Below and just to the north of the peak of the outcrop hill containing temple VMS-42, tank VMS-43, and VMS-44–47.
  Present Land Use/Disturbances: Some quarrying in and around wall.
  Site Description: Double-faced wall. This 184 m long east-west wall spans an area of sheet rock between outcropping boulders. It is associated with transport site VMS-44 and with temple complex VMS-42. A gap in the wall is located c. 5 m due south of the upper stairs of VMS-44. A short wall of roughly shaped boulders extends south from this gap, further defining the transport route over the outcrop.
  The main wall is c. 2.4 m wide with two faces and a rubble core. It is preserved up to one to two courses, and is constructed of large unmodified stones and split and shaped rectangular blocks. This wall served to channel movement over the outcrop through the central passage. It may thus have had a defensive role as well as its role in managing movement.
  Artifacts: 100% collection; no artifacts recovered.
  Temporal Affiliation: Vijayanagara.
  References: Sinopoli 1991; Morrison 1995:64, 74.
  Illustrations: Figure 3.27.

SITE: VMS-46   Block: O   Transect: 2
  Primary Site Use: Transport: stairs and associated footpaths.
  Site Dimensions: 70 × 2.8 m
  Setting: On southern face of outcrop near outcrop base. The outcrop slopes up from south to north toward site VMS-45, the long wall located near the outcrop peak.
  Present Land Use/Disturbances: Modern quarrying nearby.
  Site Description: Stairs and paths. This site consists of seven separate flights of stairs, including rock-cut and constructed steps, ascending from south to north near the base of the large outcrop containing temple complex VMS-42 and associated sites. The flights of two to six stairs each are separated by 1-12 m areas of worn sheet rock. A 16.8 m long stone pavement extends to the northeast from the topmost stairway and is constructed of irregularly placed small-medium stones, with a retaining wall on the south edge. The lowermost stairway is oriented 12° east of north and is 13.6 m long. It is paralleled by a low rubble wall that incorporates natural boulders and outcrops in its construction. The walls and stairs most likely served to regulate movement across the outcrop and to the temple complex.
  Artifacts: 100% collection; no artifacts recovered.
  Temporal Affiliation: Vijayanagara.
  References: Sinopoli 1991; Morrison 1995:64, 74.
  Illustrations: Figure 3.27.

SITE: VMS-47   Block: O   Transect: 2
  Primary Site Use: Transport: rock-cut stairs and walls.
  Site Dimensions: c. 60 × 40 m
  Setting: On north downslope side of large outcrop containing VMS-42–46. VMS-47 is located near the bottom of the slope in an area of extensive sheet rock.
  Present Land Use/Disturbances: Modern quarrying.
  Site Description: Walls and stairway. This site is located 18 m north of temple complex VMS-42/F7 on sheet rock that slopes down to the north. The southernmost feature of the site is an east-west oriented wall, constructed of large modified tightly fitted blocks. The wall is up to 1.08 m wide and two courses high. The wall extends west for 41 m, with a gap in the center, and abuts large outcropping boulders. North of the wall's east end is a stairway of three constructed steps and one natural step; an east-west wall extends to the east of the stairway and is similar in construction to the lower wall. A rock-cut stairway consisting of fifteen roughly cut and heavily worn steps, averaging 0.56 m wide × 0.26 m deep × 0.07 m high, is located c. 50 m northwest of the lower stairway.
  Artifacts: 100% collection; no artifacts recovered.
  Temporal Affiliation: Vijayanagara.
  References: Sinopoli 1991; Morrison 1995:64, 74.
  Illustrations: Figure 3.27.

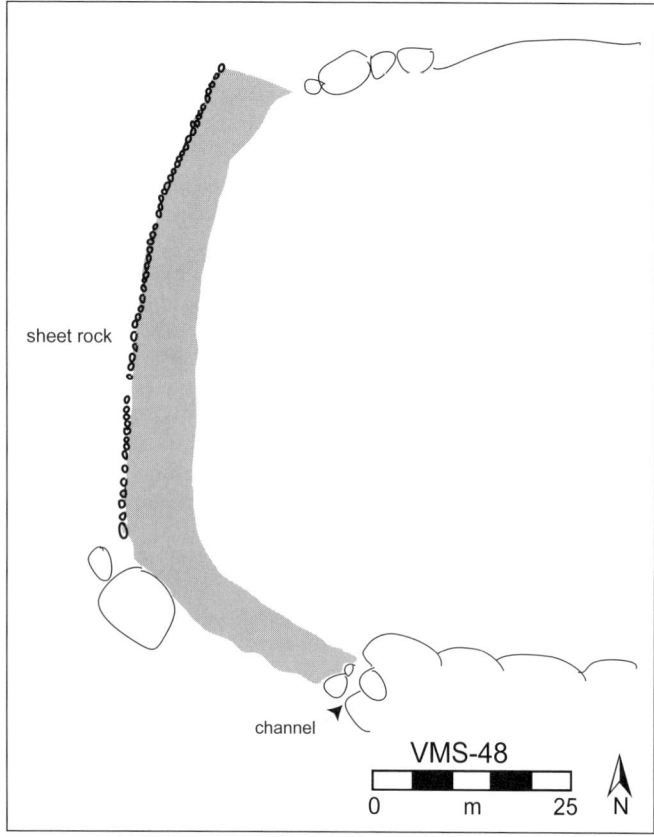

Figure 3.30. VMS-48, plan.

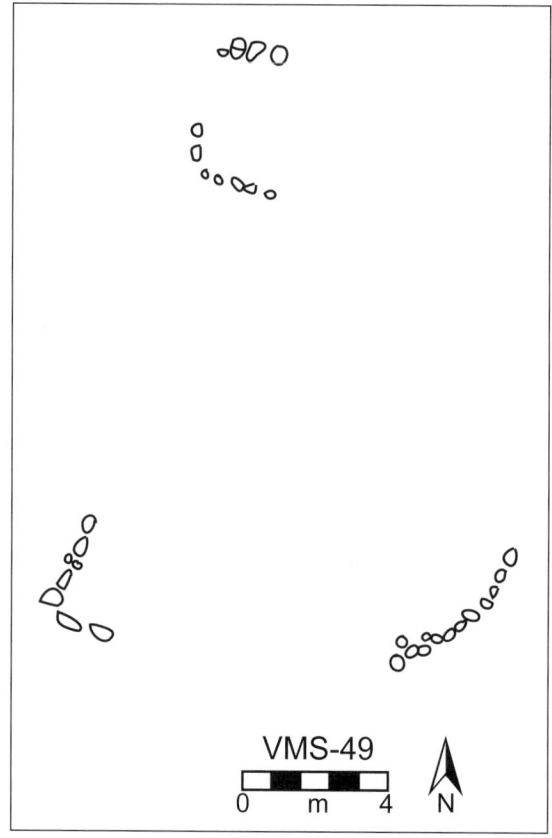

Figure 3.31. VMS-49, plan.

SITE: VMS-48 Block: O Transect: 1/2
Primary Site Use: Agricultural: earthen reservoir embankment.
Site Dimensions: 78 × 12 m
Setting: In small colluvial valley to south of high outcrop.
Present Land Use/Disturbances: Recent quarrying in area. There has been considerable slope wash and soil accumulation within embankment basin.
Site Description: Water control embankment. This low earthen embankment is predominantly oriented north-south, though it turns to the east near its south end. It extends from the south edge of a large outcrop and abuts large outcropping boulders in the south. The earthen embankment is c. 1.5 m high by 10-12 m in width. It enclosed an area, c. 65 × 80 m in extent, to the east. This 0.5 ha basin would have retained runoff from the surrounding slopes to the north, south, and east. At the base of the embankment's west face is a single course of large unmodified rounded stones (c. 1 × 0.5 m). There is no stone facing on the east.

This feature thus differs from most Vijayanagara period reservoirs in that it lacks the characteristic stepped stone facing on the catchment basin side. It likely functioned to maintain moisture within the valley to its east, rather than to channel water to the west, where there is only sheet rock. At the south end of the embankment is a 0.60 m wide channel located between outcropping boulders. This channel could have served to release excess runoff from the area impounded by the embankment.

Artifacts: 100% collection; 1 quartz/quartzite pebble core.
Temporal Affiliation: Vijayanagara.
References: Morrison 1995:89, 102; Lycett 1991; Sinopoli and Morrison 1991:68; Sinopoli 1991.
Illustrations: Figure 3.30.

SITE: VMS-49 Block: O Transect: 2
Primary Site Use: Residential?: isolated rubble walls.
Site Dimensions: 23 m × 16 m
Setting: Located in flat area with soil accumulation amid outcropping boulders. Site is situated on the north edge of a low outcrop hill, to the south of VMS-48.
Present Land Use/Disturbances: Recent canal and power station to the southwest, considerable soil accumulation from slope wash from outcrop. The site is overgrown with thick grasses; surface visibility is poor.
Site Description: Three spatially segregated areas of isolated rubble walls. The walls are constructed of medium and large loosely fit unmodified cobbles and boulders. The walls are L-shaped or semi-circular and are spaced approximately 8-10 m apart. They were likely foundation walls, and may be the remnants of a short-term residential camp. Alternately, these may have been associated with embankment VMS-48, located nearby.
Artifacts: 100% collection; no artifacts recovered.
Temporal Affiliation: Unknown.
Illustrations: Figure 3.31.

Plate 3.16. VMS-50, stairs.

Plate 3.17. VMS-51, stairs.

SITE: VMS-50 Block: O Transect: 1
   Primary Site Use: Transport: rock-cut stairs.
   Site Dimensions: 12 × 0.67 m
   Setting: On outcrop sloping down to north.
   Present Land Use/Disturbances: Modern quarrying.
   Site Description: Three stairways. These stair segments are located on the north face of the high outcrop containing temple complex VMS-42, and have a predominant orientation of 28° east of north. The top, southernmost, section is rock-cut, and consists of a flight of nine narrow steps (average dimensions: 0.48 × 0.33 × 0.08 m). The central segment, to its north, is a short segment of two parallel stairways, 0.85 m in length and 0.20 m apart. Further north is the lowermost stairway, 5.6 m long and constructed of modified rectangular blocks. This site is part of the transportation corridor over the outcrop and to temple complex, VMS-42.
   Artifacts: 100% collection; no artifacts recovered.
   Temporal Affiliation: Vijayanagara.
   References: Sinopoli 1991; Morrison 1995:64, 74.
   Illustrations: Figure 3.27; Plate 3.16.

SITE: VMS-51 Block: O Transect: 2
   Primary Site Use: Transport: stairs.
   Site Dimensions: 10 × 2 m
   Setting: On sheet rock sloping down to the north on the northeast face of the outcrop hill containing VMS-42 and associated sites.
   Present Land Use/Disturbances: None.
   Site Description: Rock-cut stairs. These stairs provide a route across an expanse of sloping sheet rock and head down to the north to the small valley containing VMS-21. Although no other sites are located in the immediate vicinity of VMS-51, this locale provides excellent visibility of the valley below. From east to west, the stairs curve around the edge of a sheet rock outcrop, oriented roughly east-west, and then turn down to the north. The fifteen steps are very well cut and are tightly spaced. They average 0.40 m wide × 0.3 m deep × 0.05-0.10 m high.
   Artifacts: 100% collection; no artifacts recovered.
   Temporal Affiliation: Vijayanagara.
   References: Sinopoli 1991.
   Illustrations: Plate 3.17.

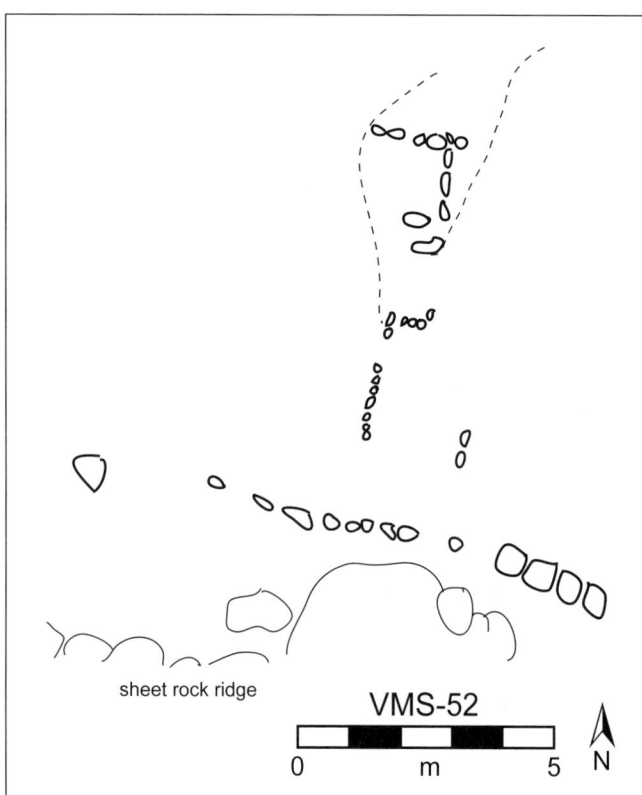

Figure 3.32. VMS-52, plan.

SITE: VMS-52   Block: O   Transect: 2
   Primary Site Use: Agricultural/transport: walls.
   Site Dimensions: 20 × 15 m
   Setting: These walls are located in an area of gently sloping colluvium along the south edge of a valley. They sit at the north base of a large outcropping hill containing Vijayanagara period temple complex VMS-42 and associated sites (VMS-43–47, 50, 51).
   Present Land Use/Disturbances: Considerable erosion and colluviation.
   Site Description: Multiple walls. This site consists of a number of walls that likely had diverse functions. On the south end of the site, along the north face of a large outcrop hill, is a large east-west trending wall. This c. 20 m long wall segment parallels the base of the outcrop, which lies some 1-5 m to its south. It is constructed of a single course of large-very large unmodified stones and is undoubtedly a continuation of VMS-53, located c. 100 m to the east. The wall most likely served to define a transport route along the base of the outcrop, though it may also have functioned to control runoff from the outcrop.
   The other component of this site consists of several walls, of smaller unmodified stones, that extend north into the valley and incorporate outcropping boulders. These walls are visible due to a deep erosional gully, and may have extended much further than presently discernible. They appear to have been associated with agricultural activities, and may have been check dams or part of a terrace system.
   Artifacts: Moderately dense ceramic scatter associated with a localized and variable distribution. Areas to the southwest (area 1) and northeast (area 2) of the long wall were collected separately.
   Area 1: 600 g ceramics; wares: 59 black plain ware, 17 red plain ware, 2 black decorated. Diagnostics: 1 lamp, 4 jars.
   Area 2: 200 g ceramics; wares: 55 black plain ware, 4 red plain ware. Diagnostics: 2 jars.
   Temporal Affiliation: Vijayanagara?
   References: Morrison 1995:89, 102.
   Illustrations: Figure 3.32.

SITE: VMS-53   Block: O   Transect: 2
   Primary Site Use: Transport: walls.
   Site Dimensions: 14 × 0.5 m
   Setting: On sheet rock near north edge of outcrop.
   Present Land Use/Disturbances: Soil deposition upslope of wall, small runoff channel down slope.
   Site Description: Wall segments. This site consists of three wall segments, oriented predominantly east-west and located along the north edge of a large outcrop. The easternmost wall segment is 7 m long and is constructed of large unmodified stones. A gap of c. 1 m separates this wall from two parallel walls to the west. The latter are oriented slightly to the north of east, and are spaced c. 2 m apart. The terrain to the south of the wall is slightly elevated above the fields to the north. This site is probably a continuation of site VMS-52, some 100 m to its west, and most likely served to define an elevated path or transport route along the base of the outcrop.
   Artifacts: Very sparse scatter of nondiagnostic ceramics. 100% collection. <50 g ceramics; wares: 4 black plain ware, 1 red decorated.
   Temporal Affiliation: Vijayanagara?
   References: Morrison 1995:89, 102.

SITE: VMS-54   Block: O   Transect: 2
   Primary Site Use: Industrial: lime processing.
   Site Dimensions: 8.5 m diameter
   Setting: Low-lying area within a fallow agricultural field.
   Present Land Use/Disturbances: Site is located within an agricultural field.
   Site Description: Circular mound of calcium carbonate. The interior of this 8.5 m diameter "ring" is depressed about 1 m below the ring's top level. It appears to be a soak pit of some sort, perhaps for leaching lime or *kankar* deposits prior to heat processing. The ring is located within a square enclosure (90 m on a side) defined by low earthen walls; these appear to be field boundaries and may be of relatively recent date.
   Artifacts: 100% collection; no artifacts recovered.
   Temporal Affiliation: Unknown.
   References: Morrison 1995:85.

SITE: VMS-55   Block: O   Transect: 2
   Primary Site Use: Unknown: wall.
   Site Dimensions: 2.5 × 0.5 m
   Setting: On north slopes of large outcrop, near its base.
   Present Land Use/Disturbances: Recent quarrying in this area has disturbed many stones; the site may have originally been much larger.
   Site Description: Wall segment. This 2.5 m long wall segment is loosely constructed of six medium to large unmodified stones. It is oriented 26° north of west. There are several possible wall segments similar to this one along the base of the outcrop, but this area has been heavily disturbed by quarrying and the original extent of these features is not discernible. Perhaps transport related or erosion control features.
   Artifacts: Sparse ceramic scatter. 100% collection. <50 g ceramics; wares: 13 black plain ware, 1 red plain ware.
   Temporal Affiliation: Unknown.
   References: Morrison 1995:89, 102.

SITE: VMS-56   Block: O   Transect: 6
   Primary Site Use: Unknown: wall.
   Site Dimensions: 5 × 0.5 m
   Setting: Low-lying area amid agricultural fields.
   Present Land Use/Disturbances: Area is being farmed. Footpaths and a recent well are located nearby.
   Site Description: North-south wall segment. This 5 m long wall segment of unknown temporal affiliation is located at the east boundary of a modern agricultural field, between the field and an area of thorny scrub and cactus. May be an earlier field boundary?
   Artifacts: 100% collection; no artifacts recovered.
   Temporal Affiliation: Unknown.

SITE: VMS-57   Block: O   Transect: 6
   Primary Site Use: Unknown: wall.
   Site Dimensions: 20 × c. 0.5 m
   Setting: Area of gently sloping terrain on edge of agricultural fields.
   Present Land Use/Disturbances: Irrigation canals in area. Some of the smaller stones incorporated into the wall have recent quarry marks and are new additions.
   Site Description: East-west wall. This 20 m long wall segment is constructed of a single course of large unmodified stones, c. 0.80 m on a side, interspersed with smaller stones. Soil accumulation to the south of the wall is greater than on the north. The wall may have had an agricultural function, in limiting soil erosion or bounding a field. The wall may turn to the north on the east edge, but only a few poorly aligned stones are evident.
   Artifacts: Light ceramic scatter. 100% collection. <50 g ceramics; wares: 8 black plain ware. Diagnostics: 2 pedestal vessels. Lithics: 1 possible quartzite flake.
   Temporal Affiliation: Unknown.

SITE: VMS-58   Block: O   Transect: 4
   Primary Site Use: Agricultural/transport: wall.
   Site Dimensions: 12 × 0.60 m
   Setting: On northwest edge of outcrop near its base, immediately above agricultural fields.
   Present Land Use/Disturbances: Extensive recent quarrying of stone and soil.
   Site Description: Wall. This wall runs along the northwest edge of a large outcrop. It is oriented 18° east of north and supports a low terrace to its east (against the outcrop) c. 1 m above the present ground level. The wall is constructed of rounded unmodified small-medium stones (0.4-0.6 m in dimension) with some modified blocks. Two courses are preserved. This is probably a retaining wall that helped to limit slope wash and control runoff from the outcrop. It may also have defined a route of movement along the outcrop edge above the nearby fields. A similarly constructed east-west wall extends c. 6 m out perpendicular to the outcrop from a point 5 m beyond the north edge of the first wall.
   Artifacts: 100% collection; no artifacts recovered.
   Temporal Affiliation: Unknown.
   References: Morrison 1995:89, 102.

SITE: VMS-59   Block: O   Transect: 4
   Primary Site Use: Agricultural: reservoir embankment.
   Site Dimensions: 22 × >12 m
   Setting: Low-lying area with outcropping boulders within reservoir bed and to east of embankment.
   Present Land Use/Disturbances: Site has been heavily disturbed by canal and road construction; much of the embankment has been destroyed. The site is located near the confluence of two major modern irrigation canals.
   Site Description: Reservoir embankment and sluice. This site consists of the fragmentary remains of what was once a very large and elaborately constructed reservoir embankment. The embankment is oriented 30° north of east. On its northeast end it abuts a hill of outcropping boulders; its west terminus has been destroyed by recent canal construction. The stepped stone south face of the embankment is preserved up to sixteen courses (c. 7 m above the current ground surface). It is constructed of roughly worked stone blocks, c. 1-1.25 m long × 0.4 m high, and incorporates large *in situ* boulders along parts of its length. The original width of the embankment is not determinable, but is at least 12-15 m.

   A large undecorated sluice gate is located near the east end of the embankment (perhaps one of several original sluices). It rises c. 8-10 m above present ground level. The upper cross-slab consists of inverted panels of angled beveled molding, separated by a horizontal panel. Corner and central pendant medallions occur on the top panel. A stone-lined outlet channel, c. 0.25 m wide, is visible in the base of the embankment.

   The construction of this site is far more formal and substantial than many of the other embankments in the region. It is not possible to measure the total length of the embankment. Given its scale and orientation, it is likely that it extended for at least half a kilometer and possibly much further. It likely supported substantial field systems to its north and east. A Vijayanagara period inscription was reported to be located on a nearby boulder (Patil and Patil 1995: insc. 407-8).
   Artifacts: Area heavily disturbed; no collections made.
   Temporal Affiliation: Vijayanagara.
   References: Morrison 1994:89, 102; Sinopoli and Morrison 1991:68.
   Illustrations: Figures 3.33, 3.34; Plates 3.18, 3.19.

SITE: VMS-60   Block: O   Transect: 4
   Primary Site Use: Agricultural/transport?: wall/terrace.
   Site Dimensions: 56 × 2 m
   Setting: Near south base of large outcrop hill.
   Present land use/disturbance: Modern canals and road nearby, some slope wash and wall collapse.
   Site Description: Crudely constructed wall or terrace. This wall is constructed of large unmodified and lightly modified stones, c. 0.6-0.8 m in dimension. Coursing is irregular with some chinking. The wall runs for c. 56 m and is oriented 40° west of north, forming a c. 2 m wide terrace on its northeast side (against the boulder). This wall may have served to prevent slope wash and control runoff into areas irrigated by reservoir VMS-59. It may also have defined an elevated route of movement along the base of the outcrop.
   Artifacts: 100% collection; no artifacts recovered.
   Temporal Affiliation: Vijayanagara?
   References: Morrison 1995:89, 102.

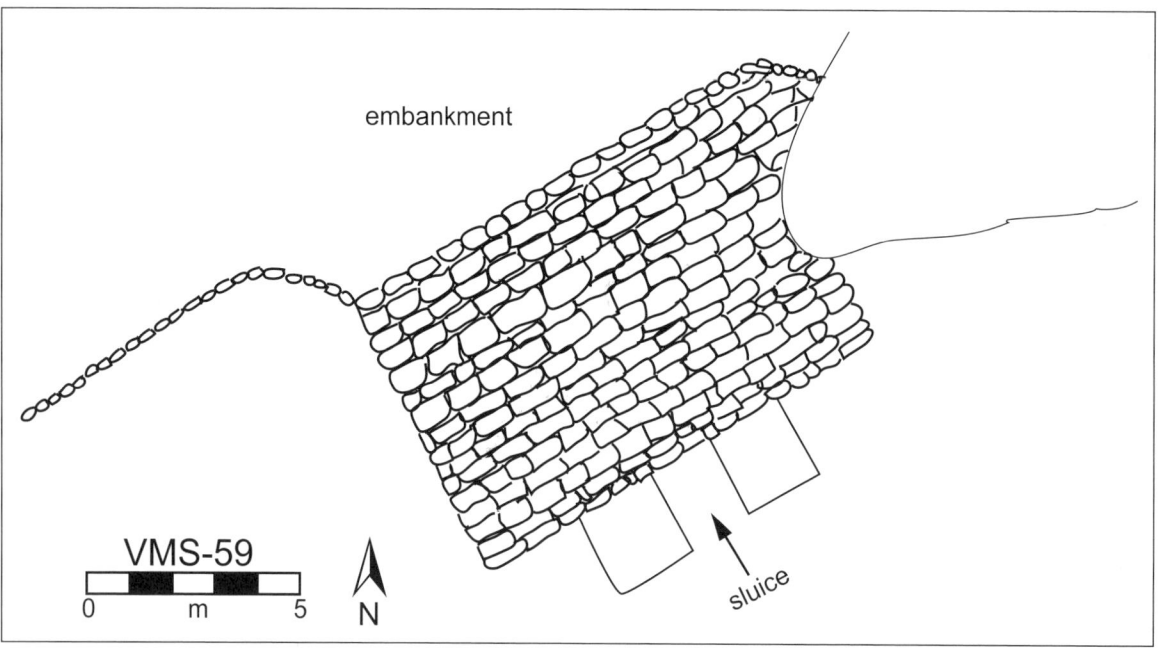

Figure 3.33. VMS-59, plan.

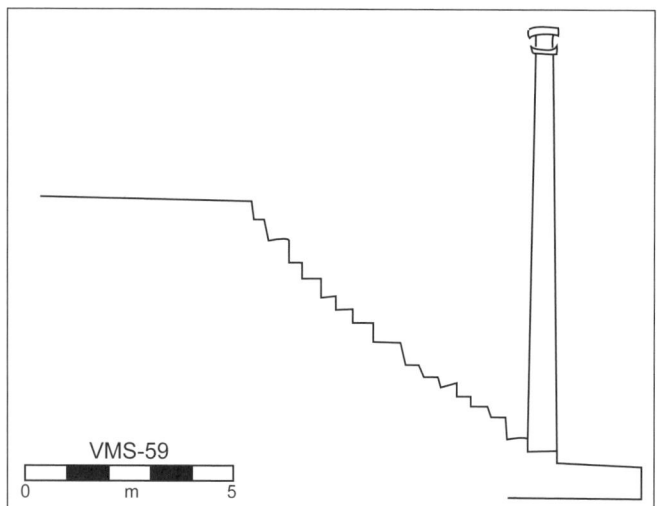

Figure 3.34. VMS-59, section.

Plate 3.19. VMS-59, reservoir, sluice and embankment detail.

Plate 3.18. VMS-59, reservoir overview.

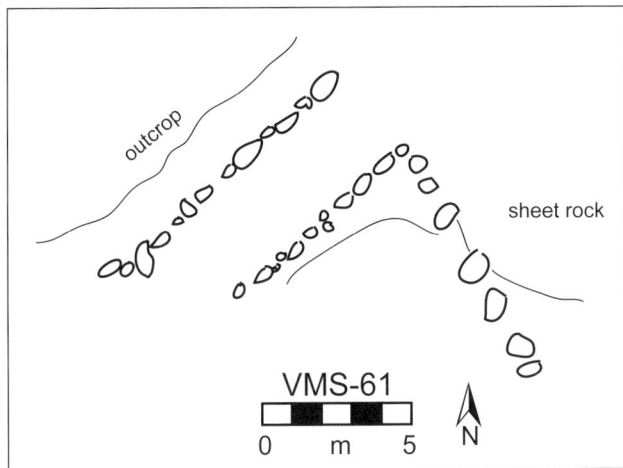

Figure 3.35. VMS-61, plan.

SITE: VMS-61   Block: O   **Transect:** 5
   Primary Site Use: Agricultural: walls.
   Site Dimensions: 12 × 10 m
   Setting: Near base east of large outcrop, in area of limited soil accumulation and exposed sheet rock.
   Present Land Use/Disturbances: Quarrying and quarry roads across sheet rock area.
   Site Description: Three wall segments. These small walls are located just east of high outcrop, with sheet rock to their north. There are two parallel single-faced, north-south oriented walls constructed of medium-large unmodified and split stones (c. 0.5 × 0.5 m in dimension). The walls are spaced c. 3.5 m apart with the west wall c. 11 m long and the east wall c. 8 m in length. A single course is visible. A third wall of similar construction is oriented perpendicular to the walls, and extends east along the south edge of sheet rock. These walls may have served to limit erosion and check runoff into fields to the south and east.
   Artifacts: 100% collection; no artifacts recovered.
   Temporal Affiliation: Unknown.
   References: Morrison 1995:89, 102.
   Illustrations: Figure 3.35.

SITE: VMS-62   Block: O   **Transect:** 5
   Primary Site Use: Defensive: embankment.
   Site Dimensions: 134 × 20 m
   Setting: Low-lying area east of large outcrop hill, exposed sheet rock to both north and south of feature.
   Present Land Use/Disturbances: Quarrying in area, soil on north face of embankment has been mostly removed, modern canal and road cut through the site on east.
   Site Description: Large wall/embankment. This roughly east-west oriented wall abuts an outcrop on the west and runs for more than 130 m to the east. The south stone face is slightly stepped and preserved up to seven courses. The wall is constructed of loosely fitted small to medium irregular unmodified and split stones with some chinking. The north face is a sloping earthen embankment. It has mostly been mined away, but stood about 1.5 m high and 15-20 m wide. Despite the structural similarity to reservoir embankments in the stepped face and embankment, there is little arable land nearby. Instead, there is a large expanse of sheet rock and outcrop c. 30 m north of the embankment and also immediately to its south. No sluices or channels are apparent. The site may have been a fortification wall spanning a low-lying area between outcrops and could have extended considerably further to the east.
   Artifacts: 100% collection; no artifacts recovered.
   Temporal Affiliation: Vijayanagara?
   References: Morrison 1995:64, 89, 102.
   Illustrations: Figure 3.36.

SITE: VMS-63   Block: O   **Transect:** 5
   Primary Site Use: Unknown: wall.
   Site Dimensions: 55 × 1.0 m
   Setting: Low-lying region near the north edge of a large outcrop hill.
   Present Land Use/Disturbances: Modern foot trails.
   Site Description: Large wall. This northwest-southeast oriented wall is constructed of unmodified irregular stones, 0.60-1.0 m in dimension. The wall runs for 40 m along its major axis and then turns further to the southeast for 4 m. It defined a transport route or could have served as an erosion control feature.
   Artifacts: 100% collection; no artifacts recovered.
   Temporal Affiliation: Unknown.
   References: Morrison 1995:89, 102.

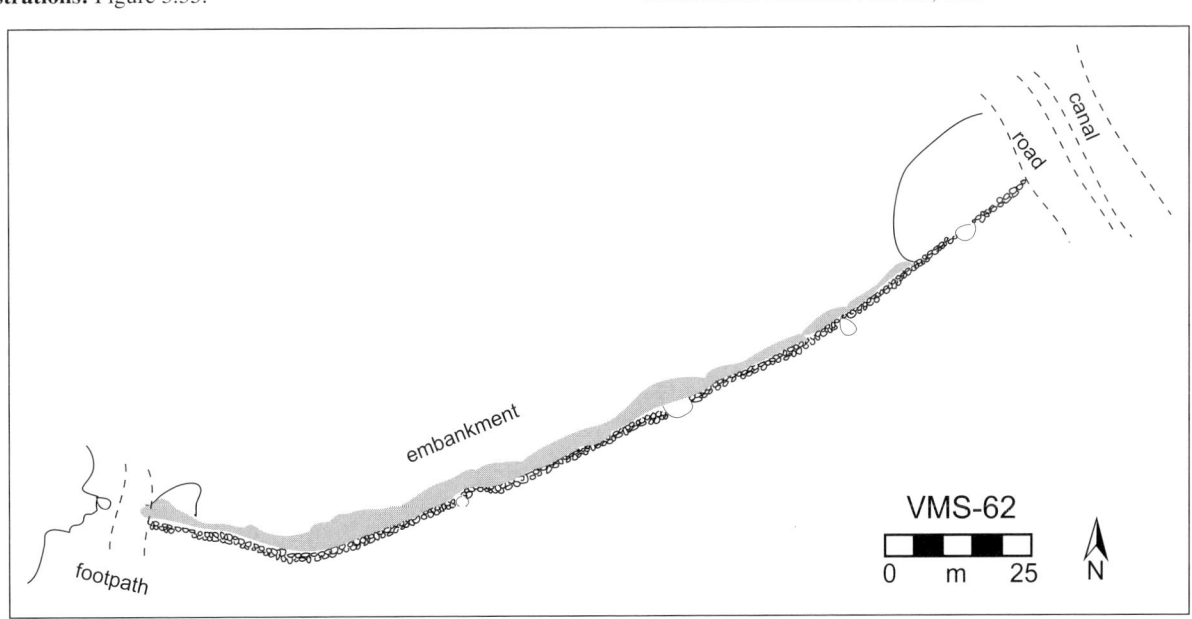

Figure 3.36. VMS-62, plan.

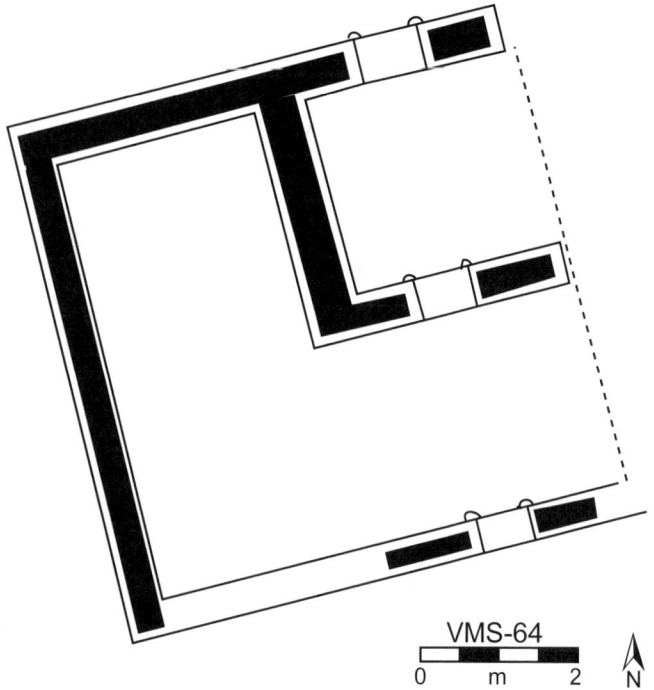

Figure 3.37. VMS-64, plan.

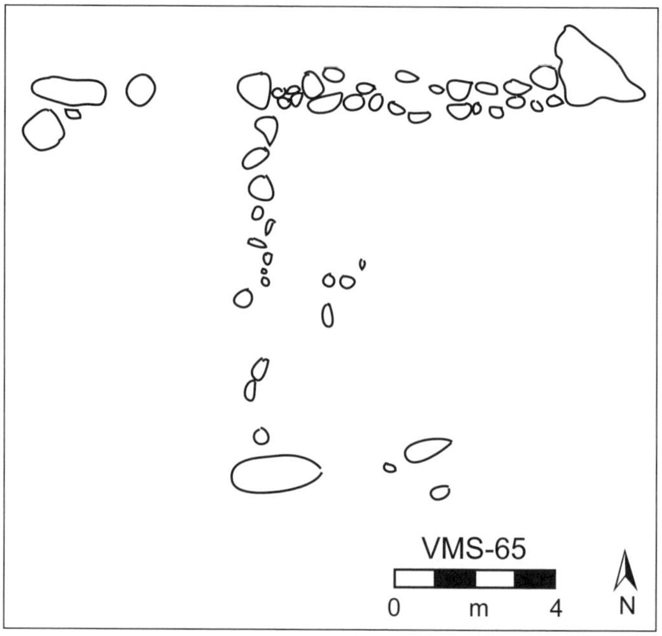

Figure 3.38. VMS-65, plan.

SITE: VMS-64   Block: O   Transect: 6
Primary Site Use: Transport/administrative: structure.
Site Dimensions: 6.4 × 6.4 m
Setting: Along Kampli Road between Venkatapur and Bukkasagara.
GPS Location: 15°19'38.9" N, 76°30'45.9" E
Present Land Use/Disturbances: Damage to the east portion of the structure. The structure has been recently occupied and used as a stable.
Site Description: Columned structure. This multi-roomed structure of post and lintel construction is built on a well-constructed c. 1 m high foundation platform without moldings. Six columns are preserved of what probably was originally a nine-column structure. The columns are square and, like the rectangular capitals, are unadorned. Three aligned doorways provide access through the structure, through its east bay (perhaps originally a central bay?). Wide rectangular slabs support lintels containing two door sockets on the north face of each door.

The west end of the structure is walled, as are the west portions of the north wall and the north half of the central axis. No walls are preserved on the east face or on the south face. The walls are constructed of horizontal slabs, c. 2.6 × 0.4 × 0.4 m, laid in well-fitted horizontal courses with no mortar or chinking. The ceiling is of east-west oriented slabs similar to the walls. The south door has a raised threshold. The building is Vijayanagara in style. It is possible that the building was symmetrical, with the doors in the center, and that the east portion has been destroyed. This well-constructed structure may have been a roadside facility, such as a rest house or way station. It was probably not residential.
Artifacts: Some probable modern ceramics within structure; very few artifacts outside the structure. 100% collection; 50 g ceramics; wares: 22 black plain ware, 4 red plain ware, 1 red decorated.
Temporal Affiliation: Vijayanagara.
References: Morrison 1995:72.
Illustrations: Figure 3.37.

SITE: VMS-65   Block: O   Transect: 4
Primary Site Use: Residential: rubble wall structure.
Site Dimensions: 7 × 5 m
Setting: On lower north slopes of large outcrop hill, area of thin soil accumulation.
Present Land Use/Disturbances: Some stone quarrying in area.
Site Description: L-shaped foundation walls. These single-course walls are located on a relatively flat area of a high outcrop. The walls are constructed of small irregular unmodified stones and were likely foundation walls for a structure of impermanent materials. Approximately 10 m to the east of the structure is a mound of stones c. 1 m high × 3 m in diameter. There is another small wall located 33 m to the southwest.
Artifacts: Sparse scatter. 100% collection. <50 g ceramics; wares: 4 black plain ware. 1 modern glass bangle.
Temporal Affiliation: Unknown.
Illustrations: Figure 3.38.

SITE: VMS-66   Block: O   Transect: 5
Primary Site Use: Residential/other: artifact scatter.
Site Dimensions: 96 × 58+ m
Setting: Low-lying irrigated fields.
Present Land Use/Disturbances: Modern canal on north edge of the scatter, in modern sugar cane field and processing area.
Site Description: Moderately dense artifact scatter. This extensive scatter (long axis oriented east-west) consists largely of ceramics, including a large number of diagnostic sherds. Some modern bangle fragments and metal pieces were also found. Some low wall fragments possibly define field borders or other features; these are probably remnants of relatively recent activities. The scatter may be associated with manuring activity or short-term residential activities in the area.

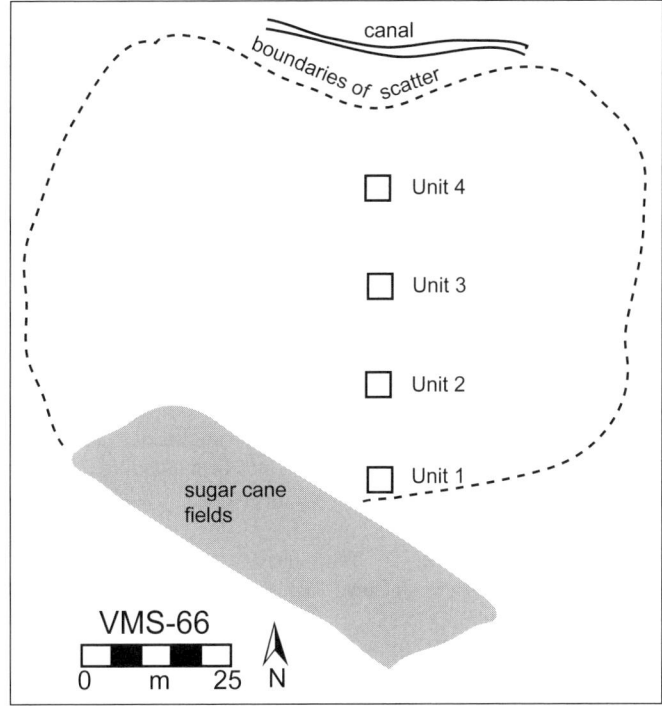

Figure 3.39. VMS-66, plan.

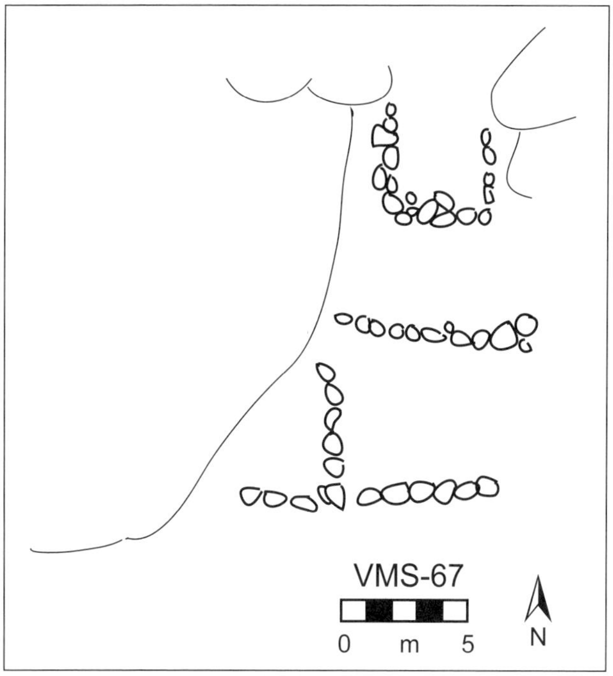

Figure 3.40. VMS-67, plan.

Artifacts: A systematic collection was made along a central north-south axis, with four 4 × 4 m units located c. 16 m apart; artifacts were recovered in units 1 and 2. A diagnostic collection was also conducted. Collection units were numbered sequentially from south to north.

Unit 1: 100 g ceramics; wares: 11 black plain ware, 2 red plain ware. Diagnostics: 2 bowls, 1 jar.

Unit 2: 200 g ceramics; wares: 17 black plain ware, 4 red plain ware, 1 red decorated. Diagnostics: 1 bowl, 6 jars.

Temporal Affiliation: Unknown; some of the ceramics are clearly recent, while others may date to Vijayanagara period.

Illustrations: Figure 3.39.

SITE: VMS-67   Block: O   Transect: 6
  Primary Site Use: Residential: walls and structure.
  Site Dimensions: 17 × 13 m
  Setting: On outcrop, structures abut outcropping boulders on west and north, in area of thin soil accumulation.
  Present Land Use/Disturbances: Some slope wash.
  Site Description: Rectangular chamber and associated walls. This three-walled structure located in a flat area on a small outcrop is 5 × 4 m in dimension and abuts outcropping boulders to the north. Its walls are single faced, of medium-large unmodified and modified stones, c. 0.6-0.8 m in dimension. The flat ground surface to the south of this structure was likely the result of terracing; three walls below and to the south of the structure served as retaining walls for terraces. The site is likely associated with short-term residential use.
  Artifacts: Localized scatter of ceramics in lower portions of the site, probably function of post-occupational slope wash and erosion. Four arbitrarily defined units were collected.

Unit 1 (upper tier and chamber): No artifacts recovered.
Unit 2 (lower terrace): 450 g ceramics; wares: 61 black plain ware, 1 red plain ware, 1 coarse ware. Diagnostics: 6 jars.
Unit 3 (lower terrace west of crosswall): 1250 g ceramics; wares: 83 black plain ware. Diagnostics: 1 jar (most sherds probably from one modern vessel).
Unit 4 (area beneath lower terrace): 300 g ceramics; wares: 126 black plain ware. Diagnostics: 1 jar.
  Temporal Affiliation: Unknown.
  Illustrations: Figure 3.40.

SITE: VMS-68   Block: O   Transect: 6
  Primary Site Use: Defensive?: wall.
  Site Dimensions: 24 × 0.5 m
  Setting: The north end of the wall abuts the base of a small outcrop; the south end terminates against an upright boulder in fallow agricultural fields.
  Present Land Use/Disturbances: Modern Kampli Road is c. 50 m to the south; fallow banana field to west.
  Site Description: Wall. This single-course wall is constructed of loosely fit, medium unmodified stones. The wall extends for 24 m north-south and is 0.40 m wide. The wall is perpendicular to the contemporary (and Vijayanagara period) Kampli Road, with which it may have been related. That is, if it had an earthen superstructure or additional stone courses, it would have served as an effective barrier to movement across this valley and would have channeled movement toward the main road course.
  Artifacts: 100% collection; no artifacts recovered.
  Temporal Affiliation: Unknown.

Plate 3.20. VMS-69, column detail.

In the courtyard are several architectural and sculpted pieces of Vijayanagara date. These include an upright column with several unusual carvings, including lingam and dancing figures. The more unusual sculptures on this column are crudely sculpted, in a "folk art" style. These include a snake charmer and stooped figure (farmer?) with a hoe or other tool over the shoulder. A round disc-shaped capital tops this column. In front of it is set a stone Nandi, four naga stones, and a carved block with a pair of feet encircled by a snake. Other small lingams, Nandi images, present in the courtyard are probably modern. Also in the courtyard is another stone Nandi, not in Vijayanagara style (probably recent).

On the east side of the courtyard facing the road along the Turtha Canal are two Vijayanagara period yali balustrades. The source of these various Vijayanagara temple elements is unknown; perhaps a larger temple once existed in this locale, or they were brought in from other collapsed temples in or near Venkatapuram.

Artifacts: Temple is in worship; no collections made.
Temporal Affiliation: Vijayanagara, plus later additions.
Illustrations: Plate 3.20.

SITE: VMS-70   Block: O   Transect: 5
Primary Site Use: Residential: rock shelter.
Site Dimensions: 4 × 3 m
Setting: On north face of small outcropping hill, with dry farmed fields to the north. Site is located to the north of Vijayanagara period (and modern) road.
Present Land Use/Disturbances: Intensive quarrying, near paved Kamalapuram-Kampli Road. Shelter is still in use as evidenced by recent hearths and artifacts.
Site Description: Rock shelter and inscribed images. This small shelter (4 × 3 m in area) is roofed by an overhanging boulder. Beneath the overhang is a flat sheet rock surface with two games pecked on it. The games are worn and patinated, and have clearly been here for some time. White and yellow dots and lines have been painted on the shelter ceiling. Defining the north edge of the shelter is an upright boulder. A lingam, c. 0.2 m high, and a well-executed Nandi are inscribed on it. These have no patina and appear to be relatively recent. The Roman letter "P" is pecked into the rock face, further supporting a recent interpretation. The stone at the cave entry has been fluted around its edges.
Artifacts: Light scatter of modern sherds, not collected.
Temporal Affiliation: Unknown. Game types familiar at Vijayanagara, although are also played today and are not temporally diagnostic.

SITE: VMS-71   Block: O   Transect: 4
Primary Site Use: Religious: displaced Vijayanagara images.
Site Dimensions: n.a.
Setting: Low-lying area near paved road between Kamalapuram and Kampli.
Present Land Use/Disturbances: Sculptures are located within modern structures.
Site Description: Vijayanagara period images. Three small recently constructed mandapas contain several Vijayanagara period images. The structures are found along the Kamalapuram-Kampli road near Venkatapuram Camp. To the north of the road is a single structure containing a large Vijayanagara striding Hanuman image carved on a slab c. 2.5 m high × 1.5 m wide × 0.5 m thick. Two shrines are located south of the road. Each contains multiple images, including Ganapati, nagas, and the goddess Nagamma (with a human torso and snake body). The original locations of these sculptures are unknown.
Artifacts: Modern ceramics and oil lamps; not collected.
Temporal Affiliation: Vijayanagara sculpture, modern structures.

SITE: VMS-69   Block: O   Transect: 7
Primary Site Use: Religious: Shaivite temple.
Site Dimensions: 25 × 25 m
Setting: Low-lying area adjacent to Turtha Canal and canal road. The temple is on the northeast edge of the contemporary settlement of Venkatapuram, and likely lay within Vijayanagara period Venkatpuram as well.
Present Land Use/Disturbances: Temple is still in worship and there have been many additions and alterations.
Site Description: Rectangular two-chamber temple. This east-facing temple is 8 × 3 columns in plan. The columns are of the mass-produced Vijayanagara style of square panels separated by recessed octagonal sections, and have simple rectangular capitals. The roof appears to be recent. The carved or sculpted plaster (?) door guardians and elephants on the lintel above the main entrance to the temple are also of recent construction. There is a small Vijayanagara carved slab with a Hanuman image in the sanctuary. The central image in the sanctuary is a lingam. The structure is so heavily plastered that its original outlines are unclear. The courtyard is probably a post-Vijayanagara addition, as is a porch attached to the structure.

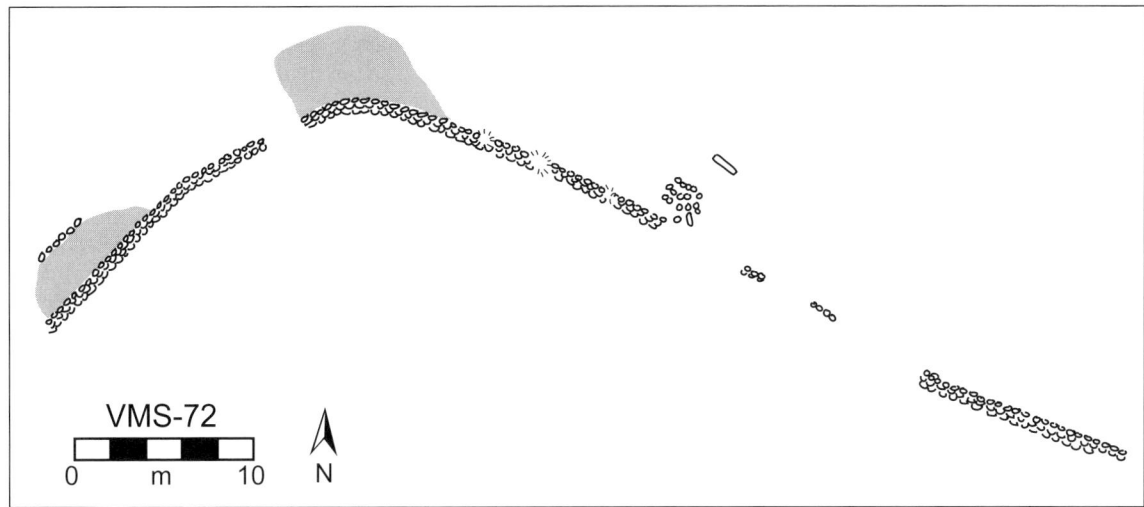

Figure 3.41. VMS-72, plan.

SITE: VMS-72   Block: O   Transect: 10
  Primary Site Use: Agricultural/water control: reservoir embankment.
  Site Dimensions: 126 × 12 m
  Setting: Gently sloping valley between two outcrops, reservoir abuts granitic outcrop on the west.
  Present Land Use/Disturbances: Much of soil and masonry of the embankment has been removed to nearby fields.
  Site Description: 126 m long reservoir embankment. The embankment faces south and is roughly semicircular, with a dominant orientation of 20° south of east. The embankment abuts a granitic outcrop on the west, but does not extend to the corresponding outcrop on the east, instead stopping c. 60 m from it. The area of impoundment is c. 80 × 100 m, encompassing the lower part of a small valley that is ringed by outcrops. The south border of settlement VMS-2 is c. 115 m to the north.
  The embankment is in very poor condition. Its south stone-lined face has up to six visible courses of stepped masonry of unmodified medium stones. At its west end, a single masonry course is evident on the north face. This may have been a foundation or retaining course for the earthen embankment. The embankment was c. 10-15 m wide.
  Eighty-two m from the west end of the embankment is the probable sluice area. Here the reservoir has been breached. To the north of the embankment is a rectangular structure, 2.8 × 1.3 m, and several large cut slabs and a few small square blocks. These are the only modified stones in the area. This feature was likely part of the water distribution system.
  To the south of the embankment near its west end is a broken column segment (c. 1 m long), with a square cross section at the base and a rounded upper section. Its original context is unknown.
  Artifacts: Area is heavily disturbed; not collected.
  Temporal Affiliation: Vijayanagara.
  References: Morrison 1995:72, 102.
  Illustrations: Figure 3.41.

SITE: VMS-73   Block: O   Transect: 10
  Primary Site Use: Residential: rectangular structure and associated wall.
  Site Dimensions: 10 × 5 m
  Setting: Near base of outcrop.
  Present Land Use/Disturbances: Modern road borders site to the north; some quarrying has occurred in the area.

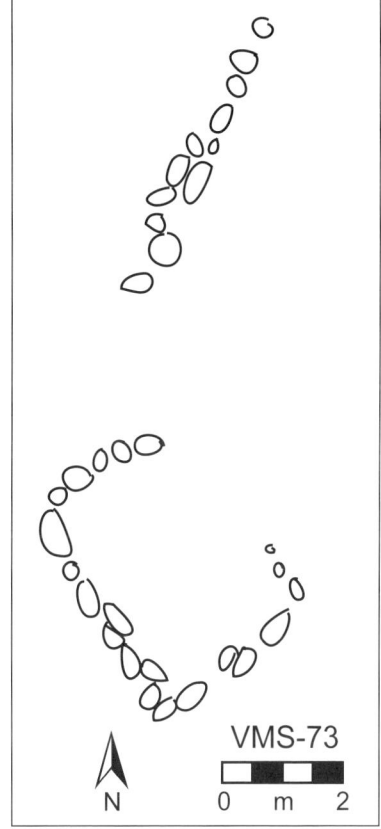

Figure 3.42. VMS-73, plan.

  Site Description: Rectangular rubble wall structure. This 4 × 3 m structure is constructed of small-medium unmodified boulders. Walls are single face, with no mortar or chinking, with one to two courses preserved. Three m to the north of the structure is a 5 m long wall fragment, oriented 20° east of north. This wall is similarly constructed, though it has two faces. It may be part of an enclosure wall or belong to a second structure. These are probably foundation walls for small residential structures.
  Artifacts: 100% collection; no artifacts recovered.
  Temporal Affiliation: Unknown.
  Illustrations: Figure 3.42.

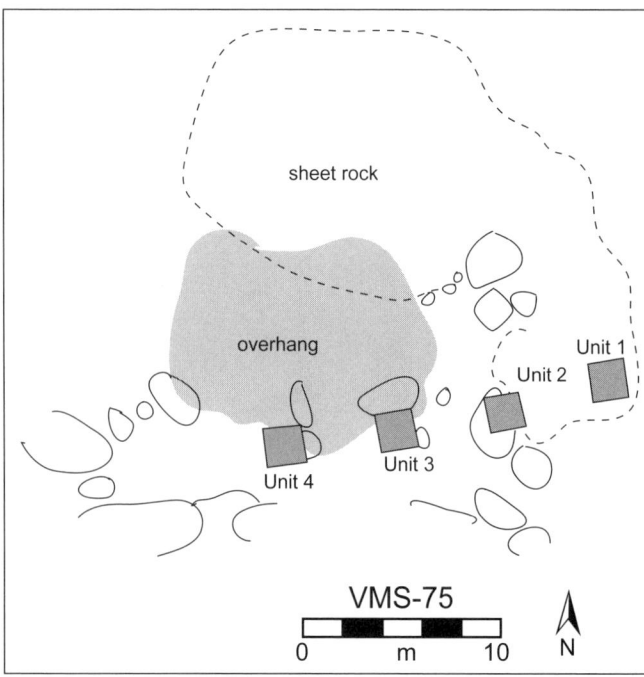

Figure 3.43. VMS-75, plan.

SITE: VMS-74 Block: O Transect: 10
Primary Site Use: Unknown: wall.
Site Dimensions: 36 × 1-1.5 m
Setting: Flat area of outcrop, c. 20 m above its north base.
Present Land Use/Disturbances: Some grazing.
Site Description: Wall. This single-course wall, oriented 26° south of east, is composed of small-medium unmodified granite stones. The wall varies in width from two to four elements. It bounds a small terrace in the outcrop to its north, defining a c. 10 × 10 m area enclosed by outcrops to the northwest and southeast. The wall continues over the outcrop to a total length of 36 m.
Artifacts: 100% collection; no artifacts recovered.
Temporal Affiliation: Unknown.

SITE: VMS-75 Block: O Transect: 10
Primary Site Use: Residential: rock shelter and lithic scatter.
Site Dimensions: 24 × 18 m
Setting: On outcrop, near northwest edge of outcrop hill.
Present Land Use/Disturbances: Modern features on north edge of site, including stone cairn or animal trap. There has been considerable slope wash in the area; all artifacts are in pockets of accumulated soil.
Site Description: Rock shelter and lithic scatter. This small south-facing rock shelter is enclosed by boulders on its north, west, and east, and roofed by a partial overhang. On the sheet rock surface is a lithic scatter; no ceramics were recovered. There is a dense scatter of lithics in the shelter area, with lower densities around the edges. Lithics include flakes, flaking debris, and shatter of varying raw materials, including basalt, cryptocrystalline stone, quartzite debris, and cobbles.
Artifacts: Four 2 × 2 m units were collected at 4 m intervals along a central transect oriented 8° south of west. A diagnostic sweep was also conducted.

Unit 1: 40 g quartz/quartzite lithics; 8 flakes, 13 pieces angular debris, 3 cores, 4 pieces bipolar debris.
Unit 2: 20 g quartz/quartzite lithics; 1 flake, 5 pieces angular debris, 2 pieces bipolar debris.
Unit 3: Total lithics 140 g. 20 g volcanic material: 3 flakes, 1 piece angular debris; 20 g chert: 3 flakes, 1 core; 100 g quartz/quartzite material: 5 flakes, 19 pieces angular debris, 1 core, 4 pieces bipolar debris.
Unit 4: Total lithics 340 g. 120 g volcanic material: 14 flakes, 14 pieces angular debris; 200 g quartz/quartzite: 11 flakes, 63 pieces angular debris, 6 cores, 11 pieces bipolar debris; 20 g chert: 1 core.
Judgment Unit: 20 g chert: 1 flake, 1 piece angular debris, 1 flake tool; 100 g quartz/quartzite: 2 pieces angular debris, 1 core, 1 piece bipolar debris, 1 tool. 1 ceramic body sherd, 1 burnt bone (large mammal radius).
Temporal Affiliation: Unknown.
References: Lycett 1991; Sinopoli and Morrison 1991:65.
Illustrations: Figure 3.43.

SITE: VMS-76 Block: O Transect: 10
Primary Site Use: Unknown: ceramic and lithic scatter.
Site Dimensions: 20 × 11 m
Setting: Flat area with soil build-up amid outcrops.
Present Land Use/Disturbances: Scattered small agricultural fields nearby; erosion and slope wash have probably been considerable.
Site Description: Artifact scatter. This is predominantly a ceramic scatter, with a small number of lithics. Artifacts are distributed evenly across the 20 × 11 m area. It is found at the base of a low rocky ridge in a relatively flat area in high and dry plateau zone. The site is perhaps the remains of a short-term residential camp.
Artifacts: 100% collection. Lithics: several quartzite cobbles with evidence for possible flaking, 1 green fine-grain quartzite core with some edge modification. Ceramics: 400 g; wares: 226 black plain ware, 25 red plain ware. Diagnostics: 3 jars.
Temporal Affiliation: Unknown.
References: Lycett 1991; Sinopoli and Morrison 1991:65.

SITE: VMS-77 Block: O Transect: 10
Primary Site Use: Transport?: walls.
Site Dimensions: 8 × 4 m
Setting: On northeast face and near the base of a large outcrop hill.
Present Land Use/Disturbances: Field wall and unpaved road on east boundary.
Site Description: Three wall fragments. These small walls are composed of basalt and granite cobbles and blocks. Up to two courses are visible. The main wall is 8 m long, and one to three elements wide. It is oriented c. 20° east of north and may have been a retaining wall or field or road boundary. A small wall segment runs parallel to it from its south end. At its north end is a perpendicular wall heading to the northwest, c. 2 m long. It appears to be a portion of a wall that bordered an old road.
Artifacts: 100% collection; no artifacts recovered.
Temporal Affiliation: Unknown.
Illustrations: Figure 3.44

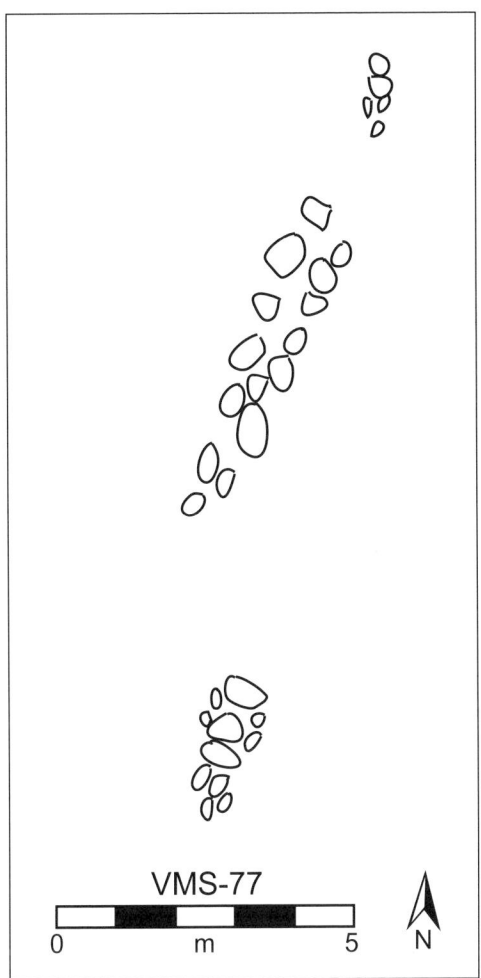

Figure 3.44. VMS-77, plan.

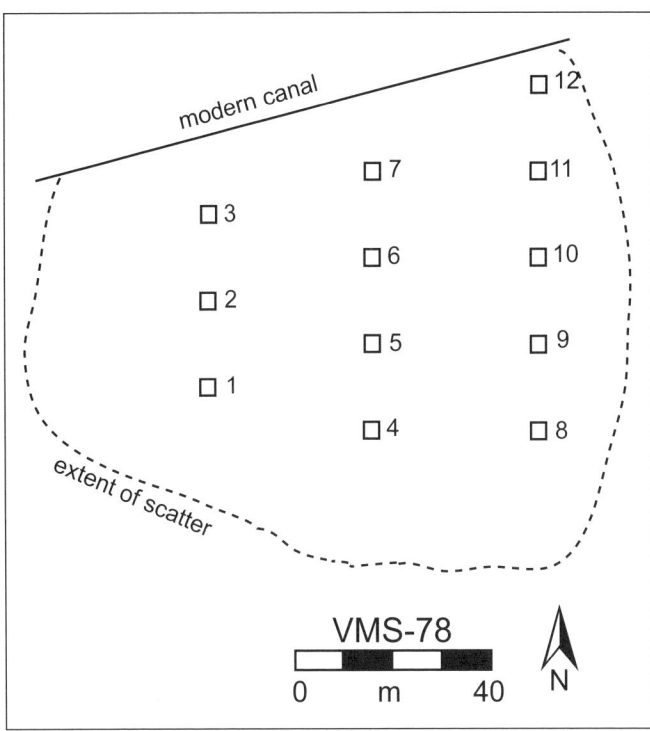

Figure 3.45. VMS-78, plan.

SITE: VMS-78   Block: O   Transect: 10
  Primary Site Use: Residential: artifact scatter.
  Site Dimensions: c. 120 m in diameter
  Setting: Low-lying area on south bank of Tungabhadra Right Bank Main Canal, and due south of large settlement VMS-2.
  Present Land Use/Disturbances: A cart path runs along the west edge of the site, and the Tungabhadra Right Bank Canal is to the north. There has been significant soil displacement due to agricultural activities and canal construction. Current ground surface level most likely considerably above Vijayanagara surfaces.
  Site Description: Artifact scatter. This large scatter is most likely associated with VMS-2 settlement site, from which it is separated by the modern canal. Given the considerable soil displacement in the area, the ceramics cannot be thought of as *in situ*. However, there is a clear clustering of materials and a distinct pattern of drop-off, suggesting that the site has some integrity. Artifacts include ceramics, iron slag, and basalt flakes. A stone mortar was also observed, suggesting a residential site. Ceramics are consistent with a Vijayanagara date.
  Artifacts: Three north-south transects were spaced 40 m apart and 4 × 4 m units spaced at 20 m intervals along each transect, for a total of twelve units.

  Unit 1: 100 g ceramics; wares: 9 black plain ware, 1 coarse ware. Diagnostics: 1 jar.
  Unit 2: 100 g ceramics; wares: 18 black plain ware, 2 red plain ware. Diagnostics: 1 jar.
  Unit 3: 50 g ceramics; wares: 2 black plain ware.
  Unit 4: 100 g ceramics; wares: 53 black plain ware, 4 red plain ware, 1 black decorated. Diagnostics: 1 jar.
  Unit 5: 250 g ceramics; wares: 96 black plain ware, 1 red plain ware, 3 black decorated. Diagnostics: 4 jars.
  Unit 6: 600 g ceramics; wares: 89 black plain ware, 19 red plain ware, 2 black decorated. Diagnostics: 8 jars.
  Unit 7: 150 g ceramics; wares: 47 black plain ware. Diagnostics: 2 jars.
  Unit 8: 50 g ceramics; wares: 10 black plain ware, 2 red plain ware. Diagnostics: 1 bowl, 1 jar.
  Unit 9: 100 g ceramics; wares: 43 black plain ware. Diagnostics: 1 jar.
  Unit 10: 100 g ceramics; wares: 45 black plain ware, 3 red plain ware. Diagnostics: 1 jar.
  Unit 11: 50 g ceramics; wares: 20 black plain ware, 1 red plain ware, 1 coarse ware.
  Unit 12: <50 g ceramics; wares: 2 black plain ware.
  Temporal Affiliation: Vijayanagara. Many of the ceramics are of typical Vijayanagara forms; there may be some later artifacts mixed in.
  References: Lycett 1991.
  Illustrations: Figure 3.45.

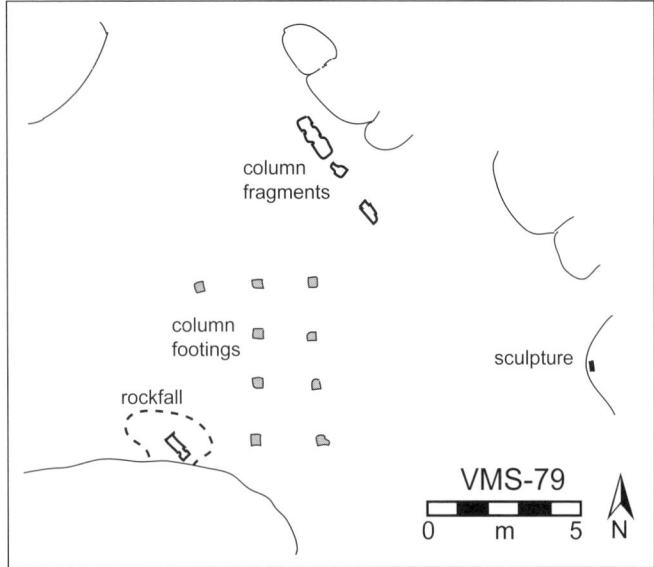

(*Left*) Figure 3.46. VMS-79, plan.

(*Above*) Plate 3.21. VMS-79, unfinished column *in situ*; note flaking debris in foreground.

SITE: VMS-79   Block: O   Transect: 10
Primary Site Use: Religious: unfinished structure.
Site Dimensions: 30 × 15 m
Setting: On low sheet rock against north face of large outcropping boulders. Located c. 20 m south of the Vijayanagara period Turtha Canal (VMS-120).
Present Land Use/Disturbances: Modern threshing floor. There is extensive modern quarrying in area. Soil accumulation partly covers portions of the site.
Site Description: Unfinished temple/structure under construction. This unfinished structure is north facing, abutting a 15 m high vertical granite outcrop to its south. The plan of the structure is evident from square depressions pecked onto the sheet rock on the north and east of the outcrop. These "footings" mark the intended locations of columns. The structure would have been 4 columns north-south (c. 6 m) × 3 columns east-west (c. 5 m).

There is considerable evidence for *in situ* column manufacture, with one complete roughly dressed column lying to the northeast of the column footings, and a broken fragment of another roughly dressed unfinished column nearby. These columns would have been square with octagonal insets, typical late Vijayanagara period column forms. To the south is a fragment of another quite different column, of similar form but with a longer octagonal inset (0.3+ m). This may have been intended as a lamp column to be placed in front of the structure.

A collapsed section of outcrop lies above a fallen column on the south boundary of the site. It appears that the collapse of the outcrop halted construction of this structure. Granite flaking debris provides evidence for *in situ* column manufacture and the unfinished nature of this structure. Brick and plaster fragments are also present, as is a slag-like material, probably fired lime, or *kankar*, which could have been ground for plaster. These materials are perhaps the remains of a stockpile for later stages of construction.

On a boulder to the east of the structure is a small two-character inscription and carving of Hanuman. No other sculpted elements are present.

This structure appears to have been intended to be a shrine or temple, and was located alongside the Turtha Canal and associated transport route that bordered the canal.

Artifacts: Ceramic scatter varies from sparse within the structure, to very heavy east of the structure. Four collections were made: unit 1, area to the east of the structure (15 × 15 m); unit 2, within structure (6 × 5 m); unit 3, west of structure (15 × 15 m); unit 4, north of structure.

Unit 1: 500 g ceramics; wares: 291 black plain ware, 1 red plain ware, 1 red decorated ware. Diagnostics: 4 bowls, 4 jars. Other artifacts: 1 piece iron, 1 piece brick, 1 piece iron ore.

Unit 2: 150 g ceramics; wares: 31 black plain ware. Diagnostics: 4 jars.

Unit 3: 50 g ceramics; wares: 7 black plain ware. Diagnostics: 1 jar.

Unit 4: 200 g ceramics; wares: 54 black plain ware, 9 black decorated ware. Diagnostics: 1 bowl, 2 jars.

Temporal Affiliation: Vijayanagara.
References: Morrison 1995:72-73; Sinopoli 2003:216-17.
Illustrations: Figure 3.46; Plate 3.21.

SITE: VMS-80   Block: O   Transect: 11
Primary Site Use: Religious: Shaivite (Nagesvara) temple complex.
Site Dimensions: 65 × 21 m
Setting: Low-lying area, near base of outcrop, constructed on sheet rock.
Present Land Use/Disturbances: Temple is still in worship, and enclosed by a modern wall; small platforms in front of the temple may be later additions.
Site Description: Shaivite temple complex. The complex consists of: (1) a walled enclosure containing a partially roofed courtyard area; (2) a roofed porch (outside the enclosure, and flanking its main entry) with raised platforms on either side of a central walkway; and (3) a small sanctuary within the enclosure.

Porch: The raised porch platforms are 4 columns east-west × 2 columns north-south, and are 0.15-0.30 m high. The columns are square with octagonal insets. They are topped by simple rectangular capitals that are spanned by lintels and roofed with long rectangular slabs. The platforms have simple beveled upper moldings and no lower moldings. The platform surfaces are paved with rectangular stones.

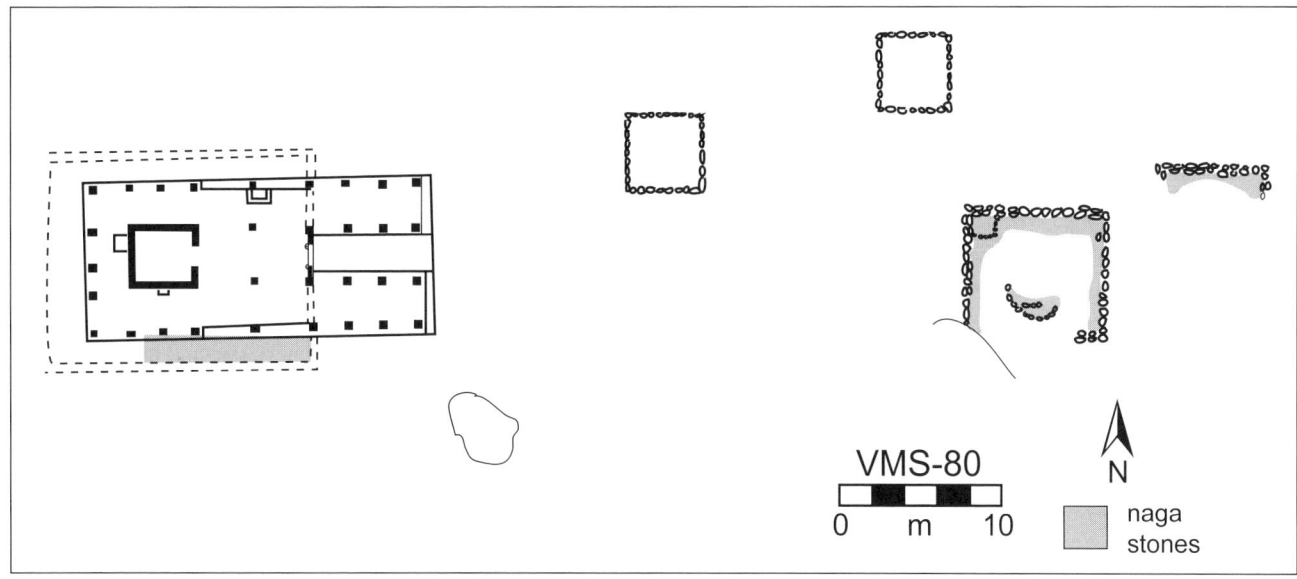

Figure 3.47. VMS-80, plan.

Enclosure: The walled enclosure is entered through a doorway at the east end of the entry path defined by the two porch platforms. The door is of the Vijayanagara period, with Shaivite door guardians. There are two door sockets in the lintel over the passage. The 20 × 8 m enclosure has Vijayanagara period columns, but the walls spanning them are modern.

The roofed inner courtyard of the enclosure is paved with rectangular stones. The two heavily plastered columns in front of the main shrine are sculpted; images include geese, cow with calf, standing human figure, seated human figure, elephant, Hanuman, naked ascetic, and seated female figure. Unlike the other columns in the courtyard, these two are set on low platforms. There are two stone troughs—one in front of the sanctuary, the other abutting the rear of the sanctuary. Along the south wall of the courtyard are hundreds of sculpted naga stones.

Sanctuary: The single-chamber sanctuary is 3 × 2 columns, walled by long rectangular slabs. One female and one male door guardian flank the sanctuary entry. They face the door, holding offerings. A lotus is sculpted on the lintel, with another on the sanctuary's ceiling. The central image is a large seven-headed cobra; associated with this are a Nandi and a smaller cobra; another cobra is carved on the wall of sanctuary.

Other Features: A well and concentration of naga stones on a small modern platform are located outside the temple complex to its northwest. The well is irregular in plan and appears to have been rock-cut, c. 6.4 × 4 m. There are walls on the west and east faces of the well depression. These are well constructed of square tightly fitted blocks.

The small platform to the east of the temple is rectangular, c. 6 × 8 m, with three walls formed by naga sculptures six to seven deep. In the center of this platform are eight more sculptures arranged in a U-shape and facing the north. To the east of the platform are some wall fragments that may be the remains of an earlier platform.

This temple is known as the Nagesvara temple. It is mentioned in the Sanskrit Pampamahatmya text stored in Hampi's Virupaksha temple and described as located along the road that ran along the Turtha Canal to Hampi (Krishna Das, pers. comm.).

Artifacts: Temple is in worship; no collections made.
Temporal Affiliation: Vijayanagara, with later additions.
References: Morrison 1995:73, 79; Sinopoli and Morrison 1991:67; Sinopoli 1993b:629.
Illustrations: Figure 3.47; Plates 3.22, 3.23.

Plate 3.22. VMS-80, view of porch and entryway into walled temple complex.

Plate 3.23. VMS-80, naga stones along the south wall of complex courtyard.

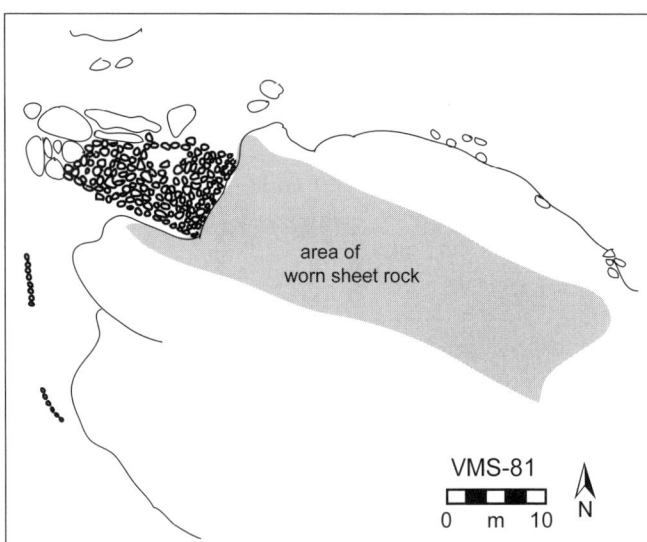

Figure 3.48. VMS-81, plan.

SITE: VMS-81   Block: O   Transect: 10/11
  Primary Site Use: Transport: road segment.
  Site Dimensions: 60 × 12 m
  Setting: Extending over sheet rock and low outcrop.
  Present Land Use/Disturbances: Recent quarrying has destroyed portions of site.
  Site Description: Stone pavement and worn sheet rock. This 60 m long road segment incorporates sheet rock in the east portion, and in the west, is constructed of unmodified stones of varying sizes. It is oriented 20° north of west and may have extended to the temple, VMS-80. Both sheet rock and constructed pavement portions are heavily worn and polished by use. A small circular depression, c. 0.25 m in diameter, is pecked into the sheet rock to the south of the pavement. The pavement served to level irregularities in the sheet rock and the road could have allowed cart passage. The path is not presently in use; a modern track lies to its west.
  Artifacts: 100% collection: one worked sherd.
  Temporal Affiliation: Vijayanagara?
  References: Morrison 1995:73; Sinopoli and Morrison 1991:67.
  Illustrations: Figure 3.48.

SITE: VMS-82   Block: O   Transect: 10
  Primary Site Use: Unknown: possible soil retention wall.
  Site Dimensions: 12 × c. 5 m
  Setting: On area of relatively flat to gently sloping terrain on north side of large outcrop hill, area of shallow soil accumulation.
  Present Land Use/Disturbances: Modern quarry road and quarrying activities c. 10 m to north of site.
  Site Description: East-west wall. This 12 m long single-course rubble wall is located on a flat spot in massive outcrop. This flat area is c. 30 m north-south × 200 m east-west, and has some soil accumulation, though it does not appear to have been recently farmed. The wall may have been a soil retention wall to prevent runoff down the steeply sloped sheet rock to the south.
  Artifacts: 100% collection; no artifacts recovered.
  Temporal Affiliation: Unknown.
  References: Morrison 1995:89, 102.

SITE: VMS-83   Block: O   Transect: 15
  Primary Site Use: Religious: Vaishnava temple complex.
  Site Dimensions: c. 390 × 150 m
  Setting: Temple is located midway up the north slopes of a moderately steep sheet rock outcrop. It is south of and overlooks settlement site VMS-101 and impounded spring VMS-84.
  Present Land Use/Disturbances: Intensive modern quarrying in area. A modern temple complex is located near the base of the outcrop to the northwest of VMS-83. Quarrying has probably destroyed the remains of a road that led to the temple gate.
  Site Description: Temple complex. This temple complex extends across the slopes of a large sheet rock and boulder outcrop. It is enclosed within massive walls that formed a flat terrace for the structures. The main temple, oriented 26° east of north, is built against the outcrop, with its shikara on the outcrop. A twelve-column gate led to the temple complex, probably from a path to the north (linked to VMS-101?), and by site VMS-84.

Two tiers of walls form the terrace upon which the temple is constructed. A lower wall defines a rectangular terrace (c. 10 × 15 m) in front of the temple. The wall is constructed of medium to large stones, loosely fitted with chinking. It incorporates outcropping boulders along its base and is up to eight courses high and 11.2 m long.

The upper wall, c. 4 m in front of the temple, is constructed of small to medium roughly dressed stones and incorporates some large boulders. The wall is eleven courses high, with irregular coursing and chinking, and is oriented roughly east-west. It runs east-west for 9 m then jags 1 m to the north, and runs another 8 m before abutting boulders and changing direction. The upper terrace continues to the west of the temple, where it is defined by a wall constructed of massive wedge-shaped blocks; another higher terrace wall is c. 8 m to the south. This uppermost wall defines a flat terrace to its south, c. 28 × 22 m in extent and paved with large flagstones. Single-course walls of large rectangular stones define the east and west boundaries of the terraces and abut the outcrop to the south. Structures may have been constructed on this large terrace, though none are now evident. Some peg holes are present, but form no clear alignments.

The main temple of the complex sits on a low platform with upper and lower simple beveled molding, and consists of a 4 × 3 column antechamber (4.5 × 8.35 m) and a small sanctuary. Entry to the antechamber was from a central stairway of three stairs. The antechamber is roofed by long rectangular slabs. It is oriented 26° east of north and backs against the outcrop. The columns are standard mass-produced Vijayanagara forms. Within the antechamber are several sculptural fragments, none in their original location, including a beautifully sculpted chlorite Vishnu image, 0.6 m tall and 0.3 m wide. A small Anjaneya Hanuman image has been placed near the sanctuary door.

Vaishnava door guardians flank the entry to the sanctuary. The sanctuary abuts the outcrop, which forms a natural ledge upon which an image could have been set. To the east of the sanctuary is a second small chamber, empty except for an image base.

The square shikara of the sanctuary is built on top of the outcrop boulder and is secured by granite pegs. The tiered shikara has a square base section, c. 4 m on a side and 3.5 m high, and narrowing toward the top. Above this is a smaller three stepped section, with a seated yogi figure below a medallion and yali. There are traces of a wall of brick and mortar on the edge of the shikara boulder.

A small 1.5 × 1.5 m platform is in front of the temple. This platform presumably was originally the base for a lamp column, of which only the base is now present. Also present is a worn chlorite sculpture of a

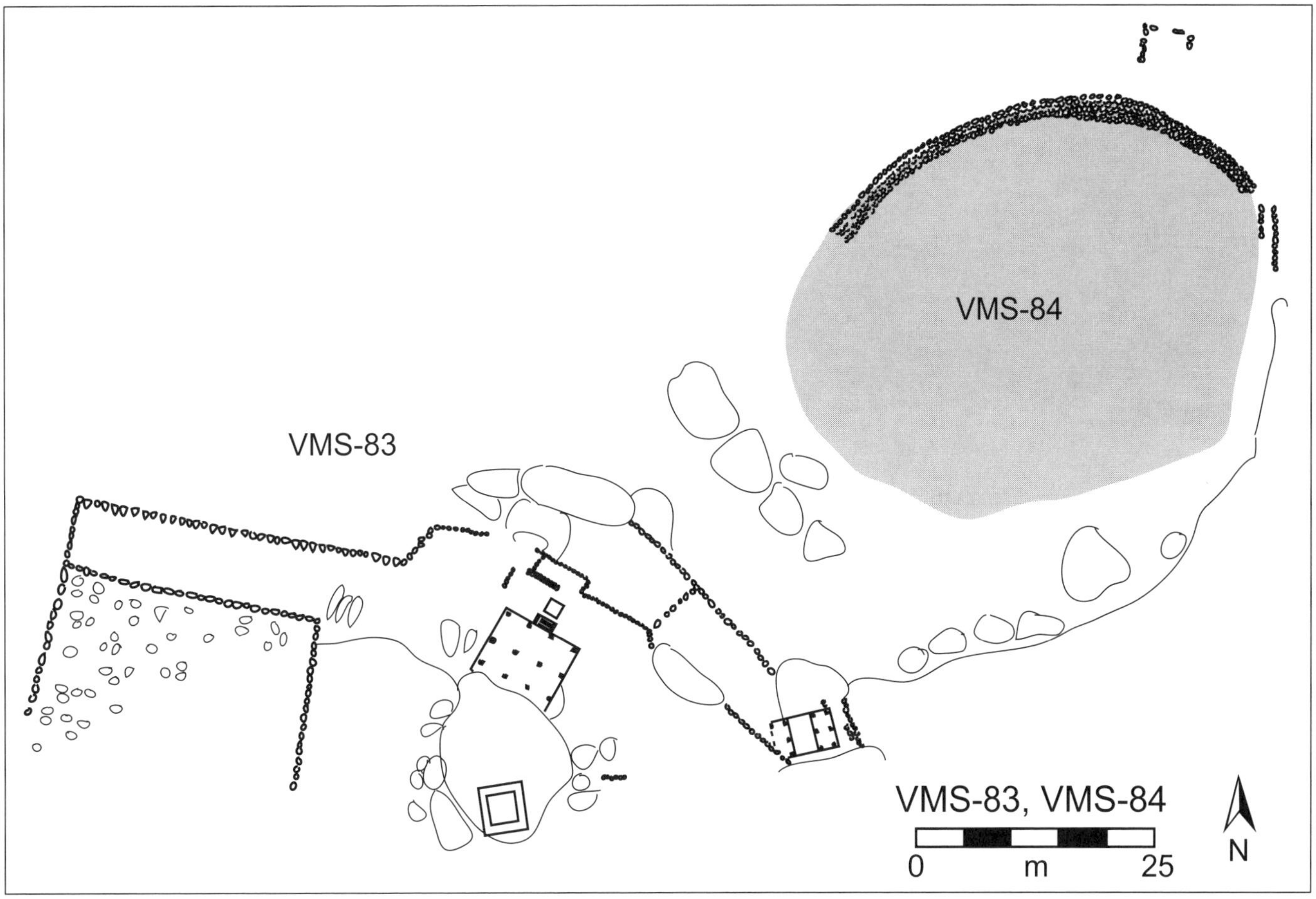

Figure 3.49. VMS-83 and VMS-84, plan.

female figure holding a swordlike object. There are two grinding slabs by the temple entrance.

A twelve-column roofed gateway is located to the southeast of the temple and provided the main entry to the complex. The gate has two platforms, each 3 × 2 columns (3.9 × 1.9 m), with a central passage, 1.7 m wide. The unsculpted columns are square and roughly dressed with rectangular capitals.

Artifacts: Ceramic scatter within and around the temple structure, low densities elsewhere. Three judgment surface collection units were defined. Visibility was variable, because of thick grasses in some areas of site (especially unit 2).

Unit 1, temple and terrace in front of temple (14 × 13 m): 350 g ceramics; wares: 161 black plain ware, 29 red plain ware, 1 black burnished ware, 1 coarse ware. Diagnostics: 2 bowls, 6 jars. Other artifacts: 1 iron fragment, 2 lithics.

Unit 2, terrace below temple (2 × 8 m): 50 g ceramics; wares: 6 black plain ware, 1 red plain ware.

Unit 3, uppermost paved terrace to west of temple (22 × 28 m): <50 g ceramics; wares: 1 black plain ware.

Temporal Affiliation: Vijayanagara.

References: Morrison 1995:64, 68, 74, 79-80; Sinopoli and Morrison 1991:66-68; Sinopoli 1993b:629.

Illustrations: Figure 3.49; Plate 3.24.

Plate 3.24. VMS-83, overview.

Plate 3.25. VMS-84, view from south.

Plate 3.26. VMS-85, fortification wall segment.

SITE: VMS-84   Block: O   Transect: 15
Primary Site Use: Water control: masonry-lined spring.
Site Dimensions: Approximately 50 m diameter.
Setting: Flat area at the base of outcrop, located due north of temple VMS-83 and on west edge of settlement VMS-101.
Present Land Use/Disturbances: Large modern temple complex c. 60-80 m to the west of the spring; the Tungabhadra Right Bank Canal is located c. 40 m to the north. The masonry surrounding the spring has eroded; some of it may have been replaced or removed. The edges of the basin are overgrown with dense aquatic vegetation.
Site Description: Impounded spring. VMS-84 is a perennial water source that has been enclosed by a stepped embankment to form a pool approximately 50 m in diameter. The stone embankment extends around the north, east, and west of the spring, with the outcrop face forming the south boundary. The c. 2 m high stepped embankment is constructed of nine courses of unmodified and roughly dressed split stones. In the southwest quadrant of the site the original embankment has been replaced by a recent vertical wall of three to four courses constructed of small to medium loosely fitted irregular and rectangular stones.

A small square structure (c. 5 m) is located to the north of the pool; three walls are preserved up to three courses. Fragments of a stone basement lie below it, and a naga stone and other sculpted Vijayanagara stone elements are found nearby. This was probably part of a larger structure that was damaged during the construction of the modern canal. Other structures may also have existed in this area, which is on the west edge of settlement VMS-101.
Artifacts: 100% collection. <50 g ceramics; wares: 3 black plain ware, 1 red plain ware.
Temporal Affiliation: Vijayanagara.
References: Morrison 1995:68, 80; Sinopoli and Morrison 1991:66.
Illustrations: Figure 3.49; Plate 3.25.

SITE: VMS-85   Block: O   Transect: 14
Primary Site Use: Defensive: bastion/wall.
Site Dimensions: 18.4 × 13.6 m
Setting: Low-lying area to west of settlement VMS-101 and impounded spring VMS-84. Feature is located to the north of outcrop containing temple VMS-83 and modern temple complex.
Present Land Use/Disturbances: Abuts modern temple complex, which may have destroyed part of feature.
Site Description: Fortification walls or bastion. These well-constructed walls are oriented at right angles to each other and are constructed of rectangular and trapezoidal blocks, several with Vijayanagara quarry marks. The walls are slightly stepped with seven courses preserved. They bound an area filled with earth and rubble and may have been part of a fortification or bastion associated with settlement VMS-101.
Artifacts: None.
Temporal Affiliation: Vijayanagara.
References: Morrison 1995:64.
Illustrations: Plate 3.26.

SITE: VMS-86   Block: O   Transect: 14
Primary Site Use: Defensive: fortification wall.
Site Dimensions: 8 × 1.3-2.6 m
Setting: On outcrop spanning gap between large boulders.
Resources: VMS-84, a spring, c. 150-200 m to northeast.
Present Land Use/Disturbances: Amid agricultural field; a modern canal encloses the area.
Site Description: Wall. This broad, well-constructed east-west wall runs between two large outcropping boulders on sheet rock slopes to the south of temple complex VMS-83. The wall blocks access across a flat area to the south of the temple. The three-course wall is constructed of medium unmodified stones in the upper two courses. The lowest course is set on sheet rock and includes several quarried rectangular slabs (one over 2 m long and 0.6 m high). The wall has two faces with an earthen fill and ranges from 1.3 to 2.6 m wide. It incorporates a small split boulder at one end. To its north is a small rock shelter containing modern artifacts.
Artifacts: Modern ceramics (water storage and cooking jar), glass, coconut husks in rock shelter. No collections made.
Temporal Affiliation: Vijayanagara?
Illustrations: Figure 3.50.

SITE: VMS-87   Block: O   Transect: 14
Primary Site Use: Transport: path and walls.
Site Dimensions: 78 × 3 m
Setting: On sheet rock sloping gently up to north on west side of outcrop hill.
Present Land Use/Disturbances: Some soil accumulation.
Site Description: Paved path and associated walls. This site consists of a path oriented 10° west of south. It is paved on the north end for c. 8 m and then continues along sheet rock for c. 78 m, turning to a more west orientation (60° west of south). The edges of the path are defined by outcrop and boulders and the sheet rock is heavily worn; a rock-cut step is found midway along the path. Above the north end of the path are two walls that join at an oblique angle. The west wall is

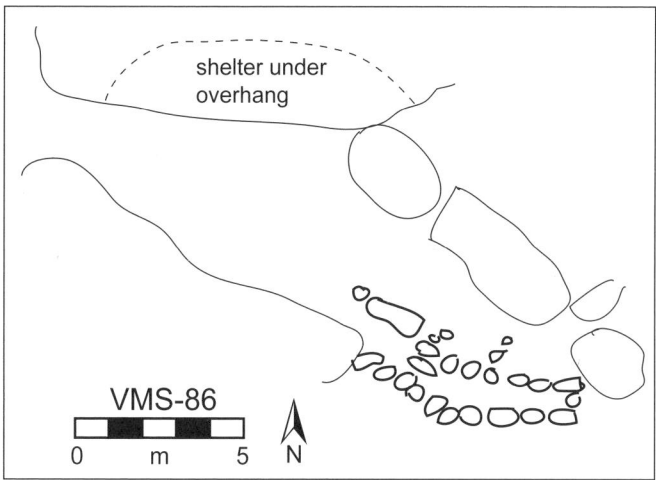

Figure 3.50. VMS-86, plan.

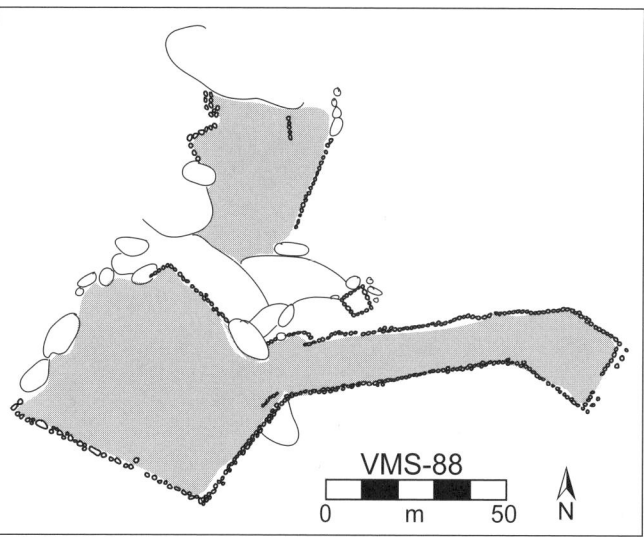

Figure 3.51. VMS-88, plan.

oriented 20° west of north and is 2.0 m long. From its southeast end a second wall extends due east. Both are constructed of a single course of unmodified and split medium stones. The site cannot be traced further as modern paths obscure it, but it may have extended to the north and east toward temple complex VMS-83 or to the modern temple on the outcrop above it. The walls may be associated with the path, forming a flat terrace along the sheet rock.

Artifacts: 100% collection; no artifacts recovered.
Temporal Affiliation: Vijayanagara.
References: Morrison 1995:74.

SITE: VMS-88   Block: O   Transect: 14
   Primary Site Use: Unknown: walls and terracing.
   Site Dimensions: 90 × 58 m
   Setting: On area of sloping sheet rock on north face of an outcrop hill, terrain slopes down to the north. Areas of soil accumulation behind terrace walls.
   Present Land Use/Disturbances: Modern shrine 60 m to east. There has been considerable slope wash and redeposition of artifacts.
   Site Description: Multiple walls, some forming irregularly shaped terraces on the gently sloping sheet rock. The south upper terrace is "lute-shaped," with a long east-west oriented arm on the east (c. 52 m long × 8 m wide) leading into a rhomboidal platform on the west (c. 35 × 35 m). The lower north terrace is much smaller (c. 24 m east-west × 16 m). There are also walls associated with a recent shrine located on the slope to the southeast of the site.
   The function of this site is unclear. Residential use is most likely. However, there are no clear structural remains, although there are some isolated wall segments on the south terrace. Site VMS-102, also consisting of walls and terraces, is located c. 10 m to the southeast of VMS-88; these two sites are probably part of a single complex.
   Artifacts: Artifact scatter consists of ceramics and one large amorphous piece of iron. Density is variable and visibility is poor; sherds are mostly small fragments of body sherds. Four arbitrarily defined units were collected. Unit 1: within rectangular area, west portion of large terrace, c. 30 × 26 m; unit 2: within overhang at west part of large terrace (9 × 3 m); unit 3: long elevated walled area of main terrace ("neck"), 50 × 6 m; unit 4: lower terrace area.
   Unit 1: 200 g ceramics; wares: 70 black plain ware.
   Unit 2: 200 g ceramics; wares: 5 black plain ware, 1 coarse ware. Diagnostics: 1 jar (modern storage).
   Unit 3: 400 g ceramics; wares: 128 black plain ware, 51 red plain ware, 1 coarse ware. Diagnostics: 1 bowl.
   Unit 4: <50 g ceramics; wares: 5 black plain ware, 1 red plain ware.
   Temporal Affiliation: Unknown.
   Illustrations: Figure 3.51.

SITE: VMS-89   Block: O   Transect: 14
   Primary Site Use: Unknown: wall.
   Site Dimensions: 30 × c. 5 m
   Setting: Flat area on ridge on high outcrop hill.
   Present Land Use/Disturbances: None.
   Site Description: Single-course wall. This 30 m long wall is constructed of small, loosely fit, unmodified stones. It has a single face and abuts a small boulder on the north and extends south for 5 m before abutting another small boulder. It is then offset to the east and extends south for another 10 m. There are several other possible wall fragments in this area. VMS-88 is c. 30-40 m to the north. The wall may have defined a route of movement across the outcrop, but its specific function is unclear.
   Artifacts: 100% collection; no artifacts recovered.
   Temporal Affiliation: Unknown.

SITE: VMS-90   Block: O   Transect: 15
   Primary Site Use: Agricultural: wall.
   Site Dimensions: 8 × 0.50 m
   Setting: In narrow valley between two outcrop hills.
   Present Land Use/Disturbances: In erosion gully; extensive soil movement and erosion has undoubtedly occurred.
   Site Description: Check dam. This two-course wall is constructed of loosely fit medium unmodified rounded stones. It is oriented 60° west of north and spans an erosion gully in a narrow valley. This feature was likely a check dam that served to limit erosion and silt deposition into the bed of reservoir embankment VMS-91, which is located below it c. 100 m to the east.
   Artifacts: 100% collection; no artifacts recovered.
   Temporal Affiliation: Vijayanagara?
   References: Morrison 1995:89, 102.

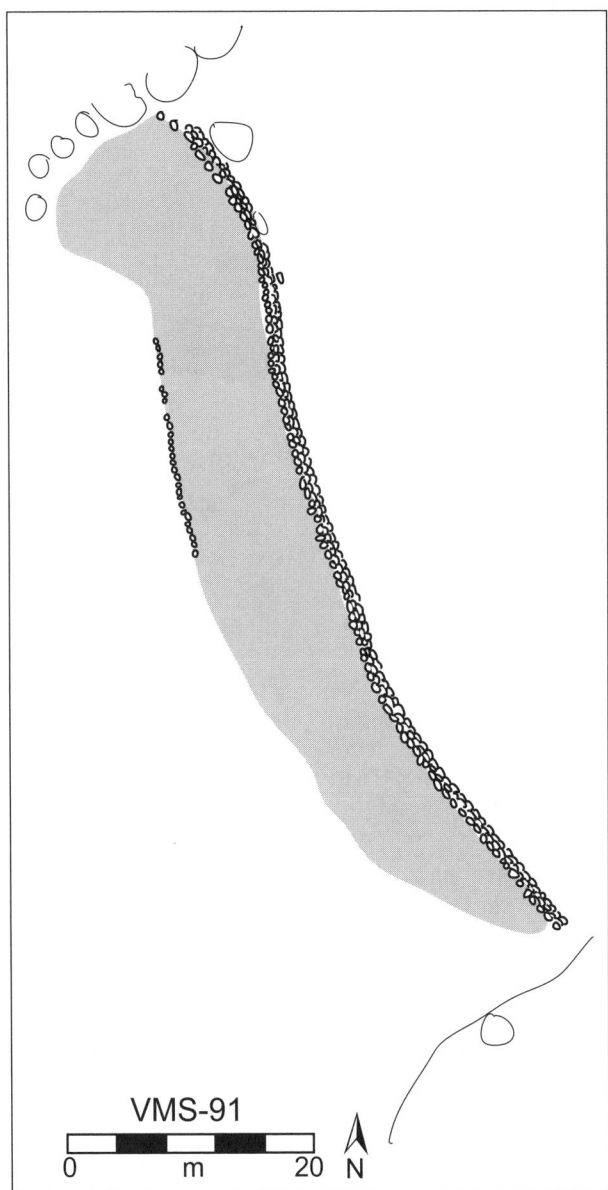

Figure 3.52. VMS-91, plan.

(*Above*) Plate 3.27. VMS-91, overview.

(*Left*) Plate 3.28. VMS-91, sluice gate.

SITE: VMS-91   Block: O   Transect: 14
  Primary Site Use: Agricultural: reservoir embankment.
  Site Dimensions: 75 × c. 13 m
  Setting: Gently sloping valley; outcrops to north, south, and east.
  Present Land Use/Disturbances: The area to the east of the embankment is being farmed and there has been considerable soil accumulation. Some quarrying in surrounding outcrop.
  Site Description: Reservoir embankment. This roughly north-south embankment captured runoff from outcrops to its east, north, and south. The area impounded by the tank is c. 250 m east-west × 70 m north-south at its maximum; the area below the reservoir (to the west) is c. 150 × 100 m. The east stone face is constructed of small (0.25 × 0.2 m) and medium (0.4 × 0.3 m) unmodified angular and rounded stones. Coursing and stepping are irregular. Up to fourteen courses are preserved. A small simple sluice gate is located c. 10 m south of the north end of the embankment. The sluice is constructed of two upright tapering coarsely dressed columns, spaced 1.5 m apart. They are spanned by a simple rectangular slab. Vijayanagara quarry marks are evident on the posts. The sluice outlet is obscured by collapsed stones.
  A possible small wall is located on the outcrop north of the embankment. Moderate ceramic densities are found here. Another reservoir (not documented) is visible c. 130 m to the east in transect 13.
  Artifacts: Ceramic fragments in flat area near base of sheet rock, iron fragment nearby.
  Site was collected in two zones. Unit 1: low-lying area to northwest of sluice; unit 2: low-lying area to west of embankment.
  Unit 1: 250 g ceramics; wares: 89 black plain ware, 4 red plain ware. Diagnostics: 1 bowl. Other artifacts: 1 iron fragment.
  Unit 2: 50 g ceramics; wares: 4 black plain ware. Diagnostics: 1 bowl.
  Temporal Affiliation: Vijayanagara.
  References: Morrison 1995:85, 89, 102.
  Illustrations: Figure 3.52; Plates 3.27, 3.28.

Plate 3.29. VMS-92, detail of rock surface.

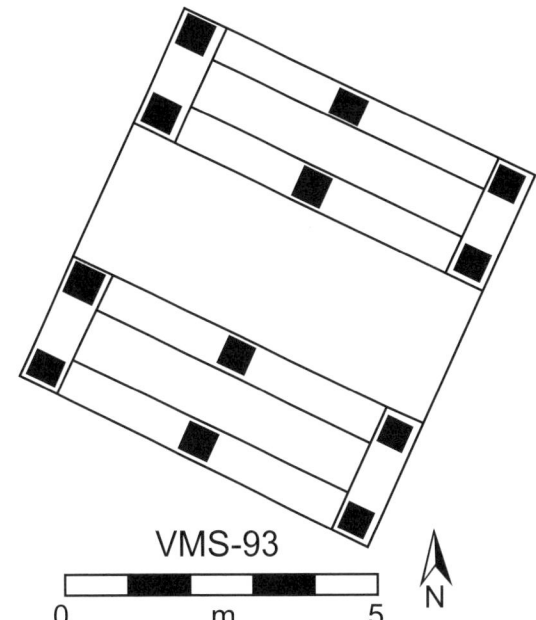

SITE: VMS-92   Block: O   Transect: 14
  Primary Site Use: Industrial: depressions on boulder, metal working.
  Site Dimensions: 4 × 2 m
  Setting: On boulder and sheet rock at northwest edge of outcrop hill.
  Present Land Use/Disturbances: Modern quarrying has resulted in the destruction of original surface of much of the surrounding sheet rock.
  Site Description: Pecked boulders. This site consists of two large boulders that abut and form a small overhang in an area of sheet rock. There are more than 100 shallow pecked depressions on the slanting upper surfaces of these stones. The largest of these boulders, and the one with the most depressions, is c. 1.5 × 1.0 m in dimension, and its upper surface is completely covered by pecked depressions. The depressions average c. 4 cm in diameter and 1 cm deep, and some are linked by shallow furrows. The surface of the outcrop slopes down slightly.
  Similar features have been observed by Hegde (pers. comm.) in western India and in that context are associated with metal working, particularly gold working. Molten metals are poured over the sloping surface, and heavier elements are deposited in these shallow depressions, while waste materials slough off. It is not clear that VMS-92 served this function, but it does resemble Hegde's sites very closely, and he has suggested that this was a common technique of processing gold bearing veins throughout ancient South Asia. If true, this is likely a late prehistoric or Early Historic site (late centuries BCE-early centuries CE).
  Artifacts: None.
  Temporal Affiliation: Unknown; possibly late prehistoric/Early Historic.
  References: Morrison 1995:85.
  Illustrations: Plate 3.29.

SITE: VMS-93   Block: O   Transect: 11
  Primary Site Use: Transport: gate.
  Site Dimensions: 6.5 × 6.5 m
  Setting: Located along the route of the Kamalapur-Kampli road between the Vijayanagara period settlements VMS-2 and Bukkasagara.
  Present Land Use/Disturbances: Site is 20 m north of Tungabhadra Right Bank Main Canal, along paved road.
  Site Description: Two-platform gate. This roofed gate consists of two 3 × 2 column platforms separated by a 2.4 m wide roofed passage.

(*Top*) Figure 3.53. VMS-93, plan.
(*Above*) Plate 3.30. VMS-93, overview.

The basement has no formal moldings, just simple rectangular outsets, above a vertical panel. The columns are square and rest on footing blocks, 0.5 m² × 0.19 m high. The columns facing the passage have insets cut away. The columns are unsculpted, with the exception of a single lotus carving on one column. They are topped by beveled cruciform capitals. The platforms and passage are roofed with long rectangular slabs (2.5 × 0.4 m) laid perpendicular to the orientation of the passage. There is no evidence for a wall or fortifications in the vicinity.
  This gate is located along the modern Kampli road about 750 m to the south of Bukkasagara. It is roughly perpendicular to the road, suggesting either that the Vijayanagara period road followed a different route than the modern one or, more likely, that there was an additional Vijayanagara period road that branched off the main road at this locale.
  Artifacts: Along modern road; no collections made.
  Temporal Affiliation: Vijayanagara.
  References: Morrison 1995:72; Sinopoli and Morrison 1991:67.
  Illustrations: Figure 3.53; Plate 3.30.

SITE: VMS-94   Block: O   Transect: 14
  Primary Site Use: Religious: inscribed boulder with Shaivite image (Ganesha).
  Site Dimensions: Boulder 2 × 3 m, image 1.5 × 1 m.
  Setting: In flat area within drainage or impoundment area of reservoir VMS-117.
  Present Land Use/Disturbances: Within modern agricultural fields; modern field wall located due north of the boulder.
  Site Description: Boulder inscribed with Ganesha and inscription. Carved on the east face of a small (c. 3 m long × 1.5 m high) outcropping boulder in the middle of an agricultural field is an image of Ganesha and an inscription. The inscription is located within an inscribed square frame (0.45 × 0.43 m) above and to the right of Ganesha. It is badly eroded and difficult to discern any characters clearly. The Ganesha image was not completed. The figure is in seated posture and is 0.75 m tall. The Vijayanagara style arch that framed the image, and the rat associated with the god, are incomplete, with only the outlines pecked in. At the top of the frame to Ganesha's right is a crescent moon and to the left is the outline of a circle (sun?).
  Artifacts: Small number of sherds in fields around boulder. 100% collection. <50 g ceramics; wares: 1 black plain ware. Diagnostics: 1 bowl.
  Temporal Affiliation: Vijayanagara.
  References: Morrison 1995:80; Sinopoli 2003:225.

SITE: VMS-95   Block: O   Transect: 14
  Primary Site Use: Agricultural: check dams.
  Site Dimensions: 41 × c. 10 m
  Setting: Near south edge of outcrop, terrain slopes down to the southwest.
  Present Land Use/Disturbances: Some quarrying in area.
  Site Description: Rubble-wall check dams. Four walls of unmodified small to medium stones span a narrow area between outcropping boulders. The walls are oriented perpendicular to the line of slope. In places, amorphous piles of stones have blocked small gaps between outcropping boulders. This site overlooks the impoundment basin of reservoir VMS-117 and may be a soil and erosion control feature that served to prevent silting of the reservoir bed during periods of heavy runoff.
  Artifacts: Sparse ceramic scatter. 100% collection. <50 g ceramics; wares: 1 black plain ware. Diagnostics: 1 bowl.
  Temporal Affiliation: Vijayanagara.
  References: Morrison 1995:89, 102.

SITE: VMS-96   Block: O   Transect: 14
  Primary Site Use: Unknown: wall.
  Site Dimensions: 13 × 2.0-2.5 m
  Setting: Low area in outcrop.
  Resources: Reservoir VMS-117 is c. 500 m to the northwest.
  Present Land Use/Disturbances: Many modern walls in vicinity.
  Site Description: Wall constructed of two faces of large unmodified stones with an earth, rubble, and stone core. The wall ranges from 2 to 2.5 m in width. Only one course is preserved. This wall is of quite different construction than the many clearly recent walls in the area. Given its width, it may be defensive or associated with a transport route.
  Artifacts: Area is heavily disturbed; no collections made.
  Temporal Affiliation: Unknown.

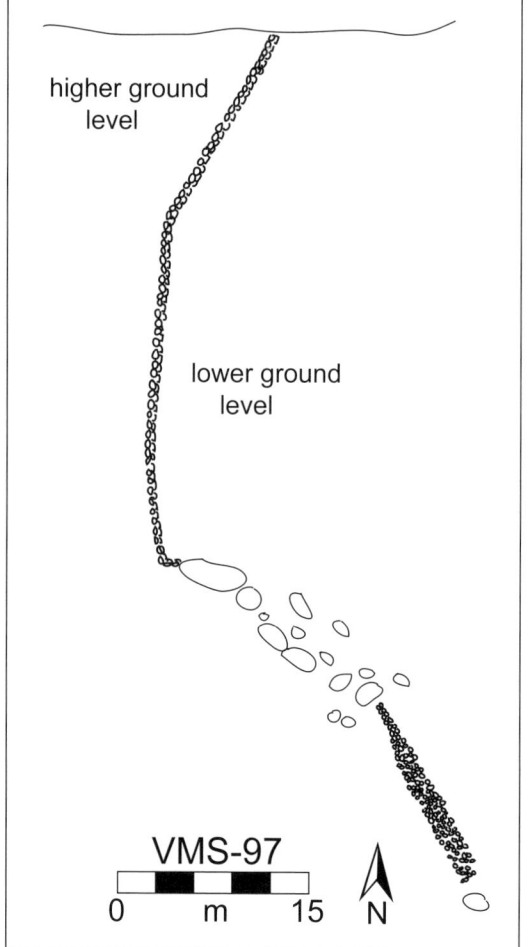

Figure 3.54. VMS-97, plan.

SITE: VMS-97   Block: O   Transect: 14
  Primary Site Use: Agricultural: water control embankment.
  Site Dimensions: 46 × 3.2 m
  Setting: In an upland valley between outcrops, the terrain slopes down to the northwest.
  Present Land Use/Disturbances: The southeast end of the embankment has been partly destroyed. The embankment is breached at various points, and the interior catchment basin has silted in.
  Site Description: Stone and earth embankment. This embankment, oriented 15° east of north, captured runoff from an outcrop to its northeast. The embankment most likely functioned to maintain soil moisture in the area to its east, rather than to channel water to fields to the west, as the latter area is at a higher elevation (c. 2 m) than the land within the embankment. Three stepped courses of small-medium unmodified stones are visible on the east face of the embankment. The northeast end abuts a large outcrop, while in the south the embankment turns to the east for c. 2 m before abutting an outcropping boulder.
  Artifacts: 100% collection; no artifacts recovered.
  Temporal Affiliation: Unknown.
  References: Morrison 1995:89, 102.
  Illustrations: Figure 3.54.

SITE: VMS-98   Block: O   Transect: 14
  Primary Site Use: Agricultural: erosion control wall.
  Site Dimensions: 8 × 0.6 m
  Setting: Area of gently sloping dry farmed agricultural fields in dry upland zone amid high outcrops. Located near the edge of a drainage channel that slopes down to the west, near a large erosion gully.
  Present Land Use/Disturbances: Slope wash.
  Site Description: Small single-faced wall. This roughly north-south wall is constructed of two courses of unmodified medium stones. The wall probably served to limit erosion from the fields into the drainage, or functioned as a runoff control feature.
  Artifacts: 100% collection; no artifacts recovered.
  Temporal Affiliation: Unknown.
  References: Morrison 1995:89, 102.

SITE: VMS-99   Block: O   Transect: 15
  Primary Site Use: Water control: catchment basin.
  Site Dimensions: 15 × 8 m
  Setting: Near base of outcrop at edge of high valley. Located on the south side of a large drainage channel cutting through valley between outcrops (sloping down to east).
  Present Land Use/Disturbances: Vegetation along drainage channel is fairly lush.
  Site Description: Masonry-walled basin. This rectangular basin is bounded by masonry-lined stepped walls on three sides, with vertical sheet rock on the other. The c. 2 m wide north-east wall of the embankment is 15 m long and is constructed along the edges of a down-cut erosion channel. This wall is faced by stepped masonry courses on each side and is c. 1.5 m high. The drainage channel itself is masonry lined in this area.

  The two side walls are 8-10 m in length and extend from the ends of the long wall southwest to the outcrop. These walls are constructed of medium modified stones and are much narrower than the long wall described above. Three to four courses are visible. They are also stepped, but only on the interior face.

  This water storage basin would have captured runoff from the outcrop above it. It is located at the extreme west end of a long valley that extends down to the east. While arable land is present in this valley, there are no areas flat and rock-free enough to be farmed within 150 m or so of the feature.
  Artifacts: Encounter with cobra at this site prevented any collections from being made.
  Temporal Affiliation: Vijayanagara?
  References: Morrison 1995:90.
  Illustrations: Figure 3.55.

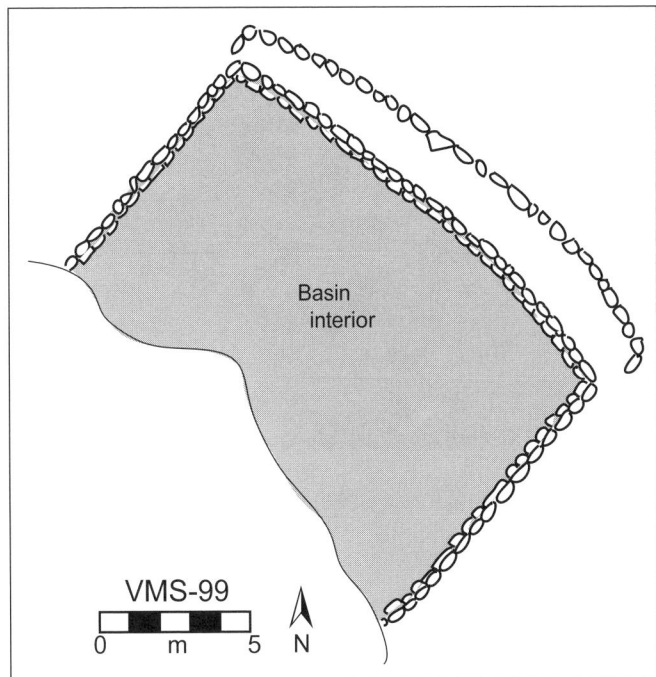

Figure 3.55. VMS-99, plan.

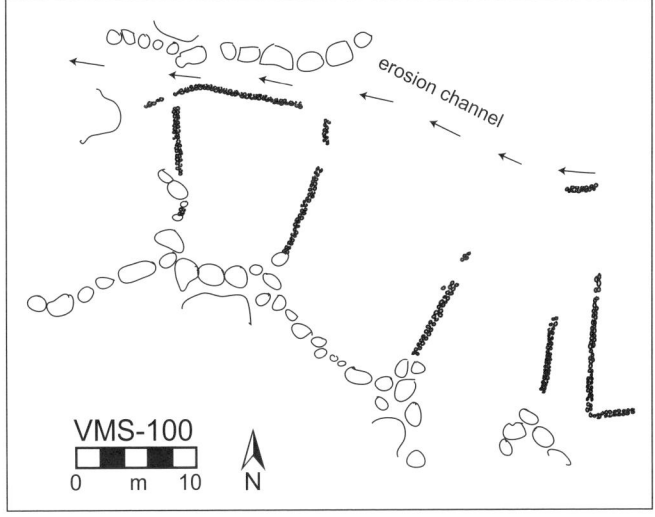

Figure 3.56. VMS-100, plan.

SITE: VMS-100   Block: O   Transect: 15
  Primary Site Use: Agricultural: check dams.
  Site Dimensions: 94 × 33 m
  Setting: Gently sloping area in high rugged plateau zone, sloping down to the west.
  Resources: None.
  Present Land Use/Disturbances: Some walls are broken.
  Site Description: Seven linear arrays of rubble ranging from 1 to 2 m wide and spaced from 10 to 25 m apart. These "walls" functioned to control runoff and prevent soil erosion in this gently sloping area. Five of the walls are roughly perpendicular to the nearby outcrops to the north and south that define a small valley; the other runs along the base of the outcrops in two discontinuous segments. Together these alignments comprise a check dam or small terrace system for rain-fed agriculture.
  Artifacts: 100% collection; no artifacts recovered.
  Temporal Affiliation: Unknown.
  References: Morrison 1995:89, 102; Sinopoli and Morrison 1991:68.
  Illustrations: Figure 3.56.

Plate 3.31. VMS-101, wall segment.

Plate 3.32. VMS-101, bedrock mortars, one unfinished.

SITE: VMS-101   Block: O/J   Transect: 14-17
  Primary Site Use: Residential: settlement.
  Site Dimensions: 800 × 400 m (minimally)
  Setting: Low-lying region to north of large outcrop hill, and to east of settlement of Bukkasagara.
  Present Land Use/Disturbances: Tungabhadra Right Bank Main Canal cuts through the site. The excavation for the canal has undoubtedly destroyed many features. A modern Shaivite monastery may be covering earlier structures; there is also a recent cemetery and quarrying activities. It is unknown to what extent contemporary Bukkasagara overlies VMS-101 ("Old Bukkasagara"); there are Vijayanagara period temples throughout the contemporary village.
  Site Description: Extensive Vijayanagara period settlement. This site has been badly disturbed and is partly obscured by recent construction. When visited in 1988 several features were visible (described below). We were unable to map the site in 1988 due to time constraints, and when the site was revisited in 1996 with the intention of mapping, much of the area had been converted to rice paddies and little of the site remained.
  Structural details visible in 1988 included evidence for multiple spatially dispersed square or rectangular mounds in which well-constructed rubble walls were sometimes visible. Walls ranged in width from 0.6 to 1 m. Only a few unambiguous multi-room structures were discernible; one of these appears to have four to five rooms and plastered walls. Three block mortars were observed; one of these was unfinished. There are at least two very long rubble walls associated with the settlement that may have bordered routes of movement to the town or the settlement itself. One of these runs approximately east-west, paralleling the canal. The other is at the east end of the site, near the mouth of a small valley.
  This settlement was at least partially fortified. The bastionlike structure, VMS-85, may be associated with this site, and the remains of a small fort (VMS-650) are visible in the outcrops to its north in Block J.
  Wall materials are variable, ranging from small to large angular unmodified stones. No moldings or finished architectural elements were observed, but several quarried blocks, with Vijayanagara period quarry marks, were noted. Nearly all walls have two faces, some with rubble and earth cores. Several structures with superimposed floors can be seen, though strata visible in excavated areas do not appear very deep.
  The site is associated with and probably contemporary to temple complex VMS-83 and impounded spring VMS-84.
  Artifacts: The artifact scatter is variable and density is highest in the western area of the site. There is evidence for modern dumping, particularly near the modern cemetery.
  Eight 4 × 4 m collection units were spaced at 50 m intervals along a central east-west axis. A general diagnostic collection was also made. A total of 1700 g of ceramics were collected.
  Diagnostic collection includes 10 other bowls, 1 lamp, 6 flange rim jars, 9 straight rim jars, and 4 round rim jars. Additional diagnostics were recovered from the collection units. Many are of recent forms, though others likely date to the Vijayanagara period.
  Unit 1: 250 g ceramics; wares: 39 black plain ware, 3 red plain ware. Diagnostics: 1 bowl, 1 jar.
  Unit 2: <50 g ceramics; wares: 2 black plain ware.
  Unit 3: 50 g ceramics; wares: 3 black plain ware, 1 red plain ware. Diagnostics: 1 bowl.
  Unit 4: 300 g ceramics; wares: 58 black plain ware, 1 coarse ware. Diagnostics: 2 jars.
  Unit 5: No artifacts recovered.
  Unit 6: 50 g ceramics; wares: 10 black plain ware, 2 red plain ware.
  Unit 7: 300 g ceramics; wares: 136 black plain ware, 15 red plain ware, 1 red burnished ware, 1 black decorated. Diagnostics: 1 bowl, 3 jars.
  Unit 8: 700 g ceramics; wares: 219 black plain ware, 37 red plain ware. Diagnostics: 3 bowls, 8 jars.
  Temporal Affiliation: Vijayanagara (with later additions).
  References: Morrison 1995:63, 64, 68, 69, 79, 80, 99; Sinopoli and Morrison 1991:66, 67; Sinopoli 1997:481; Sinopoli 2003:237.
  Illustrations: Plates 3.31, 3.32.

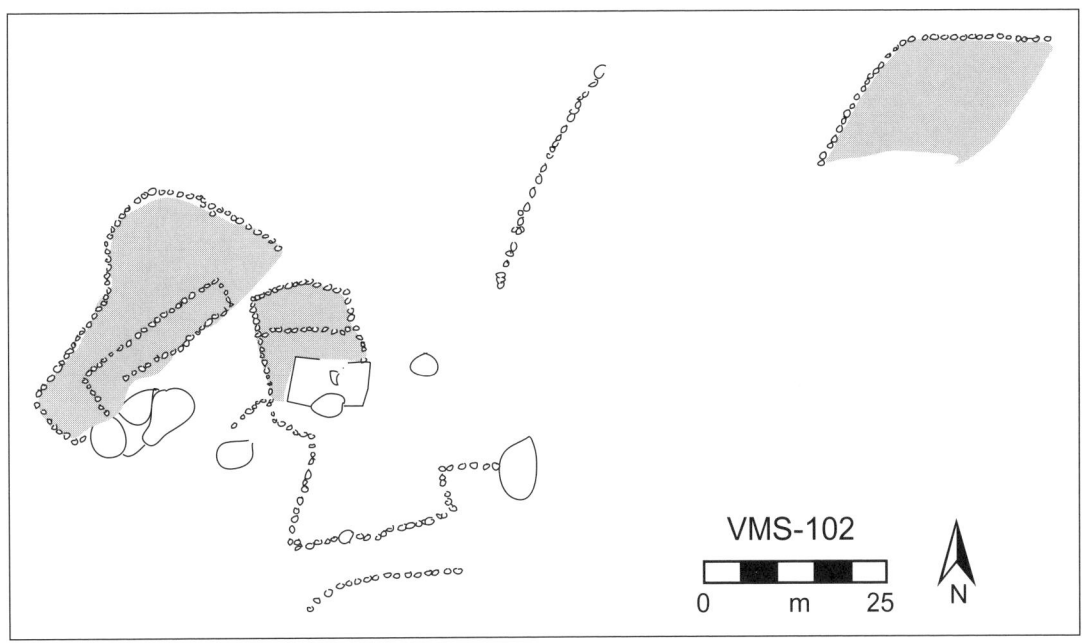

Figure 3.57. VMS-102, plan.

SITE: VMS-102   Block: O   Transect: 15
  Primary Site Use: Religious/residential?: terraces and shrine.
  Site Dimensions: 140 × 70 m
  Setting: On sloping sheet rock surface of outcrop; terrace walls enclose small flat areas of gravelly soil.
  Present Land Use/Disturbances: Modern abandoned shrine to west of site; some portions of the terrace wall have been breached by erosion. Slope wash and redeposition of artifacts has been considerable.
  Site Description: Two artificial terraces and associated walls. This site is located c. 25 m to the south of the crest of the large outcrop hill south of Bukkasagara and VMS-101. The east terrace consists of a semicircular rock wall up to 1.8 m high, with a radius of 10 m. There is a very light ceramic scatter on this terrace.
  Thirty m to the west is a 32 m long wall composed of a single line of large granite stones; its southwest end incorporates a number of massive boulders. Twelve m to the west of the south end of this wall is a shrine, now abandoned, but clearly post-Vijayanagara in date. It contains a Nandi image and an empty image base. A series of walls are located to the south and southwest of the shrine; these form small terraces and retain soil. A stairway leading to the crest of the outcrop is located c. 20 m southwest of the shrine. Another terrace system is located due west of the shrine and consists of four parallel and semicircular walls that define terraces. The four terraces span an elevation of 5-7 m from the sheet rock in the north to the highest (s) terrace.
  A moderate to dense ceramic scatter is visible. Terraces designated as site VMS-88 are located c. 10 m northwest of this area, and these two sites may best be conceived of as a single complex.
  Artifacts: Sparse ceramic scatter on the east terrace; moderate to dense scatter on the west terrace. The ceramic density is very heavy on the small terrace directly north of the shrine. A 100% collection was conducted on that terrace only. 3100 g ceramics; wares: 1092 black plain ware, 103 red plain ware, 4 black burnished, 9 black decorated, 3 red decorated. Diagnostics: 1 bowl, 15 jars. Lithics: one flake tool, of translucent green glass.
  Temporal Affiliation: Unknown, some construction (perhaps all) post-Vijayanagara.
  References: Lycett 1991.
  Illustrations: Figure 3.57.

SITE: VMS-103   Block: O   Transect: 12
  Primary Site Use: Religious: sati image and displaced Vijayanagara elements.
  Site Dimensions: c. 10 × 10 m
  Setting: Along paved Kamalapuram-Kampli Road, which is also the course of Vijayanagara period road. Site is near Vijayanagara period gate, VMS-93.
  Present Land Use/Disturbances: Sculpture is found within a recent structure.
  Site Description: Vijayanagara period images in a recent structure. This two-chamber shrine is recent in date, but incorporates older architectural and sculptural elements. These include a sati memorial stone with an image of a woman with her right hand upraised. Above her head are small images of a lingam, two seated figures, and a sun and moon. Around the shrine are other displaced Vijayanagara period elements, including an image base, column base, and some dressed stones with Vijayanagara quarry marks.
  Artifacts: Modern structure; no collections made.
  Temporal Affiliation: Images are Vijayanagara period, structure is recent.

Plate 3.33. VMS-104, shrine.

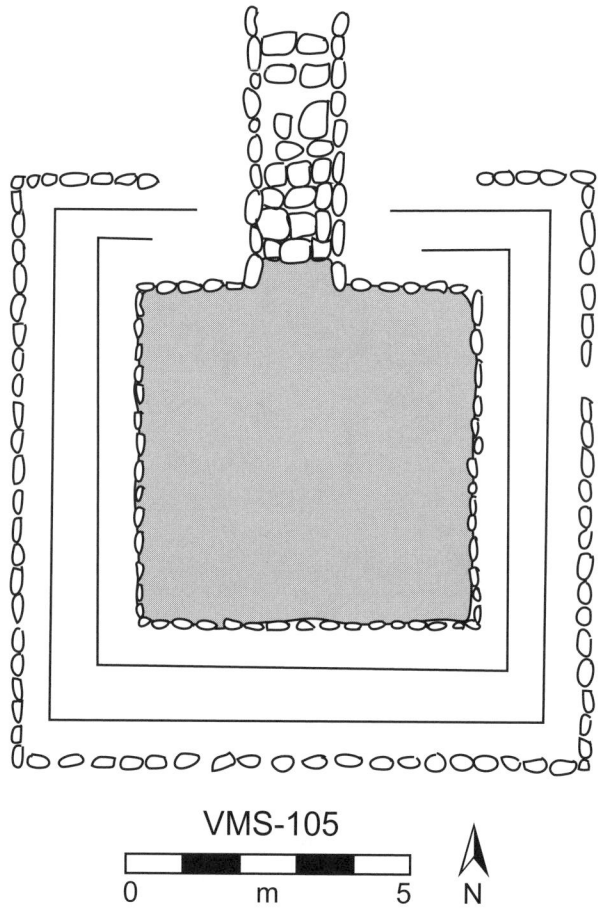

Figure 3.58. VMS-105, plan.

SITE: VMS-104 Block: O Transect: 18
  Primary Site Use: Religious: shrine.
  Site Dimensions: 4 × 3.2 m
  Setting: On gentle slope in high valley.
  Resources: None nearby; site is located in runoff channel.
  Present Land Use/Disturbances: Shrine is in worship.
  Site Description: Single-chamber shrine. This 2 × 2 column shrine is constructed of roughly dressed unadorned columns with rectangular capitals. It abuts an outcropping boulder, which forms its rear wall, and is oriented 28° east of south. The other walls are constructed of large rectangular slabs with Vijayanagara quarry marks. The roof is of the offset square plan. No image is present.
  Artifacts: Very light sherd scatter in fields in front of shrine; not collected.
  Temporal Affiliation: Vijayanagara.
  References: Morrison 1995:73.
  Illustrations: Plate 3.33.

SITE: VMS-105 Block: O Transect: 18
  Primary Site Use: Water control: step well.
  Site Dimensions: 6.5 × 5.25 m
  Setting: In dry farmed field at base of outcrop in high valley.
  Present Land Use/Disturbances: Modern fields, erosion in valley.
  Site Description: Square step well. This well is located at the base of an east-west outcrop in a narrow flat valley. It is presently dry but is in good condition. The feature was situated at the edge of a drainage channel to capture runoff from the outcrop. It is c. 4.5 m deep, with interior dimensions of 3 × 3.2 m, and exterior dimensions of 5.25 × 5.25 m. The walls are composed of undressed granite blocks with mortar and chinking stones, with up to twenty-seven courses visible. The walls are stepped outward (from bottom to top) at approximately 1 m intervals, forming four tiers. Access steps are located at the north end of the well and are composed of unmodified granite slabs. Two parallel walls flank the steps.
  Artifacts: Low density ceramic scatter in general area, extending across valley; not collected.
  Temporal Affiliation: Vijayanagara.
  References: Morrison 1995:73.
  Illustrations: Figure 3.58.

SITE: VMS-106 Block: O Transect: 18
  Primary Site Use: Agricultural/transport: wall.
  Site Dimensions: 39 × c. 5 m
  Setting: Sloping area near west edge of outcrop hill.
  Present Land Use/Disturbances: Modern dirt road along edge of site.
  Site Description: Crudely constructed wall. This wall is located at the northwest base of a large outcrop, which it parallels at an orientation of 28° north of east. It most likely served as a runoff control device and may also have bordered a path that ran along the base of the outcrop and linked shrine VMS-104 with well VMS-105. The wall is constructed of two loosely fitted courses of medium to large unmodified stones.
  Artifacts: Very light scatter in surrounding fields; not collected.
  Temporal Affiliation: Unknown; if associated with shrine and well probably Vijayanagara.
  References: Morrison 1995:73, 89, 102.

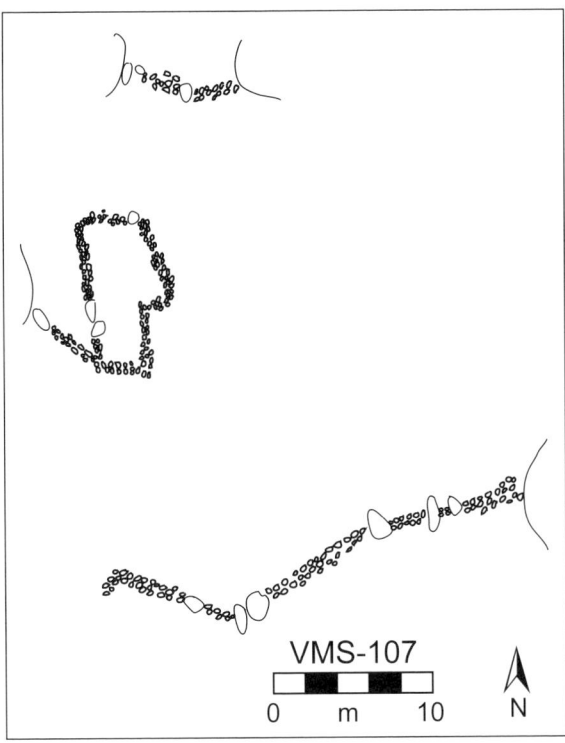

Figure 3.59. VMS-107, plan.

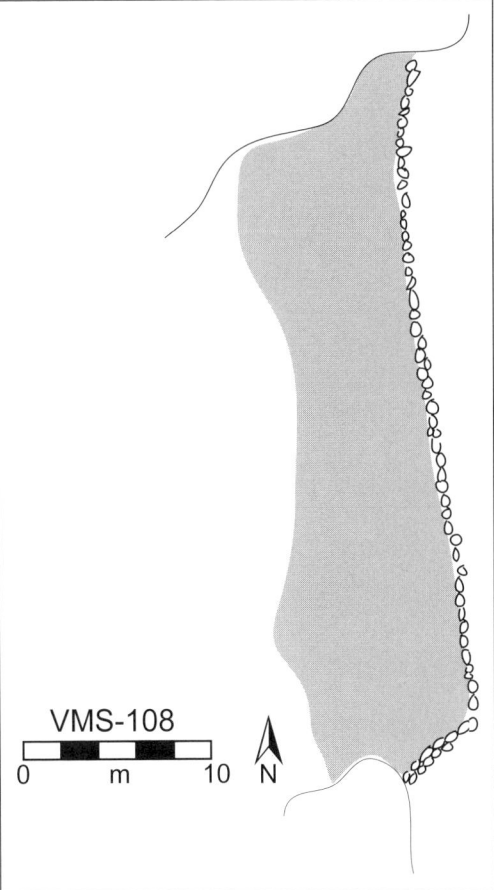

Figure 3.60. VMS-108, plan.

Plate 3.34. VMS-108, detail of embankment construction.

SITE: VMS-107   Block: O   Transect: 18
   Primary Site Use: Unknown/residential?: rubble walls.
   Site Dimensions: 36 × 30 m
   Setting: Flat area of outcrop, shallow soil accumulation around walls.
   Present Land Use/Disturbances: Some recent burning in area.
   Site Description: Rubble walls. Three walls constructed of small and large unmodified stones piled between outcrops. The elements are variable in size and random in orientation. No chinking or mortar is evident. The northeast wall is c. 5 m long and spans the gap between two outcropping boulders. It is situated at the edge of a runoff channel. Approximately 8 m to the south is an irregularly shaped chamber c. 4 m east-west × 9 m north-south. The southernmost wall is located c. 14 m to the south of this structure and spans the entire width of the outcrop saddle, with a small gap. The wall is informal and jagged, consisting of piled rubble; its width varies from one to five elements. The site likely is the remains of a short-term residential camp, perhaps occupied by pastoralists.
   Artifacts: 100% collection; no artifacts recovered.
   Temporal Affiliation: Unknown.
   Illustrations: Figure 3.59.

SITE: VMS-108   Block: O   Transect: 18
   Primary Site Use: Agricultural: reservoir embankment.
   Site Dimensions: 36 × c. 10 m
   Setting: Spans a drainage channel amid high outcrops.
   Present Land Use/Disturbances: Some modern footpaths; embankment is breached by an erosion channel.
   Site Description: Embankment with stepped stone east face and earthen west face. The stone face is informally constructed of unmodified small stones. Up to six courses are preserved and coursing is irregular and loosely fit. The embankment functioned to capture runoff from the outcrops to the east. The area to the west consists of sheet rock, so only the c. 60 × 60 m impounded area to the site's east could have been farmed.
   Artifacts: 100% collection. <50 g ceramics; wares: 3 black plain ware. One gray chert tool.
   Temporal Affiliation: Vijayanagara?; not recently maintained.
   References: Lycett 1991; Morrison 1995:89, 102.
   Illustrations: Figure 3.60; Plate 3.34.

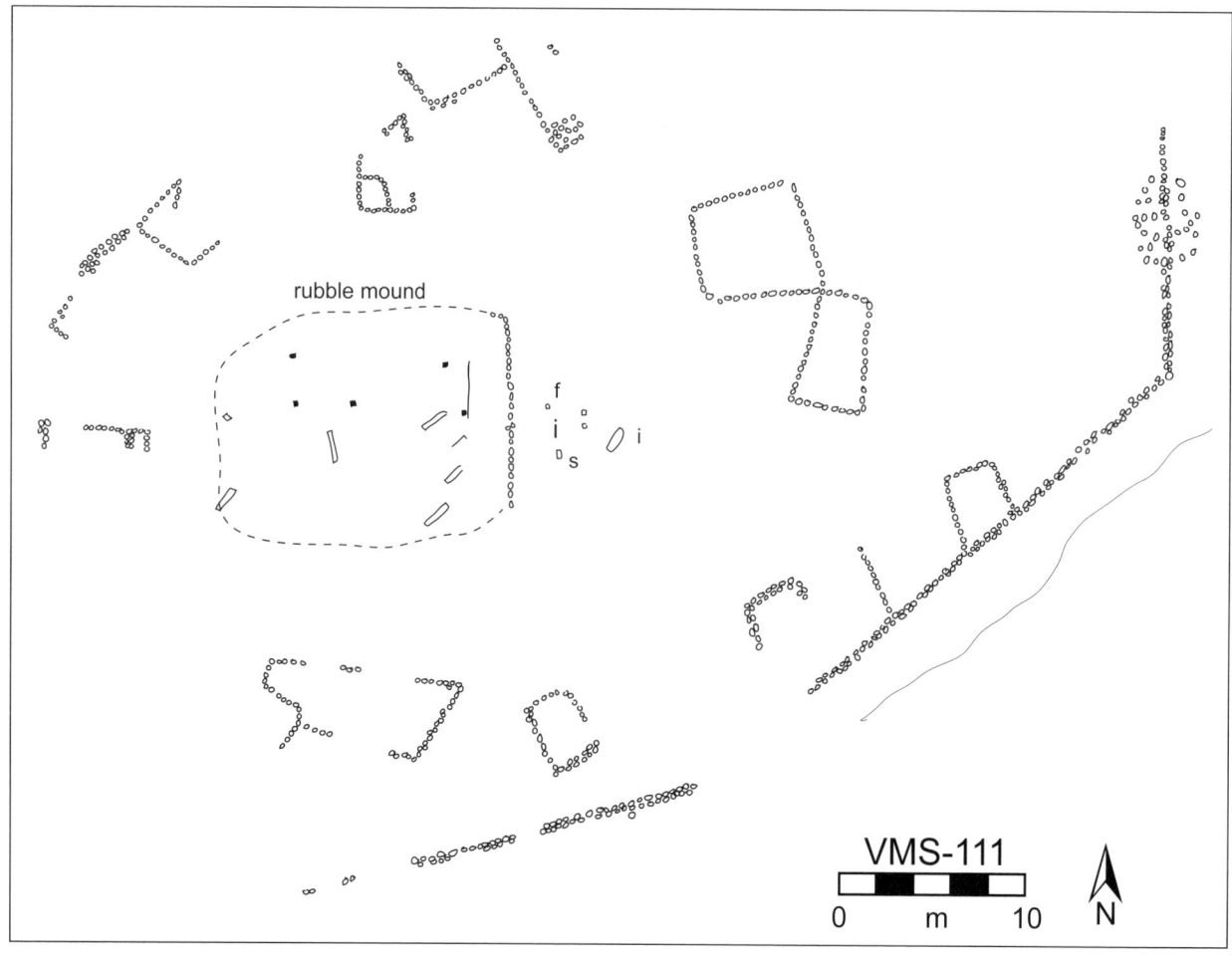

Figure 3.61. VMS-111, plan.

SITE: VMS-111   Block: O   Transect: 12
  Primary Site Use: Religious: Shaivite temple complex.
  Site Dimensions: 66 × 48 m
  Setting: On sheet rock on low outcrop above Kamalapuram-Kampli Road.
  Present Land Use/Disturbances: Near modern canal and irrigated fields. The site is heavily eroded; some looting pits have been dug into the shrine's foundation; columns have been displaced.
  Site Description: Shrine with associated rooms and walls. This site consists of a small shrine with at least ten associated rooms and an enclosure wall. All of the features are built on sheet rock. The shrine was 3 × 2 columns and was constructed on a low platform. Only five unsculpted columns are still standing and several fallen capitals are present. Three long slabs are located south of the shrine, and may have been part of a porch or a plinth around the platform.
  Several image fragments are found on the sheet rock to the east of the shrine. These include a portion of a trident and two blocks depicting feet encircled by a naga. A four-line inscription is pecked on nearby sheet rock, in Kannada script. The inscription is dated on paleographic grounds to the sixteenth century. It refers to the erection of a column (?) to the Shaivite god Mailara by an individual named Honaaya. The inscription is poorly written and several of the characters are garbled, indicating that the carver may have been illiterate (C.S. Patil, pers. comm.). An inscribed image of a devotee is located on the sheet rock nearby, with the name Honaaya associated with it.
  There are several small square and rectangular rooms south of the shrine, built on the sheet rock over a shallow layer of soil. They are constructed of double-faced rubble walls. A long, well-constructed, double-faced rubble wall, 0.5 m wide, encloses the site on the east and south. Several rooms are built against this wall. In the center of the enclosed area are two freestanding rooms. The rooms are of uniform size, and may have served to house travelers or devotees.
  Artifacts: There are a small number of highly fragmented sherds in the limited patches of soil on the outcrop; no collections made.
  Temporal Affiliation: Vijayanagara, probably sixteenth century, on basis of inscription.
  References: Morrison 1995:72, 80; Morrison and Sinopoli 1992; Patil and Patil 1995: insc. 391-92; Sinopoli 1994; Sinopoli 1993b:629-30; Sinopoli 2003:234-35; Sinopoli and Morrison 1991:67.
  Illustrations: Figure 3.61; Plates 3.35-3.37.

Plate 3.35. VMS-111, standing column.

Plate 3.36. VMS-111, inscription.

Plate 3.37. VMS-111, sculpted block.

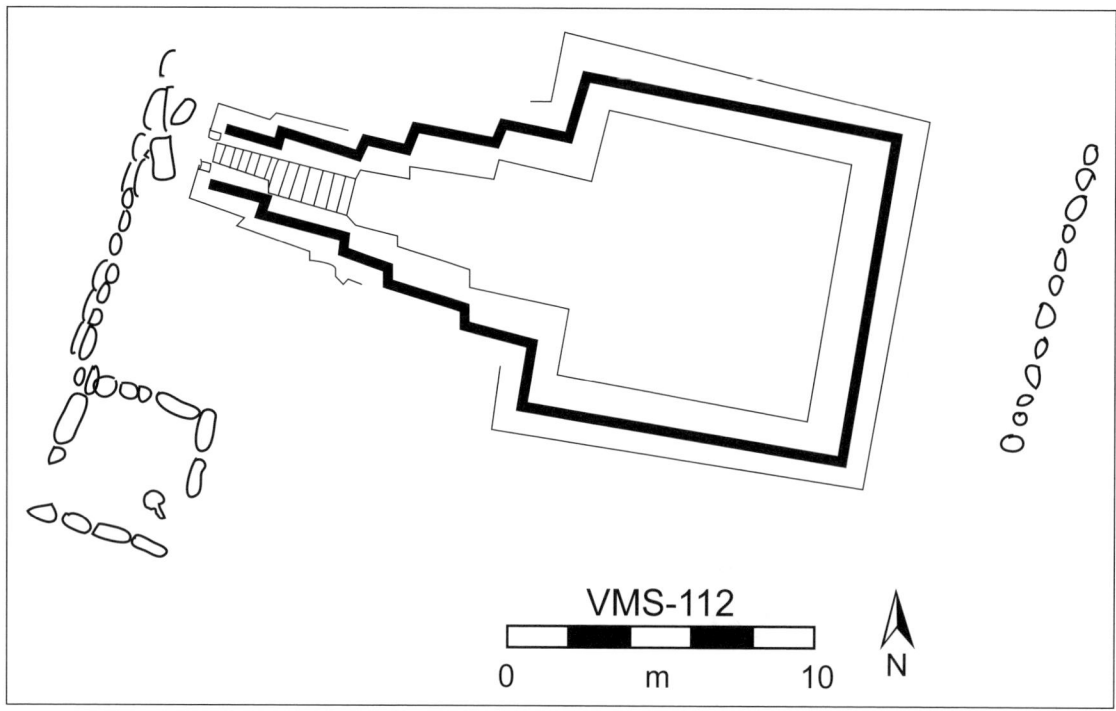

Figure 3.62. VMS-112, plan.

SITE: VMS-112   Block: O   Transect: 13
   Primary Site Use: Water control: step well and associated features.
   Site Dimensions: 64 × 40 m
   Setting: In broad low valley along Kamalapuram-Kampli Road; probably along ancient road course.
   Present Land Use/Disturbances: Tungabhadra Canal and paved road nearby.
   Site Description: Step well and associated features. This site consists of: (1) a recent tree enclosure west of the well; (2) a retaining wall to the east of the well; (3) disturbed fragments of a possible shrine; and (4) Vijayanagara period step well.
   1. The tree enclosure, of recent construction, is constructed of Vijayanagara architectural elements that must have come from a no longer existing nearby structure. It is located to the southwest of the step well and is constructed of well-dressed slabs and rectangular blocks of variable size and shape. A low north-south wall extends from the northwest corner of the platform to the columns flanking the well (see below).
   2. Retaining wall to the east of the step well is constructed of one course of large unmodified stones that spans a small wash. Its temporal affiliation is unclear.
   3. Architectural fragments: located c. 20 m to the south of the well entry (not shown on map) are fragments of Vijayanagara period stone molding and slabs; these may be the remains of a small shrine structure.
   4. Step well: this elaborate well is constructed of well-dressed granite elements. Two columns with inset octagonal sections and lotus bud motifs are located at the northwest terminus of the well, flanking the stairway. They define a gate to the well, and in form closely resemble an elaborate reservoir sluice gate. These c. 5 m tall columns are visible from a considerable distance. A boundary wall runs from the columns to the tree enclosure. The columns are topped by a granite slab lintel. The lintel is shaped, on its external face, with a sculpted linear groove running across the midsection, broken by a rectangular outset panel in the center. Two sculpted stone Nandis sit atop the lintel, facing out toward the road. Just inside this gate six large rectangular slab steps lead down into the well. Below them is a small platform, from which five more steps head down to the current water level. The stairway is enclosed by the exterior walls of the well.
   The well is keyhole shaped with a stepped expanding long axis. The roughly square main chamber of the well is c. 10 × 10 m. On the ground surface is an enclosing wall of end-set slabs that follows the plan of the walls of the well basin. Within this wall is a course of large blocks and slabs that form a slightly protruding shelf over the well interior. The walls are extremely well constructed of long rectangular slabs, tightly fit with little chinking and no mortar. Ten courses are visible. This is a very formal and elegant construction.
   Artifacts: 100% collection; no artifacts recovered.
   Temporal Affiliation: Vijayanagara.
   References: Morrison 1995:72, 83.
   Illustrations: Figure 3.62; Plates 3.38, 3.39.

Plate 3.38. VMS-112, well overview.

Plate 3.39. VMS-112, columned gate, entry to well.

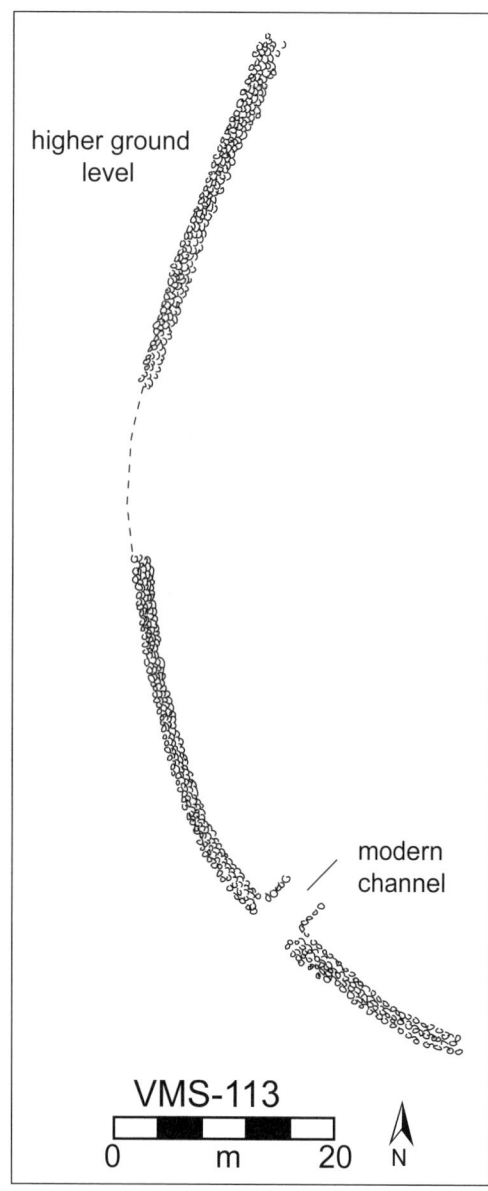

Figure 3.63. VMS-113, plan.

seven stepped stone courses on its east face. The stone facing is of small to medium unmodified and coarsely dressed stones; coursing is irregular and sinuous. This is a crude construction, similar to nearby embankment VMS-91. The embankment is semicircular in plan and served to capture runoff from the outcrops to the north and east, with a catchment area of c. 120 × 150 m. The flat zone to the west is c. 250 × 100 m. No clear earthen embankment is presently identifiable on the west of the stone face, as soil levels on this side are even with the top of the stone face.

Artifacts: Moderate artifact scatter along footpath that runs along interior of embankment; no collections were made.

Temporal Affiliation: Vijayanagara.
References: Morrison 1995:89, 102.
Illustrations: Figure 3.63.

Site: VMS-114   Block: O   Transect: 11
Primary Site Use: Transport mounded area and road wall.
Site Dimensions: 21 × 14 m mound, 54 m long wall
Setting: In a flat area near east base of high outcrop hill, c. 15 m to the north of the paved Kamalapuram-Kampli road.
Present Land Use/Disturbances: Paved Kampli Road is c. 15 m to the south of the site. The Tungabhadra Right Bank Main Canal is c. 40 m to the south. The site has been severely damaged by the construction of these features.
Site Description: Mounded area and associated wall. This site consists of a low (c. 0.6-0.7 m high) artificial mound, 21 × 14 m in dimension, oriented 35° south of west. The mound may have been bounded by masonry; there are a few large slabs with Vijayanagara quarry marks and one square block (column footing?) associated with it, but none are *in situ*.

On the south side of the mound is a long roughly east-west wall constructed of large unmodified stones. This wall likely bordered the route of the Vijayanagara period road, along the same course of the modern paved road. Portions of the same road wall were recorded as site VMS-652. The mound may be the remains of a roadside structure.

Artifacts: Light ceramic scatter over mounded area; no collections were made.
Temporal Affiliation: Vijayanagara.
References: Morrison 1995:2.

SITE: VMS-113   Block: O   Transect: 13
Primary Site Use: Agricultural: reservoir embankment.
Site Dimensions: 140 m × 2.5+ m
Setting: In low broad valley to the east of the Kamalapuram-Kampli road and step well VMS-112. Embankment VMS-91 is located in the same valley c. 150 m to the southeast.
Present Land Use/Disturbances: Embankment has been breached by farmers to create a water channel to agricultural fields. A field wall overlies the embankment. There has been considerable soil accumulation to the west.
Site Description: Reservoir embankment. This stepped stone construction has a predominant roughly north-south orientation and has

SITE: VMS-115   Block: O   Transect: 11
Primary Site Use: Residential/transport?: rectangular structure on low mound.
Site Dimensions: 20 × 5 m
Setting: Flat area to the south of the Kamalapuram-Kampli road, along Vijayanagara period road course.
Present Land Use/Disturbances: Modern paved road is c. 5 m west of the site; modern canal nearby.
Site Description: Structure on mound. Site consists of an 8 × 5 m rectangular structure built atop an earthen mound. The mound is 20 × 5 m in area and oriented 35° south of west. The outlines of the structure are only partly discernible; no internal divisions are visible. Rectangular dressed slabs define the edges of the structure; there are some plaster fragments visible. This site may be associated with Vijayanagara period road and the VMS-111 temple complex to the east.
Artifacts: A few body sherds on mound; not collected.
Temporal Affiliation: Unknown/ Vijayanagara?
References: Morrison 1995:72.

SITE: VMS-116   Block: O   **Transect:** 15
   Primary Site Use: Religious: Vaishnava temple complex.
   Site Dimensions: c. 75 × 75 m
   Setting: Along road in the settlement of Bukkasagara.
   Present Land Use/Disturbances: Temple is in worship; many modifications have been made to structures, including the placing of a concrete slab inscribed with "1967" inside the temple. Heavy plaster obscures many details.
   Site Description: Walled temple complex. This complex includes a number of Vijayanagara and later structures enclosed within a modern compound wall. Structures include the temple, five associated shrines, and a possible well.

   The main temple has four chambers: a 4 × 4 column antechamber with entry from the south, and three sanctuaries, each entered directly from the antechamber. Two of the sanctuaries are on the south side of the structure; the third is on the east. Elephant balustrades flank the central stairway to the raised antechamber. The columns are square in plan with octagonal insets and cruciform capitals. The outermost columns are sculpted, with Shaivite and Vaishnavite images; the antechamber has a lotus panel ceiling. There has clearly been considerable modification of the temple and a concrete slab marked with the year 1967 is on the wall. The doors to the sanctuaries were closed and locked, preventing their documentation.

   A small two-chamber shrine is located in the northwest corner of the compound. It has a 4 × 2 column antechamber and 2 × 2 column sanctuary with modern shikara. Much of the structure is of the Vijayanagara period. Sculptures within the shrine's sanctuary include a large Anjaneya Hanuman, a small striding Hanuman, a naga, and a Ganesha (in antechamber). The sanctuary has Vaishnava door guardians, and an offset square ceiling.

   To the east of this shrine is a smaller 2 × 2 column single-chamber shrine containing an image of Ganesha. The columns probably date to the Vijayanagara period; the walls are recent. Four m to the east is a possible well, c. 1.5 m in diameter, defined by roughly shaped granite blocks. This is no longer in use, but its construction suggests that it is probably post-Vijayanagara. A displaced Nandi is found nearby.

   Another small shrine with possible Vijayanagara elements is located to the east of the temple. It contains cast iron images of nine anthropomorphic deities, each associated with an animal, including deer, raptor, two horses, goose, burro, pigeon, lion, and elephant.

   There is a small shrine to the south of the one abutting the main complex; it contains a recent stone Nandi and lingam. The columns are of the Vijayanagara period and its walls are of recent construction.

   Another small shrine with old columns and modern walls is located outside and across the street from the walled complex. This has Vaishnavite door guardians with a Nandi image in the main chamber. Outside the shrine is a large stone trough, with a Nandi and lingam carved on the face. The shrine also contains an elephant balustrade, which appears to be in worship.
   Artifacts: Temple is in worship; no collections made.
   Temporal Affiliation: Vijayanagara with later modifications. Many of the Vijayanagara images are likely not in their original location, and have been moved to this complex from elsewhere.
   References: Morrison 1995:69, 79, 89; Sinopoli 1993b:629.

SITE: VMS-117   Block: O   **Transect:** 12-14
   Primary Site Use: Agricultural: reservoir embankment.
   Site Dimensions: 90 × 6 m
   Setting: Embankment encloses a small runoff-fed valley encircled by outcropping hills on the southern side.
   Present Land Use/Disturbances: A modern stone quarry road runs through the reservoir's catchment basin. A recent irrigation canal lies c. 70 m to the north.
   Site Description: Reservoir embankment. This approximately east-west embankment is faced with irregularly coursed masonry on its southern side. Stones are medium sized; most are unmodified, though some have been split. Coursing ranges from seven visible courses on the eastern side to thirteen visible courses near the center, where the embankment reaches a maximum height of 3 m. A large outcropping boulder is incorporated into the embankment near its center. The eastern end does not extend to the outcropping rock face, leaving a gap of 10-12 m, through which livestock now pass. Despite this gap, water is still held in the enclosure, even relatively late into the dry season. The catchment basin, c. 120 × 80 m, is in some areas floored by exposed sheet rock, though in other areas considerable sediment accumulation is evident. On its western end, the embankment extends to the outcrop, curving slightly to the south. There is no indication of a sluice. The northern earthen face of the embankment is faced on its external edge by a single-coursed, single-faced wall of large unmodified stones.

   The embankment's catchment basin is, as noted, c. 130 × 80 m in extent. The area below the embankment (to the north) is even smaller (c. 100 × 60 m), and is also bordered by outcrops, though a small channel at the northern end of this zone could have allowed water to flow further north.
   Artifacts: No collections made.
   Temporal Affiliation: Vijayanagara and later.

SITE: VMS-119   Block: O   **Transect:** 14
   Primary Site Use: Religious: Vaishnava temple.
   Site Dimensions: 15 × 12 m
   Setting: On south edge of Bukkasagara along the Kamalapuram-Kampli road.
   Present Land Use/Disturbances: The temple is currently in worship; recent modifications have been made, and the site is located within a recent enclosure wall.
   Site Description: Temple within a recent enclosure. The temple faces west toward the main road leading into Bukkasagara. It has a 4 × 2 column antechamber and a 2 × 2 column sanctuary. The columns are elaborately sculpted with Vaishnavite and Shaivite iconography. They are square with octagonal insets, and have cruciform capitals. The ceiling has carved lotus motif panels. The roof has slanted slabs on the east end of the structure.

   The sanctuary has Vaishnava door guardians. The stone panels framing the door are carved with serpentine (or vine) motifs, with a Lakshmi figure over the doorway. The interior ceiling is of offset squares, with a lotus medallion in the center. The central image is a large striding Hanuman that is incorporated into the rear wall of the shrine. Six small heavily worn (and unidentifiable) carved images have been placed within the antechamber, as have several column fragments.

   The south bay of the antechamber has been walled off, forming a small room now being used as a kitchen. This wall is of post-Vijayanagara (recent?) date. To the southeast of the temple is a well surrounded by modern masonry. A platform is located 12 m to the east of the temple; on this is a circular granite column with an inverted lotus bud and quarter medallion capital.
   Artifacts: Structure is in worship; no collections made.
   Temporal Affiliation: Vijayanagara with later modifications.
   References: Morrison 1995:69, 79.
   Illustrations: Plate 3.40.

Plate 3.40. VMS-119, temple entry.

SITE: VMS-120   Block: M, N, O, J

Primary Site Use: Agricultural: Turtha Canal.

Site Dimensions: Linear distance of c. 9.5 km, although actual length is significantly longer due to the canal's winding course. Canal width ranges from c. 2 to 6 m.

Setting: The canal winds through low-lying areas south of the Tungabhadra River in an irregular and opportunistic course that meanders around the base of outcropping hills and areas of higher terrain. Nowhere is the canal more than 1.5 km from the river.

Present Land Use/Disturbances: The canal remains in use today and has been considerably modified since its initial construction. No obvious original facing is visible.

Site Description: Irrigation canal. The Turtha Canal channels water from the southern bank of the Tungabhadra eastwards across the northern portions of Blocks M, N, O, and J. At its western end, the canal originates in Block M in a series of seven diversion weirs, or *anicuts*, recorded as site VMS-472. The canal then winds through low-lying areas along the river to the east, and empties into the river in Block J (in transect 5). In Block N, the zone around the canal has been termed the "irrigated valley" by John Fritz et al. As discussed in Chapter 1, this canal separates the Vijayanagara "urban core" from its "sacred center." Several small feeder channels along the canal route flow into the Tungabhadra to handle overflow during periods of high water levels. In Block O, as elsewhere, the Turtha Canal has been continuously repaired and maintained, with no original facing evident. Other than the route, little can be said about the Vijayanagara period construction.

Artifacts: No collections made.

Temporal Affiliation: Vijayanagara. A story recounted by the sixteenth-century Portuguese visitor to Vijayanagara, Fernao Nuniz (Sewell 1900:300-310), suggests that a canal that could be the Turtha was constructed quite early in the city's history, under one of the early Sangama rulers (possibly Bukkaraya II, CE 1399-1406), though this description is not supported by dated inscription or other contemporary records of its construction. A late fourteenth- to early fifteenth-century date is thus possible, but not confirmed.

References: Morrison 1995:88.

SITE: VMS-229   Block: O   Transect: 12

Primary Site Use: Agricultural: reservoir embankment.

Site Dimensions: 82 × 6 m

Setting: A flat gently sloping area at the base of an outcrop; the reservoir abuts outcrop on both ends. This embankment cuts off the northeast flowing section of a long Y-shaped valley between granite outcrops. VMS-72 is located in a parallel position in the northwest part of the valley.

Present Land Use/Disturbances: Several small footpaths cut the embankment. A contemporary shrine consisting of painted red and white stripes and offerings of green glass bangles is located on the outcrop to the southeast of the reservoir. The reservoir bed is completely silted in, and a modern flow-sluice of sorts has cut it near the center. The stonework is in very poor condition.

Site Description: Reservoir embankment. The masonry of the south face of this embankment is constructed of unmodified and split large granite stones. Coursing is irregular; up to three stepped courses are visible near its eastern end. The masonry is generally in poor condition. The reservoir is almost completely silted in, so that only the top of the masonry is visible, and the reservoir bed is at a much higher level than the area below (1-2 m). Almost all the original earthen embankment has been cut away—only small remnants remain near its east end. At the east end, the masonry turns abruptly toward the south. Here there is a gap in the earthen embankment and a line of large boulders. South of the latter is a low wall of a single course of cobbles. This may have been a water outlet; no formal sluice gate is preserved.

Approximately 100 m upstream of the reservoir, a c. 50 m long terrace wall extends across the valley. It is constructed of earth, with a masonry facing (height about 10 cm).

Artifacts: Sparse ceramic scatter above and below reservoir wall. No collections made due to extensive post-use colluviation and disturbance.

Temporal Affiliation: Vijayanagara.

References: Morrison 1995:89, 102.

Illustrations: Figure 3.64.

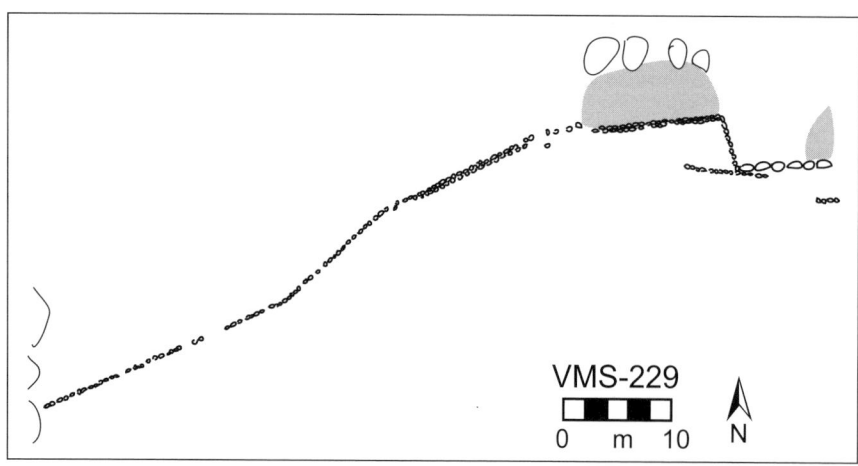

Figure 3.64. VMS-229, plan.

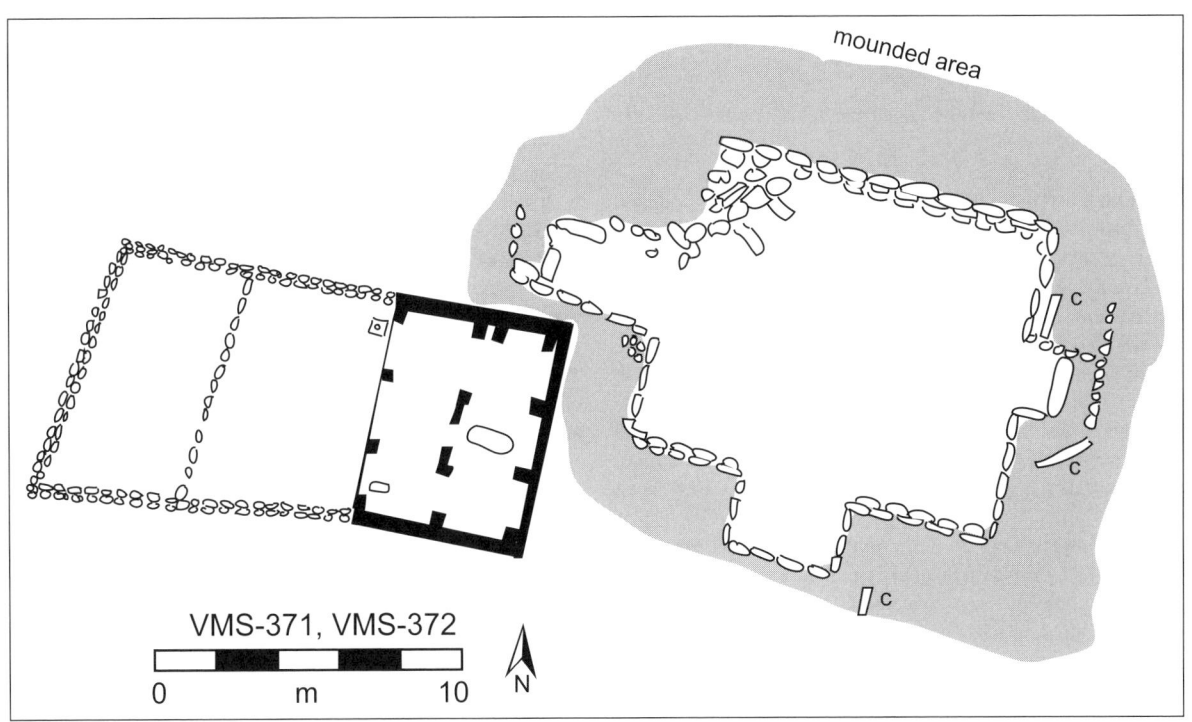

Figure 3.65. VMS-371 and VMS-372, plan.

SITE: VMS-371   Block: O   Transect: 7
Primary Site Use: Religious: Shaivite temple.
Site Dimensions: 16 × 8 m
Setting: Temple is located within irrigated rice and sugar cane fields; step well VMS-372 is located directly to the east.
GPS Location: 15°19'55.2" N, 76°31'05" E
Present Land Use/Disturbances: Temple is located within a modern enclosure wall and is presently in worship. Structure has been whitewashed.
Site Description: Nandi temple. This small Vijayanagara period temple is located within a recent enclosure. The temple is a 4 × 3 column rectangular structure (7 × 6 m) on a low platform with simple beveled molding. The west-facing sanctuary is the central rear bay in the structure interior. The front row of four columns all have square bases above which are, from bottom to top, octagonal, sixteen-sided and octagonal panels and a square top. The columns are painted and plastered; no sculptural details are evident. The rear columns include simple square columns and square columns with rectangular insets. The walls of the temple postdate the columns and images.

The sanctuary faces west, with a formal doorway flanked by Shaivite door guardians; a small Ganesha image is inscribed on the lintel. No north or south walls are present. The central image in the sanctuary is a large granite Nandi. At his feet is a small headless Ganesha. In the northeast corner of the structure is a displaced image base on which sits a small image of Vishnu. Nearby is a small image of three seated figures, and five naga stones. In the southwest corner of the structure is a beautifully sculpted chlorite Nandi; a stone block mortar is near the northwest corner. Circa 5.5 m to the west of the temple within the modern compound wall is a low foundation wall, of which a single course is visible (perhaps the remains of an earlier enclosure wall?).

This temple is quite unusual in plan, particularly in the absence of a separate sanctuary chamber. It is likely that this Vijayanagara period

Plate 3.41. VMS-371, view of temple.

structure has been subject to considerable modification and that the original plan has been altered.

Artifacts: Sparse and localized artifact scatter. Artifacts are visible in localized clusters to the north and south of the temple, especially in mounded earth against the north and south compound walls, which probably results from recent rice paddy construction. Many of the ceramics appear modern. 100% collection. 750 g ceramics; wares: 59 black plain ware, 1 red plain ware, 9 brown plain ware, 2 coarse ware. Diagnostics: 1 bowl, 4 jars.
Temporal Affiliation: Vijayanagara with later modifications.
Illustrations: Figure 3.65; Plate 3.41.

SITE: VMS-372   Block: O   Transect: 7
Primary Site Use: Water control: step well.
Site Dimensions: 22 × 16 m
Setting: Within irrigated rice and sugar cane fields; temple VMS-371 is located directly to the west.
GPS Location: 15°19'56.2" N, 76°31'1.7" E
Present Land Use/Disturbances: Site is surrounded by mounded soil resulting from excavations of surrounding rice fields. The west side of the well has been heavily modified; remaining sides are overgrown. Modern walls and field rubble surround the well.
Site Description: Step well. This well is located directly to the east of temple VMS-371. The square water basin has outset sections on the east and south sides. The disturbed steps are on the west. The north wall of the well consists of four visible tiers of granite blocks; these are slightly stepped. The blocks decrease in size from the water level to the ground surface (from large, c. 1 m long × 0.4 m high, to medium, c. 0.45 m long × 0.2 m high). The west face and stairway have been heavily modified.

A large block projects into the basin on the northwest corner. This block has a depressed groove on its upper end, and was likely part of a pulley water-lifting device. Near the rectangular (2 × 2 m) outset section of the basin along the east side of the well is a standing column on a low platform. Two fallen columns lie nearby. These columns are of common Vijayanagara form, with square panels separated by octagonal insets. No columns are clearly associated with the south outset section (also 2 × 2 m), although a fallen column lies near the well's southeast corner. To the southeast of the well is a large mound of brick, stone, and mortar. This may comprise structural remains from the shikara of temple VMS-371.

Despite recent disturbance, it is evident that this Vijayanagara period well was quite substantial and formally constructed. The fallen columns and platforms around it suggest that it may once have been surrounded by a colonnade or been associated with now collapsed mandapas, perhaps associated with the nearby temple.

Artifacts: Light ceramic scatter, even distribution around well, though dense vegetation limits visibility. Distinctive molded ceramic fragment of human face. 100% collection. Diagnostics: 5 jars, 1 molded jar fragment, with human face.
Temporal Affiliation: Vijayanagara with later modifications.
Illustrations: Figure 3.65.

SITE: VMS-604   Block: O   Transect: 5
Primary Site Use: Mortuary: rock shelters with megalith and artifact scatter.
Site Dimensions: 52 × 27 m
Setting: On south face of sloping outcrop (sloping down to south), shelter is defined by numerous boulders and is partly roofed by overhang, with small pockets of eroding granite and sandy soil.
GPS Location: 15°20'59.7" N, 76°30'35.4" E
Present Land Use/Disturbances: Rice fields at the base of the slope to the south of site. Modern artifacts are found inside the shelter. Slope wash has probably disturbed the site somewhat.
Site Description: Rock shelter with megalith and artifact scatters. The site may be divided into four areas: (1) a shallow south-facing shelter on the east; (2) the site's main shelter, oriented northwest/southeast; (3) an enclosed chamber to the northeast of and entered via the main shelter; and (4) a small south-facing west chamber. A linear cairn megalith is located between the main chamber and the northeast chamber. In the flat area to the southwest of the shelter there is a small scatter of sherds.

The east chamber is c. 8 × 5 m in dimension, and is partly roofed by an overhang. There is a sparse ceramic scatter within the chamber and on a boulder to the southeast of the opening is a grinding slick, c. 20 × 0.15 m.

The main chamber of the large shelter is c. 26 × 8 m and oriented roughly 40° west of north. There are numerous boulders within the shelter, in places narrowing it to only a meter wide, with changes in elevation. Six small cupules have been inscribed on the sloping sheet rock near the shelter entrance. These are shallow circular depressions, ranging from 0.06 to 0.10 m in diameter and 0.01 to 0.03 m deep. Two similar cupules are found within the shelter near the entrance.

Between the main shelter and the northeast shelter is a cairn megalith, 2.6 m long × 2 m wide, with a central passage, 0.35 m wide × 0.25 m high, that runs the length of the cairn. The stones comprising the chamber are medium to large modified boulders. No quarry marks are evident; instead, the stones were flaked.

The northeast chamber is roughly 14 × 6 m in area, with variable surface elevations (higher in the northwest than in the east). There is a moderately dense scatter of ceramics, slag droplets, and fired daub in the southeast quadrant of this chamber. Elsewhere, artifacts are sparsely distributed.

The west chamber is more open to the light and has a sparse artifact density of sherds and a single iron fragment.
Artifacts: Include both prehistoric and recent ceramics, iron, slag, daub, and one fragment of brick. The daub may be part of a furnace lining, suggesting metal processing may have occurred nearby. Two 2 × 2 m judgment units were placed in areas of high density; a diagnostic sweep was made.
Unit J1: 350 g ceramics; 100 g slag.
Unit J2: 450 g ceramics; 400 g slag.
Temporal Affiliation: Iron Age/Early Historic with later occupation.
References: Sinopoli and Morrison 2006b:515-16, 519.
Illustrations: Figure 3.66; Plate 3.42.

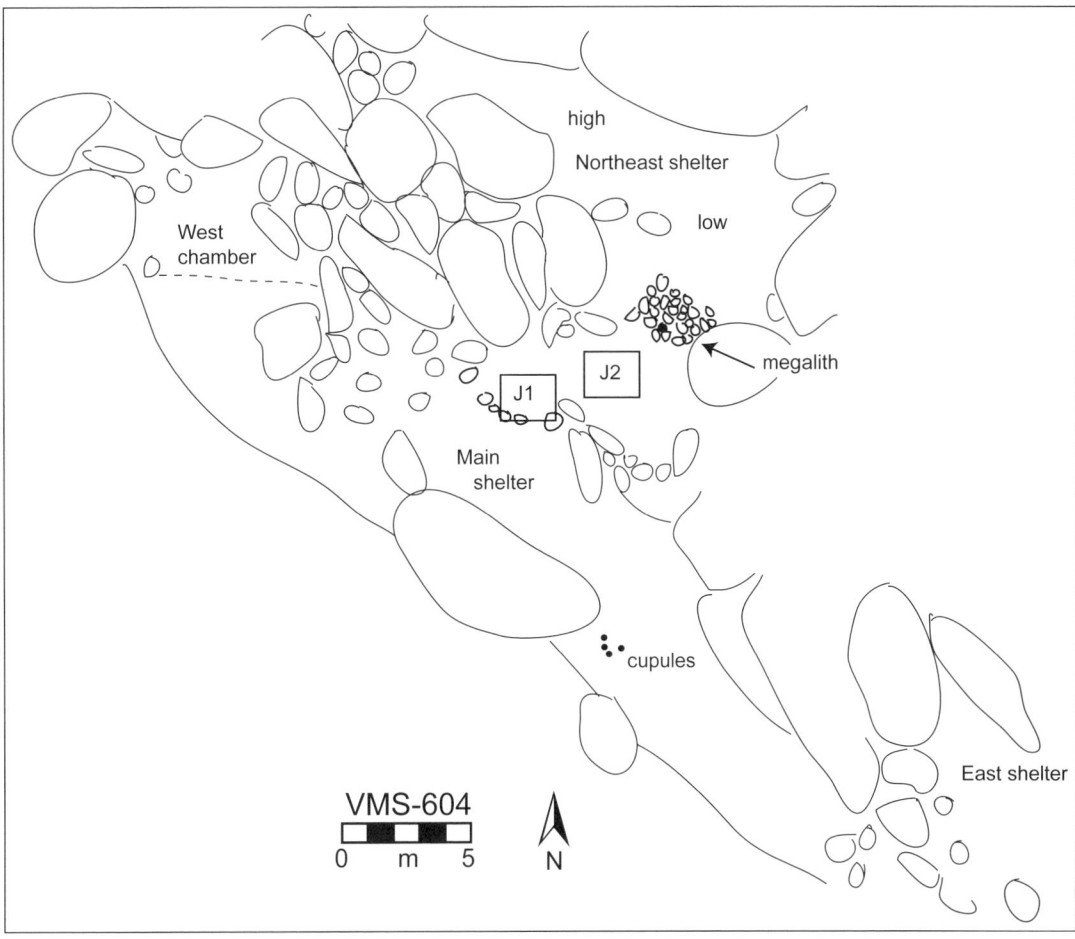

Figure 3.66. VMS-604, plan.

Plate 3.42. VMS-604, detail of pecked cupules.

Plate 3.43. VMS-607, sculpture in modern shrine.

SITE: VMS-607   Block: O   **Transect:** 13
Primary Site Use: Religious: sculpture.
Site Dimensions: n.a.
Setting: Within a small recently-constructed shrine of granite slabs in an irrigated field, c. 60 m south of the Turtha Canal near the village of Bukkasagara.
GPS Location: 15°20'56.5" N, 76°31'44.5" E
Present Land Use/Disturbances: In fallow field on modern structure; lower portion of sculpture is buried.
Site Description: Sculpture. Vijayanagara period sculpture placed in a modern shrine. The sculpture depicts two male devotees, each with palms together. Both are wearing dhotis and have their hair arranged in a large bun on the right side of their heads.
Artifacts: Recent artifacts in fields around shrine; not collected.
Temporal Affiliation: Vijayanagara period image in modern shrine.
Illustrations: Plate 3.43.

SITE: VMS-652   Block: O   **Transect:** 12-13
Primary Site Use: Transport: road wall.
GPS Location: Southwest end 15°19'38.0" N, 16°30'37.8" E; near VMS-64 15°19'38.9" N, 76°30'45.9" E; northeast end, 15°19'40.6" N, 76°30'46.0" E.
Site Dimensions: 312 × 1 m
Setting: Wall runs along the west side of paved Kamalapuram-Kampli Road.
Present Land Use/Disturbances: Site has been disturbed. It is discontinuous in some areas and has boulders piled against it in others, where it reinforces modern field walls.
Site Description: Road wall. This long wall is constructed of a single course of large unmodified and split boulders (c. 80-1.00 m on a side), spaced in a line with gaps of 10-20 cm between them. The wall parallels the course of the modern paved road, and also the course of the Vijayanagara period road. Site VMS-64, a small mandapa, is located at the midpoint of the wall; site VMS-114 includes another segment of the same wall.
Artifacts: No collections made.
Temporal Affiliation: Vijayanagara.
References: Sinopoli and Morrison 2006b:515-16.

Plate 3.44. VMS-653, Ganesha shrine on boulder.

SITE: VMS-653   Block: O   **Transect:** 2
Primary Site Use: Religious: Shaivite shrine (Ganesha).
Site Dimensions: 3 × 2 m
Setting: On north-facing boulder on edge of outcrop. Along Kamalapuram-Kampli Road.
GPS Location: 15°19'19.2" N, 76°30'14.2" E
Present Land Use/Disturbances: Circa 18 m to the south of modern paved road; plastic and other recent trash in area.
Site Description: Ganesha image. Image and niches are carved into a small north facing of a boulder along the Vijayanagara period roadway. Seven small (0.10 × 0.05 m) rectangular depressions have been carved into the boulder, four beneath the image and three to its right. These may be shelves for oil lamps or offerings. Many boulders in the vicinity have Vijayanagara period quarry marks. There is no evidence that there was ever a more substantial structure around the image.
Artifacts: Modern debris in area. No collections made.
Temporal Affiliation: Vijayanagara.
References: Sinopoli and Morrison 2006b:515, 517, 524.
Illustrations: Plate 3.44.

– 4 –
Block T: Site Summaries

SITE: VMS-136 Block: T Transect: 1

Primary Site Use: Agricultural/transport: water catchment basin.
Site Dimensions: 80 × 80 m
Setting: On a gentle slope lying north/northeast of an area of granite outcrops. Modern dry fields lie to the north of the reservoir, between it and the Tungabhadra Right Bank Main Canal.
Present Land Use/Disturbances: The site is located c. 200 m south of the Tungabhadra Right Bank Main Canal. The reservoir is breached in two locations at its southeast end. A section of the inner west wall has collapsed c. 20 m south of the northwest corner. A section at the midpoint of the north wall has collapsed.
Site Description: Water catchment feature. This large water catchment feature is associated with elevated road system VMS-137 (in Block S), which it abuts. The basin is fed by runoff from the outcrops to the south/southwest. The subrectangular basin abuts an outcrop on its east side, with the west, north, and south walls constructed of medium and large modified and unmodified stones. Each wall has two stepped faces, separated by an earthen core. The north wall is 6 m wide at its top. Ten to twelve courses are visible; elements range in size from c. 1 × 1 × 1 m to c. 0.50 × 0.50 × 0.50 m, and decrease in size from bottom to top. At the northeast corner, a double-faced small wall extends north from the exterior face of the north wall for 8 m and then turns to the east and continues for another 5 m. This may be associated with an overflow channel for the basin. Other than this channel, there is no evidence for a sluice or other outlet, suggesting this feature did not channel water to agricultural fields (to the north). The site was likely primarily a water source associated with the road.
Artifacts: 100% collection. Very sparse scatter; however, edge of artifact scatter VMS-135 (Block S) is <50 m north from the exterior face of the north wall. <50 g ceramics; wares: 2 black plain ware. Diagnostics: 1 jar.
Temporal Affiliation: Vijayanagara.
Illustrations: Figure 4.1.

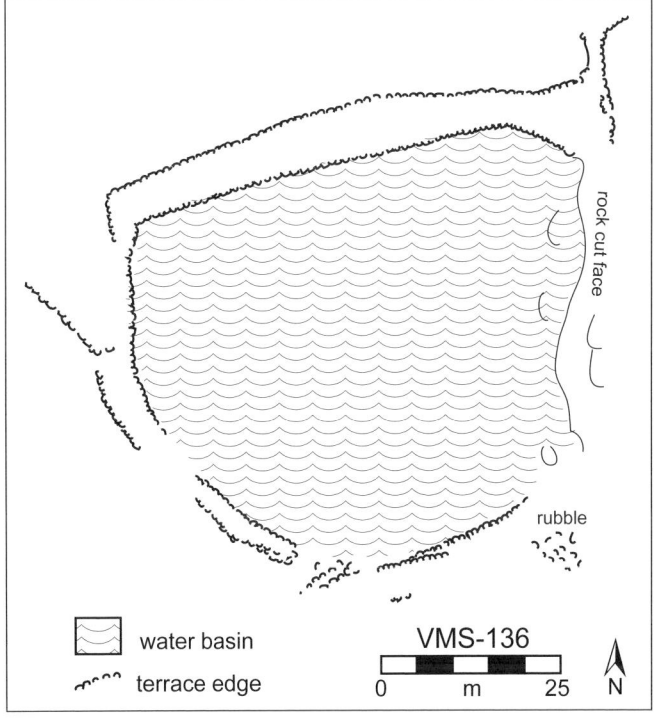

Figure 4.1. VMS-136, plan.

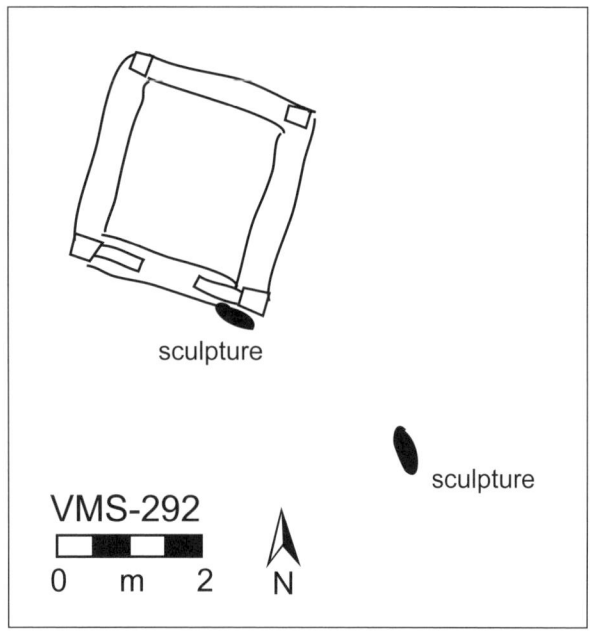

Figure 4.2. VMS-292, plan.

Plate 4.1. VMS-292, shrine overview.

SITE: VMS-292   Block: T   Transect: 5
  Primary Site Use: Religious: shrine and sculptures.
  Site Dimensions: 9 × 4 m
  Setting: Low mound amid agricultural fields. Site is located just north of village of Sitaram Tanda.
  Present Land Use/Disturbances: In agricultural fields near modern settlement. Sculptures are not in their original locations.
  Site Description: Shrine and sculptures. This 2 × 2 column south-facing shrine is located on a low mound. The square unsculpted columns taper slightly and have Vijayanagara quarry marks. Columns are spanned by partly preserved horizontal slab walls; the ceiling is of east-west oriented horizontal slabs, c. 0.4 m wide. The door lintel has two interior sockets. A standing lamp column with square base and octagonal shaft and an inscribed devotee figure on the north side is located c. 8 m south of the shrine. Three displaced sculptures are outside the shrine: a small carved slab depicting male and female devotees with folded hands beneath a Vijayanagara style arch; a Nandi image (missing the head); and a block sculpted with two feet encircled by a snake. Fifty meters south of the shrine is a displaced column c. 1.2 m tall with a small, sculpted Nandi (c. 0.40 m long) on top (boundary marker?).
  Artifacts: A sparse scatter of ceramics within and around the structure; no collections made.
  Temporal Affiliation: Vijayanagara.
  References: Sinopoli and Morrison 2006a:441, 458.
  Illustrations: Figure 4.2; Plates 4.1, 4.2.

Plate 4.2. VMS-292, sculpted panel depicting male and female devotees.

SITE: VMS-293 Block: T Transect: 6
  Primary Site Use: Religious: Shaivite temple.
  Site Dimensions: 40 × 16 m
  Setting: Flat terrain surrounded by agricultural fields, on outskirts of village of Sitaram Tanda.
  Present Land Use/Disturbances: Agricultural fields with modern field walls to north of structure.
  Site Description: Temple with associated lamp column and sculpted stone basin. The structure is presently in worship and consists of an open roofed porch, an antechamber, and a sanctuary. It is constructed on a raised basement, c. 1 m high, with simple single-angle moldings on top and bottom. The 4 × 2 column porch is walled on the west and east sides, with long horizontal slabs c. 0.80 m high × 1.5-2.0 m long. The front central columns are square with octagonal insets and lack sculptures. The outer front columns are square, with simple insets on the exterior front corner. The columns rest on square bases with some beveling. A mortar is set into the floor of the porch. A small opening into the antechamber (1.3 m high × 0.6 m wide) is located on the west side. The parapet consists of unsculpted plastered brick with simple angled stone eaves, though it may once have had Nandi images on the corners.

  The antechamber is square (2 × 2 column, c. 4 × 4 m) with a Ganesha image sculpted over the lintel and door sockets on the interior of the entryway. The walls and floor are of horizontal slabs. A lizard is sculpted on the ceiling with a large naga carved on the exterior of the east wall. The square 2 × 2 column sanctuary (c. 4 × 4 m) contains a modern image base. A floor drain runs from the center of the chamber out through the base of the west wall. The ceiling is constructed of offset square panels. The central image (in worship) appears to be a heavily damaged Nandi placed atop a slab (probably currently worshipped as a lingam). The shikara is simple in form and consistent with an early Vijayanagara date; it is composed of plastered brick, with poorly preserved floral carved plaster motifs.

  Circa 10 m northwest of the temple is a large rectangular stone basin (2 m long × 1.5 m wide × 1.5 m high) on a low informal (disturbed) stone platform. Carved on its north face are (from left to right) three devotees facing a Nandi and lingam. Two holes penetrate the basin below the sculpted panel; a crescent moon and sun are located in the upper left and right, respectively.

  A tall Vijayanagara lamp column (resting on a later column base) is located c. 20 m in front of the temple entry. The column is c. 4 m tall, and has six square panels with octagonal insets; a small Nandi is sculpted on the south side, facing the temple. A displaced Vijayanagara image base is incorporated into the modern field wall, just north of the structure.
  Artifacts: 100% collection; no artifacts recovered.
  Temporal Affiliation: Vijayanagara.
  References: Morrison 1995:8; Sinopoli and Morrison 2006a:441, 452.
  Illustrations: Figure 4.3; Plates 4.3, 4.4.

SITE: VMS-294 Block: T Transect: 6
  Primary Site Use: Water control: step well.
  Site Dimensions: 10 × 6 m
  Setting: Flat terrain in agricultural fields.
  Present Land Use/Disturbances: Heavily overgrown by thorny scrub and grasses.
  Site Description: Step well. This small well is oriented 16° east of north and is located c. 30 m south of Shaivite temple VMS-293. The well is very overgrown and its precise plan cannot be determined. The stairs are located on the north, descending to a c. 6 × 6 m² water chamber. Chamber walls are constructed of rectangular slabs 0.6-0.8

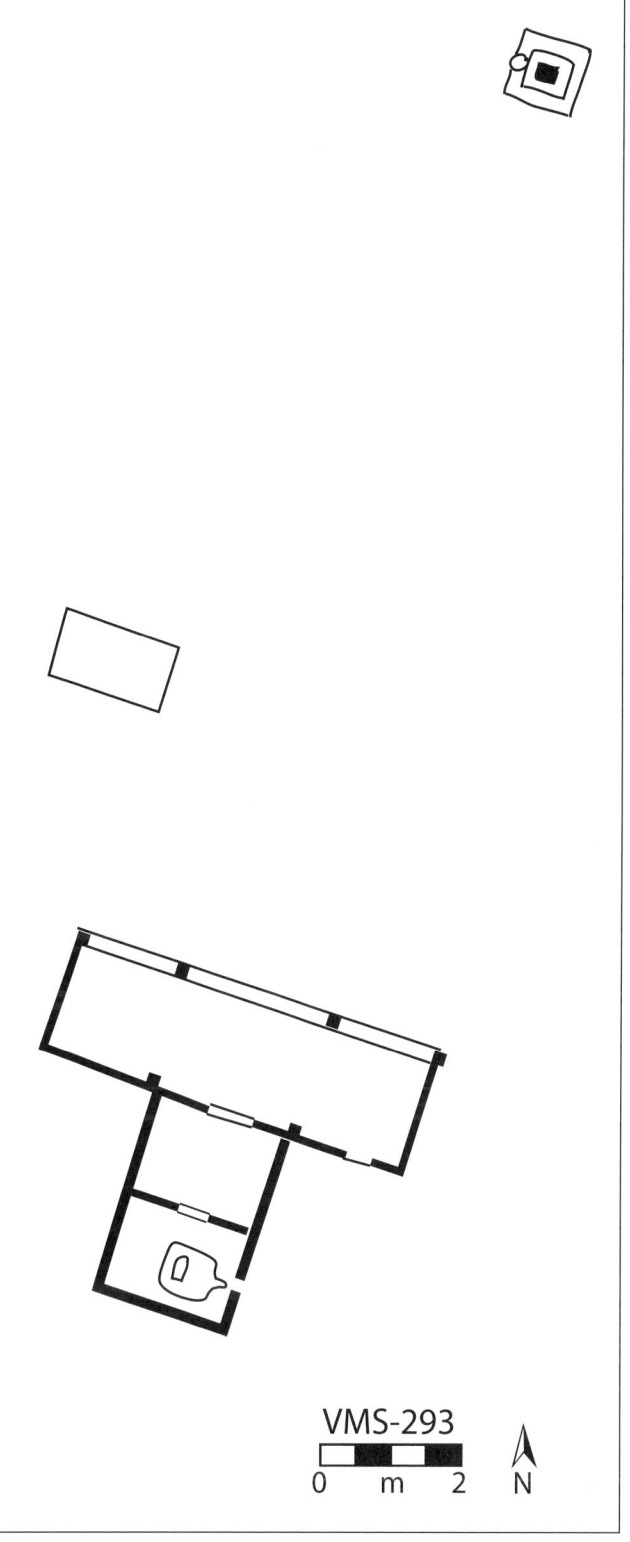

Figure 4.3. VMS-293, plan.

Plate 4.3. VMS-293, temple from west.

Plate 4.5. VMS-295, detail of inscription; edge of lingam to left of scale.

Plate 4.4. VMS-293, sculpted stone basin located northeast of the temple.

Plate 4.6. VMS-296, bedrock inscription.

m long × 0.3 m high. Six horizontal courses with some chinking are visible above the water level.
    Artifacts: 100% collection. <50 g ceramics; wares: 1 black plain ware.
    Temporal Affiliation: Vijayanagara, probably associated with temple VMS-293.
    References: Morrison 1995:84.

SITE: VMS-295   Block: T   **Transect:** 6
    Primary Site Use: Religious: Shaivite inscription.
    Site Dimensions: 1.10 × 0.40 m
    Setting: Boulder in irrigation canal in area of agricultural fields.
    Present Land Use/Disturbances: Areas on either side of the canal are cultivated; boulder part of modern footpath.
    Site Description: East-west oriented inscription located on a sheet rock boulder in an irrigation canal. The inscription consists of a lingam below a crescent moon and sun. A brief inscription in Kannada script is located to the right of the lingam. This may be a field marker. The inscription and image are fairly worn and patinated and do not appear to be recent.

    Artifacts: None observed; no collections made.
    Temporal Affiliation: Vijayanagara?
    References: Sinopoli and Morrison 2006a:44.
    Illustrations: Plate 4.5.

SITE: VMS-296   Block: T   **Transect:** 5
    Primary Site Use: Religious: Shaivite carving on sheet rock.
    Site Dimensions: 0.5 × 0.5 m
    Setting: Sheet rock outcrop near agricultural fields.
    Present Land Use/Disturbances: Next to threshing floor at edge of plowed fields.
    Site Description: A small lingam on pitha inscribed on outcropping sheet rock, with a crescent moon above it on the left and a sun on the right. No associated features observed. Inscription is worn and patinated; it does not appear to be recent. Perhaps a field boundary? May be associated with VMS-295.
    Artifacts: 100% collection; no artifacts recovered.
    Temporal Affiliation: Unknown.
    References: Sinopoli and Morrison 2006a:441, 453.
    Illustrations: Plate 4.6.

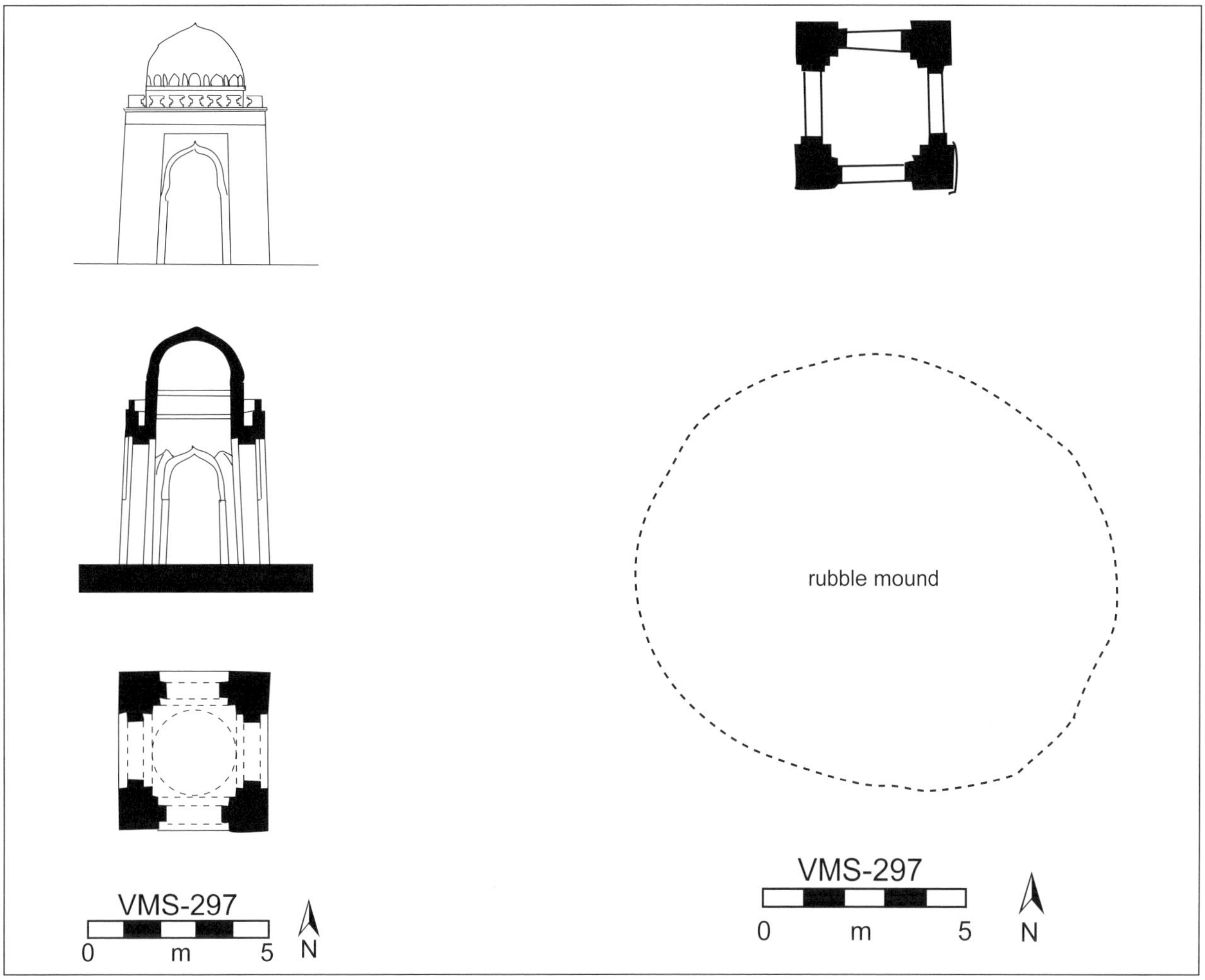

Figure 4.4. VMS-297, plan.

SITE: VMS-297   Block: T   Transect: 8
Primary Site Use: Religious/mortuary: tomb.
Site Dimensions: 16 × 11 m
Setting: Flat area amid agricultural fields; low outcrop hill c. 60 m to the north of feature.
Present Land Use/Disturbances: Cultivated area; rubble mound in front of tomb may be remains of destroyed structure.
Site Description: Tomb. This small open structure (c. 4 m on a side) has four arched doorways topped by a dome; it closely resembles tombs in the Islamic quarter of the urban core and in Kadirampur (Block M, VMS-387). The walls taper slightly and are constructed of plaster-covered rectangular granite blocks with Vijayanagara quarry marks; the dome is of fired brick. The dome's interior and exterior bases are plastered and decorated with small arches and columns. The roof is edged with a brickwork parapet, much of which has broken off. Interior arches frame each entry. To the south of the tomb is a mounded rubble pile in which can be seen the remnants of a collapsed structure, including a possible arch with mortar and stones with Vijayanagara quarry marks (perhaps the remains of a second tomb?).
Artifacts: 100% collection; no artifacts recovered.
Temporal Affiliation: Vijayanagara.
References: Michell 1992:146; Morrison 1995:81, 95; Sinopoli and Morrison 2006a:441-42, 458.
Illustrations: Figure 4.4; Plate 4.7.

Plate 4.7. VMS-297, tomb overview; note rubble mound to left of structure.

SITE: VMS-298   Block: T   **Transect:** 5
   Primary Site Use: Water control: step well.
   Site Dimensions: 13 × 9 m
   Setting: Flat terrain amid irrigated fields.
   Present Land Use/Disturbances: Well still in use with some modern additions, steps now blocked.
   Site Description: Step well. The upper portion of this functioning step well has been recently constructed of small square blocks. However, the lowest visible course is quite different in construction, with large rectangular blocks with Vijayanagara quarry marks. Entry was from the south, with four long granite slab steps (c. 1.5 × 0.4 × 0.15 m) visible.
   Artifacts: 100% collection; no artifacts recovered.
   Temporal Affiliation: Vijayanagara, with later modifications.
   References: Morrison 1995:84; Sinopoli and Morrison 2006a:456.
   Illustrations: Figure 4.5.

SITE: VMS-299   Block: T   **Transect:** 5-6
   Primary Site Use: Agricultural: terrace system.
   Site Dimensions: 210 × 75 m
   Setting: Gentle to moderate terrain, sloping down to east/northeast. Located along the north edge of sheet rock in a narrow upland valley.
   Present Land Use/Disturbances: Irrigation channel with elevated metal water pipe. There has been some recent trenching near the site's northeast edge. A cart path has cut through the walls on the west edge of the site.
   Site Description: Terrace system. This site consists of several low rubble walls or stone piles ranging from 0.1 to 0.4 m high and 0.5 to 1.0 m wide. For the most part, these are not formal walls, but instead are linear piles of small to medium unmodified stones. On the east edge of the system are several boulders with recent petroglyphs, including snakes, sun, and several Kannada letters. The site may be associated with terrace system VMS-300, located c. 50 m to its north.
   Artifacts: 100% collection; no artifacts recovered.
   Temporal Affiliation: Unknown; inscriptions are recent, but the path cutting through the walls suggests that the terrace system has not been in use for some time.
   References: Morrison 1995:94, 102.
   Illustrations: Figure 4.6.

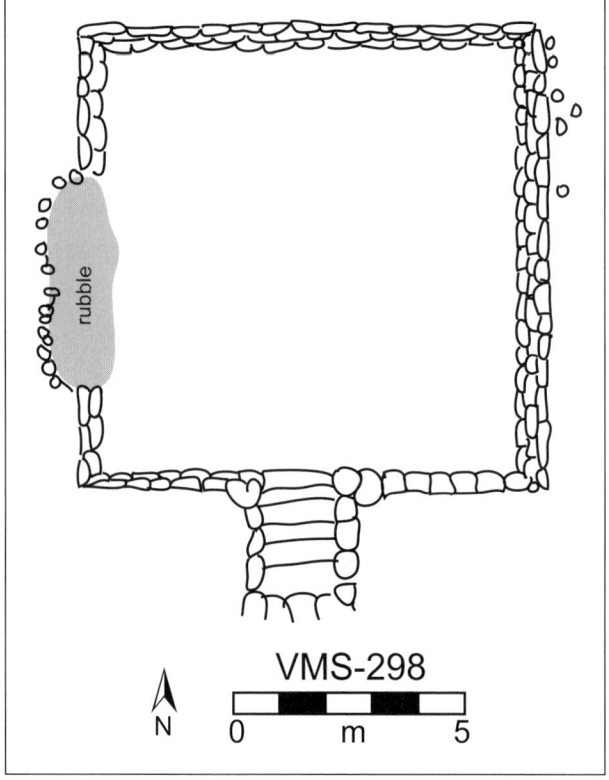

Figure 4.5. VMS-298, plan.

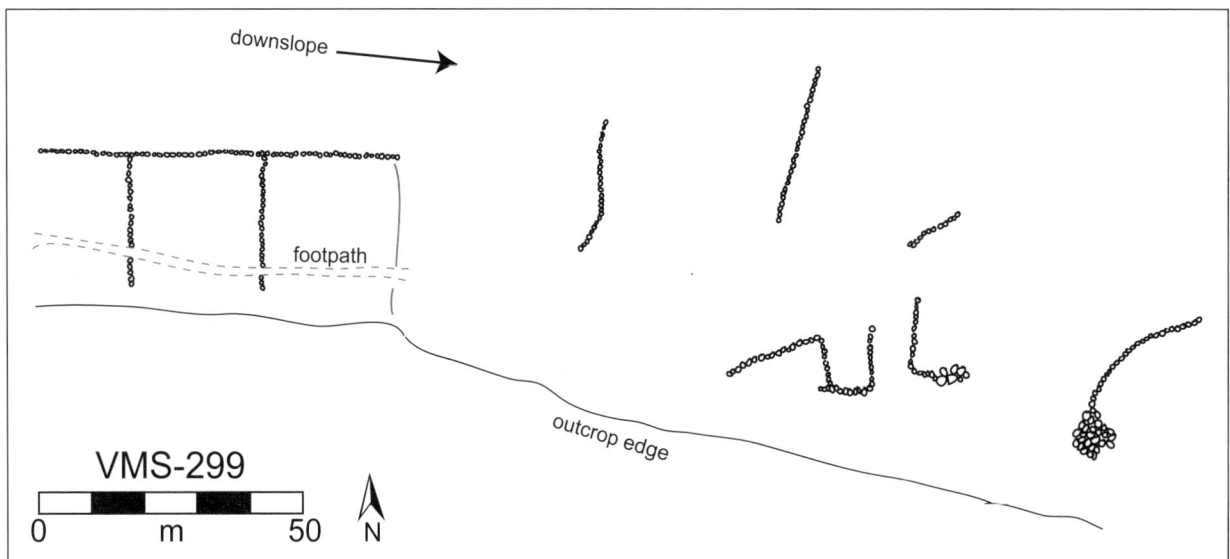

Figure 4.6. VMS-299, plan.

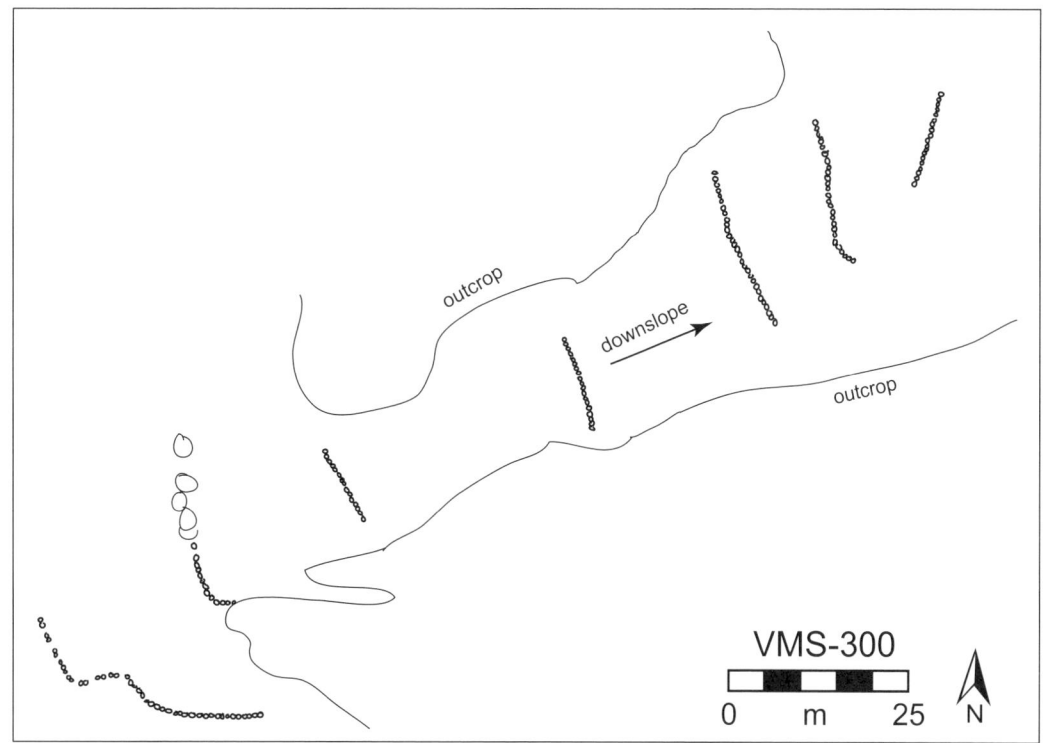

Figure 4.7. VMS-300, plan.

SITE: VMS-300   Block: T   Transect: 5
  Primary Site Use: Agricultural: terrace system.
  Site Dimensions: 150 × 30 m
  Setting: Gentle to moderate terrain sloping down to northeast, in narrow upland valley with outcrops to the north and south.
  Present Land Use/Disturbances: Uncultivated or fallow; terraces breached in some places.
  Site Description: Small terrace system. This site is located c. 50 m due south of terrace system VMS-299, which is found in the next narrow valley. A low outcropping ridge separates the two systems, and a higher ridge is located to the south of VMS-300 (beyond which is another field system). The valley slopes up to the southwest and narrows, turning toward the south near the top and intersecting the south set of fields. The system consists of seven low "walls" or rubble piles (c. 1 m wide) constructed of small to large unmodified stones. These are roughly level with the ground surface on the upslope (southwest) side and c. 0.5 m above the downslope ground surface. There are several recent naga petroglyphs on outcrops to the south.
  Artifacts: 100% collection; no artifacts recovered.
  Temporal Affiliation: Unknown; however, the fields are quite overgrown and the system has not been maintained for some time.
  References: Morrison 1995:94, 102.
  Illustrations: Figure 4.7; Plate 4.8.

Plate 4.8. VMS-300, overview of terrace walls.

SITE: VMS-301   Block: T   Transect: 6
  Primary Site Use: Agricultural: reservoir embankment.
  Site Dimensions: 125 × ~10 m
  Setting: Embankment abuts outcrop in the northeast. The area is presently under dry farm agriculture. The terrain slopes gently down to the northwest.

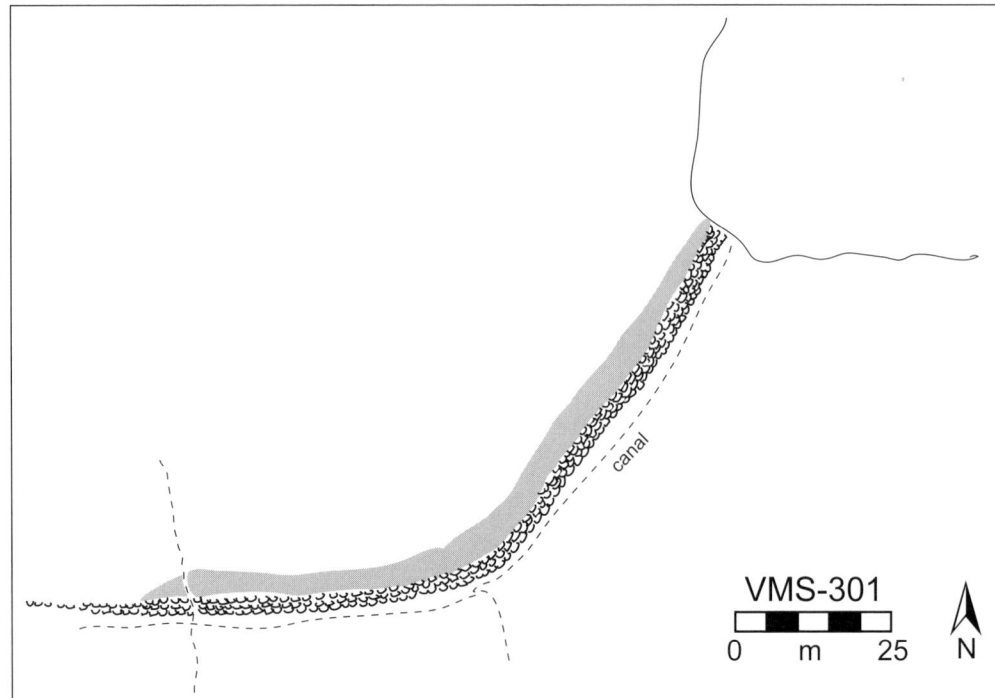

Figure 4.8. VMS-301, plan.

Present Land Use/Disturbances: The area around the embankment is cultivated and the site has been heavily damaged by post-use agricultural activities. It is heavily overgrown; a modern water channel cuts through it on the west.

Site Description: Reservoir embankment. This 125 m long embankment abuts an outcrop at the northeast; its west termination is less clear due to disturbances. The embankment captured runoff from the outcrops to the northeast, south, and east. Eight stepped irregular courses of unmodified small to medium stones face its north side. The earthen face has been disturbed by agricultural activities and its precise width is not measurable. No sluices are present.

Artifacts: 100% collection; only one modern vessel observed.
Temporal Affiliation: Vijayanagara.
References: Morrison 1995:102.
Illustrations: Figure 4.8.

SITE: VMS-302   Block: T   Transect: 6
Primary Site Use: Agricultural: reservoir embankment.
Site Dimensions: 75 × 26 m
Setting: Area slopes down gently to northwest. The reservoir abuts an outcrop on its north end.
Present Land Use/Disturbances: The south end of the site tapers into plowed agricultural fields and may have been considerably disturbed. The site's original dimensions cannot be determined.
Site Description: Reservoir embankment. The stepped stone eastern face of this predominantly north-south oriented embankment is constructed of medium unmodified and modified stones, with seven to eight courses visible. Some stones have Vijayanagara quarry marks and there is evidence for quarrying in nearby outcrops. A single course double-faced (1 m wide) stone retaining wall bounds the edge of the earthen embankment to the west.

Artifacts: 100% collection; no artifacts recovered.
Temporal Affiliation: Vijayanagara.
References: Morrison 1995:102.
Illustrations: Figure 4.9.

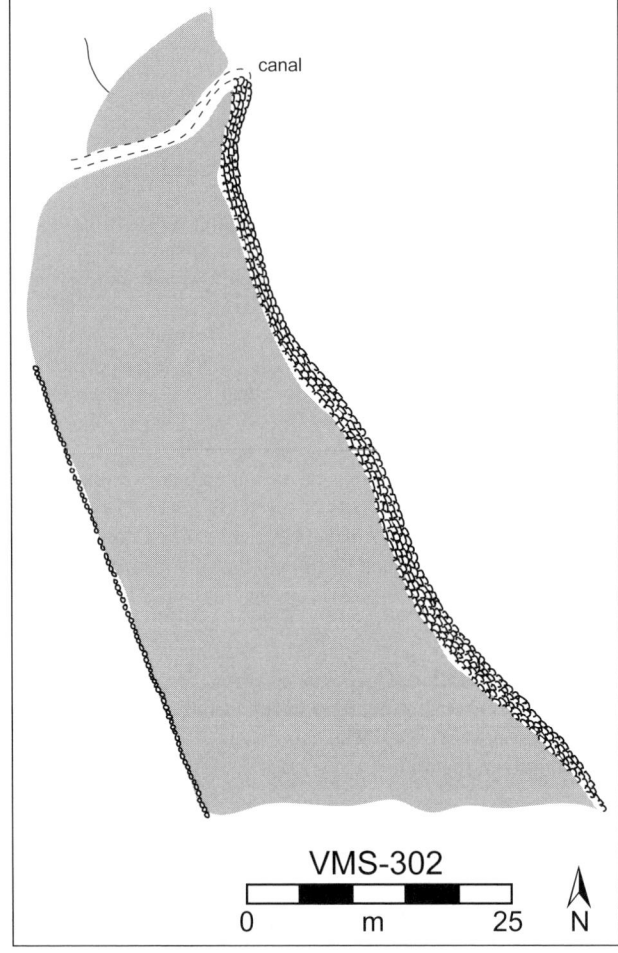

Figure 4.9. VMS-302, plan.

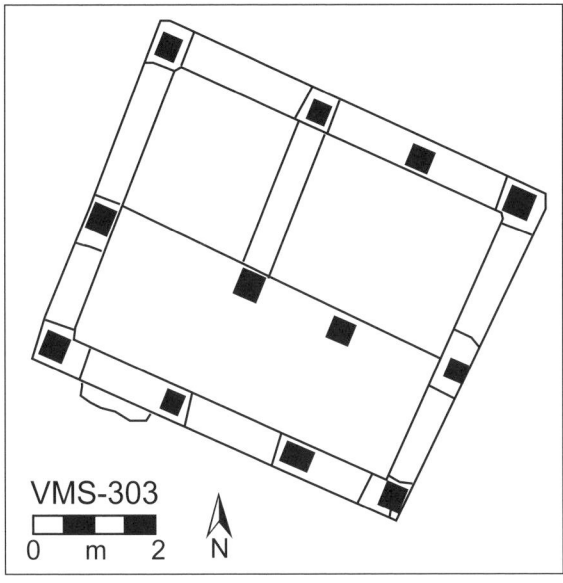

Figure 4.10. VMS-303, plan.

Plate 4.9. VMS-303, overview.

SITE: VMS-303 Block: T Transect: 7
Primary Site Use: Transport: mandapa.
Site Dimensions: 7 × 6 m
Setting: Located in flat terrain in area of dry farmed agricultural fields, near northwest end of road wall VMS-325 and probably associated with transport route.
Present Land Use/Disturbances: Dirt road alongside mandapa.
Site Description: Unwalled 3 × 4 column mandapa on a low stone basement. Seven of the columns are square and unsculpted. The remainder have square panels separated by octagonal insets; three have crude sculpted motifs, including sun, moon, conch, trident and chakra. The columns rest on crudely shaped rectangular bases, linked by long stone slabs. Half of the ceiling is preserved and is constructed of well-fit stone slabs with Vijayanagara quarry marks and some traces of mortar. The floor of the structure is stepped, with the south half and the northwest quadrant raised slightly above the northeast quadrant. Although not conforming to the plan of a typical Vijayanagara gate, this seems the most probable function, and the structure is likely associated with a Vijayanagara transport route, either as a gate or way station.
Artifacts: 100% collection; no artifacts recovered.
Temporal Affiliation: Vijayanagara.
References: Sinopoli and Morrison 2006a:440.
Illustrations: Figure 4.10; Plate 4.9.

SITE: VMS-304 Block: T Transect: 6
Primary Site Use: Religious/defensive: Shaivite shrine and associated structure.
Site Dimensions: c. 50 × 10 m
Setting: On a steep outcrop. The shrine is located on a high boulder, c. 8 m above the outcrop ledge containing the structure. This site is located at a point of excellent visibility to the north toward the major Vijayanagara period road leading east from the urban core.
Present Land Use/Disturbances: The shrine is still in worship with recent painting on images. Recent quarrying on outcrop.
Site Description: Small Shaivite shrine and associated structure. The north-facing shrine is located on a ledge under an overhang near the top of a high outcrop. Access to the shrine is difficult, requiring a climb of c. 8 m up a nearly vertical outcrop from the lower portion of the site. From the shrine there is a view to the north across the valley containing the large Vijayanagara road designated as sites VMS-326, 360, 361.

The shrine floor is defined by a triangular projecting boulder bordered by a low enclosure wall. An overhanging boulder projects over the entire feature. A sculpted image of two feet encircled by a cobra is inscribed on the flat outcrop immediately inside the enclosure wall. At the rear is a vertical rock face on which images are carved. The main images are Shiva and Parvati seated beneath a Vijayanagara style arch. Above their heads is a scroll of stylized images, perhaps script or snakes. Three stylized human heads/skulls are carved beneath their feet. A small plastered wall projects out from the vertical rock face to the right of the arch. The shrine is located c. 8 m above and to the east of an outcrop ledge on which is located a small poorly preserved square structure or platform (c. 6 m on a side). This structure is constructed of double-faced rubble walls with rubble fill. On top is a long granite slab with Vijayanagara quarry marks that may have been part of a roof or column. It is likely that this structure was a platform associated with an outpost or watch tower.
Artifacts: 100% collection on ledge containing structure; no artifacts recovered.
Temporal Affiliation: Vijayanagara.
References: Morrison 1995:81.
Illustrations: Figure 4.11; Plate 4.10.

106 *The Vijayanagara Metropolitan Survey*

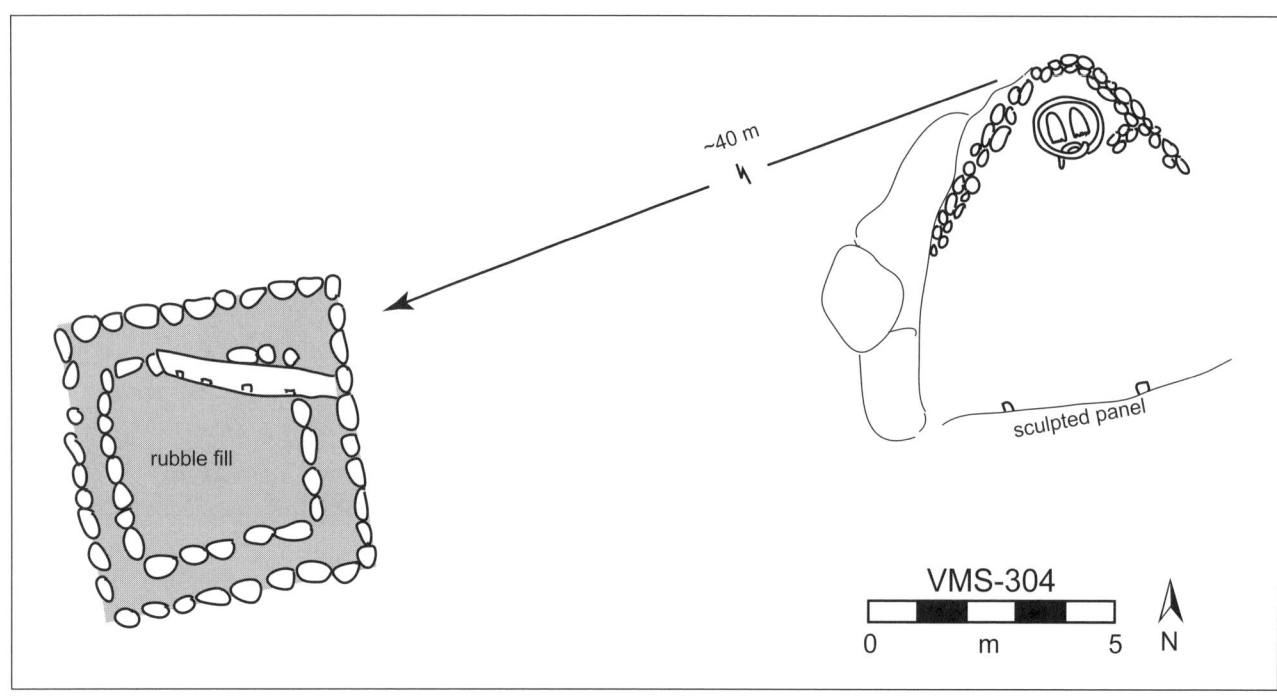

Figure 4.11. VMS-304, plan.

Plate 4.10. VMS-304, sculpted panel beneath overhang.

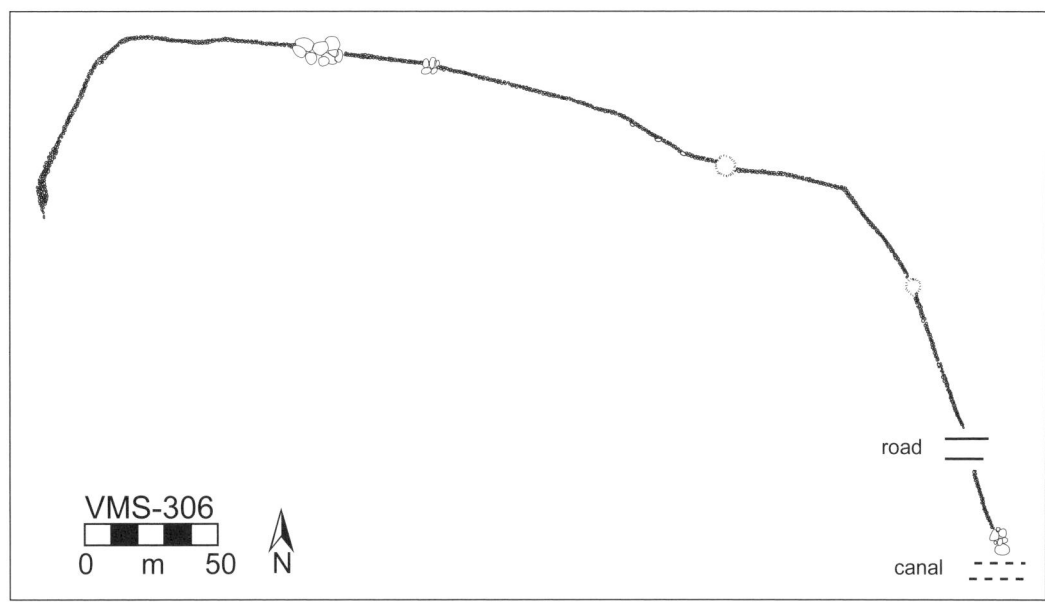

Figure 4.12. VMS-306, plan.

SITE: VMS-305   Block: T   Transect: 5-6
   Primary Site Use: Transport/defensive?: earthen embankment.
   Site Dimensions: 120 × 20 m
   Setting: Low flat area between two outcrops, irrigated fields to the north and south.
   Present Land Use/Disturbances: Rice paddies surround site.
   Site Description: Embankment. This long earthen embankment, oriented 10° south of west, crosses a low area between two outcrops. Some of the earth of the embankment may be derived from excavation of nearby rice fields. However, the embankment is also well situated to serve defensive functions, inhibiting movement across this valley, or transport related functions, and thus may considerably predate rice field construction.
   Artifacts: 100% collection on embankment; no artifacts observed.
   Temporal Affiliation: Unknown.

SITE: VMS-306   Block: T   Transect: 7-8
   Primary Site Use: Defensive/unknown: wall.
   Site Dimensions: 500 × 1 m
   Setting: Along ridge of low outcrop hills, area of moderate to steep slopes.
   Present Land Use/Disturbances: Tungabhadra High Level Canal is located just south of the site, as are several small residential structures associated with its construction.
   Site Description: Large wall of undetermined function. This wall is predominantly oriented east-west and runs along the crest of an outcrop ridge; at both the east and west extremes the wall turns south down the slope of the ridge. The east end appears to continue on the opposite bank of the canal (and may be part of the same features as VMS-339). Preservation of the wall is variable. The better preserved sections of the wall are c. 1-1.2 m high × 1 m wide, with two faces of unmodified medium to large stones, with infill of small cobbles. Six to eight irregularly laid

Plate 4.11. VMS-306, rubble wall (in center of photo).

courses are visible. The unmodified stones are either of granite or basalt, depending upon the material composing the outcrop ridge at different sections along its length. This structure may have served defensive or fortification functions; its location on a stony outcrop makes it unlikely to be a field boundary or enclosure.
   Artifacts: No collections made; no artifacts observed.
   Temporal Affiliation: Probably Vijayanagara.
   References: Morrison 1995:66, 79; Sinopoli and Morrison 2006a:440.
   Illustrations: Figure 4.12; Plate 4.11.

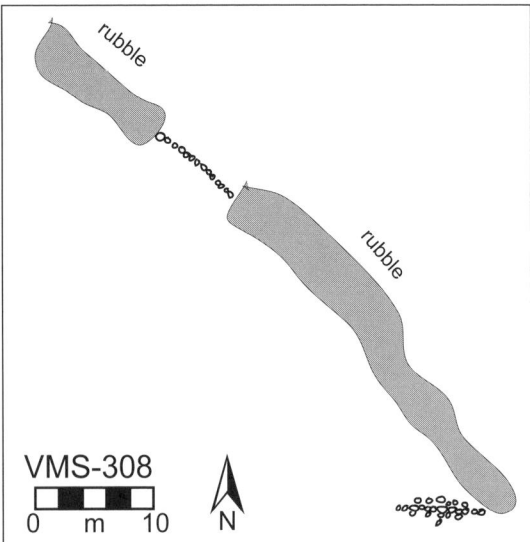

Figure 4.13. VMS-308, plan.

SITE: VMS-307   Block: T   Transect: 5
   Primary Site Use: Agricultural: soil control walls.
   Site Dimensions: 90 × 65 m
   Setting: Valley between two large hills of outcropping boulders; area slopes up to north and south with isolated outcropping boulders and thorny scrub.
   Present Land Use/Disturbances: Modern fallow fields, walls breached by small drainage channels in places.
   Site Description: Crudely constructed stone walls. This pair of unconnected stone walls are oriented roughly perpendicular to one another in a shallow valley that slopes gently upward to the north and south. The longer east-west wall is constructed of unmodified small-medium stones (0.10-0.50 m) and is c. 1 m wide and rarely more than a single course in height, incorporating outcropping boulders. The shorter north-south wall is similarly constructed. At its south end this wall crosses a shallow runoff gully. The north edge abuts a small boulder outcrop. These walls appear to serve to control soil erosion and may have been associated with a larger recent terrace system to the west (not recorded), though site VMS-307 is not currently maintained.
   Artifacts: 100% collection; no artifacts recovered.
   Temporal Affiliation: Unknown.
   References: Morrison 1995:102.

SITE: VMS-308   Block: T   Transect: 6
   Primary Site Use: Agricultural: soil control walls?
   Site Dimensions: 7-8 × 1 m (total site may be c. 40 m long)
   Setting: Narrow valley between two outcrop hills.
   Present Land Use/Disturbances: Plowed and fallow fields.
   Site Description: Wall of unmodified small to medium stones. This wall is oriented c. 45° west of north and is located southwest of a modern field. It is c. 0.8 m wide and up to 0.5 m high and incorporates several large outcropping boulders. It has two faces with an additional row of cobbles in between; two courses are visible. The wall appears to be a soil control device, perhaps associated with the nearby agricultural field. It may originally have extended further to the northwest and southeast as indicated by the location of a slightly raised area of rubble and thorny scrub, which follows its course.
   Artifacts: 100% collection; no artifacts recovered.
   Temporal Affiliation: Unknown.
   References: Morrison 1995:102.
   Illustrations: Figure 4.13.

SITE: VMS-309   Block: T   Transect: 6
   Primary Site Use: Agricultural: reservoir embankment.
   Site Dimensions: 350 × 20 m
   Setting: Located in flat area, to south of a low outcrop hill; area is presently under rainfall agriculture. The terrain slopes down to the north.
   Present Land Use/Disturbances: Embankment is overgrown with brush and thorny scrub; sluice gate has been displaced and is in worship. The earthen embankment has been removed in the area near the sluice, revealing a basal stone pavement.
   Site Description: Reservoir embankment. This long, low reservoir embankment is oriented c. 10° south of east. Its south stone face is primarily constructed of unmodified small to medium stones, though some are split, and have Vijayanagara quarry marks. Up to twelve stepped courses are visible. The earthen embankment reaches a maximal width of c. 18 m. A single sluice gate is present c. 90 m from the embankment's east edge. It has been displaced and is flush against the stepped embankment and no longer aligned with the sluice channel (c. 2 m to its east). It consists of two coarsely dressed rectangular columns (0.4 × 0.5 × 2.6 m) spaced 1.36 m apart. Two rectangular stone lintels span the top of the columns (the top smaller than the bottom but with no visible molding). These are pierced by a central circular hole. A crosspiece set tongue in groove into the uprights is located midway down the columns. Immediately behind the sluice gate a portion of the earthen embankment has been removed, revealing a stone pavement above a stone-lined sluice channel. The pavement extends the entire width of the embankment (18 m from north to south) and many of the exposed stones exhibit Vijayanagara quarry marks. At its north end the opening of the sluice channel is 0.60 m high and 0.42 m wide.
   Artifacts: 100% collection; no artifacts recovered.
   Temporal Affiliation: Vijayanagara.
   References: Sinopoli and Morrison 2006a:440-41.
   Illustrations: Figure 4.14; Plate 4.12.

SITE: VMS-310   Block: T   Transect: 6
   Primary Site Use: Agricultural: terrace system.
   Site Dimensions: 120 × 35 m
   Setting: Terrain slopes gently down to the southwest; the site abuts a low outcrop to its south.
   Present Land Use/Disturbances: Fallow fields, recent quarrying, and recent petroglyphs; footpaths cross through breaks in walls.
   Site Description: Agricultural terrace system. This site consists of a series of five unconnected roughly parallel walls, which are oriented northwest/southeast, perpendicular to the line of the slope, and spaced at intervals ranging from 15 to 40 m. Two other walls border the site on the northwest edge; these parallel the line of slope. These informal walls are one to two courses high and 0.6-0.8 m wide. They are composed of linear piles of small-medium unmodified stones, lack clear faces, and incorporate small outcropping boulders. The walls are overgrown and heavily silted in.
   Artifacts: 100% collection; no artifacts recovered.
   Temporal Affiliation: Unknown.
   References: Morrison 1995:102.
   Illustrations: Figure 4.15.

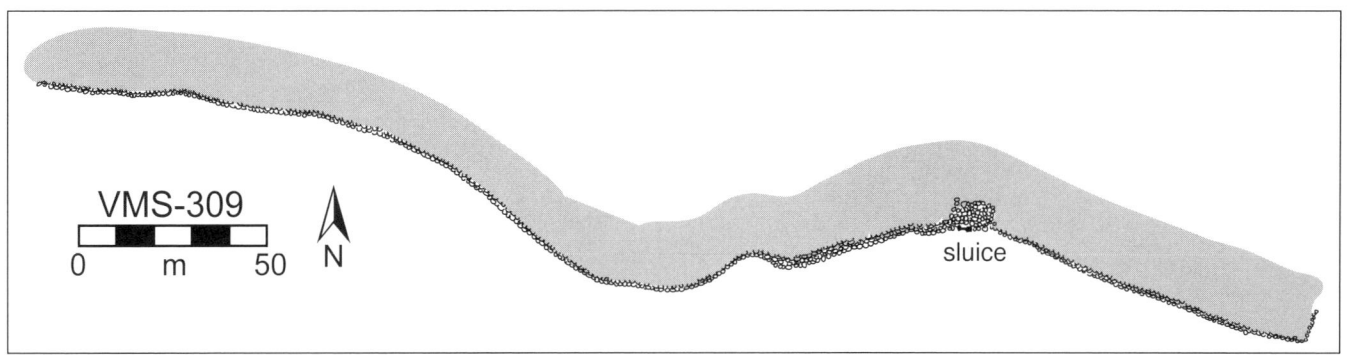

(*Above*) Figure 4.14. VMS-309, plan.

(*Left*) Plate 4.12. VMS-309, pavement and sluice.

(*Below*) Figure 4.15. VMS-310, plan.

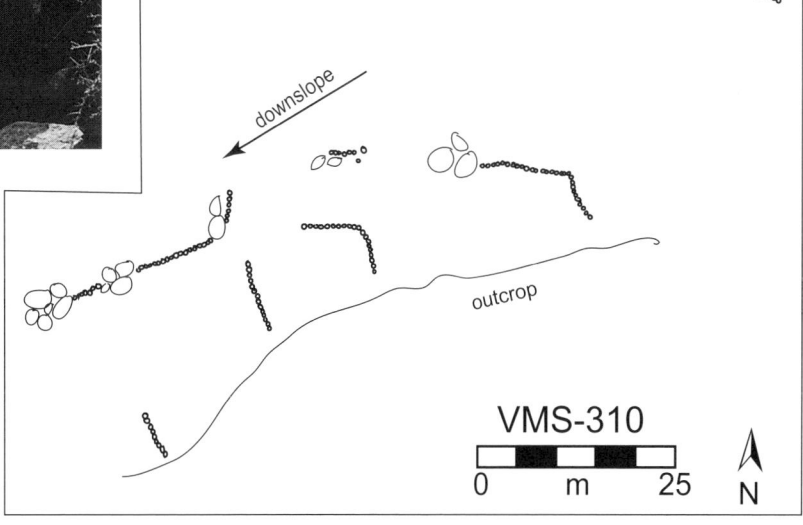

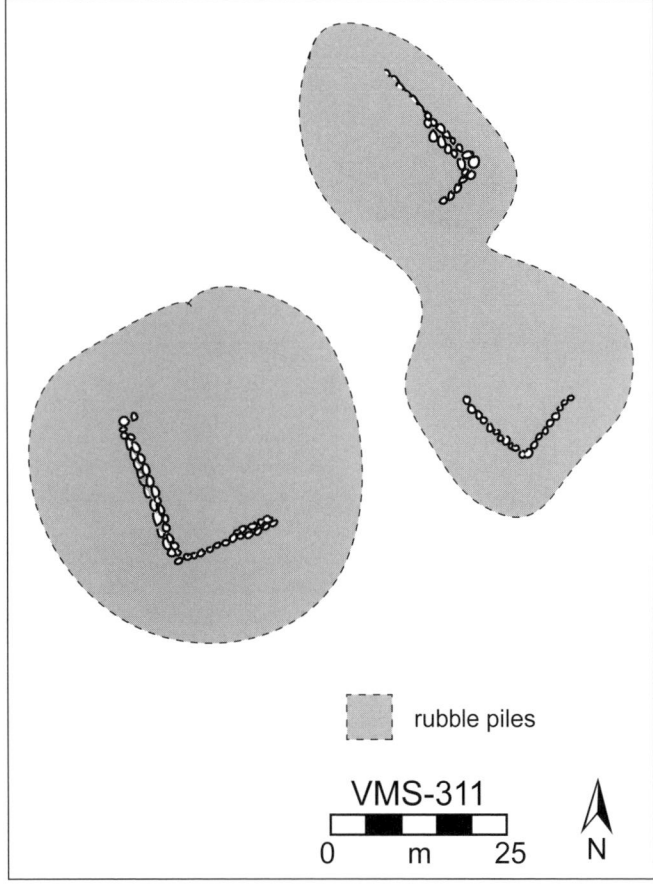

Figure 4.16. VMS-311, plan.

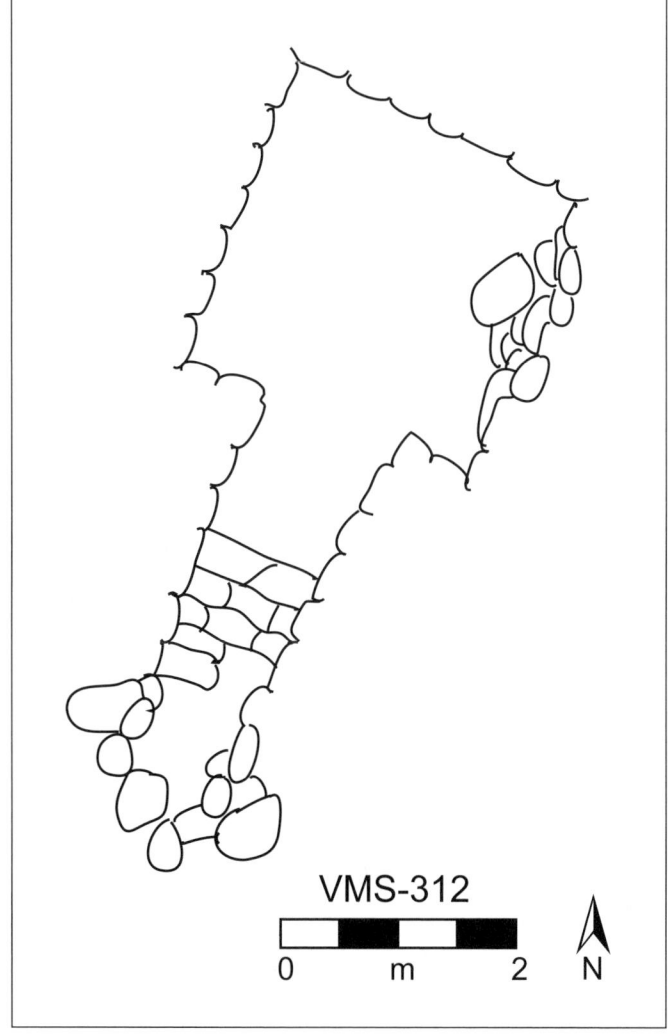

Figure 4.17. VMS-312, plan.

SITE: VMS-311   Block: T   Transect: 7
   Primary Site Use: Unknown/residential?: structural remains.
   Site Dimensions: 18 × 17 m
   Setting: Flat terrain amid dry farmed agricultural fields.
   Present Land Use/Disturbances: Surrounding area is cultivated; the site is overgrown with thorny scrub.
   Site Description: Three closely spaced low mounds. These mounds are comprised of earth and unmodified small-medium cobbles and appear to be the remains of collapsed rectangular structures. They are 9 × 9 m (west pile), 4.5 × 7 m (north) and 6 × 6.5 m (south) in dimension. In each rubble mound, small portions of vertical wall faces are visible, each with clear corners.
   Artifacts: 100% collection; no artifacts recovered.
   Temporal Affiliation: Unknown.
   Illustrations: Figure 4.16.

SITE: VMS-312   Block: T   Transect: 7
   Primary Site Use: Agricultural: step well.
   Site Dimensions: 3.3 × 3.15 m
   Setting: Flat terrain amid dry farmed agricultural fields.
   Present Land Use/Disturbances: Vegetation obscures part of site; east face of well basin has collapsed. The site is presently in worship.
   Site Description: Step well. This site is constructed of angular granite slabs. A stepped passage (five steps visible) on the south descends to a square water chamber, c. 3 m on a side. Up to eleven courses of modified and unmodified medium to large stones (c. 0.15 m high × 0.50 m across) are visible on the south wall of the chamber, forming a vertical face. Coursing is regular and horizontal, with some chinking stones. The silt-filled chamber is currently 1.6 m deep; red and white painted designs on the south wall indicate its present use as a shrine. This site is located a few m from VMS-311 and may be associated with it.
   Artifacts: 100% collection; no artifacts recovered.
   Temporal Affiliation: Unknown.
   References: Morrison 1995:84.
   Illustrations: Figure 4.17.

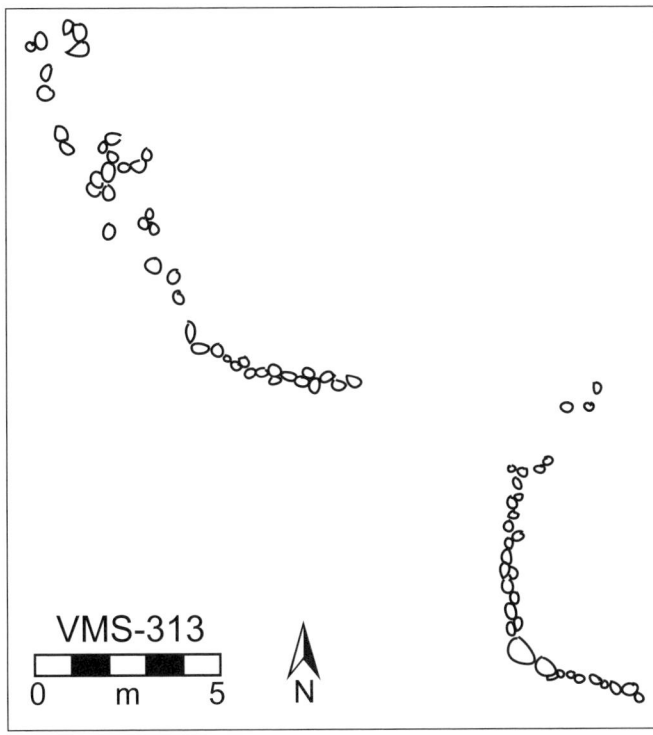

Figure 4.18. VMS-313, plan.

SITE: VMS-313 Block: T Transect: 7
   Primary Site Use: Agricultural: isolated soil control walls.
   Site Dimensions: 22 × 6 m
   Setting: Flat to gently sloping area between rock outcrops.
   Present Land Use/Disturbances: Overgrown cart track parallels the west wall of the site.
   Site Description: A pair of isolated roughly semicircular walls in a flat area between two large outcrops. The northwest wall is c. 13 m long, with a single course of small-medium unmodified stones visible. Ground surface is c. 0.2 m higher on the east side of the wall. The south wall, c. 6.5 m in length, is much less clearly constructed, and is identified by a line of small stones along the edge of a large flat outcrop. The walls may have served to control erosion and soil displacement.
   Artifacts: 100% collection; no artifacts recovered.
   Temporal Affiliation: Unknown.
   Illustrations: Figure 4.18.

SITE: VMS-314 Block: T Transect: 7
   Primary Site Use: Agricultural: isolated wall.
   Site Dimensions: 8.6 × 0.5 m
   Setting: High relatively flat area of arable soils in high area among granite outcrops.
   Present Land Use/Disturbances: Area is uncultivated.

   Site Description: Isolated wall. This 8.6 m long east-west wall is located c. 60 m north of soil control walls, VMS-313. Along part of its length, natural outcrops are incorporated as a footing for the wall that is constructed of unmodified medium stones. It is at most two courses high, c. 0.5 m wide, and except for a few stones, is single faced. It spans an area between two outcrops and may have been a soil retaining wall.
   Artifacts: 100% collection; no artifacts recovered.
   Temporal Affiliation: Unknown.
   References: Morrison 1995:102.

SITE: VMS-315 Block: T Transect: 12-13
   Primary Site Use: Agricultural: reservoir embankment.
   Site Dimensions: 500 × 20 m
   Setting: Low-lying area sloping gently down toward the southeast; the site abuts outcrops on its north end.
   Present Land Use/Disturbances: Banana and rice fields may have resulted in some destruction of earthen face of embankment; small modern shrine on top of the embankment; a c. 15 m wide breach near its north end. An enormous banyan tree, probably several centuries old, with a modern shrine, is found near the center of the embankment; footpath runs across top of embankment (may well have been Vijayanagara transport route).
   Site Description: Reservoir embankment. This large reservoir is oriented c. 30° west of north and is c. 500 m in length. The reservoir is still functional and it is evident from the staining on the stone face that the water sometimes reaches heights within 2-2.5 m of the top of the c. 8 m high embankment. The reservoir abuts natural boulder outcrops to the north and extends across a low area to the southeast. It captured runoff from higher slopes to the south and west. Terrace system VMS-344 is located upslope (to the west/northwest) and may have served to limit silt accumulation in the reservoir bed.
   The southwest stepped stone face of the embankment rises c. 8 m above modern ground surface and consists of six to fifteen visible courses of unmodified or split medium to large stones (0.4-1.0 m in dimension). Horizontal slabs or steps project out from the stepped embankment at several points. The earthen face of the embankment is 12-15 m wide and is partially bounded near its midpoint by a c. 50 m long stepped stone retaining wall with six visible courses.
   A sluice is found near the midpoint of the embankment and an overgrown channel near the south end may constitute evidence for a second sluice channel. The extant sluice gate consists of two square tapering columns spaced 1.08 m apart (0.35 m^2 at the base × 3.2 m high). The columns are coarsely dressed, unsculpted with no quarry marks visible. A horizontal crosspiece is set tongue in groove between the columns about halfway up their length. The columns are linked at the top by two stacked slabs forming a lintel. The lower of these slabs is roughly beveled with projecting corners. The upper slab is beveled on the southeast side. A circular hole, 0.20 m in diameter, penetrates the three cross slabs. A stone-lined channel c. 0.5 m wide (now blocked off) extends from the columns into the embankment face. The channel outlet is visible on the opposite side of the embankment.
   Artifacts: No collections made.
   Temporal Affiliation: Vijayanagara.
   References: Morrison 1995:81, 94-96, 102; Sinopoli and Morrison 2006a:442, 454.
   Illustrations: Figure 4.19; Plate 4.13.

112 *The Vijayanagara Metropolitan Survey*

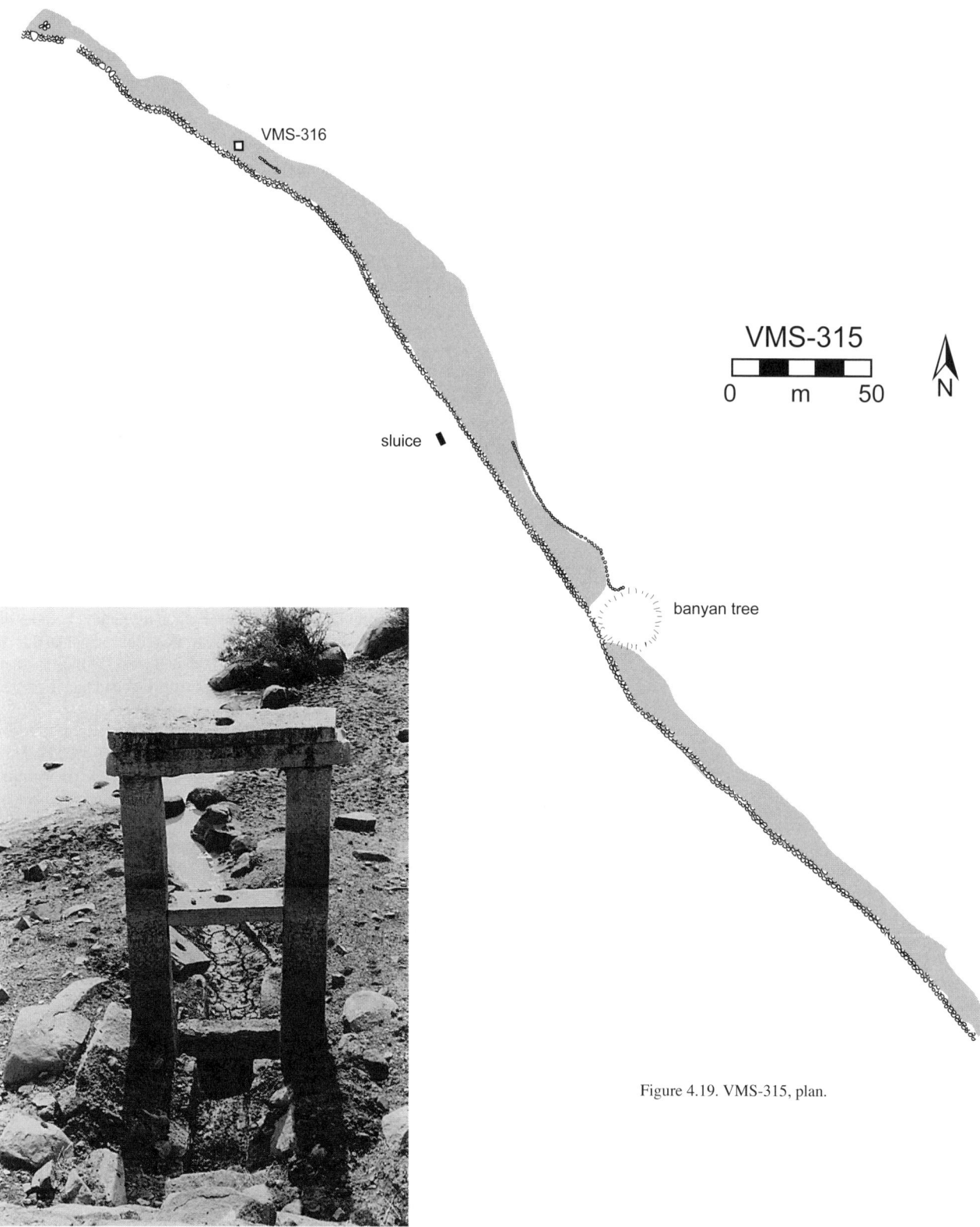

Figure 4.19. VMS-315, plan.

Plate 4.13. VMS-315, sluice gate; note maintained sluice channel and standing water in rear.

SITE: VMS-316   Block: T   Transect: 12
   Primary Site Use: Religious: modern shrine with image.
   Site Dimensions: 4 × 6 m
   Setting: On top of embankment VMS-315, near north end.
   Present Land Use/Disturbances: Modern structure in worship.
   Site Description: Modern shrine containing stone lingam of unknown date. The lingam and its base are composed of a single stone, with circular base. Behind the shrine is a small columnar block c. 0.15 m² × 0.6 m high with Vijayanagara quarry marks.
   Artifacts: No collections made.
   Temporal Affiliation: Structure is modern; the image possibly dates to the Vijayanagara period.
   References: Sinopoli and Morrison 2006a:442.
   Illustrations: Figure 4.19.

SITE: VMS-317   Block: T   Transect: 3
   Primary Site Use: Religious: Shaivite temple and associated mandapas.
   Site Dimensions: 60 × 50 m
   Setting: Flat terrain to north of modern paved road, on near course of Vijayanagara period road.
   Present Land Use/Disturbances: Amid agricultural fields; main temple is now being used as a stable.
   Site Description: Temple complex consisting of a central east-facing temple (F1) and five associated mandapas (F2-F6). The complex does not appear to have been walled and was probably constructed over a considerable period, from the fourteenth through the sixteenth century. In particular, the temple (F1) is of fourteenth-century construction, while several of the surrounding mandapas were likely constructed later in the Vijayanagara period. The temple is located along Vijayanagara period east-west road, leading east from the capital (the modern Nallapur Road).

   Feature 1: Early Vijayanagara east-facing Shaivite temple consisting of 3 chambers: a large and small antechamber, and a sanctuary. The temple is built on a low basement with simple angled tripartite moldings. Exterior walls are of two courses of horizontal slabs (c. 8 m high) separated by a single course that projects slightly outward.

   The large outer antechamber is 4 × 4 columns in plan and was entered from doors on the south, east, and north. Each door is flanked by Shaivite door guardians. Doorways are finely sculpted with angled bands surrounding the entry and a lotus on the lintel. The walls of the antechamber are double faced with rubble fill, and the outer columns are paired, with a single capital spanning them.

   Only the four inner columns of the antechamber are sculpted. These define a raised floor area; the remaining columns are simple dressed square columns with some quarry marks evident. The four central columns rest on square column bases with miniature basement tripartite beveled moldings. They are of early Vijayanagara form and date to the fourteenth century. The lowermost section of the columns is square with projecting corner buds on top; above this is a band of two sixteen-sided segments separated by an octagonal segment; another square sculpted segment is above this inset, above which is another octagonal section. The upper portion tapers slightly and is topped by a double capital with a circular lower segment and an upper segment that is circular at the bottom and square on top with downward projecting corner lobes. Above this are cruciform brackets. Images sculpted on the columns include: lotus, peacock, the saint Matsyendranatha crouching on fish, a bearded warrior with sword, ascetics, goose, star, and monkey. The ceiling in the central bay is of rotated square plan. In other bays the ceiling is of slabs that alternate orientation (by bay) from north-south to east-west.

   The entry to the small inner antechamber is also flanked by Shaivite door guardians though it is less ornate than the outer doors of the structure. This chamber is 3 columns long × 2 columns wide, with slightly inward projecting square unsculpted columns spanned by walls. Some plaster/paint is visible on the walls.

   The 2 × 2 column sanctuary has a finely sculpted entryway, with Shaivite door guardians and a goddess over the lintel. The ceiling is of offset square form, with a central lotus medallion. A large image base is in the sanctuary, and a floor drain extends out through its north wall. The stepped temple shikara projects over the inner antechamber. It is of stone construction, with six inset squares, with projecting square lobes evenly placed along each face. The domed top is plastered; no sculpture is evident. The shikara, columns, and plan of the outer antechamber are consistent with an early Vijayanagara (fourteenth century) date.

   Feature 2: 2 × 2 column unwalled mandapa (c. 2.8 m on a side) on raised basement (c. 8 m) located c. 6 m to the east of the main temple. The tripartite basement moldings have upper and lower beveled panels with corner medallions. The unsculpted columns rest on square footings and are of the common late Vijayanagara form of square panels separated by octagonal insets. Seven Shaivite images have been placed on the mandapa; these include four granite naga images (three single, one double), feet surrounded by a naga, and a Bhairava image. Also present is a chlorito-schist sculpted column fragment. A fallen granite column segment lies to the west of the mandapa; to its east is a low rubble mound, possibly the remains of another small structure.

   Feature 3: 2 × 2 column mandapa on low platform located c. 40 m east of Feature 1. The platform is built of three courses of loosely fit medium to large crudely modified stones, with long rectangular blocks on top. Traces of a plaster floor are present. The slightly tapering columns are square in plan, with no sculptures or insets. They are topped by rectangular brackets, spanned by beams. The roof is of offset squares. No images are present.

   To the north of this feature is a depressed gully, c. 8 m wide. It is partially lined with stones, some with Vijayanagara quarry marks; on the west side the bedrock appears to have been excavated. This feature may be the remains of a well, but is partially obscured by modern agricultural activities and vegetation, so a precise identification is not possible.

   Feature 4: Long east-west 4 × 2 column mandapa and associated standing columns, north of Feature 1. Basement is obscured by overgrown rubble mound. Columns vary in plan; the south columns are crudely dressed and square in plan with no insets. The north columns have three panels with octagonal insets; none are sculpted. The columns are topped by rectangular or T-shaped brackets spanned by crossbeams. These beams project out to the north some 0.40 m beyond the columns, and are sculpted with angled eaves and a lingam on top. The ceiling is of horizontal slabs, oriented north-south in the center bay and east-west in the other bays. A similar mandapa may have stood to the west of this one, now evidenced by a low mound and three standing columns.

   Feature 5: Poorly preserved mandapa, c. 10 m north of Feature 1. The feature is a small rubble mound with a single standing column and three fallen slabs or columns. Probably a 2 × 2 column mandapa; a heavily eroded Bhairava image rests on the mound.

   Feature 6: 2 × 2 column mandapa in poor state of preservation located south of Feature 1. It appears to have been constructed on a low basement, with unsculpted square columns, only three of which are standing. No sculptural elements.

   Feature 7 (not illustrated): Low mound c. 6 m north-south × 3 m east-west located southwest of Feature 6. The mound consists of outcropping stones on the south and decaying brick and fired earth on the north. Although iron slag is presented at the site, it is not especially abundant at

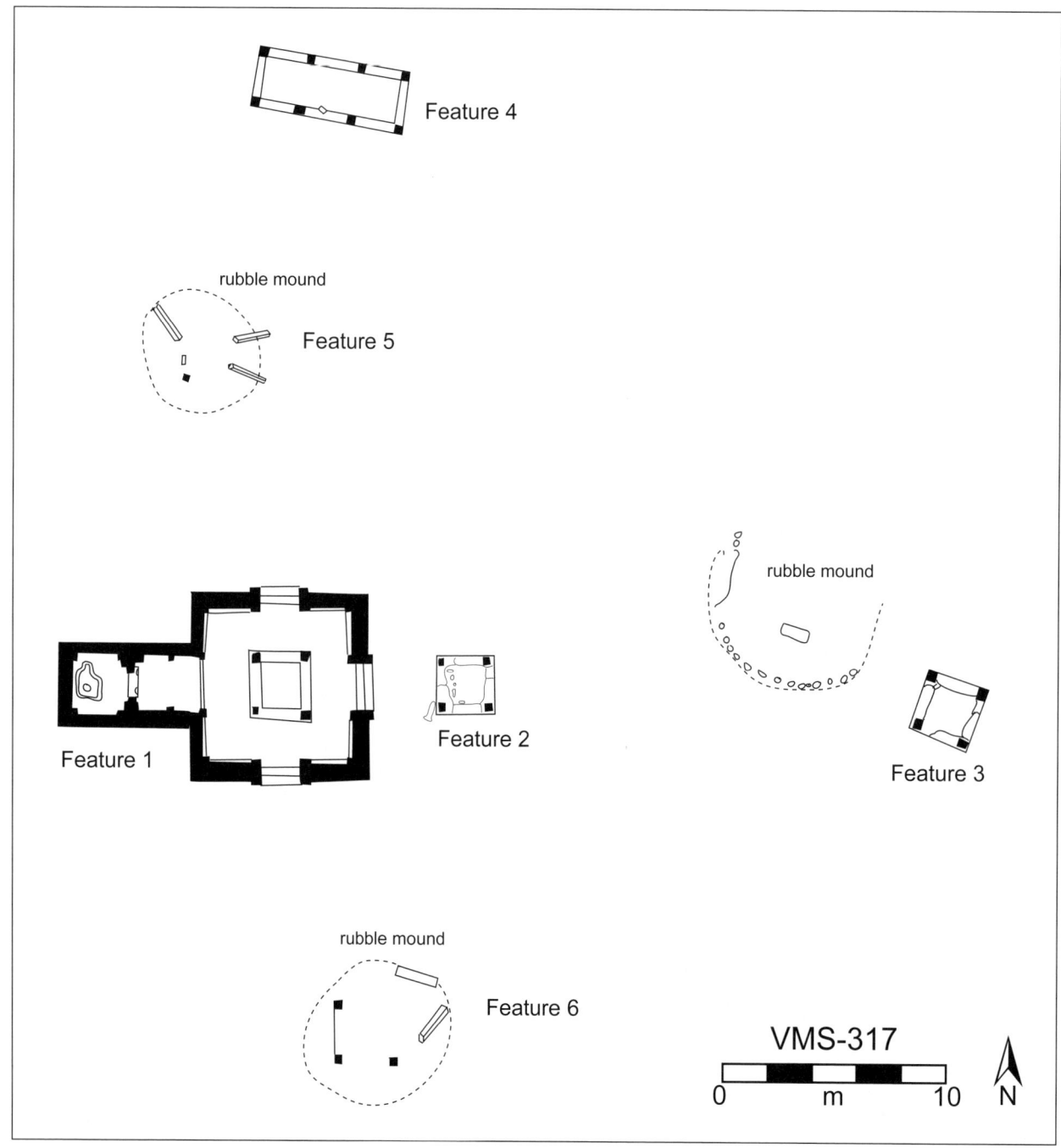

Figure 4.20. VMS-317, plan.

this feature. It may nonetheless be associated with iron working, though its chronological relation to the temple is unclear.

Artifacts: Moderate dense and localized scatter of ceramics and iron slag in plowed fields surrounding the structures; slag is highest in areas to east and south of the main temple; a diagnostic surface collection of ceramics was conducted, and a total collection of visible iron slag was made, yielding 6.2 kg.

Temporal Affiliation: Main temple dates to early or pre-Vijayanagara; mandapas are most likely later Vijayanagara additions.

References: Morrison 1995:79, 81, 86, 99; Sinopoli 1996; Sinopoli 2003:197; Sinopoli and Morrison 2006:439, 443.

Illustrations: Figure 4.20; Plates 4.14-16.

Plate 4.14. VMS-317, Feature 1: temple.

Plate 4.15. VMS-317, Feature 4.

Plate 4.16. VMS-317, Feature 3, with main temple to left, and Feature 4 in rear.

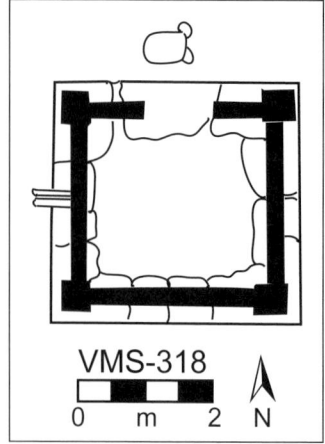

Figure 4.21. VMS-318, plan.

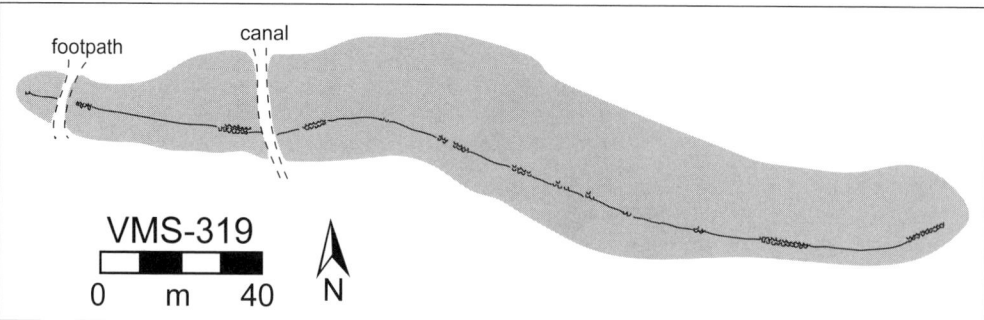

Figure 4.22. VMS-319, plan.

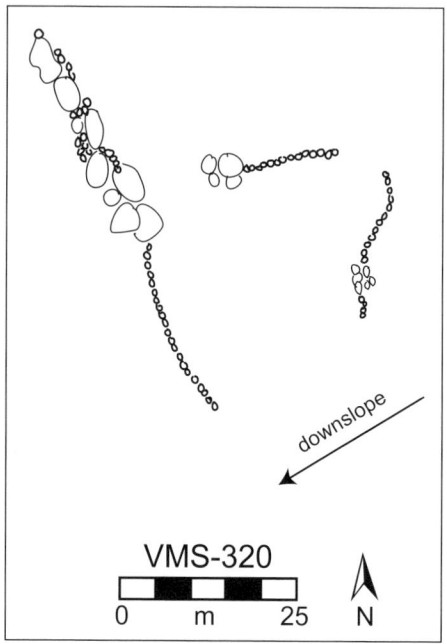

Figure 4.23. VMS-320, plan.

SITE: VMS-318 Block: T Transect: 4
Primary Site Use: Religious: shrine.
Site Dimensions: 3.4 × 3.15 m
Setting: Circa 30 m to the south of paved Nallapur Road, which follows the Vijayanagara period road course that today is an earthen path.
Present Land Use/Disturbances: Shrine is surrounded by rice paddies.
Site Description: 2 × 2 column walled mandapa. This walled mandapa is constructed on a 0.8 m high basement with simple single angle moldings and corner medallions. The two crudely dressed square columns (0.4 m across at base × 1.7 m tall) rest on square footings. The west, south and east walls are constructed of four courses of closely fitted horizontal slabs (0.55-0.30 m high, decreasing in size from bottom to top). A turtle image is sculpted on the exterior of the south wall and a drain extends through the center of the west wall. The north doorway is flanked by two vertical stone slabs; a lotus is sculpted on the lintel and two carved door sockets are on the lintel interior. The walls of the shrine are penetrated by two square holes (0.15 m on a side) in the southeast and southwest upper corners, which may have served to allow light in or smoke out of the structure. The ceiling is of offset square plan with central lotus medallion.
Artifacts: 100% collection; no artifacts recovered.
Temporal Affiliation: Vijayanagara.
Illustrations: Figure 4.21.

SITE: VMS-319 Block: T Transect: 7-8
Primary Site Use: Agricultural: reservoir embankment.
Site Dimensions: 240 × 35 m
Setting: Flat area, terrain slopes gently down to the north.
Present Land Use/Disturbances: Embankment has been robbed of stones and may have been much larger; rubble has been piled on the overgrown embankment; modern canals cut through site, as does a cart track on the west edge.
Site Description: Reservoir embankment. This low stone-faced and earthen embankment has up to eight stepped courses of unmodified small to medium stones visible on the south face. Mounding suggests that the south face may have originally extended out roughly 4 m beyond its present edge. No clear boundary is visible on the north earthen face of the embankment due to disturbance by modern cultivation. No sluices are preserved.
Artifacts: 100% collection; only two black plain ware body sherds observed.
Temporal Affiliation: Vijayanagara.
References: Morrison 1995:79, 82, 102.
Illustrations: Figure 4.22.

SITE: VMS-320 Block: T Transect: 9
Primary Site Use: Agricultural: terrace system/soil control walls.
Site Dimensions: 60 × 40 m
Setting: Gentle to moderate terrain sloping down to southwest with outcropping boulders, surrounded by higher rock outcrops.
Present Land Use/Disturbances: Uncultivated.
Site Description: Three retaining walls and associated rubble piles formed around natural outcrops. The informal walls are composed of loosely laid small to medium unmodified stones and incorporate natural outcropping stones. In some areas, two to three courses are visible, with wall width ranging from c. 0.4 to 1 m. The walls likely served to define terraces and/or limit soil erosion.
Artifacts: 100% collection; no artifacts recovered.
Temporal Affiliation: Unknown.
References: Morrison 1995:95, 102.
Illustrations: Figure 4.23.

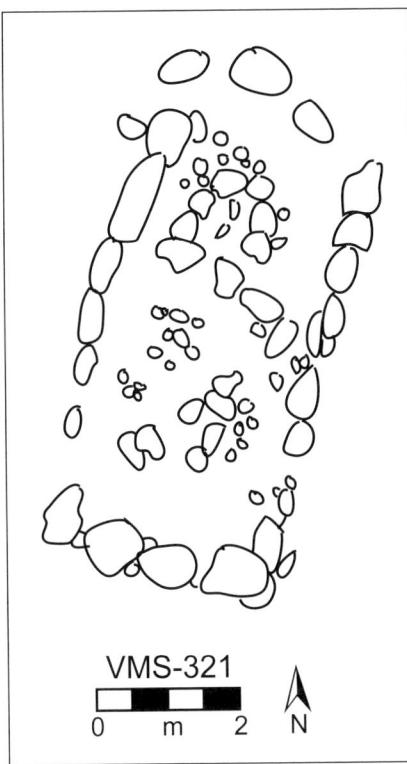

Figure 4.24. VMS-321, plan.

SITE: VMS-321   Block: T   Transect: 9
  Primary Site Use: Defensive/transport: isolated wall.
  Site Dimensions: 7.5 × 3.5 m
  Setting: Flat terrain between low-lying agricultural fields to north and edge of an outcrop spur to the south.
  Present Land Use/Disturbances: Threshing floor and rice fields appear to have destroyed portions of the site.
  Site Description: Wall segment. This is a 7.5 m long segment of a massive 3.5 m wide double-faced block/boulder wall with rubble infill. Boulders forming the single-course wall range from 0.6 × 0.4 × 0.4 m to 1.0 × 0.35 × 0.40 m. The south end may be faced, possibly defining a gate or passage. Located in a narrow area between outcrops and low-lying agricultural fields, the wall may have defined a transport route, and is quite similar in construction to the nearby Vijayanagara road, VMS-326, to which it may be connected.
  Artifacts: One basalt flake.
  Temporal Affiliation: Vijayanagara.
  References: Morrison 1995:65, 79.
  Illustrations: Figure 4.24.

SITE: VMS-322   Block: T   Transect: 8-9
  Primary Site Use: Agricultural: reservoir embankment.
  Site Dimensions: 170 × 15 m
  Setting: Terrain slopes down to north with large outcrop ridges to east and west.
  Present Land Use/Disturbances: Area around site is under cultivation. An irrigation canal has cut into the north face of the embankment. Two modern structures and a well to the west of the embankment may have resulted in some destruction; there is a large breach in the embankment near its midpoint.
  Site Description: Reservoir embankment. This east-west oriented reservoir (12° south of east) captured runoff from higher terrain to its south. The stepped stone south face is constructed of unmodified medium to very large granite stones and is preserved to a height of c. 1.5 m, with six courses visible. The northern earthen face of the embankment has probably been disturbed by more recent activity and is presently c. 15 m wide. No sluice is preserved.
  Artifacts: None.
  Temporal Affiliation: Vijayanagara.
  References: Morrison 1995:102.
  Illustrations: Figure 4.25.

SITE: VMS-323   Block: T   Transect: 9
  Primary Site Use: Agricultural: wall.
  Site Dimensions: 30 × 0.6 m
  Setting: Terrain slopes down to the northwest; boulder outcrops to southeast.
  Present Land Use/Disturbances: Fallow fields, footpaths along north end of the site.
  Site Description: Erosion control wall. This wall is located at the edge of an agricultural field and abuts outcrops on its south end (oriented 32° west of north). The ground surface is significantly lower on the northwest side of the wall, with considerable soil accumulation on the southeast side, suggesting that the feature has been in place for some time. The wall appears to be double faced; three courses of medium-large unmodified stones are visible on the lower face, and natural outcropping boulders are incorporated in some areas.
  Artifacts: 100% collection. <50 g ceramics; wares: 1 black plain ware. Diagnostics: 1 jar. One lithic.
  Temporal Affiliation: Unknown; soil accumulation suggests wall is not recent.
  References: Morrison 1995:102.
  Illustrations: Figure 4.26.

SITE: VMS-324   Block: T   Transect: 8
  Primary Site Use: Agricultural: reservoir embankment.
  Site Dimensions: 65 × 15 m
  Setting: Terrain slopes down to the north and west.
  Present Land Use/Disturbances: Area is presently under cultivation. Field walls and a recent shrine abut the embankment.
  Site Description: Reservoir embankment. The east stepped stone face of this small reservoir embankment (orientation 37° west of north) is c. 1 m high and composed of up to six courses of loosely laid small stones with a small number of larger stones. Most are unmodified, but one has Vijayanagara quarry marks. A channel is visible near the north end of the embankment and may have served as an outlet.
  Artifacts: A few fragmented nondiagnostic sherds were observed. No collections were made.
  Temporal Affiliation: Vijayanagara.
  References: Morrison 1995:102; Sinopoli and Morrison 2006a:440.
  Illustrations: Figure 4.27.

118 *The Vijayanagara Metropolitan Survey*

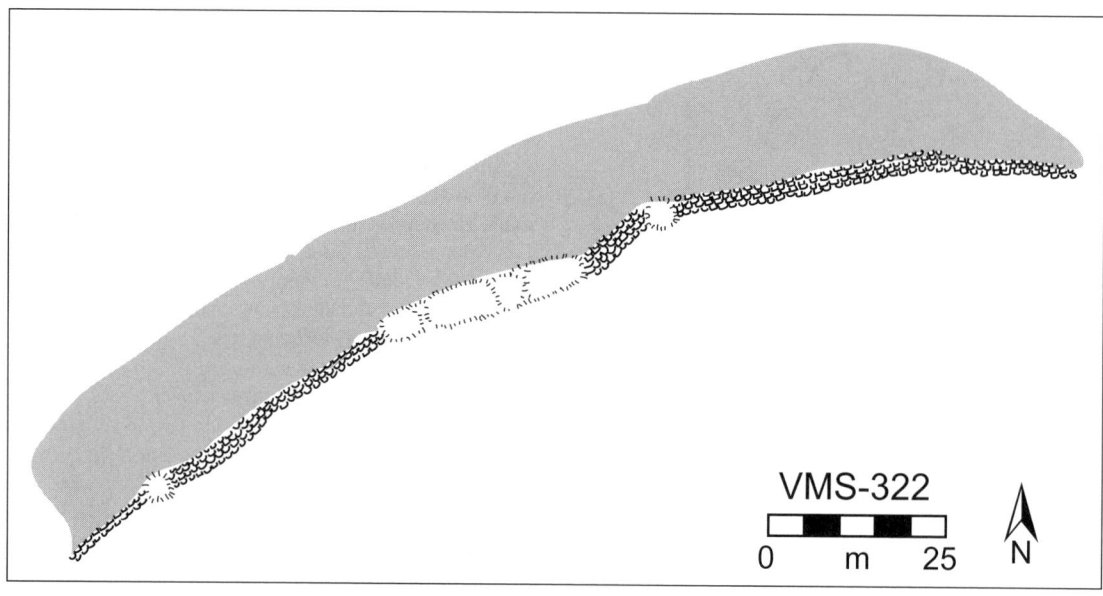

Figure 4.25. VMS-322, plan.

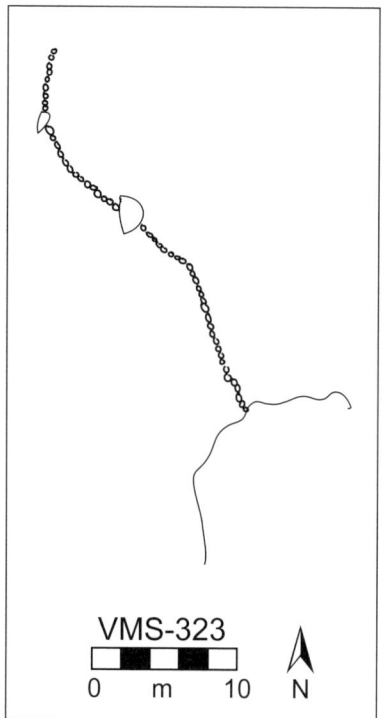

Figure 4.26. VMS-323, plan.

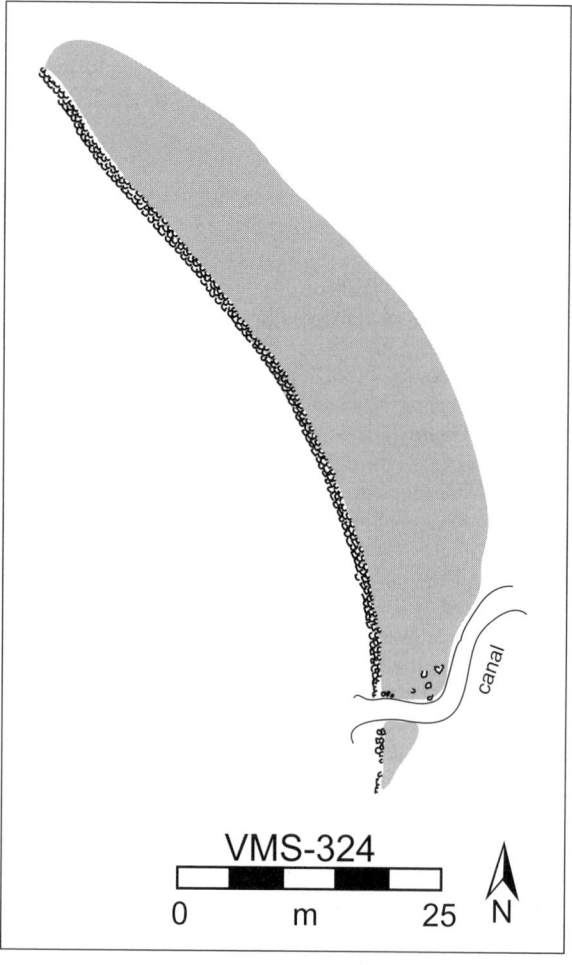

Figure 4.27. VMS-324, plan.

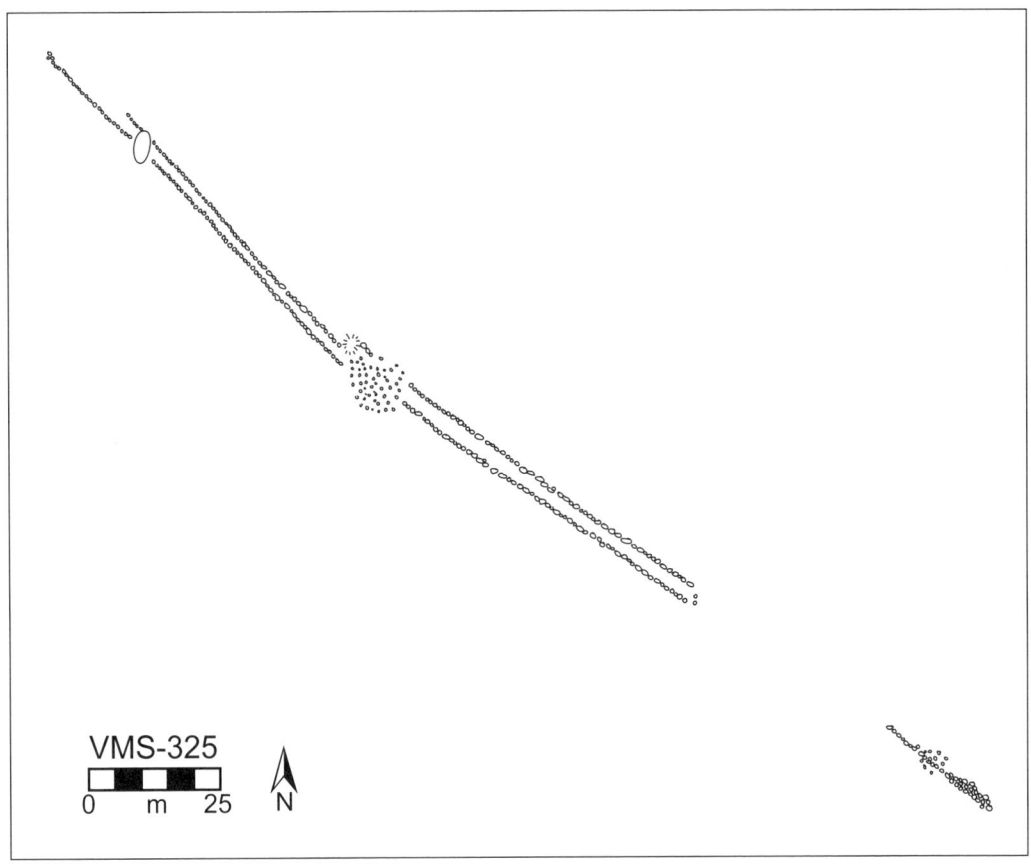

Figure 4.28. VMS-325, plan.

SITE: VMS-325   Block: T   Transect: 8
   Primary Site Use: Transport: wall.
   Site Dimensions: 250 × 2.5 m
   Setting: In area of moderate slopes and small outcropping boulders, terrain slopes down to the northwest. Site is located to the east of gate VMS-303 and to the north of reservoir VMS-324.
   Present Land Use/Disturbances: The site is overgrown by thorny scrub and cacti; a cart track runs parallel to the wall. Agricultural field walls and other recent construction may have led to some displacement and gaps.
   Site Description: Road wall. This large wall extends for c. 250 m in a northwest/southeast direction (40° north of west). It incorporates small outcropping boulders in places. The wall is double faced with rubble infill. It is c. 2 m wide × 0.8 m high and is composed of unmodified medium to large stones. Up to three courses are visible, with some chinking. Circa 175 m from its northwest terminus is a gap of c. 48 m, after which the wall continues for another 26 m to the southeast. The west end of the wall is aligned with site VMS-303, a Vijayanagara mandapa and probable gate. The wall may have lined the edge of a broader road or, more likely, defined the road bed itself.
   Artifacts: 100% collection; no artifacts recovered.
   Temporal Affiliation: Vijayanagara.
   References: Morrison 1995:66, 79; Sinopoli and Morrison 2006a:440.
   Illustrations: Figure 4.28; Plate 4.17.

Plate 4.17. VMS-325, road wall.

Plate 4.18. VMS-326, overview to west; overgrown elevated area in left center marks route of road.

Plate 4.19. VMS-326, detail of road construction.

SITE: VMS-326 Block: T Transect: 9-14
  Primary Site Use: Transport: road system.
  Site Dimensions: 1200 × 50 m
  Setting: Low-lying area to the south of and parallel to the Nallapur road. VMS-326 connects with site VMS-360 to its east. In some areas the site abuts outcropping slopes.
  Present Land Use/Disturbances: Area surrounding road is partly cultivated and partly overgrown; modern cart tracks, field walls, and plowing activities have disturbed portions of the site.
  Site Description: Road system. This site is a segment of a large road system that is c. 100 m south of and roughly parallel to the modern paved (Nallapur) road. The Vijayanagara road extended southeast from the city core. An eastern segment of the road was designated as VMS-360. A number of sites were recorded along the road: watchtower/bastion VMS-327, step well VMS-328, and settlements VMS-329 and VMS-361, among other features.
  The site is defined by two parallel rows of large stone boulders (c. 0.65 × 0.50 × 0.50 m) spaced 30 to 40 m apart. Along many sections, these walls are formed by dual lines of stones, 2-3 m apart with rubble and earth fill. Along the road c. 660 m from its west end is a massive outcropping boulder (Feature 1; c. 30 m across × 5 m high). Features found on this boulder include: extensive Vijayanagara quarry marks; two pecked stone game boards; a pecked circular depression; and, on a high point beneath an overhang, a row of eleven pecked ovoid depressions, c. 0.04-0.11 m across. This area may have been a shrine as the overhang has natural reddish and white streaks reminiscent of the painting on contemporary shrines. The outcrop would have provided a good vantage point of the road, as well as a convenient and shaded resting place for travelers. VMS-326 is most likely a portion of a major road that extended east from the Vijayanagara city core, perhaps toward the Daroji Valley (and gate VMS-370). Segments of this route have been recorded in Block S.
  Artifacts: Some modern ceramics observed near Feature 1; elsewhere, scatter was light to none. No collections were made.
  Temporal Affiliation: Vijayanagara.
  References: Morrison 1995:65, 79; Sinopoli and Morrison 2006a:440.
  Illustrations: Plates 4.18-4.20.

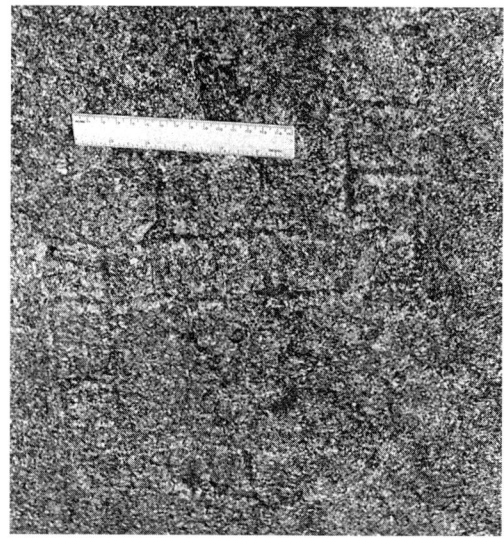

Plate 4.20. VMS-326, game board on outcrop along route of road.

SITE: VMS-327 **Block:** T **Transect:** 13
Primary Site Use: Defensive: watchtower.
Site Dimensions: 26 × 12 m
Setting: On outcrop near east end of road section VMS-326 and above settlements VMS-329 and VMS-361, and step well VMS-328.
Present Land Use/Disturbances: Overgrown by brush and grasses. There has been considerable erosion and slope wash on the outcrop; artifacts and building materials appear to have washed down the slopes of the outcrop, especially to the north.
Site Description: Watch tower or bastion. This site consists of the remains of a circular structure or platform and an associated wall located on a conical outcrop immediately overlooking Vijayanagara road VMS-326. The circular structure is c. 10 m in diameter and up to 2 m high. Up to six loosely fitted courses of its circular wall are preserved, to a height of 1.5 m. The walls are constructed of shaped granite blocks, c. 0.40 m across × 0.25-0.30 m high, with Vijayanagara quarry marks. Some chinking is evident. An accumulation of earth and rubble is mounded above the extant wall.

A light scatter of pottery is found on and near the structure and extends down the rubble slopes of the outcrop. An associated wall extends from the structure down the slope of the outcrop, oriented 15° east of north. Although disturbed, it appears to have been double faced and c. 0.6 m wide. Only one course of small-medium unmodified stones is visible. A stone with Vijayanagara quarry marks is found near the north end of the wall. The location and form of this site suggest that it served as a watchtower or lookout point, perhaps to monitor traffic along road VMS-326. The structure was solid, with rubble fill, and could not have served as a granary or storage facility.
Artifacts: Sparse scatter of ceramics, some modern debris. Diagnostic collection from structure and surrounding slopes.
Temporal Affiliation: Vijayanagara, with later reuse of some materials.
References: Morrison 1995:65, 71, 78; Sinopoli and Morrison 2006:439.
Illustrations: Figure 4.29.

SITE: VMS-328 **Block:** T **Transect:** 13
Primary Site Use: Residential/agricultural: step well.
Site Dimensions: 14 × 9 m
Setting: Flat area to east below outcrop containing VMS-327. Site is associated with road VMS-326 and settlements VMS-329 and VMS-361.
Present Land Use/Disturbances: Site is overgrown and the walls and stairway are partly collapsed; east wall has recent repairs.
Site Description: Step well. The access to this well was from its southwest corner, and involved a change in direction, with upper steps oriented roughly to the north, and lower steps to the east. The site is overgrown and the steps are not presently visible. The well still contains water and only the upper four to five courses of medium to large rectangular blocks with Vijayanagara quarry marks are visible. A ground stone mortar is located near the southwest corner of the well.
Artifacts: Light sherd scatter surrounding the well was collected as part of VMS-329.
Temporal Affiliation: Vijayanagara.
References: Morrison 1995:71, 84; Sinopoli and Morrison 2006:439-40.
Illustrations: Figures 4.30, 4.31.

SITE: VMS-329 **Block:** T **Transect:** 13-14
Primary Site Use: Residential/religious: structural foundations.
Site Dimensions: 54 × 50 m
Setting: Flat area around low outcrop containing VMS-327; step well VMS-328 is located within site area, which is also associated with VMS-361 and road VMS-326.
Present Land Use/Disturbances: Area is under cultivation. The site has been heavily disturbed by canal and field construction. According to an informant, several ancient structures in the area have been leveled over the past forty years.
Site Description: Disturbed area with evidence for the foundations of several structures. The site is located along transport route VMS-326 at the east base of an outcrop topped by a watchtower VMS-327. Visible architectural elements include rectangular dressed granite slabs with Vijayanagara quarry marks. In the southwest edge of the site, and disturbed by a modern canal, a low basement with a simple single angle molding is partly exposed in a rubble mound. To its northeast is a 15 m long area of eight exposed flat slabs; these may be pavement or foundation stones. In the southeast portion of the site, a single square irregularly dressed column (c. 0.4 m² at base) stands on a small rubble mound. The north end of the site consists of partly buried low slabs, perhaps defining a small structure. Other modified stones are visible here and there in the fields and a stone block mortar is found at the southwest corner of the well. These remains may constitute part of the settlement recorded as VMS-361.

Given the heavily disturbed nature of the site it is not possible to identify what kinds of structures were originally found here. However, these do not appear to be the remains of typical house foundations, and may instead be the remains of more formal temple or administrative structures.
Artifacts: Moderate to heavy scatter of ceramics in fields below VMS-327 and on slopes. A diagnostic collection was made (see Chapter 6).
Temporal Affiliation: Vijayanagara.
References: Morrison 1995:71; Sinopoli 1997:481, 484; Sinopoli and Morrison 2006:439-40.
Illustrations: Figure 4.31.

The Vijayanagara Metropolitan Survey

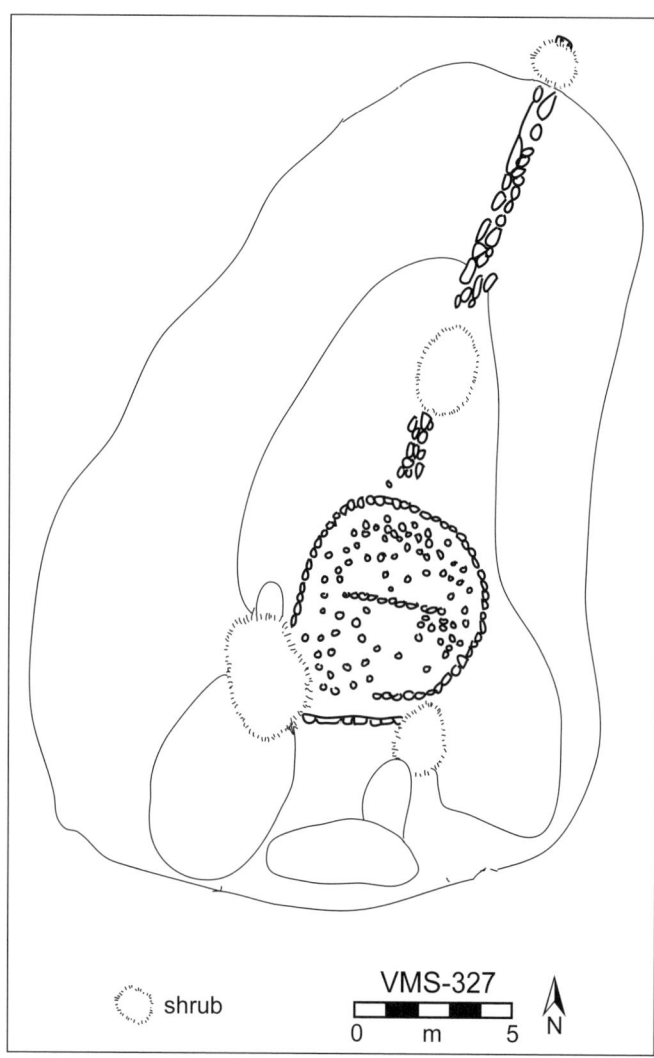

Figure 4.29. VMS-327, plan.

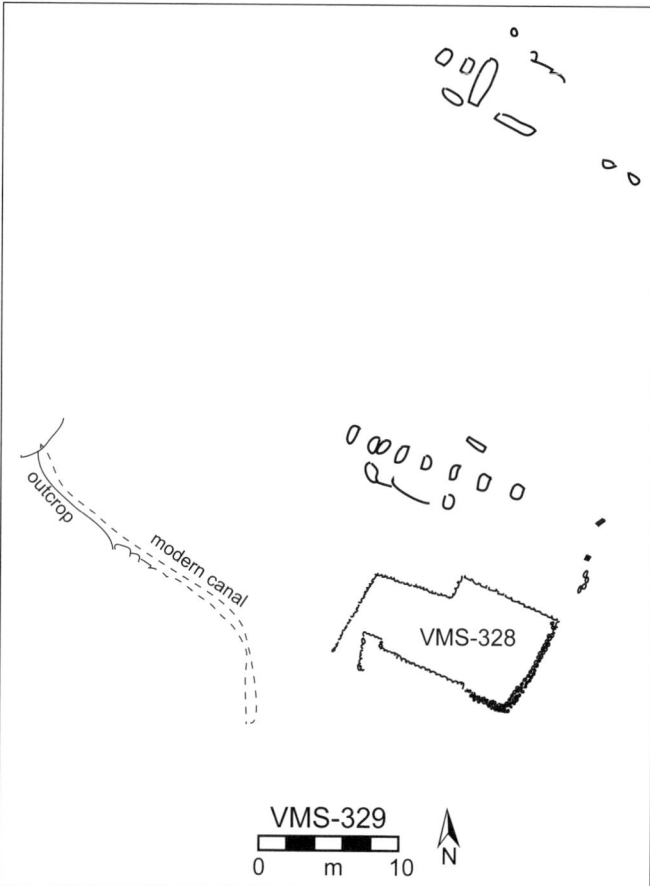

Figure 4.31. VMS-329 and VMS-328, plan.

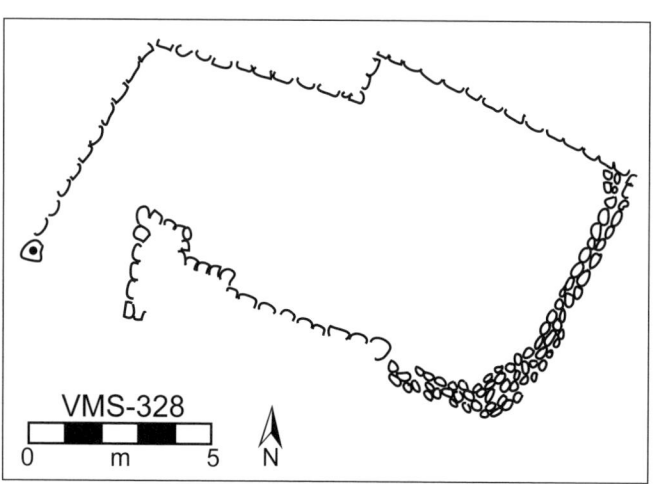

Figure 4.30. VMS-328, plan.

Block T: Site Summaries 123

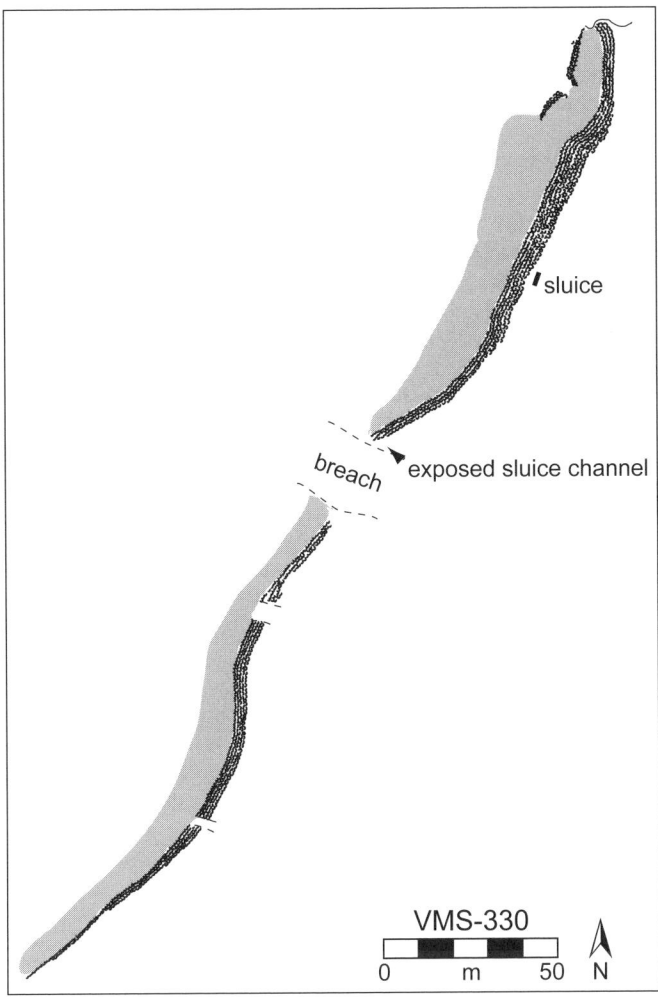

Figure 4.32. VMS-330, plan.

Plate 4.21. VMS-330, detail of exposed sluice channel.

Plate 4.22. VMS-330, close-up of eastern stone face of embankment.

SITE: VMS-330   Block: T   Transect: 13-14

Primary Site Use: Agricultural: reservoir embankment.

Site Dimensions: 650 × 60 m

Setting: Flat terrain in agricultural fields, abuts low outcrops on its north end, and terminates in the south at Vijayanagara road VMS-326.

Present Land Use/Disturbances: Agricultural fields surround site. The embankment is overgrown and has been disturbed by quarrying, modern canals, and a road along the top.

Site Description: Reservoir embankment. This long embankment (oriented 20° east of north) spans a broad valley and is bordered on the south by Vijayanagara road system VMS-326. Isolated walls, VMS-331, are at the northeast boundary of the site. The east stepped stone face of the c. 50 m wide embankment is preserved to c. 10 m high, with up to twenty courses of large unmodified or split blocks.

A modern canal cutting through the embankment near its midpoint has exposed a massive sluice gate and water channel. The channel was lined with rectangular blocks (2.5-3 m long × 0.66 m high) enclosed within brick and plaster. The channel dimension cannot be estimated. The fallen sluice columns that lie near the channel are 4.3 m high, with base dimensions c. 0.55 m², tapering slightly toward the top. A pierced crosspiece (1.20 × 1.65 × 0.22 m, 0.23 m diameter central hole) is nearby. The top crosspiece is also present, with single bevel molding and corner and medial (1/3 across) quarter lobe medallions.

Fragments of a second sluice are located c. 130 m from the northeast end of the embankment. These include a fallen column, crosspiece, and top slab, c. 2 m long × 0.3 m high, with six projecting medallions spaced 0.2 m apart on the single visible face. Near the northeast end, both sides of the embankment are stone faced, with up to thirteen courses visible. A number of large slabs with Vijayanagara quarry marks are incorporated into the west embankment face or are located to its west. Some of these form a low platform or pavement, c. 2 × 3 m in dimension; this may be a portion of a walkway along the base of the outcrop. Vijayanagara quarry marks are visible on the outcrop slopes to the northwest of the embankment.

At its north end, the defensive aspects of the embankment are especially visible, as the double-faced wall is in effect a fortification wall. The embankment itself and, during some times of year, the water pooled to its east would have effectively served to restrict movement across this broad and otherwise easily traversed valley, such that travelers were restricted to the course of the main road to its south (VMS-326).

Artifacts: No collections made.

Temporal Affiliation: Vijayanagara.

References: Morrison 1995:71, 95, 102; Sinopoli and Morrison 2006:439.

Illustrations: Figure 4.32; Plates 4.21, 4.22.

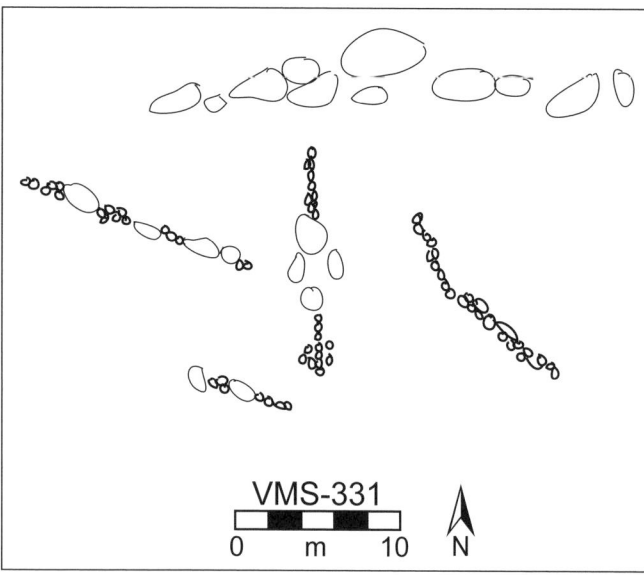

Figure 4.33. VMS-331, plan.

SITE: VMS-331   Block: T   Transect: 14
  Primary Site Use: Agricultural: erosion control walls.
  Site Dimensions: 38 × 23 m
  Setting: Area of gentle slopes with outcropping boulders c. 25 m north of north end of reservoir VMS-330.
  Present Land Use/Disturbances: Uncultivated.
  Site Description: Isolated walls. This site consists of isolated wall segments constructed of small to medium unmodified stones that have been piled between outcropping boulders. There are no formal courses; in parts, sections of the walls are a single course high although they are often several stones wide (up to 0.5 m). These informal features most likely served to prevent or slow runoff and erosion down into bed of reservoir, VMS-330.
  Artifacts: 100% collection; no artifacts recovered.
  Temporal Affiliation: Unknown, but associated with Vijayanagara period reservoir, VMS-330.
  Illustrations: Figure 4.33.

SITE: VMS-332   Block: T   Transect: 14
  Primary Site Use: Agricultural: soil control walls and embankment.
  Site Dimensions: 33 × 7 m, 20° south of east
  Setting: In a narrow runoff channel on southeast slopes of large outcrop. The terrain slopes down to the southwest. The site abuts outcrop on its east and west ends.
  Present Land Use/Disturbances: Partly overgrown, the long wall has been breached by an erosion gully.
  Site Description: Long wall and associated features. This site consists of a long double-faced wall and three associated features that cross a natural drainage channel sloping down to the south/southwest. The long wall is more than c. 33 m long × 1 m wide and is constructed of three to six courses of unmodified medium-sized stones (c. 0.3-0.6 m in dimension). The west segment of the wall is oriented roughly east-west; to the east it turns to a southeast orientation (45° south of east). South of the east end of the wall is a low earthen embankment (oriented 45° south of east), c. 6 m wide and bordered on its south by a wall of medium unmodified stones, c. 4.5 m long and one course high. This may be the remnant of a retaining wall. A wall, 4 m long, extends to the south from the west end of the main wall. VMS-332 was most probably used to prevent erosion from the field to the north, although a defensive function is also possible.
  Artifacts: 100% collection; no ceramics. A fragment of an apparent ground stone pestle was photographed but not collected.
  Temporal Affiliation: Unknown; large wall is breached and no longer in use.
  References: Morrison 1995:95, 102.
  Illustrations: Figure 4.34.

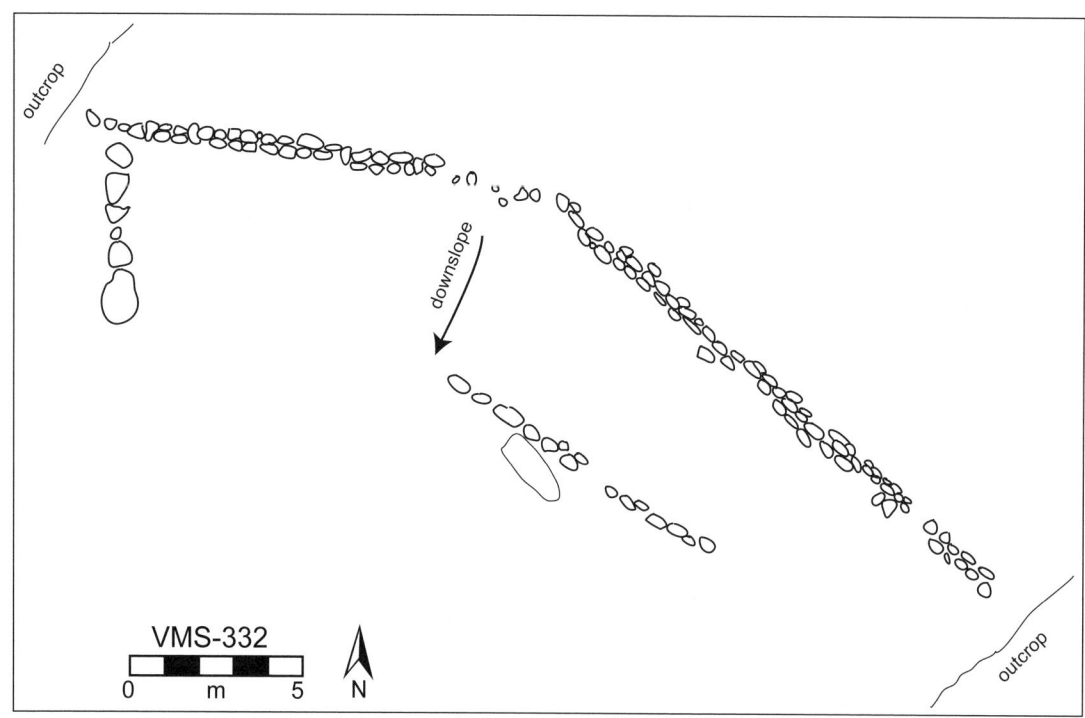

Figure 4.34. VMS-332, plan.

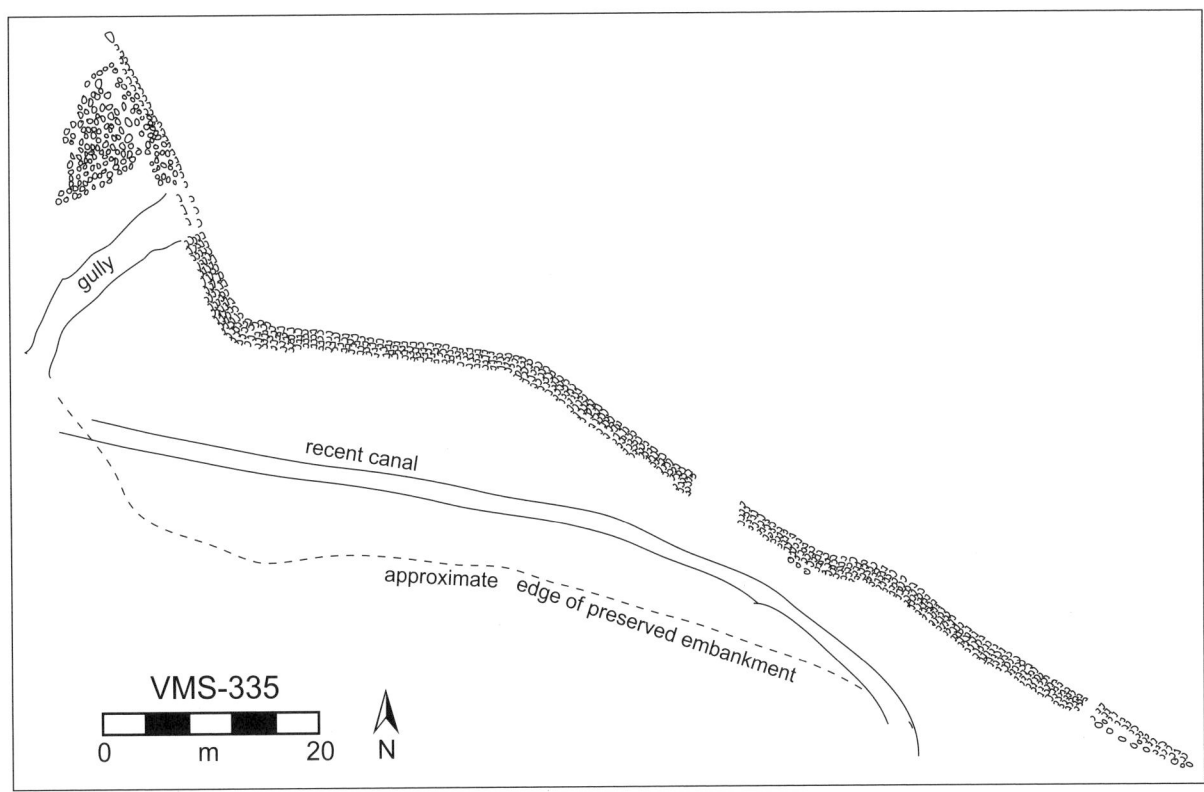

Figure 4.35. VMS-335, plan.

SITE: VMS-333   Block: T   **Transect:** 14
   Primary Site Use: Boundary marker: stone cairn.
   Site Dimensions: 1.3 m diameter
   Setting: Located on outcrop.
   Present Land Use/Disturbances: Uncultivated.
   Site Description: Small circular stone cairn. This cairn is c. 1.3 m in diameter × 1.2 m high and constructed of angular unmodified small-medium stones with irregular coursing and chinking stones (five to eight courses visible) and appears to be solid throughout. It is most probably a modern boundary marker for the reserved forest to the north.
   Artifacts: No collections made.
   Temporal Affiliation: Recent.

SITE: VMS-334   Block: T   **Transect:** 12
   Primary Site Use: Boundary marker: stone cairn.
   Site Dimensions: Circular, 1.5 m diameter
   Setting: On outcrop.
   Present Land Use/Disturbances: Uncultivated.
   Site Description: Small stone cairn or marker, c. 1.5 m in diameter × 1.0 m high, constructed of angular unmodified medium-large stones with irregular courses. This cairn is located to the west of VMS-333, with a similar cairn visible to the east in transect 13. Most probably a recent boundary marker for the reserved forest.
   Artifacts: No collections made.
   Temporal Affiliation: Recent.

SITE: VMS-335   Block: T   **Transect:** 12
   Primary Site Use: Agricultural: reservoir embankment.
   Site Dimensions: 130 × 25 m
   Setting: Spans a small valley gently sloping down toward the southeast; sites abuts outcrop on both ends.
   Present Land Use/Disturbances: Embankment has been breached by a modern canal at several points; parts of the earthen embankment have been removed.
   Site Description: Reservoir embankment. This embankment is oriented 40° north of west and spans a small valley, abutting low outcropping boulders on either end. The stepped stone embankment on the northeast face is constructed of up to seven uneven and irregular courses of medium to large (0.25-0.80 m) unmodified rounded and angular stones. No sluices are visible. There is a possible water channel on the west end (where the embankment turns north) but the stones have been considerably disturbed here. The catchment basin to the north of the reservoir could have covered an area some 80 × 100 m east-west and watered extensive low-lying fields to the southwest.
   Artifacts: Light ceramic scatter southeast of the embankment and within the reservoir bed. A diagnostic collection (see Chapter 6) was made but because of the extensive disturbance in area, no systematic collections were conducted.
   Temporal Affiliation: Vijayanagara.
   References: Morrison 1995:102.
   Illustrations: Figure 4.35.

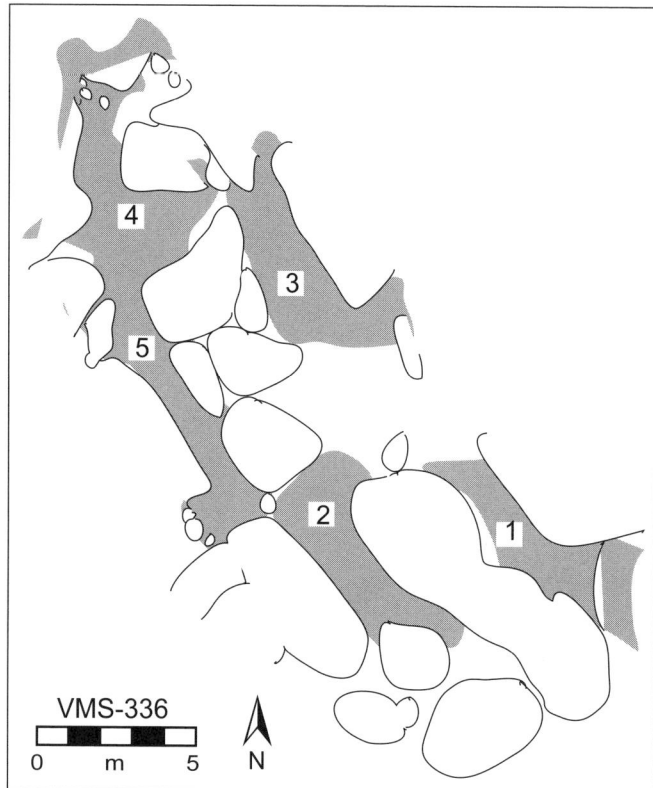

Figure 4.36. VMS-336, plan.

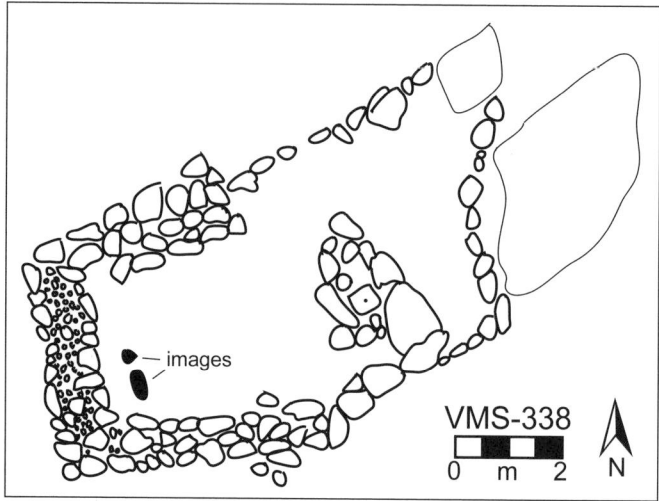

Figure 4.37. VMS-338, plan.

SITE: VMS-336   Block: T   Transect: 11
  Primary Site Use: Residential: rock shelter.
  Site Dimensions: 20 × 8 m
  Setting: Small interconnected shelters formed by overhanging boulders near crest of small outcrop hill.
  Present Land Use/Disturbances: Extensive modern quarrying in outcrop; modern artifacts and animal droppings present.
  Site Description: Interconnected rock shelters. The shelters are formed in the interstices of massive boulders with several openings providing entry into them. There are five distinct chambers divided by boulders or open areas overgrown with vegetation. Surfaces consist of loose dirt scattered with stones, ceramics, and animal droppings. The density of pottery and sherd size varies considerably from chamber to chamber.
  Artifacts: Ceramic scatters in different chambers, also some pieces of plastic, bone, and coprolites. Ceramics appear to be from large storage jars and most, if not all, are post-Vijayanagara (recent) in date. 100% collections were made in chambers 1 and 5, diagnostic collections in chambers 2-4. Ceramics were recovered in chamber 1 only.
  Chamber 1: 5900 g ceramics; wares: 177 black plain ware, 1 red plain ware. Diagnostics: 8 jars.
  Temporal Affiliation: Recent occupations, possibly with some earlier use.
  References: Morrison 1995:66; Sinopoli and Morrison 2006:439.
  Illustrations: Figure 4.36.

SITE: VMS-337   Block: T   Transect: 11
  Primary Site Use: Boundary marker: stone cairn.
  Site Dimensions: Circular, 1.5 m in diameter

  Setting: On outcrop.
  Present Land Use/Disturbances: Uncultivated.
  Site Description: Small stone cairn, c. 1.4 m in diameter × 1.5 m high, constructed of ten courses of angular modified and unmodified small-large stones. The diameter decreases somewhat toward the top where there appear to be some capping stones. This cairn is similar to VMS-333 and VMS-334 but is somewhat better preserved.
  Artifacts: No collections made.
  Temporal Affiliation: Recent.

SITE: VMS-338   Block: T   Transect: 11
  Primary Site Use: Religious: hill-top shrine (Shaivite).
  Site Dimensions: 9 × 5.5 m
  Setting: On top of a steeply sloped high hill of outcropping boulders and cobbles.
  Present Land Use/Disturbances: Shrine is currently in worship; modern oil lamps, flowers, and banners are present.
  Site Description: Small shrine. This small rectangular shrine is located on top of a very high hill of granitic and gabbro cobbles and outcropping boulders. The hilltop has been leveled with rubble infill forming a low platform. More rubble is located downslope to the south and west; it is unclear whether this is wall fall or deliberately placed, but it does not appear to define a pathway. On the platform is a small unroofed three-sided east-facing structure constructed of angular unmodified medium to large stones. The walls are double faced with rubble infill (up to 1.1 m wide) and reach a height of 1.25 m. The structure is still in use and its date is uncertain. Inside are two worked stones: a small finely sculpted chlorite architectural fragment (c. 0.2 × 0.2 × 0.1 m) with a yali and floral motif, and a heavily eroded granite slab with Vijayanagara quarry marks (0.65 × 0.35 × 0.15 m) (any image that existed on this slab has since been eroded). The shrine is Shaivite, indicated by modern banners with trident designs associated with a small standing modern granite pillar, designated as Virabhadra by an informant.
  Artifacts: Modern oil lamps were present near images; no older artifacts were observed. No collections were made.
  Temporal Affiliation: Unknown/perhaps Vijayanagara as well as recent use.
  References: Morrison 1995:81.
  Illustrations: Figure 4.37.

Plate 4.23. VMS-339, overview of wall from southern end to the northwest.

Plate 4.24. VMS-339, detail of wall construction at southern end.

SITE: VMS-339 Block: T Transect: 8-12
Primary Site Use: Defensive: fortification wall.
Site Dimensions: 2000+ × 2-6 m
Setting: Extends over long area that includes several zones of outcropping boulders and dry farm fields and terminates in south at high outcrop hill.
Present Land Use/Disturbances: Largely uncultivated with some fallow areas. The wall has collapsed in some areas and is cut in several locations by footpaths and roads; north terminus of wall at Tungabhadra High Level Canal; may connect with VMS-306 to north of canal.
Site Description: Fortification wall. This massive linear wall extends for more than 2 km across survey transects 8-12 at a dominant orientation of 60° south of east. It is constructed of unmodified medium to large granitic angular rounded stones (0.3-0.8 m). Preservation varies considerably; in the north the wall is used as modern field walls and has been both built upon and quarried for stones. Near this end it ranges from 3.5 to 6.0 m wide and from c. 0.5 to 1 m high. At points, the wall runs along the west edge of outcrops, becoming quite broad along such sections (10-15 m). In some sections the wall incorporates outcropping boulders 1-2 m across.

Circa 900 m from its north terminus, the wall becomes 1.25 m wide and double faced; this appears to be a better preserved section that may be representative of the original construction. At the southeast end, the wall extends up the slopes of a steep outcrop and is c. 4 m wide × 2 m high. This section of the wall is well preserved with clear faces on either side. No Vijayanagara quarry marks were noted along the course of the wall although a fragment of a soapstone pencil was found. Considering its massive construction, this wall seems likely to have been constructed for defensive purposes, perhaps to restrict or slow movement through the valley.

Artifacts: Light scatter of ceramics noted in the fallow fields near the north end of site, denser scatters among the rocks on the east side of the wall. Artifact distribution was clustered and irregular. A surface collection was made in one fairly dense 5 × 5 scatter near the midpoint of the well. 700 g ceramics; wares: 106 black plain ware, 9 red plain ware. Other: 1 steatite pencil fragment.
Temporal Affiliation: Vijayanagara.
References: Morrison 1995:65-66, 79, 81, 84, 94-95, 97, 99; Sinopoli and Morrison 2006a:440, 457.
Illustrations: Plates 4.23, 4.24.

SITE: VMS-340 Block: T Transect: 8
Primary Site Use: Defensive/residential: circular structure and three rectangular structures.
Site Dimensions: 48 × 46 m
Setting: Round structure on low outcropping boulder; others in surrounding fields. Site is located in a high area with excellent views of valleys to the southwest, northwest, northeast, and southeast.
Present Land Use/Disturbances: In area of fallow agricultural fields.
Site Description: Structural foundations. This site consists of the remains of one circular and three rectangular structures. The circular structure (structure 1) is farthest to the east and consists of six to seven courses (1.3 m high) of modified medium stones set upon a footing course on a low sheet rock outcrop. The core of the structure is filled with earth and rubble. It thus does not appear to have been a storage structure, but may instead have been a watch tower.

A c. 4 m long wall is located to the northwest of structure 1; only one course is visible. Structure 2, c. 10 m to the west of structure 1, is c. 5 m east-west × 8 m north-south in dimension (though it may consist of two closely spaced structures separated by a narrow alley); only a single course of foundation stones is preserved. Structure 3 (c. 10 m north-south × 4 m east-west) is located c. 24 m west of structure 2. The one to two course double-faced foundation walls are c. 0.65 m wide and constructed with modified and unmodified small-medium stones.

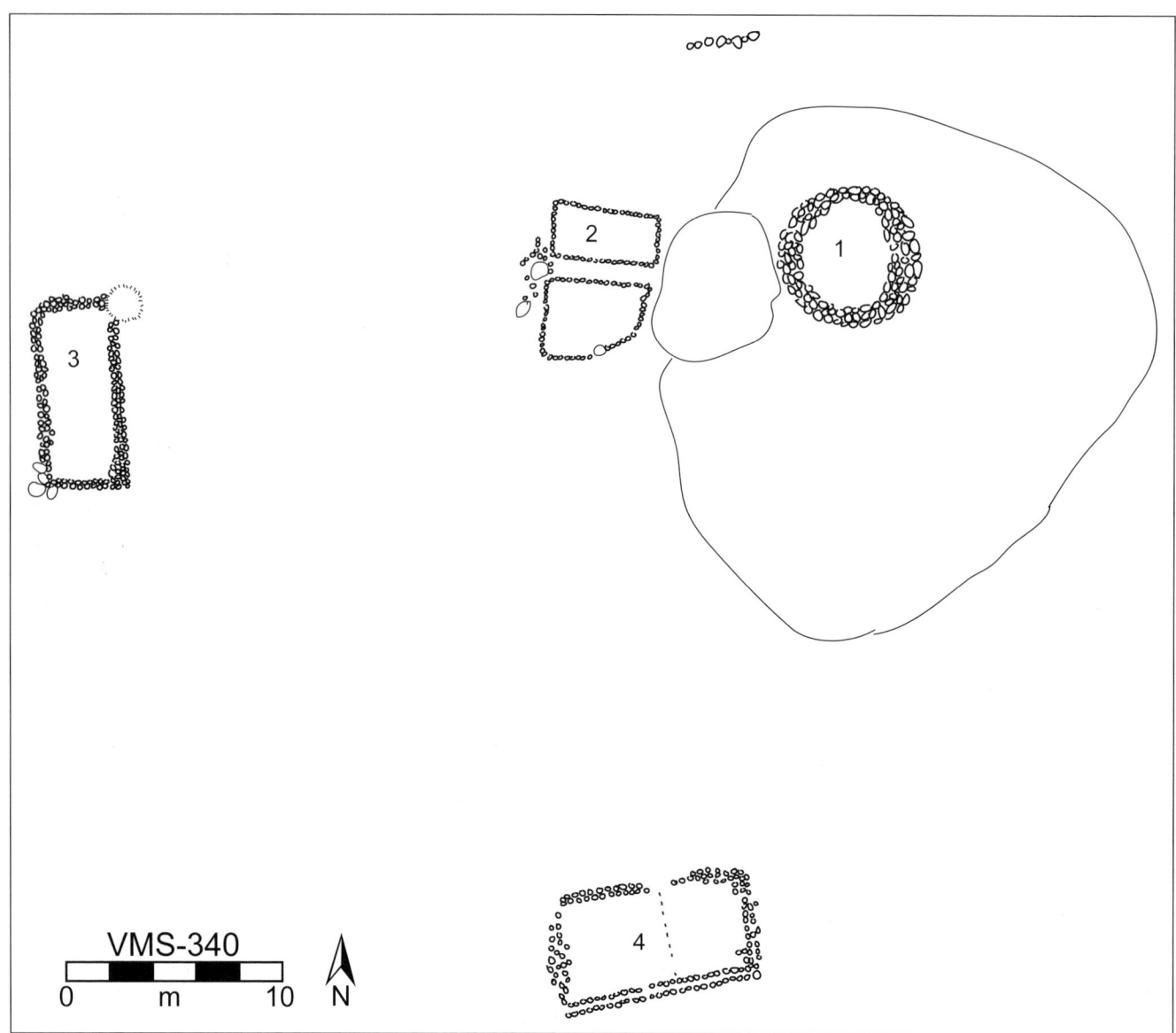

Figure 4.38. VMS-340, plan.

Structure 4, located c. 24 m south of structure 2, is c. 12 m east-west by 6 m north-south. A single course of double-faced walls of unmodified cobbles, c. 0.5 m wide, is visible.

The location of this site on a relatively high area with extensive views in several directions and the presence of a circular structure (watchtower?) suggest that this site may have been a military outpost. The site is located c. 350 m southwest of the center of VMS-339, a probable fortification wall restricting access from the northeast. From this location, it would have been possible to maintain surveillance over most if not the entire length of the wall.

Artifacts: Sparse scatter of sherds throughout the area around the structures. Four separate collections were made: (1) in an area of somewhat denser scatter (with several rims probably deriving from the same vessel) on the rock outcrop to the south of the circular structure, (2) in the open area between structures 1-4, (3) in the area immediately around structure 3, and (4) in the area around structure 4. In addition, a stone block fragment with part of a socket hole was noted southwest of the circular structure.

Unit 1: 250 g ceramics; wares: 11 black plain ware. Diagnostics: 1 jar (remains of a single vessel in small scatter).

Unit 2: 100 g ceramics; wares: 15 black plain ware, 1 red plain ware. Diagnostics: 2 jars.

Unit 3: 50 g ceramics; wares: 12 black plain ware. Diagnostics: 2 jars.

Unit 4: 50 g ceramics; wares: 4 black plain ware, 2 red plain ware; 1 jar.

Temporal Affiliation: Vijayanagara, some of the pottery is later.

References: Morrison 1995:71; Sinopoli and Morrison 2006:439-40.

Illustrations: Figure 4.38.

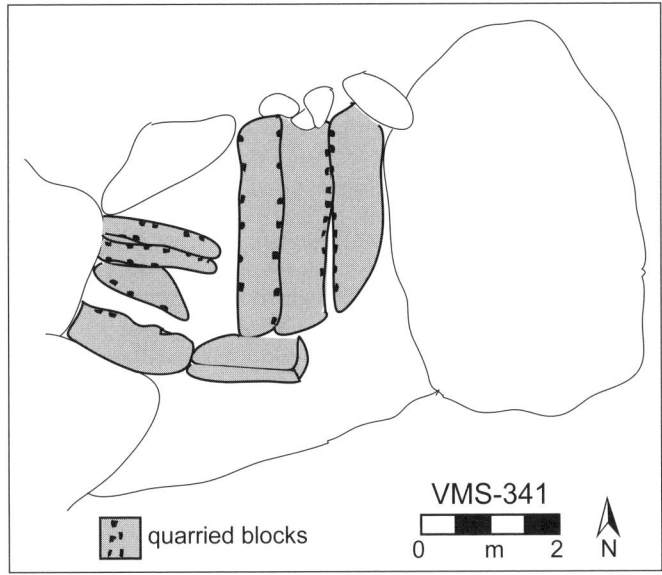

(*Left*) Figure 4.39. VMS-341, plan.
(*Above*) Plate 4.25. VMS-341, view of quarried slabs.

SITE: VMS-341   Block: T   **Transect:** 9
  Primary Site Use: Industrial: quarry site.
  Site Dimensions: 23 × 7 m
  Setting: On sheet rock outcrop.
  Present Land Use/Disturbances: Recent quarrying in area, c. 40 m to the west of the site.
  Site Description: Stone quarry site. Quarrying activities ceased in progress as several slabs have been partly cut and left *in situ*. The site consists of a large sheet rock outcrop, one portion of which has been cut into three slabs. Nearby are three additional quarried boulders. Each has distinctive Vijayanagara style quarry marks, ranging from 0.03 to 0.06 m wide × 0.03-0.05 m deep and spaced 0.15-0.25 m apart. In many cases, multiple shallow pick marks are found between quarry marks. Ceramics were found under the quarried slabs of the sheet rock and in the cracks between the slabs, with a second scatter located *c.* 12 m to the northeast of the quarried area.
  Artifacts: 100% collection of both ceramic scatters. 2150 g ceramics; wares: 87 black plain ware, 49 brown plain ware. Diagnostics: 6 jars.
  Temporal Affiliation: Vijayanagara; some pottery may be associated with recent quarrying.
  References: Sinopoli and Morrison 2006a:442.
  Illustrations: Figure 4.39; Plate 4.25.

SITE: VMS-342   Block: T   **Transect:** 9
  Primary Site Use: Agricultural/water control: reservoir embankment.
  Site Dimensions: 62 × 13 m
  Setting: Area slopes gently down to north and east; embankment spans area between boulder outcrops.
  Present Land Use/Disturbances: South of Tungabhadra High Level Canal; embankment is cut by a small breach and is partially obscured by canal construction debris.
  Site Description: Reservoir embankment. This roughly east-west embankment spans an area between two boulder outcrops. The stone-faced south side is preserved to c. 1-1.2 m tall, with four to six courses of medium to large rounded and angular unmodified stones. The earthen north face is c. 10 m wide and incorporates a long line of large outcropping boulders. The catchment area enclosed by the embankment is relatively small, c. 60 × 60 m. This feature likely functioned to retain soil moisture in that basin rather than to channel water to fields to the north, where there are numerous outcropping boulders and little arable land.
  Artifacts: 100% collection; no artifacts recovered.
  Temporal Affiliation: Vijayanagara.
  References: Morrison 1995:102.
  Illustrations: Figure 4.40.

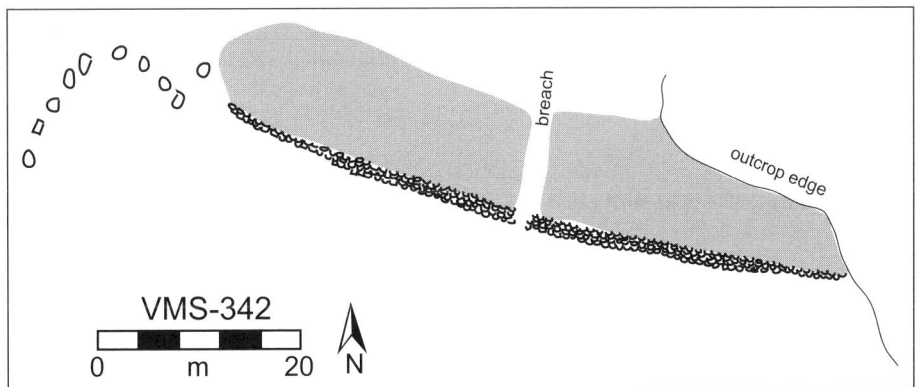

Figure 4.40. VMS-342, plan.

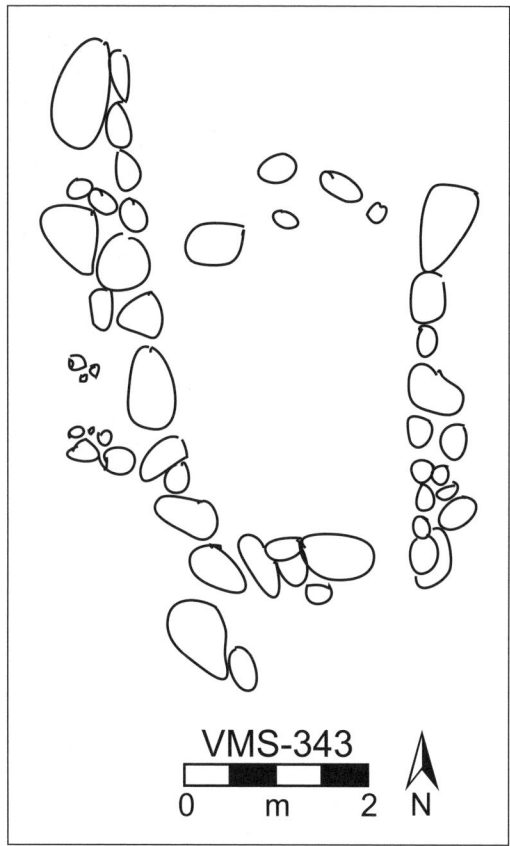

Figure 4.41. VMS-343, plan.

SITE: VMS-343   Block: T   Transect: 9
  Primary Site Use: Residential: rectangular structure.
  Site Dimensions: 8 × 5 m
  Setting: Flat area amid fallow fields.
  Present Land Use/Disturbances: In fallow fields, cart track c. 10 m south of site.
  Site Description: Single-room rectangular structures. This structure consists of two parallel north-south walls of medium-large unmodified stones, possibly linked by a third wall at their south end. The parallel walls are c. 8 m long and c. 5 m apart and consist of only one to two visible courses. They may have been a footing course for walls of impermanent materials. A cart track oriented in an east-west direction is 10 m to the south of the structure. Cobbles and boulder rubble are piled on either side of the track that heads toward reservoir embankment VMS-315 to the east.
  Artifacts: None noted.
  Temporal Affiliation: Unknown.
  References: Morrison 1995:71, 94; Sinopoli and Morrison 2006:439.
  Illustrations: Figure 4.41.

SITE: VMS-344   Block: T   Transect: 9-11
  Primary Site Use: Agricultural: terrace system.
  Site Dimensions: 320 × 280 m
  Setting: Slopes gently down toward east; site is located upslope from (to the west) reservoir embankment VMS-315, with which it was possibly associated.
  Present Land Use/Disturbances: Area is largely fallow, with a small part uncultivated.
  Site Description: Extensive terrace system. This site consists of five long parallel roughly north-south oriented walls spaced from 30 to 50 m apart and extending for a length of c. 150 m. These walls are bounded to the north and south by perpendicular east-west walls. On the northeast side, two parallel east-west walls form boundaries for a cart track that runs between them (unmapped). The walls consist of one to two courses of unmodified, small-medium stones and are partly silted in and buried in some areas.

  Although these features are clearly still being maintained and may define contemporary field boundaries, their location relative to reservoir embankment VMS-315 suggests they may have a long history of use; the north-south walls in particular are well situated to slow the rate of runoff into the reservoir basin and hence, limit silt accumulation in the reservoir bed. The walls defining the cart track are spaced 12 m apart; the track may extend as far west as fortification wall VMS-339.

  Several small rectilinear structures are associated with the terrace system. A small structure is found in the southwest corner of the site in an area of outcropping stones and sheet rock. It consists of three walls (west, south and east) constructed of large (0.50-0.80 m) unmodified and split stones, with small cobbles used as chinking. It is c. 4.5 m north-south by 2.5 m east-west, and the single course of stones is likely a foundation wall for a seasonal residence. A second better preserved and more recent looking structure (c. 4 × 2.5 m) is located in the south central area of the site. It is constructed of rubble, with mud infill, and survives to a height of five to six irregular courses of small-large unmodified stones. Two other similar rubble wall structures in varying states of preservation are also present.
  Artifacts: A few body sherds were seen in the fields of the system, but were not collected. One black body sherd was found near the structure in the southwest corner of the system (structure 1) as well as an angular basalt fragment with a circular groove, 4 cm in diameter, cut into it. Two sherds were noted near structure 2, as well as some drilled basalt pieces similar to that found near structure 1. No systematic collections were made.
  Temporal Affiliation: Although currently maintained, this terrace system probably dates to the Vijayanagara period, and was associated with VMS-315.
  References: Morrison 1995:94-95, 102; Sinopoli and Morrison 2006:439, 442.
  Illustrations: Figure 4.42; Plate 4.26.

Figure 4.42. VMS-344, plan.

Plate 4.26. VMS-344, small structure on west edge of terrace system.

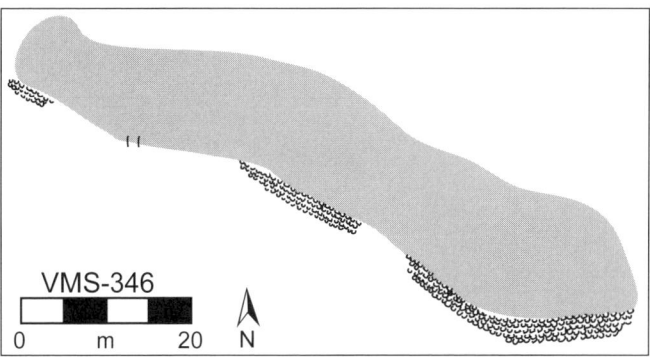

Figure 4.43. VMS-346, plan.

SITE: VMS-345   Block: T   Transect: 9-11
   Primary Site Use: Transport?: wall.
   Site Dimensions: c. 750 × 3 m
   Setting: Wall skirts the northeast side of an outcrop ridge near the base of its steeper slopes. Terrain slopes down to north of wall to narrow valley with fallow fields.
   Present Land Use/Disturbances: Collapsed in places.
   Site Description: Walls. This long stone wall skirts the northeast side of an outcrop ridge near the base of its steeper slopes. It is composed of medium and large unmodified stones and incorporates natural boulders in places. Near its west end, it may reach four to five courses in height (c. 0.95 m); to the east there are no more than one to two courses and the wall is much less distinct.

In most places, the area to the south of the wall (upslope) is characterized by a flat or roughly level surface often three or more meters wide, suggesting that the wall may have been a retaining wall for a path or cart track, useful for circumnavigating the low-lying agricultural fields during the rainy season and for providing access to settlement VMS-365 to the east. The site is very likely associated with similar sites VMS-353 and VMS-348.
   Artifacts: No collections made. A few nondiagnostic body sherds were noted.
   Temporal Affiliation: Vijayanagara, probably associated with settlement VMS-365.
   References: Morrison 1995:66, 79; Sinopoli 2006b:525-26, 532; Sinopoli and Morrison 2006a:440.

SITE: VMS-346   Block: T   Transect: 10
   Primary Site Use: Agricultural: reservoir embankment.
   Site Dimensions: 72 × 15 m
   Setting: Narrow valley sloping down toward northeast.
   Present Land Use/Disturbances: Fallow fields surround embankment; a c. 15 m wide channel has been cut through the embankment near its west end.
   Site Description: Reservoir embankment. The stepped stone south face of this reservoir embankment (oriented 26° north of west) is c. 1.4 m high, with up to seven courses of unmodified small to medium stones. The embankment reaches a maximum width of c. 12 m. A portion of a stone-lined water channel is evident near the west end of the embankment and may be original. The embankment may have been a water/soil control feature rather than a formal reservoir.
   Artifacts: 100% collection. No artifacts observed.
   Temporal Affiliation: Vijayanagara.
   References: Morrison 1995:97, 102.
   Illustrations: Figure 4.43.

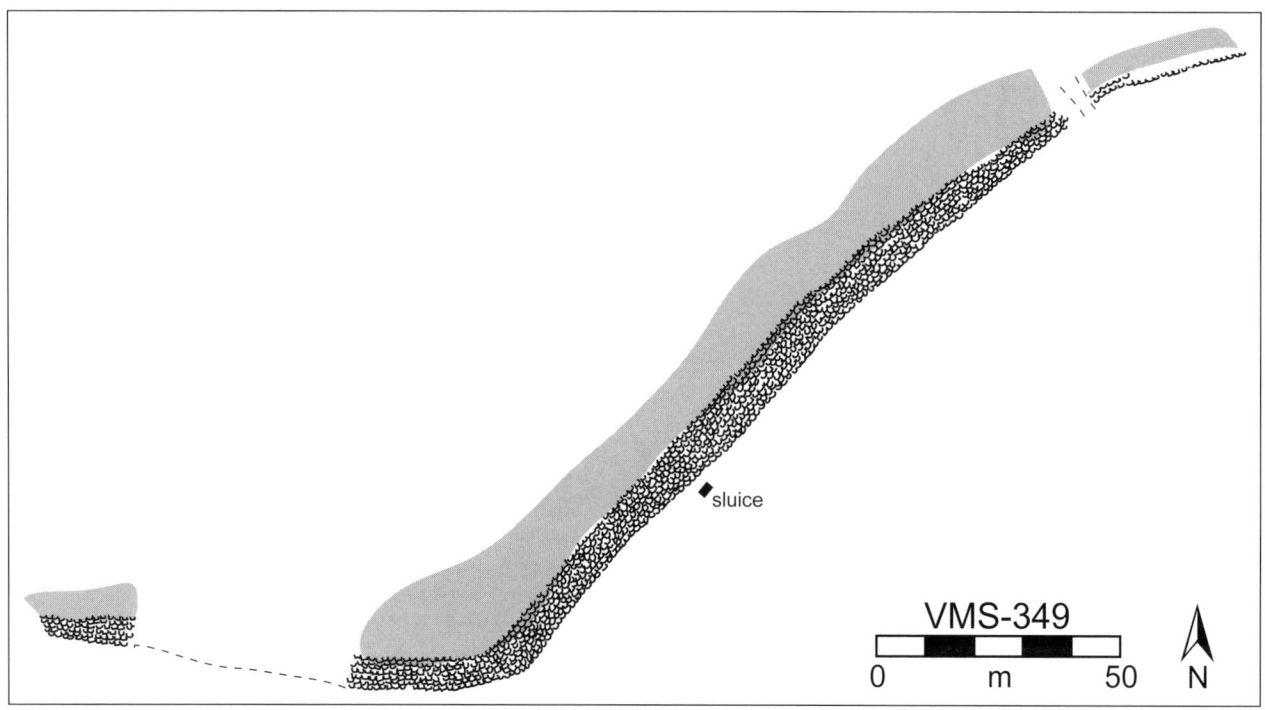

Figure 4.44. VMS-349, plan.

SITE: VMS-347   Block: T   Transect: 11
Primary Site Use: Agricultural: soil control walls.
Site Dimensions: c. 120 × 110 m
Setting: In drainage basin, terrain slopes gently down to northeast.
Present Land Use/Disturbances: Surrounding area is uncultivated; gaps in walls due to erosion.
Site Description: Soil retention walls. Two walls that cross a shallow drainage, located just east of the long fortification wall VMS-339 and perhaps contemporary with it. The walls are spaced c. 100 m apart (with a possible third wall between them) and are oriented perpendicular to the drainage slope (26° north of west). They incorporate large boulders in places and are constructed of angular and rounded medium sized stones, only two to three courses high (0.3-0.4 m). The walls are heavily silted and largely covered with grass and both are broken or eroded in places by the course of the modern drainage gully. They likely functioned as small terrace or soil control walls.
Artifacts: 100% collection. <50 g ceramics; wares: 1 brown plain ware.
Temporal Affiliation: Unknown; heavy silting of walls suggests that a Vijayanagara date is possible. May be part of system associated with reservoir VMS-315.
References: Morrison 1995:95, 97, 102.

SITE: VMS-348   Block: T   Transect: 12-13
Primary Site Use: Transport: wall/roadway.
Site Dimensions: 260 × 1 m
Setting: Along north base of outcrop to the west of settlement VMS-365.
Present Land Use/Disturbances: Wall is breached in a few places and has been cut by a footpath; parts may have been mined to form a later animal pen.
Site Description: Long wall. This wall runs along the north base of a high outcrop forming a low flat terraced area to its south. It is likely associated with similar walls VMS-345 and VMS-353. The single-faced wall is constructed of medium to large unmodified angular and rounded granite stones (c. 0.4-1.0 m). Up to four irregular courses are preserved in some areas. The wall likely defined the north edge of a pathway that skirted the outcrop and led to settlement VMS-365.
Artifacts: No artifacts observed; no collections made.
Temporal Affiliation: Vijayanagara.
References: Morrison 1995:66, 79; Sinopoli 2006b:525-26, 532; Sinopoli and Morrison 2006a:440.

SITE: VMS-349   Block: T-Y   Transect: 13-15
Primary Site Use: Agricultural: reservoir embankment.
Site Dimensions: 300 × 20 m
Setting: Embankment spans a valley between high outcrop ridge on the west and slightly higher ground with scattered outcrops to the east. The valley slopes down from southeast to northwest.
Present Land Use/Disturbances: A road cuts through the embankment near its east end; a large breach is found near west end.
Site Description: Reservoir embankment. This embankment extends in a broad arc from southwest to the northeast, with a predominant orientation of 40° north of east. At its highest, along the more west section, the stepped stone southeast face of the embankment is c. 4 m high, with ten to twelve courses of large unmodified stones. Stepping is pronounced; in some areas, courses are offset by as much as 0.5 m from the one below them.

A sluice gate is located near the midpoint of the embankment. Its columns are dressed but unsculpted and are spaced 1.16 m apart; the lintel and cross slab are missing. A fallen slab lies in front of the columns.
Artifacts: 100% collection; no artifacts recovered.
Temporal Affiliation: Vijayanagara.
References: Morrison 1995:71, 95, 102; Sinopoli 1993a; Sinopoli 2006b:525, 527, 532, 535.
Illustrations: Figure 4.44.

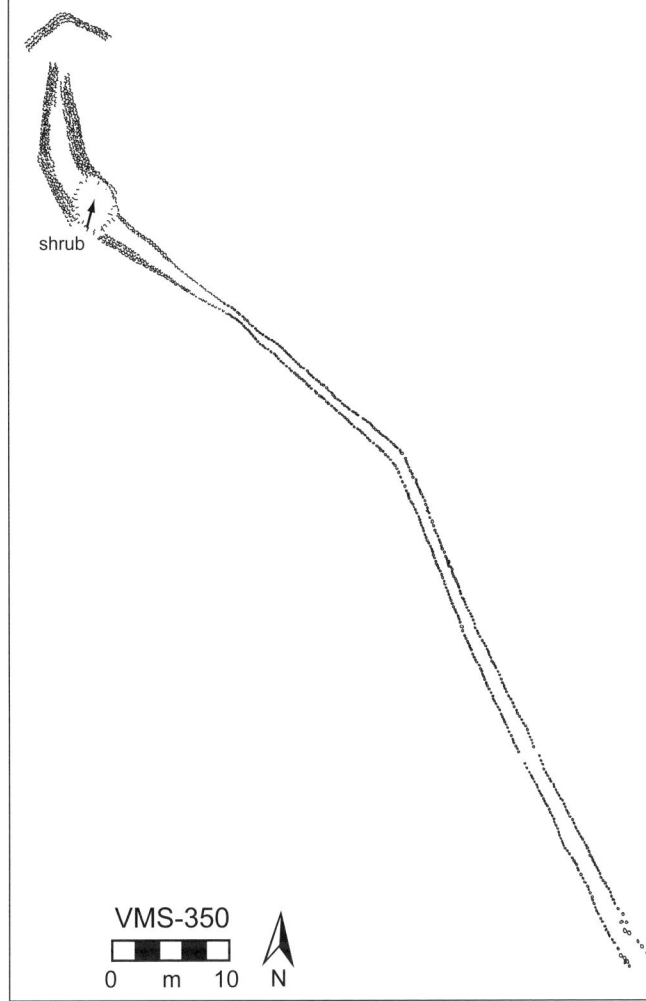

Figure 4.45. VMS-350, plan.

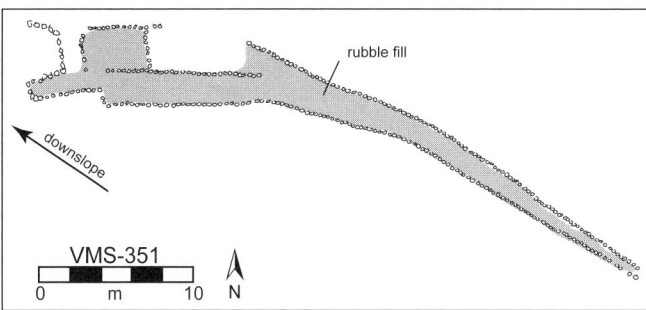

Figure 4.46. VMS-351, plan.

SITE: VMS-350 **Block:** T **Transect:** 12
Primary Site Use: Transport/agricultural?: wall.
Site Dimensions: 94 × 6 m
Setting: On a low flat-topped ridge to the east of drainage leading into basin of reservoir VMS-315.
Present Land Use/Disturbances: Some stones have been removed; walls are partly collapsed and overgrown in places.
Site Description: Double-faced wall with earth and rubble fill. This long wide wall has a dominant orientation of 30° west of north. In the southeast, the wall is one course high (c. 0.35 m high) and 1.2-1.4 m wide. Toward the northwest, as the wall extends down the slope of the ridge, three to five courses are present (1 m high) and the wall expands to 5 m wide and is stepped on both faces. A small stepped and angled 8 m long wall is located 4 m north of the northeast end of the main wall. The function of the wall is unclear; it may have helped to channel water into the basin of VMS-315 or may have defined a transport route.
Artifacts: Some modern ceramics observed, not collected.
Temporal Affiliation: Probably Vijayanagara.
References: Morrison 1995:95-96, 102.
Illustrations: Figure 4.45.

SITE: VMS-351 **Block:** T **Transect:** 12
Primary Site Use: Agricultural?: wall and platform.
Site Dimensions: 40 × 5 m
Setting: Low rise above drainage sloping down to northwest toward reservoir VMS-315.
Present Land Use/Disturbances: Disturbed and overgrown.
Site Description: Walls and platform. This complex of associated walls and a platform is located on a low rise above a natural drainage channel. The dominant feature is a long double-faced rubble-filled wall oriented roughly east-west and c. 40 m long. The wall ranges from 0.8 to 2.5 m wide and from one to three courses high. At its west end it abuts the southeast corner of a rectilinear platform, c. 4 m on a side. Only the northeast and southeast walls of the platform are well preserved. A low mounded area west of the platform is bounded by a single-faced north-south wall of eight horizontal courses. Other small wall fragments extend to the west. These are also single faced with up to six visible courses. The precise function of this site is unknown. It may be associated with agricultural activities, in particular, with lifting water from the drainage to fields at a higher elevation (it is possible that the long wall defined the edges of a canal channel).
Artifacts: Very sparse scatter of ceramics. 100% collection. <50 g ceramics; wares: 2 black plain ware. Diagnostics: 1 jar.
Temporal Affiliation: Unknown; the site is clearly not in use and overgrown; may date from the Vijayanagara period.
References: Morrison 1995:96, 102.
Illustrations: Figure 4.46.

SITE: VMS-352 **Block:** T **Transect:** 12
Primary Site Use: Transport: wall.
Site Dimensions: 16 × 1 m
Setting: Gently sloping area at the north base of a high outcrop ridge.
Present Land Use/Disturbances: Fallow fields to north, uncultivated slopes to south.
Site Description: Isolated wall. This single-faced wall segment, oriented 45° north of east, consists of one course of large unmodified boulders at the northeast base of a sloping area. It may be associated with similar walls to its east and west (VMS-345, VMS-353, VMS-348) and may form the boundary of a transport route skirting the base of the high outcrop to its south.
Artifacts: None noted; no collections made.
Temporal Affiliation: Vijayanagara.
References: Morrison 1995:97; Sinopoli 2006b:525, 532.

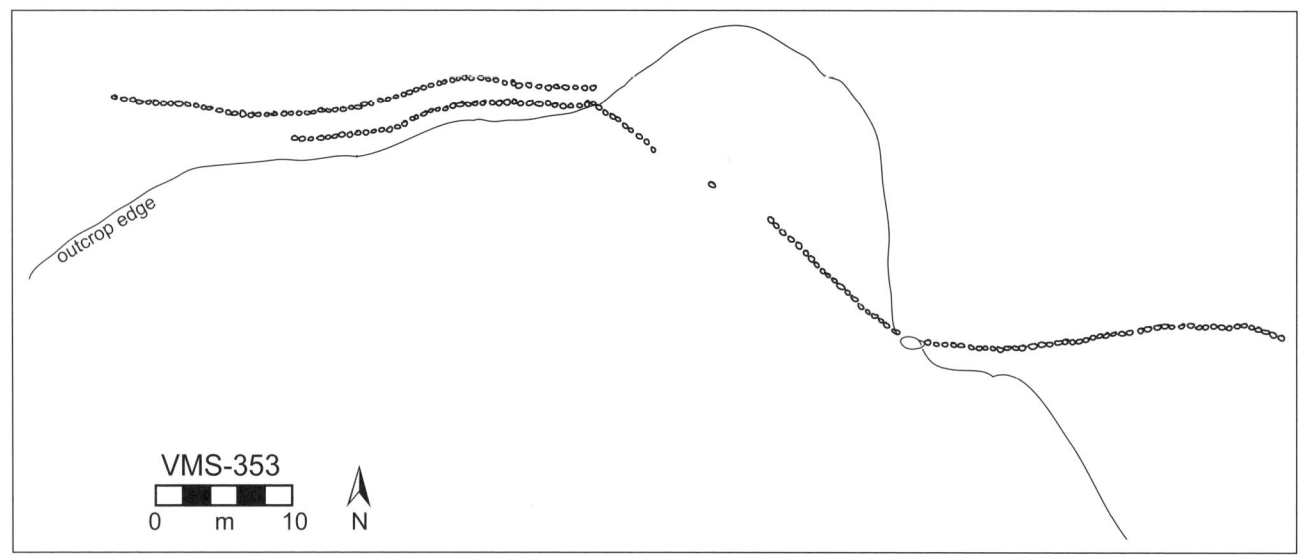

Figure 4.47. VMS-353, plan.

SITE: VMS-353   Block: T   Transect: 12-13
   Primary Site Use: Transport: walls.
   Site Dimensions: 170 × 3.5 m
   Setting: This site is located on the lower slopes near the northeast margin of large outcrop hill to the northwest of settlement VMS-365.
   Present Land Use/Disturbances: Area is uncultivated. There are some footpaths and evidence for recent quarrying.
   Site Description: Road walls. These walls are part of a larger complex of walls that ring the north base of a large outcrop hill (VMS-345, VMS-348, VMS-352). In the west third the site consists of two parallel walls spaced between 2 and 3.5 m apart, while in the east two-thirds there is a single wall. A flat earthen surface between the two walls or between the wall and the sheet rock appears to have defined a path. The walls incorporate naturally outcropping boulders and are constructed of up to four courses of medium-large unmodified or partly modified angular and rounded stones (0.5-1.0 m). Some have Vijayanagara quarry marks; there are also quarry marks on nearby sheet rock.
   Artifacts: None observed; no collections made.
   Temporal Affiliation: Vijayanagara.
   References: Morrison 1995:79; Sinopoli 2006b:525-26, 532; Sinopoli and Morrison 2006a:440.
   Illustrations: Figure 4.47.

SITE: VMS-354   Block: T   Transect: 14
   Primary Site Use: Transport?: U-shaped walls.
   Site Dimensions: 23 × 6 m
   Setting: Flat area amid modern agricultural fields.
   Present Land Use/Disturbances: Surrounding area is heavily overgrown with thorny scrub and large cacti.
   Site Description: A double-faced wall with a central U-shaped projection. This feature is oriented 35° west of north; in most places both faces of the main wall are visible, and the walls survive to a height of c. 1 m (four to five courses). The portions of the wall forming the central "U" are c. 0.6 m thick while the "wings" on either side are wider (c. 1.6 m). The projection is c. 5.5 m wide × 4.5 m deep. It does not appear to have had rubble infill, though there is considerable wall collapse and rubble accumulation so this cannot be ruled out. An isolated line of single large cobbles/boulders is located about 80 m to the southeast. This site is situated in a location that affords views in most directions, and may

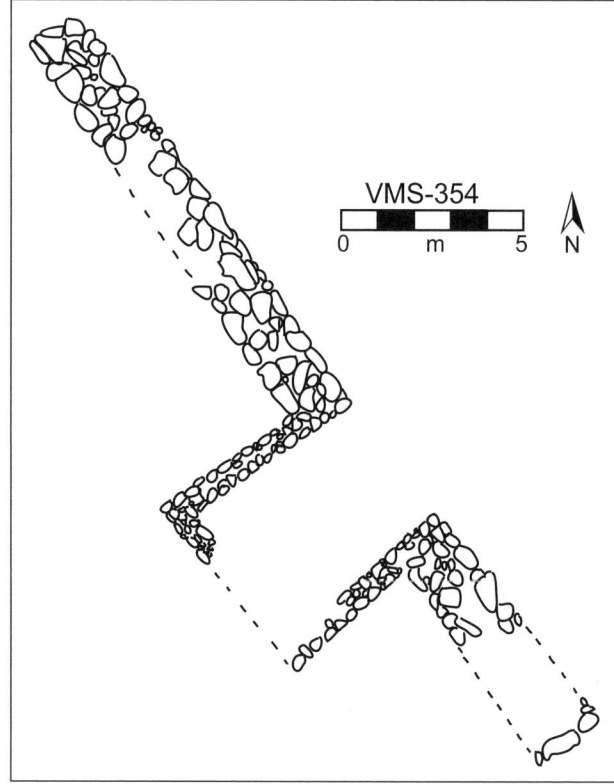

Figure 4.48. VMS 354, plan.

have been part of a line of walls or borders with defensive purposes or that defined a transport route from the southeast to northwest, perhaps between VMS-365 settlement and across embankment VMS-315. A very similar site, VMS-356, is located some 250 m to the southeast. If these sites were associated, they form a line parallel to long wall VMS-339.
   Artifacts: 100% collection; no artifacts recovered.
   Temporal Affiliation: Probably Vijayanagara.
   References: Morrison 1995:79.
   Illustrations: Figure 4.48.

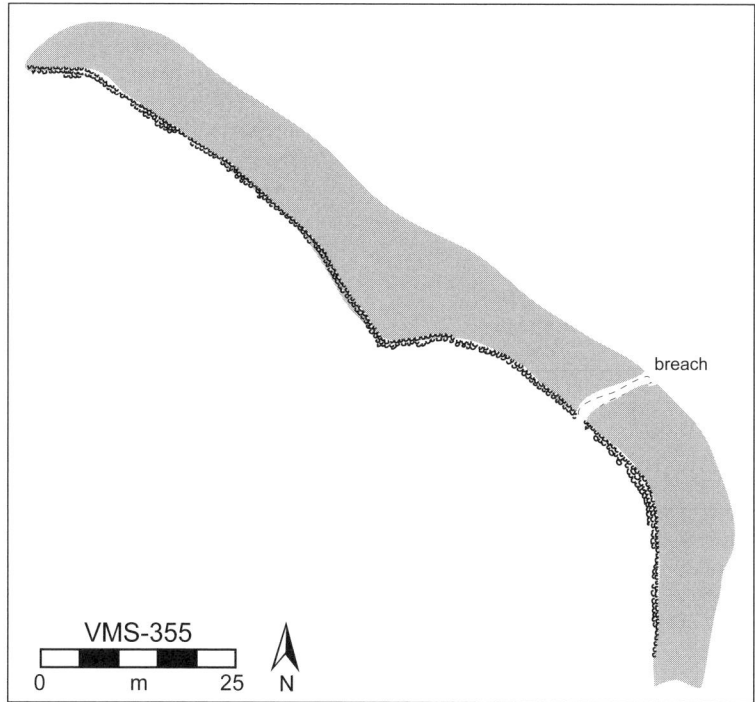

Figure 4.49. VMS-355, plan.

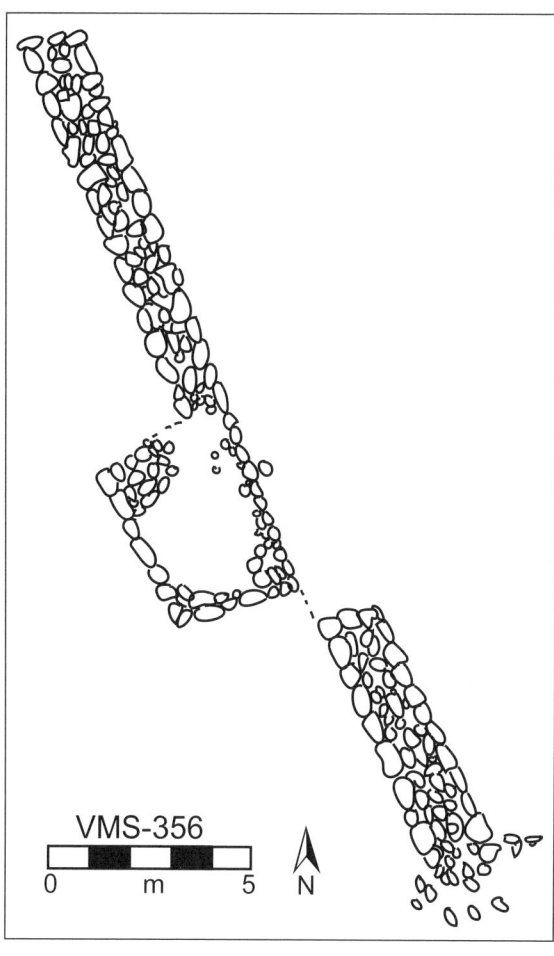

Figure 4.50. VMS-356, plan.

SITE: VMS-355   Block: T   **Transect:** 15
   Primary Site Use: Agricultural: embankment.
   Site Dimensions: 120 × 8 m
   Setting: Surface slopes gently downward to northeast.
   Present Land Use/Disturbances: Collapsed in places and breached by modern irrigation channel.
   Site Description: Embankment. This small embankment is oriented 40° south of east. Its stepped stone southwest face is up to five courses (1 m) high and constructed of small-medium unmodified stones. The earthen embankment ranges from 8 to 11 m wide. There is no sluice outlet and this site appears to have served to maintain moisture within the catchment basin rather than channel it to the northwest.
   Artifacts: Light scatter of recent artifacts (including glass and ceramics) from manuring activities in fields to east of embankment. No collections made.
   Temporal Affiliation: Vijayanagara.
   References: Morrison 1995:95, 102.
   Illustrations: Figure 4.49.

SITE: VMS-356   Block: T   **Transect:** 15
   Primary Site Use: Transport?: U-shaped walls.
   Site Dimensions: 24 × 4 m
   Setting: Flat area amid fallow fields.
   Present Land Use/Disturbances: Cart track along the east side of site; plant growth on walls has resulted in some disturbance.
   Site Description: Wall and U-shaped projection. This feature consists of two short double-faced walls oriented 25° west of north and separated by a rectangular projection or platform that extends out to the southwest. The two walls are offset slightly. Construction is of double-faced rubble-filled walls, up to 1.6 m wide, with up to four courses of unmodified angular medium-large stones. It is unclear whether the projecting structure was walled on all sides, or if it was open to the east. There is a low course of stones on this side, but it may have defined the edge of a platform rather than the base of a higher wall. VMS-356 is similar to VMS-354, which is constructed at a similar orientation, some 300 m to the northwest. A local farmer stated that VMS-356 had been a Nandi shrine. It is more probable that this structure may have lined a transport or defensive route leading to the small walled settlement to the south (VMS-365).
   Artifacts: 100% collection; no ceramics recovered; a possible quartzite core.
   Temporal Affiliation: Vijayanagara.
   References: Morrison 1995:79.
   Illustrations: Figure 4.50.

SITE: VMS-357   Block: T   **Transect:** 15/16
   Primary Site Use: Agricultural/water control: reservoir embankment.
   Site Dimensions: 250 × 20 m
   Setting: Area slopes down to the northwest.
   Present Land Use/Disturbances: Heavily disturbed; much of stone facing of embankment has been removed.
   Site Description: Reservoir embankment. This heavily disturbed reservoir embankment has a dominant orientation of 48° east of north. At its southwest end, the embankment is oriented north-south and then

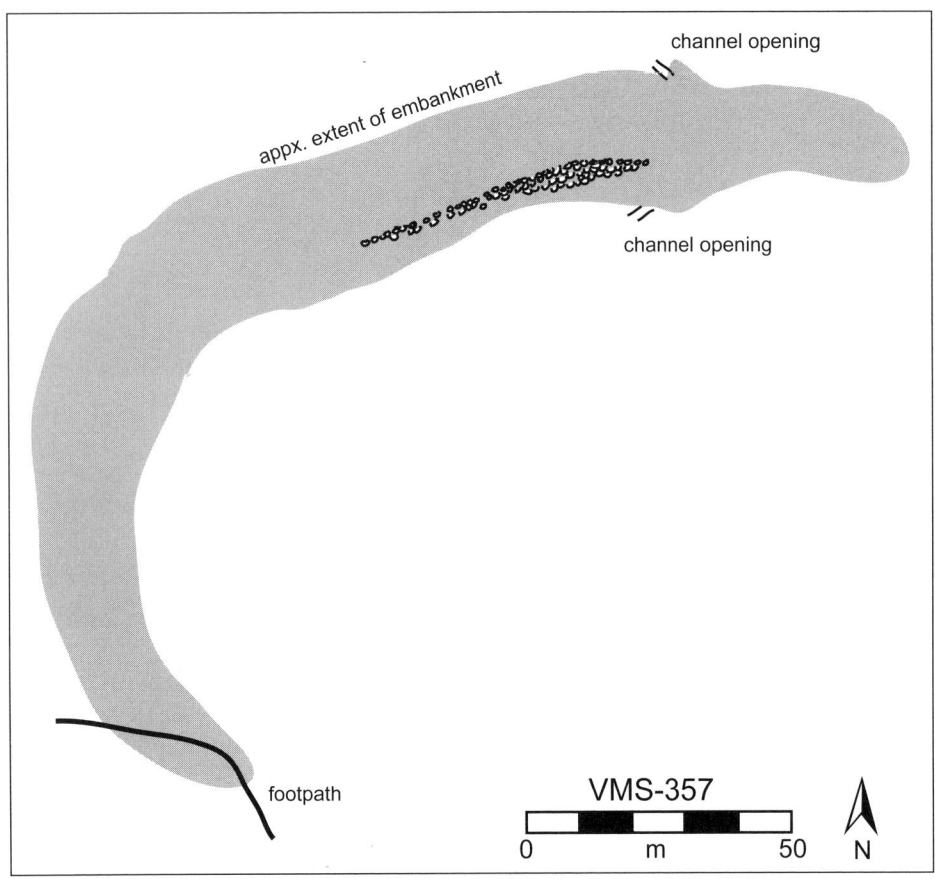

Figure 4.51. VMS-357, plan.

gradually arcs toward the east. Except for a short stretch along the east half the stone embankment face has been removed from its southeast face. Where it is intact, up to thirteen courses of small-medium unmodified stones are visible on the c. 3 m high and c. 22 m wide embankment. An outlet channel lined with flat quarried slabs with Vijayanagara quarry marks is located near the northeast end of the feature.
Artifacts: 100% collection; no artifacts recovered.
Temporal Affiliation: Vijayanagara.
References: Morrison 1995:95, 102.
Illustrations: Figure 4.51.

SITE: VMS-358   Block: T   Transect: 14
Primary Site Use: Transport: isolated walls.
Site Dimensions: c. 400 × 200 m
Setting: Flat terrain within an uncultivated zone located to south and east of settlement VMS-361, and parallel to east end of road segment VMS-326.
Present Land Use/Disturbances: A cart track runs along long wall to its south. Informants stated that there were once a number of structures here that were removed following the construction of the Tungabhadra dam (1950s) when the area was converted into agricultural fields.
Site Description: Road walls. Several long walls define transport routes that were likely associated with road VMS-326 (c. 150 m to north) and with a small Vijayanagara settlement, VMS-361. The longest wall is oriented roughly east-west. In the east part of the site, fragments of two to three large north-south walls are visible. Construction is of unmodified and modified medium to large stones; in some areas the walls are double faced. Two parallel east-west walls, spaced c. 20 m apart, are found in the west end of the site. They appear to incorporate modern and Vijayanagara elements, including some stones with Vijayanagara quarry marks near Feature 1, a collapsed Vijayanagara structure, c. 70 m from the west end of the site. The feature is a rubble mound, c. 8 m in diameter, with quarried stones, a column fragment, and a displaced sculptural element depicting Lakshmi flanked by elephants (perhaps a lintel fragment). This is mostly likely the remains of a small shrine. There are traces of other rubble piles that may demarcate cleared structural material, but no clear patterns. Toward the east end, the wall circles around the base of a small outcrop, and becomes more fragmentary.
Artifacts: Light scatter of ceramics in fields to north of the wall and between walls near the west end of site. Collections near settlement area were designated as VMS-361.
Temporal Affiliation: Vijayanagara.
Illustrations: Figure 4.52.

SITE: VMS-359   Block: T   Transect: 13
Primary Site Use: Unknown: structure on outcrop.
Site Dimensions: 40 × 20 m
Setting: Large outcrop boulder amid agricultural fields. Site is located c. 300 m due south of the outcrop containing bastion VMS-327.
Present Land Use/Disturbances: Modern quarrying on outcrop.
Site Description: Structural fragments located atop an outcropping boulder. The outcrop boulder is oriented east-west and is c. 40 m east-west × 20 m north-south and c. 12 m high; it slopes up gradually from the northwest, while the southeast face is much steeper. Few structural

Figure 4.52. VMS-358, plan.

Plate 4.27. VMS-359, column footing on outcrop.

remains are preserved. On top of the outcrop is a long slab (1.5 × 0.40 × 0.40 m) with Vijayanagara quarry marks. A similar slab lies c. 5 m to the north and two to three other fallen blocks with Vijayanagara quarry marks were noted on the southeast slope of the outcrop. Also found on the relatively flat upper surface are pecked column or slab foundations; three of these are fairly clear, defining a line 6 m long and oriented c. 25° east of north. No clear pattern for a structure is evident. Three small (c. 0.20 × 0.25 m) grinding slicks are located slightly downslope and c. 10 m east of the structure, suggesting the occurrence of food processing activities. There is a small mounded rubble area (c. 2 m diameter × 0.4 m high) on top of the outcrop. This site may have been a look-out or shrine, associated with sites VMS-326–329, VMS-358, and VMS-361.

Artifacts: 100% collection on outcrop slopes and top. <50 g ceramics; wares: 6 black plain ware. Other artifacts: 1 over-fired ceramic disk or crucible fragment.

Temporal Affiliation: Vijayanagara.
Illustrations: Plate 4.27.

SITE: VMS-360   Block: T   **Transect:** 16-18
Primary Site Use: Transport: road.
Site Dimensions: 800 × 30 m
Setting: Flat area amid cultivated or fallow fields; the eastern extension of the road was recorded as VMS-326 (above).
Present Land Use/Disturbances: Walls are disturbed and disrupted in parts.
Site Description: Road wall. This is an easterly extension of road VMS-326. Like that site, VMS-360 is parallel and to the south of the paved Nallapur road. It consists of two parallel double-faced walls, spaced c. 20-30 m apart. Near its east end is a masonry-lined spring, c. 50 × 25 m, which abuts, to the south, outcropping boulders. There is some evidence for Vijayanagara period quarrying and pecking among the boulders. In the west, the site is more disturbed. The walls defining the road are constructed of medium-large unmodified rounded stones, with one course visible. These two rows of double-faced "walls" or boundaries most likely lined a major Vijayanagara east-west road that extended from the royal center and probably toward Daroji.

Artifacts: 100% collection; no artifacts recovered.
Temporal Affiliation: Vijayanagara.
References: Morrison 1995:78, 84; Sinopoli and Morrison 2006a:440.

SITE: VMS-361   Block: T   **Transect:** 13
Primary Site Use: Residential: settlement.
Site Dimensions: 85 × 70 m
Setting: Low rise with numerous small boulder outcrops and areas of sheet rock. Associated with bastion VMS-327, step well VMS-328, and site VMS-329.
Present Land Use/Disturbances: Surrounding area is largely fallow; only foundation walls of the settlement are preserved. Rubble piles suggest many more structures originally present. Structures in arable areas were removed in the 1950s and 1960s, according to an informant.
Site Description: Settlement. This site consists of a cluster of low walls outlining the foundations of structures of a small settlement. The site is located c. 100 m south of the east-west Vijayanagara road, VMS-326, and is c. 30-40 m south of watchtower VMS-327. The site is probably associated with step well VMS-328 and foundations VMS-329, and with portions of road VMS-358 that connects the settlement with the main east-west road through the area.

The settlement is situated on a low gently sloping rise with numerous small boulder outcrops. Extant foundations are bounded on the northwest, north, and northeast by a fairly continuous wall incorporating natural boulders. Similar walls bound the area (somewhat less clearly) on the southeast. The latter abut a more substantial banked and somewhat overgrown angled wall, 5-7 m wide, at the southeast corner of the area. Although limited stretches have two faces, the boundary walls are generally single faced and composed of small-medium stones one to two courses high. Within this walled area are several wall segments. Some partition the area into smaller enclosures or compounds, while others clearly demarcate foundations of structures. At least four chambers are identifiable; three are contiguous with the northeast chamber abutting the north wall of the settlement area. The fourth, located some 10 m to the south/southwest, contains a large boulder with a mortar ground into its flat surface. The considerable amount of stone rubble within the settlement area suggests many more structures were present, though relatively few intact walls can be identified. It is likely that this area was part of a larger settlement.

Artifacts: Ceramics were present throughout the area; the scatter was heaviest in the large open area southeast of the room containing the mortar and along the north stretch of the road documented as VMS-358. Fourteen collections were made: eight within bounded walled areas (J1-J8, including a diagnostic sweep in the walled area J7; see site plan) and six 2 × 2 m units along two north-south transects in the fields southeast of major structural remains.

J1: <50 g ceramics; wares: 1 black plain ware. Diagnostics: 1 jar.
J2: <50 g ceramics; wares: 2 black plain ware, 3 red plain ware.
J3: 50 g ceramics; wares: 11 brown plain ware, 4 red plain ware. Diagnostics: 1 jar.
J4: 50 g ceramics; wares: 10 black plain ware, 5 brown plain ware, 5 red plain ware. Diagnostics: 3 jars.
J5: 150 g ceramics; wares: 58 black plain ware, 3 brown plain ware, 10 red plain ware, 3 red burnished ware. Diagnostics: 1 bowl, 5 jars.

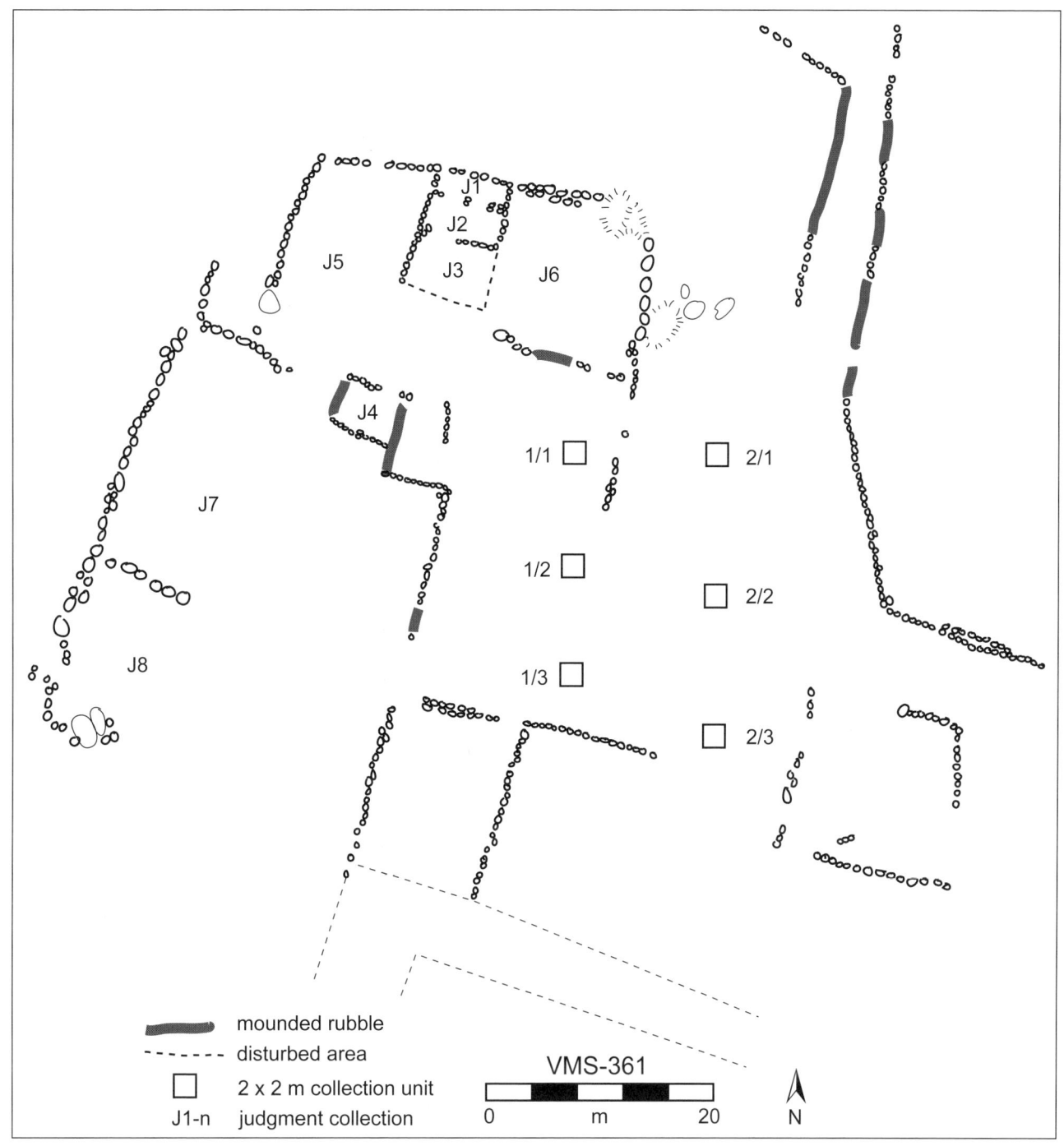

Figure 4.53. VMS-361, plan.

J6: 50 g ceramics; wares: 3 black plain ware, 17 brown plain ware, 4 red plain ware.

J7: Diagnostic collection only.

J8: 100 g ceramics; wares: 13 black plain ware. Diagnostics: 4 jars.

Transect 1 Unit 1: 700 g ceramics; wares: 293 black plain ware, 9 red plain ware.

Transect 1 Unit 2: 700 g ceramics; wares: 186 black plain ware, 10 red plain ware.

Transect 1 Unit 3: 300 g ceramics; wares: 30 black plain ware, 1 red plain ware.

Transect 2 Unit 1: 300 g ceramics; wares: 79 black plain ware, 1 red plain ware.

Transect 2 Unit 2: 150 g ceramics; wares: 64 black plain ware, 5 red plain ware.

Transect 2 Unit 3: <50 g ceramics; wares: 18 black plain ware.

Temporal Affiliation: Vijayanagara.

References: Morrison 1995:78, 84, 95, 99; Sinopoli 1997:481, 484; Sinopoli and Morrison 2006:439-40.

Illustrations: Figure 4.53.

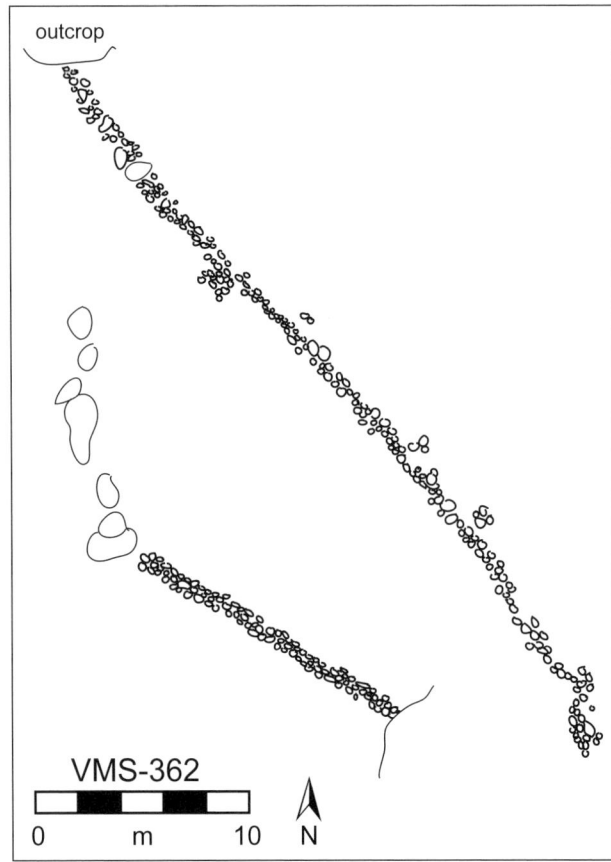

Figure 4.54. VMS-362, plan.

SITE: VMS-362   Block: T   **Transect:** 17
   Primary Site Use: Agricultural: soil control walls.
   Site Dimensions: 40 × 14 m
   Setting: Terrain slopes down to south toward a drainage channel.
   Present Land Use/Disturbances: Amid fallow fields; the southeast wall probably postdates the northeast wall. The latter is heavily silted in and has been cut by footpaths and modern runoff channels.
   Site Description: Terrace system. Two parallel walls form a small terrace system above and north of a drainage channel. The walls are oriented southeast/northwest. The north wall, though silted in to a considerable degree, is well preserved in parts, with up to four irregular courses. It is constructed of medium-large (c. 0.4-0.7 m) unmodified rounded stones. In a few places, the wall is cut by footpaths and drainage channels. The southeast wall appears to be more recent; it is not silted in and is only one to two courses high. In the hills to the north and west of the site are many terrace walls, most of which appear to be of recent construction. To the southeast is a recent (?) well and channel with abandoned field houses (not recorded). The entire area of upland slopes south of the modern High Level Canal is extensively terraced—though clearly maintained and many walls are probably recent; some walls overlay canal fill.
   Artifacts: 100% collection. <50 g ceramics; wares: 1 black plain ware.
   Temporal Affiliation: Mostly recent, perhaps with some earlier components.
   References: Morrison 1995:94, 102.
   Illustrations: Figure 4.54.

SITE: VMS-363   Block: T   **Transect:** 17
   Primary Site Use: Agricultural: soil retention wall.
   Site Dimensions: 85 × 2 m
   Setting: Area of gentle to moderate slopes; terrain slopes down to the southwest, above a natural drainage channel (northwest/southeast).
   Present Land Use/Disturbances: Channel to the west is uncultivated; fallow fields lie to the east. A road cuts through the wall in the northeast.
   Site Description: Soil retention wall. This wide wall parallels a natural drainage channel, at an area where the terrain changes slope. The wall abuts outcrop boulders on its north end. It is c. 2 m wide and oriented 16° west of north, and is stepped slightly on its west face, with up to four steps visible. In some areas it has been recently maintained, with new stones added to span breaches formed by erosion gullies. Construction is of medium-large unmodified, rounded stones, without clear coursing. The wall extends from a low outcrop on the north, c. 80 m to the south on the edge of a low rise; it acts to retain soil and limit erosion from the fields to the east. Although quite broad, it does not appear to be a road segment or fortification feature.
   Artifacts: 100% collection; no artifacts recovered.
   Temporal Affiliation: Unknown; clearly in use for some time.
   References: Morrison 1995:96, 102.

SITE: VMS-364   Block: T   **Transect:** 18
   Primary Site Use: Agricultural: reservoir embankment.
   Site Dimensions: 190 × 45 m
   Setting: Spans a narrow valley whose terrain slopes down to the north. The embankment extends between two outcrop hills.
   Present Land Use/Disturbances: Surrounding area is uncultivated. There is a large breach in the embankment with a cart track running through it. Boundary walls for the nearby reserved forest abut the embankment at its east and west edges.
   Site Description: Reservoir embankment. This high reservoir embankment spans a narrow valley between outcrops to the northeast and southwest. The embankment (oriented 35° east of north) incorporates outcropping boulders on either end. Toward the center (now largely removed) it is quite high. At least twenty-one courses of large-very large (0.50-1.2 m) angular blocks form the east stone face of the embankment. Most are unmodified, but several are roughly shaped with Vijayanagara quarry marks. Flat stone steps project out from the embankment at irregular intervals.

   A stone-lined sluice channel (0.5 m across) is located c. 30 m from the northeast end and projects c. 5 m into the reservoir bed. It is lined with rectangular granite slabs, with a semicircular slab above the top piece and covered with a 0.08 m layer of mortar and plaster and pebbles; more stone blocks are laid on top of the mortar. No sluice gate or columns are present. The top of the embankment is quite broad (c. 15 m across), and the embankment base reaches a width of 50 m and a height of c. 10-11 m. A low stone wall (two to three courses high) defines the edge of the earthen embankment on the northwest side. On this side, beyond the northeast end of the embankment, is an area of gently sloping sheet rock. Along the rock, oriented c. 30 east of north, are two parallel low retaining walls (three to four courses high) spaced 2 m apart. They define a low flat area of sheet rock, but other than quarry marks, there is no evidence for use or habitation, and their function is unknown. These walls continue beyond the embankment along the northwest face of the outcrop.

   Near the north end of the earthen embankment is a square structure, constructed of large rectangular slabs set on end (c. 2 m long × 0.60 m high × 0.20 m across) on a low platform of plaster and brick. There are several long fallen slabs with traces of plaster nearby. Other partly

Block T: Site Summaries 141

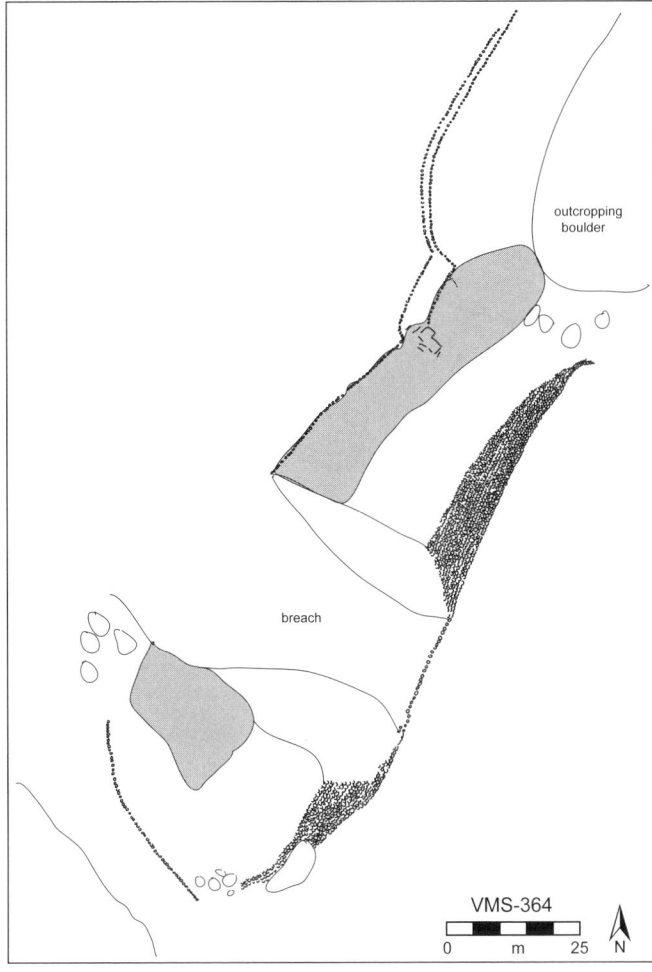

Figure 4.55. VMS-364, plan.

Plate 4.28. VMS-364, detail of embankment face.

Site Description: Walled settlement. This small settlement consists of three main areas: (1) the settlement core: a walled circular area containing densely packed rubble wall structures; (2) a smaller settlement area to the northwest; and (3) a small embankment to the northeast of the walled area. Also associated with this site are sites VMS-348 and VMS-353, long walls that define paths along the outcrop to the northwest of the settlement, and reservoir embankment VMS-349.

Area 1: The settlement core is c. 140 m in diameter and enclosed within a massive double-faced enclosure wall, 1-2 m wide, which abuts and incorporates the granite hill to the south and west of the settlement, and extends to the edge of reservoir VMS-349 in the southeast. South of the settlement, a similarly constructed rectangular enclosure extends south from the main wall. Inside the enclosure are a number of rubble mounds and platforms, with numerous wall segments, suggesting the presence of a large number of structures (estimates are difficult because of abundant wall fall and disturbance). The area appears to have been divided into several large compounds by rubble walls. Fragments of plaster flooring and ceramic water pipes are visible. In the northeast quadrant of the settlement core is a modern structure containing a large heavily painted Hanuman image. The image is obscured by layers of paint, so its features cannot be clearly discerned; it may be of Vijayanagara age. The structure incorporates some Vijayanagara architectural elements, including slabs with quarry marks and a molding or lintel fragment with corner medallions. On the northwest boundary of the circular enclosure walls are found additional wall sections, some of which appear to define modern agricultural fields. Low mounds are present in the fields, suggesting the remains of structures. This area is also characterized by high surface densities of ceramics.

Area 2: Area of structures located northwest of the core settlement area on a relatively flat expanse of sheet rock and enclosed by enclosure and terrace walls, constructed of large unmodified boulders. At least ten structures are visible; all consist of a single course of unmodified small-medium stones, suggesting that these were foundation courses. Structures range in size from c. 5 × 5 to 5 × 11 m. A circular stone mortar was noted near one of the structures.

Area 3: To the northeast of the main settlement area is a small east-west embankment that spans a gully. It is c. 1.2 m tall, with its stepped stone south face constructed of up to five courses of unmodified medium-large stones. North of the embankment is an area of sheet rock, suggesting this was primarily a water retention feature rather than an agricultural reservoir.

buried slabs define a channel toward the embankment. This structure probably overlies the brick- and plaster-lined water channel where it comes out of the edge of the earthen embankment and may be associated with a basin for water distribution. On its south end, the embankment is terminated by a faced wall (seven courses high and oriented c. 30° west of north), c. 40 m long. It may define a road or passageway across the outcrop above the reservoir.

Artifacts: 100% collection. <50 g ceramics; wares: 3 black plain ware.
Temporal Affiliation: Vijayanagara.
References: Morrison 1995:102; Sinopoli and Morrison 2006a:440, 442, 455.
Illustrations: Figure 4.55; Plate 4.28.

SITE: VMS-365   Block: T   Transect: 13/14
Primary Site Use: Residential: settlement.
Site Dimensions: 425 × 220 m
Setting: Located on the east edge of a large outcrop hill, the settlement incorporates a portion of the outcrop and areas of sheet rock as well as low-lying open space.
Present Land Use/Disturbances: Foot and cart paths pass through the site. There has been recent quarrying of rubble wall foundations. A modern shrine incorporates a Vijayanagara Hanuman image; portions of the settlement may be disturbed by agricultural activities.

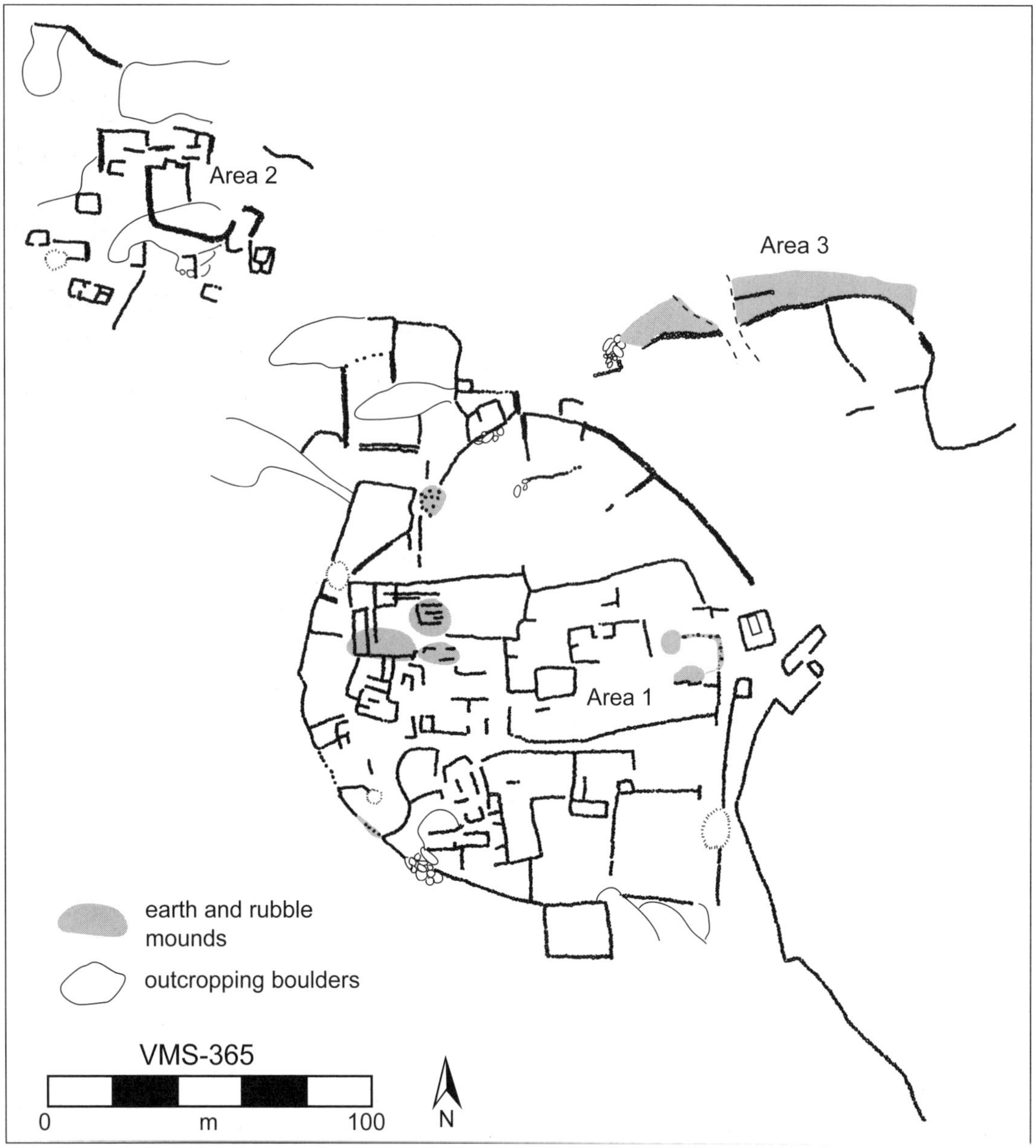

(*Left*) Figure 4.56. VMS-365, plan.

(*Below*) Plate 4.29. VMS-365, enclosure wall of main settlement area.

Artifacts: All surface ceramics were collected from a rubble wall mound in the core area (J1). A surface collection of diagnostic sherds was made in the agricultural fields to the north of the walled core area. The ceramics are consistent with a Vijayanagara date.

J1: 350 g ceramics; wares: 94 black plain ware, 8 red plain ware, 1 coarse ware, 1 black burnished ware, 1 red burnished ware. Diagnostics: 3 bowls, 5 jars.

Diagnostic Collection: n = 110. Forms documented include: shallow bowls (5), other bowls (6), flange rim jars (43), straight rim jars (23), and round rim jars (4). Ceramics appear to be Vijayanagara in date. One stone bowl fragment also collected.

Temporal Affiliation: Vijayanagara.

References: Morrison 1995:66-67, 78-79, 95, 99; Sinopoli 1997:481, 484; Sinopoli 2006b; Sinopoli and Morrison 2006:439-40, 443.

Illustrations: Figure 4.56; Plates 4.29-4.31.

(*Above*) Plate 4.30. VMS-365, rubble wall structure in northern area of site.

(*Below*) Plate 4.31. VMS-365, striding Hanuman image in modern shrine.

Plate 4.32. VMS-366, Ganesha and large Nandi image; smaller Nandi is to left of Ganesha.

SITE: VMS-366   Block: T   Transect: 4
   Primary Site Use: Religious: isolated sculptures.
   Site Dimensions: 16 × 11 m
   Setting: Flat area amid agricultural fields, south of low outcrop hill.
   Present Land Use/Disturbances: Structure is of recent construction. The images are painted and in worship.
   Site Description: Vijayanagara period sculptures. This site consists of a recently constructed shrine containing Vijayanagara sculptures and a lamp column and platform. Within a three-walled structure that opens to the south are images of a striding Hanuman (c. 1 m high), a broken image of which only the feet and the base molding remain intact (c. 0.2 m high), Nandi (0.65 m long × 0.6 m high), Ganesha (0.18 m high × 0.30 m wide), and smaller Nandi (0.25 m wide × 0.20 m high). Fifteen naga images are located some 2 m west of the structure. A small stone wall runs to the south of these images. A stone grinding wheel (c. 0.75 m in diameter) is c. 2 m northeast of the structure. The platform and lamp column are 3 m south of the structure. The platform has a rectilinear base (1.5 m^2) surmounted by a painted, octagonal column, with a square base (0.5 m across).
   Artifacts: Sparse to moderate scatter of sherds. One piece of slag recovered. The scatter appears to extend into the fields in most directions, suggesting this may have been a denser area of settlement during Vijayanagara times. Diagnostic collection was made within a radius of 5 m around the shrine and lamp column.
   Temporal Affiliation: Vijayanagara with later construction.
   Illustrations: Plate 4.32.

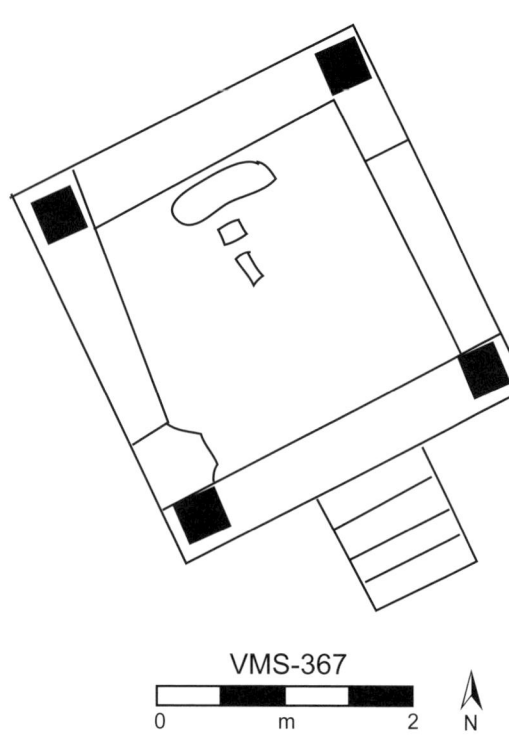

(*Left*) Figure 4.57. VMS-367, plan.

(*Right*) Plate 4.33. VMS-367, columned structure.

SITE: VMS-367   Block: T   **Transect:** 3
  Primary Site Use: Religious: shrine.
  Site Dimensions: 3.4 × 3.3 m
  Setting: Flat area amid cultivated rice fields.
  Present Land Use/Disturbances: Threshing floor next to structure; images are in worship.
  Site Description: 2 × 2 column mandapa. The columns of this small structure, c. 3.4 × 3.3 m (oriented 26° west of north), rest on a low platform (0.8 m high) with simple beveled moldings on top and bottom and corner medallions. The unsculpted columns are square, c. 0.35 m at the base and 1.7 m high. They are irregular, with dressing and quarry marks visible, and are topped by rectangular brackets linked by cross-slabs. The roof is of rectangular slabs. On the south side, four steps lead up to the platform. Two displaced Vijayanagara sculptures are within the structure. The first is a slab, probably once embedded in a wall, c. 0.4 m high, sculpted with images of Rama and Sita. A small headless Nandi sits facing the slab.
  Artifacts: 100% collection; no artifacts visible.
  Temporal Affiliation: Vijayanagara.
  Illustrations: Figure 4.57; Plate 4.33.

SITE: VMS-368   Block: T   **Transect:** 3
  Primary Site Use: Religious: temple.
  Site Dimensions: 11 × 11 m
  Setting: Flat area within agricultural fields.
  Present Land Use/Disturbances: Husks and straw piled within the antechamber. The structure is heavily disturbed; many of the wall slabs have been removed; columns have fallen and several ceiling slabs are missing.
  Site Description: Three-chamber temple. This northeast-facing temple has a 4 × 4 column antechamber, a 2 × 2 column double-walled sanctuary, and a 3 × 2 column chamber, apparently a later addition, which abuts the structure on the west. The columns of this addition are not quite aligned with the main antechamber.
  The structure is built on a low platform, now buried. The columns of the antechamber are square with octagonal insets. They are unsculpted, except for one unfinished (?) lotus medallion panel. The central two rows of columns have cruciform brackets, while atop the remainder are rectangular blocks. The ceiling is preserved over four bays; the central bay had an offset square ceiling, while elsewhere it consists of east-west oriented rectangular slabs, c. 2 m long × 0.40 m wide. There may have been projecting eaves in the front, as the cross beams are angled down and project out c. 0.50 m. Within the antechamber is a displaced granite image base (c. 0.56 × 0.56 m), and a slab with a sculpted Vaishnava image of the deity Srinivasa-Tiruvengalanatha (0.70 × 0.55 × 0.21 m).
  The 2 × 2 column sanctuary has double-faced slab walls, with brick fill. A lotus medallion is sculpted over the lintel. The ceiling was of offset square plan, though central portions are missing, providing a view into the shikara. The brick and plastered shikara is c. 7 m high. Sanctuary interior walls were plastered.
  The west chamber of the structure is a 3 × 2 column addition that abuts the west side of the antechamber. Its columns are square in plan and are plastered. There is no formal doorway or lintel.
  Artifacts: 100% collection; no artifacts recovered.
  Temporal Affiliation: Vijayanagara.
  Illustrations: Figure 4.58; Plate 4.34.

Block T: Site Summaries

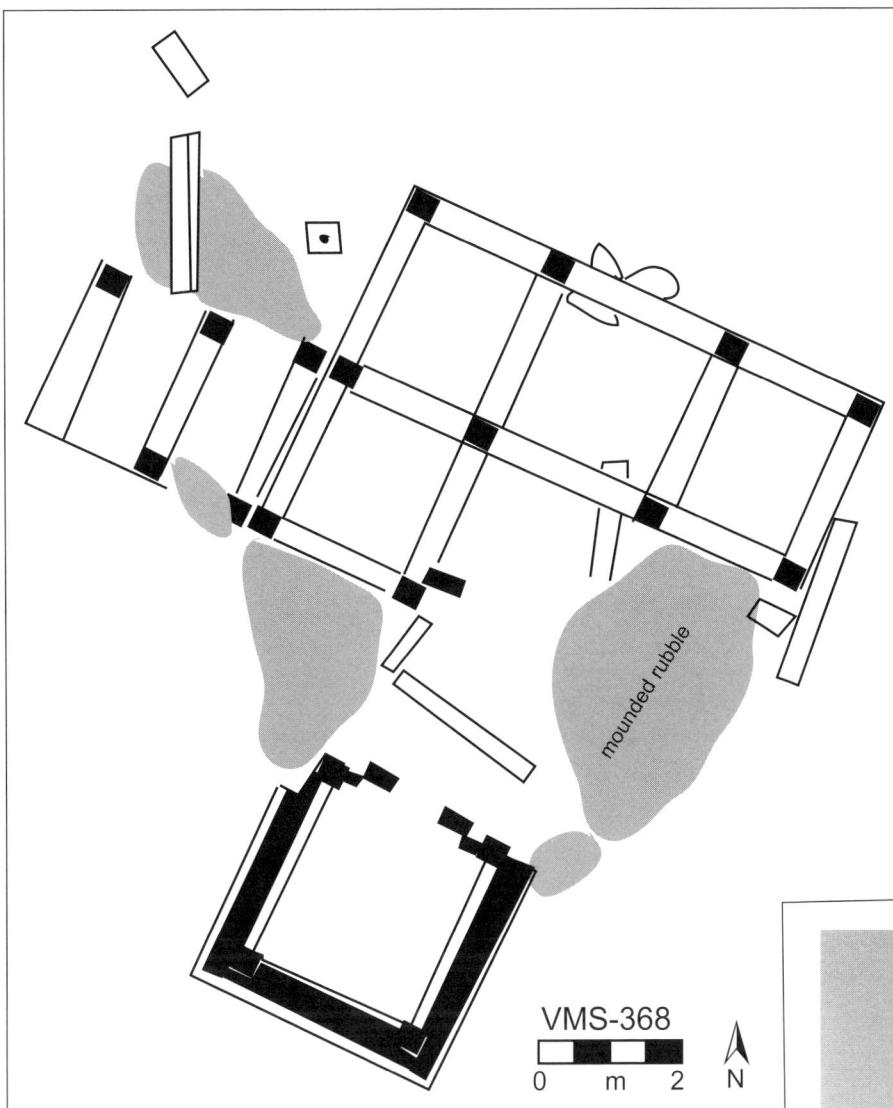

Figure 4.58. VMS-368, plan.

Plate 4.34. VMS-368, temple shikara and sanctuary.

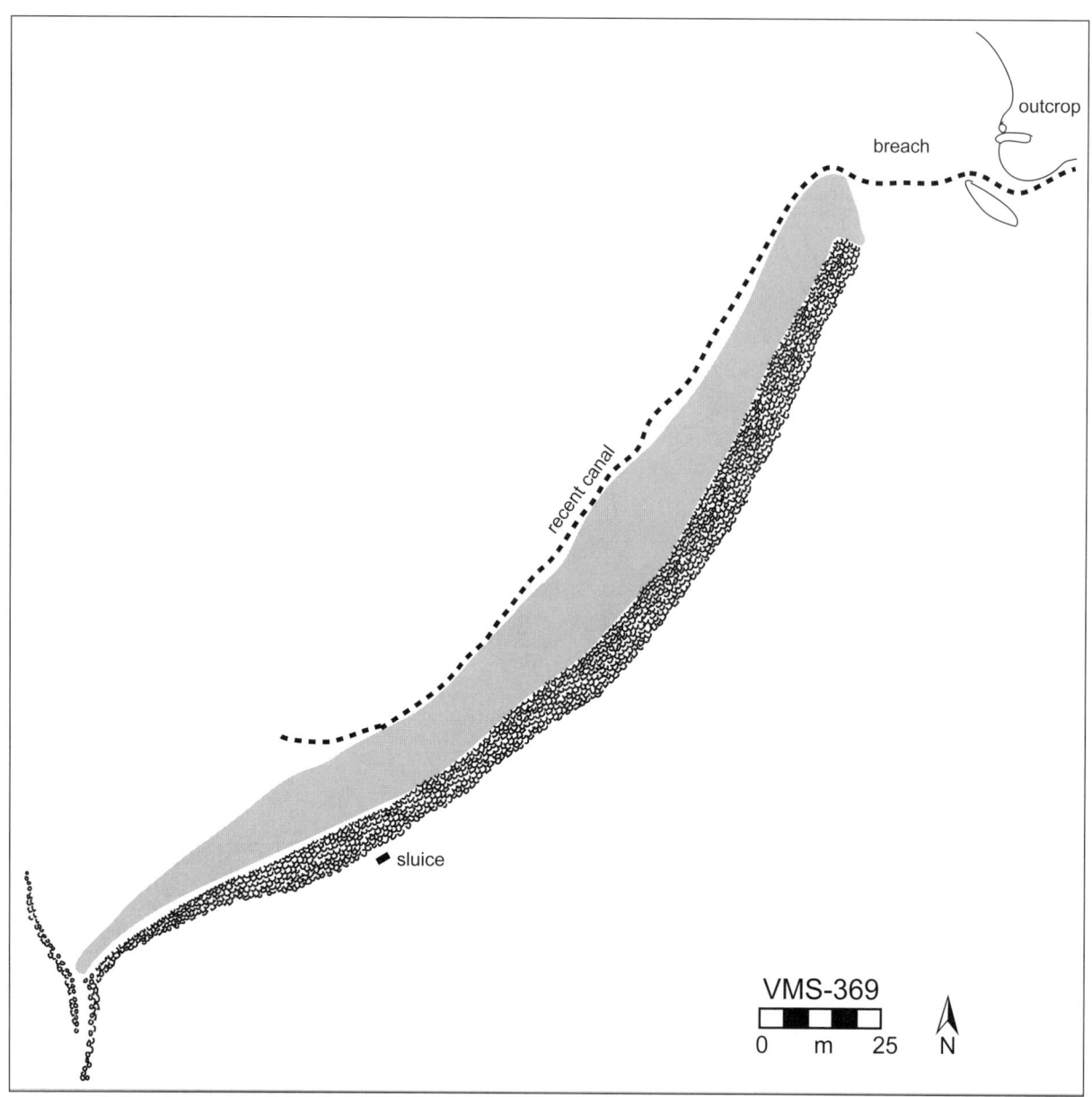

Figure 4.59. VMS-369, plan.

SITE: VMS-369   Block: T   Transect: 2
Primary Site Use: Agricultural: reservoir embankment.
Site Dimensions: c. 260 × 30 m
Setting: Reservoir abuts outcrop on the northeast, and spans a gently sloping valley with terrain sloping down to the southwest.
Present Land Use/Disturbances: Area around embankment is under cultivation. A modern canal cuts through northeast edge of the embankment, a footpath runs along the top, and the sluice gate is currently in worship. Some mining of the earthen embankment has occurred, forming a breach near the northeast end. The sluice channel has been cleared and is still operational (though the gate is not).
Site Description: Reservoir embankment. This southwest/northeast embankment channeled water from slopes to the southeast. The stone southeast face is constructed of unmodified medium-large stones (c. 0.40-1.0 m); fifteen courses are visible (5 m high). The embankment is both overgrown and silted, and it is likely that at least five more courses were originally present and are now obscured. The embankment was c. 20 m wide. On its southwest end, the stone face of the embankment extends c. 40 m to the north, to create an erosion control wall that retained soil.

A sluice gate is located c. 80 m from the southwest end of the site. The two columns and central crosspiece still stand, and the uppermost molding/crosspiece lies fallen and partly buried nearby. The columns are 3.1 m tall, square in plan, and tapering toward the top. The crudely carved fallen upper crosspiece of the sluice gate has a single bevel with corner and central medallion. The outlet of the sluice channel is visible and has been cleared with the upper slabs removed. This reservoir embankment is located in the same drainage and upslope from embankment VMS-132.
Artifacts: 100% collection; no artifacts recovered.
Temporal Affiliation: Vijayanagara.
References: Morrison 1995:95, 102.
Illustrations: Figure 4.59.

– 5 –
Block S: Site Summaries

SITE: VMS-7   Block: S   Transect: 11
  Primary Site Use: Religious: temple.
  Site Dimensions: 22 × 22 m
  Setting: Located amid level dry farmed agricultural fields.
  Present Land Use/Disturbances: The site is surrounded by agricultural fields. Vegetation is growing on the temple platform and modern walls surround the structure, extending up to the west wall of the platform. In 1993, after the following description was written, the structure was conserved by the Karnataka Directorate of Archaeology and Museums (KDAM). It has been extensively rebuilt and its core is no longer visible.
  Site Description: Temple. This large elevated temple of formal construction is built on a raised stepped platform, 2.26 m high, which provides a commanding view of the surrounding region. This platform in turn rests on an outer basement with a simple molding 0.62 m high, which extends 3 m beyond the base of the main platform. The main platform is constructed of rectangular finely dressed stones, 0.35-0.40 m in height, and ranging from 0.80 to >3.0 m in length. There are seven courses of stones, tightly fitted together without mortar or cement, capped by a 0.3 m high ledge, which juts out slightly from the platform. The platform and the structure it supports have a cruciform plan, 8 columns (north-south) by 6 columns (east-west), with the sanctuary on the north. The entry to the structure was to the south, from a now-collapsed stairway.

  The columns of the structure are very roughly finished with quarry and chisel marks evident. There are no sculptures. Two column types are present: square with octagonal insets (mostly on the west side of the structure) and simple rectangular columns (column height 2.9 m). Capitals are cruciform and roughly finished. Ceilings, where preserved, consist of north-south beams, c. 2 × 0.5 m, covered by brick and mortar. A lotus panel is carved over the door to the sanctuary; no door guardians are present. A stone doorjamb with sockets lies in the west chamber, and a grinding slick has been worn into the floor of the central portion of the structure. Portions of a drain lie amid the debris of the collapsed southern end of the structure. The temple is associated with a step well, VMS-8, which lies c. 40 m to the northwest.

  Artifacts: The temple is located c. 60 m from iron processing site VMS-121. Its platform is filled with material from that site, including slag, ceramic crucible fragments, and stone. Abundant slag is found in the fields surrounding the structure, extending over several thousand square meters. Other artifacts include a small number of ground stone implements, possibly hammer stones and hoes. Ten 2 × 2 m units were collected along four north-south transects located out at 15 m intervals (numbered from 1-4, east to west; only one unit was collected on transect 1, no materials recovered). Transect 3 intersected with the western boundary of the platform. Units were collected at 20 m intervals along each transect. Artifact densities were highest to the east and south of the structure, much lower to the north and west.
  Transect 2 Unit 1: 250 g ceramics; wares: 38 black plain ware, 4 red plain ware, 4 coarse ware. Diagnostics: 4 jars, 1 unidentifiable rim. Other artifacts: 250 g brick/furnace fragments, 2250 g slag.
  Transect 2 Unit 2: 200 g ceramics; wares: 48 black plain ware, 3 red plain ware, 2 black burnished ware. Diagnostics: 1 bowl, 2 jars. Other artifacts: 1700 g slag.
  Transect 2 Unit 3: 200 g ceramics; wares: 20 black plain ware, 1 red plain ware, 2 black burnished ware. Diagnostics: 2 bowls, 3 jars. Other artifacts: 1 over-fired sherd, 1350 g slag.
  Transect 2 Unit 4: 100 g ceramics; wares: 32 black plain ware, 2 red plain ware. Diagnostics: 5 jars. Other artifacts: 1 tuyere fragment, 650 g slag.
  Transect 2 Unit 5: 200 g ceramics; wares: 33 black plain ware, 1 red burnished ware. Diagnostics: 2 bowls, 5 jars. Other artifacts: 1750 g slag, 450 g brick, 100 g over-fired ceramics/furnace fragments.
  Transect 3 Unit 1: 300 g ceramics; wares: 17 black plain ware, 2 red plain ware. Diagnostics: 1 bowl, 1 jar. Other artifacts: 550 g slag, 200 g over-fired ceramics/furnace fragments.
  Transect 4 Unit 1: 50 g ceramics; wares: 10 black plain ware. Diagnostics: 1 jar. Other artifacts: 200 g slag, 1 brick fragment.
  Transect 4 Unit 2: <50 g ceramics; wares: 3 black plain ware. Diagnostics: 1 jar. Other artifacts: 250 g iron slag.
  Transect 4 Unit 3: <50 g ceramics; wares: 4 black plain ware. Other artifacts: 250 g iron slag, 1 quartzite core.

Plate 5.1. VMS-7, overview from west.

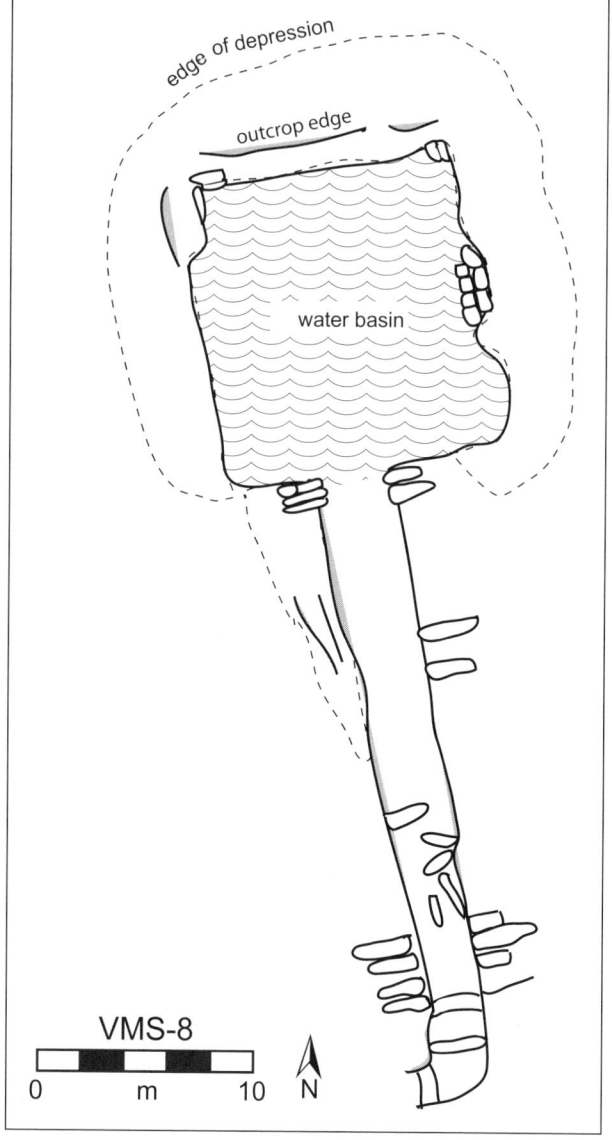

Figure 5.1. VMS-8, plan.

Transect 4 Unit 4: 50 g ceramics; wares: 10 black plain ware. Diagnostics: 2 jars. Other artifacts: 300 g slag, 100 g over-fired ceramics/furnace fragments.

Temporal Affiliation: Elaborate moldings suggest late Vijayanagara period date. VMS-7 postdates the initial use and perhaps abandonment of VMS-121.

References: Morrison 1995:85; Morrison and Sinopoli 1996:70; Sinopoli 2003:197.

Illustrations: Plate 5.1.

SITE: VMS-8   Block: S   Transect: 11
Primary Site Use: Religious/water storage: step well.
Site Dimensions: 44 × 14 m
Setting: Gently sloping, dry farmed fields.
Present Land Use/Disturbances: Fields have been cleared all around the well and a large portion of the quarried masonry blocks have slumped and fallen into the well basin; some may have been robbed. The well is heavily overgrown but still holds water.
Site Description: Large step well. The well itself is approximately square and is reached through a 28 m long sloping entry corridor. The lower part of the well is rock-cut, but its upper portion consists of regularly coursed quarried granite blocks (up to seven courses). Blocks are undressed, many with visible quarry marks. Block sizes vary greatly. Some chinking stones have been used, but no plaster or mortar is visible. The highest course of masonry is composed of long, east-west oriented slabs that project c. 0.4 m toward the interior of the well. This deep open well is entered by rock-cut steps and steps made of long stone slabs, which curve around to the west at the south end of the long entry corridor. It is likely associated with the temple, VMS-7.
Artifacts: Sparse, localized scatter of earthenware ceramics and some slag. 100% collection of area up to 5 m around the well. 100 g ceramics; wares: 9 black plain ware, 1 red plain ware, 1 brown plain ware. Diagnostics: 1 bowl, 2 jars. Other artifacts: 250 g iron slag with ceramic slag.
Temporal Affiliation: Vijayanagara.
References: Morrison 1995:85.
Illustrations: Figure 5.1; Plate 5.2.

Plate 5.2. VMS-8, view to the south looking toward VMS-7.

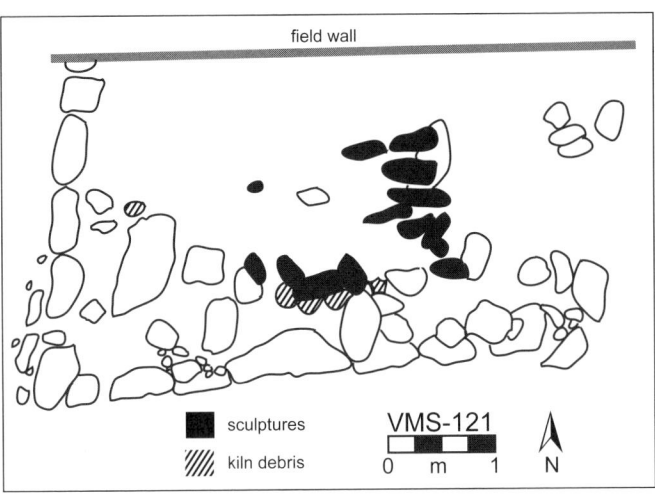

Figure 5.2. VMS-121, plan.

Plate 5.3. VMS-121, naga stones on platform.

SITE: VMS-121 Block: S Transect: 12

Primary Site Use: Industrial: iron working, religious/ritual secondary use.

Site Dimensions: 3 × 5 m (platform), surrounded by more extensive surface scatter.

Setting: Level dry farmed fields.

Present Land Use/Disturbances: A modern field wall has truncated the north edge of the structure, and plowing has dispersed the artifact and slag scatter. Power lines run to the north of the site and an unpaved road is c. 30 m to its east.

Site Description: Iron working furnace converted into a shrine. The central element of this site is a small square platform or structure bounded by cobble walls (now clearly preserved only on the south and west sides), one to two elements wide and one to two courses high. The walls define an apparently solid structure with a level upper surface c. 0.5 m above the modern ground surface. Atop the structure lies a semicircle of eleven worn naga stones and small cobbles. Set back from the naga stones is a ground stone fragment that may be intended to be a lingam. Iron, iron slag, vitrified ceramics, and parts of three tuyeres can be seen beneath the naga stones. Near the south edge of the structure is a semicircular area of smelting debris including iron, slag and vitrified ceramic. Much of the debris from this site was associated into the basement fill of the nearby temple, VMS-7. Like many other iron working sites, VMS-121 is associated with water sources (reservoirs VMS-122 and VMS-190 and the step well VMS-8).

Artifacts: Very dense scatter of iron slag and ash with a low density of ceramics surrounds the structure, but densities are particularly high to the south. The scatter extends c. 80 m north of the structure, 120 m south, 20 m east, and 80 m west, encompassing both VMS-7 and VMS-8. Area was collected as VMS-7 (see above).

Temporal Affiliation: Predates late Vijayanagara temple, VMS-7.

References: Lycett 1994; Morrison 1995:85; Morrison and Sinopoli 1992:347; Morrison and Sinopoli 1996:69-70; Sinopoli and Morrison 1995; Sinopoli 2003:196-99.

Illustrations: Figure 5.2; Plate 5.3.

SITE: VMS-122 Block: S Transect: 11

Primary Site Use: Agricultural: reservoir embankment.

Site Dimensions: 80 × 7 m

Setting: Gently sloping, dry farmed fields.

Present Land Use/Disturbances: This small reservoir has been so heavily disturbed and dismantled that it is almost unrecognizable. The disturbance appears to be a result of field clearing. The modern power canal is c. 225 m to the west; its construction blocked runoff to this small facility.

Site Description: Reservoir embankment. The embankment is visible only as a low linear earthen mound and masonry wall. The north end is higher and at this end are visible two courses of the masonry that once faced the embankment on its east side. Most of the earthen fill is now spread onto the fields on the west. The masonry on the east face is discontinuous. The lower course of stones consists of unshaped small boulders and although the upper course is heavily disturbed, it seems to consist of large cobbles. There is a more continuous single course of large stones on the west (downstream) side of the reservoir. This was either the edge of the embankment or was part of its internal structure. Four fragments of sluice gate uprights, moved from their original locations, now lie to the east of the embankment.

Step well VMS-8 is located just below the reservoir. Although this pattern of association is common, in this case the well is much larger and more elaborate than those generally associated with reservoirs. If VMS-8 and VMS-121 were contemporaneous, the iron processing site would have been situated on or near the edge of the water.

Artifacts: Dense artifact scatter with a moderate to high density of ceramics and low to moderate density of iron slag. The scatter is continuous with that of VMS-121 and VMS-7, and was not collected separately.

Temporal Affiliation: Construction is consistent with Vijayanagara affiliation. VMS-122 may predate the late Vijayanagara temple (VMS-7) and step well (VMS-8).

References: Morrison 1995:85, 91, 102.

Plate 5.4. VMS-123, bastions southeast of Penukonda gate (VMS-217).

Plate 5.5. VMS-123, wall construction detail.

SITE: VMS-123   Block: S   Transect: 18
Primary Site Use: Defensive: outer city wall and gate.
Site Dimensions: c. 6.5 km × 10 m
Setting: This long, well-constructed fortification wall traverses a range of topographic settings, crossing low-lying agricultural fields as well as higher outcrop hills.
Present Land Use/Disturbances: Agricultural activities in low-lying areas; some stone robbing has damaged wall in other areas; relatively little disturbance in upland sections of the wall.
Site Description: Fortification wall and bastions. VMS-123 is a massive fortification wall that roughly parallels the walls of the Vijayanagara urban core in the southeast quadrant of the city, and is located approximately 1.5 to 2 km to the south and east of the inner urban core walls. Starting in the southwest, the wall extends c. 2.2 km to the southeast before turning to a northeasterly orientation, for another c. 4 km. Near the southwest edge of this wall, a smaller, similarly constructed wall projects to the north for approximately 500 m. The construction of this feature is likely associated with the sixteenth-century expansion of the Vijayanagara settlement in the northeast quadrant of Block S. As such, the wall is part of a larger complex of sites forming the outer perimeter of the urban core, including VMS-451 (Block R); VMS-455, VMS-505, and VMS-510 (Block M); the Kamalapuram reservoir (VMS-231) in Block S; and VMS-10 to the north in Block O. The wall transverses the varied topography of the region, in some areas spanning agricultural fields, and in others incorporating outcropping boulders on outcrop hills. Throughout it is well constructed of quarried granite blocks of trapezoidal form in its outer (south, east) faces, with rubble fill. The pieces are generally well fitted, with minimal use of chinking. The interior face is less finely constructed, with a combination of quarried block and small to large unmodified boulders.

Twenty-nine square bastions project from this wall; these are more widely spaced in the south, and become quite regular, at intervals of c. 250 m, in the northern section of the wall. The bastions typically range from 6 to 8 m² at their base, and abut the wall. Construction is similar, though in some cases, bastions exhibit considerably more chinking stones than evident in the wall section against which they abut. Access through VMS-123 was achieved via three entries, all simple, narrow passages rather than formally constructed gates. Likely, these primarily served the needs of local residents who required access to fields or production areas beyond the walls.
Artifacts: No formal collections made. One lithic recovered, utilized flake of dark red brown chert (commonly associated with Neolithic and Iron Age lithics in the region).
Temporal Affiliation: Vijayanagara, sixteenth century.
References: Brubaker 2004:81-97; Morrison and Sinopoli 1996:61.
Illustrations: Plates 5.4, 5.5.

SITE: VMS-124   Block: S   Transect: 18
Primary Site Use: Unknown: isolated walls/small structure.
Site Dimensions: 36 × 18 m
Setting: Gently sloping area with exposed rock.
Present Land Use/Disturbances: Site lies inside a modern cement-walled enclosure in an area that has been heavily disturbed. There are numerous pits and large piles of stones.
Site Description: Several masonry walls of unknown function. Segment *a* runs east-west, is 0.64 m wide, and consists of two faces of small-medium unshaped and some split stones. Only one course is visible. At the west end, wall *a* is aligned with several small boulders; it appears to continue west of the boulders and possibly turns to the south. Wall segment *b* is perpendicular to *a*, running to the north. However, the two do not now meet. Wall *b* is 0.41 m wide and consists of medium-large split stones. The stones have been chipped to create a flatter face. Segment *c* runs parallel and 1.14 m to the east of *b*. It is similarly constructed, but with smaller stones. Segment *d* is parallel to *a*, which is about 26 m to its south. It, too, is constructed of medium and medium-large stones, some split and some unshaped. Only the south face of this 5.34 m long wall is visible (present width 0.39 m).
Artifacts: Modern earthenware ceramics. All except one sherd are located on or near wall segment *a*. 100% collection of site area and c. 5 m around the walls. 200 g ceramics; wares: 15 black plain ware. Diagnostics: 2 jars (1 modern).
Temporal Affiliation: Unknown (recent?).
Illustrations: Figure 5.3.

Figure 5.3. VMS-124, plan.

SITE: VMS-125   Block: S   Transect: 18
  Primary Site Use: Agricultural: reservoir embankment.
  Site Dimensions: 728 × 45 m
  Setting: Sloping area with a few outcropping boulders, sheet rock at west end.
  Present Land Use/Disturbances: Extensive disturbance. The (unpaved) Nallapur road runs along the top of much of this reservoir embankment. The embankment has been breached in several places by leveling and by the extension of modern irrigation canals that feed rice and vegetable fields in the old reservoir bed. Modern quarrying has pockmarked the sheet rock at its west end, and calcium carbonate ($CaCO_3$) mining, road construction, and repairs have created large pits where fill has been robbed from the embankment. Fill from the embankment has been smeared out into the fields on the north, making the width difficult to determine.
  Site Description: Reservoir embankment. This 728 m long embankment extends from west to east across a gently sloping area; two sluices are currently preserved (described below). The west end of the embankment runs over sheet rock. Although the modern road has breached the embankment, seven stepped courses of small, unshaped boulders and some quarried blocks, irregularly coursed, are visible at this end. Some 70 m from the west end, large boulders are incorporated into the embankment and it is breached by a modern irrigation ditch. A second breach, the result of a road, is located to the east of the western sluice, Feature 2 (below). Near the eastern sluice (Feature 3), a significant concentration of calcium carbonate is visible in the embankment fill; this has mostly been mined out, presumably for lime processing. Circa 20 m to the west of Feature 3, the embankment incorporates several large boulders. Atop these boulders are three column footings, forming three sides of a square, and suggesting the presence of a small structure 5 m (east-west) by 3 m (north-south). The east end of the reservoir becomes lower and narrower; there is no outcrop or hill on this end.
  Feature 1: Feature 1 is a rectangular platform c. 11 m long (east-west) × 3 m wide (north-south) located atop the embankment near its west end. Three sets of masonry steps, extending along the entire side of the platform, lead up to it from the north. The platform is constructed of large, rectangular flat but unshaped boulders. On the southwest corner, seven large boulders create a flat surface. There are no associated artifacts. The masonry face of the embankment is c. 3 m to the south of the platform.
  Feature 2: Feature 2 is the west sluice gate of the embankment. Only the two uprights remain. The uprights are square in cross section (0.36 × 0.20 and 0.45 × 0.40 m) and are roughly dressed with some visible quarry marks. Although the square peg holes for the lower cross bar are visible 0.65 m above the present ground surface, neither cross bar is present nor can the tunnel be seen. The uprights are 1.96 m (east) and 2.02 m high (west).
  Feature 3: Feature 3 is the second sluice, 200 m east of Feature 2. This feature consists of two uprights, square in section (0.44 × 0.44 and 0.46 × 0.45 m) and joined by a lower cross bar and two (now displaced) upper bars. The uprights are more finely dressed than Feature 2. The lower cross bar (1.27 × 0.49 × 0.16 m) has a 0.16 m circular perforation in its center. This perforation is unusual in that a larger opening is cut around it on the top of the cross bar to a depth of about 0.2 m. The two uppermost cross bars are displaced and lie to the north of the uprights; these elements are roughly dressed and plain, with no moldings. Because this sluice is being used as part of a modern irrigation system, a lower, subterranean cross bar is visible (also with an inset larger circle above the perforation), and the passageway under the embankment is intact and paved with flat, quarried, rectangular stones. The uprights are now 3.71 m high.

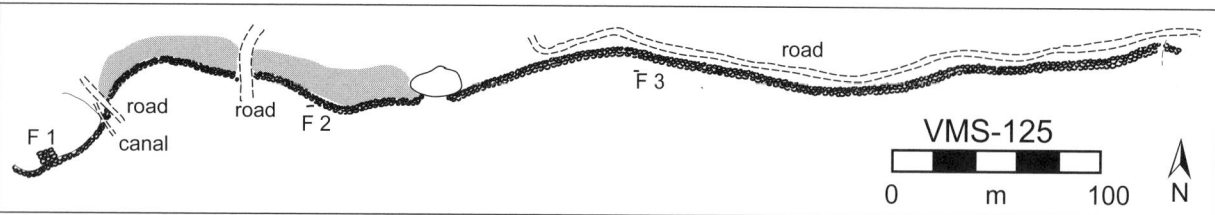

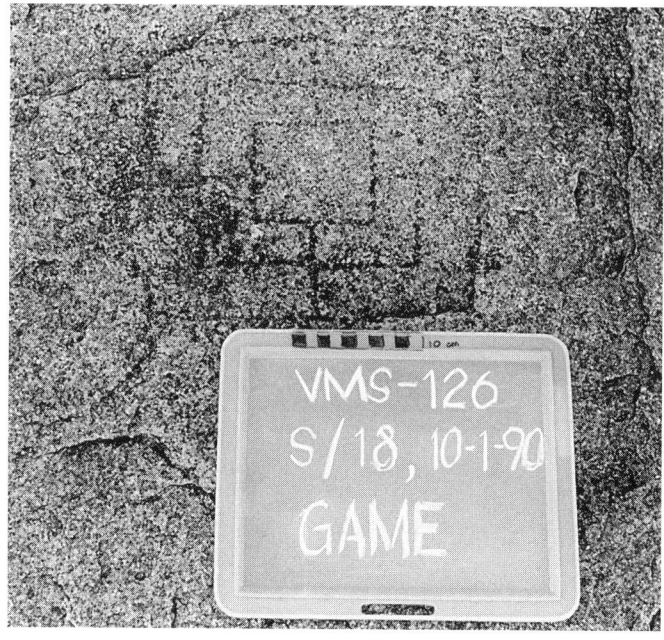

(*Top*) Figure 5.4. VMS-125, plan.
(*Left*) Plate 5.6. VMS-125, Feature 3, eastern sluice.
(*Above*) Plate 5.7. VMS-126, concentric square game board.

Artifacts: Moderate to dense ceramic scatter in the dry fields near the west end of the embankment and a dense ceramic scatter on its north. Dense vegetation on the east obscures artifact patterning. An east-west transect was laid out north of the embankment with 2 × 2 m units collected every 30 m along it (units 1-4). A judgment unit was placed on the reservoir embankment. Two separate diagnostic collections were made, to the south and north of the embankment, respectively. Two pieces of slag were recovered in the southern diagnostic collection. Only the following units contained cultural materials.

Transect 1 Unit 4: 100 g ceramics; wares: 21 black plain ware. Lithics: 1 flake (cryptocrystalline stone).

Transect 2 Unit 2: <50 g ceramics; wares: 2 black plain ware.

J1: 50 g ceramics; wares: 7 black plain ware.

Temporal Affiliation: Vijayanagara.

References: Morrison 1995:79, 91, 95, 102; Morrison and Sinopoli 1996:71.

Illustrations: Figure 5.4; Plate 5.6.

SITE: VMS-126   Block: S   Transect: 18
   Primary Site Use: Other: peg holes, game boards.
   Site Dimensions: 12 × 6 m
   Setting: Low, flat outcrop.
   Present Land Use/Disturbances: Modern petroglyphs, Kannada graffiti, and quarrying.
   Site Description: Peg holes and games have been cut into a low, flat outcrop just above the western end of VMS-125. The outer city wall, VMS-123, is located c. 50 m to the west. The seven peg holes indicate the possible existence of walls; however, no structural debris remains. There are three peg holes in linear arrangement (3° north of east); the two on the ends are 0.06 × 0.06 m. The center peg hole is diamond shaped and smaller (0.03 × 0.035 m). A second peg hole of the latter type is located just north of the first. An isolated peg hole is located 4 m (40° west of north) from the linear arrangement of three and one. This fifth peg hole is of the larger type. A sixth peg hole is located 1 m (10° north of west) and a seventh is located 10 m along the same orientation—both are of the 0.06 m × 0.06 m type. In addition to the peg holes, two game boards are located at the southwest end of the outcrop in the shade of a large boulder. The first consists of an incised grid pattern; corner and end squares contain X's. The second consists of three concentric squares, 0.27 × 0.25 m. Both modern and non-recent quarry marks appear throughout the area.
   Artifacts: None observed; no collections made.
   Temporal Affiliation: Unknown.
   Illustrations: Plate 5.7.

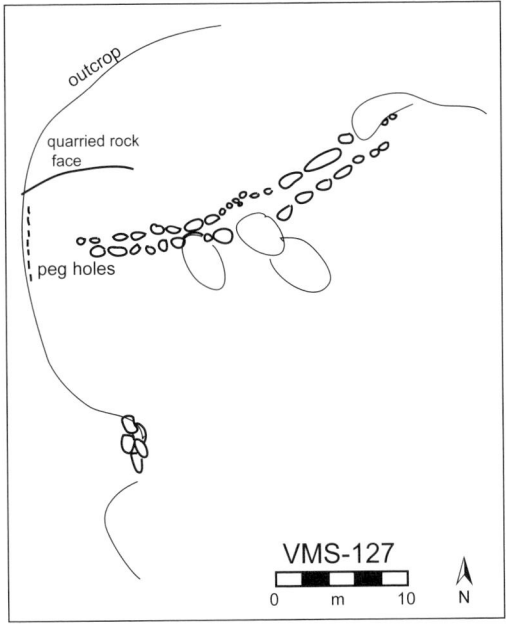

Figure 5.5. VMS-127, plan.

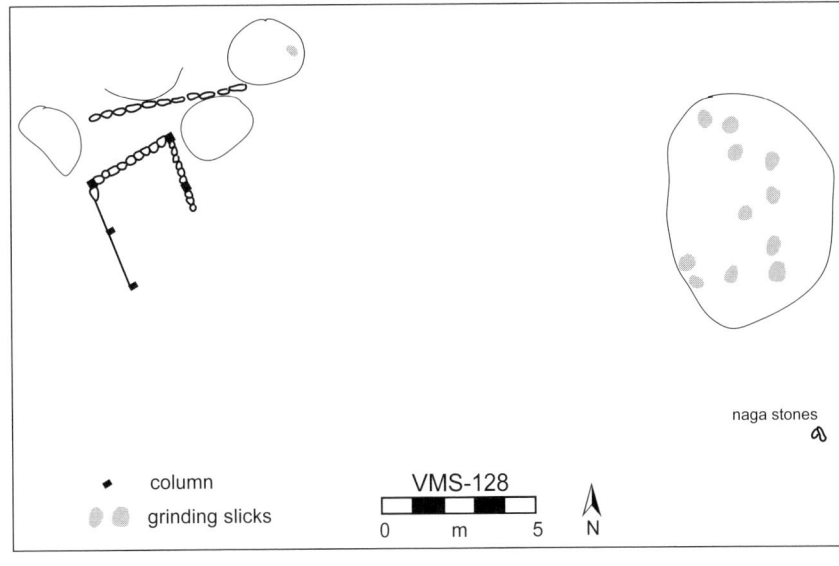

Figure 5.6. VMS-128, plan.

SITE: VMS-127   Block: S   Transect: 18
Primary Site Use: Unknown: isolated walls.
Site Dimensions: 30 × 20 m
Setting: Small granite outcrop lying just above modern irrigated fields.
Present Land Use/Disturbances: A small modern building, now in ruins, lies 20-25 m from VMS-127. Modern quarrying has occurred on the outcrop containing the site.
Site Description: Wall and associated pile of granitic rubble. The rubble accumulation forms a "plug" between two large, naturally occurring boulders on the west edge of the outcrop. The elements are medium to large and unmodified. The plug is perpendicular to the main wall, two to three elements wide, and three to four "courses" high. The arrangement does not suggest a formal wall.

The main east-west wall (1.25 m wide) consists of unmodified granitic cobbles and blocks. A single course is visible; elements are placed with their long axes parallel to the long axis of the wall. This wall has two faces separated by an earthen core and incorporates existing outcrops. A linear arrangement of seven peg holes cut into the outcrop lies at the west terminus of this wall, perpendicular to its long axis.

Evidence of non-recent quarrying occurs on the outcrop, with several quarrying areas situated just north of the main wall. Several quarried elements, which were at least minimally modified, are scattered over the site area. If these were ever structural elements, they are now displaced and dispersed. Two isolated peg holes are located c. 15 m south of the main wall on the southwest edge of the outcrop.

Artifacts: Low density, dispersed ceramic scatter clustered along edge of rice paddy on north edge of the outcrop. 100% collection. Ceramics: 100 g; wares: 4 black plain ware, 7 brown plain ware.
Temporal Affiliation: Unknown, probably Vijayanagara.
Illustrations: Figure 5.5.

SITE: VMS-128   Block: S   Transect: 18
Primary Site Use: Religious or residential: mandapa.
Site Dimensions: 24 × 9 m
Setting: Amid outcropping boulders near irrigated fields.
Present Land Use/Disturbances: The leveling of fields for rice and banana fields around the site has led to the accumulation of large piles of earth on and near the boulders containing the structure, possibly obscuring additional features.
Site Description: Columned structure (mandapa). This 3 × 2 column mandapa is set among boulders, including one outcrop that contains numerous grinding slicks. The structure is built upon a surface held stable by a 5 m long retaining wall of unmodified cobbles. The mandapa is constructed of roughly dressed columns (0.25 × 0.25 m section) with visible quarry marks. Rubble walls join the columns. A displaced architectural element, part of a molding or lintel, lies nearby. Fragments of plastered cement lie scattered around the structure. A boulder near the mandapa contains a grinding slick; there are an additional eleven slicks on another boulder some 16 m east of the structure. Near this boulder are two naga stones. This area may have been used for food or plaster processing, perhaps associated with the temple VMS-129.
Artifacts: Sparse ceramic scatter around structure. A judgment collection was made around exposed parts of the structure, avoiding areas of recent disturbance. <50 g ceramics; wares: 5 black plain ware.
Temporal Affiliation: Vijayanagara.
References: Morrison 1995:76; Morrison and Sinopoli 1996:67.
Illustrations: Figure 5.6.

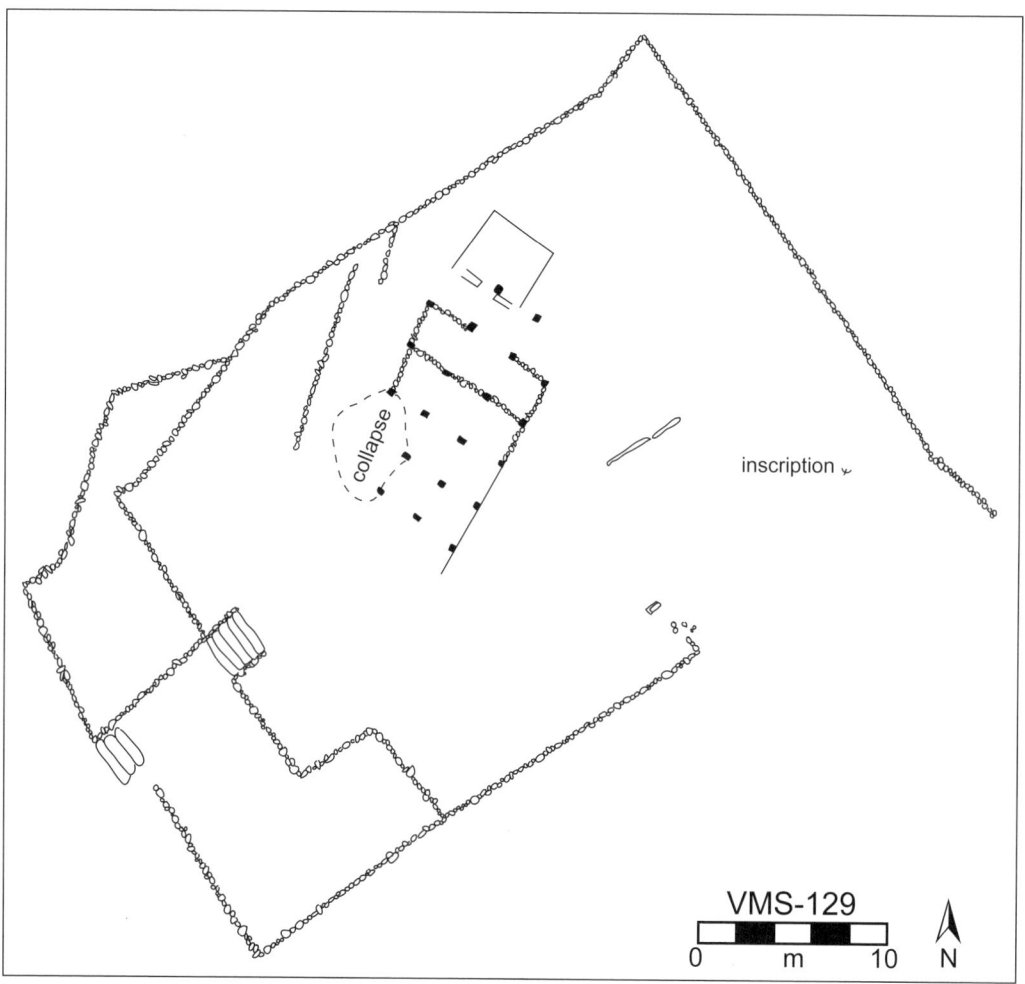

Figure 5.7. VMS-129, plan.

SITE: VMS-129   Block: S   Transect: 18
   Primary Site Use: Religious: Vaishnavite temple.
   Site Dimensions: 45 × 30 m
   Setting: On an outcrop hill.
   Present Land Use/Disturbances: The shrine is still in worship. Some architectural elements are displaced, but there is no major disturbance.
   Site Description: Small temple. The structure is built atop a low hill on a surface stabilized by two tiers of terraces defined by retaining walls. The entrance to the temple was from the south, by means of two stairways. The lower terrace is smaller, extending only across the south side of the complex. The upper terrace is larger, and irregular in shape, bounded by a wall five courses high, built of irregularly shaped stones.
   The south side of the temple consists of a porch of 4 × 4 columns, open on the south and walled on other sides. The inner columns are square in section, with inset octagons. The outer columns are plain, undressed, and square in section. One remaining wall slab contains a crudely executed carving of the Vijayanagara boar emblem. A large rectangular image base lies in the middle of the porch. An antechamber one column deep abuts the porch. This area was walled with long horizontal slabs up to 2 m long. A carved and socketed doorway with Vaishnavite door guardians separates the antechamber from the 2 × 2 column sanctuary to its north. The ceiling of the sanctuary, built of rotated squares, is partly collapsed, exposing the brick and plaster shikhara above it. Outside the sanctuary, the temple is roofed with long horizontal beams oriented north-south along the central aisle, and east-west along the side aisles. Column iconography includes depictions of a trident, flowers, sages, a six-sided star with a circle in its center, crescent moon, Garuda, lingam, and a female devotee, among others. The southwest corner of the temple has collapsed.
   There are traces of rubble walls west of the temple and some possible foundations to the east. A displaced column and a slab with a four-line Kannada inscription are found in this area. West of the shrine are the foundations of a north-south wall running across sheet rock.
   Artifacts: 100% collection; no artifacts recovered.
   Temporal Affiliation: Vijayanagara.
   References: Morrison 1995:76; Morrison and Sinopoli 1996:67.
   Illustrations: Figure 5.7; Plates 5.8, 5.9.

(*Above*) Plate 5.8. VMS-129, view from south.

(*Left*) Plate 5.9. VMS-129, doorway to sanctuary with Vaishnava door guardians.

SITE: VMS-130   Block: S   **Transect:** 18
Primary Site Use: Unknown: isolated wall.
Site Dimensions: 50 × 2 m
Setting: Level irrigated fields.
Present Land Use/Disturbances: Rubble mounds at the west end of the wall may be a product of field clearance. The site is just north of a dirt road.
Site Description: Isolated wall. This poorly preserved feature appears to be remnants of a border or retaining wall rather than part of a structure. This wall is located c. 10 m south/southwest of the outcrop on which VMS-129 is situated. It may, thus, have been an exterior wall for the temple complex and/or may have defined a transport route to the temple. The wall is composed of unmodified cobbles laid in a single course end to end. It has two faces with an earthen core (0.35-2.3 m wide) for most of its length, although near its southeastern end, it is composed of a single line of elements. A single, poorly preserved crosswall is located at the northwest end of the wall.
Artifacts: No collections made.
Temporal Affiliation: Unknown; if associated with temple VMS-129, it is likely Vijayanagara in date.
References: Morrison 1995:76; Morrison and Sinopoli 1996:67.
Illustrations: Figure 5.8.

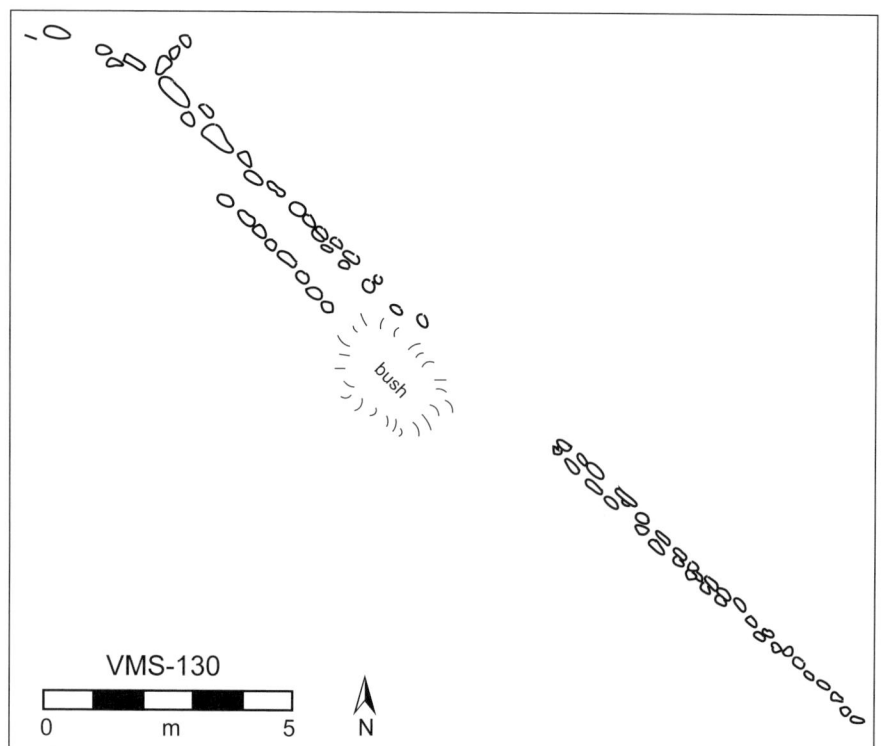

(*Above*) Figure 5.8. VMS-130, plan.

(*Right*) Figure 5.9. VMS-131, plan.

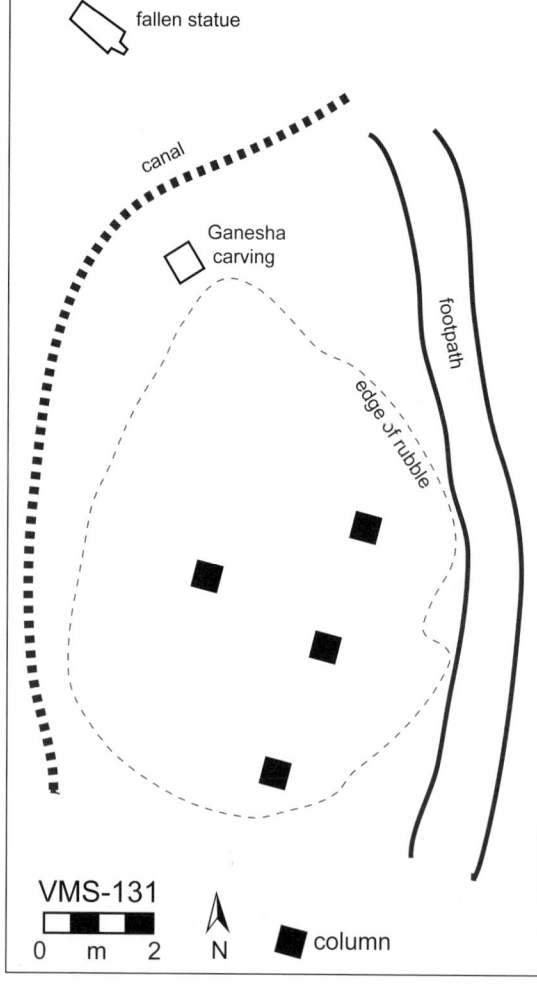

SITE: VMS-131   Block: S   Transect: 18
  Primary Site Use: Religious: shrine.
  Site Dimensions: 12 × 8 m
  Setting: Level irrigated fields.
  Present Land Use/Disturbances: Modern road to the north. Piles of rubble from field clearing surround the structure. Columns have been broken and displaced, as has the image.
  Site Description: Shrine. Fragmentary remains of a 4 × 2 column mandapa located on the south side of the road leading to the Penukonda gate. Three columns remain upright. These are square in cross section (one with inset octagons) and roughly finished. One column has carvings of a crescent moon, chakra, and circular flower. Foundation slabs are visible on the northwest corner, but are buried elsewhere. A facedown, headless, and heavily weathered sculpture of Ganesha lies northwest of the structure.
  Artifacts: 100% collection; no artifacts recovered.
  Temporal Affiliation: Vijayanagara.
  Illustrations: Figure 5.9.

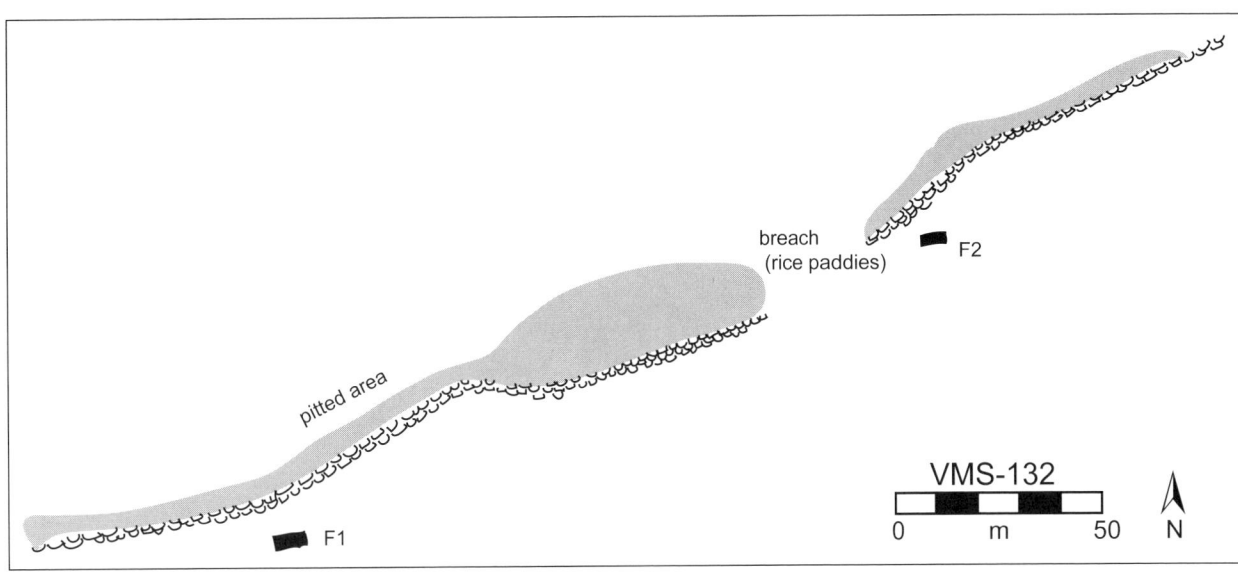

(*Above*) Figure 5.10. VMS-132, plan.

(*Right*) Plate 5.10. VMS-132, reservoir embankment, view from south.

SITE: VMS-132   Block: S/T   Transect: 18/1
Primary Site Use: Agricultural: reservoir embankment.
Site Dimensions: 290 × 20 m
Setting: Nearly level irrigated fields.
Present Land Use/Disturbances: Extensive damage to the reservoir embankment caused by clearing and leveling for irrigated fields. An unpaved road lies immediately north of the embankment and a footpath runs along its top. The sluices are in worship.
Site Description: Reservoir embankment. Water was impounded to the south of this large earth and stone embankment. The heavily damaged earthen embankment is faced with eleven courses of masonry on its south side, composed of small irregularly shaped blocks. Two sluices are visible. Local topography suggests that this facility retained runoff from a large area. The basin south of the embankment is roughly 500 m north-south.
Feature 1: West sluice, located c. 55 m from the embankment's west end. The sluice consists of two roughly finished uprights, rectangular in section (height 1.75 m above present ground surface) and joined only by a central cross bar (0.70 m long × 0.1 m high × 0.45 m deep). There is no upper cross bar. A stone (0.55 × 0.25 m), in worship, is found beneath the crosspiece. Behind this stone, only rubble is visible. The sluice is set 4 m from the edge of the embankment.
Feature 2: East sluice, located c. 50 m from the east end of the embankment. The sluice consists of two roughly dressed uprights, square in section (0.3 × 0.3 m, height 2.5 m above the present ground surface). Slots for a central cross bar are present, and a broken fragment of the latter lies nearby. What seems to be the upper crosspiece is also displaced (1.5 × 0.55 m). Although it is partly obscured by vegetation, it appears to have central and corner medallions and thus probably also has simple moldings. The sluice is set 6 m in front of the embankment.
Artifacts: Sparse and variable scatter of earthenware ceramics. Collection of area 5 m from edge of the embankment on the south side only. 150 g ceramics; wares: 30 black plain ware, 3 red plain ware. Diagnostics: 7 jars.
Temporal Affiliation: Vijayanagara.
References: Morrison 1995:75, 91, 95, 102; Morrison and Sinopoli 1996:63.
Illustrations: Figure 5.10; Plate 5.10.

Plate 5.11. VMS-133, terrace system, long double-faced wall in southeast of site.

SITE: VMS-133   Block: S   **Transect:** 16-18
   Primary Site Use: Agricultural: terraces.
   Site Dimensions: 375 × 375 m
   Setting: Gentle to moderate slopes interspersed by low granitic outcrops.
   Present Land Use/Disturbances: Although there are some dry farmed fields in the area, most of the site is not cultivated but is used for grazing and wood gathering. Erosion has disturbed many alignments; however, the systematic dismantling of terraces in dry farmed fields is the most significant disturbance. The extent of this activity is unknown. In 1993, after the following description was written, the area was incorporated into the grounds of Kannada University and hundreds of tree-planting holes were excavated into the site and several paved roads were constructed, one cutting through the west edge of the site.
   Site Description: Agricultural terrace system. This system of connected agricultural terraces is located in a long, narrow valley with gently sloping sides (referred to as the east and west slopes). Drainage in the valley runs from south to north. On the south is an east-west ridge of outcrops; a gap in this ridge is spanned by a reservoir embankment, VMS-226. South of this ridge, drainage runs from north to south (VMS-134). Most of the terraces are concentrated on the east slope. The walls, some quite long, form enclosed areas in which there is up to 1.5 m of soil development. The west slope is mostly covered with dry farmed fields, but a few terraces are found there. The soil is very rocky and there are numerous spits of sheet rock and outcrops. Further downstream (to the north), the large reservoir VMS-132 is fed by runoff from VMS-133. Water from VMS-226 must have fed crops on these terraces and in turn, the terraces controlled erosion in the catchment of VMS-132. Reservoirs and terraces are thus integrated features in this area. There do not appear to be any terraces in the flat area between VMS-133 and VMS-132.
   The walls of this terrace system are variable in construction. The most simple are no more than linear raised concentrations of gravel. Most walls are single-faced alignments of unmodified cobbles, gravel, and large boulders. In many cases, walls abut outcrops or fingers of sheet rock. Outcrops are also augmented by stones piled in the gaps. Of particular interest, however, are the large numbers of formally constructed walls. Some have two faces, with earth and rubble cores, and range from 1 to 2 m wide. These are clustered in the southeast portion of the system in a relatively steep area. Other walls have up to four irregular courses. These multi-course walls are all long east-west walls, which appear to separate the area into three long east-west strips (on the east slope of the drainage).
   Of note is the large number of very long walls in the system, both parallel to and perpendicular to the drainage. Most of these long walls are continuous, or are broken only where they connect raised islands of outcrops, and thus do not appear to be the product of accretional construction. Most of the walls retain soil behind them, forming flat areas for plant growth. A few walls or check dams are found in the drainage channel itself at the base of the slope.
   This terrace system was first recorded in 1990, and was identified as a potential site for a future test excavation to explore the efficacy of the terraces for improving soil conditions for agriculture. In 1994, we revisited the site and found that subsequent to the acquisition of the land by Kannada University, hundreds of tree-planting holes had been excavated, each c. 50 × 50 cm and spaced more or less regularly across the site area. With the permission of the University, these holes allowed observations of sediment profiles across a portion of the site. Sixty-one profiles were documented from the exposed faces.
   Artifacts: One modern pot break. There is a very low density ceramic scatter between VMS-132 and VMS-133. No surface collections were made at the site; very few artifacts were noted on the surface.
   Temporal Affiliation: Vijayanagara.
   References: Morrison 1993; Morrison 1995:92-93, 102; Morrison and Sinopoli 1996:71; Morrison and Sinopoli 2006a:429; Morrison and Sinopoli 2006b:464.
   Illustrations: Figure 5.11; Plate 5.11.

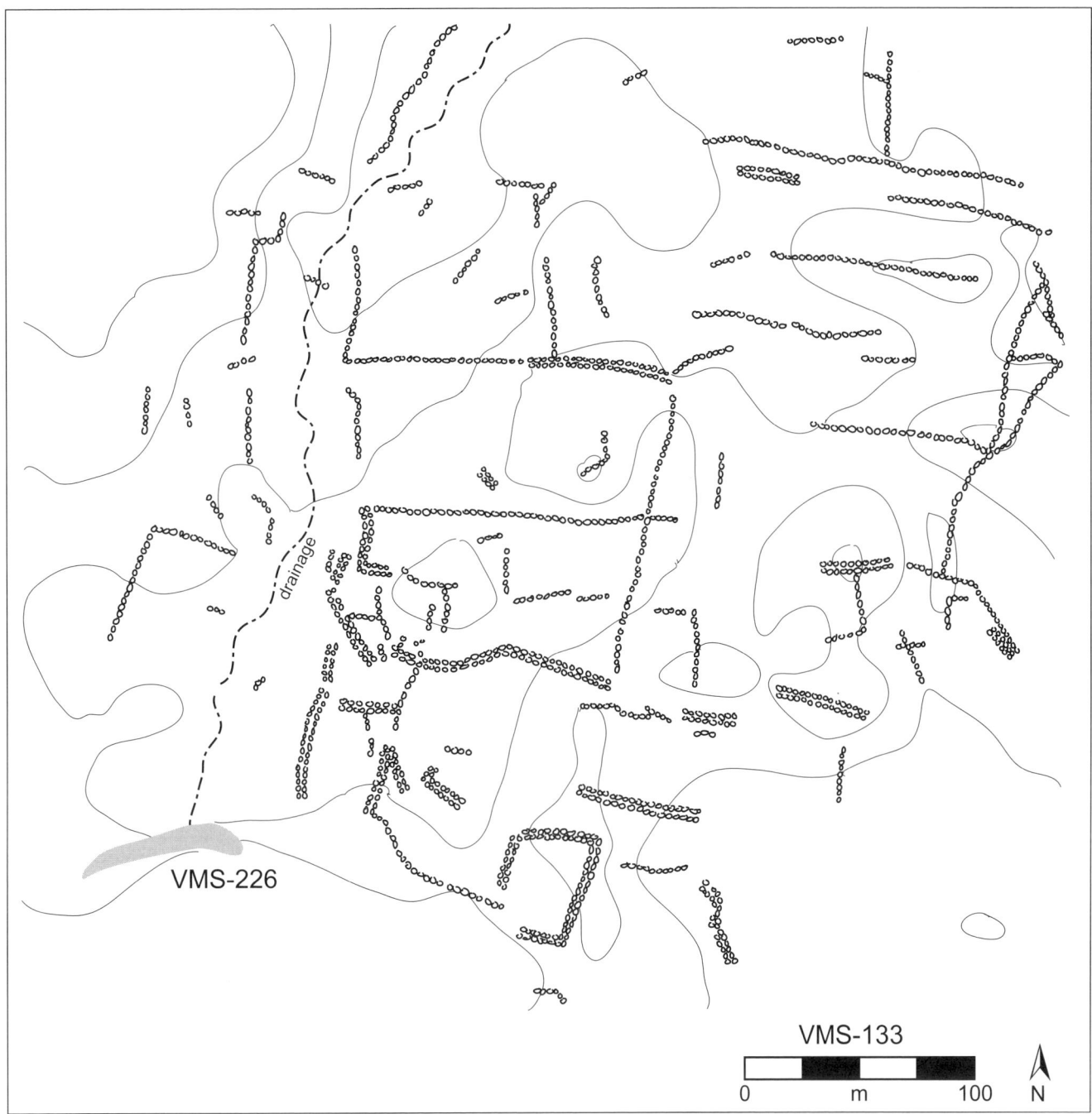

Figure 5.11. VMS-133, plan (VMS-226 in lower left).

SITE: VMS-134   Block: S   **Transect:** 18
  Primary Site Use: Agricultural: terrace system.
  Site Dimensions: 100 × 150 m
  Setting: Gentle slopes amid outcrops.
  Present Land Use/Disturbances: Modern canal construction debris truncates the site on the south, and a cart track runs along its west side. Some breaches in terraces appear to be due to erosion; very little farming takes place in this area.
  Site Description: Agricultural terrace system. Because a modern canal has truncated its south end, the original extent of this system is unknown. The site is situated on a gently sloping south-facing hillside with relatively flat, arable areas, but with numerous rocky outcrops. VMS-134 lies just south/southeast of terrace system VMS-133, but is part of a separate drainage system that flows south. VMS-134 is similar in construction and materials to VMS-133. All terraces are made of unmodified granitic cobbles and pebbles varying widely in size and shape. Most are one to two elements wide. The northernmost wall has two faces (0.9 m wide), with smaller stones used as fill between the faces. Other terraces are less substantial, and none is more than one course high.
  Artifacts: No surface collections were made at the site; only one black plain ware sherd was observed on the site's surface.
  Temporal Affiliation: Vijayanagara?
  References: Morrison 1995:92, 102; Morrison and Sinopoli 1996:71.

SITE: VMS-135   Block: S   **Transect:** 18
  Primary Site Use: Residential: ceramic scatter.
  Site Dimensions: 120 × 40 m
  Setting: Flat to moderately sloping dry fields.
  Resources: 80 m northwest of reservoir VMS-136.
  Present Land Use/Disturbances: Plowing.
  Site Description: Earthenware ceramic and slag scatter. This scatter lies within the bed of a small reservoir, VMS-136. The densest area of scatter is approximately 40 × 120 m, with sherds visible in an unplowed field. Fields to the north and east have recently been ploughed and artifact visibility, if not density, is lower in these fields.
  Artifacts: Earthenware ceramics, slag. Two north-south transects were laid out, spaced 2 m apart (T1 in west; T2 in east); a diagnostic sweep was made of the entire site area. The following units contained cultural materials.
  Transect 1 Unit 2: <50 g ceramics; wares: 1 black plain ware.
  Transect 1 Unit 3: <50 g ceramics; wares: 1 black plain ware.
  Transect 2 Unit 2: <50 g ceramics; wares: 1 black plain ware.
  Transect 2 Unit 4: <50 g ceramics; wares: 3 black plain ware, 1 coarse ware.
  Transect 2 Unit 5: <50 g ceramics; wares: 1 black plain ware.
  Temporal Affiliation: Vijayanagara.
  Illustrations: Figure 5.12.

SITE: VMS-137   Block: S/T   **Transect:** S18/T1
  Primary Site Use: Transport: road.
  Site Dimensions: 380 × 130 m
  Setting: Gentle to moderate slopes with sheet rock.
  Present Land Use/Disturbances: Area of occasional dry cultivation. Parts of the road wall have been incorporated into field boundaries while others have been removed. A modern canal cuts the north end of the road and a ditch flows down its center.
  Site Description: Road segment. This feature borders reservoir VMS-136. This road presumably once extended further north. Site seg-

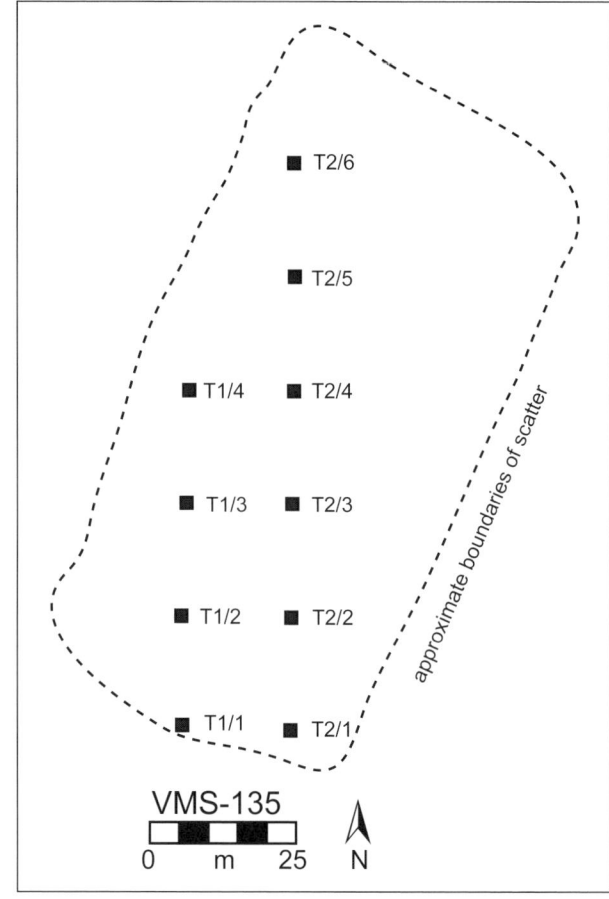

Figure 5.12. VMS-135, plan.

ments are described from north to south. The northernmost wall segment consists of a raised earthen walkway 8 m wide and bounded by masonry walls. This c. 90 m long segment is oriented northeast-southwest, and becomes narrower at its northern end. Only one face is visible along the western face where the structure is incorporated into modern field boundaries. At the south end of the northern segment, the road is broken by a gap and then turns toward the southeast, and becomes a masonry-faced raised causeway. The causeway rises about 1.5 m above the level fields to the north and east, consists of several roughly parallel walls, and may have been repaired or remodeled several times. Several small crosswalls are visible, perhaps support walls. The southern portion of this stretch of road abuts with reservoir VMS-136, on its east. In some areas, particularly near the base of the reservoir, the road walls are terraced, and at this point, the road becomes quite broad (16 m).

The southernmost section of the road follows the west face of the reservoir before diverging to the southwest, where it intersects with sheet rock. A steeply sloping pavement of irregularly shaped flat stones (20 m wide) has been laid to even out the sheet rock. Beyond the pavement, worn sheet rock continues for c. 40 m.
  Artifacts: Survey team walked a collection transect along the center of the road bed and recovered no artifacts. The only region with materials present was in ploughed fields along the edge of the ceramic scatter, VMS-135, previously collected.
  Temporal Affiliation: Vijayanagara.
  References: Morrison 1995:74-75; Morrison and Sinopoli 1996:63.
  Illustrations: Figure 5.13; Plate 5.12.

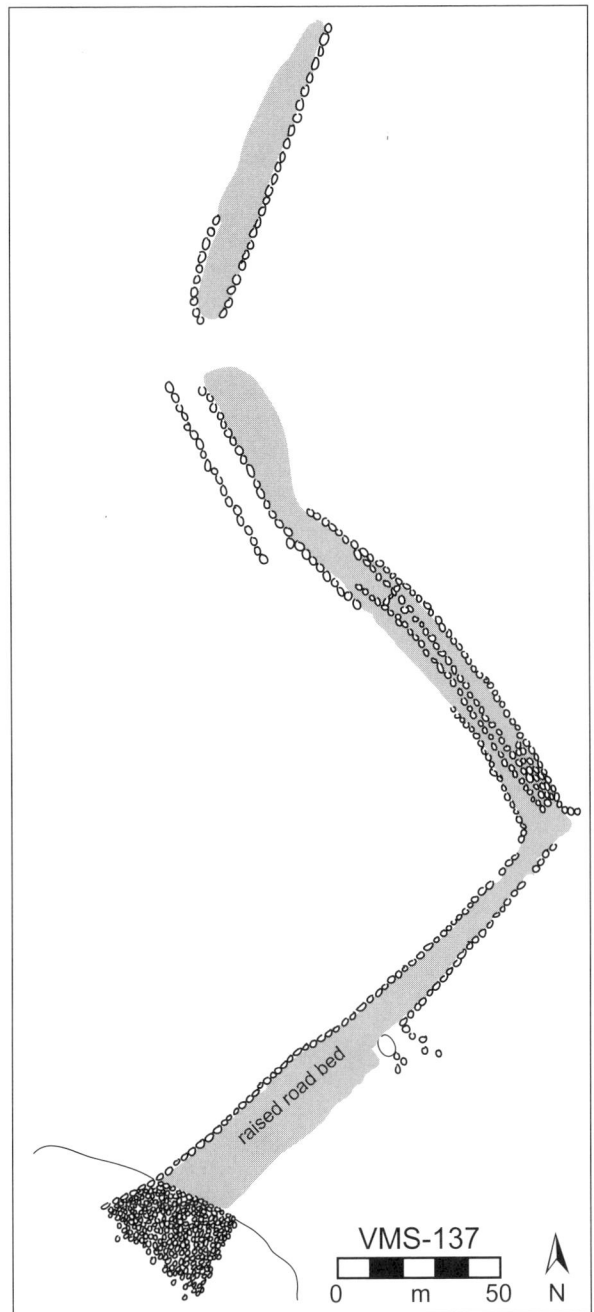

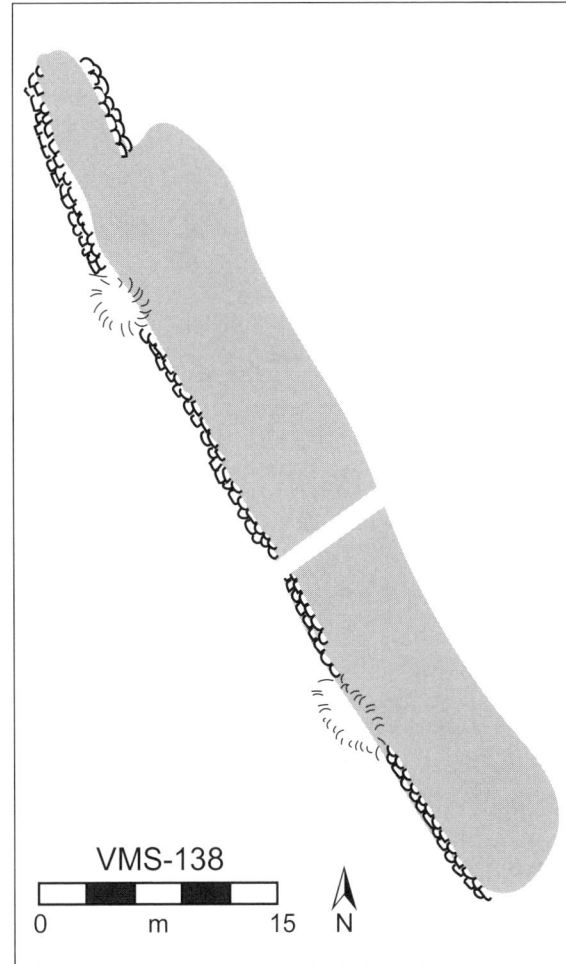

(*Left*) Figure 5.13. VMS-137, plan.

(*Below Left*) Plate 5.12. VMS-137, raised road bed.

(*Above*) Figure 5.14. VMS-138, plan.

SITE: VMS-138   Block: S   Transect: 18
  Primary Site Use: Agricultural: reservoir embankment.
  Site Dimensions: 50 × 10 m
  Setting: Base of gentle slope in dry farmed area.
  Present Land Use/Disturbances: Two recently repaired breaches.
  Site Description: Reservoir embankment. This c. 50 m long earthen and stone embankment is oriented northwest-southeast and captures runoff within 60 × 50 m catchment basin to its southeast. Six to seven stepped masonry courses of unmodified cobbles bound the eastern face of the low earthen embankment. At least two breaches near the northwest end of the embankment have been filled with cobbles. There are no sluices extant, but a waste weir may have been present where the structure is now breached.
  Artifacts: 100% collection of embankment and area within 5 m surrounding it. Lithics recovered; <50 g ceramics (not recorded).
  Temporal Affiliation: Unknown, probably Vijayanagara.
  References: Morrison 1995:91, 92, 102.
  Illustrations: Figure 5.14.

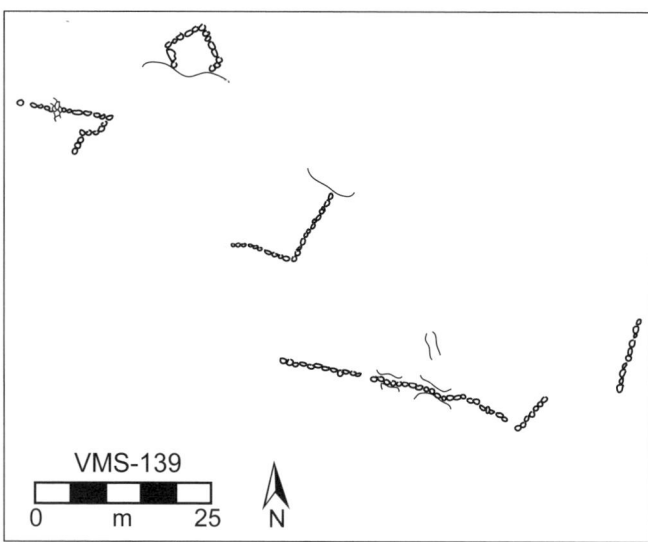

Figure 5.15. VMS-139, plan.

SITE: VMS-139 Block: S Transect: 17
Primary Site Use: Agricultural/residential: check dams and one-room structure.
Site Dimensions: 85 × 40 m
Setting: West slope of a low outcrop in dry farmed area, in an area with good soil development. A natural drainage channel runs west down the slope of the outcrop.
Present Land Use/Disturbances: Vegetation is growing around the structures; many stones are displaced or missing.
Site Description: Wall alignments. VMS-139 consists of several long walls oriented approximately perpendicular to the natural drainage channel, which flows down from east to west. These walls likely served to slow runoff and erosion and to define the borders of agricultural fields. They are constructed of a single course and a single face of unmodified small to medium sized cobbles. The site area does not appear to have been recently used. Near the top of the slope on the north edge of the channel is a small square single-room structure, similarly constructed. This site may have once been part of a much larger Vijayanagara period dry field system.
Artifacts: 100% collection within entire site area. A scatter of earthenware ceramics was documented around the room. 50 g ceramics; wares: 9 black plain ware.
Temporal Affiliation: Vijayanagara.
References: Morrison 1995:92-93, 102; Morrison and Sinopoli 1996:71.
Illustrations: Figure 5.15.

SITE: VMS-140 Block: S Transect: 18
Primary Site Use: Residential: settlement.
Site Dimensions: 195 × 135 m
Setting: Level irrigated area.
Present Land Use/Disturbances: Heavily disturbed by piled-up debris from a modern canal. Modern cement walls bisect the site. The original site boundaries are not distinguishable.
Site Description: Settlement area. The site, located just inside the Vijayanagara city wall (VMS-123), consists of earthen and masonry mounds with a few visible wall alignments and displaced sculptural elements. This was probably an area of ephemeral structures, and may have been part of a broader zone of settlement in this region associated with the sixteenth-century Vijayanagara period suburb of Varadadevi-ammana-pattana. A bedrock mortar was noted. A Vijayanagara period temple to the north, in Block N, may be associated with this settlement, as may VMS-124.

A basalt dyke outcrops nearby and although only one wall is constructed of this material, it has obviously been extensively used, perhaps for manufacturing pegs or other objects, as the site is littered with flaked basalt. The chipping debris is concentrated in the mounded areas. Several large basalt boulders in this area have Vijayanagara quarry marks.

Other than the temple, there is no formal architecture. However, several granite sculptural elements are situated atop a rubble mound, and three displaced sculptural elements are gathered into a modern shrine. These include images of Hanuman, a naga, and a hero stone; all are of Vijayanagara period date. A block containing an inscribed game lies next to the latter.
Artifacts: South of the modern canal is an extensive scatter of earthenware ceramics extending c. 50 m south and c. 60 m east of VMS-140. Collections were made along three north-south transects placed 50 m apart and collected at 30 m intervals. An additional 2 × 2 m unit (J1) was placed along transect 1, and a second (J2) was located c. 5 m south of an isolated sati stone. Diagnostic collections were made across the entire mapped area: D1 consists of lithics, slag, and so on; D2 consists of ceramics. Unit D3 contains ceramics from a scatter located south of the modern canal.

The following units contained cultural material:
Transect 1 Unit 1: 50 g ceramics; wares: 2 black plain ware, 1 red plain ware, 1 brown plain ware.
Transect 2 Unit 2: 50 g ceramics; wares: 9 black plain ware. Diagnostics: 1 jar.
Transect 2 Unit 4: 50 g ceramics; wares: 7 black plain ware, 1 brown plain ware.
Transect 3 Unit 1: 50 g ceramics; wares: 3 black plain ware. Diagnostics: 1 jar.
Transect 3 Unit 2: 50 g ceramics; wares: 2 black plain ware, 2 red plain ware, 2 brown plain ware. Diagnostics: 1 jar.
Transect 3 Unit 3: 50 g ceramics; body sherds: 8 black plain ware, 2 brown plain ware. Diagnostics: 1 jar.
J1: 50 g ceramics; wares: 3 black plain ware, 1 brown plain ware.
J2: 50 g ceramics; wares: 2 black plain ware, 1 brown plain ware. Diagnostics: 1 jar.
D1: Lithics: 2 quartz cores.
Temporal Affiliation: Vijayanagara.
References: Morrison 1995:85; Sinopoli 2003:151, 236.
Illustrations: Figure 5.16.

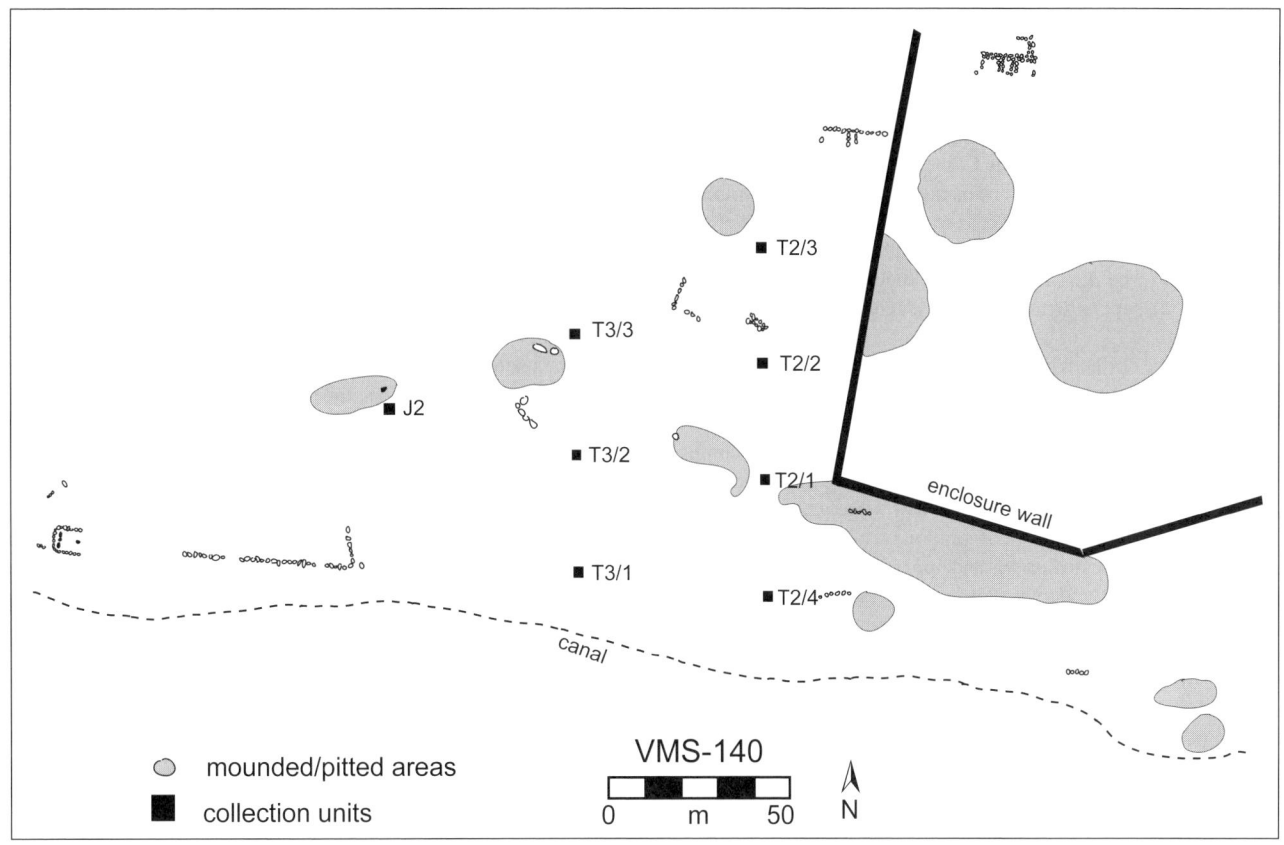

Figure 5.16. VMS-140, plan.

SITE: VMS-141　Block: S　Transect: 17
Primary Site Use: Unknown: reused slabs and naga stone.
Site Dimensions: 10 × 10 m
Setting: Level dry farmed fields.
Present Land Use/Disturbances: None of this site is *in situ*. A recent burial that incorporates a few quarried blocks is located nearby; a column footing and many quarried blocks are used in a farmer's wall 40 m west of the well.
Site Description: Well with displaced blocks. Two long dressed slabs (2.71 m × 0.36 m × 0.26 m) and numerous quarried blocks have been incorporated into an apparently modern well. Circa 50 m south is a small sheet rock outcrop with a mortar set into a shallow square depression. Approximately 35 m northwest of the well is a naga stone with two intertwined nagas.
Artifacts: Earthenware ceramics, slag, chipped basalt, and granite. The scatter may be an extension of the larger scatter that extends over transects 18 and 17 north of the modern road. No collections made.
Temporal Affiliation: Vijayanagara elements in recent structures.

SITE: VMS-142　Block: S　Transect: 16
Primary Site Use: Religious: Vaishnavite temple complex.
Site Dimensions: 95 × 50 m
Setting: Level area surrounded by dry farmed fields.
Present Land Use/Disturbances: Heavily overgrown with vegetation; structure not in use.
Site Description: Vaishnava temple complex. This large temple complex is enclosed in massive enclosure walls and contains two shrines—the larger to the south, aligned with the enclosure doorways, and the smaller to the north/northwest. There are three entries into the temple enclosure. Those to the east and south are simple doors in the wall. The north entry (Feature 4) is a major gateway. Two small mandapas are located in the northeast and southeast corners of the enclosure. Many small rubble-walled rooms line the enclosure walls along the south, west, and north. There thus seems to have been some associated settlement inside and outside the temple walls. The east gate of the temple aligns with a gate in the city wall (VMS-651), such that when one stands in the sanctuary of the main shrine and faces east, the temple gateway exactly frames this distant gate.

Feature 1: The northern mandapa (10 × 10 m), located in the northeast corner of the enclosure. The structure is quite simple with no carvings and plain square columns. The basement moldings have two steps with angled bevel and corner quarter medallions. In the center of the roof is a small elevated section that would allow smoke from cooking fires to escape, also roofed and with angled eaves.

Feature 2: The southern mandapa (10 × 10 m), located in the southeast corner of the enclosure. The structure has 16 × 16 columns, and a central, elevated roof section with angled eaves like that of Feature 1.

Feature 3: Shrine located in the northwest corner of the complex. The shrine consists of an outer chamber and inner sanctuary. The shrine faces east and is set on a stone basement. Carved balustrades flank five steps on the east side of the structure. The mandapa of the outer chamber has sixteen columns, square with circular inset octagons. The outer walls and door to the outer chamber are carved with pilasters and miniature temple elements. The door leading to the sanctuary is decorated very simply. The brick superstructure over the sanctuary is preserved but no plaster remains.

Feature 4: The northern gateway and enclosure wall. The monumental gateway is located directly north of the north entry of the main shrine (Feature 5). The enclosure wall abuts both sides of the gate. The south side of the gate is built on a square footing course that carries a complex molding sequence. The lower molding is three step with convex bevel, lotus petal, and lower wavy outline. It has a projecting beveled molding on the outer edges and yali-faced decoration on the inner. Above this is a flat section with decorated panels and upper yali-decorated moldings. Above this lower and wider part of the basement moldings are four more sets of moldings supporting the main south facade. This portion is decorated with attached columns and "flower pots." Above this is a large convex molding decorated with scrollwork, and then, above a flat masonry course, the brick superstructure begins. The superstructure has three main tiers, each with a central window, and miniature gopura motifs, in brick. Above the third tier is a barrel-shaped brick vault.

To the east and west of the south gate entrance are many small carved figures including a horse, *rishi* (sage), goose, Krishna with chakra, lion, turtle, yali, Rama, Krishna with flute, and makaras with foliate designs emerging from them.

The interior of the gate consists of two main bays. Posts and lintels separate each bay; Yaksha figures are carved on each post. The whole interior is elaborately decorated with foliate designs, lotuses, and scalloped edging. In the south bay are two inset rooms or niches, atop a foundation of three horizontal slabs. In the center of each, along the passage, are square columns with inset sections and upwardly projecting lotus buds. Separating the two chambers is a second post and lintel, elaborately carved with Yaksha figures. On each side are Vaishnavite door guardians. Both sides of the doorway have sculptures of different avatars of Vishnu. North of the door guardians are two inscriptions (see below).

The north side of the gate is constructed so that its platforms face north. The elaborate facade, similar to the south corner pillars, has a detached lunette carved out of the same block. Curved eaves overhang the north entrance.

Feature 5: Main temple. This large east-facing temple sits on a raised basement with elaborate moldings identical to those on the north gate of the complex (Feature 4). The structure consists of four east-west oriented rooms, with the sanctuary on the west. The doorway to each room becomes progressively smaller as one moves from the east entrance toward the sanctuary.

The outer, east room is square and has exterior doors on the east, south, and north. The east stairway is missing; avatars of Vishnu are carved on panels near the door. There are porches with elaborately carved pillars outside both the north and south entrances. This outer chamber is walled, with twelve columns, four of which are freestanding. The columns are square with circular decorative insets and cruciform capitals with pendant lotus buds. Carvings on the columns consist exclusively of Vaishnava motifs. The columns support stone beams with geometric carvings. The flooring incorporates large, rectangular stone slabs. Columns inset into walls are more irregular with few carvings.

A central two step stairway leads through a wide entry to the first antechamber, the floor of which is slightly elevated. The doorway to the second antechamber is elaborately carved, Vaishnava door guardians and lotus panels on lintels and threshold. Within this room, the uppermost wall panel is carved.

The entry into the sanctuary has no carvings. The image base has fallen over, and grass and shrubs are growing inside the sanctuary. A portion of the brick gopuram is preserved, but the central section has collapsed.

Feature 6: Circa eleven small (c. 7 × 5 m) rooms that abut the complex's south, west, and north interior enclosure walls. The rooms were probably residential chambers, kitchens, and storage rooms. The rooms are mostly clustered behind the temple and shrine, but two are situated near Feature 2. All rooms are overgrown. A large grinding machine base is also located behind the main structure.

Feature 7: A massive enclosure wall (*prakara*). The wall is c. 2 m wide and is constructed of horizontally placed dressed slabs that contain a brickwork core. The uppermost masonry course is of small square blocks, which project slightly over the wall. Up to a meter of brick superstructure is visible above the highest masonry course. Small holes appear at intervals where the masonry ends and brickwork begins. There are many small images carved into the wall including fish, Hanuman, boar, turtle, goose, and sun. On the south and east are simple doorways. A massive doorway (Feature 4) is on the north side, perhaps indicative of a major road along this side of the complex.

Artifacts: The surrounding fields contain a sparse to moderate density scatter of chipped basalt and granite, ceramics, and slag, continuous with an extensive scatter some 750 m east-west that lies north of the paved road. Inside the complex is a sparse scatter of ceramic and slag. The scatter is densest in the vicinity of the rubble-walled rooms (F6), and includes several large pieces of slag. Nine 2 × 2 m judgment units were placed in functionally diverse areas of the complex (J1-J9); a diagnostic sweep was also made. Units containing cultural materials are:

J1: <50 g ceramics; wares: 2 black plain ware, 1 brown plain ware.

J3: 50 g ceramics; wares: 5 black plain ware, 2 brown plain ware.

J4: <50 g ceramics; wares: 1 brown plain ware.

J5: 450 g ceramics; wares: 61 black plain ware, 11 brown plain ware. Diagnostics: 6 jars, 10 unidentifiable. Other artifacts: <50 g slag.

J8: 50 g ceramics; wares: 8 black plain ware, 3 brown plain ware. Diagnostics: 1 jar, 1 unidentifiable.

Temporal Affiliation: This complex dates to the Tuluva dynasty and reign of Achyutadevaraya (A.D. 1530-1542); this dating is based on multiple lines of evidence. The inscriptions have been published in South Indian Inscriptions (SII), IV, No. 256-257, and in Annual Report on South Indian Epigraphy (ARIE), 27-28 of 1889 (also Filliozat and Filliozat 1988). The inscription, repeated also at the Vitthala and several other temples in the sacred center, is in Sanskrit, in both Kannada and Nandinagari script. It consists of two verses, recording the *anandanidhi* or "deposit of felicity" of the emperor Achyutadevaraya. The date corresponds to 26 August 1539. The ornate style of carving and the absence of any Shaivite motifs also demonstrate that this is a late temple, built within the Varadadevi-ammana-pattana suburb, which was constructed by Achyutadevaraya in the 1530s.

References: Filliozat and Filliozat 1988; Morrison 1995:80, 85; Morrison and Sinopoli 1996:67, 69; Sinopoli 1993b; Sinopoli 2003:154.

Illustrations: Figure 5.17; Plates 5.13-5.16.

Block S: Site Summaries

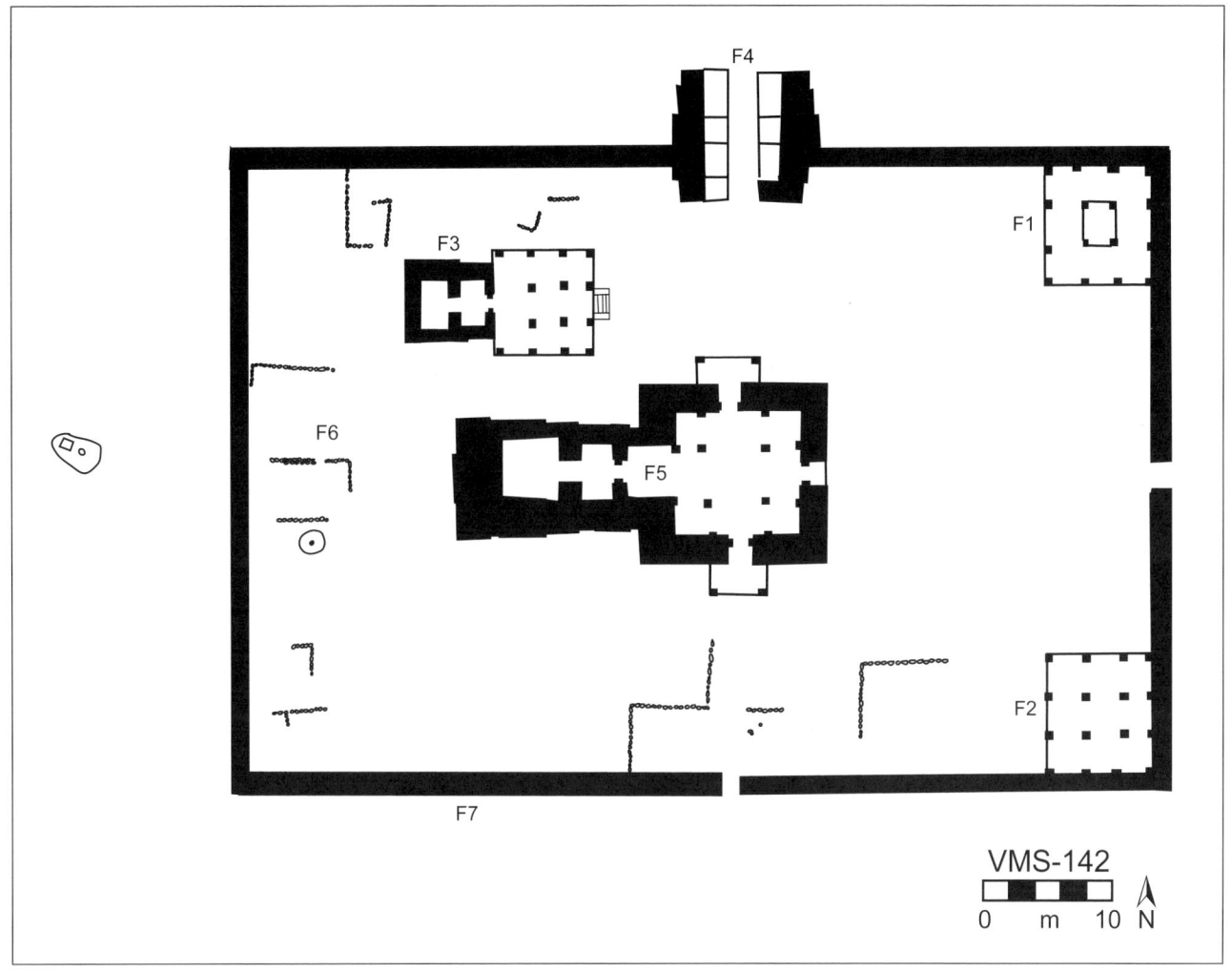

Figure 5.17. VMS-142, plan.

(*Top Left*) Plate 5.13. VMS-142, northern gopuram.

(*Left*) Plate 5.14. VMS-142, Feature 3, sanctuary and shikara of shrine in northwest corner of complex.

(*Top Right*) Plate 5.15. VMS-142, Feature 4, sculptural details on northern gate to complex, Vaishnava images.

(*Above*) Plate 5.16. VMS-142, Feature 6, grinding machine in residential area within complex.

Plate 5.17. VMS-143, overview of north side.

SITE: VMS-143   Block: S   **Transect:** 16
  Primary Site Use: Religious, transport: well.
  Site Dimensions: 15 × 16 m
  Setting: Level dry farmed fields.
  Present Land Use/Disturbances: 10 m from paved road. The well is badly collapsed and filled in with sediment and vegetation.
  Site Description: Rock-cut and masonry well, associated with temple complex VMS-142. The lower portion of this well (c. 1 m is visible) is rock-cut; the upper portion is of masonry. The latter is composed of square and rectangular undressed blocks, loosely fit together and incorporating some chinking stones. A square feature constructed of two slabs laid crosswise over two other slabs projects out over the well on its north side. The slabs used in this projection are reused chlorite moldings.

  The masonry sides of the well are preserved to nine courses and are stepped back every third course. Footholds project from the south, east, and north walls. There is a gradual decline from the west side (stairs?) into the well depression, which appears to constitute the main entrance to the well. The entrance turns 90° to the south, creating an L-shaped opening. Some of the stonework lining the north-south section of the entrance is still visible. This well is associated with the temple VMS-142. Two ornate chlorite-schist moldings are visible nearby.
  Artifacts: Located amid the transect 16-18 residential scatter; in this area artifact densities are moderate, and consist exclusively of earthenware ceramics. No artifacts are visible within or immediately surrounding the well, and no collections were made.
  Temporal Affiliation: Vijayanagara.
  Illustrations: Plate 5.17.

SITE: VMS-144   Block: S   **Transect:** 16
  Primary Site Use: Religious: temple complex.
  Site Dimensions: 75 × 75 m
  Setting: Level dry farmed fields.
  Present Land Use/Disturbances: Hearths and modern ceramics indicate recent site use. Structures are generally poorly preserved.
  Site Description: Vaishnava temple. This small three-chambered temple faces 20° east of north. Its front facade is the most ornate; the others are relatively plain. The outer porch, an east-facing columned hall, is walled with long, horizontal dressed slabs, and sits on a stone basement with elaborate molding. A staircase with curving, geometric "elephant trunk" balustrades is located on the east side of the temple.

  Vaishnava door guardians flank both the main entrance and the entrance to the antechamber. Above the door to the latter is a carving of Lakshmi between two elephants. Carved on the columns are yalis, tortoises, fish, lotus medallions, geese, devotees, lingam, naga, and conch.

  Collapsed building elements and mounded soil obscure the west side of the basement. The south side has a different design; a basement and lower molding support ornate columns with detached columnettes, atop a sitting yali. The east facade has elaborately curving eaves. There are three superstructures; these gopura are partially collapsed but plaster figures can be seen between the towers. This facade evidently extended all around the structure at one point. The beams supporting the roof are also carved.
  Feature 1: A 2 × 2 m mandapa, c. 40 m west of the temple. This small structure is badly disturbed; only the plinth, two columns, and portions of the basement remain. A fallen cruciform capital lies between the standing columns.
  Feature 2: Consists only of architectural elements, but may have been either a small shrine or lamp column platform. The 12 m long feature is oriented east-west and situated directly in front of the main temple. Along the east edge of the structures are aligned slabs, next to which is a column footing and a half-buried block with a sculpted Vishnu image.
  Feature 3: Heavily disturbed and overgrown platform southeast of the main temple. The platform is built with long, rectangular dressed blocks. The corner blocks are two stepped with angled bevel moldings and quarter corner medallions. This feature may actually consist of two platforms and was perhaps a gate.
  Feature 4: Small square well c. 15 m northeast of the main temple. The well is overgrown, but up to eight courses of small blocks are visible on all sides. A steep and narrow staircase is centered on the south side. No water is presently visible.
  Feature 5: Platform c. 10 m northeast of the main temple. This 3 × 3 m platform is constructed of long, rectangular dressed granite blocks.
  Artifacts: This site is located within the artifact scatter that extends across the northeast quadrant of Block S, which constitutes the remains of Achyutadevaraya's suburb, Varadadevi-ammana-pattana. Three east-west transects were laid out at intervals of 30 m (transect 1 on the south, transect 3 to the north), with units located every 15 m along them. A diagnostic sweep was made of the entire site area.
  Transect 1 Unit 1: 100 g ceramics; wares: 9 black plain ware, 1 red plain ware, 15 brown plain ware. Diagnostics: 2 bowls, 3 jars. Other artifacts: 1 piece slag (<50 g).
  Transect 1 Unit 2: 100 g ceramics; wares: 35 black plain ware, 1 brown plain ware. Diagnostics: 2 jars.
  Transect 1 Unit 3: <50 g ceramics; wares: 1 brown plain ware.
  Transect 1 Unit 4: 100 g ceramics; wares: 18 black plain ware, 8 brown plain ware. Diagnostics: 1 jar. Other artifacts: lithics, 150 g.

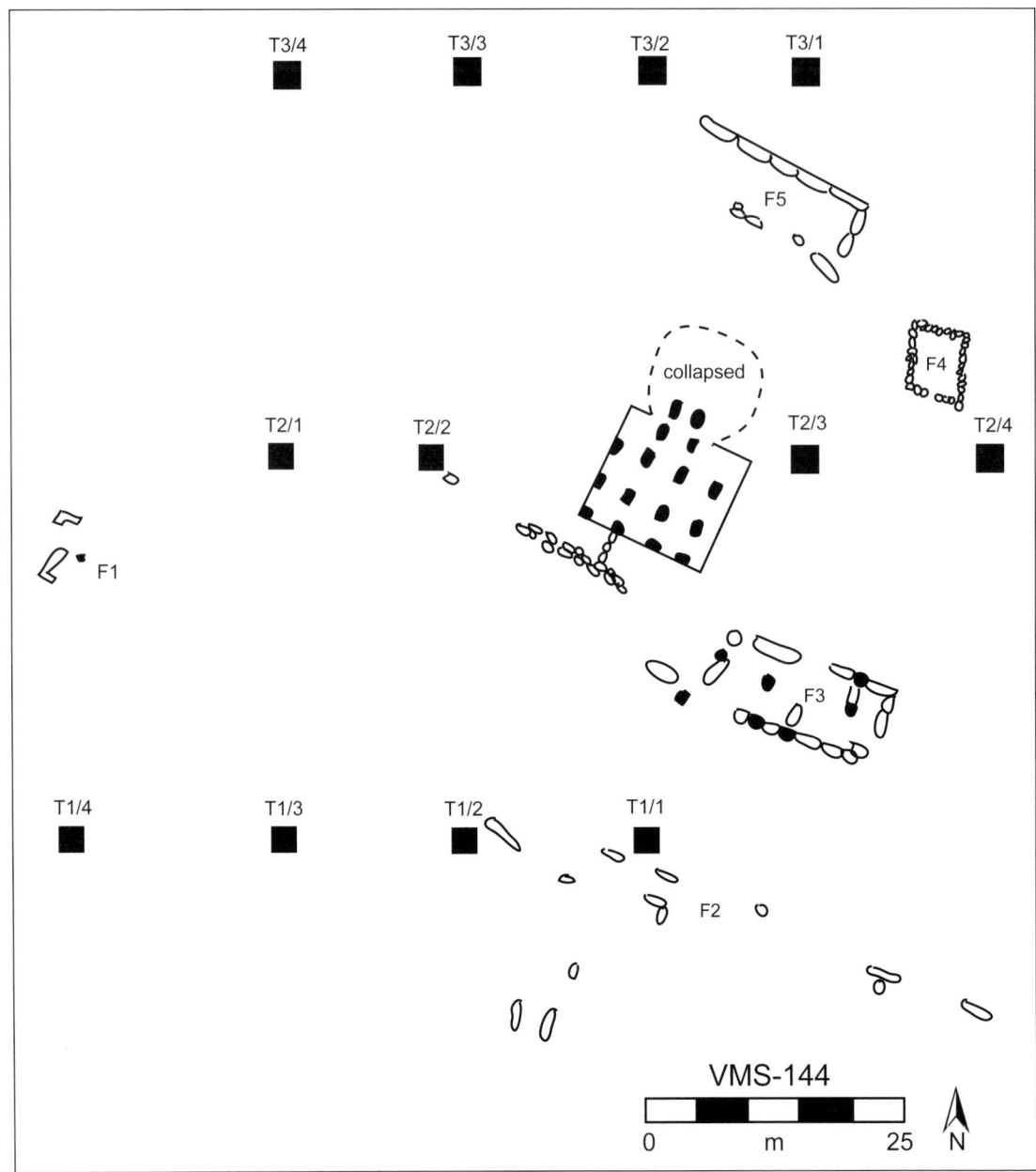

Figure 5.18. VMS-144, plan.

Transect 2 Unit 1: 150 g ceramics; wares: 27 black plain ware, 4 red plain ware, 6 brown ware, 1 coarse ware. Diagnostics: 3 jars, 7 unidentifiable.

Transect 2 Unit 2: 150 g ceramics; wares: 23 black plain ware, 3 brown plain ware. Diagnostics: 2 jars, 2 unidentifiable.

Transect 2 Unit 3: 100 g ceramics; wares: 53 black plain ware, 17 brown plain ware, 1 coarse ware. Diagnostics: 1 bowl, 3 jars, 9 unidentifiable.

Transect 2 Unit 4: 200 g ceramics; wares: 51 black plain ware, 14 brown plain ware. Diagnostics: 1 jar, 3 unidentifiable. Other artifacts: 2 fragments slag (20 g).

Transect 3 Unit 1: 150 g ceramics; wares: 22 black plain ware, 2 red plain ware, 11 brown plain ware. Diagnostics: 2 jars, 2 unidentifiable.

Transect 3 Unit 2: 300 g ceramics; wares: 72 black plain ware, 10 brown plain ware. Diagnostics: 1 bowl, 1 jar, 8 unidentifiable.

Transect 3 Unit 3: 200 g ceramics; wares: 22 black plain ware, 1 red plain ware, 5 brown plain ware. Diagnostics: 2 bowls, 2 unidentifiable.

Transect 3 Unit 4: 200 g ceramics; wares: 47 black plain ware, 6 red plain ware, 35 brown plain ware. Diagnostics: 7 jars, 9 unidentifiable. Other artifacts: 1 piece slag (100 g).

Temporal Affiliation: Late Vijayanagara (sixteenth century). Date indicated by detached column and curved eaves of the main shrine.

References: Morrison 1995:80; Morrison and Sinopoli 1996:69; Sinopoli 2003:151.

Figure: Figure 5.18.

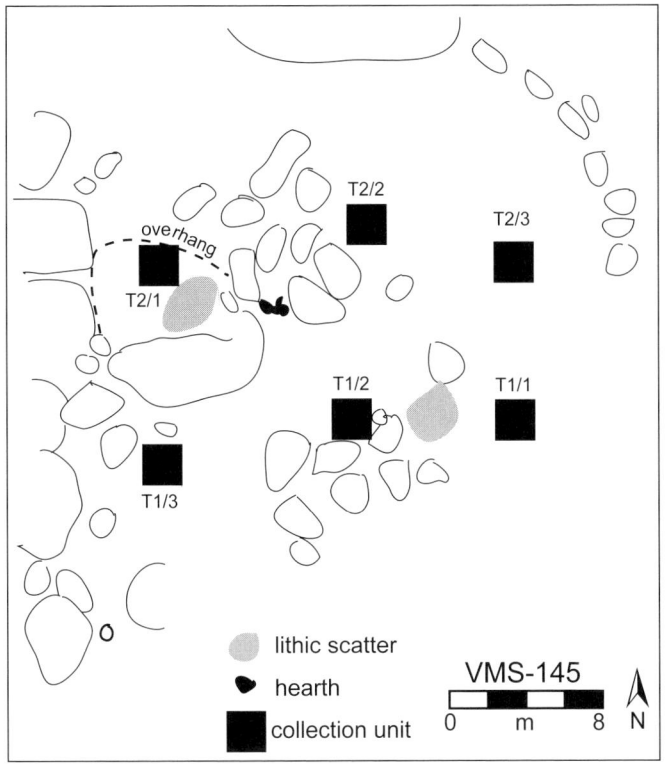

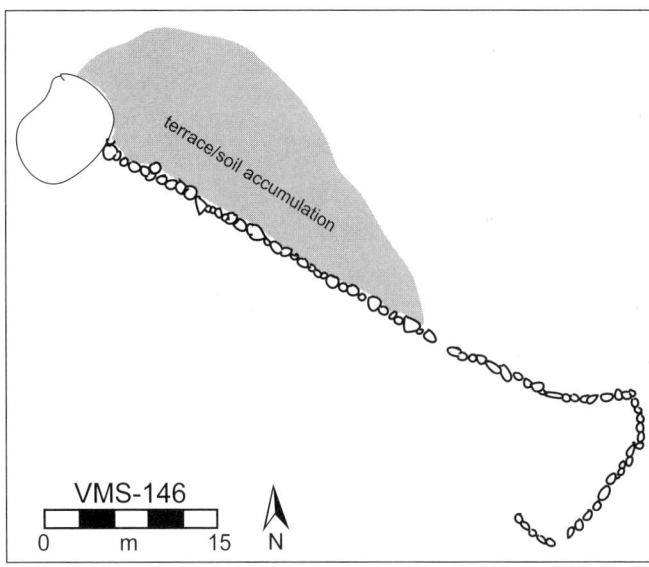

Figure 5.20. VMS-146, plan.

Figure 5.19. VMS-145, plan.

SITE: VMS-145   Block: S   Transect: 17
  Primary Site Use: Residential: rock shelter.
  Site Dimensions: 24 × 23 m
  Setting: Moderately sloping outcrop above a dry farmed plain.
  Present Land Use/Disturbances: Disturbed by modern quarrying. A modern hearth and the presence of bottle glass in the rock shelter attest to recent use.
  Site Description: Rock shelter. This north-facing natural shelter probably functioned as a shelter over many different periods. The ceiling has collapsed in the southwest corner of the rock shelter, covering a large number of artifacts. A recent broken earthenware storage jar cached beneath a boulder was designated as Feature 1.
  Artifacts: A moderate to high density lithic and ceramic scatter is concentrated at the shelter's drip line. Lithics appear in small 0.5 m clusters. Two east-west transects spaced at 10 m intervals, with collections every 10 m; a total of six units collected along the transects. In addition, three diagnostic collections were made—D1: inside shelter, ceramics; D2: outside shelter, all; D3: inside shelter, lithics.
  Transect 1 Unit 1: 1250 g ceramics; wares: 176 black plain ware, 86 brown plain ware. Diagnostics: 4 jars.
  Transect 1 Unit 2: 250 g ceramics; wares: 35 black plain ware, 40 brown plain ware.
  Transect 2 Unit 1: 1 lithic, utilized flake, translucent white quartz.
  Transect 2 Unit 2: 50 g ceramics; wares: 12 black plain ware, 1 brown plain ware.
  Transect 2 Unit 3: 50 g ceramics; wares: 12 black plain ware. Lithics: 94 flakes (90 quartz, 2 cryptocrystalline, 2 volcanic stone), 83 fragments angular debris (quartz), 3 cores (2 quartz, 1 cryptocrystalline), 11 bipolar cores (quartz).
  Temporal Affiliation: Pre-Vijayanagara, Vijayanagara, and recent.
  Illustrations: Figure 5.19.

SITE: VMS-146   Block: S   Transect: 17
  Primary Site Use: Agricultural: retaining wall.
  Site Dimensions: 120 × 75 m
  Setting: Base of outcrop on sheet rock.
  Present Land Use/Disturbances: None.
  Site Description: Retaining wall. The wall is constructed of unmodified cobbles piled atop sheet rock. The wall is situated at the base of a small outcrop, at an oblique angle to an east-west trending ephemeral water course that emerges from the outcrop at the southeast end of the wall. A terrace of sandy soil c. 10 m wide has formed behind the wall. The terrace is well developed but there is no evidence of recent maintenance or use. This feature is part of a larger system of soil and water control features interspersed throughout the area. Some of these features show evidence of recent maintenance and use, while others are in disrepair or linked to Vijayanagara period facilities.
  Artifacts: A dense, localized ceramic scatter is found on the terrace behind the wall and in the boulders southwest of the wall. 100% collection within 10 m of the wall. 400 g ceramics; wares: 171 black plain ware, 161 brown plain ware. Diagnostics: 4 jars.
  Temporal Affiliation: Unknown. It is probable that the land use system in the area today is similar to that of the Vijayanagara period, even if some components of the system are different.
  Illustrations: Figure 5.20.

Plate 5.18. VMS-147, overview.

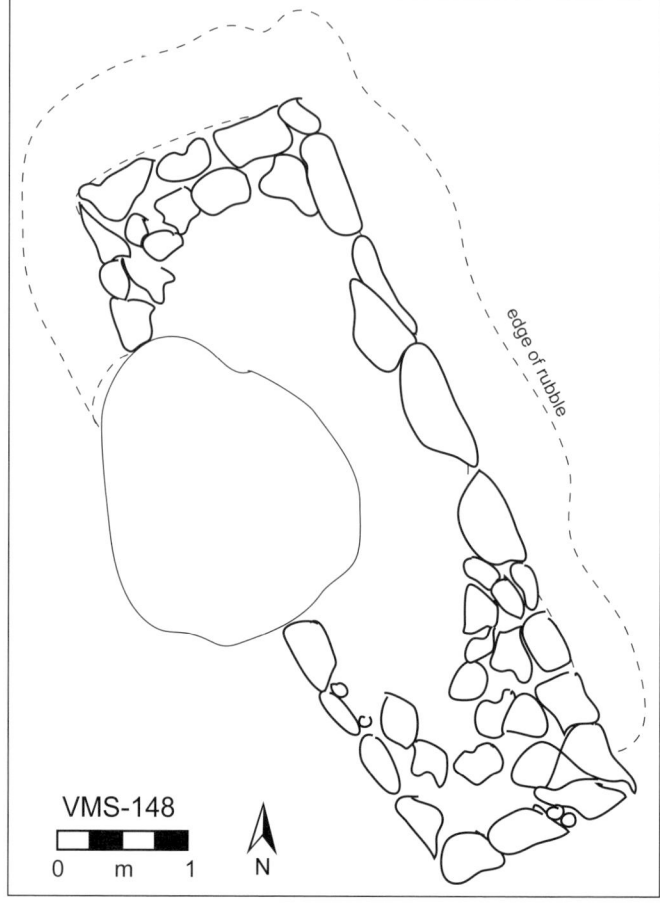

Figure 5.21. VMS-148, plan.

SITE: VMS-147   Block: S   Transect: 17
   Primary Site Use: Residential: rock shelter.
   Site Dimensions: 2 × 1.4 m
   Setting: Under boulders, sheet rock nearby.
   Present Land Use/Disturbances: None.
   Site Description: Rock shelter. This locale is created by two large granite boulders that lean together, forming a triangular shelter. Both ends of the shelter are open but neither entrance is large enough for human passage. The smaller boulder has a flat, worn, table-like surface. The shelter is located c. 25 m north of VMS-146.
   Artifacts: Moderate, even ceramic scatter within the shelter and around the shelter's entrance to a 10 m radius from the shelter. Most of the ceramics were in the outcrops north of the rock shelter. 100% collection. 1150 g ceramics; wares: 252 black plain ware, 112 brown plain ware. Diagnostics: 2 bowls, 6 jars.
   Temporal Affiliation: Unknown.
   Illustrations: Plate 5.18.

SITE: VMS-148   Block: S   Transect: 17
   Primary Site Use: Agricultural: one-room structure.
   Site Dimensions: 3.5 × 6.5 m
   Setting: Gently sloping dry farmed fields.
   Present Land Use/Disturbances: Minimal.
   Site Description: One-room structure. The structure is composed of four masonry walls built into a large boulder located on the southeast edge of the watershed of the reservoir VMS-194. Roughly dressed blocks and unmodified cobbles are laid end to end, up to five courses high. The north wall is largely collapsed. This structure is quite substantial for a field house/day-use facility, and there is no evidence of domestic activities. It may have been used for storage. An ephemeral wash runs along the north side of the site.
   Artifacts: None observed; no collections made.
   Temporal Affiliation: Unknown.
   Illustrations: Figure 5.21.

SITE: VMS-149   Block: S   Transect: 16
   Primary Site Use: Other/residential: artifact scatter.
   Site Dimensions: 17 × 15 m
   Setting: Outcrop amid gently sloping dry farmed fields.
   Present Land Use/Disturbances: Dry farmed fields. A bullock cart track runs past the north side of the site. A threshing floor is located 30 m west of the scatter. Fields to the west are irrigated, but these are lower lying than VMS-149.
   Site Description: Ceramic scatter around a large outcrop. Perhaps the remains of residential or dumping activities.
   Artifacts: Localized, dense clusters of sherds within a 17 × 15 m area. The scatter is centered on a small east-west oriented outcrop that forms the border between two fields. Some modern glass is also found here. Two north-south transects were placed at intervals of 10 m, collections taken at 10 m intervals along each transect. A diagnostic sweep was also made. The following units contained artifacts:
   Transect 1 Unit 1: 250 g ceramics; wares: 43 black plain ware, 16 red plain ware. Diagnostics: 1 jar.
   Transect 1 Unit 2: <50 g ceramics; wares: 1 black plain ware.
   Transect 2 Unit 2: 100 g ceramics; wares: 3 black plain ware. Diagnostics: 2 jars.
   D1: 350 g ceramics; wares: 6 black plain ware, 10 brown plain ware. Diagnostics: 2 bowls, 6 jars, 16 unidentifiable.
   Temporal Affiliation: Unknown.

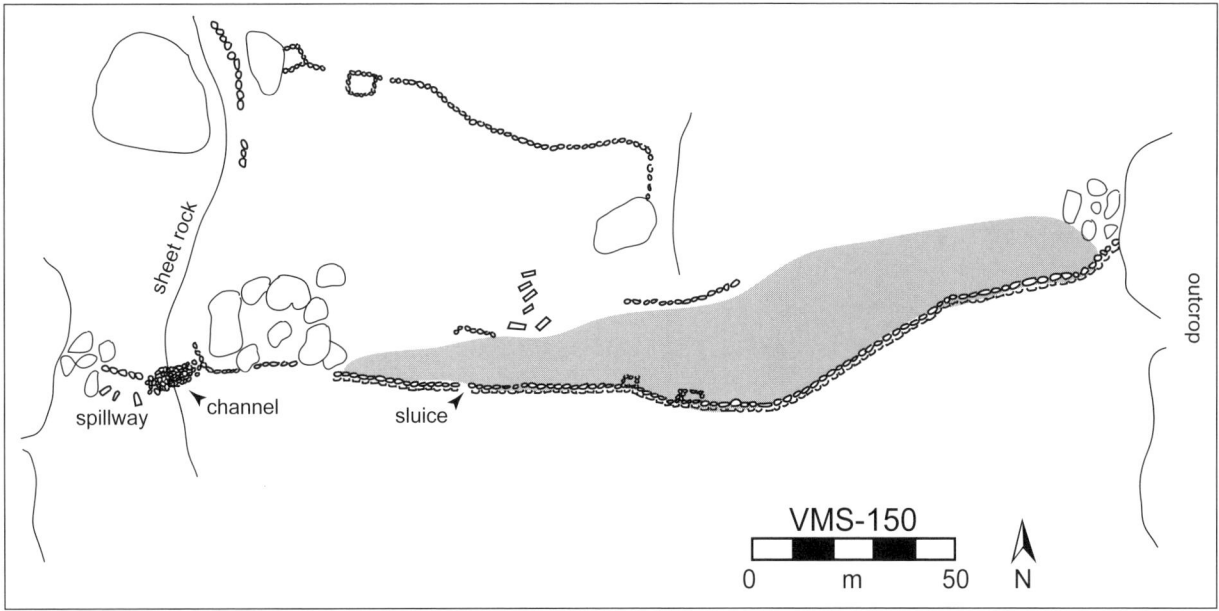

Figure 5.22. VMS-150, plan.

SITE: VMS-150   Block: S   Transect: 16
Primary Site Use: Agricultural: reservoir embankment.
Site Dimensions: 240 × 90 m
Setting: Flat and gently sloping sheet rock, outcrop, and hilltop.
Present Land Use/Disturbances: Above the embankment are dry farmed fields. Below the embankment are wet and dry fields. A footpath runs along the embankment; overall disturbance is minimal.
Site Description: Reservoir embankment. The long embankment varies greatly in width and height as it is incorporated into natural outcrops and hills at several points along its course. Atop the embankment are several short wall alignments and a single small, square room.

The west end consists of an earthen embankment faced on its south face with four to five stepped courses masonry composed of unmodified and split small-medium boulders. There is a narrow strip of masonry on the north side as well. This reservoir is unusual for its double stepped masonry. Near the east end of the embankment, each course is stepped back, but after c. 5 m, the lower steps are each two courses high. These double-course steps appear and disappear, but along most of the embankment at least one step is disproportionately high. The boulders are larger toward the middle of the embankment and the steps widen as the structure curves. Several long, unmodified slabs are incorporated into this center portion, in which chinking stones are interspersed with quite massive masonry. As the embankment makes a sharp turn to the west, the masonry becomes much smaller, more irregularly coursed, and the steps that were clear elsewhere are not evident in this segment, which may represent a later repair. Further west, the configuration of deep steps continues with a few split stones incorporated into the masonry. Near the west end of the embankment, a channel has been excavated in the field to the south. An opening underneath the embankment is visible at this point, although no gate remains. The opening is simply constructed of split blocks, now painted red and white. Traces of the channel are visible on the north side.

At its west end, the embankment incorporates a large granite outcrop. Here, there is no earthen embankment; the masonry face is built up against the outcrop. Within the outcrop is a channel, c. 1.5 m wide and apparently natural, with a base of stone. There is no evidence how or if the flow of water through this channel was controlled. It is now piled up with cobbles, small boulders and quarried blocks. At the west end of the embankment, some masonry curves around to the north, forming an east edge to the bedrock channel. This channel may have served as a waste weir or safety overflow outlet. West of the channel are more outcrops; some aligned stones may indicate a partial extension of the south masonry. On this side are three quarried 2-2.5 m long slabs of unknown function. Water would have cascaded over several natural rock steps and into several natural cisterns before flowing into the drainage channel on the north, debouching out onto sheet rock. On the north side of the embankment, just east of the incorporated hill, are three more quarried slabs. Like the ones on the west, they are lying horizontally and approximately parallel, but have no clear function.

Downstream (north) from the embankment is a rocky area, its north edge flanked by a wide rubble wall that incorporates a small room. Near the west end of the wall is a north-south alignment of boulders set atop the sheet rock to help channel water from the stone channel.

There is a probable second sluice east of the first, where masonry is found on the north side of the embankment, and where a channel emerges near the lower rubble wall. A well, VMS-151, lies near this channel. The water-retaining area of this feature forms a closed basin c. 300 m (north-south) × 240 m (east-west).

Artifacts: Three plain ware sherds near west end of embankment. On north side, near the horizontal slabs, is a lithic and ceramic scatter c. 19 m in diameter. The scatter is of uniformly high density, with well defined edges, and contains debris from the bipolar reduction of vein quartz. A transect was laid along the long axis of the scatter, and two 2 × 2 m units were placed at 10 m intervals. A diagnostic collection was also taken at this scatter; one utilized artifact—a scraper of white quartz.

Transect 1 Unit 1: 250 g ceramics; wares: 81 black plain ware, 5 brown plain ware. Diagnostics: 2 jars.

Transect 1 Unit 2: 900 g ceramics; wares: 112 black plain ware, 1 brown plain ware. Diagnostics: 1 jar.

Temporal Affiliation: Vijayanagara and later (?).
References: Morrison 1995:91, 102.
Illustrations: Figure 5.22.

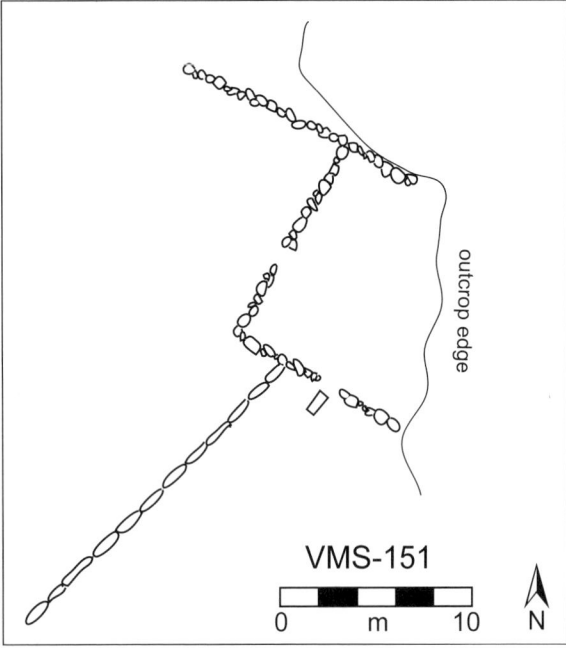

Figure 5.23. VMS-151, plan.

SITE: VMS-151   Block: S   Transect: 16
   Primary Site Use: Agricultural: well.
   Site Dimensions: 10 × 9 m
   Setting: Base of low outcrop.
   Present Land Use/Disturbances: Fields adjacent to the well are irrigated. Some of the masonry is displaced; several blocks at the bottom of the well. A tree growing inside the well has been uprooted and is now resting on the southeast wall. Immediately to the southeast is a small modern shrine; circa 15 m to the northeast is another modern shrine.
   Site Description: Well. The well is adjacent to and below reservoir VMS-150. It is located at the base of an outcrop that forms its north and east sides. Long, dressed rectangular granite blocks form the other two walls. A long wall extends south from the southwest edge of the well. The walls are generally well preserved. The well has a lower course of long rectangular blocks over which smaller blocks and unmodified stones have been placed more recently, perhaps to form a field wall. The well is deep but has a low water level.
   The modern shrine next to the well consists of a small rock at the base of a tree; the shrine to the northeast of the well is concealed from view by large trees and vines and is nestled in a small (2 m high) gap in the face of the outcrop. Lamps, bangles, and vermillion marks indicate recent use.
   Artifacts: A small, localized ceramic scatter was found on the slope southeast of and 5 m from the well. 100% collection. 650 g ceramics; wares: 112 black plain ware. Diagnostics: 7 jars.
   Temporal Affiliation: Vijayanagara.
   Illustrations: Figure 5.23.

SITE: VMS-152   Block: S   Transect: 16
   Primary Site Use: Transport: road.
   Site Dimensions: 110 × 35 m
   Setting: Saddle between two outcrops.
   Present Land Use/Disturbances: A recent field wall intersects the road on the south; the Right Bank High Level Canal is c. 20 m to the north.

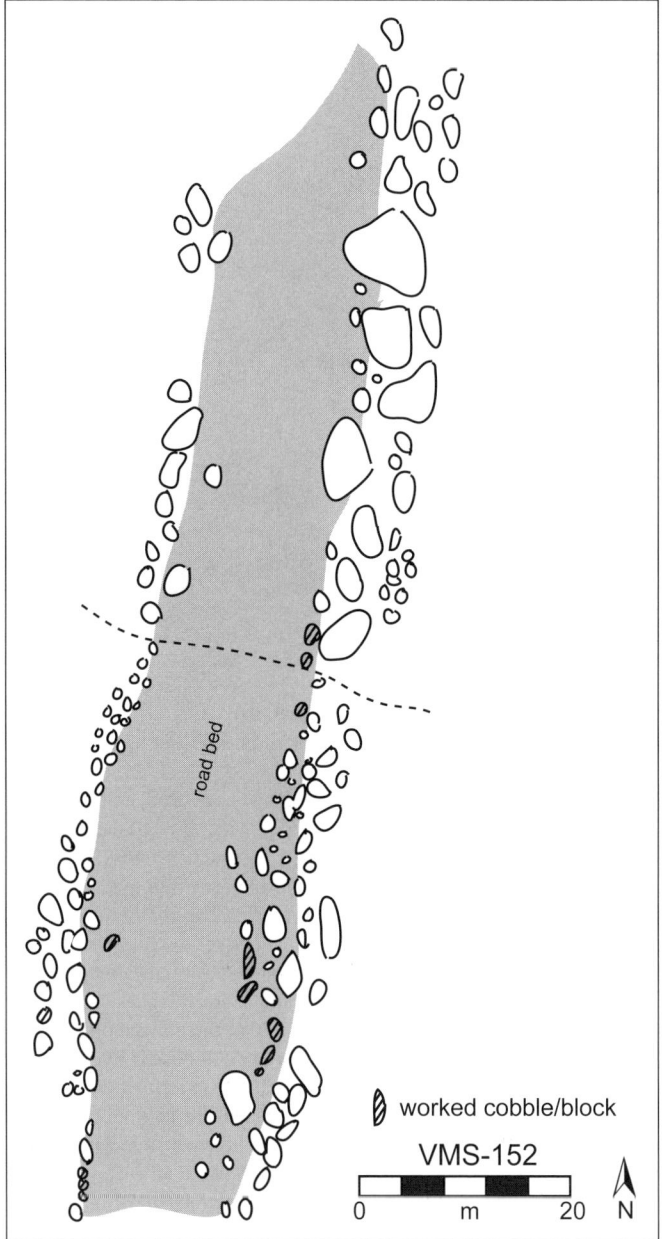

Figure 5.24. VMS-152, plan.

   Site Description: Isolated road segment constructed as a level terrace between granitic outcrops. The roadway runs roughly north-south and consists of a terrace cleared of cobbles and walled on both sides. The 0.2 m wide walls consist of the natural outcrop augmented by a single course of unmodified cobbles. Another possible wall segment consisting of a single line of five irregular, unmodified elements is located 22 m east of the road segment.
   Artifacts: Modern ceramic scatter; not collected.
   Temporal Affiliation: Unknown.
   References: Morrison 1995:75; Morrison and Sinopoli 1996:63-64.
   Illustrations: Figure 5.24.

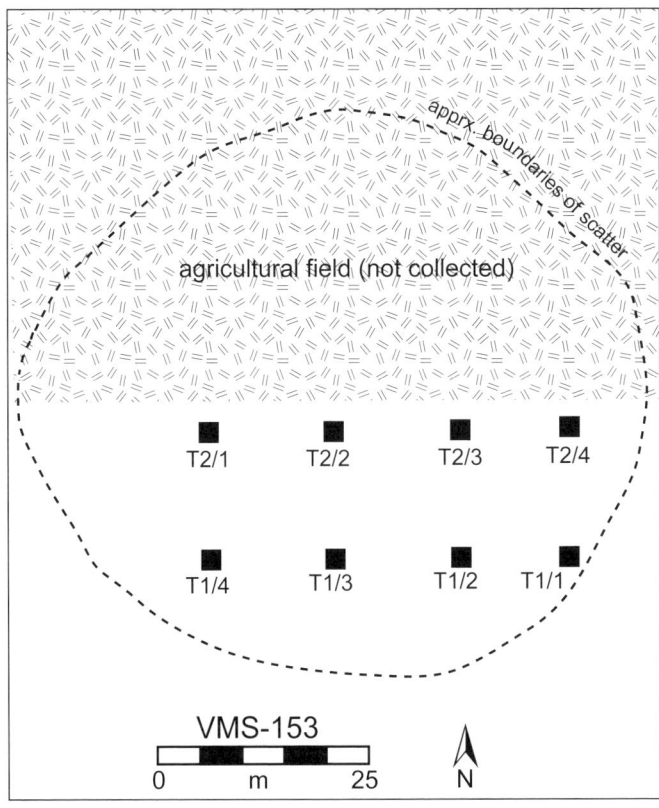

Figure 5.25. VMS-153, plan and location of collection units.

SITE: VMS-153 Block: S Transect: 16

Primary Site Use: Unknown/residential: artifact scatter.
Site Dimensions: 70 × 62 m
Setting: Level dry farmed fields.
Present Land Use/Disturbances: Dry farming, grazing. Northern half of site was planted in cotton when recorded and could not be collected.
Site Description: Artifact scatter. Site is located c. 150 m north of the east end of the embankment of VMS-150. The scatter is in the area that would have been watered by the reservoir. Probably the remains of residential debris.
Artifacts: Sparse, oval-shaped scatter of ceramics with some chunks of slag, occasional lithics, and a single round granite stone with evidence of battering. Two east-west transects were laid out, spaced 15 m apart in southern half of site, with 2 × 2 m collection units placed at 15 m intervals; a total of eight units were collected.
Transect 1 Unit 1: <50 g ceramics; wares: 3 black plain ware.
Transect 1 Unit 2: <50 g ceramics; wares: 2 black plain ware.
Transect 1 Unit 3: 50 g ceramics; wares: 7 black plain ware, 1 brown plain ware.
Transect 1 Unit 4: <50 g ceramics; wares: 6 black plain ware, 1 brown plain ware.
Transect 2 Unit 1: 100 g ceramics; wares: 13 black plain ware, 1 coarse ware.
Transect 2 Unit 2: <50 g ceramics; wares: 3 black plain ware.
Transect 2 Unit 3: <50 g ceramics; wares: 1 red plain ware.
Transect 2 Unit 4: <50 g ceramics; wares: 2 black plain ware, 2 brown plain ware.
Other: Lithics: 1 utilized flake of gray-white chert, 1 quartz core.
Temporal Affiliation: Unknown.
Illustrations: Figure 5.25.

SITE: VMS-154 Block: S Transect: 16

Primary Site Use: Religious: displaced sculptures.
Site Dimensions: n/a
Setting: Level coconut grove.
Present Land Use/Disturbances: Site consists of displaced Vijayanagara period sculptures in a modern shrine.
Site Description: Vijayanagara period sculptures placed in front of a small, cinder block temple. Inside the shrine is a post-Vijayanagara female Shaivite deity with a naga hood, holding trident and drum. On the outside platform are the older carvings. These include a four-armed Shiva holding a trident and drum; a lingam of a dark, fine-grained material; two naga stones; and a Nagamma. In front of the shrine are a lingam and a carving depicting two feet surrounded by a ring next to two carved devotees, possibly male, with severed heads. One head has a side knot of hair; the other is a cow head. A disused block mortar lies near the temple. Vijayanagara-type quarried elements lie in a canal to the south.
Artifacts: No collections made.
Temporal Affiliation: Vijayanagara and later.

SITE: VMS-155 Block: S Transect: 18

Primary Site Use: Water storage: cistern.
Site Dimensions: 0.6 × 1.1 m
Setting: Steeply sloping sheet rock.
Present Land Use/Disturbances: Minimal; there is some modern quarrying in nearby irrigated fields.
Site Description: Rock-cut cistern. This small square cistern (0.6 × 1.1 × 0.23 deep) is cut into sheet rock near the base of a large outcrop and just below an extensive expanse of sheet rock. This facility captures runoff from the sheet rock. Vijayanagara-type dressing marks and heavy mineral staining mark the depression.
Artifacts: None observed; no collections made.
Temporal Affiliation: Vijayanagara.

SITE: VMS-156 Block: S Transect: 18

Primary Site Use: Religious: inscribed slab.
Site Dimensions: 0.5 × 0.2 × 1.4 (high)
Setting: Level irrigated field.
Present Land Use/Disturbances: None.
Site Description: Isolated inscribed slab, possibly from temple VMS-129. Three pecked designs, possibly of lotus and/or chakra, are depicted on the slab. A second uninscribed but dressed and quarried slab is located c. 100 m to the north.
Artifacts: None observed; no collections made.
Temporal Affiliation: Vijayanagara.

Plate 5.19. VMS-157, inscribed sheet rock.

SITE: VMS-157   Block: S   Transect: 18
  Primary Site Use: Other: inscribed sheet rock.
  Site Dimensions: 4 × 2 m
  Setting: Sloping sheet rock.
  Present Land Use/Disturbances: A recent dirt road running to the Penukonda gate is located c. 25 m south of the site, which is surrounded by irrigated fields. Some of the rock face has been chipped away.
  Site Description: Pecked games, figures, and a single word in Kannada on very smooth, rounded sheet rock at the base of the outcrop bearing temple VMS-129. The designs include several games, one anthropomorphic figure, and an ornate design (chakra?). Near the figures the outcrop shows signs of pre-modern quarrying.
  Artifacts: None observed; no collections made.
  Temporal Affiliation: Vijayanagara (?).
  Illustrations: Plate 5.19.

SITE: VMS-158   Block: S   Transect: 18
  Primary Site Use: Defensive, transport: road and "horse stones."
  Site Dimensions: 160 × 40 m
  Setting: Level area near foot of outcrop.
  Present Land Use/Disturbances: Extensively disturbed by grazing, plowing, and stone robbing for irrigation ditches and farmers' walls, and by the dirt road leading out from the Penukonda gate, which bisects the site along its north boundary. A telephone line cuts across the site to the south, while modern irrigation ditches form west and northeast boundaries.
  Site Description: Vijayanagara roadway with associated features. The road led out from the Penukonda gate (VMS-217). Its course is followed, in part, by the modern road. The site is situated at the foot of the outcrop containing VMS-129, lying on a broad, flat, plain, at the east edge of the outcrop bearing the outer city walls (VMS-123) of Vijayanagara. A shrine (VMS-131) lies 45-50 m to the east, along the course of this road. VMS-130, a possible boundary wall or road segment, may be a continuation of this roadway.
  Area 1: The south boundary wall of the road segment closest to the Penukonda gate. It consists of a massive, double-faced cobble wall, of which c. 25 m remains intact. This wall is cut by fields, irrigation ditches, and the dirt road. It is c. 1.5 m wide, one to two elements high (0.5-1 m), and is composed of very large unmodified cobbles.

Area 2: Lies perpendicular to the road wall and is an alignment of widely spaced small boulders, eight to twelve elements wide. This feature is badly disturbed. Although the boulders are mostly oriented east-west, there are also several north-south alignments. These may be the remnants of fortifications, such as those barriers near city walls designed to slow or stop mounted soldiers, known as "horse stones" (Sewell 1900). The boulders in this area are either unmodified or split, exhibit a wide variation in size, and are irregularly placed and oriented.

The north exterior of the alignment is formed by larger boulders and slabs placed upright. These uprights form part of a modern field wall, and may thus be a recent modification. An irrigation ditch runs along these uprights. Several modern carvings, pecked into the upright slabs, are visible at either end of the alignment. On the east are what appear to be a conch and several unfinished religious motifs. Adjacent to this recent carving is a naga stone with Vijayanagara-type quarry marks. At the west end of the alignment is an upright slab with Vijayanagara-type quarry marks and an inscribed lingam with sun and moon. This design is highly weathered and is more deeply pecked than the recent ones.

Area 3: A mounded area at the northeast edge of the site containing a roughly shaped and dressed upright (possible column), and a well-dressed, horizontal slab. Only a small portion of the slab is visible on the surface. The nature and function of this structure are unknown; it may be a column footing.
  Artifacts: Extremely diffuse and sparse scatter of ceramics with most sherds from plowed area to east of site. 100% collection over entire site area. 250 g ceramics; wares: 22 black plain ware, 1 red plain ware, 11 brown plain ware. Diagnostics: 5 jars.
  Temporal Affiliation: Vijayanagara.
  References: Morrison 1995:65, 76; Morrison and Sinopoli 1996:67.
  Illustrations: Figure 5.26.

SITE: VMS-159   Block: S   Transect: 17-18
  Primary Site Use: Agricultural: reservoir embankment.
  Site Dimensions: 170 × 15 m
  Setting: Amid rice paddies on a low rise.
  Present Land Use/Disturbances: Heavily disturbed and largely overgrown. Massive soil movements have changed the land surface and the embankment is both cut and eroded. The area is planted in irrigated rice and bananas and the embankment is being used as a cart track. Irrigation ditches run along the south side of the embankment and cut its east and west ends.
  Site Description: Reservoir embankment. This small, badly disturbed reservoir embankment is located southwest of the Penukonda gate road and south/southeast of the city wall. The reservoir is situated on an undulating plain crossed by low east-west trending outcrops. Both the construction and location are consistent with a Vijayanagara period temporal affiliation, perhaps early. The area appears to be colluviated. There is no evidence of an actual sluice, but one of the recent irrigation channels breaching the embankment passes through the likely sluice location. The embankment is faced by stepped masonry on the north side, with some masonry also visible on the south side. The masonry consists of up to six courses of unmodified large granitic cobbles laid end to end.
  Artifacts: 100% collection. One black plain ware body sherd recovered.
  Temporal Affiliation: Vijayanagara (?).
  References: Morrison 1995:91, 102.
  Illustrations: Figure 5.27

Block S: Site Summaries

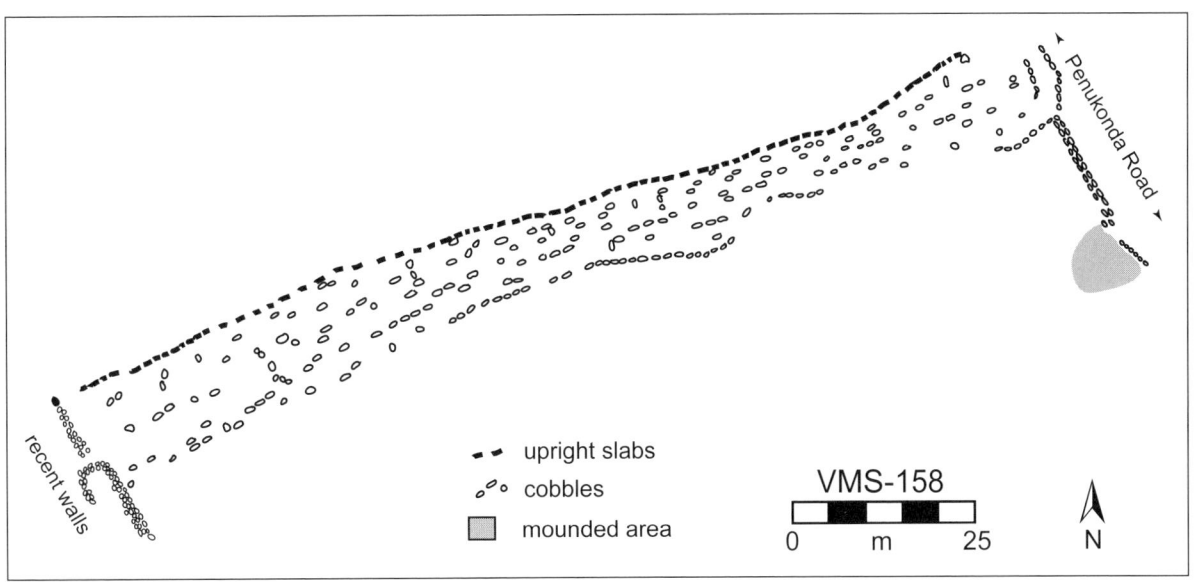

Figure 5.26. VMS-158, plan.

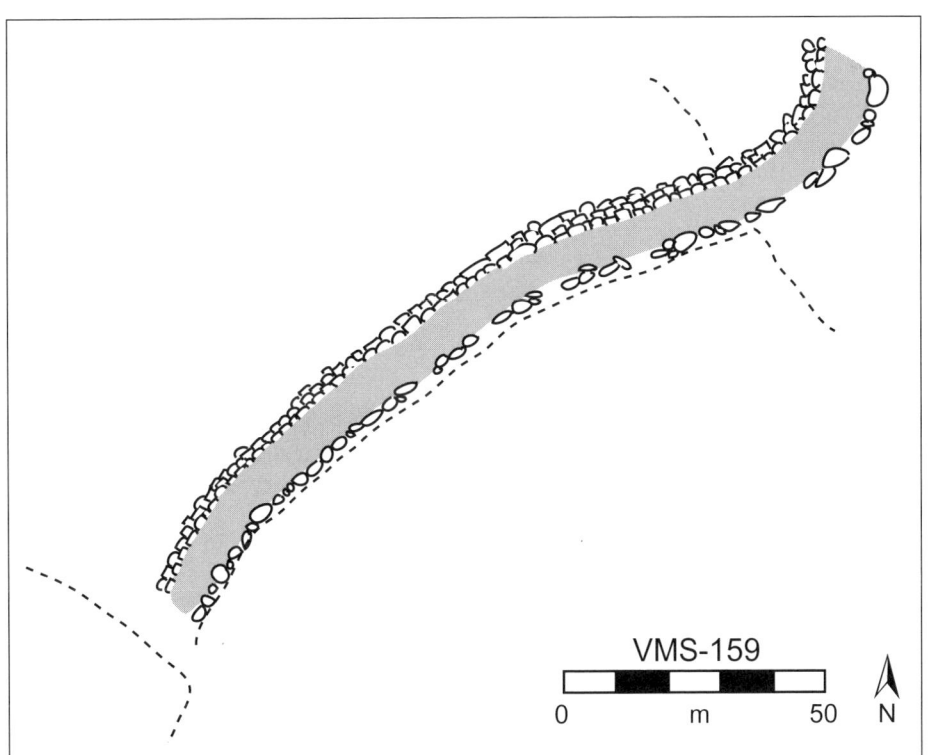

Figure 5.27. VMS-159, plan.

Plate 5.20. VMS-160, alignments.

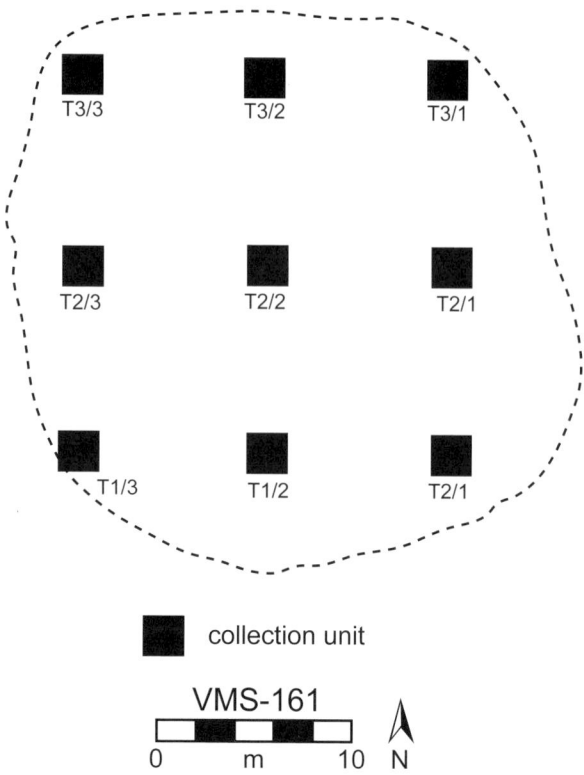

Figure 5.28. VMS-161, plan, approximate site boundaries, and collection units.

SITE: VMS-160   Block: S   Transect: 18
  Primary Site Use: Transportation: road.
  Site Dimensions: 80 × 60 m
  Setting: Level area surrounded by fields.
  Present Land Use/Disturbances: Recent dirt road and road wall truncate site on the south. Grazing, plowing, stone robbing, and recent quarrying have significantly modified the site.
  Site Description: Road segment with small shrine (Feature 1). This site is located 1 km south of the outer city wall and may be a continuation of VMS-137. The surface of this north-south road is c. 30 m wide and is bounded by two parallel earthen-core walls or low platforms. These walls are roughly built of unmodified split cobbles and boulders. The stone alignments are two elements wide and one to two courses high, with c. 6 m wide bordering embankments. Several cobble crosswalls span the road platforms. North and east of the east platform is an east-west wall formed by a single line of large cobbles; recent disturbance has obscured the relation of this wall, if any, to the roadway. The temple complex VMS-164 lies 200 m to the west.
  Feature 1: A small shrine near the south end of the west embankment. This shrine is placed in one of a series of small rooms. The others lie to the south of Feature 1 and are all rubble filled. Feature 1 is a raised area, c. 4 m on a side, defined by quarried foundation slabs and blocks. It is occupied by a displaced, decapitated Vijayanagara period statue, apparently of Lakshmi.
  Artifacts: Very low density ceramic scatter throughout area. 100% collection within road area and embankment. 50 g earthenware ceramics. Wares: 6 black plain ware, 3 brown plain ware. Other diagnostics: 1 piece of Chinese blue-on-white porcelain found near south edge of site.
  Temporal Affiliation: Vijayanagara.
  References: Morrison 1995:75; Morrison and Sinopoli 1996:63-64.
  Illustrations: Plate 5.20.

SITE: VMS-161   Block: S   Transect: 17-18
  Primary Site Use: Residential: ceramic scatter.
  Site Dimensions: 35 × 25 m
  Setting: Level fields, on a low rise adjacent to outcrops.
  Present Land Use/Disturbances: Irrigated fields surround the site and an abandoned irrigation ditch runs through its center.
  Site Description: Small, localized ceramic scatter located in the broad, irrigated plain southeast of the city walls. The highest ceramic concentration occurs in the center of the site, in a north-south oriented oval, with a diffuse scatter continuing to the edges of the site. Some slag occurs southeast of the ceramic concentration.
  Artifacts: Three east-west transects, 10 m apart, collections every 10 m; a total of nine units were collected. Diagnostic collection of entire site area. The following units contained artifacts:
  Transect 1 Unit 1: <50 g ceramics; wares: 6 black plain ware. Other: 1 fragment slag.
  Transect 1 Unit 2: 100 g ceramics; wares: 12 black plain ware, 4 brown plain ware. Diagnostics: 1 jar.
  Transect 1 Unit 3: 100 g ceramics; wares: 4 black plain ware, 2 brown plain ware. Diagnostics: 1 jar.
  Transect 2 Unit 2: 100 g ceramics; wares: 10 black plain ware, 3 brown plain ware.
  Transect 2 Unit 3: 50 g ceramics; wares: 7 black plain ware, 2 brown plain ware.
  Transect 3 Unit 1: 50 g ceramics; wares: 7 black plain ware, 2 brown plain ware.
  Transect 3 Unit 2: 100 g ceramics; wares: 4 black plain ware, red plain ware, 1 brown plain ware. Diagnostics: 1 jar.
  Transect 3 Unit 3: 150 g ceramics; wares: 12 black plain ware, 1 red plain ware, 1 brown plain ware. Diagnostics: 1 bowl.
  Temporal Affiliation: Vijayanagara.
  Illustrations: Figure 5.28.

Plate 5.21. VMS-162, images.

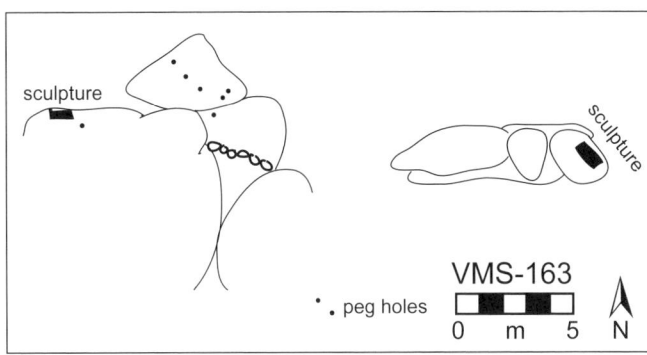

Figure 5.29. VMS-163, plan.

SITE: VMS-162   Block: S   Transect: 17
Primary Site Use: Religious: displaced sculptures.
Site Dimensions: 5 × 5 m
Setting: Level, rice paddies.
Present Land Use/Disturbances: Sculpture has been moved to a modern shrine, not *in situ*.
Site Description: Displaced sculptures. Two Vijayanagara-style sculptures placed on an elevated modern masonry platform. The smaller is a Ganesha image, with a broken head and shoulder. The larger is a female figure with hair in a bun, seated with one leg folded under her. Her right hand holds a staff or mace, while her left hand holds a circular object. Two drilled depressions are found on either side of her head.
Artifacts: No collections made.
Temporal Affiliation: Recent shrine with displaced Vijayanagara sculptures.
Illustrations: Plate 5.21.

SITE: VMS-163   Block: S   Transect: 16
Primary Site Use: Religious: rock shelter and carved relief.
Site Dimensions: 23 × 11 m
Setting: Rock shelter in outcrop.
Present Land Use/Disturbances: Recent irrigation has caused large-scale soil movement. Quarrying has also modified the site, which includes recent cultural features such as hearths and a retaining wall across the mouth of the shelter. The shelter is currently in use as a field house and the carving is in worship.
Site Description: Rock shelter and associated sculpture. The rock shelter is now in use as a field house and contains a hearth and modern ceramics. The mouth of the shelter is 3 m across and faces north. There are a series of Vijayanagara-style peg holes (0.04 × 0.04 m) northwest from the interior of the shelter. In addition to the alignment of peg holes, a striding Hanuman figure is pecked into the outcrop west/northwest of the shelter. This figure is half completed with only the head and right arm visible.

Circa 15 m east of the rock shelter is a carved hero stone with Vijayanagara-style quarry marks. This is an elaborate bas-relief with five figures and a horse. From left to right: (1) female standing, right arm raised, half moon with circles above head; (2) male, standing, facing horse with both arms outstretched, palms together; (3) horse with two seated figures. The first is male (?), right arm raised, bent at the elbow, and wearing a headdress; the second is female, seated behind. The last figure (4) is a male, depicted walking behind the horse and holding a raised staff. Above this are three small quarry marks (0.01 m^2), and 0.15 m above these are several larger quarry marks. This carving is now in worship, decorated with red paint, green bangles, and flowers.

Artifacts: A low density ceramic scatter extends throughout nearby fields. Much of this material appears to be water transported. Nevertheless, the density of ceramics north and east of the rock shelter exceeds the background density. This latter material may be modern. A single north-south transect was placed along the mouth of the shelter, with three 2 × 2 m collection units spaced at 10 m intervals. A diagnostic collection was also made.

Transect 1 Unit 1: 100 g ceramics; wares: 21 black plain ware, 1 red plain ware, 1 brown plain ware.

Transect 1 Unit 2: 50 g ceramics; wares: 8 black plain ware, 2 brown plain ware. Diagnostics: 1 jar.

Transect 1 Unit 3: 100 g ceramics; wares: 8 black plain ware, 6 brown plain ware.

Temporal Affiliation: Vijayanagara and recent.
References: Morrison 1995:75; Morrison and Sinopoli 1996:64.
Illustrations: Figure 5.29; Plates 5.22, 5.23.

Plate 5.22. VMS-163, unfinished Hanuman image.

Plate 5.23. VMS-163, sculpted panel.

SITE: VMS-164   Block: S   Transect: 16
Primary Site Use: Religious: temple complex.
Site Dimensions: 50 × 60 m
Setting: Level irrigated fields.
Present Land Use/Disturbances: Located amidst irrigated fields, the complex itself is uncultivated and heavily overgrown. The sanctuary of Feature 3 is collapsed, as is a possible lamp pillar in front of this feature. Some of the numerous rubble-walled rooms filling the complex's enclosure walls incorporate dressed blocks and slabs. As such, they may have been constructed later than the main phase of temple construction/use, taking advantage of the structure's decay. A recent shrine has been built into the east gateway (Feature 1) and a dirt track runs north-south along the east edge of the enclosure wall.

Site Description: Temple complex. Original construction of the complex dates to the first half of the Vijayanagara period, though many changes were made in the structure and use of this site during the Vijayanagara period and subsequently. In its original configuration, the complex was probably enclosed, as suggested by the two gates and mandapa. However, the current enclosure wall is probably not original. The later construction of the interior rooms possibly involved some shift in emphasis from a more typical temple to a pilgrim center, school, or residential area. The shrine itself was not converted, however, suggesting that the basic religious function of this feature was retained.

The complex is located amidst irrigated fields watered by reservoir VMS-190, is visible from the city walls to the north, and is located along the fairly narrow north-south corridor between two reservoirs (VMS-190 and VMS-165). The temple may be associated with the road VMS-160. To its north is a small mandapa (VMS-215) as well as a sculpture (VMS-163). These sites all appear to be oriented to the road segment VMS-183. Also associated with the temple is a step well and the nearby road walls of VMS-214, which lead directly to the temple complex.

The complex consists of an informal enclosure (recent?) wall, containing a central temple (Feature 3) and associated mandapa (Feature 2), and is entered through two gateways, on the east (Feature 1) and north (Feature 4). Outside the complex, to the north and east of the east gateway, is a square platform built around an anthill and Neem tree. This platform has probably been recently built to enclose these two sacred features. On the platform is a broken piece of circular column with eighteen facets, probably part of one of the lamp column uprights. It is possible that there were two lamp columns: one inside and one outside the complex. The base (0.52 × 0.57 m) of one of these column fragments lies near the road in front of the temple. This rectangular fragment contains curled motifs on the corners, surmounted by an octagonal section. It may be that the eighteen-faceted piece was set atop this, followed by a fancy capital.

The entire complex is surrounded by an informally constructed enclosure wall consisting of two faces of unmodified cobbles and rubble, with only occasional quarried blocks. This wall is in variable condition, being more poorly preserved on the east side, adjacent to the dirt track. Here it abuts the east edge of the eastern gate (Feature 1), and runs east of and parallel to the east edge of the mandapa (Feature 2). Oddly, these two features do not line up, though one would expect the mandapa and the gate both to be built into/up against the enclosure wall. The present enclosure wall is almost definitely a later construction, as it incorporates some formal architectural elements such as capitals and dressed blocks (0.83 m wide on the south side). Almost nothing remains of the enclosure wall on the west. A modern farmer's wall here runs north-south, turning to the east at its north end and obliterating the northwest corner of the site. Some sections of enclosure wall are present on the north side of the complex, however, beginning east of the north gateway (Feature 4). The wall is wider here (1.16 m) though it continues to be a mixture of rubble construction with some formal blocks and slabs.

Many rubble-walled rooms are located within the complex. Often these are bonded to the enclosure walls and, like them, sometimes incorporate formal architectural elements such as moldings, dressed slabs, and blocks. One wall abuts the sanctuary of the temple; others block access to the mandapa (Feature 2) from the west. In fact, there are so many rooms that it would have been quite difficult to get around. Access into the complex is now only possible through the eastern gate; the north gate is currently blocked with construction fragments, including column fragments, a capital element, and at least four large, square flat slabs with elaborate, well-dressed moldings that probably are the remains of a very elaborate basement.

Feature 1: The east gateway of the temple complex, situated 14 m to the east of the main shrine and c. 8 m south of the mandapa (Feature 2). The gate is approached by four to five steps. Two open but covered platforms (c. 1 m high) of long rectangular granite blocks flank the entrance. On each, three pairs of columns support the superstructure. The platforms have two stepped angled bevel moldings with corner quarter medallions. Between the moldings are large rectangular dressed blocks. Neither the moldings nor the blocks have carvings, with the exception of the central blocks between the moldings on either side of the entrance. These are sculpted with yali figures enclosed by floral designs. The columns at the entrance are square with inset octagonal sections. The outer columns on the east edge of the gate are faceted only on the outer side and are capped by cruciform capitals. Near the entry, the inner columns are plain with rectangular capitals. They flanked a door now indicated by a lintel with a figure of Lakshmi and carved door sockets, and a raised threshold. The columns support long rectangular beams that in turn support a roof of rectangular granite slabs, some unevenly cut. Eaves project on all sides and there is some brickwork atop the roof indicating a collapsed superstructure.

The northern gate platform has recently been enclosed to form a shrine, containing displaced sculptural elements, including a sculpted floral motif and an indistinguishable figure. Other displaced elements presently in worship include a Hanuman, naga, a seated male figure, a cross-legged seated figure, and fragments of a badly damaged chlorite image.

Feature 2: The mandapa located in the southeast corner of the temple complex. Unlike similar structures in many complexes, it does not fit into the corner of the outer wall, but is freestanding. The base is a platform of long rectangular blocks with a simple tripartite molding. Some of the blocks have been displaced and the structure is overgrown with thorny scrub. Four pairs of columns, two with cruciform and six with square capitals, support a flat roof made of long slabs. Only three columns are faceted. There is evidence for extensive post-construction repair work. A probable image base lies alongside the mandapa to its west.

Feature 3: The central temple of the complex. It consists of a columned porch, two antechambers, and a sanctuary. The temple has plain exterior walls, with little ornamentation. Its basement consists of a simple tripartite molding with corner bosses.

A columned porch of 4 × 2 columns forms the entrance to the temple. A flight of two or more steps leads onto the porch, which is open on three sides. The columns consist of three parts: a base, a shaft, and a capital, each carved out of a different block and placed on top of each other. The bases are plain cubes. Above them, the shafts are square in section with inset octagons and with petal motifs at the base. The shafts are carved near the top with depictions of yalis, floral designs, conches, a Hanuman, a trident, a turtle, meditating sages, a female figure having four arms and holding weapons, some seated figures, dancing figures, Krishna with the snake Kala, and male figures holding weapons. The cruciform capitals have scrolled ends; the capitals support long stone beams that carry the roof.

The lintel over the doorway to the outer antechamber is carved with a floral design. This walled, square, columned chamber is 4 × 4 columns. Some of the large stone slabs forming the floor have been ripped out. The columns set into the walls are unadorned slabs topped by truncated cruciform capitals. The four central columns differ from the others and the uppermost portions of their central shafts are carved into a graceful curved form, characteristic of early Vijayanagara construction. This rounded form tops a square column with inset faceted discs, decorative petals at the corners of the lower square section, and several carvings, including Ganesha, Krishna with snake, Vishnu with Lakshmi seated on his thigh, a dancing couple, a Trimurti figure, dancing women, Rama, a Nandi, and Narasimha. The composite capitals are composed of three elements: a lower disk, followed by a curved piece with a square top and pendant buds, and a cruciform capital with scrolled edges. The capitals support long beams that bear the flat roof. The central bay has a ceiling of rotated squares with a lotus design.

The entrance to the inner antechamber is marked by a double set of door frames that create a step up into the small enclosed room. The first door is decorated with entwined lotus flowers; the second is flanked by Vaishnavite door guardians.

A plain doorway leads into the sanctuary. This room is mostly collapsed, but still contains an image base with a carved Garuda. It once had a ceiling of rotated squares. Only traces of the brickwork superstructure remain. There is a spout on the outer side of the remaining wall, but the spout is in poor condition, making its original shape unclear.

Feature 4: The north gate of the temple complex. It has been heavily disturbed and is overgrown. The gate consists of two platforms flanking an entrance passage. Long rectangular dressed granite blocks were used for the simple tripartite moldings that adorn the platforms. These are not well constructed and the inset vertical faces between upper and lower moldings are made of rubble. The upper surfaces of some of the moldings have square column footings, but there is now only one fragment of a column with some sculpture. The platforms are mounded with earth and rubble.

Artifacts: A moderately dense ceramic scatter covers the complex. There were eight collection units along two east-west transects: Transect 1 was located to the south of the main temple, and Transect 2 to its north. The 2 × 2 m collection units were placed at intervals of 15 m; a total of seven units were collected (not illustrated on site plan). Two 2 × 2 m judgment units were collected. A diagnostic collection was also made. Several mortars lie about in the complex, including a broken one in the farmer's wall and grinding slicks on Feature 1. The following units contained artifacts:

Transect 1 Unit 1: 100 g ceramics; wares: 4 black plain ware, 1 brown plain ware, 2 black burnished ware. Diagnostics: 1 jar.

Transect 1 Unit 3: 150 g ceramics; wares: 31 black plain ware, 1 red plain ware. Diagnostics: 1 bowl, 1 jar.

Transect 1 Unit 4: 100 g ceramics; wares: 17 black plain ware.

Transect 2 Unit 1: 150 g ceramics; wares: 44 black plain ware, 2 brown plain ware, 1 burnished ware. Diagnostics: 1 bowl, 1 jar.

Transect 2 Unit 2: 50 g ceramics; wares: 10 black plain ware, 1 red plain ware, 1 brown plain ware. Diagnostics: 1 jar.

Transect 2 Unit 3: <50 g ceramics; wares: 1 brown plain ware.

J1: 50 g ceramics; wares: 10 black plain ware, 1 brown plain ware.

J2: 100 g ceramics; wares: 13 black plain ware, 1 brown plain ware. Diagnostics: 4 jars.

Temporal Affiliation: The original elements of the complex probably date to the first half of the Vijayanagara period. Other elements (the internal rooms) are apparently later additions.

References: Morrison 1995:75, 80; Morrison and Sinopoli 1996:71.

Illustrations: Figure 5.30; Plates 5.24-5.26.

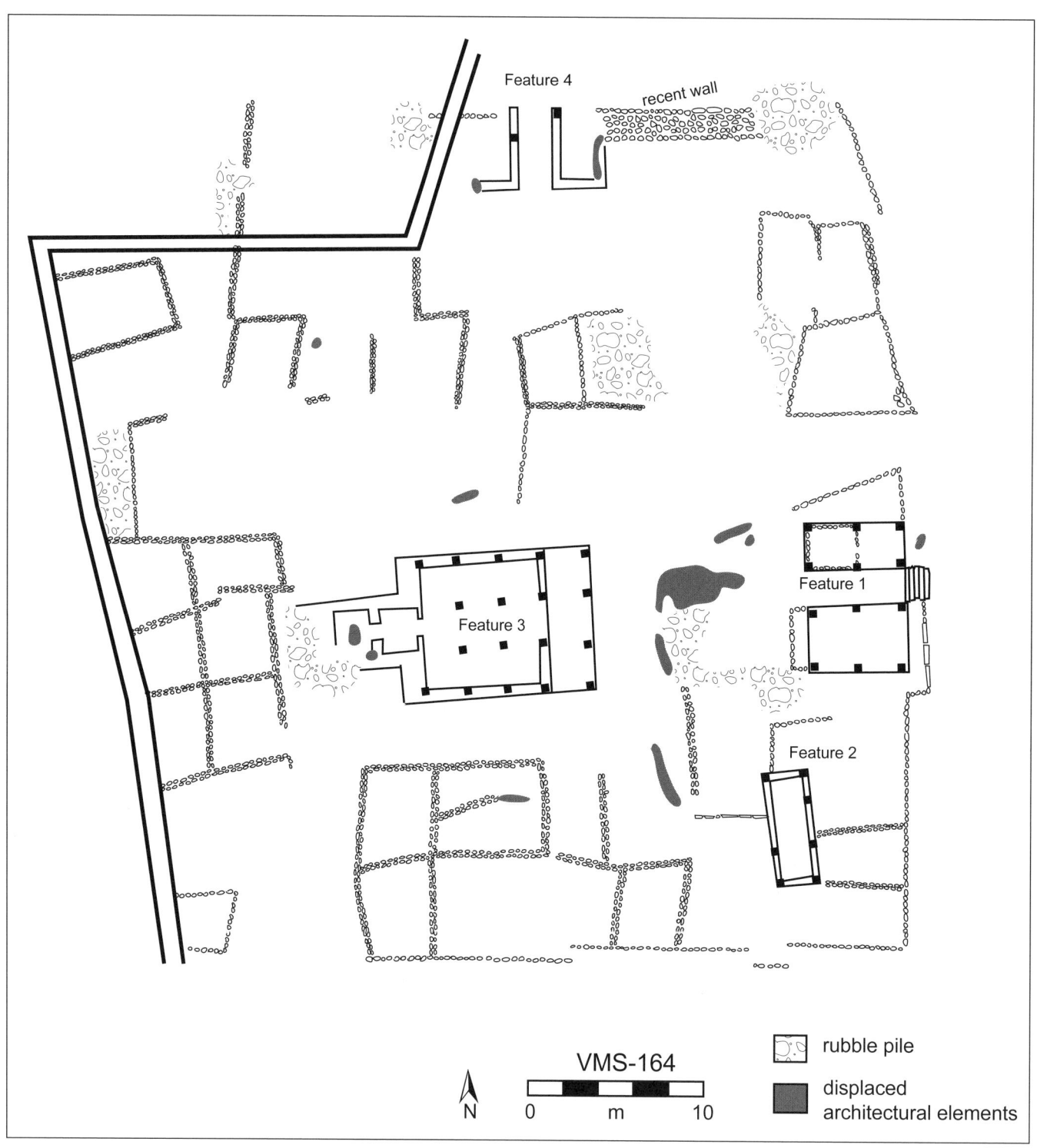

Figure 5.30. VMS-164, plan.

Plate 5.24. VMS-164, Feature 1, eastern gate.

Plate 5.25. VMS-164, temple (Feature 3).

Plate 5.26. VMS-164, interior column in temple, early Vijayanagara.

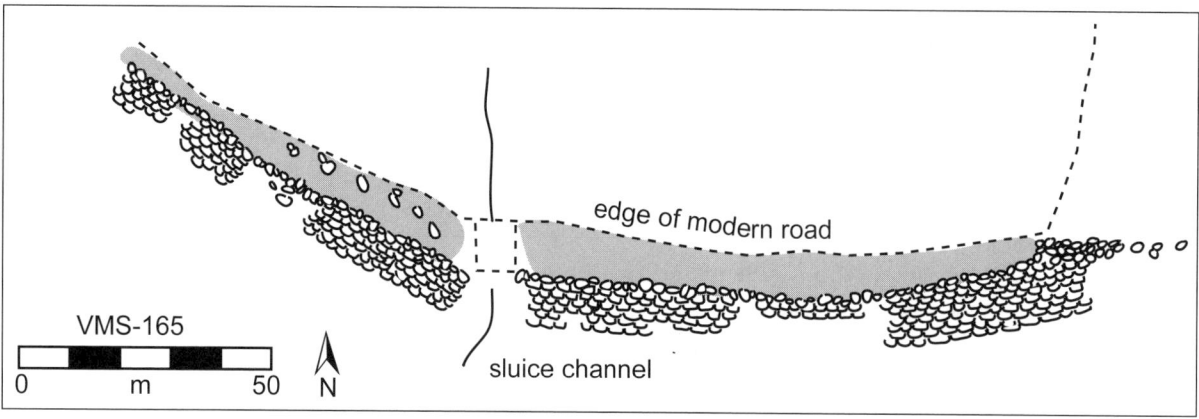

Figure 5.31. VMS-165, plan.

SITE: VMS-165   Block: S   Transect: 16-17
Primary Site Use: Agricultural: reservoir embankment.
Site Dimensions: 220 × 20 m
Setting: Level fields in irrigated area.
Present Land Use/Disturbances: Heavily disturbed by a road that cuts off the entire north edge of the embankment and by modern irrigation ditches that have breached it. The embankment is in poor condition and is overgrown with thorny scrub.
Site Description: Reservoir embankment. This reservoir is part of a complex of large embankments including VMS-132, VMS-231, and VMS-190 that form a northwest-southeast oriented line across Block S. The embankment is in poor condition and only the remnants of a tunnel are visible, incorporated within a modern wall that crosses a breach. This tunnel may have been reassembled. The south side of the embankment is faced with up to eight courses of stepped masonry composed of unmodified cobbles and boulders. Some quarried blocks and slabs lie scattered, but there are no clear indications of a sluice gate.
Artifacts: Dense scatter of ceramics along the embankment west of the breach in irrigated bean and peanut fields. 100% collection. 200 g ceramics; wares: 25 black plain ware. Diagnostics: 1 jar.
Temporal Affiliation: Vijayanagara.
References: Morrison 1995:75, 91, 102; Morrison and Sinopoli 1996:63.
Illustrations: Figure 5.31.

SITE: VMS-166   Block: S   Transect: 17
Primary Site Use: Unknown/agricultural?: isolated wall.
Site Dimensions: 28 × 1 m
Setting: Gently sloping dry fields.
Present Land Use/Disturbances: A recent shrine is located at the north end of this overgrown wall, which is paralleled by a farmer's wall 20 m to the west.
Site Description: Wall segment. This feature is of unknown function and temporal affiliation, though it may have been associated with soil and water control. The wall is composed of large, unmodified and roughly shaped cobbles, blocks, and chinking stones. The wall stands to a height of four courses along its west face and three courses on its east face. The two faces of the wall are separated by a 1 m wide earthen core.
Artifacts: 100% collection; none observed.
Temporal Affiliation: Unknown.
Illustrations: Figure 5.32.

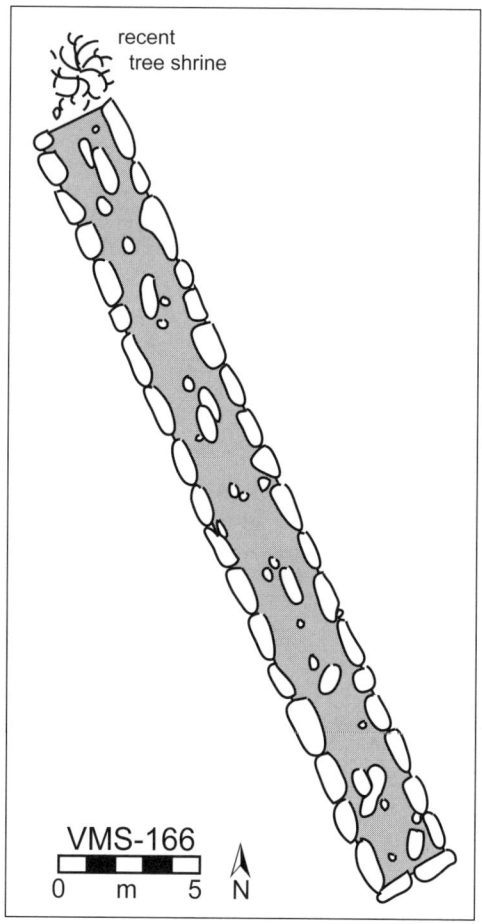

Figure 5.32. VMS-166, plan.

SITE: VMS-167   Block: S   Transect: 16
Primary Site Use: Residential: isolated wall.
Site Dimensions: 8 × 0.5 m
Setting: Steep outcrop with a 30-40° slope.
Present Land Use/Disturbances: Outcrop currently in use by herders.
Site Description: Isolated boulder "wall" in front of a small outcrop. The wall consists of a line of unmodified boulders of all shapes

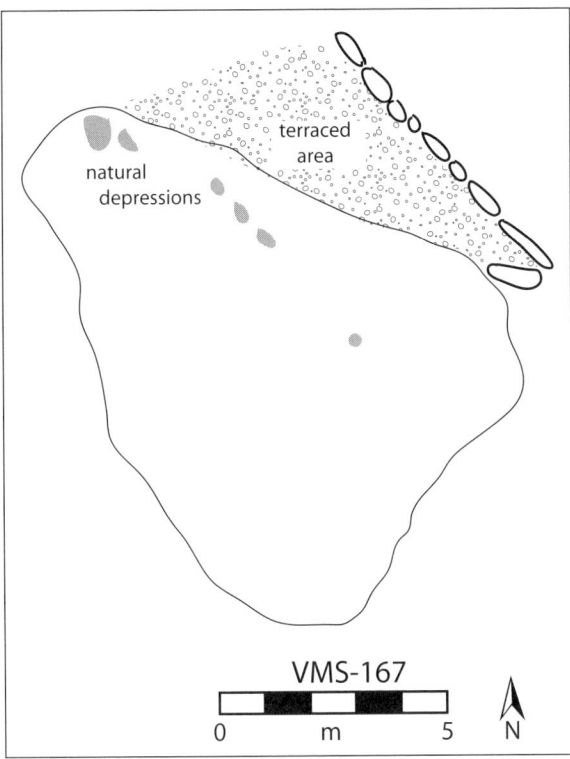

Figure 5.33. VMS-167, plan.

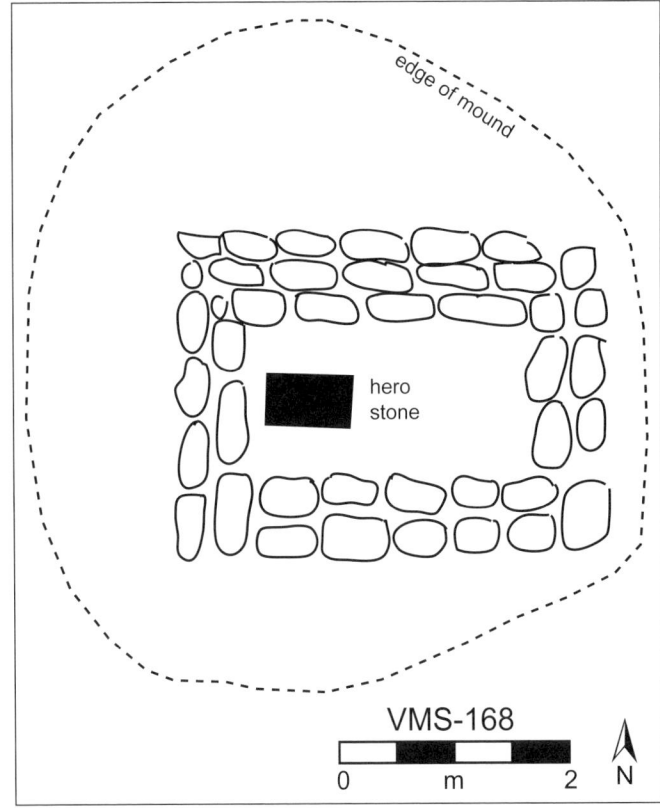

Figure 5.34. VMS-168, plan.

and sizes. The individual elements are placed in random orientations forming more of a pile than a wall. This alignment forms a small terrace next to the outcrop. This site may be a day-use shelter for goat herds or farmers. Four small circular natural depressions that hold water occur in the outcrop behind the wall. The site lies on the south edge of a steep outcrop overlooking dry fields.

Artifacts: Moderately dense lithic and ceramic scatter near the wall. One lithic core was found. 100% collection. 1100 g ceramics; wares: 161 black plain ware, 13 brown plain ware. Diagnostics: 14 jars. Other artifacts: 1 lithic: core of light gray volcanic stone.

Temporal Affiliation: Unknown.
Illustrations: Figure 5.33.

SITE: VMS-168   Block: S   Transect: 16
Primary Site Use: Religious: structure and hero stone.
Site Dimensions: 4.75 × 2.5 m
Setting: Level dry farmed fields.
Present Land Use/Disturbances: Traces of blue paint on the sculpture are probably recent. The sculpture is surrounded by thick overgrowth and some stones are missing or displaced.
Site Description: Square structure containing a hero stone. The structure rests on a low mound. Its walls consist of three courses of unmodified granitic cobbles, two elements wide. Wall fall lies around this small structure. Inside the low enclosure is a sculpture on a dressed granitic block. It depicts a horse with two riders—a man and a woman. To the right and the left are two circles, broken, but probably suns or moons. Also to the left is a naga. The riders display common Vijayanagara hairstyles and jewelry. Both have right hands raised, the man holding a sword over his head, common poses for deceased warriors and satis. The

Plate 5.27. VMS-168, hero stone.

lower quarter of the block bears three lines of inscriptions, not clearly legible. Two flower-holes are present on either side of the block.

Artifacts: A well-defined small cluster (0.5 m diameter) of ceramics is located near the southeast corner of the wall fall. 100% collection. 50 g ceramics; wares: 7 brown plain ware.

Temporal Affiliation: Vijayanagara.
Illustrations: Figure 5.34; Plate 5.27.

SITE: VMS-169   Block: S   Transect: 15-16
   Primary Site Use: Residential: artifact scatter.
   Site Dimensions: 150 × 150 m
   Setting: Level upland between two reservoirs.
   Resources: Site is located between reservoirs VMS-165 and VMS-190.
   Present Land Use/Disturbances: Road over the embankment of VMS-190 forms the north boundary of the scatter, a cart road the east boundary, and a canal the south boundary. The area is under cultivation.
   Site Description: Large diffuse artifact scatter located in a flat, upland plain between two large Vijayanagara period reservoirs. VMS-164, a temple complex, lies just to the north. This site is probably the product of a complex occupational history, as indicated by multiple overlapping distributions of several artifact classes, including ceramics, worked sherds, lithics of several raw material types, slag, ground stone of pink granite, a pestle, and kiln debris. Some of this material may be midden debris from the temple complex. Much of the material is certainly a product of iron smelting in proximity to one or both reservoir embankments. Other materials may relate to other activities requiring water for processing, or agriculture, or both. A modern trash scatter is associated with the threshing floor and a foot/cow path that crosses the site. Several modern pot breaks are also associated with the threshing floor. Plowing has spread the scatter and broken up any ancient features (e.g., kilns). Larger artifacts and rocks are found on the borders between fields while smaller ones cluster on the uncultivated edge of the embankment of VMS-190.
   Artifacts: Sparse to moderate scatter of ceramics, lithics and slag spread over a large area of fallow dry fields. There is much overlap in artifact class distributions; however, lithic visibility/density is higher in the west half, while ceramic and slag densities are higher in the east half. Collections were made along five north-south transects, spaced 30 m apart, with 2 × 2 m units placed every 30 m. Total of twenty-four units plus diagnostic collection.
   Transect 1 Unit 1: <50 g ceramics; wares: 5 black plain ware, 2 brown plain ware. Diagnostics: 2 jars. Other: 100 g iron slag.
   Transect 1 Unit 2: No ceramics. Other: 50 g iron slag.
   Transect 1 Unit 3: 50 g ceramics; wares: 3 black plain ware, 2 brown plain ware. Other: 100 g iron slag and furnace debris.
   Transect 1 Unit 4: <50 g ceramics; wares: 1 black plain ware. Other: 50 g iron slag.
   Transect 1 Unit 5: <50 g ceramics; wares: 3 black plain ware. Other: 100 g iron slag.
   Transect 2 Unit 1: <50 g ceramics; wares: 4 black plain ware, 2 brown plain ware.
   Transect 2 Unit 2: <50 g ceramics; wares: 1 black plain ware. Other: 50 g iron slag.
   Transect 2 Unit 3: 50 g ceramics; wares: 6 black plain ware, 1 brown plain ware. Other: 50 g iron slag.
   Transect 2 Unit 4: 50 g ceramics; wares: 8 black plain ware, 2 brown plain ware. Other: 50 g iron slag.
   Transect 2 Unit 5: <50 g ceramics; wares: 6 black plain ware, 2 brown plain ware. Other: 50 g iron slag.
   Transect 3 Unit 1: 50 g ceramics; wares: 11 black plain ware, 2 brown plain ware. Diagnostics: 1 jar. Other: 400 g iron slag.
   Transect 3 Unit 2: 50 g ceramics; wares: 11 black plain ware, 1 coarse ware. Diagnostics: 1 jar. Other: 300 g iron slag and furnace debris.
   Transect 3 Unit 3: <50 g ceramics; wares: 2 brown plain ware. Other: <50 g iron slag.
   Transect 3 Unit 4: No ceramics. Other: 50 g iron slag.
   Transect 3 Unit 5: <50 g ceramics; wares: 1 black plain ware.
   Transect 4 Unit 1: <50 g ceramics; wares: 1 black plain ware. Other: <50 g iron slag.
   Transect 4 Unit 2: <50 g ceramics; wares: 4 black plain ware, 3 brown plain ware. Other: 150 g iron slag.
   Transect 4 Unit 3: <50 g ceramics; wares: 9 black plain ware. Diagnostics: 1 bowl, 2 jars. Other: 100 g iron slag.
   Transect 4 Unit 4: <50 g ceramics; wares: 2 black plain ware. Diagnostics: 1 jar. Other: 50 g iron slag.
   Transect 4 Unit 5: <50 g ceramics; wares: 3 black plain ware.
   Transect 5 Unit 1: <50 g ceramics; wares: 4 black plain ware, 2 brown plain ware.
   Transect 5 Unit 2: <50 g ceramics; wares: 4 black plain ware, 2 brown plain ware. Other: 50 g iron slag.
   Transect 5 Unit 3: <50 g ceramics. Other: 50 g iron slag.
   Transect 5 Unit 4: <50 g ceramics; wares: 4 brown plain ware.
   Lithics (all): 21 flakes (18 quartz, 3 volcanic), 4 utilized flakes (2 quartz, 1 chert, 1 volcanic), 1 scraper (black variegated chert), 1 denticulate (1 gray volcanic), 4 fragments angular debris (quartz), 9 fragments bipolar flaking debris (8 quartz, 1 cryptocrystalline).
   Temporal Affiliation: Vijayanagara and later, possibly earlier as well.
   References: Sinopoli 2003:197.
   Illustrations: Figure 5.35.

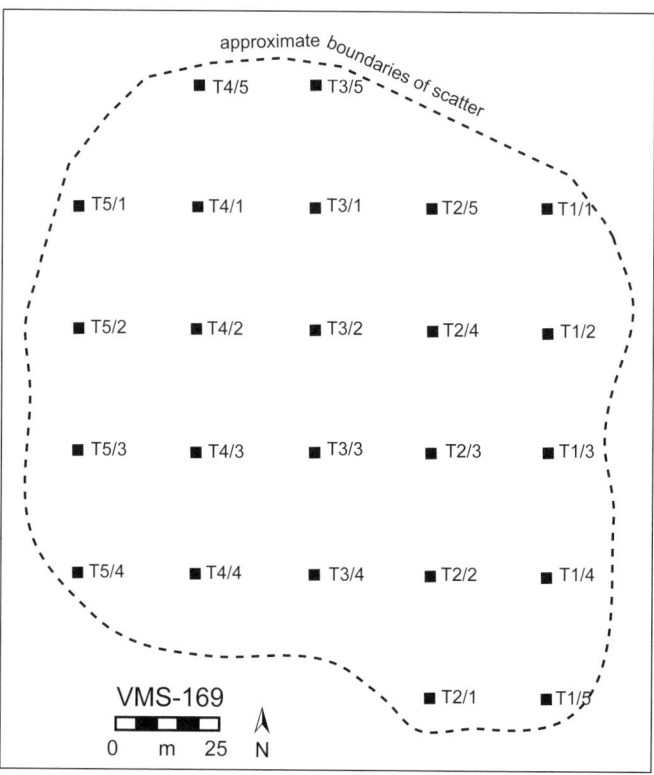

Figure 5.35. VMS-169, plan, approximate site boundaries, and collection units.

Plate 5.28. VMS-170, "horse-tie."

Plate 5.29. VMS-171, displaced sculptures, naga and Nandi images.

SITE: VMS-170   Block: S   Transect: 18
Primary Site Use: Residential: rock shelter and "horse tie."
Site Dimensions: 7.1 × 3.8 m
Setting: Outcrop with rock shelter.
Resources: Circa 250 m northwest of reservoir VMS-125.
Present Land Use/Disturbances: Extensive modern quarrying in the area. A paved road runs c. 80 m to the north. There has been minor rock fall within the shelter.
Site Description: Rock shelter and associated features. This small west-facing rock shelter is formed by overhanging granitic boulders. On a flat rock near the exterior of the shelter is a small square hole, 0.03 × 0.03 m, along with several game boards and an incised groove, 0.16 m long. Approximately 45 m from the entrance of the shelter is a "horse tie" cut into a small outcropping boulder. This feature was located along a Vijayanagara period road that led from the large gate in the city wall (VMS-123/Feature 1), toward the Pattabhirama temple (VMS-237). The shelter probably served as a temporary resting place or habitation, and likely has a long history of use.
Artifacts: Moderate scatter of ceramics and one lithic inside the shelter, none outside the drip line. A diagnostic collection was made.
Temporal Affiliation: Vijayanagara and possibly later.
Illustrations: Plate 5.28.

SITE: VMS-171   Block: S   Transect: 17
Primary Site Use: Religious: displaced sculptures.
Site Dimensions: 40 × 20 m
Setting: Level area in dry fields.
Present Land Use/Disturbances: Located amid fields along a paved road; the sculptures are not *in situ*.
Site Description: Displaced sculptures. This site consists of a number of images, placed around and under a thorny shrub. The images include eleven to twelve naga stones and a small Vijayanagara-style Nandi. Two meters to the southwest is a second, somewhat larger, Nandi. A block mortar lies in a field 16 m southwest of the naga stones, and a few quarried blocks have been incorporated into a nearby modern wall. The only element in place is a small outcropping boulder with a single square peg hole in the top.
Artifacts: Site is surrounded by the immense residential artifact scatter which covers the north end of transects 16-18. Ceramics, some slag, and a few concentrations of quartzite pebbles were noted. No collections made.
Temporal Affiliation: The Nandi sculptures date to the Vijayanagara period; the other elements are consistent with a Vijayanagara date.
Illustrations: Plate 5.29.

SITE: VMS-172   Block: S   Transect: 17
Primary Site Use: Commercial, residential, defensive, or other: elevated platforms.
Site Dimensions: 87 × 35 m
Setting: Level dry farmed fields.
Present Land Use/Disturbances: Disturbed by field clearing and plowing; adjacent to a recent dirt road leading east from the Penukonda gate.
Site Description: At least eight small stone and rubble-filled platforms. The highest now stands c. 1.50 m above the level of the surrounding fields, with stone walls three courses high. Almost all are surrounded on at least one side by areas of earth and rubble wall collapse. The platforms are not in any particular alignment, but are all quite square and uniform in size (2.5 × 2.5 m). Several are massively constructed while others are built of rubble. Construction elements include both quarried blocks and unmodified stones. Several platforms appear to have been internally divided and one (number 4) has two exterior wall faces, c. 0.1

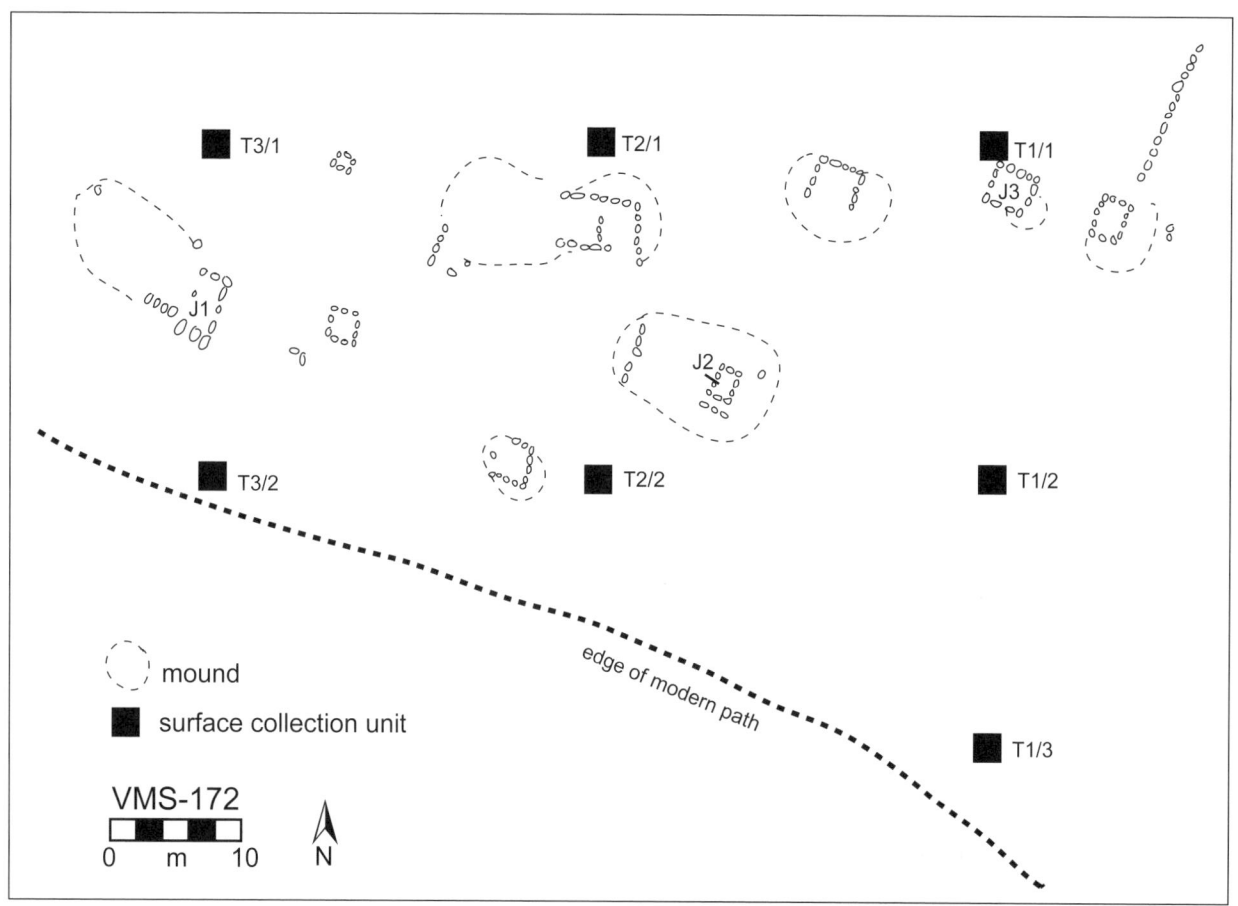

Figure 5.36. VMS-172, plan and location of collection units.

m apart. Perhaps there were originally two platforms very close together here. Atop one platform, a patch of flat cement is visible.

The platforms' location just outside the Penukonda gate and associated city wall and along the Penukonda road is suggestive. Perhaps they served a commercial function or were associated with the control of traffic. A residential use seems unlikely. A few pieces of broken basalt and a possible basalt peg are associated with Platforms 1 and 3, respectively.

Artifacts: The immense artifact scatter covering the north end of transects 16-18 fades out just inside the city wall, c. 60 m north of VMS-172. The area around the platforms has a very sparse scatter of ceramics but more are found on top of them. Collections were made along three transects spaced 30 m apart, with units spaced every 20 m. A total of seven units were collected along transects plus three judgment units placed on structures. Not all contained artifacts.

Transect 1 Unit 3: <50 g ceramics; wares: 8 black plain ware, 2 brown plain ware.

Transect 2 Unit 1: <50 g ceramics; wares: 2 black plain ware, 1 brown plain ware.

Transect 3 Unit 1: <50 g ceramics; wares: 1 brown plain ware.

Transect 3 Unit 2: <50 g ceramics; wares: 2 brown plain ware.

J1: <50 g ceramics; wares: 1 black plain ware.

J2: <50 g ceramics; wares: 3 black plain ware, 1 brown plain ware.

J3: 150 g ceramics; wares: 29 black plain ware, 13 brown plain ware. Diagnostics: 1 jar.

Plate 5.30. VMS-172, platform detail.

Temporal Affiliation: Unknown, probably Vijayanagara.
References: Morrison 1995:76; Morrison and Sinopoli 1996:67.
Illustrations: Figure 5.36; Plate 5.30.

SITE: VMS-173   Block: S   Transect: 17
   Primary Site Use: Religious: temple.
   Site Dimensions: 21.3 × 15 m
   Setting: Level area amid dry farmed fields. Well VMS-200 is located c. 25 m to the southeast.
   Present Land Use/Disturbances: Located on the south edge of the modern Penukonda dirt road, which approximates the course of the ancient roadway. The temple has been extensively modified. The present owner purchased the place in the 1960s and constructed the exterior wall and a few walls near the present entrance, and also plastered and whitewashed the structure. Other post-Vijayanagara walls are earlier. The gopuram and perhaps the central image of Virabhadra are also post-Vijayanagara; a decapitated Shaivite image is lying in an unlit and unused area to the west of the sanctuary.
   Site Description: Temple. This large Shaivite temple faces northeast, toward the road. Although quite impressive in detail, this temple is constructed of rather simple materials. Its columns are of the "mass-produced" type common in the city and there are no moldings on the basement. In front of the temple but not aligned with it is a 5 × 5 m platform edged by reworked walls of quarried slabs and rubble. One slab bears a curved molding. On a small outcropping boulder west of this platform are carvings of Rama (bow slung over his left shoulder) and Sita. A few blocks and slabs lie about in the roadway; one has a rounded top with carved chakras, sun and moon, and a bident. The lower section is broken off and may be lying face down nearby. The whole is shaped like an inscription slab, but the lower portion could not be turned over. In this area is a surface composed of heavily worn small square stones, just like the cobbled surface near the Penukonda gate, 150 m to the west.

The original form of this temple is somewhat difficult to determine, given the number of modern walls around it and the subsequent lack of lighting. It is a structure of 8 × 10 columns set on a basement and divided by older and newer walls into distinct areas. Beginning on the north, the side of the original entrance, is a square roofed porch that extends out beyond the main structure. A segment of well-worn rectangular slabs leads up to the porch. The porch is followed by a columned hall, which was apparently originally open on the sides. A U-shaped wall defines an enclosed space that contains the antechamber and sanctuary; the open walkway or *pradakshina* (circumambulation) route around the walled interior rooms has been recently walled in. The original configuration of interior rooms is difficult to determine, but the placement of doorways suggests that the antechamber was a partially walled area (open on the north) of 6 × 3 columns and the sanctuary a large room of 4 × 6 columns. However, this space may have been divided into subsidiary shrines or other rooms.

The basement is simply constructed of horizontal, rectangular, and quarried but undressed slabs loosely fit, with many chinking stones. Several of the elements on the north edge of the basement appear to be reused; one is an eroded door guardian, another, a mortar. This basement may have been repaired, but it is clearly original as it supports Vijayanagara columns and a Vijayanagara superstructure.

Columns are, for the most part, square with octagonal insets. The capitals are simple rectangular blocks with cutouts. Some columns are carved. On the small porch are a turtle, lotus, sun, and moon. A slab with a carved image of a striding Hanuman has been set into a recent wall. In this wall is a new doorway, partly framed by a column more elaborate than most, having inset sections with more facets and with a central band. This column has a carved chakra, lotuses, a bident, and Yaksha figures. Just inside this recent door is a ceiling section of rotated squares.

There seems to have been a step up to the interior rooms, indicated by a long worn sill of rectangular slabs. Columns along this sill have carvings such as a lotus in a ring, and a dancing female figure wearing only a pointed hat. The columns built into the wall itself are more massive; on one is a crouching yali figure. The *pradakshina* walls themselves are constructed of four courses of long horizontal roughly dressed slabs. Set atop them is a course of very thin slabs into which a sort of rounded molding has been incised. Inside the walled area, the ceiling is about 0.4 m lower; the columns are much shorter, and the floor is slightly higher.

What appears to be the original doorway between the antechamber and the sanctuary is obscured by modern plasterwork, but there are traces of door guardians of uncertain affiliation. As noted, a modern (?) Virabhadra image is in the sanctuary. Behind it is a large slab with a Nandi and lingam and empty space below. A Vijayanagara Nandi is in front of the shrine and in this same area is a Bhairavi image (with characteristic trident, drum, sword, three heads, etc.). Leaning against Bhairavi is a small, well-carved lion head (yali) and stuck into a modern wall is a carved ram-headed figure. All of these features are so heavily plastered that it is difficult to make out details.

The superstructure consists of a plaster and brick facade around all four sides of the temple. Sculpted on its north face is a row of small figures (now headless) that flank niches with larger figures. Nandis face diagonally outward on the northeast and northwest corners of the structure. The façade is lower around the rest of temple, consisting of plaster merlons. Simple eaves slope down from the roof. The gopuram is modern.

   Artifacts: As this temple is being actively used, there is a modern scatter all around it. A sparse pre-modern background scatter of ceramics is also present. No collections were made.
   Temporal Affiliation: Vijayanagara with later modifications.
   References: Morrison 1995:76; Morrison and Sinopoli 1996:67.
   Illustrations: Figure 5.37; Plate 5.31.

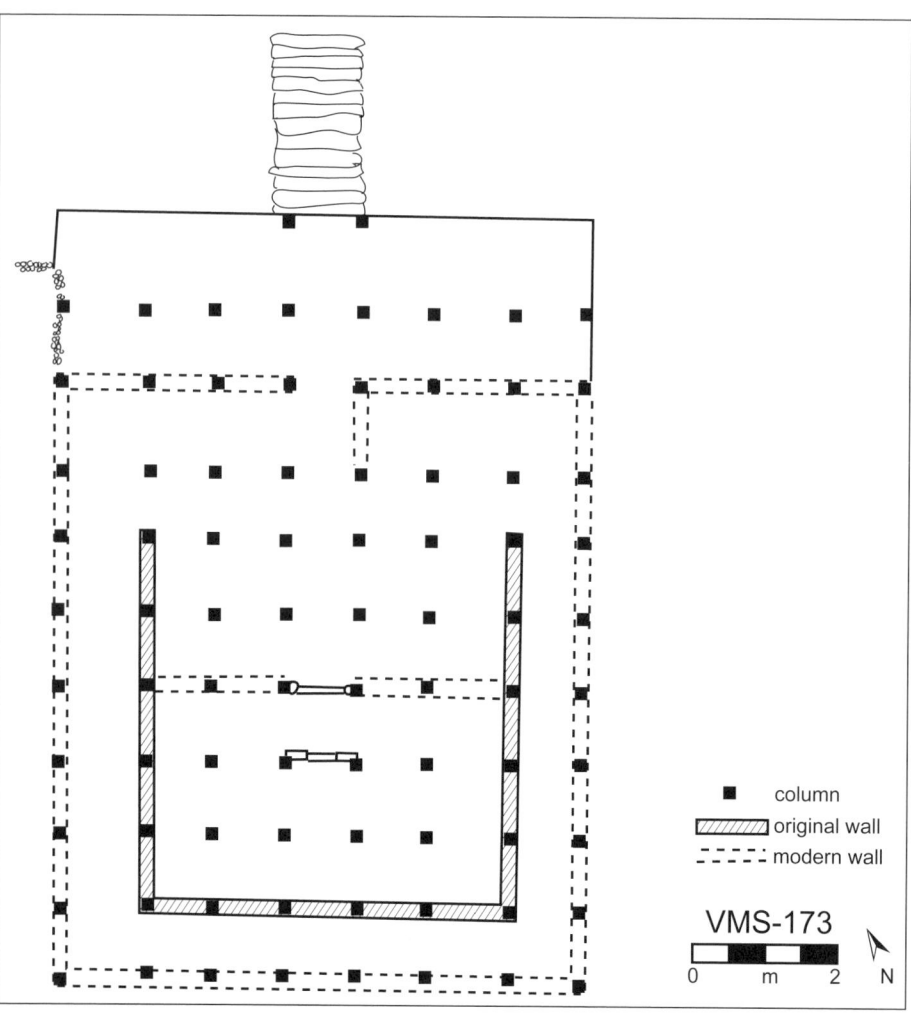

Figure 5.37. VMS-173, plan.

Plate 5.31. VMS-173, temple entry.

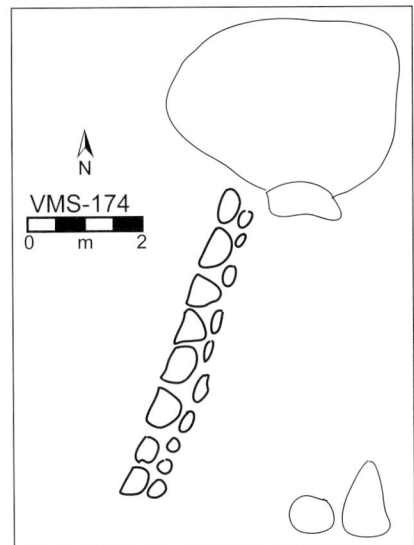

Figure 5.38. VMS-174, plan.

SITE: VMS-174   Block: S   **Transect:** 17
Primary Site Use: Transport: wall along passage.
Site Dimensions: 5 × 0.75 m
Setting: On a saddle between two outcrops.
Present Land Use/Disturbances: The outcrop shows evidence of extensive quarrying, both recent and older. Nearby farmers' walls may have robbed stone from the site.
Site Description: Wall. This north-south oriented wall is located just inside outer city wall, VMS-123, near the entrance from gate VMS-123/ Feature 1. The wall is parallel to a broad passageway between two low outcrops and may have served to define this natural route. Unmodified boulders form the west face of this one-course wall, while the east face is of rubble. A small battered basalt cobble is integrated into the wall. The other side of this passage, some 10 m to the west, is edged by a short north-south rubble wall segment, which is oriented parallel to VMS-174 and located adjacent to a low outcrop.
Artifacts: There is sparse ceramic scatter across the entire outcrop. Although the site lies inside VMS-123, the background scatter is somewhat lower here than to the east. 100% collection. 150 g ceramics; wares: 10 black plain ware, 23 brown plain ware. Diagnostics: 2 bowls, 5 jars.
Temporal Affiliation: Unknown.
Illustrations: Figure 5.38.

SITE: VMS-175   Block: S   **Transect:** 17
Primary Site Use: Residential: well.
Site Dimensions: 9 × 7 m
Setting: Gently sloping dry fields.
Present Land Use/Disturbances: A paved road runs c. 60 m north of the site, which has been subject to extensive quarrying (modern and ancient). The structure itself is overgrown with vegetation.
Site Description: Well or room. This structure forms a shallow depression that collects water during the rainy season. It is located in an area of high density Vijayanagara period occupation. The structure is constructed of split and unmodified large stones. The east wall is three courses high and meets an outcrop at its north end. The south wall also has three courses, but it either ends to make an opening or has slumped where the southwest corner of the feature would be expected. The west wall is two courses high. It joins the outcrop on one end and turns a corner on the other to create a sort of foyer to the main "room." This shape is suggestive of wells found elsewhere in the region. No cementing material is used in the walls.

Artifacts: A dense ceramic scatter is located west of the structure; a sparse scatter extends along the south and east sides. 100% collection. 250 g ceramics; wares: 43 black plain ware, 11 brown plain ware. Diagnostics: 1 bowl, 7 jars. Other: 100 g iron slag.
Temporal Affiliation: Unknown/Vijayanagara?
References: Morrison 1995:84.

SITE: VMS-176   Block: S   **Transect:** 17
Primary Site Use: Residential: terraces.
Site Dimensions: 87 × 65 m
Setting: Gently sloping sheet rock and outcrops adjacent to the outer city wall.
Present Land Use/Disturbances: Dry farmed fields surround the site and extensive modern quarrying is present. Rubble piles rest against the low outcrops that dot this area; much cultural material has eroded from the sheet rock at the south end of the site.
Site Description: Residential terraces. The c. 200 m wide area between the modern paved road and the Vijayanagara city wall is replete with walls, evidence of quarrying, artifacts, and mortars, all indicative of a dense zone of occupation. The ground surface rises toward the city wall, providing an easy view over the wall from the inside while preserving the height of the wall on the outside. This site consists of two east-west terrace walls that shore up the gradual slope between the city walls and the road. A third lower wall lies c. 20 m north of the north wall of VMS-176, and is recorded with VMS-174. Both terrace walls retain soil and are well preserved in sections though other portions are covered with rubble from field clearing. At the south edge of the site on a large, low expanse of sheet rock is a wall stub and occupational debris. Near the base of this outcrop is a chunk of coarse (Vijayanagara-type) cement. There was probably a small room or structure here. Further west on the heavily quarried sheet rock are two games, a column footing, a mortar, and a rectangular rock-cut cistern. There is what may be another terrace wall c. 20 m to the south. Close to this is a low expanse of sheet rock containing another bedrock mortar.

That this area was residential is suggested by its location inside the city walls, its dense artifact scatter, the large number of walls in the area (although many are temporally ambiguous), and the high degree of surface modification and control.

The north terrace wall is constructed of one course of unmodified cobbles. Two faces are visible on the east end, but the west end is more disturbed and ambiguous. At the east end, a short wall segment extends south, but it is in poor condition and it is not clear if the terraces were once connected. The south wall is more solidly constructed, with the central section made of one to two courses of rectangular quarried blocks that are inset 0.25 m and may have served as steps. The other sections are built of unmodified and split stones and cobbles. At the south end of the site, atop the sheet rock, is a short east-west rubble wall segment, with cement debris. A rock-cut cistern lies within this site.

Artifacts: As elsewhere within the city walls, there is a sparse background scatter of ceramics and slag. This scatter is more dense east of VMS-176 and drops off almost entirely south of the city walls. A single piece of blue-on-white Chinese porcelain was found atop the sheet rock with the wall, games, and occupational debris. Two north-south transects were placed at intervals of 20 m, with units collected every 20 m. A judgment sample (J1) was placed within a room in the southern area of the site.

Transect 1 Unit 1: 100 g ceramics; wares: 11 black plain ware, 2 brown plain ware.
Transect 1 Unit 2: <50 g ceramics; wares: 1 black plain ware.
Transect 1 Unit 3: 50 g ceramics; wares: 4 black plain ware, 1 brown plain ware.
Transect 2 Unit 1: 50 g ceramics; wares: 7 black plain ware, 2 brown plain ware.

Transect 2 Unit 2: 100 g ceramics; wares: 9 black plain ware, 3 red plain ware. Diagnostics: 1 jar.

Transect 2 Unit 3: 100 g ceramics; wares: 12 black plain ware, 1 red plain ware. Diagnostics: 3 jars.

J1: 100 g ceramics; wares: 22 black plain ware.

Temporal Affiliation: Late Vijayanagara period, possibly others.
Illustrations: Figure 5.39.

SITE: VMS-177   Block: S   **Transect:** 16
Primary Site Use: Religious: sculpture.
Site Dimensions: 10 × 5 m
Setting: Middle of Penukonda Road.
Present Land Use/Disturbances: The sculpture is covered in recent applications of blue and green paint. Freshly broken and quarried blocks and rubble have been piled up around the sculpture on the platform.
Site Description: Hanuman sculpture on low platform in Penukonda Road. The platform is constructed of two courses of quarried square and rectangular granite blocks. The sculpture itself is carved from a large boulder, around which the platform was constructed. A 5 m long wall projects toward the west and is in alignment with the south face of the platform. The entire area is mounded, suggesting that the platform was once larger and may have had a dividing wall. The striding Hanuman sculpture measures 1.20 × 1.04 m. A conch shell and chakra are sculpted on the upper corners of the boulder. A small fragment of a chlorite image has been placed on the platform.
Artifacts: None observed; no collections made.
Temporal Affiliation: Vijayanagara.
References: Morrison 1995:77; Morrison and Sinopoli 1996:67.
Illustrations: Figure 5.40; Plate 5.32.

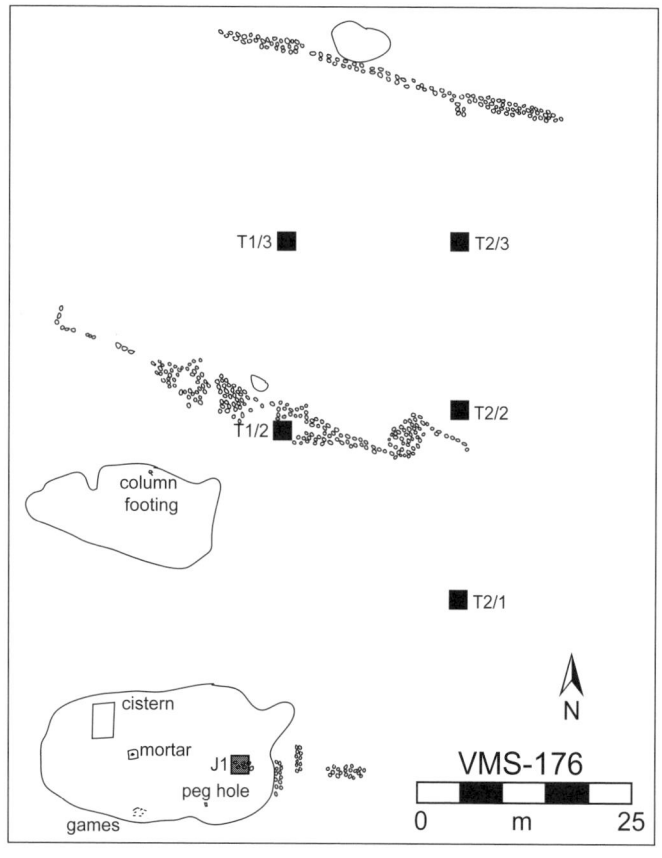

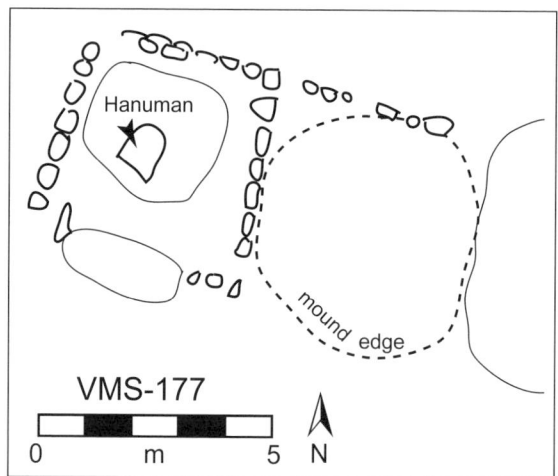

(*Above Left*) Figure 5.39. VMS-176, plan and location of collection units.

(*Above Right*) Figure 5.40. VMS-177, plan.

(*Left*) Plate 5.32. VMS-177, Hanuman image on boulder.

SITE: VMS-178   Block: S   Transect: 16
   Primary Site Use: Residential: structure and artifact concentration.
   Site Dimensions: 80 × 100 m
   Setting: Gently sloping area inside city wall.
   Present Land Use/Disturbances: Field clearing, quarrying. The Penukonda road runs along the south edge of the site.
   Site Description: Residential area. This site is rather arbitrarily defined from the area of high density occupation debris inside the city walls. It has a high artifact density, numerous possible wall foundations, many bedrock mortars, and a grinding slick. The low outcropping boulders are extensively modified by quarrying; many have single or paired peg holes. This area seems to have contained numerous ephemeral structures, indicated only by indistinct rubble wall fragments now preserved only near field borders. This area includes a large depression (c. 50 × 50 m) that may have been a tank or well. It is not bounded by walls, but near its east edge is a broken chlorite architectural element, either a capital or a column footing.
   Artifacts: Variable density ceramic scatter with sparse slag and lithic component. This site lies within the continuous artifact scatter found inside the city walls. A single north-south transect was laid out, placed due north of VMS-177. Four collection units were placed at 20 m intervals along this transect. A diagnostic collection was also made.
   Transect 1 Unit 1: 100 g ceramics; wares: 7 black plain ware, 7 brown plain ware. Diagnostics: 1 jar.
   Transect 1 Unit 2: 50 g ceramics; wares: 9 black plain ware, 2 brown plain ware. Other artifacts: 1 piece slag, <50 g.
   Transect 1 Unit 3: 100 g ceramics; wares: 10 black plain ware, 7 brown plain ware; 1 coarse ware. Other artifacts: 1 piece slag, <50 g.
   Transect 1 Unit 4: 100 g ceramics; wares: 35 black plain ware, 8 brown plain ware. Diagnostics: 4 jars.
   Temporal Affiliation: Vijayanagara.

SITE: VMS-179   Block: S   Transect: 16
   Primary Site Use: Industrial: iron working.
   Site Dimensions: 50 × 35 m
   Setting: Level to gently sloping dry fields.
   Present Land Use/Disturbances: Extensive disturbance. The land has been cleared for cultivation and there are mounds of rubble around the site area and around an electric pole on the east side of the site.
   Site Description: Iron processing site. This was the location of an iron smelting workshop as indicated by a very high density of iron slag and what appear to be tuyere fragments in a localized area. There are no clear indications of the location of the furnace although chunks of fired brick are scattered in one portion of the site. Lying within the city walls, this facility was situated in an area of high residential density. Several mortars are located in the vicinity. There is a large temple complex (VMS-142) c. 60 m north of the site and a step well, VMS-143, c. 75 to the northwest.
   Artifacts: High background density ceramic scatter. The density of ceramics on the site is consistent with that of nearby areas. There is, however, a heavy to very heavy scatter of iron slag and other indications of iron processing. Two north-south transects were collected at intervals of 15 m, with units placed at 20 m intervals. The following units contained artifacts:
   Transect 1 Unit 1: 100 g ceramics; wares: 12 black plain ware, 11 brown plain ware. Diagnostic sherds: 1 jar. Other artifacts: 2300 g slag, 100 g furnace fragments.
   Transect 1 Unit 2: 100 g ceramics; wares: 15 black plain ware, 3 red plain ware, 12 brown ware. Diagnostics: 1 jar. Other artifacts: 3700 g slag, 100 g furnace fragments.

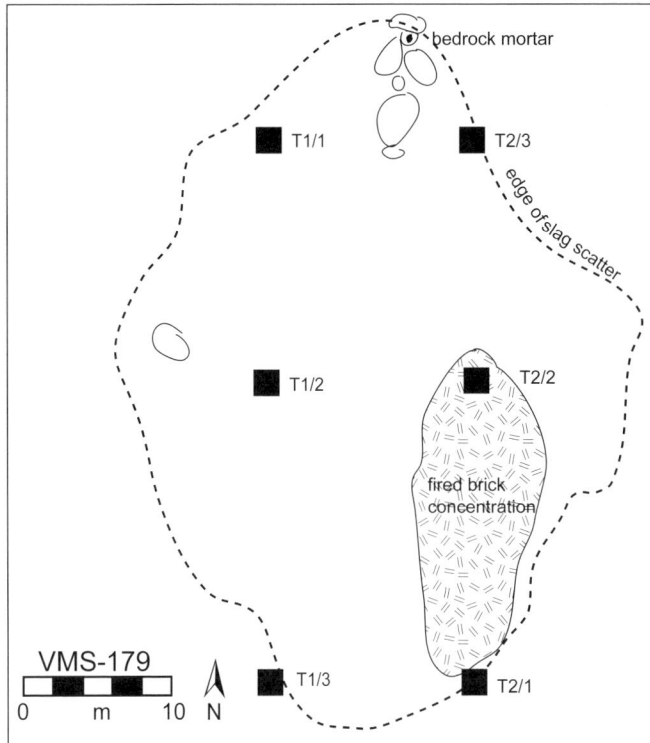

Figure 5.41. VMS-179, plan, approximate site boundaries and collection units.

Plate 5.33. VMS-179, iron slag on site surface.

   Transect 1 Unit 3: 50 g ceramics; wares: 3 black plain ware, 6 brown plain ware. Other artifacts: 1450 gm slag, 50 g furnace fragments.
   Transect 2 Unit 2: <50 g ceramics; wares: 5 black plain ware, 1 brown plain ware. Diagnostics: 1 jar. Other artifacts: 2150 g slag, 200 g furnace fragments.
   Transect 2 Unit 3: 50 g ceramics; wares: 8 black plain ware, 1 red plain ware, 7 brown plain ware. Diagnostics: 1 bowl, 2 jars. Other artifacts: 1000 g slag, 50 g furnace fragments.
   Temporal Affiliation: Vijayanagara.
   References: Morrison 1995:85; Morrison and Sinopoli 1996:63, 71; Sinopoli 2003:197.
   Illustrations: Figure 5.41; Plate 5.33.

SITE: VMS-180 Block: S Transect: 16
Primary Site Use: Residential/transport: step well.
Site Dimensions: 17 × 17 m
Setting: Level dry farmed fields.
Present Land Use/Disturbances: Heavily disturbed by field clearing and possibly by paved road c. 30 m to the north.
Site Description: Probable step well. What was probably a square step well defined by quarried granite blocks is now indicated by a depression with three blocks lying along its south side, two on its north, and one on its west side. The rest of the masonry is covered by soil and vegetation; some may also have been robbed. The depression is about 3 m deep and is dry but has palm trees and bushes growing in it. The site lies on the road from VMS-123/Feature 1 to the Pattabhirama temple (VMS-237).
Artifacts: Located in an area of a large, continuous artifact scatter, the artifact density in the area surrounding the site is relatively lower than the area surrounding VMS-179. 100% collection. 600 g ceramics; wares: 120 black plain ware, 3 red plain ware, 38 brown plain ware. Diagnostics: 1 bowl, 15 jars.
Temporal Affiliation: Vijayanagara.

SITE: VMS-181 Block: S Transect: 16
Primary Site Use: Agricultural: embankments and terraces.
Site Dimensions: 160 × 140 m
Setting: Sloping outcrops and sheet rock.
Present Land Use/Disturbances: Both dry farmed and irrigated fields surround the site. The channels and walls are being actively maintained and used. There is evidence of both older and more recent quarrying.
Site Description: Soil and water control feature. This site consists of a series of large and small embankments, most constructed of mounded earth. These are designed to impound runoff from the north slope of the southwest/northeast trending outcrop on which they are situated as well as to create a complex series of terraces and basins in which crops are grown. The construction date of this series of features is unclear. Although some embankment sections are clearly older than others and a few quarried blocks of apparent Vijayanagara affiliation are integrated into some walls, the system is clearly used and maintained at present.

More than half of the slope of this outcrop is sheet rock. The wider and broader passages between the sheet rock are blocked by wide, sinuous earthen embankments, the narrower and steeper passages by shorter, higher embankments shored up on the downstream side with rubble walls. The masonry on the latter is not stepped back, as is generally the case for Vijayanagara period features of this kind. There are two large embankments. Above the higher south embankment are small paddy fields terraced up the slope and separated by low earth and cobble borders. A stone-lined channel, similar to those found in Vijayanagara reservoirs, is cut near the east end of the embankment. This channel does, however, incorporate a recently quarried block and it is not possible to say if this indicates a recent date for its construction or simply a recent repair. Attached to the east end of the embankment is a smaller earthen embankment, running approximately north-south, that prevents water from the channel from dispersing.

Downstream (north) from the large embankment, the steep and rather constricted passage is terraced with two masonry-faced earth walls. Thus, this feature integrates elements of both reservoir and terrace construction into a single interlocking system. Downstream and to the north is a second lower earthen embankment, similar to the upper. A channel is cut into this embankment; water flow is controlled with piled up stones.
Artifacts: Sparse artifact scatter, part of the continuous low density scatter found across an extensive area. No collections made.

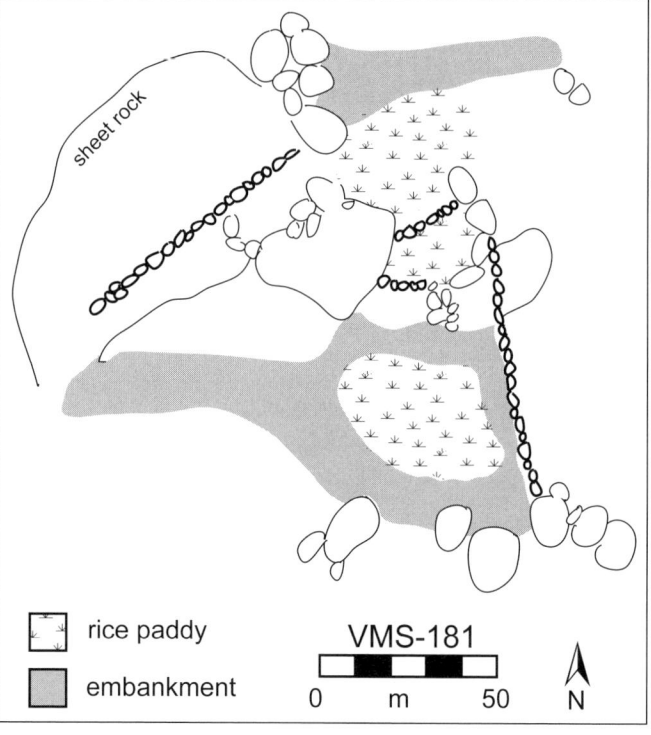

Figure 5.42. VMS-181, plan.

Temporal Affiliation: Unknown. Some recent components.
References: Morrison 1995:92, 102.
Illustrations: Figure 5.42.

SITE: VMS-182 Block: S Transect: 16
Primary Site Use: Transport/religious: road and shrines.
Site Dimensions: 90 × 60 m
Setting: Gently sloping route between outcrops.
Present Land Use/Disturbances: Dry farmed fields have obliterated the north section of the road. A drainage channel cut through the outcrop follows the course of the road, destroying most of the road edge and cobble pavement.
Site Description: Road segments and associated shrines. This paved and walled road segment 2.2-2.5 m wide extends north from an opening in the outer city wall (VMS-123) through a natural opening in a southwest/northeast trending outcrop. The road course defined by this site joins the road leading outward through the Penukonda gate and, in the other direction, into the city, heads almost directly to temple complex VMS-142. The well-worn cobble paving consists of small unmodified stones set close together. Double-faced walls of small unmodified boulders and an occasional quarried block flank the road. The walls are 1.6-1.9 m wide. Quarried blocks and a single column footing located near the north end of the wall suggest that small structures may have been built along the road.

Several shrines and sculptures line this road. From north to south and on the west side of the road they include: (1) a displaced (?) Virabhadra and Bhairavi, and a stone with two pairs of feet encircled by a naga; (2) an *in situ* quarried boulder with a column footing cut into it and next to it a large block with two pairs of feet encircled by a naga; (3) a Nagamma sculpture; and (4) a 2 m high naga made out of a natural rock forma-

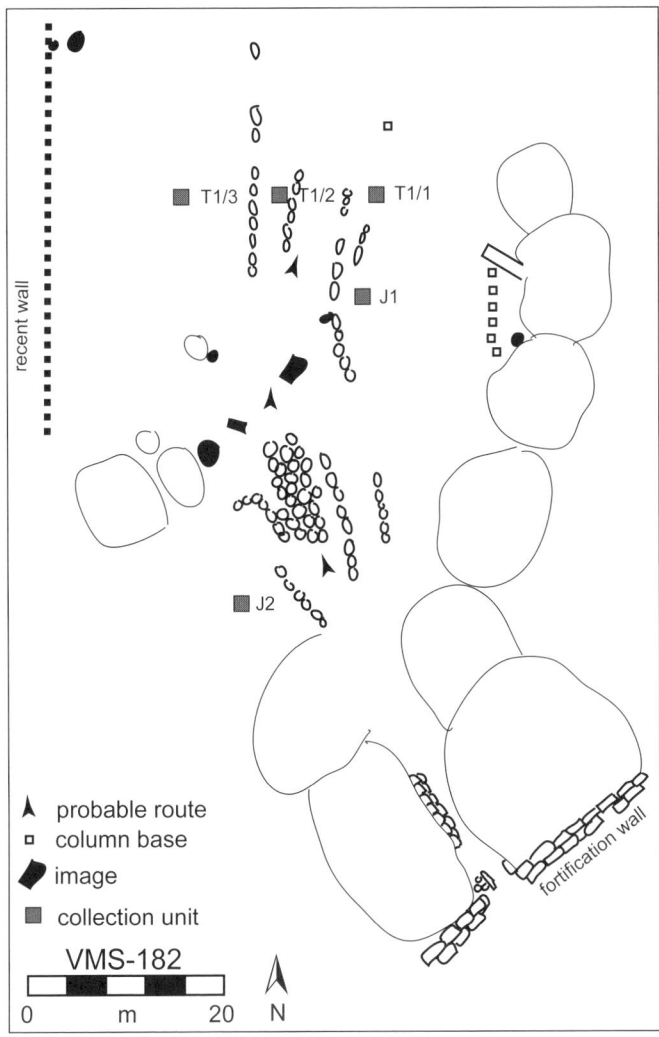

Figure 5.43. VMS-182, plan and location of collection units.

Plate 5.34. VMS-182, road bed.

Plate 5.35. VMS-182, large naga carved from natural rock formation.

tion, the coils and head enhanced by carving. There is no road wall in front of this large naga, which either was approached by steps or else had a low platform around it (a few aligned blocks remain). Moving to the east side of the roadway, associated features include: (1) a long naga stone and a square block, possibly a complement to the column footing on the west side of the road; (2) a rectangular stone with two shallow oval niches cut into one face; and (3) an outcropping boulder with three deep rectangular niches cut into it. Set up against a boulder, c. 3 m east of the road, is a small shrine into which several sculptures have been piled. That its original function was a shrine is clear from the well-carved panels of Virabhadra and Bhairavi carved into the face of the boulder. Leaning against another boulder is a slab or column fragment with a standing Nandi flanked by linga and facing a trident, with a single-line inscription below; this was likely a boundary marker. A nearby dressed rectangular slab has two more lines of text. A partly buried outcrop nearby carries a carved female figure. Lying next to her on a block is what appears to be another Virabhadra, as well as a series of sculptures including a naga stone, a few unsculpted stones, a sculpture of a male holding a sword, the lower half of a Ganesha image, two sculptures of males holding staffs or long bows and swords, and an inscribed boundary stone with a small, headless Nandi.

The road continues south of the gap in the city walls, where it is designated as VMS-183.

Artifacts: In an area with moderately high density ceramic scatter, but density here is locally higher. One east-west transect was laid out, with units placed every 10 m (3 units total). Two 2 × 2 m judgment units were collected, and a diagnostic collection was made. Ceramics (totals): 175 g; wares: 11 black plain ware, 3 brown plain ware, 4 jars.

Temporal Affiliation: Vijayanagara.
References: Morrison 1995:75; Morrison and Sinopoli 1996:65.
Illustrations: Figure 5.43; Plates 5.34-5.37.

194   *The Vijayanagara Metropolitan Survey*

Plate 5.36. VMS-182, images of Virabhadra and Bhairavi. In front of them is a stone sculpted with two pairs of feet encircled by a naga.

Plate 5.37. VMS-182, sculpted Nandi, lingam and inscription on slab or column fragment.

SITE: VMS-183   Block: S   Transect: 16
   Primary Site Use: Transport/religious: road and temple.
   Site Dimensions: 225 × 115 m
   Setting: Level area adjacent to outcrops and sheet rock, just outside city wall.
   Present Land Use/Disturbances: Modern drainage channel has been constructed along course of road and incorporates a road wall near Feature 1. The area around the opening in the city wall is very disturbed and Feature 1 is partially collapsed.

Site Description: Road segment and associated temple, Feature 1. This site is the south extension of the road VMS-182, and passes through the outer city wall (VMS-123) through two square bastions that face south, on either side of a natural pass through the outcrops. The opening is not a formal gate, but more a doorway with flat, finished faces in the 6 m wide wall on either side of the 2.5 m wide opening. The original level of the passage is difficult to discern, but the walls must have loomed at least 4 m above its base. As one passes out of the city walls to the broad open valley on the south, sheet rock outcrops flank the passage on either side for c. 60 m.

Just inside (north) the city wall, a small, square, rubble-walled platform perches on sheet rock to the east of and above the passage. Immediately to the south of the long, narrow passageway outside the city wall is a stepped masonry wall 25 m long, now truncated by field clearing. This embankment, now consisting of five irregular courses of small boulders and cobbles, probably collected runoff from the outcrop to its west, ponding up the water for use by travelers and worshipers at the nearby temple, and keeping water off the road. To the south of the stepped wall, the drainage channel meets two parallel walls, apparently two sides of a structure that bordered the west side of the road. Each is 0.6-0.8 m wide and constructed of unmodified cobbles; a distance of 0.8-0.85 m separates the two walls. The west wall of this pair abuts the enclosure wall of Feature 1, a small temple built upon a high walled terrace (described below). There are indications of what may be steps running, however, right over the parallel walls. It is possible, then, that rather than defining a structure, these walls actually define subsurface drains. The east wall widens to 2.5 m, forming a low platform. Its two faces diverge, with the west side eventually disappearing and the east side forming the west face of a massively constructed wall (or platform) of three parallel faces, each having up to five courses of large unmodified and split masonry elements.

Beginning approximately opposite Feature 1 is a long wall, constructed of two faces of large cobbles and small unmodified and split boulders, that forms the east edge of the roadway. In the wide part of the roadway are several well worn cobbles, evidently remnants of paving. Although the south end of this wall disappears into cleared and irrigated fields, the west road wall continues, curving around to the west and following the base of the outcrop. A second wall, c. 2 m away and closer to the outcrop, emerges out of a pile of boulders and parallels the west road wall until both are chopped up by irrigated fields. The area between the two walls is now depressed, suggesting that this may have been a drainage channel. Like the northern channel, however, this function could be recent and perhaps these walls simply define the course of the road, running along the base of the outcrop. Further west are a series of runoff control walls and check dams near the edge of an outcrop.

Feature 1: A small east-facing temple overlooking the roadway of VMS-183. It is located outside the city walls on an earthen terrace enclosed by masonry walls. Steps appear to have connected it with the roadway and the stepped-back wall to its north may have gathered runoff into a small pond for the use of the temple. The enclosure wall, now at most four courses high, is constructed of unmodified stones of all sizes, from pebbles to large boulders.

The shrine itself appears to have had an outer chamber to its east, now represented by three partly buried slabs aligned north-south in front of the standing antechamber and by two walls extending east from the antechamber. A step up to the west leads to the antechamber, open on the east and walled on other sides by horizontal dressed slabs, some more than 2 m long. Instead of columns in the exterior walls, there are slightly protruding triangular blocks. These, as well as two column footings cut into the east basement of the antechamber, indicate that it probably had 2 × 2 standing columns. There are now two freestanding columns, rectangular in section with simple square cutouts, leaning against the door frame of the sanctuary. The latter is simply carved with a square pilaster. The door guardian is not well preserved and its affiliation is unclear. The sanctuary itself is undecorated, but plastered, with no image or image base.

The temple is built partly on cut sheet rock and partly on a footing course of square blocks. A great deal of apparently original plaster still adheres to the structure. The simple brick and plaster shikhara is in poor condition. Patches of concrete suggest a paved area east of the outer mandapa.

Artifacts: Artifact densities outside the city wall are lower than they are inside the wall. Ceramic density around this site is very low. One long north-south transect was laid in the possible road area to the east of the small parallel walls. Judgment units were placed on platform 1, in an unplowed but cobbled area of the road, and near the east side of the step well. A diagnostic collection was made. Ceramics (all units): 700 g; wares: 91 black plain ware, 4 brown plain ware.

Temporal Affiliation: Vijayanagara.

References: Morrison 1995:75; Morrison and Sinopoli 1996:65.

Illustrations: Figure 5.44; Plate 5.38.

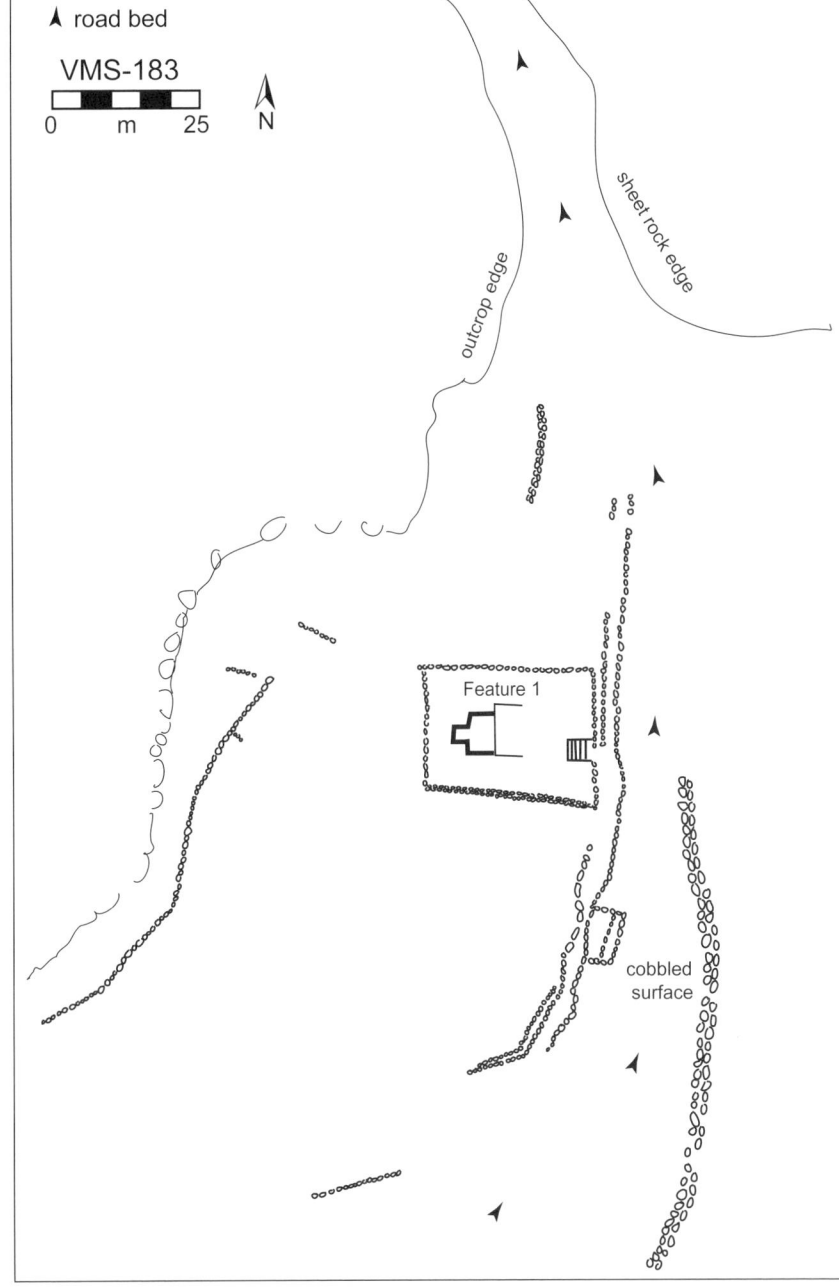

(*Right*) Figure 5.44. VMS-183, plan.

(*Below*) Plate 5.38. VMS-183, Feature 1: temple; bastion of VMS-123 (outer city wall) on right.

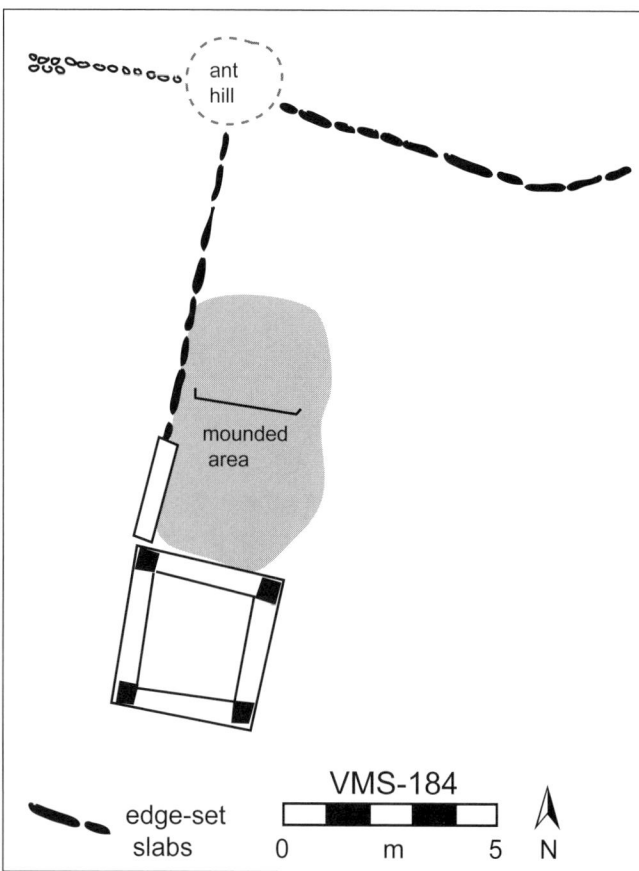

Figure 5.45. VMS-184, plan.

SITE: VMS-184   Block: S   Transect: 16
Primary Site Use: Transport/other: mandapa on road.
Site Dimensions: 3.5 × 3.5 m
Setting: Level dry farmed area.
Present Land Use/Disturbances: Plowing and field clearance have disturbed this structure, located 15 m south of the still-used Penukonda road.
Site Description: Mandapa. This square 2 × 2 column structure is constructed of dressed granite slabs surrounding a brick floor. The unroofed structure has basement moldings, two stepped with angled bevel and a corner quarter medallion. Sitting atop plain rectangular columns are capitals of simple rectangular blocks. Nearby are two displaced formal architectural elements of unknown function. The structure has apparently been partly dismantled and perhaps remodeled. A long flat slab extends from the structure to the north, in line with a row of slabs set on edge that extends to the road. A mounded area and the edge of another flat slab suggest another room, structure, or defined space north of the mandapa itself. Some slabs and cobbles now defining the road might have been robbed from this structure.
Artifacts: This site is within the high density artifact scatter inside the city walls, but ceramic densities are lower here. A low density of slag was noted. 100% collection. 75 g ceramics; body sherds: 31 black plain ware, 6 brown plain ware, 4 red plain ware. Diagnostics: 1 bowl.
Temporal Affiliation: Vijayanagara.
References: Morrison 1995:77; Morrison and Sinopoli 1996:67.
Illustrations: Figure 5.45.

SITE: VMS-185   Block: S   Transect: 16
Primary Site Use: Agricultural: wall.
Site Dimensions: 5 × 0.33 m
Setting: Base of outcrop.
Present Land Use/Disturbances: Dry farmed agricultural fields.
Site Description: Isolated north-south wall segment located below and outside the city wall, at the base of an area of sheet rock. This 5 m long wall is at least 0.33 m wide; earth is piled up on the west side of the wall. It is constructed of small cobbles and a few quarried blocks and apparently served as a retaining wall to control erosion and runoff.
Artifacts: 100% collection; no artifacts observed.
Temporal Affiliation: Unknown.
References: Morrison 1995:75, 102; Morrison and Sinopoli 1996:65.

SITE: VMS-186   Block: S   Transect: 16
Primary Site Use: Administrative/religious: platform.
Site Dimensions: 30 × 28 m
Setting: Level area near VMS-183.
Present Land Use/Disturbances: Dry fields surround the structure while irrigated fields lie some 25 m to its south. The lower platform and parts of the southwest and southeast enclosure walls have been disturbed by field clearance.
Site Description: Platform. This unusual, large two-tiered, apparently open platform is a visually impressive structure that may have had either administrative or religious functions. Inside a lower and larger square walled platform, now 0.3 m higher than the surrounding fields, is a higher (1.52 m higher) central square platform. The latter appears to be divided into two sections by an interior wall. The area north of this wall is somewhat higher and has an intact section (3 × 3 m) of cement and plaster floor. The area south of the wall is slightly lower and is slumped toward the south. The structure is located about 60 m east of road VMS-183 and opposite the temple VMS-183/Feature 1 and is probably associated with them. The layout of this structure is unlike any known residential or religious structure. The absence of any quarried or dressed elements in such a large structure of such formal layout is striking.

The double-faced walls of the lower platform range from 0.9 to 1.1 m wide. The outer face is constructed of small to medium unmodified boulders with their flattest surfaces facing outward. Many are set on end and even though there is now only a single course preserved, the wall stands up to 0.75 m above ground level. The exterior walls of the upper platform consist largely of natural bedrock, sometimes quarried square, but more often unmodified, making the edge rather irregular. Where there is no bedrock, small boulders and cobbles form double-faced walls. The interior wall of the high platform is mostly a squared-off basaltic outcrop.
Artifacts: Light ceramic scatter on lower and upper terrace, but where fill is eroding out of upper terrace, ceramic density is moderate. Several basalt pegs were found near the structure. A single north-south transect, with three collection units placed at 20 m intervals. Two judgment units were collected: J1 on the lower terrace, J2 on the site's upper terrace. A diagnostic collection was made on the lower terrace. Only the following units contained artifacts:
Transect 1 Unit 3: <50 g ceramics; wares: 3 black plain ware, 1 brown plain ware.
J2: <50 g ceramics; wares: 5 black plain ware.
Temporal Affiliation: Unknown; probably Vijayanagara.
References: Morrison 1995:75; Morrison and Sinopoli 1996:65.
Illustrations: Figure 5.46; Plate 5.39.

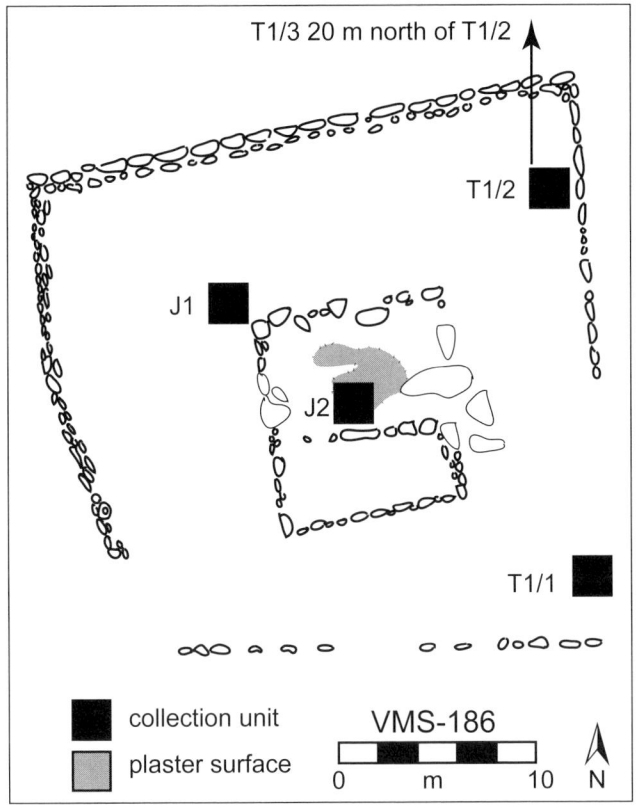

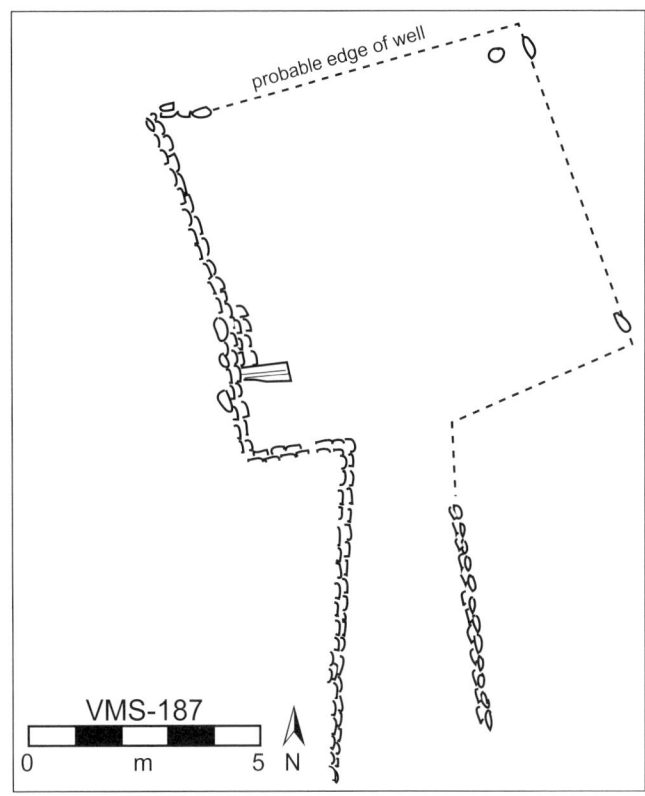

(*Above Left*) Figure 5.46. VMS-186, plan and location of collection units.

(*Above Right*) Figure 5.47. VMS-187, plan.

(*Left*) Plate 5.39. VMS-186, overview of platform from north.

SITE: VMS-187   Block: S   Transect: 16
Primary Site Use: Transport/residential: step well.
Site Dimensions: 12 × 9 m
Setting: Level dry farmed fields.
Present Land Use/Disturbances: A modern channel incorporating elements from this structure runs along its south edge, leading to irrigated fields 10 m south. This area is heavily grazed and there are many piles of cobbles from field clearance.
Site Description: Well. This T-shaped step well is associated with the road and temple, VMS-183. The platform, VMS-186, lies 80 m to the northeast. The well is constructed of up to seven stepped courses of quarried rectangular, square, and a few triangular granite blocks with some cobble chinking interspersed. The well is entered from the south, along a narrow passage that once flanked stairs (no longer visible) that led down to the water chamber. The grassy surface of the silted-in well is now 2 m below the modern ground surface. It slopes up to the south toward the entrance.

A small platform extends out over the well on its west side. Atop this platform is a long horizontal slab with an irregular depression cut in its upper surface. The platform and slab facilitated the hauling of water containers out of the well. In the area east and northeast of the well, where fields have not been cleared, there are numerous possible walls, evidence of possible additional structures. In this area, some 20 m east of the well, are two small boulders, one with an inscribed sun, moon, conch and chakra, and the other with a short inscription. Both inscriptions appear to be recent.

Artifacts: Moderate density scatter of extremely small ceramics around the platform and near the south edge of well. No artifacts visible in or around the north or east sides of the well. No collections made.
Temporal Affiliation: Vijayanagara.
References: Morrison 1995:75; Morrison and Sinopoli 1996:65.
Illustrations: Figure 5.47.

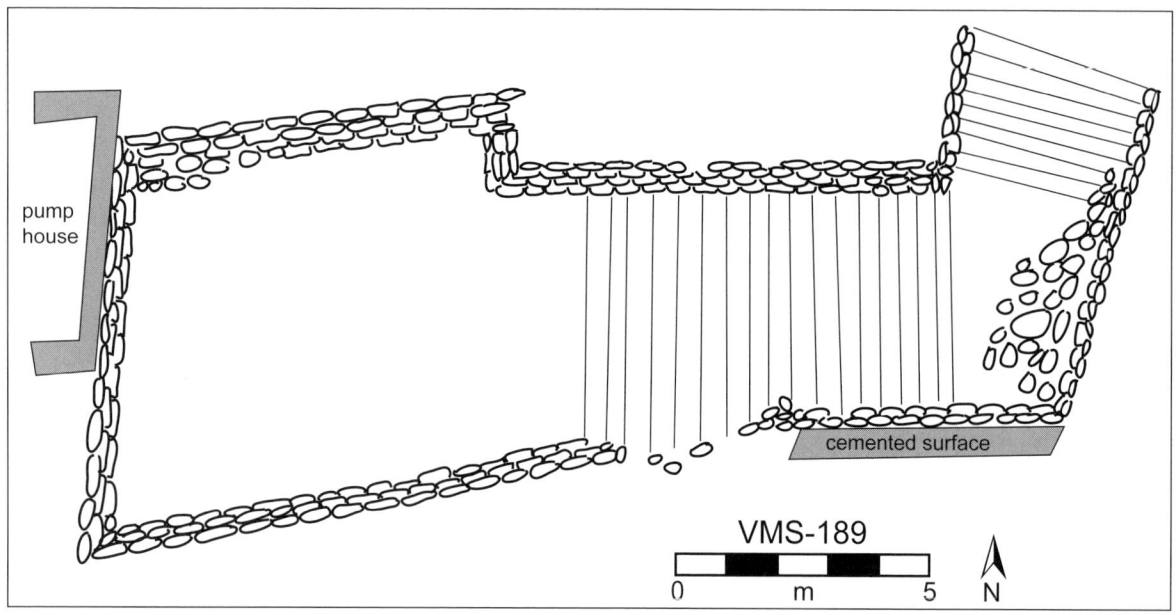

Figure 5.48. VMS-189, plan.

SITE: VMS-188   Block: S   Transect: 16
   Primary Site Use: Unknown/residential: isolated room.
   Site Dimensions: 3 × 2.5 m
   Setting: Slope near base of outcrop.
   Present Land Use/Disturbances: Uncultivated area subject to colluviation.
   Site Description: Isolated single-room 3 × 2.5 m structure consisting of east and west walls perpendicular to an outcrop that forms the north wall. The west wall consists of two slightly stepped courses of small boulders; the east wall is in poor condition but may have been similarly constructed. The interior of the structure is mounded; this structure may have been used for storage.
   Artifacts: 100% collection. <50 g ceramics; a single black plain ware sherd was recovered.
   Temporal Affiliation: Unknown.

SITE: VMS-189   Block: S   Transect: 17
   Primary Site Use: Residential/agricultural/transport: step well.
   Site Dimensions: 19 × 10 m
   Setting: Level area near base of outcrop.
   Present Land Use/Disturbances: Part of this structure is recent; an old step well has been converted into a tube well with an electric pump set. A power line runs along the edge of the site, near the contemporary road. The well has been significantly deepened, and most of its west half is new construction. Slabs with non-recent quarry marks serve as steps going all the way down to the water level, considerably deeper than that of the ancient well. Thus, these have probably been added.
   Site Description: Step well. This well-constructed masonry, brick and plaster well is located along the Penukonda road. There is some indication that a paved and plastered surface defined by a low wall may have once extended all the way around the well. The modern construction appears to have preserved the well's overall shape, just changing the alignment of walls at its west end. The T-shaped step well has a staircase facing east that, after a sizeable landing, turns to the north to face the road. The older parts of the well are constructed of quarried square blocks with some angular chinking stones. The walls consist of four tiers, each composed of three masonry courses, and each set back by 0.15 or 0.2 m. Remnants of brick and plaster remain and indicate that the entire well was bricked and plastered to create a smoothly stepped effect. The base of the original well was rock-cut, apparently no more than about 0.5 m deep. The well now has a rock-cut section some 3 m deep.
   Artifacts: Piles of earth and construction debris cover the area around the well, obscuring artifact patterning. Ceramic densities are low, similar to the background artifact density in the area. No collections made.
   Temporal Affiliation: Vijayanagara and mid- to late twentieth century.
   References: Morrison 1995:76; Morrison and Sinopoli 1996:67.
   Illustrations: Figure 5.48.

SITE: VMS-190   Block: S   Transect: 13-15
   Primary Site Use: Agricultural: reservoir embankment.
   Site Dimensions: 684 × 20 m
   Setting: Level area below gently sloping uplands.
   Present Land Use/Disturbances: This reservoir is still in use and has some minor recent modifications. A road runs across the top of the embankment and the second sluice gate has been fitted with a metal walkway extending from the top of the embankment to the top of the sluice where a metal control rod is located. A platform has been constructed around the sluice and its lower portion cemented.
   Site Description: Reservoir embankment. This massive nearly 700 m long earthen embankment is faced with masonry on the south side, retaining what is now a year-round water supply, partly fed by a recent canal. Before the construction of this canal, the water supply in this reservoir may have been more seasonal. The masonry consists of up to twenty-four stepped courses of unmodified small rounded boulders of black volcanic material, gray granite, and unmodified and roughly quarried pink granite. These different color materials are arranged in alternate bands of gray, pink, and black, creating a striking overall striped effect. Occasional long, horizontal slabs extend out from the masonry. Two of these have circular holes (one broken) cut through them and one has a ground surface.
   Sluice 1: The east sluice lies about 9 m south of the embankment and is no longer in use, having been replaced by a new concrete and metal sluice located adjacent to the embankment. This ornate sluice is c. 7 m high and consists of dressed uprights and a cross bar, capped by a well-dressed lintel slab. This is in turn capped by a lower molding, two stepped with convex bevel and numerous ornate yali head medallions. Atop this is a smaller upper molding, three stepped with angled bevel

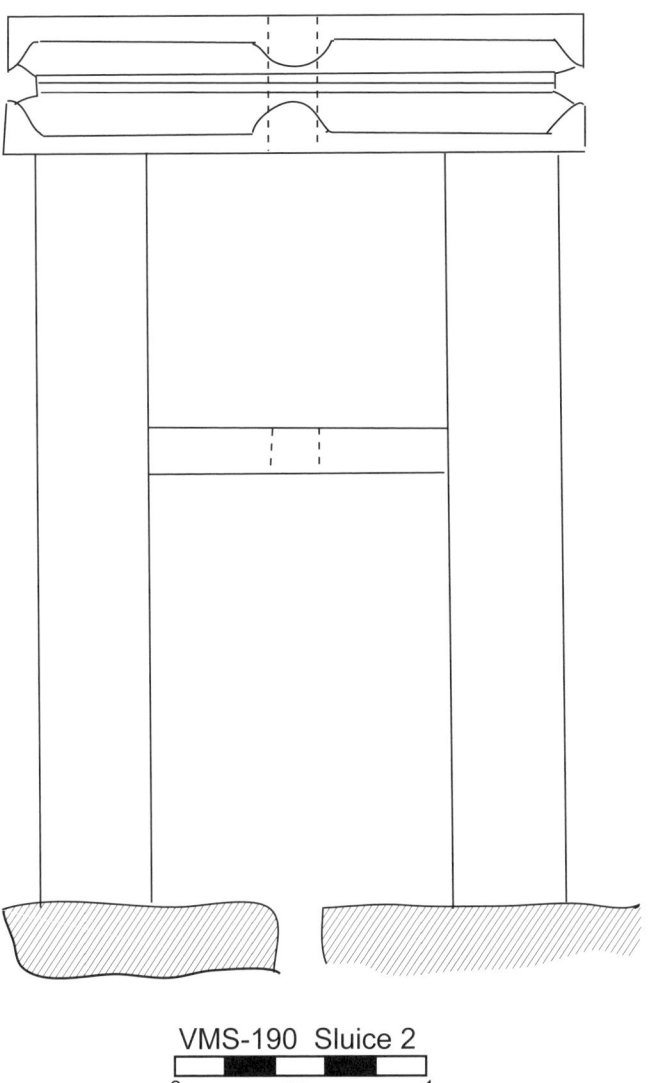

Figure 5.49. VMS-190, sluice 2, section.

Plate 5.40. VMS-190, sluice 1.

Plate 5.41. VMS-190, masonry detail from above; protruding slab with lingam carving.

bearing a highly eroded central carving of what appears to be Lakshmi with two elephants. The upper molding seems to be somewhat too small for its location and may be reused. There is an unusually high proportion of quarried blocks, as well as a number of protruding slabs in the masonry near this sluice.

Sluice 2: The west sluice, still in use. It differs from sluice 1 in that the well-dressed uprights are capped by a simpler molding sequence of lower and upper moldings, two stepped with angled bevel with corner quarter medallions, and central half medallions. This sluice is also shorter (3.6 m) and more compact than sluice 1 and is probably earlier.

The north side of the reservoir is also partly faced with stepped masonry, consisting of two to three courses of unmodified cobbles, somewhat smaller than the elements used in the south masonry, but with the same regularity of coursing (straight, continuous, with essentially no chinking). Atop the embankment c. 120 m east of sluice 2 are several walls and a number of small features, which may be graves. Further east, a protruding slab features a lingam carved in low relief, surrounded by a shallow channel, and with a sun carved in the upper right corner.

Artifacts: None observed; no collections made.

Temporal Affiliation: Early Vijayanagara and later Vijayanagara, continuing use until present.

References: Morrison 1995:75, 91-92, 102; Morrison and Sinopoli 1996:63, 65.

Illustrations: Figure 5.49; Plates 5.40, 5.41.

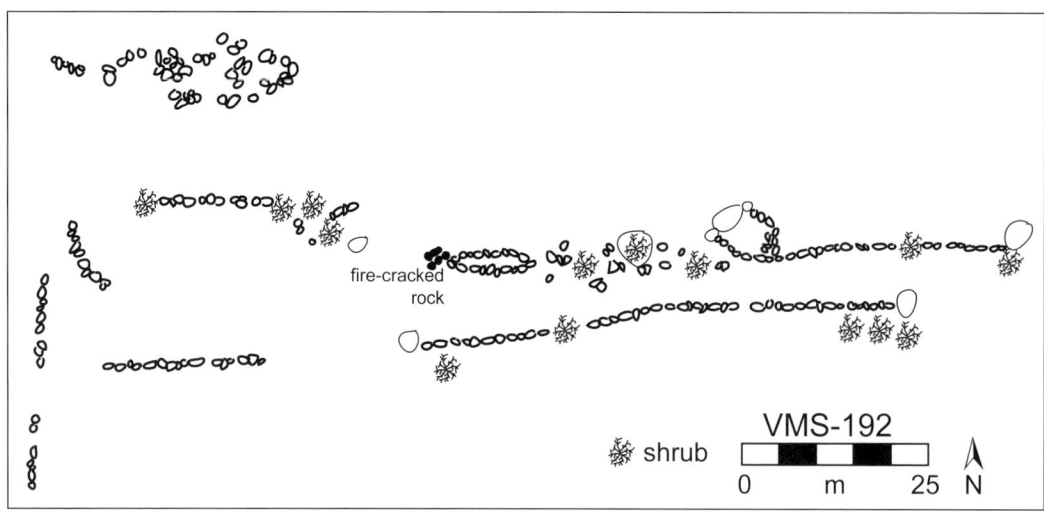

Figure 5.50. VMS-192, plan.

SITE: VMS-191   Block: S   **Transect:** 14
   Primary Site Use: Agricultural: terraces.
   Site Dimensions: c. 125 × 125 m
   Setting: Gentle slopes amid low outcrops.
   Present Land Use/Disturbances: Minimal. This area is occasionally dry farmed, but little clearing has taken place and a little-used cart track runs through the area.
   Site Description: Agricultural terraces and check dams. This terraced area lies just above (in the catchment) of the reservoir VMS-190. Most of the walls consist of a single course of a single face of cobbles, in some cases piled rather than coursed. Some segments incorporate *in situ* sheet rock and boulders; others have been made partly of large unmodified boulders. Most walls are placed perpendicular to the flow of runoff. However, since some of the terraced areas are completely enclosed, other walls run parallel to the drainage. Two major drainage systems are terraced, one extending north-south and draining directly into the reservoir, and one extending east-west and joining the north-south drainage just before its empties into VMS-190. The overall slope is gentle and there does not seem to be very deep soil development behind the terraces. These terraces evidently served to control water and especially soil in the catchment of VMS-190. They are an integral part of its operation and, as such, may be contemporaneous with it.
   Artifacts: Scatter of heavily eroded small earthenware ceramics, more dense near the water's edge. No collections made.
   Temporal Affiliation: Unknown; possibly Vijayanagara.
   References: Morrison 1995:92, 102; Morrison and Sinopoli 1996:71.

SITE: VMS-192   Block: S   **Transect:** 14
   Primary Site Use: Unknown/residential?: walls and possible structures.
   Site Dimensions: 13 × 50 m
   Setting: Sloping area amid outcrops.
   Present Land Use/Disturbances: A bullock cart path runs along the long axis of the wall, between the wall and the rooms. Walls of rooms have unclear alignments and appear to be badly disturbed.
   Site Description: A series of rock alignments built into natural granite outcrops. The major feature of this site is a long east-west wall paralleled by a series of smaller walls to the north, some of which appear to form small rooms or enclosures in the outcrops. These smaller walls also run east-west, and they and the long east-west wall are broken through in approximately the same places. The walls do not appear to be agricultural features and may be structural foundations. The long wall and the room walls are constructed of single courses of unmodified granitic cobbles; a third wall segment is built into the outcrops further north. Near the west end of the site is a north-south wall or check dam. A number of fire-altered granite boulders are located adjacent to a narrow enclosure in the center of the site; there is no evidence for a modern hearth.
   Artifacts: Lithic and ceramics. A highly localized (c. 1 m diameter) ceramic scatter is situated south of the main east-west wall; a dense lithic scatter reflecting bipolar and core reduction also lies south of the long wall but it is segregated from the ceramic scatter. 100% collection for ceramics, with systematic collection in area of dense lithic scatter for range of material types and production techniques. Two east-west transects were spaced 10 m apart, with collections placed at 10 m intervals. The following units contained lithics (ceramics data are presented as summary data).
   Transect 1 Unit 2: 1 utilized flake (gray quartz).
   Transect 1 Unit 3: 33 flakes, 72 fragments angular debris, 8 bipolar cores (all of quartz).
   Transect 2 Unit 2: 4 flakes (quartz), 20 fragments angular debris, 3 fragments bipolar cores (quartz).
   Transect 2 Unit 3: 31 unutilized flakes (quartz), 4 utilized flakes (1 chert, 3 gray quartz), 128 fragments angular debris (quartz), 11 fragments bipolar debris (quartz).
   Diagnostic Sweep: 26 unutilized flakes (quartz), 9 utilized flakes (gray quartz), 1 scraper (gray quartz), 90 fragments angular debris (quartz), 1 core (quartz), 6 fragments bipolar flaking debris (quartz).
   Ceramics (Summary Data): 250 g; wares: 69 brown plain ware. Diagnostics: 1 bowl.
   Temporal Affiliation: Unknown.
   Illustrations: Figure 5.50.

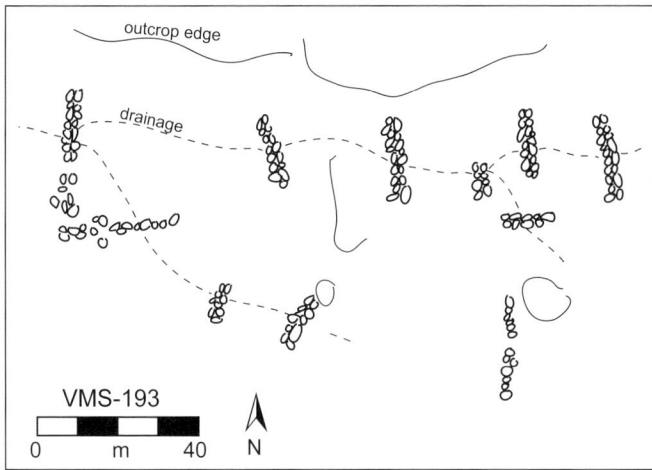

Figure 5.51. VMS-193, plan.

SITE: VMS-193   Block: S   Transect: 14/15
Primary Site Use: Agricultural: check dams.
Site Dimensions: 140 × 60 m
Setting: Moderate slope near base of outcrop.
Present Land Use/Disturbances: Largely enclosed by a modern wall, part of this area is cultivated in cotton and eucalyptus. The outcrop in the middle of the enclosure has been recently quarried.
Site Description: Small check dams. A single branching drainage channel is crossed by eleven small dams constructed of unmodified small cobbles. Although much of the land within the recent enclosure walls has been cleared, the terraces themselves seem to be relatively undisturbed except where a recent wall is superimposed over them. Some of the check dams show evidence of recent maintenance.
Artifacts: Sparse, dispersed ceramic scatter with a single vein quartz lithic flake fragment. Collections along an east-west oriented transect with two units collected; a diagnostic collection was also made.

Transect 1 Unit 1: <50 g ceramics; wares: 1 black plain ware, 1 red plain ware, 4 brown plain ware. Diagnostics: 2 jars.
Transect 1 Unit 2: <50 g ceramics; wares: 1 black plain ware, 1 red plain ware, 1 brown plain ware.
Transect 1 Unit 3: Lithics: 1 utilized white quartz "chunk," 1 utilized flake (opaque white quartz).
Temporal Affiliation: Unknown, not recent.
References: Morrison 1995:92, 102.
Illustrations: Figure 5.51.

SITE: VMS-194   Block: S   Transect: 13-15
Primary Site Use: Agricultural: reservoir embankment.
Site Dimensions: 300 × 10 m
Setting: Valley between two large outcrops.
Present Land Use/Disturbances: A large part of this reservoir has been dismantled. It is currently surrounded by and incorporated into agricultural fields; irrigation ditches crisscross the site. A modern road runs c. 100 m to the south. The area appears to be heavily colluviated.
Site Description: Reservoir embankment. This badly disturbed site is located upstream from VMS-190, in the same drainage. The embankment is situated in a small valley between two large outcrops, in an area now irrigated by the modern Right Bank High Level Canal originating at the Tungabhadra reservoir. Only the east and west ends of the masonry facing remain; the extant masonry (from the south side of the embankment) consists of two to four stepped courses of large, unmodified boulders. In between these preserved wall stubs, the masonry has been dismantled and everywhere its earthen core has been spread out into the fields. There are no traces of sluice gates.
Artifacts: The artifact scatter around this feature appears to be entirely recent. No collections made.
Temporal Affiliation: Vijayanagara.
References: Morrison 1995:91-92, 102.
Illustrations: Figure 5.52.

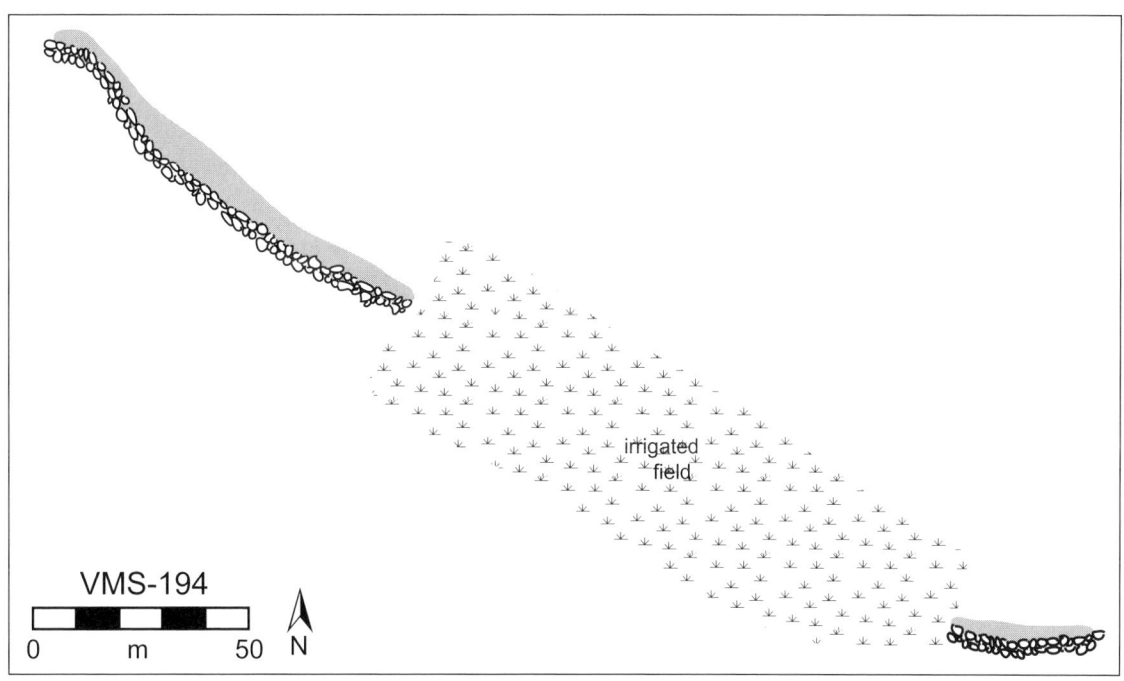

Figure 5.52. VMS-194, plan.

SITE: VMS-195   Block: S   **Transect:** 14
   Primary Site Use: Residential: lithic and ceramic scatter.
   Site Dimensions: 25 × 40 m
   Setting: Level dry farmed fields.
   Present Land Use/Disturbances: Located in a fallow field, a modern field camp and threshing floor are located on the east and northeast edges of the site.
   Site Description: Artifact scatter. This small lithic scatter is located just south of the bed of the reservoir VMS-194. This scatter may be superimposed by a very sparse ceramic scatter, or the two might be associated. There are no associated features.
   Artifacts: The scatter is diffuse and even, probably a product of repeated plowing. The dominant raw material type is vein quartz, which occurs locally in cobbles weathered from the nearby granitic outcrops. Flakes, angular debris, bipolar debris, and cores were noted, but no formal tools were observed. Two east-west transects were laid out at 10 m intervals, with a total of five units collected at 20 m intervals. The following units contained ceramics.
   Transect 1 Unit 2: Ceramics: <50 g, 1 brown plain ware, 1 jar.
   Diagnostic Collection: Lithics: 4 flakes (2 quartz, 1 cryptocrystalline), 10 angular debris (quartz), 1 core and 2 bipolar cores (quartz).
   Temporal Affiliation: Unknown.

SITE: VMS-196   Block: S   **Transect:** 14
   Primary Site Use: Unknown: isolated walls.
   Site Dimensions: 100 × 34 m
   Setting: Sloping area amid outcrops.
   Present Land Use/Disturbances: Although the site area itself is uncultivated, irrigated fields lie to the south and a recent shrine c. 50 m to the southeast. The walls are fragmentary and badly disturbed; cow and foot paths have cut through some walls.
   Site Description: Walls. These long walls are constructed of single courses of unmodified cobbles. Most run east-west and are built into and over boulders on a low east-west trending outcrop. The outcrops and walls have helped to form a low earthen terrace to the north of the outcrop. This terrace does not seem to be agricultural, nor is there any evidence for residential structures. There is one fragmentary north-south crosswall. VMS-196 lies just west of VMS-192, which is similar in layout and construction, having seemingly nonagricultural retaining walls built into an outcrop.
   Artifacts: Sparse lithic and ceramic scatter. Some of the ceramics are highly eroded. 100% collection. 550 g ceramics; wares: 64 black plain ware, 2 red plain ware, 82 brown plain ware. Diagnostics: 3 jars. Lithics: 9 flakes, 1 utilized flake, 13 fragments angular debris, 1 core, 8 bipolar cores (all of quartz).
   Temporal Affiliation: Unknown.

SITE: VMS-197   Block: S   **Transect:** 14
   Primary Site Use: Residential: artifact scatter.
   Site Dimensions: 100 × 10 m
   Setting: Atop low sloping outcrop.
   Present Land Use/Disturbances: Uncultivated; paths pass to the north and south of site.
   Site Description: Lithic and ceramic scatter. The scatter is located within a low east-west trending granitic outcrop c. 100 m long, consisting of a central area of sheet rock, with large boulders at the east and west ends. Several small natural cisterns occur in the sheet rock. VMS-197 is c. 25 m north of VMS-196 (isolated walls) and c. 25 m northwest of VMS-192 (artifact scatter and isolated walls and rooms) and is probably associated with these sites. A quartz vein runs east-west through the outcrop and may be the raw material source for many of the lithics in the surrounding area.
   Artifacts: The artifact scatter consists of several very dense patches located within areas of large boulders, surrounded by a diffuse, sparse lithic and ceramic scatter. A low density ceramic and lithic scatter extends south toward VMS-196 and VMS-192. A single east-west oriented transect was laid across the site, with units collected at 15 m intervals. A diagnostic collection was also made. The following units contained artifacts:
   Transect 1 Unit 2: Ceramics: 1350 g; wares: 161 black plain ware, 1 red plain ware, 38 brown plain ware. Diagnostics: 6 jars.
   Transect 1 Unit 3: Ceramics: <50 g; wares: 1 brown plain ware. Lithics: utilized flake (translucent white quartz).
   Diagnostic Collection: Lithics: 16 flakes, 50 fragments angular debris, 3 cores, 4 bipolar cores.
   Temporal Affiliation: Unknown.

SITE: VMS-198   Block: S   **Transect:** 14
   Primary Site Use: Agricultural: check dams.
   Site Dimensions: 200 × 80 m
   Setting: Broad plain between two outcrops.
   Present Land Use/Disturbances: The site area is uncultivated and has been disturbed primarily by cow paths.
   Site Description: Check dams. The four widely-spaced check dams in a narrow drainage impede erosion on to a broad plain and help prevent silt accumulation in the reservoir to the north (VMS-190). The walls themselves are constructed of single courses of unmodified cobbles. The check dams have helped create flat terraces, which form excellent ground for dry farming, although the land seems to have lain fallow in recent times. The two west check dams show evidence of recent maintenance while the others are defunct. Northwest of the site is a small rock shelter and ceramic scatter.
   Artifacts: Sparse, but localized ceramic and lithic scatter concentrated in the west half of the site. 100% collection in the narrow drainage containing the check dams. 200 g ceramics; wares: 10 black plain ware, 26 brown plain ware. Diagnostics: 1 bowl, 1 jar. Other artifacts: lithics: 1 quartz flake, 1 quartz bipolar core.
   Temporal Affiliation: Unknown.
   References: Morrison 1995:92, 102.
   Illustrations: Figure 5.53.

SITE: VMS-199   Block: S   **Transect:** 14
   Primary Site Use: Agricultural: check dams.
   Site Dimensions: 100 × 75 m
   Setting: Slope in drainage channel amid outcrops.
   Present Land Use/Disturbances: Grazed area south of a modern canal. The area has been subject to erosion and is crossed by numerous cow paths.
   Site Description: Check dams. These six soil and water control features are situated on an open sloping plain, rising to the south to a zone of rocky uplands. Smaller outcrops dot the landscape, forming a number of small drainage systems, including that associated with VMS-199. The terrace walls are constructed of a single course of unmodified cobbles and boulders, laid end to end. Low outcrops are incorporated into some of the check dams and the soil in the terraces created by these walls is shallow and rocky. Similar terraces are found in other small drainages throughout this area.

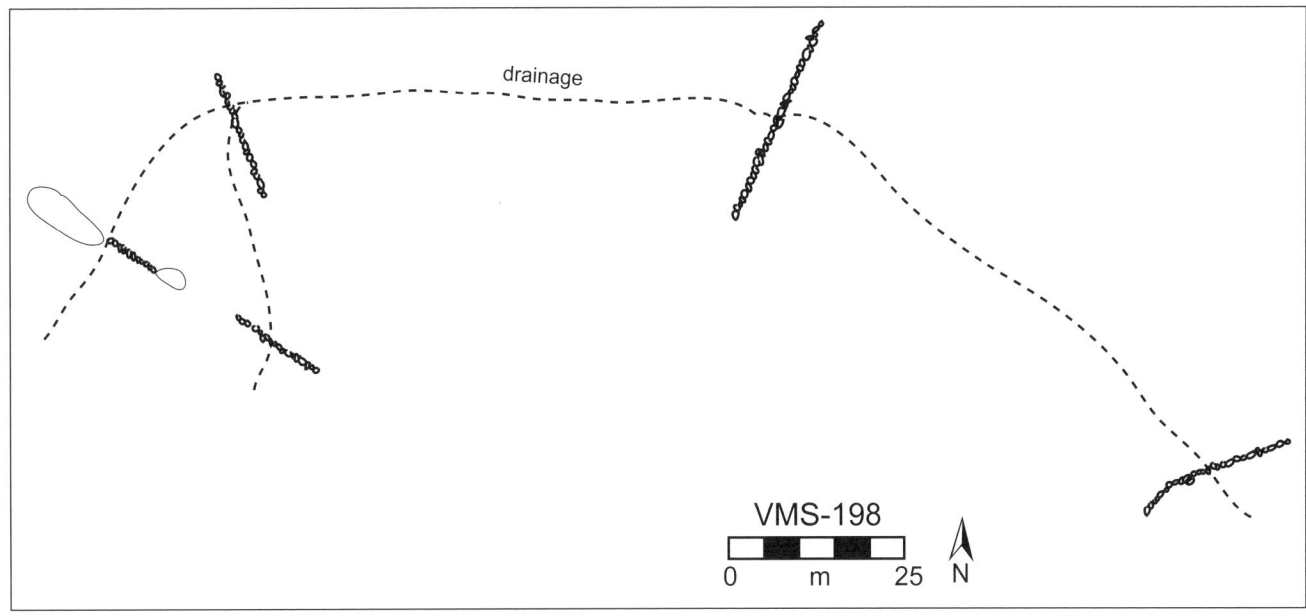

(*Above*) Figure 5.53. VMS-198, plan.

(*Right*) Figure 5.54. VMS-199, plan.

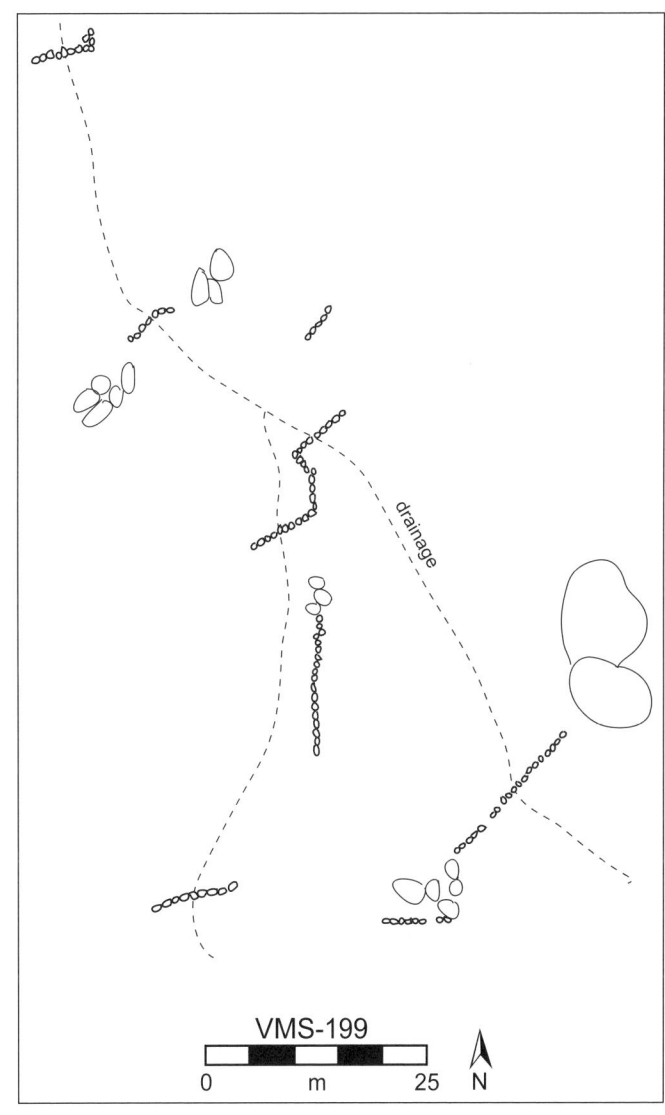

Artifacts: Low density, diffuse ceramic and lithic scatter. 100% collection in drainage area. Ceramics: <50 g, 3 black plain ware. Lithics: 1 flake, 1 angular debris, 1 core (all of quartz).
Temporal Affiliation: Unknown, not recent.
References: Morrison 1995:92, 102.
Illustrations: Figure 5.54.

SITE: VMS-200   Block: S   Transect: 17
Primary Site Use: Residential/religious: well.
Site Dimensions: 12 × 10 m
Setting: Level irrigated area.
Present Land Use/Disturbances: Modern irrigation canals lead into this heavily overgrown and partly filled in well.
Site Description: Well. The sides of the well are constructed of square quarried undressed blocks and small boulders with many chinking stones. Four courses of masonry are visible above the water level on the south, but only the south third of the east and west walls remain. There are traces of an entrance with three steps made of long quarried slabs on the north side of the well. This well appears to be associated with the Vijayanagara temple, VMS-173, and its entrance faces the temple. Eight meters south of the steps is a large granite block into which a circular basin (0.61 m diameter and 0.12 m deep) has been carved.
Artifacts: Some highly fragmented sherds are visible in the few small open patches in the dense vegetation. No collections made.
Temporal Affiliation: Vijayanagara.
Illustrations: Figure 5.55; Plate 5.42.

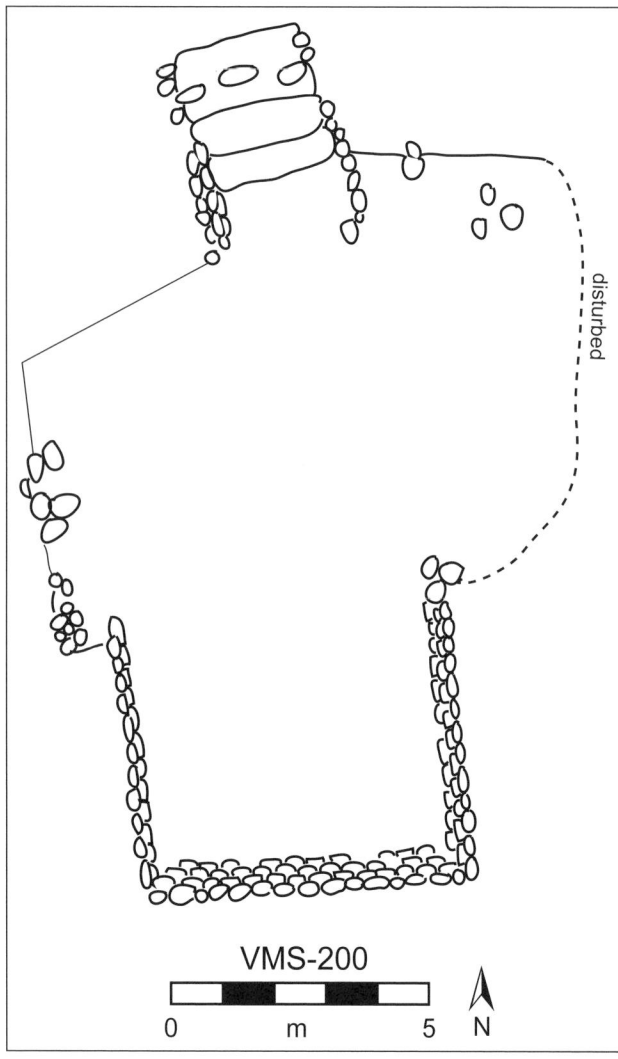

Figure 5.55. VMS-200, plan.

Plate 5.42. VMS-200, stone basin.

SITE: VMS-201   Block: S   **Transect:** 13-15
Primary Site Use: Transport: road and platforms.
Site Dimensions: 340 × 60 m
Setting: Level dry farmed fields, inside city wall.
Present Land Use/Disturbances: A contemporary dirt road runs almost exactly along the course of the old Penukonda road. The road and associated features are truncated by fields on the east and by the paved Nallapuram road on the west. A modern platform with sun shade is constructed of architectural elements from Vijayanagara structures.
Site Description: Road and associated features. This site consists of a linear series of features defining the course of the Penukonda road inside the outer city wall (VMS-123). This road enters the city through the Penukonda gate (VMS-217). Some features along the road are religious while others may be commercial and/or residential. The road is c. 30 m wide and is oriented northwest-southeast. The current west end of this road segment is intersected by the paved Nallapur road, which leads toward the Pattabhirama temple and Kamalapuram. An old road must have run along the south side of the temple complex VMS-142, as the Nallapur road now does, but the orientation of ancient structures suggests that the older road was oriented more nearly east-west; it probably intersected the Penukonda road closer to the Pattabhirama temple. This road is situated in an area of high Vijayanagara period residential density.

The south side of the road is defined by a linear alignment of earth and rubble, containing some stubs of walls and a few small unmodified boulders and bricks. Lying atop this linear mound is a broken piece of sculpture (a fragment of Hanuman's tail), a grinding slick, and a small block with two carved feet. Set back a few meters south of the road is a small, square room (c. 2.5 × 3 m) enclosed by double-faced rubble walls (0.5 m wide). The field to the west of this room contains at least ten large (2-3 m high) piles of rubble, suggesting that there were once many more structures here.

The road surface itself is lower than the platforms on either side and consists primarily of low worn outcrops of very coarse-grained yellowish brown granite, which does not hold a polish.

The platforms and walls defining the north side of the road are better preserved than those on the south, though its east end is truncated by a coconut plantation. In this plantation is a large (1.4 m high × 1.1 m wide) striding Hanuman with a broken tail. Long slabs in this area may have been scavenged from features along the road. About 35 m west of the Hanuman is an upright slab with incised lingam, sun, and moon, facing the road. A sherd of Chinese porcelain was found nearby. This upright marks the east end of an intermittent rubble wall paralleling the road. A second smaller wall is set back to the north and contains at least one possible footing. These may be indications of columned platforms lining the road. Thirty meters further west is a second upright slab, also with a carved lingam. Moving west, the linear mound gets higher and there are several small, square rubble-walled rooms (c. 2 × 2 m) built into it. Midway down the north side of the road are two square platforms that face the street. The platforms (c. 3.5 east-west by 5 m north-south) are 2.5 m apart and are defined by long dressed slabs laid horizontally. These slabs apparently originally extended around all the sides of the platform, but now are only partially preserved.

To the west of the twin platforms is a badly disturbed foundation of what may have been a temple, indicated by dressed slabs, a column footing, and displaced architectural elements, including a section of a molding (two stepped with angled bevel and a corner quarter medallion). North of the foundation is a large rectangular image base with three notches for images and a carved Garuda on its south face.

Figure 5.56. VMS-201, plan.

West of the temple foundation, the linear mound is cut into by cotton fields and becomes quite narrow. The terminus of VMS-201 is a temple, designated as Feature 1 and described below. Some 20 m to the east of Feature 1 is a large (12 m diameter) circular depression about 1.5 m deep. This may be a well. One long dressed slab with a spiral carving suggesting a balustrade lies near its edge.

Feature 1: This small Shaivite temple consists of a 4 × 4 pillared antechamber and an enclosed sanctuary. The temple is oriented to the road, facing southwest. It is entered via three (original) steps with yali balustrades. The temple is set on a raised basement; the outer columns rest on the upper moldings of the basement, and the inner four columns are connected at floor level by long dressed slabs, laid to form a c. 3 × 3 m^2 area in the center of the mandapa. Columns are square in section with square cutouts; capitals of the four center columns are cruciform with pendant lotus buds, as are those facing the road on the south. Elsewhere, the capitals are plain rectangular blocks. Columns on the south side and inside the structure contain carvings, including both Vaishnavite and Shaivite images. These include a snake charmer, female lion, elephant pulling up a tree, a goose, a figure with an upper human half and lower animal half, two Krishnas with flute, several Nandis, a rishi, Ganesha, several linga, a figure with a whip and short staff, a saint, elephant, water carrier, a conch, and a male figure on a boat with an axe.

There are three formal doorways in this small structure, and one less formal opening. The latter is on the south, where the staircase abuts the structure. There is a doorway (slab-edged) on the east side, with Shaivite door guardians on the exterior. On the north, a doorway leads into the centrally located sanctuary. Shaivite door guardians flank this doorway, and a smaller donor portrait is also carved on the left post. On each side of the door to the sanctuary are two more doorways carved with identical floral motifs. These may have led into subsidiary shrines. However, there is no clear indication of enclosed areas north of these doorways; at present they open directly to the exterior. Perhaps these were entrances to a circumambulation passage (*pradakshina patha*), either open or of brick or some ephemeral material. The roof is constructed of long horizontal granite slabs laid across connecting beams of similar slabs. One roof slab has a lotus carved on it (in the center of the structure). Traces of brick and plaster remain atop the stone roof.

Artifacts: Earthenware ceramics, Chinese porcelain, ground stone, brick. The roadway contains a very high density scatter of highly fragmented sherds. Artifact densities are also high in the surrounding fields. A long transect was laid parallel to the course of the road, along its north side. The orientation was not constant, varying with road orientation and to avoid thick thorny vegetation. Units were collected every 30 m. The following units contained artifacts.

Transect 1 Unit 1: <50 g ceramics; wares: 6 black plain ware.

Transect 1 Unit 2: <50 g ceramics; wares: 11 black plain ware. Diagnostics: 2 jars.

Transect 1 Unit 3: 50 g ceramics; wares: 20 black plain ware, 2 brown plain ware. Diagnostics: 2 jars.

Transect 1 Unit 4: <50 g ceramics; wares: 4 black plain ware.

Transect 1 Unit 6: <50 g ceramics; wares: 1 brown plain ware.

Transect 1 Unit 8: 50 g ceramics; wares: 13 black plain ware, 2 red plain ware, 5 brown plain ware. Diagnostics: 1 bowl, 1 jar.

Transect 2 Unit 1: 150 g ceramics; wares: 22 black plain ware, 6 red plain ware, 9 brown plain ware. Diagnostics: 5 jars.

Transect 2 Unit 2: 100 g ceramics; wares: 29 black plain ware, 5 brown plain ware. Diagnostics: 3 jars.

Transect 2 Unit 3: 100 g ceramics; wares: 24 black plain ware, 2 brown plain ware. Diagnostics: 2 jars.

Transect 2 Unit 4: 250 g ceramics; wares: 37 black plain ware, 2 red plain ware, 4 brown plain ware. Diagnostics: 2 jars.

Transect 2 Unit 5: 100 g ceramics; wares: 12 black plain ware, 4 brown plain ware. Diagnostics: 1 jar.

Transect 2 Unit 6: 100 g ceramics; wares: 8 black plain ware, 2 brown plain ware. Diagnostics: 1 jar.

Temporal Affiliation: Vijayanagara.

References: Morrison 1995:69, 76-77; Morrison and Sinopoli 1996:67.

Illustrations: Figures 5.56, 5.57; Plate 5.43.

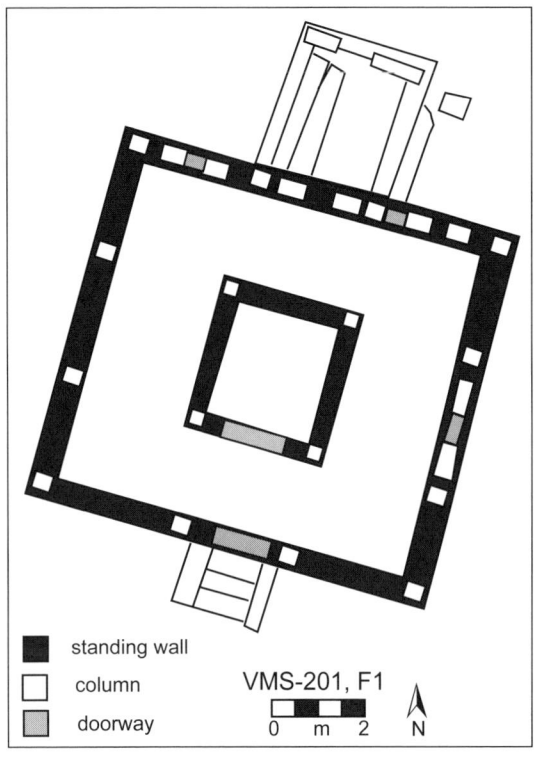

Figure 5.57. VMS-201, Feature 1, plan.

Plate 5.43. VMS-201, Feature 1, Shaivite temple.

SITE: VMS-202   Block: S   Transect: 14
   Primary Site Use: Residential: artifact scatter.
   Site Dimensions: 250 × 150 m
   Setting: Level dry farmed fields.
   Present Land Use/Disturbances: Field clearance has obliterated all architecture and destroyed layout information, sparing only some sculptures and artifacts.
   Site Description: Surface scatter. This area is part of the densely occupied residential area located south of the Penukonda road and north of the long outcrop carrying the city wall. The area has been cleared for dry farming; fields here contain at least fifteen large rubble piles, remnants of many informal structures. All that now remain are islands of features—a heap of ten naga stones, a Nagamma, the feet of a chlorite image, a stone basin (0.36 m diameter × 0.09 m deep) cut into a block, a large striding Hanuman with pointy architectural element in front, an upright molding (two stepped with convex bevel and "lotus leaves"), three block mortars, and many possible wall segments. There is at least one bedrock mortar and two grinding slicks in this area.
   This site is arbitrarily defined out of a much larger area that was also densely settled. It is similar to VMS-178 in that it is an area of particularly high architectural (i.e., masonry) density. It is likely that there are other areas inside the outer city wall that had a similar population density but more perishable architecture. VMS-202 is separated from VMS-222 by an irrigated field; the two may be contiguous.
   Artifacts: Extensive moderate density ceramic scatter with several pieces of ground stone. One north-south transect laid out to supplement data from collections from nearby VMS-201. Three units collected at 20 m intervals.

Transect 1 Unit 1: 50 g ceramics; wares: 8 black plain ware, 1 brown plain ware. Diagnostics: 2 jars.
Transect 1 Unit 2: 150 g ceramics; wares: 17 black plain ware, 2 red plain ware, 19 brown plain ware. Diagnostics: 4 jars.
Transect 1 Unit 3: 200 g ceramics; wares: 19 black plain ware, 4 red plain ware, 5 brown plain ware, 1 coarse ware. Diagnostics: 3 jars.
   Temporal Affiliation: Late Vijayanagara, with subsequent agricultural use.
   Illustrations: Plate 5.44.

SITE: VMS-203   Block: S   Transect: 14
   Primary Site Use: Residential/commercial: platform.
   Site Dimensions: 8 × 8 m
   Setting: Gently sloping sheet rock at base of outcrop bearing city wall VMS-123.
   Present Land Use/Disturbances: Modern quarrying in the area; an enclosed irrigated area lies 30 m to the west. Erosion off the north-south sloping sheet rock must be significant, but the room itself is not obviously disturbed.
   Site Description: Circa 1.5 m high platform built on sheet rock outcrop. Located on the edge of artifact scatter VMS-202, this could have been a residential or commercial structure. The small square structure is bounded by rubble walls that enclose mounded earth and incorporate several small outcrops. The walls are constructed of a single course and a single face of unmodified cobbles and rubble. There is no clear trace of a south wall, but there is a small terrace here. Circa 8 m southeast of the southeast corner of the structure is a long wall running at the same

Block S: Site Summaries

Plate 5.44. VMS-202, naga stones.

orientation as the east wall of the structure. This wall is constructed on its east face of medium-sized boulders and on the west by small cobbles. Abutting this c. 10 m long wall on the west is a shallow (0.02-0.06 m) layer of compacted soil overlying sheet rock.

Artifacts: Adjacent to VMS-202, area of large and moderate ceramic scatter. The latter continues up the sheet rock on which this structure is located. Ceramics were also found in the fill of the room. 100% collection within structure. 300 g ceramics; wares: 42 black plain ware, 6 red plain ware, 9 brown plain ware. Diagnostics: 1 bowl, 5 jars.

Temporal Affiliation: Vijayanagara?
Illustrations: Figure 5.58.

SITE: VMS-204 Block: S Transect: 14
Primary Site Use: Water storage: basin.
Site Dimensions: 10 × 6 m
Setting: Gently sloping sheet rock outcrop.
Present Land Use/Disturbances: Recent quarrying.
Site Description: Water catchment basin. A natural depression in the sheet rock has been partially modified to form a 10 × 6.5 m basin that collects rainwater and surface runoff. The south, east, and west sides of the basin have been edged with boulders that would help check sediment washing into the feature. These three sides of the basin are lined with up to four irregular courses of unmodified cobbles and boulders. This facility must have catered to the needs of some of the people residing near VMS-202. Five naga stones lie on the north edge of the basin, as do a square block with devotee feet carved on it, the head of a chlorite Vishnu (probably the upper half of the image found on VMS-202), a hero stone, a carving of an unidentifiable figure wearing a pointed headdress, and a carved lower half of a human figure wearing a long robe and sandals.

Artifacts: Very sparse ceramic scatter. 100% collections along edges of the basin. 150 g ceramics; wares: 15 black plain ware, 3 red plain ware. Diagnostics: 2 jars.

Temporal Affiliation: Vijayanagara.
Illustrations: Figure 5.59; Plate 5.45.

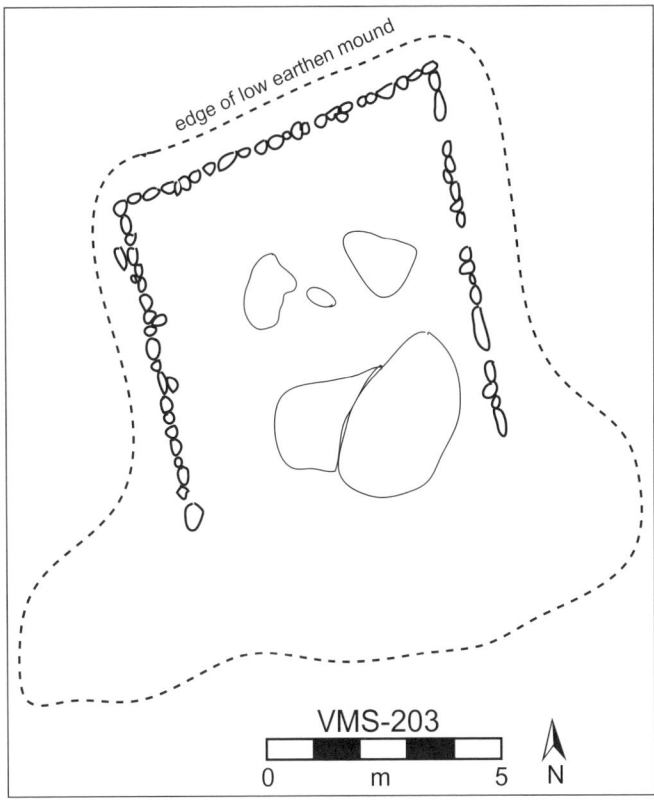

Figure 5.58. VMS-203, plan.

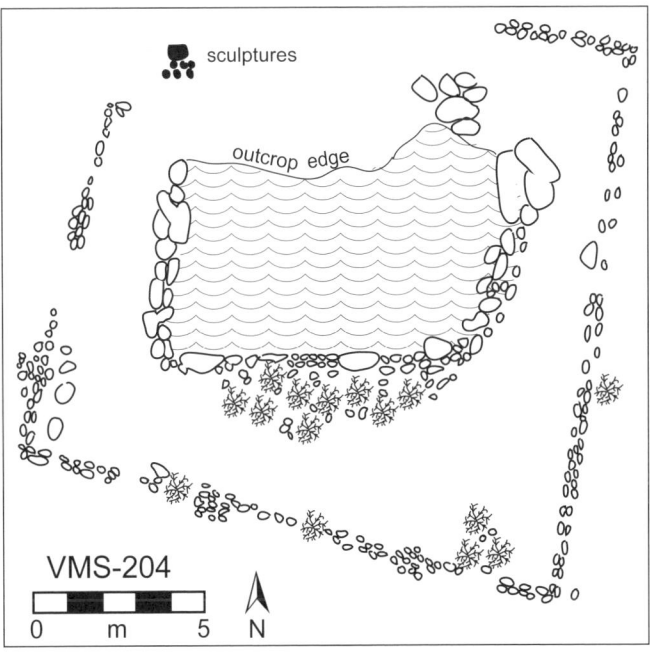

Figure 5.59. VMS-204, plan.

Plate 5.45. VMS-204, displaced images.

SITE: VMS-205   Block: S   Transect: 14
  Primary Site Use: Agricultural: terraces.
  Site Dimensions: 200 × 75 m
  Setting: Gently sloping plain, uncultivated area.
  Present Land Use/Disturbances: Recent boundary wall at the east end of the site; heavily disturbed by field clearing and erosion.
  Site Description: Terrace system. This series of terraces runs both east-west and north-south; the south edge of the system is marked by a length of outcrop. Terrace walls are poorly preserved. The embankment of reservoir VMS-206 lies just to the northeast and was probably part of the same system, serving to protect the reservoir from slope wash and runoff. The terraces are not in use and show no signs of maintenance. Walls are constructed of cobbles, which have been piled rather than coursed; most have only a single face. The west edge of the system is marked by sheet rock after which another terrace system (VMS-207) begins.
  Artifacts: Very sparse ceramic scatter, one lithic. 100% collection. No ceramics recovered; lithics: utilized flake (translucent white quartz).
  Temporal Affiliation: Unknown; possibly associated with Vijayanagara reservoir VMS-206.
  References: Morrison 1995:92-93, 102; Morrison and Sinopoli 1996:71.
  Illustrations: Figure 5.60.

SITE: VMS-206   Block: S   Transect: 14
  Primary Site Use: Agricultural: reservoir embankment.
  Site Dimensions: 200 × 20 m
  Setting: Gently sloping dry fields.
  Present Land Use/Disturbances: Modern canal and fields lie just to the north of the reservoir embankment, as does a recent dirt road.
  Site Description: Reservoir embankment or catchment basin. The embankment is remarkably square, consisting of two stone and earth embankments, which meet at right angles. It is bordered on the south by outcropping sheet rock, and on the west by a small wall. The basin captured runoff from upslope areas to the southwest, where terrace system VMS-205 is located.
  The major constructed features of the site are two well-preserved walls. The shorter of these defines the northern edge of the site and extends approximately east-west, incorporating outcropping boulders. The western end of the east-west wall now forms a terrace. Four stepped courses of masonry are visible on the south face of this wall. At the site's northwest corner is an informal breach or channel, a c. 10 m wide opening filled with piled stones. A small wall segment extends south from this area for about 1.75 m. It is unclear if this is a breakwater, or a portion of what was once a longer western boundary to the site.
  At its eastern end in the northeast corner of the site, the northern wall joins a longer oriented embankment, which extends some 60 m to the southeast. There is a second breach, possibly recent or possibly an original, located at this corner. At the southern end of this wall, its stepped masonry (western) face is constructed of eight stepped courses of small boulders with occasional quarried blocks. The width of this masonry is almost 3.5 m. The feature is probably still in use seasonally, since as noted above, a breach has been made at the north end of the northwest/southeast wall. Rocks have been piled up in the breach to control the flow of water through it. The channel created by the breach winds down to the south and east across outcrops for more than 80 m. Its route is indicated by some heavily worn sheet rock, and in some areas by small lines of rocks that may have been placed to direct the flow of water.
  Artifacts: Modern pot break. No other artifacts noted, though soil is quite gravelly and visibility is poor. No collections made.
  Temporal Affiliation: Vijayanagara.
  References: Morrison 1995:91-93, 102; Morrison and Sinopoli 1996:71.
  Illustrations: Figure 5.60.

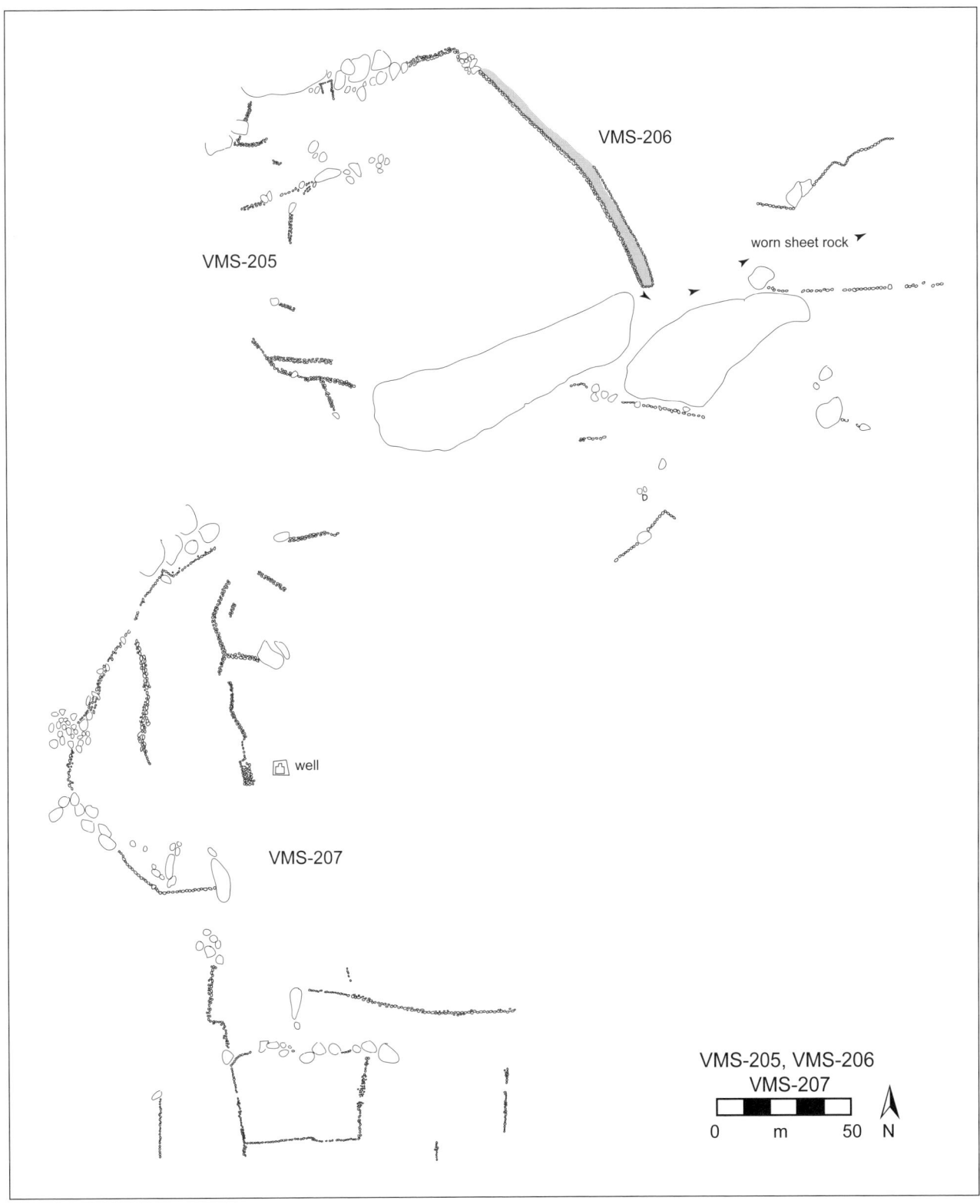

Figure 5.60. VMS-205, VMS-206, and VMS-207, plan.

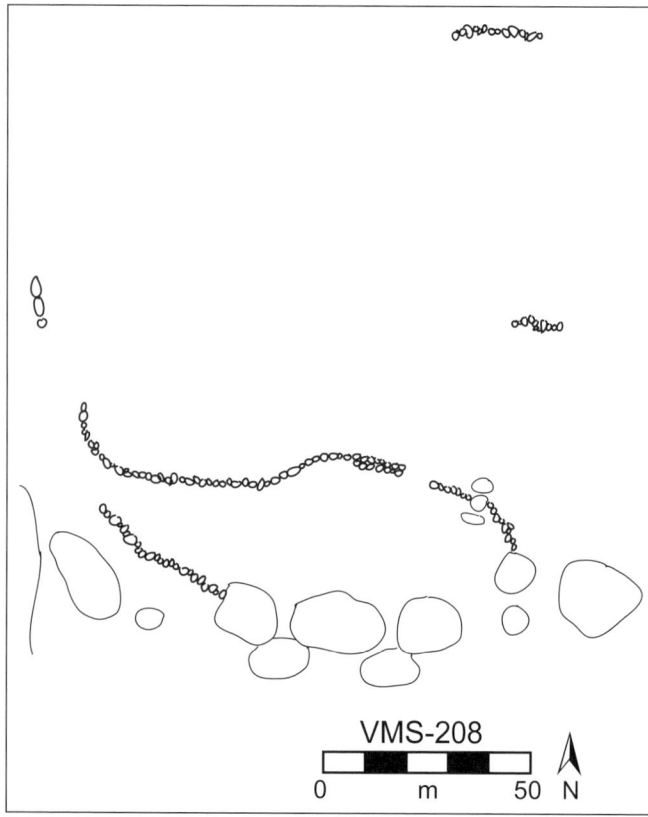

Figure 5.61. VMS-208, plan.

Plate 5.46. VMS-208, overview of alignments from west.

a single face, single course alignment of medium-large unmodified cobbles and boulders. To this basic construction may be added additional stone alignments or simply piles of cobbles and even boulders. Many walls incorporate the outcropping boulders that cover nearly half the ground surface.

A small step well is located near the center of the site in a basin among the outcrops. This well has an enclosure wall constructed of a single face of rubble. The well itself is T-shaped, with three quarried steps leading down from the north. Up to three courses of masonry (cobbles, split cobbles, and a few rough blocks) ring the now colluviated and dry well. Above the stairs on the north are two upright undressed and irregularly shaped slabs.

Artifacts: Very sparse, clustered ceramic scatter throughout the area. Some sherds found in erosion channels. 100% collection within site area; 100 g ceramics; wares: 16 black plain ware, 7 brown plain ware. Diagnostics: 1 bowl, 3 jars.

Temporal Affiliation: Unknown.

References: Morrison 1995:92-93, 102; Morrison and Sinopoli 1996:71.

Illustrations: Figure 5.60.

SITE: VMS-207   Block: S   Transect: 13
   Primary Site Use: Agricultural: terraces and well.
   Site Dimensions: 400 × 165 m
   Setting: Gently sloping area between outcrop and sheet rock.
   Present Land Use/Disturbances: Erosion has been severe and some of the terraces have apparently been washed out.
   Site Description: Agricultural terraces. This site consists of several series of walls, which served as soil and water control devices in the catchment southwest of reservoir VMS-206. As such, 205, 206, and 207 form an integrated system, though 205 and 207 are located in separate drainages. VMS-207 contains two distinct areas, characterized by different slope and distinctive construction. In the north half of the site, the terrain slopes down from west to east. The western edge of the site is bordered by a long curved terrace wall that encloses a relatively rock-free area. There is little soil built up to the west of the terrace; instead, the wall apparently served to slow runoff from the granitic outcrop to the west. Two more linear terraces walls are built below (east) this long one. East of the second is a small well.

In the second area, in the southern portion of the site, the terrain slopes down from south to north, with lesser drainages funneling in from both east and west. In this area are a series of enclosed areas, surrounded by terrace walls on two to four sides, suggesting field boundaries as well as runoff control. Many of the walls are breached and none are maintained. The map of VMS-207 is partial; at least three major additional sets of terraces are situated upslope (to the south), and one more on both east and west.

The walls themselves are variable in construction, with some wider and more sturdily built than others. Most, however, are built around

SITE: VMS-208   Block: S   Transect: 14
   Primary Site Use: Agricultural: walls and check dams.
   Site Dimensions: 60 × 70 m
   Setting: Gently sloping plain north of outcrops, under fallow dry fields.
   Present Land Use/Disturbances: The post-1950 Tungabhadra Right Bank High Level Canal runs c. 100 m north of the site and a recent irrigation ditch bisects it. The two check dams are breached.
   Site Description: Walls and check dams. These isolated walls and check dams are located in the area between reservoirs VMS-205 and VMS-194. Two walls channel runoff from the outcrops to the south into the modern irrigation ditch. Northeast of the ditch are two small east-west oriented check dams. Both are in disrepair and one is badly breached. Both the check dams and the walls are composed of unmodified boulders and cobbles, one to two elements wide, and one element high.
   Artifacts: Evenly distributed, sparse ceramic scatter, mostly confined to fallow fields. 100% collection in area enclosed by walls. One unmeasurable rim sherd recovered.
   Temporal Affiliation: Unknown.
   References: Morrison 1995:92, 102.
   Illustrations: Figure 5.61; Plate 5.46.

SITE: VMS-209   Block: S   Transect: 14
   Primary Site Use: Transport: road.
   Site Dimensions: 180 × 60 m
   Setting: Gentle-moderate slopes with outcrops.
   Present Land Use/Disturbances: Heavily disturbed in places by power line, quarrying, and erosion.
   Site Description: Road. This road begins inside Vijayanagara, somewhere at the base of the high east-west trending outcrop bearing the outer city wall VMS-123, runs up to and along the wall, and continues on the south side of it. The clear indication of road begins with two sets of steps made by placing small boulders on the naturally formed steps on the sheet rock. Above the steps, the road is cobbled, using material from the dyke of dark colored gabbro, which runs all along the fortification wall. This well-made path is built of worn, rounded, flat cobbles and small boulders closely fit together. The route runs through an opening (3-6 m wide) in city wall VMS-123 on top of the outcrop. Immediately south of the wall, the paved road becomes a cobbled ramp and subsequently a flat paved surface again; in this area only 23 m of the road surface can be traced; two step wells are placed near this end.

Beyond the long road segment are two additional staircases, neither with more than three steps, located on the north side of the outcrop. These lead the path off to the west, across sheet rock where it abuts the east edge of the outcrop containing VMS-211. An additional section of paving is visible here adjacent to VMS-211 (not on map), an area of residential terraces.

Feature 1: A small somewhat triangular step well c. 25 m southwest of the opening in the city wall and associated with the road. It is built of quarried blocks and occasional unmodified boulders. The north wall has caved in due to pressure caused by runoff and subsequent colluviation. The south and east walls are formed partly by outcrops and partly by a block wall of six courses. The maximum dimensions of the well are 8 × 6 m. The entrance may be from the southwest, but this is unclear. In this area south of the city wall, a natural depression/channel at the base of the outcrop forms a moatlike feature; this is bounded by a long wall of aligned boulders.
   Artifacts: No artifacts observed on outcrop, but artifact scatter from VMS-212 is adjacent to the west side of Feature 1. A low density scatter is present along the north side of outcrop (inside city walls). No collections made.
   Temporal Affiliation: Vijayanagara, probably late.
   References: Morrison 1995:75; Morrison and Sinopoli 1996:65.
   Illustrations: Figure 5.62; Plate 5.47.

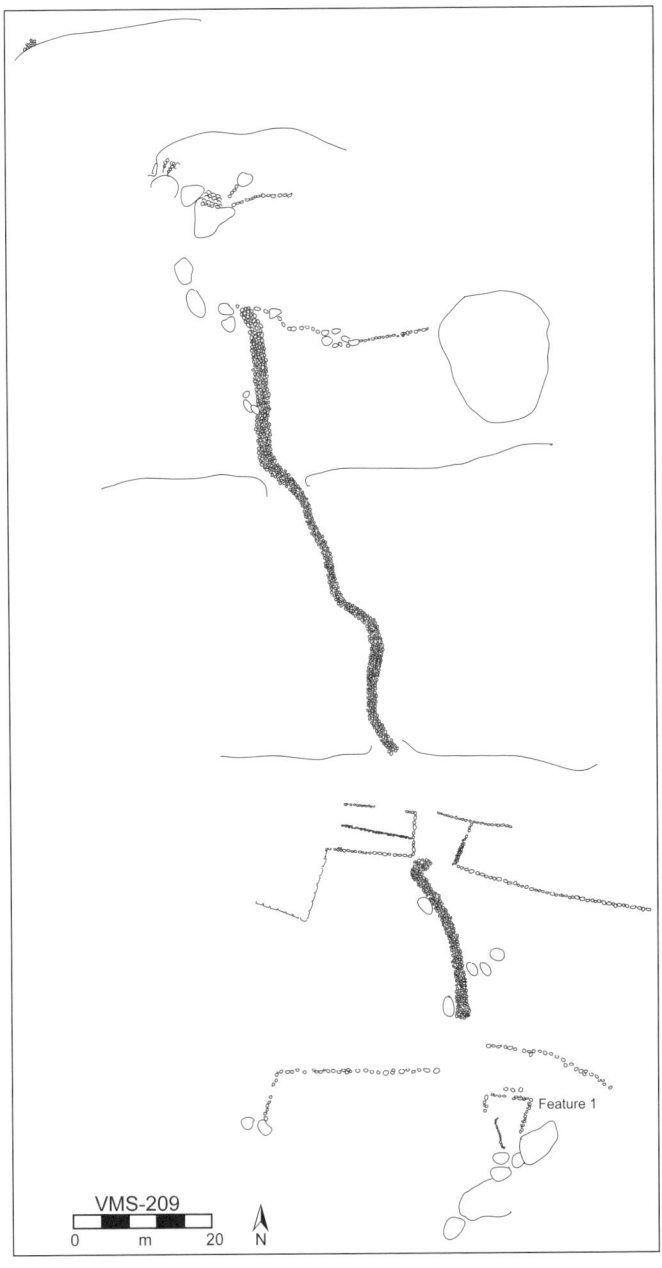

(*Above Right*) Figure 5.62. VMS-209, plan.

(*Right*) Plate 5.47. VMS-209, section of paved road.

SITE: VMS-210   Block: S   Transect: 14
   Primary Site Use: Residential/transport: step well.
   Site Dimensions: 28 × 16 m
   Setting: Near base of outcrop carrying city wall, VMS-123.
   Present Land Use/Disturbances: Displaced and collapsed elements on the north edge of well, colluviation.
   Site Description: Step well consisting of walls on three sides and an unmodified granite outcrop on the fourth (east) side. This well is located c. 50 m south of the outer city wall (VMS-123), along a narrow but well-constructed pathway to the city (VMS-209), and is situated on a natural terrace on the outcrop bearing the city wall. The well is fed entirely by runoff from the surrounding outcrop; staining on the interior indicates that it regularly fills to about 50% of capacity.
   The west interior wall is stepped eastward in three sections, narrowing toward the staircase on the south end. This wall is constructed of eight to twelve courses of unmodified and split cobbles with some chinking stones. Some quarried blocks are used in the south end. This wall is stepped back twice. The first step (0.25 m) occurs at three courses from the bottom, the second at seven courses. A level terrace, 1.5 m wide, is formed between the top of this wall and the exterior wall. The north wall is of the same construction as the west wall. However, it is badly eroded with no more than four courses visible. Only east and west stubs of this wall remain; the lack of wall fall indicates that these stubs may never have been connected, allowing a channel for runoff to enter the well.
   The east interior face consists of outcrop capped with two courses of masonry. The staircase contains ten worn block and slab steps, some elements with Vijayanagara-style quarry marks. Remnants of a border wall between the east outcrop and the staircase are visible. This wall consists of a single line of elements placed perpendicular to and abutting the staircase. Up to two courses are standing.
   A boundary wall runs all the way around the well, except on the north side, creating a level area c. 1.5 m wide. This wall is of the same general construction as the others. No more than two courses are visible, with insufficient wall fall to suggest that it was ever any higher. The exterior wall has an opening opposite the staircase, flanked by two upright slabs with inscribed symbols.
   A smaller step well, of less formal construction (VMS-209/Feature 1), is located between VMS-210 and the city wall. The primary use for both was probably as a water source for the domestic areas just inside the city wall.
   Artifacts: None observed in association with site. A sparse-moderate ceramic scatter is found in fields to the north of the well. No collections made.
   Temporal Affiliation: Vijayanagara.
   References: Morrison 1995:75, 84.
   Illustrations: Figure 5.63.

SITE: VMS-211   Block: S   Transect: 14
   Primary Site Use: Residential: terraces.
   Site Dimensions: 80 × 30 m
   Setting: Base of outcrop, moderately sloping sheet rock.
   Present Land Use/Disturbances: Erosion channels have cut through the terrace walls. Recent quarrying to the east and along the northeast edge of the sheet rock.
   Site Description: Terraces on sheet rock. The path VMS-209 comes down to the east edge of the sheet rock; a paved segment runs along its southeast edge. The single-course terrace walls are constructed of unmodified cobbles of varying sizes and a few irregularly shaped quarried blocks. Toward the southeast, three to four steplike elements could be a series of walls forming a ramplike structure or steps leading to a residential terrace. The terrace walls, which hold in the soil on the sheet rock, could either define residential terraces or be foundations for more ephemeral structures. There are several crosswalls and, in the sheet rock, a bedrock mortar.
   Artifacts: Ceramic and lithic scatter located where platform fill is eroding. An east-west transect was laid across the terrace surface, with three units collected at 20 m intervals; a 2 × 2 m judgment unit was collected. The data for these collections have been lost.
   Temporal Affiliation: Unknown.
   References: Morrison 1995:92, 102.
   Illustrations: Figure 5.64.

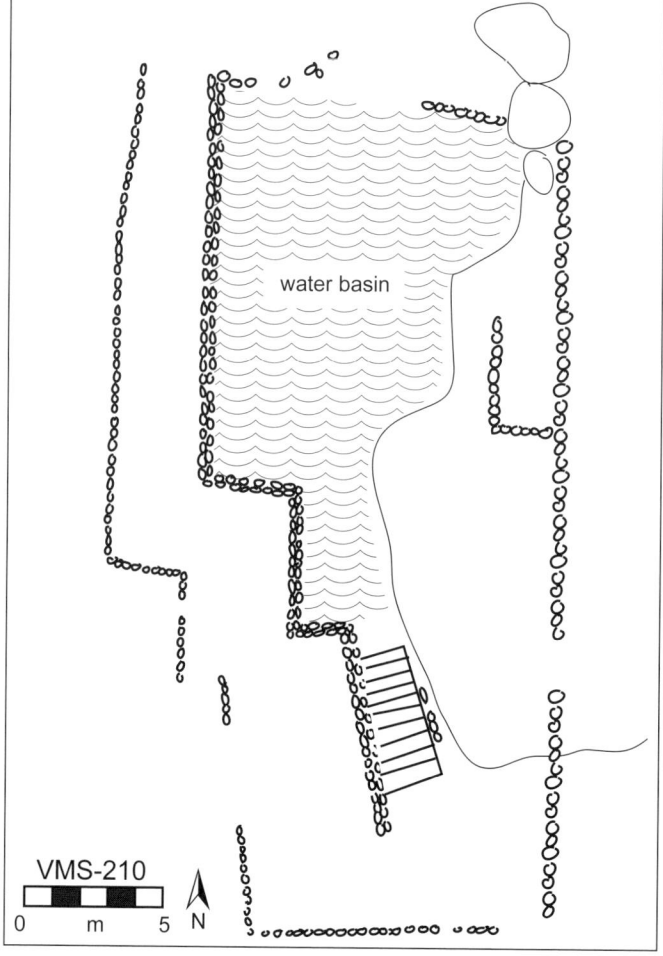

Figure 5.63. VMS-210, plan.

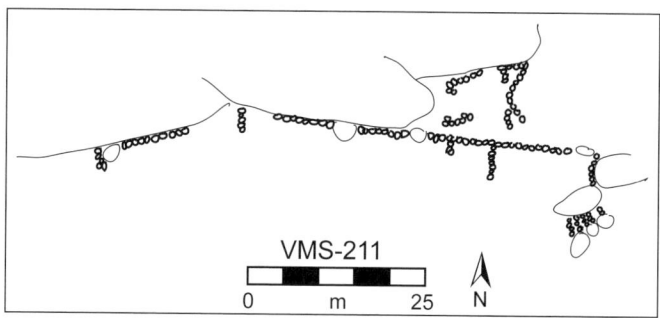

Figure 5.64. VMS-211, plan.

SITE: VMS-212   Block: S   Transect: 14
  Primary Site Use: Residential: artifact scatter.
  Site Dimensions: 96 × 35 m
  Setting: Level area at the base of an outcrop.
  Present Land Use/Disturbances: Dry farmed field. Power line runs c. 120 m to the east.
  Site Description: Vijayanagara period artifact scatter running along the base of the east-west trending outcrop that carries the outer city wall, VMS-123. It is located immediately south of the "moat" (a bounded depression/channel running along the base of the outcrop on its south side), between the latter and a low outcrop. The west edge of the scatter is the least clear; it is here defined as the edge of a ploughed field. On the east it abuts VMS-209/Feature 1 and VMS-210. In addition to ceramics and lithics, the scatter contains a low density of iron slag and kiln debris as well as one steatite pencil. There are no structures here other than the wells, the city wall, and the walls bounding the "moat."
  Artifacts: Scatter includes range of materials, including ceramics, lithics, and slag. Two east-west transects spaced at 20 m apart, with units spaced at intervals of 30 m. Separate diagnostic sweeps were made for ceramics (D1) and lithics (D2); no utilized lithics were recovered.
  Transect 1 Unit 1: <50 g ceramics; wares: 14 black plain ware, 1 brown plain ware. Diagnostics: 1 jar. Other artifacts: 1 piece iron slag.
  Transect 1 Unit 2: 100 g ceramics; wares: 15 black plain ware, 1 brown plain ware. Other artifacts: 1 piece slag.
  Transect 1 Unit 3: 150 g ceramics; wares: 11 black plain ware, 6 brown plain ware. Diagnostics: 1 bowl, 3 jars. Other artifacts: 1 piece iron slag.
  Transect 2 Unit 1: <50 g ceramics; wares: 3 black plain ware.
  Transect 2 Unit 2: 100 g ceramics; wares: 18 black plain ware, 1 red plain ware.
  Transect 2 Unit 3: <50 g ceramics; wares: 7 black plain ware, 1 red plain ware.
  Diagnostic Collection 2: Lithics: 10 flakes, 20 fragments angular debris, 6 bipolar cores (all of quartz).
  Temporal Affiliation: Vijayanagara.

SITE: VMS-213   Block: S   Transect: 14
  Primary Site Use: Water storage: cistern or well.
  Site Dimensions: 10 × 8 m
  Setting: Level area at the base of an outcrop, within city walls.
  Present Land Use/Disturbances: Dry farmed fields bordered by succulent hedge row. Grazing and field clearance have destroyed the area around this feature.
  Site Description: Cistern or well. Site VMS-213 is a small depression, enclosed by outcrops, that has been modified by the addition of walls on the east and west to form a more enclosed space. The walls consist of a single face of unmodified cobbles with a few modified square blocks and one triangular quarried block. This feature probably served to capture water, either as a well or cistern. The present ground level is depressed about 0.5 m below the surrounding ground and supports a dense mat of grass. A short east-west wall segment lies south of the feature, with an additional spur to the east. Five block or bedrock mortars are visible in the immediate vicinity of the feature.
  Artifacts: Sparse ceramic scatter in surrounding fields, continuous with VMS-202. A single piece of slag was recovered from inside the well/cistern, as was a broken lamp. 100% collection; no other artifacts recovered.
  Temporal Affiliation: Unknown.
  Illustrations: Figure 5.65.

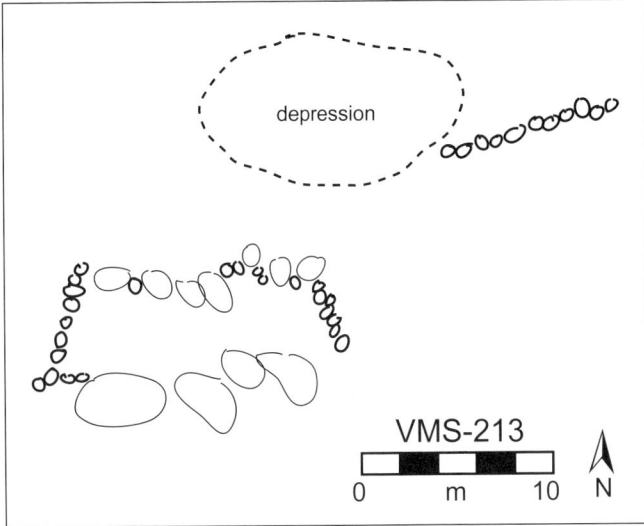

Figure 5.65. VMS-213, plan.

SITE: VMS-214   Block: S   Transect: 16
  Primary Site Use: Religious/transport: step well and road wall.
  Site Dimensions: 32 × 30 m
  Setting: Flat-gently sloping area.
  Present Land Use/Disturbances: Well is bounded by two threshing floors, a cemented canal, irrigated fields, and a dirt track. The cemented canal may incorporate masonry from the north well wall.
  Site Description: Step well and associated road feature. The step well is constructed of square, rectangular, and wedge-shaped quarried blocks. It appears to have been associated with temple complex VMS-164, and the road that led past it. The well is constructed of eight sinuous courses of masonry; there are large gaps between blocks, but only a moderate amount of chinking. On the south and east sides, the upper course is set back to form a ledge. The lowest course of masonry also juts out (c. 0.2 m), forming a lower ledge.
  To the west of the well, two massively constructed walls define a north-south oriented road. The best preserved wall extends for approximately 30 m. It and the associated walls are c. 1.9 m wide, built of two faces separated by a rubble core, and composed of up to five courses of large, dark colored boulders. Two bonded east-west walls are attached to this long wall, one near its present north end and the other forming a clear corner at its south end. There is a column footing cut into the corner boulder. The entrance to the well was clearly on the northwest. The ground level is higher on the east side of the wall, suggesting that the east road wall also defined a platform, a possibility supported by a parallel wall segment 6 m east of this long wall.
  About 9 m to the west of the long wall is a shorter segment of a parallel wall. This segment has been heavily disturbed and was likely originally much longer. Only the west face remains but construction is similar to the east road wall. The road leads directly to the east gate of VMS-164.

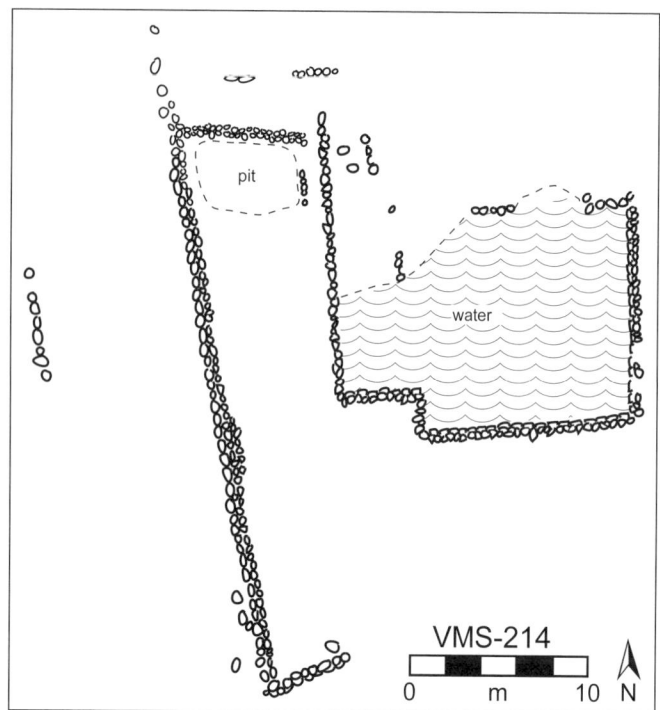

Figure 5.66. VMS-214, plan.

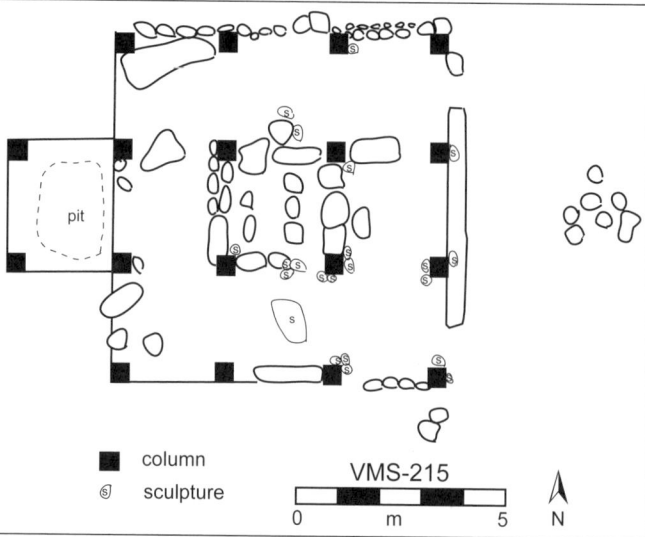

Figure 5.67. VMS-215, plan.

Plate 5.48. VMS-215, mandapa, currently in worship.

Artifacts: Ceramic scatter immediately around the well consists mostly of highly fragmented sherds. In an area where a pit has been recently excavated, both density and sherd size are higher. Ceramics include red and black burnished ware and one large coarse ware rim with "pie crust" pinch design on top. One piece of slag. Only a diagnostic collection was made.
Temporal Affiliation: Vijayanagara.
References: Morrison 1995:75, 80; Morrison and Sinopoli 1996:63-64, 69.
Illustrations: Figure 5.66.

SITE: VMS-215   Block: S   Transect: 16
Primary Site Use: Religious: mandapa.
Site Dimensions: 11 × 8 m
Setting: Level irrigated fields.
Present Land Use/Disturbances: Surrounded by fields. A recent path runs near the structure and irrigation channels run along its west, north, and east edges. Despite considerable disturbance, the structure is in worship and has been painted. Several ceiling slabs are missing, columns have slumped, and a pit has been dug between two columns.
Site Description: Columned structure, 4 × 4 column. Two additional columns stand outside the structure (on its west side); this was probably the original entrance. The columns are square with octagonal insets. In the center of the mandapa is a small square platform made up of square blocks. Most of these have been displaced, but one side retains two courses, the lower composed of a rectangular slab, and the upper of square blocks. The ceiling above this spot is made of rotated squares while the remainder is built of horizontal stone beams. The construction is haphazard and the columns poorly matched. This shrine is an example of Vijayanagara "mass production" at its worst.

There are numerous sculptures scattered around the mandapa, including fourteen naga stones, a female deity holding a snake in each of her hands, a Bhairavi, and other unidentifiable elements. This mandapa lies just north of the temple complex VMS-164 on the road defined by VMS-214.
Artifacts: 100% collection inside the structure and within 2 m of its walls. No artifacts recovered.
Temporal Affiliation: Vijayanagara.
References: Morrison and Sinopoli 1996:64.
Illustrations: Figure 5.67; Plate 5.48.

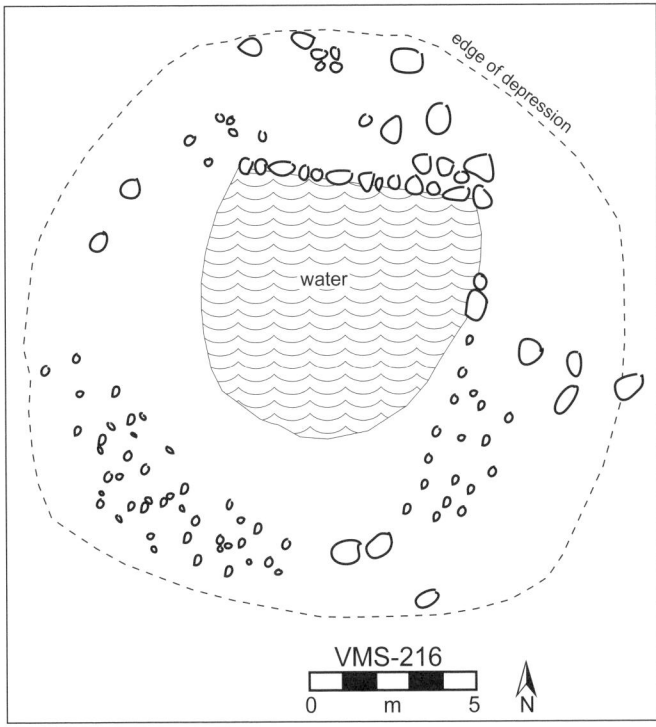

Figure 5.68. VMS-216, plan.

SITE: VMS-216 Block: S Transect: 16
Primary Site Use: Agricultural: well.
Site Dimensions: 18 × 19 m
Setting: Broad, open plain with irrigated fields.
Present Land Use/Disturbances: A recent canal and bullock cart road run just north of the site; debris from canal construction lines the south bank. The well is in poor condition, colluviated, overgrown, and partially collapsed.
Site Description: Small well located c. 50 m west of VMS-164, a temple complex, and VMS-214, a road segment. This well is fed by runoff entering on the north, east, and west. Portions of the west and south walls may have been rock-cut; a single fired brick fragment, possibly from VMS-164, lies among the debris. This well may have served as a domestic water supply, an agricultural supply, or both.

Remnants of masonry walls occur on the north, east, and west sides, but much of the layout is obscured by fallen elements. The walls are composed of unmodified large boulders and roughly dressed blocks, some with Vijayanagara-style quarry marks. Displaced and dispersed elements of an enclosing wall are visible to the north and east, along a raised bank, c. 2 m higher than the basin of the well. These walls are composed of small cobbles.
Artifacts: None observed. 100% collection.
Temporal Affiliation: Vijayanagara.
Illustrations: Figure 5.68.

SITE: VMS-217 Block: S Transect: 17
Primary Site Use: Defensive/transport/religious: Penukonda gate complex.
Site Dimensions: 53 × 45 m
Setting: Level dry farmed fields.
Present Land Use/Disturbances: A recent dirt track runs through the Penukonda gateway and several modern farmers' walls abut the older walls and structures. This area has been conserved by the ASI. A number of architectural elements are lying by the side of the road, near the west edge of VMS-217.
Site Description: Elaborate gateway complex containing late Vijayanagara temples, shrines, and gate platforms. Although these structures are known to be late, they are relatively simple. There are, for example, no detached columnettes, curved eaves, or fancy capitals. There is no evidence of remodeling and their consistent styles suggest a single phase of construction. This gate regulated traffic at the point where the Penukonda road passes through the city wall.

At the exterior (east) end of the complex are two elaborate gate platforms north and south of the road: the northern one contains a "guard room." Architectural moldings on the gate platforms are two stepped with angled bevel (no medallions). A cobbled road surface extends a short way (c. 5 m) beyond (east of) the gate platforms. On the south side of the road are two temples. The east one (Feature 2) is a small shrine, and the west one (Feature 1) is a larger structure with three rooms, a mandapa, and a circumambulation path (*pradakshina patha*) enclosed in a high wall. Propped up against Feature 1 is a slab bearing a long Kannada inscription. Opposite Feature 2, on the north side of the road, is an open space where architectural elements have been piled, as has part of a huge mortar/grinding machine. Also on the north side of the road is Feature 3, a small shrine with pillared porch that faces Feature 1. Further west (there is no corresponding structure in this position on the south side of the road) is Feature 4, a small open mandapa. Between Features 1 and 3, several low platforms paved with a square surface of small, flat, square, worn blocks extend into the road. These would constrict wheeled traffic to a narrow passage 4.5-5 m wide.

Feature 1: This multi-chambered temple is the largest and most complex structure in the gate complex. Its entrance is from the north. Above a basement course, which extends out into the street 2.5 m before stepping down c. 0.1 m to the worn cobbled surface, is an inset vertical course, followed by an upper molding (two stepped with angle bevel). It is fairly clear that this basement once supported an open columned area in front (north) of the present enclosed columned room (below). Some of the columns (six originally) that were once set up here are now lying northwest of Feature 1, adjacent to the road. These columns are more elaborately carved than the ones inside the structure and are much taller (as they stood on a lower basement). This open colonnade was attached via roof beams to the main structure; the slots for those beams are clearly visible. Thus, the north face of this temple would have been flush with that of adjacent shrine Feature 2 and the two would have presented an almost continuous facade of colonnade. On the roof of the enclosed porch are large, round merlons of brick and plaster, one each facing east and west. Perhaps there was originally also a north-facing row on the edge of the now-defunct north colonnade.

The first preserved room on the north side is a 6 × 2 columned mandapa. On the north side, plastered brickwork connects three pillars on each side, creating a central doorway. Plastered slabs wall in the rest of this porch. The columns facing the road are square in section with insets decorated with upturned leaf-like designs. Carvings are all of lotuses and other flowers. Capitals are plain rectangles with lower beveled edges. Inside this enclosed porch, columns are plain dressed square posts with rectangular capitals. The south row of columns is also walled, with three small doorways (only 1.22 m high × 0.61 m wide) built into the wall. The second column from each end is carved with part of a door frame design. Thus, as one enters the first chamber from the north, one moves into an enclosed room (no freestanding pillars except ASI ones) with three doors. The central door leads to the antechamber and then to the sanctuary. The side doors lead to an enclosed circumambulation path, which is clearly contemporaneous with the rest of the structure. The present steps up to the exterior door are not original. The antechamber was extensively modified by the ASI in the early part of the twentieth century, reducing the size of the sanctuary, and supporting its door with I-beams. There is an elaborate door frame; the door is made to look like a miniature temple. The uprights are made of blocks carved in foliate designs, with pseudo-capitals. The lintel is made to look like a molding (two step with convex bevel and lotus leaves and yali-face shaped medallions). To each side of the doorway are carved pilasters—the bases of which are similar to "flower-pots." Below the pilasters is an elaborate representation of a temple basement.

As one passes through the small doors on either side of the entrance to the sanctuary (there are door jambs on the south side of each) to the *pradakshina patha*, one steps down from the elevated basement of the enclosed interior to ground level. The latter is at about the same level as the dirt track to the north. This whole area is contained within a well-constructed enclosure wall consisting of two faces of long horizontal well dressed slabs separated by a brick core and capped with an elaborate plaster and brick coping. In this enclosure wall are four openings: the two doors noted above, the door described below, and a door on the east side near the southeast corner of the enclosed area. This door leads into a long, approximately north-south oriented, very solidly built room, built up against the enclosure wall. Although the room abuts the enclosure wall, it is of identical construction (even to the coping). The door (1.12 m long) has a little shelf on the lintel on the east side, which opens to the exterior. This room has three rectangular holes cut into the blocks of the roof, all near its southeast corner, which admit light and air. Lying in the room is an image base (0.6 × 0.6 m). On the west side, in the enclosure wall, is the fourth door, near the middle of the wall. It has door sockets on the interior side. This door is now filled in with stone on the exterior and brick on the interior, possibly by the ASI.

The exterior temple basement in the circumambulation passage is very elaborately carved, with stick dancers, hunting scene, yoga/contortionists, contemplative figures, wrestlers, geese, and other figures. Above a basement course are two sets of moldings (the lower has four steps with a convex bevel and lower inset jeweled bands). Then, the inset vertical face is divided into panels with carvings of dancers, yogi/contortionists, a hunting scene, a few people sitting, and several yalis. Above this is an approximately seven step molding with a convex bevel and jeweled bands with elaborate yali-head medallions. This is followed by a further molding (two steps with lower wavy outline and a bevel followed by a vertical face with carved geese, wrestlers, sages, and yalis). In this course on the east side of the building is a yali-faced spout, above which are two more protruding geometric moldings.

The front of the temple presents a simpler facade. The walls contain attached, carved temple representations (containing little image niches), pilasters, and pilasters set on "flower pots," all set on a carved representation of a temple basement. Above this are two more sets of moldings, then a stone base for the brick and plaster shikara. The latter is round at the top, with designs on the round part, and four tiers of miniature temple designs with well-preserved plasterwork figures. On the walls between pilasters are two long inscriptions on the east side and one on the west. Outside Feature 1 is an enclosure wall of rubble approximately eight courses high; this may be a recent construction.

Feature 2: Shrine, located on the south side of the road, adjacent to a gate platform and Feature 1. The basement slab of this small shrine is a continuation of the platform slabs in front of Feature 1. The structure is 4 m (east-west) × 5.5 m (north-south) and rectangular in plan. It consists of an enclosed shrine with a roofed, two column entry porch. The columns, square in plan with two elaborately decorated inset sections, are well dressed and decorated on three sides. Carved motifs are Vaishnavite, and include Narasimha, geese, conch, lotus, and several other figures. The capitals have three-dimensional pendant lotus bud motifs facing the sanctuary, and bas-relief pendant lotus buds facing the road. A plastered brick wall extends from the unfinished south face of the columns to the exterior (north) face of the porch. These enclosing walls consist of three rows of copiously mortared bricks running from basement to ceiling. The ceiling is built of long stone slabs set over stone beams.

The basement of the sanctuary consists of large well dressed blocks above the level of the basement slab on which the entry columns rest. A basement molding (two stepped with convex bevel) sits atop these blocks. The door to the shrine is built of large, well-dressed slabs devoid of decoration, save for a lotus motif on the sill. The shrine is enclosed on the east, west, and south sides by brick walls identical to those described above. The shrine has four undecorated columns. Capitals are cruciform with inset, beveled corners. The lintel over the entrance to the sanctuary has stone door sockets. The ceiling is constructed in the same way as that of the porch; the brick is in poor condition. However, portions retain elaborate plaster work.

The shrine contains a broken chlorite Ganesha sculpture, decidedly out of place among the Vaishnavite iconography. The image sits atop a granite image base with a large rat carved onto the north face. The interior walls are lined with triangular wall niches.

Feature 3: Shrine, located on the north side of the road directly opposite Feature 1. Feature 3 is a small, south-facing shrine similar in plan, dimensions, and construction to Feature 4 (below). However, unlike the latter, it is in excellent condition. The shrine consists of two rooms, the first consisting of an open porch of 2 (east-west) × 4 columns (north-south). Only the columns facing the road are decorated. Carvings include lotuses, other flowers, Narasimha, saints, and unidentifiable figures. Exterior columns are square in plan with two center insets, while interior columns are square. Exterior capitals are rectangular with beveled insets at each corner. Interior capitals are simple rectangles. The basement moldings are two stepped with convex bevel; a staircase extends south from the south face of the structure.

The sanctuary is formed by the addition of two central columns to the north side of the mandapa. The shrine is enclosed on three sides by walls built of well-dressed slabs placed between the columns. The ceiling is built of flat slabs; a decaying shikara of brick and plaster lies atop the shrine. The door to the shrine is flanked by Vaishnavite door guardians and by interior door sockets. Between this feature and the contemporary road is a raised platform composed of quarried and dressed blocks worn smooth by use. This platform extends 3 m to the east and to the west, beyond the edges of the structure (6 m north-south × 12.5 m east-west). An identical platform lies on the south side of the road, north of Feature 1 and Feature 2 (above). An inverted lamp column base, one of several displaced structural elements in the area, lies atop the platform south of Feature 3. This structure has been conserved by the ASI, and modern cement is visible between structural elements.

Feature 4: Shrine on the north side of the road, at the west end of the gate complex, 12 m west of Feature 3. This shrine is similar to Feature 3 (4 columns east-west × 2 north-south, with two additional center columns on the north forming a small shrine). The structure is constructed of the same kinds of columns as Feature 3; however, no roof slabs or evidence of a superstructure are present. Two of the columns facing the road are sculpted, one with Nandi, the other Ganesha. The basement moldings (two stepped with angle bevel) are visible only on the north side of the structure; one molding of this type has been reused as a roof support. The floor and basement are now buried in colluvium and the structure is surrounded by rubble on all sides.

Artifacts: Ceramic scatter is moderately dense west of the gate, less dense east of (outside) gate. No collections were made since the area lies along the route of a modern road.

Temporal Affiliation: Late Vijayanagara.

References: Morrison 1995:75; Morrison and Sinopoli 1996:67, 69; Sinopoli and Morrison 2006:440.

Illustrations: Plates 5.49-5.52.

Plate 5.49. VMS-217, paved roadbed to the east of the gate.

Plate 5.50. VMS-217, Feature 1.

Plate 5.51. VMS-217, Feature 2.

Plate 5.52. VMS-217, Feature 3.

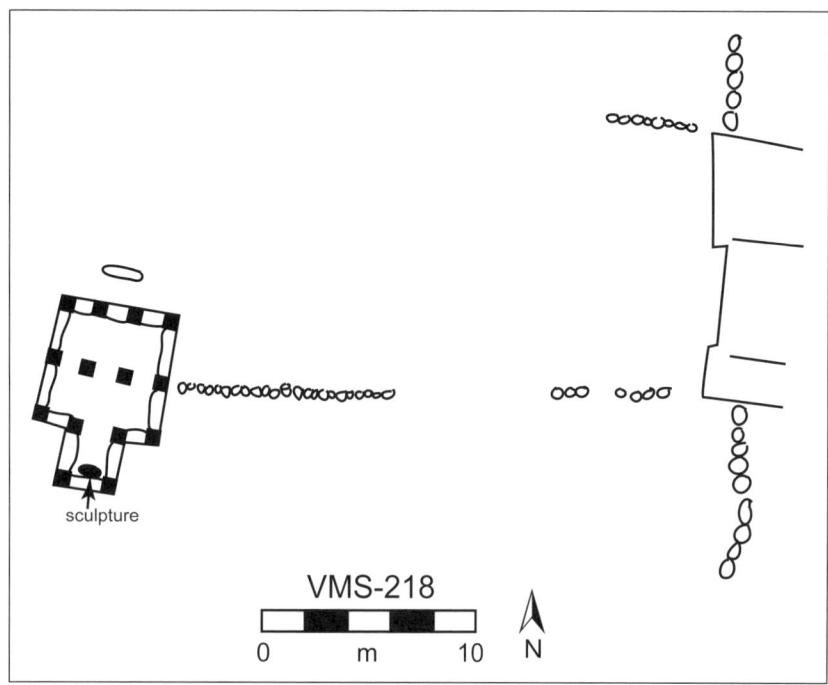

Figure 5.69. VMS-218, plan.

SITE: VMS-218   Block: S   Transect: 17
   Primary Site Use: Religious: shrine.
   Site Dimensions: 16 × 10 m
   Setting: Level dry farmed fields, inside outer city wall (VMS-123).
   Present Land Use/Disturbances: Shrine is currently in worship.
   Site Description: Shrine located on the transportation route between a gateway in the Kamalapuram circuit of the city wall (VMS-123/Feature 1) and VMS-142, a large temple complex. The shrine, which sits on a low rubble mound, contains a boldly decorated striding Hanuman sculpture (1.65 m × 0.85 m). An east-west oriented wall runs from the east side of the shrine toward the gate in the city wall.

   This north-facing shrine is composed of a columned porch and a sanctuary. The porch, 4 columns east-west × 3 columns north-south, is constructed of roughly dressed slabs and quarried columns. The capitals are similarly rough blocks. Above these are long rectangular stone beams overlain by horizontal roof slabs. Recent cobble and mortar walls enclose the mandapa and sanctuary on all sides except the north. The basement (visible only on the north side) consists of a single molding (two stepped with angled bevel). The sanctuary is made by adding two more columns to the south side of the structure; its constituents are similar to those of the mandapa. There is no evidence of a superstructure, but remnants of slab floors are visible in several places.

   There are two appended exterior walls, both in poor condition. The first is appended to the central column on the east side of the mandapa. It consists of large, roughly dressed blocks and unmodified cobbles. Two courses are visible, although the height of the mound suggests at least three courses. The wall runs toward VMS-123/Feature 1 for c. 9 m. The second wall appears to be recent.
   Artifacts: Low density ceramic scatter throughout area. The density is much higher west of the shrine. Ceramics on the north and east sides of the site are highly fragmented. 100% collection. 600 g ceramics; wares: 59 black plain ware, 7 brown plain ware, 2 coarse ware. Diagnostics: 2 jars.
   Temporal Affiliation: Vijayanagara.
   Illustrations: Figure 5.69.

SITE: VMS-219   Block: S   Transect: 13
   Primary Site Use: Agricultural: terraces.
   Site Dimensions: 94 × 136 m
   Setting: Steeply sloping outcrop inside city wall.
   Present Land Use/Disturbances: Uncultivated. Portions of the terrace system are badly eroded and gullied; however, it is in generally good condition.
   Site Description: Terrace system, located on the north face of the outcrop bearing the outer circuit of the city wall (VMS-123). It begins at the top of the flat terrace behind the wall and continues downslope for c. 94 m. There are six major east-west terrace walls with smaller check dams interspersed throughout. Construction is massive and terraces are relatively deep and well developed. Wall height varies from 0.5 to 1.5 m, and terrace areas vary from c. 25 to 100 m^2. This system is built in an area of exposed dolerite dykes and incorporates some natural outcrops. The main area of terraces is c. 94 × 35 m. A massive north-south wall, 3 m wide, occurs between the second and third terraces from the top of the slope. Terraces tend to follow the natural contours of the hillside and some are slightly stepped. Another large north-south wall is found between the fifth and sixth terraces. The sixth terrace begins at the east terminus of the main terraced area, but continues beyond the west terminus, to a total length of 136 m. This terrace follows the natural contour of the hillside to form a long retaining wall about 80 to 100 m downslope from the top of the outcrop. Although some terrace walls have been recently maintained, the well-developed soil accumulations behind them suggest a venerable origin for the system as a whole. Soils in these terraces are shallow and rocky, and set at an acute gradient. These walls are clearly retaining walls to prevent colluviation of the intensively settled valley below.
   Artifacts: Very sparse ceramic scatter. 100% collection within the area enclosed by walls. <50 g ceramics: 4 red plain ware. Diagnostics: 3 jars.
   Temporal Affiliation: Unknown; not recent.
   Illustrations: Figure 5.70; Plate 5.53.

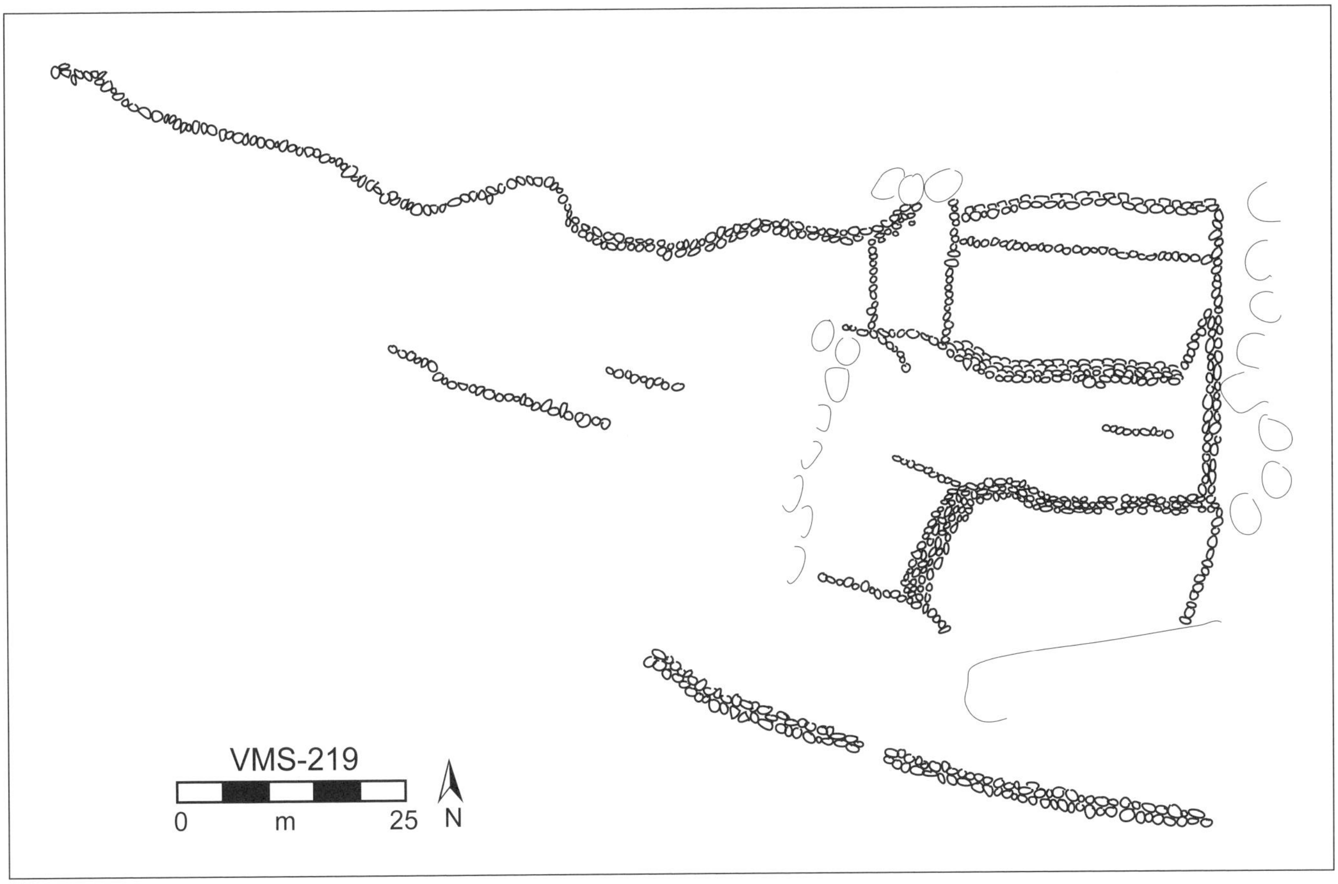

Figure 5.70. VMS-219, plan.

Plate 5.53. VMS-219, terrace wall.

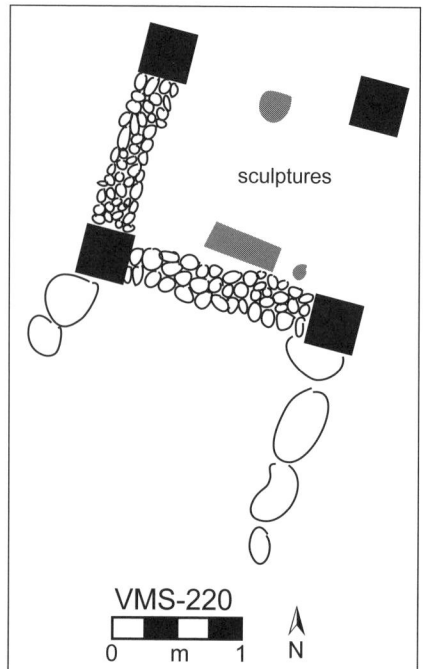

(*Left*) Figure 5.71. VMS-220, plan (square blocks indicate columns).

(*Above*) Plate 5.54. VMS-220, mandapa.

SITE: VMS-220   Block: S   **Transect:** 13
   Primary Site Use: Religious/transport: mandapa.
   Site Dimensions: 2.1 × 2.2 m
   Setting: Sheet rock on outcrop slope.
   Present Land Use/Disturbances: Cobbles are piled on the structure; these are currently being broken up. One sculpture is broken and a roof slab is missing.
   Site Description: Mandapa with 2 × 2 columns. The structure sits directly on sheet rock, set into rock-cut column footings. The square columns are quarried but not dressed (c. 1.7 m high). Each is topped by a capital made of a horizontal rectangular slab. Four long slabs join the pillars; these carry the stone roof beams. A small Shaivite sculpture and a broken sculpture of a male torso are found inside the shrine. In front of the Shiva figure is a small block with two carved feet. There is a short boulder alignment south of the mandapa.
   There appears to have been a road running along the base of the outcrop in this area. As such, the mandapa would have been located quite close to the road and within a densely occupied residential area.
   Artifacts: There are no artifacts on the sheet rock, but a moderately dense scatter lies in the fields to the north. No collections made.
   Temporal Affiliation: Vijayanagara.
   Illustrations: Figure 5.71; Plate 5.54.

SITE: VMS-221   Block: S   **Transect:** 13-14
   Primary Site Use: Residential: settlement area.
   Site Dimensions: 117 × 276 m
   Setting: Level dry farmed fields at the base of an outcrop.
   Present Land Use/Disturbances: Extensive field clearing, colluviation from the rocky outcrop to the south.
   Site Description: Residential area, arbitrarily divided from surrounding areas for recording convenience. Its boundaries are VMS-211 on the east, the outcrop containing the outer city wall (and VMS-219) to the south, the low sheet rock outcrop (part of VMS-222) on the north, and the north-south wall VMS-223 on the west. The south and west boundaries are the least ambiguous, as there is a sharp topographic separation on the south and a distinct cultural separation on the west.
   Beginning on the east is a long east-west terrace wall 25 m north of the base of the outcrop, perpendicular to runoff flow. At the east end it is little more than a linear rubble pile, but near the center it becomes a solidly-built cobble wall with two faces and rubble infill (1.49 m wide). South of this long wall and east of its dogleg, the plowed fields end about 30 m north of the base of the high outcrop. In this gently sloping boulder-strewn area are thousands of small round cobbles. Some of these form short wall stubs. In this area are a worn block mortar, a bedrock mortar, and four circles ground into the bedrock. Northwest of the long east-west wall is a similar east-west wall in poor condition. It seems to curve to the north at its west end, where it degenerates into a rubble pile. A long north-south linear rubble pile runs north from the curved end of this wall. This one does appear to be modern. Further north are remnant piles from field clearance. A possible room corner, a few quarried blocks, and a short (2 m) wall alignment can be seen here.
   Continuing west from the west end of the second wall is a low (0.15 m high, 0.3 m wide) earthen mound that is associated on the west with a linear rubble alignment, a worn block mortar, and a low outcropping boulder with a row of at least four peg holes, two with stubs of basalt pegs wedged in them. This long east-west alignment extends all the way to VMS-223. Perhaps this and the other two east-west walls were originally all part of one long, stepped retaining wall. At this west end of the site are two parallel retaining walls hugging the base of the outcrop. The south one is loosely constructed of cobbles while the north one is more massively constructed, incorporating outcropping boulders and employing large cobbles and small boulders.
   Artifacts: Within the continuous moderate density scatter of ceramics and slag found throughout this area. Some burnished red ware noted. No formal collections made. One lithic recovered, utilized flake (milky white quartz).
   Temporal Affiliation: Vijayanagara.

Plate 5.55. VMS-222, boundary column with Nandi image.

SITE: VMS-222   Block: S   Transect: 13

Primary Site Use: Residential: settlement area.
Site Dimensions: 250 × 180 m
Setting: Gently sloping sheet rock. Irrigated fields lie to the north and northeast with dry farmed fields on the other sides.
Present Land Use/Disturbances: Recent quarrying has cut away a significant portion of the outcrop, which is currently being used to process dry crops. Most cultural features visible on the surface are in areas not currently farmed. Where pits expose architecture, there is 0.5-0.6 m of colluvium above the tops of the walls, suggesting that many structures are buried.
Site Description: Area of Vijayanagara period settlement within the city walls. The borders of this site, located within an extensive area of Vijayanagara settlement, have been arbitrarily defined as that area on and near a high sheet rock outcrop, which lies north of the outcrop containing the city wall. An outlet of the High Level Canal cuts off the north side of this area. The west boundary is the wall VMS-223, the south the edge of the outcrop. VMS-221 and 222 are thus continuous.

Atop the outcrop are traces of past settlement, including wall stubs, mortars, and artifact-rich fill. The south and southwest portions of outcrop have been recently quarried away. The north side is terraced by a number of small retaining walls. Most are simply constructed of two faces of cobbles (0.2-0.4 m wide). A few are more substantially built of small boulders. Near the corner of wall VMS-223 are two parallel walls constructed of widely spaced large boulders. Some rubble lies scattered between the boulders, suggesting that the walls were originally more solid.

North and northeast of the outcrop is a level uncultivated area cut by the paved Nallapuram road and the modern canal, among other recent features. Where there has been recent pitting along the roadside one can see numerous wall segments and artifact-rich fill. A number of block mortars are located nearby and in the northeast are two upright boundary posts. The north has a carved Nandi atop it, but no inscription. The presence of boundary stones suggests some formal demarcation of space. There are also numerous block mortars in the area. One wall on the north edge of the outcrop is partially built into the sheet rock. One can see a shallow rock-cut trench as well as several peg holes for footing and anchoring the wall.

The west side of the site is, as noted, demarcated by the wall VMS-223. The latter makes a 90° turn to the west at its north end. Just east of this point are two parallel lines of boulders, loosely spaced, running approximately north-south. Perhaps these related to the channeling of traffic in this area.
Artifacts: Variable density artifact scatter (ceramics, ash, bone) with highest densities in exposed profiles and surrounding fields. No collections were made due to time constraints.
Temporal Affiliation: Vijayanagara.
References: Morrison 1995:71.
Illustrations: Plate 5.55.

SITE: VMS-223   Block: S   Transect: 12

Primary Site Use: Defensive/transport: wall.
Site Dimensions: 364 × 82 m
Setting: South part of the wall runs over an outcrop, the north half through level dry farmed fields.
Present Land Use/Disturbances: Breached by the Nallapuram road and the Right Bank Main Canal. North of the canal, the wall is obliterated by irrigated fields.
Site Description: Massive double-faced wall. VMS 223 is constructed of two faces of unmodified, mostly rounded boulders and cobbles (up to six courses) with a rubble core. This long wall abuts the city wall on the south. It is massively and solidly built, running over very steeply sloping outcrops along its south portion. One hundred meters from its juncture with outer city wall VMS-123, there is a gap (probably not original). Here the outcrop ends, and the wall is reduced to one or two courses in height, although there is a scatter of masonry on either side. Where it runs across this flat area, the wall is constructed of smaller

Plate 5.56. VMS-223, fortification wall viewed from south.

cobbles and a few split and quarried blocks. Larger elements are used in the sections of the wall running over the outcrop. Near its juncture with the city wall, VMS-223 is 1.4 m wide, achieving a width of 1.6 m along the steep part of the outcrop. Here the courses are discontinuous and somewhat stepped due to steepness of the outcrop. One hundred and ninety meters from the city wall is a possible opening c. 2 m wide. At 268 m is a stub of east-west rubble wall extending to the east. At 364 m, the wall turns 90° to the west; the corner is bonded. This east-west segment is similarly constructed and is broken up by modern features. This one- to three-course wall can be traced for 82 m before it is cut by the modern road and canal. Sections can be traced across the latter, however. There are a few possible traces of the wall beyond these features.

This wall may be an enclosure wall setting off part or all of the suburb Varadadevi-ammana-pattana associated with the Pattabhirama temple (VMS-237).

Artifacts: The wall is surrounded by a sparse to moderate density ceramic scatter. There are some highly fragmented sherds in the core of the wall. No collections made.
Temporal Affiliation: Vijayanagara.
References: Morrison 1995:71, 77; Morrison and Sinopoli 1996:63, 67.
Illustrations: Plate 5.56.

SITE: **VMS-224**   Block: S   Transect: 11-12
Primary Site Use: Transport: road and well.
Site Dimensions: 314 × 8 m
Setting: Level area near the base of an outcrop amid dry farmed fields, inside city wall.
Present Land Use/Disturbances: Colluviation, plowing, and field clearance have destroyed much of the road surface and any features once found along the road. There is heavy pitting at the west end.
Site Description: East-west road segment running along the base of the outcrop bearing outer city wall, VMS-123. On the east, the road begins 12 m west of the long north-south wall segment. The road dead-ends here with a north-south crosswall. The latter is bonded to the road walls, single-course, single-face, east-west alignments of cobbles (0.6 m wide). A few rounded cobbles in the road (8 m wide here) could be remnant paving elements. One hundred and fifty-two meters from its east end, the south side of the road is defined by a wide (1.3 m) wall, which consists of a double-faced cobble and small boulder wall abutted by a single line of small boulders on the south. The north road wall is poorly preserved here. About 15 m further west are two parallel cobble alignments in the roadway, about 2 m apart. There are traces of these alignments in the road further west. Two hundred and seventy-three meters from the east end, a hedge cuts across the road; west of this is a pitted area on the edge of Kamalapuram. The road walls continue—they stand several courses high in the fragments that remain—but the damage in this area is severe. The area south of the south road wall has a very high density of ceramics.

Feature 1: Rock-cut well. The well is roughly square (4 × 4 m) and c. 3.5 m deep. It is fed by runoff from the outcrop to the south. Quarry marks are visible on the interior faces. Although a masonry wall of at least one course once ran around the top of the well, only three elements (large, unmodified, and roughly dressed cobbles) remain in place. Feature 1 is located on a small flat terrace south of the road. The fill of this terrace has a high density of ceramics. South of the well and parallel to the roadway is a wall constructed of large cobbles, running along the base of the outcrop. This may have been an exterior wall for the well or a retaining wall to impede erosion from the outcrop. The well is in poor condition due to erosion, colluviation, and collapse of the surrounding wall.

Artifacts: Moderately high density ceramic scatter with artifact densities particularly high in the terrace fill of Feature 1. No collections made.
Temporal Affiliation: Vijayanagara.
References: Morrison 1995:77; Morrison and Sinopoli 1996:67.

SITE: **VMS-225**   Block: S   Transect: 11-12
Primary Site Use: Transport: road.
Site Dimensions: 10 × 16 m
Setting: Level dry farmed fields; partly on sheet rock.
Present Land Use/Disturbances: The Right Bank Main Canal, canal construction debris, and the Nallapuram road cut into this heavily disturbed site.
Site Description: Road segment. This north-south oriented road segment is located within the enclosed settlement area (VMS-228) south of the Pattabhirama temple (VMS-237). The road is directly aligned with the south entrance of the temple. The east and west borders of the road are formed by double-faced single-course walls with earthen cores. Each face is constructed of unmodified or split cobbles placed end to end. The road surface runs over sheet rock; there are eroding patches of cobble paving. This road is associated with the Pattabhirama temple and may have had ritual functions, perhaps serving as the chariot street of the temple.
Artifacts: Moderate density ceramic scatter with a few pieces of slag. No collections made due to time constraints.
Temporal Affiliation: Vijayanagara.
References: Morrison 1995:77; Morrison and Sinopoli 1996:63, 67.
Illustrations: Figure 5.72.

SITE: **VMS-226**   Block: S   Transect: 18
Primary Site Use: Agricultural: reservoir embankment.
Site Dimensions: 99 × 6.5 m
Setting: Gently sloping, dry farmed fields amid outcrops.
Present Land Use/Disturbances: A channel has been cut through the east end of the embankment. In 1992, a paved road was built through this area.
Site Description: Reservoir embankment. This 3 m high embankment lies at the top of a small south-north drainage on the west edge of terrace system VMS-133. The bed of the reservoir is c. 100 m (east-west) × 70 m (north-south). About 20 m east of the outcrops that define the east edge of the embankment is a short rubble wall segment (8 m) five

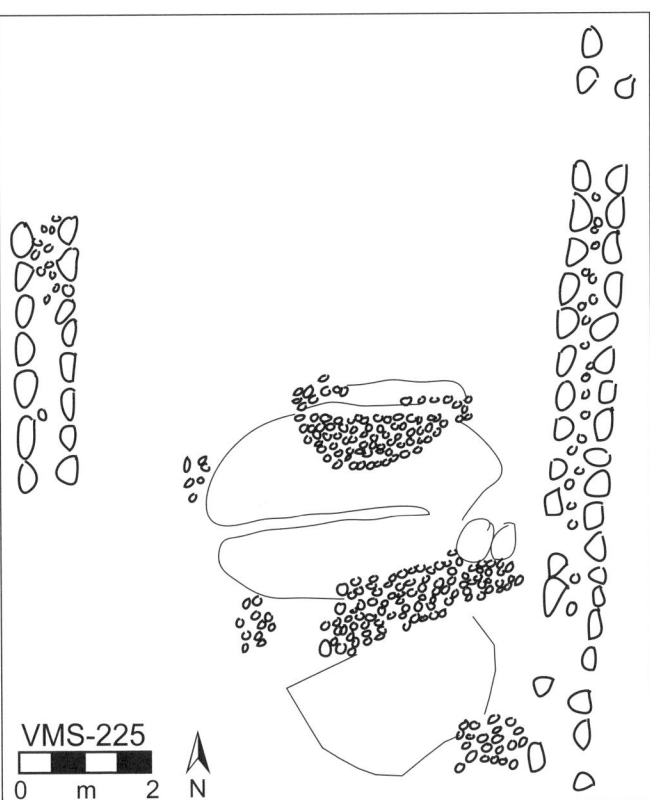

Figure 5.72. VMS-225, plan.

courses high. This wall may have served to slow runoff from the outcrop. The reservoir meets outcrops on the east but ends in a level area on the west, perhaps the former location of a breached sluice.

The earthen reservoir embankment is faced on both sides with steep masonry of unmodified and split boulders. Unusually, the masonry on the upstream (north) side is quite substantial, five to six courses. On both sides of the embankment the masonry is nearly vertical, only slightly stepped out near its base. From the western edge of the site, the south masonry rises slowly from two courses near its edge to a maximum of eleven visible courses, punctuated by several long unshaped protruding horizontal slab steps. West of the embankment is a section of wall that might originally have been part of the reservoir, though there is no earthen embankment behind it, and it may be simply a solid wall with masonry very like that found on the south side of the embankment. This wall has a recent shrine at its south end (red and white stripes, green bangles, and a small painted stone under an Acacia tree).

Artifacts: 100% collection. A single coarse ware body sherd was recovered.

Temporal Affiliation: Vijayanagara.

References: Morrison 1995:91, 102; Morrison and Sinopoli 1996:71.

Illustrations: Mapped with VMS-133; see Figure 5.11.

SITE: VMS-227   Block: S   Transect: 15
  Primary Site Use: Residential: well.
  Site Dimensions: 8 × 9 m
  Setting: Level dry farmed fields.

Present Land Use/Disturbances: Piles of recently cut granite blocks lie near the well. The masonry edging around the top of the well is almost entirely gone and the center is silted in.

Site Description: Rock-cut well. This deep (c. 3-5 m) rock-cut well is located within a residential area inside Vijayanagara's outer city wall. It is entered from the south via a ramp that parallels the south face of the well near the bottom and then turns to the east to cut into the south edge of the rock. Thus, in entering the well from above, one would walk north down a steep ramp, then turn right (east) down a shorter more gradually sloping ramp to the water level. A short, c. 3 m long segment of masonry runs along the north side of the well, near its northeast corner. It consists of three courses of rectangular quarried but undressed blocks, and is possibly modern.

Artifacts: Well is situated in an area of moderate density scatter of ceramics, slag, and lithics. No collections made due to time constraints.

Temporal Affiliation: Unknown.

SITE: VMS-228   Block: S   Transect: 12
  Primary Site Use: Residential: settlement area.
  Site Dimensions: 300 × 250 m
  Setting: Level dry farmed valley below a low sheet rock outcrop.
  Present Land Use/Disturbances: This area has been considerably disturbed by the construction of the Right Bank Main Canal, the paved Nallapuram road, a power line, and field clearance.
  Site Description: Settlement. This area has been designated as separate from nearby settlement area VMS-222 because of the division of space by the long north-south wall VMS-223. Only fragments of walls remain in this area, which is heavily disturbed by cultivation and by the post-1950 Right Bank Main Canal and its offshoot. The clearest indication that this was a densely settled area is the high concentration of artifacts visible on the surface. The site is bounded by VMS-223 on the east and north, the city wall (VMS-123) on the south, and the canal on the west. The current boundaries of the village of Kamalapuram begin on the west edge of the canal. However, rather than part of Vijayanagara period Kamalapur, this walled settlement area was more likely associated with the named suburb of Varadadevi-ammana-pattana attached to the Pattabhirama temple. If so, it may have extended to the west, past the modern canal. VMS-224, a road and well, are contained within the site area. Only a few scattered rubble wall fragments remain in the area; many connect expanses of flat sheet rock.
  Artifacts: Dense ceramic scatter on surface including variety of earthenwares, both plain and burnished. Area was covered with dense vegetation when documented; no systematic collections were possible at the time.
  Temporal Affiliation: Vijayanagara.

SITE: VMS-230   Block: S   Transect: 13
  Primary Site Use: Agricultural: reservoir embankment.
  Site Dimensions: 26 × 4 m
  Setting: Gently sloping outcrops.
  Present Land Use/Disturbances: The road connecting Papinayakahalli with Kamalapuram runs along and cuts the northwest edge of the reservoir. This area is now used for grazing and wood collecting. Borrow pits and footpaths cut into the embankment.
  Site Description: Reservoir embankment. This masonry and earthen embankment incorporates a north-south outcrop. Situated among low east-west trending outcrops, VMS-230 straddles a small rocky drainage adjacent to and west of the drainage containing a reservoir (VMS-206) and its associated terrace system (VMS-207). The catchment area of this feature is small, rocky, and irregular. No cultivable fields lie directly

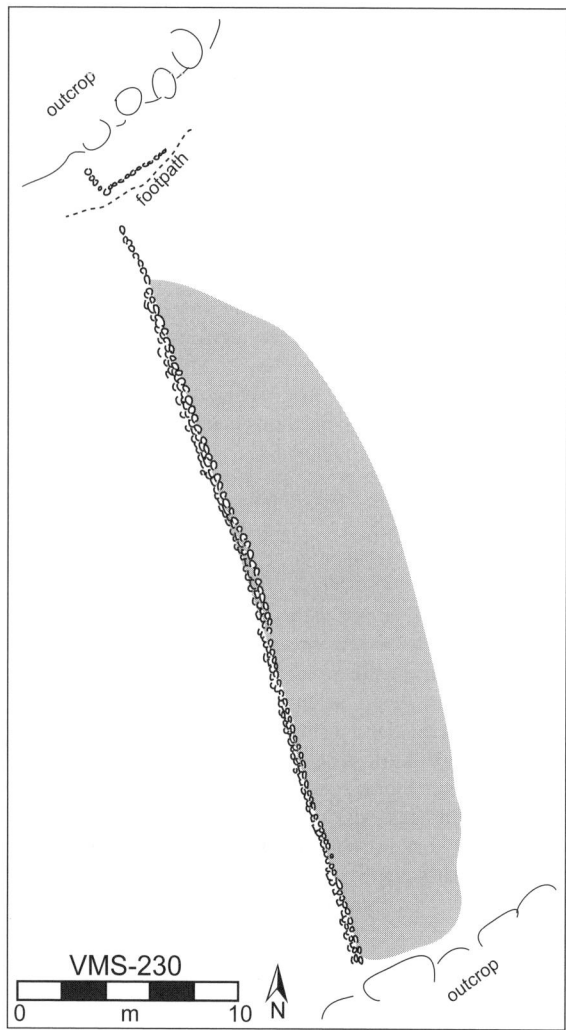

Figure 5.73. VMS-230, plan.

below the facility. Thus, cultivation would have been carried out within the bed of the reservoir itself. The south masonry facing consists of up to six courses of large cobbles laid in irregular courses. Near the center is a north-south oriented cobble crosswall (up to three courses standing).

Artifacts: 100% collection. One unidentifiable sherd, too small to collect.

Temporal Affiliation: Placement and construction are consistent with Vijayanagara period features.

References: Morrison 1995:91, 93, 102; Morrison and Sinopoli 1996:71.

Illustrations: Figure 5.73.

SITE: VMS-231   Block: S   Transect:
Primary Site Use: Agricultural: reservoir embankment.
Site Dimensions: 2 km × 1.5 km
Setting: Flat, low-lying fields.
Present Land Use/Disturbances: This canal-fed reservoir is still in use. The top of the embankment is a paved road bed; both ends of the reservoir have been extended with concrete walls. Modification to sluice channels and outlets.
Site Description: Kamalapuram reservoir. This massive reservoir embankment dominates the northwestern portion of Block S. It is supplied by the Raya Canal from the Tungabhadra River, providing a year-round source of water for irrigation. Although no inscriptions are directly associated with the canal, Morrison (1995) has argued that it most likely dates to the early fifteenth century. The original headworks of the Raya Canal are now submerged beneath the Tungabhadra dam. The Kamalapuram reservoir appears to have been constructed in the fourteenth century, suggesting that it might have once been fed by seasonal runoff; even today the reservoir collects a significant amount of runoff from the Sandur Hills to the south, as well as from the canal. The reservoir embankment is nearly 2 km long, but the easternmost 300 m or so appear to be a recent addition. The embankment height is at least 6 m on its exterior, northern face. The masonry on the south side of the embankment is much repaired, consisting of quarried and shaped blocks in the upper courses and unmodified boulders in the lowest courses.

There are at present four sluice gates, of which two are from the Vijayanagara period. The original sluices are fairly simple, containing two stepped with angled bevel moldings with half medallions. Both of the Vijayanagara period sluices are associated with stone settling basins, located below the embankment. The westernmost basin is a square stone basin, c. 5 × 5 m in dimension, which creates a "holding area" for water flowing under the embankment through the western sluice. It is constructed of long, dressed rectangular slabs set above a protruding course of similar slabs, which are currently under water. Above the visible slabs is a course of horizontally laid large dressed rectangular slabs, which protrudes over the lower face by 5 to 10 cm. On it, and set back approximately 50 cm, are carved "back rests." Three square openings are present on the north, east, and west faces of the basin, though the east face is now blocked off. A modern cement-lined channel takes water off through the west opening. There are paving slabs around the basin on the north and west sides. This pavement terminates on the north in a curving wall, defining the boundaries of the agricultural fields to the north; the elevation of the fields drops sharply here. Water flows out through the north opening of the basin through a channel that passes through this northern wall. It thus appears that the basin was likely constructed on a semicircular platform.

The broad raised embankment was the road bed for the primary route that linked the city of Vijayanagara with settlement to the west, passing through a now largely dismantled gate (VMS-452) at its western edge. The embankment is integrated into the outer city wall, supporting a small square bastion at its eastern end, near the staircase leading down to the easternmost sluice, and a much larger square bastion near its western end. The latter faces north, over the field watered by the reservoir, while the former faces south, over the water itself. A small shrine is located on the peak of the embankment, near its center. This is a 3 × 2 column shrine with an enclosed sanctuary; all around the base of the shrine is a procession of carved elephants. Although the elements appear to be of Vijayanagara date, it has been reconstructed and the structure may not be in its original location. Architectural elements include simple square columns with octagonal insets.

In addition to the major road along the embankment, a small road branched off this route toward the north. Except for this route, the area to the north of the reservoir appears to have been used exclusively for agriculture. The area watered by VMS-231 was estimated at 182 ha in 1904 (Francis 1904:282).

Artifacts: No collections made.
Temporal Affiliation: Vijayanagara to modern; first constructed early in Vijayanagara period.
References: Morrison 1995:63, 65, 69, 77, 90-91, 99, 108, 139-41; Morrison 2006; Morrison and Sinopoli 1996:71; Davison-Jenkins 1997:48-52.
Illustrations: Figures 5.74, 5.75; Plates 5.57-5.59.

Block S: Site Summaries

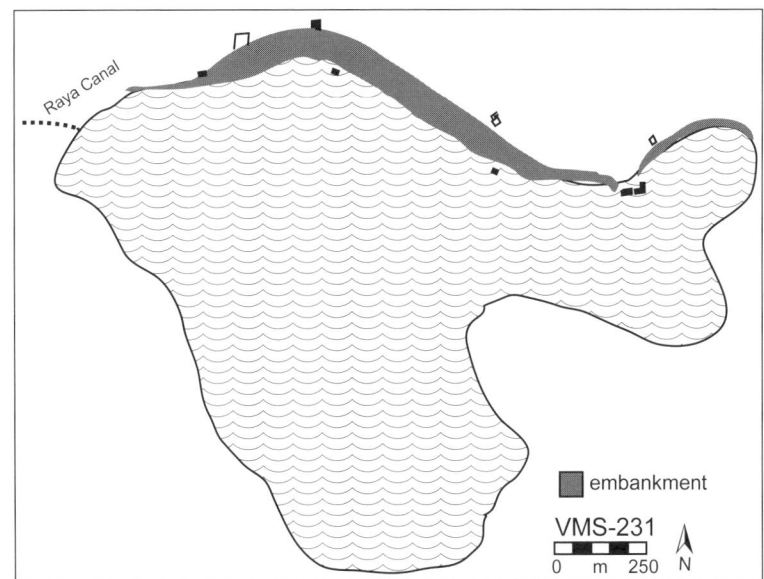

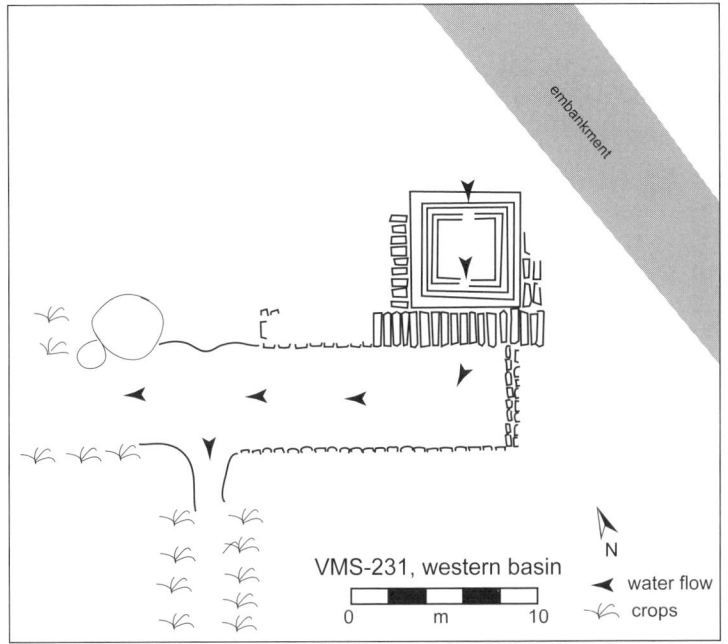

(*Above*) Figure 5.74. VMS-231, Kamalapuram reservoir plan.

(*Left*) Figure 5.75. VMS-231, western basin of Kamalapuram reservoir.

(*Below*) Plate 5.57. VMS-231, Kamalapuram reservoir; stone basin associated with outlet for the western sluice.

(*Left*) Plate 5.58. VMS-231, Kamalapuram reservoir; channel of western sluice on projecting from the earthen face of embankment.

(*Lower Left*) Plate 5.59. VMS-231, Kamalapuram reservoir, view.

SITE: VMS-232   Block: S   **Transect:** 14
  Primary Site Use: Religious: sculptures.
  Site Dimensions: n/a
  Setting: Level irrigated fields.
  Present Land Use/Disturbances: Heavily disturbed; displaced elements from nearby agricultural fields have been piled up in one place.
  Site Description: Displaced sculpture and architectural elements. Older quarried blocks and slabs have been incorporated into a modern well. It is not clear if an old well has been adapted, or another structure dismantled. Adjacent to the well is a pile of sculptures and architectural elements. These include a block with two pairs of carved feet encircled by a naga, a small naga stone, a large chunk of Vijayanagara concrete, and a two-pronged fork (bident) in a pointed arch with a chakra and conch on either side. Other elements include a rectangular block carved with a Vishnu in an arch flanked by kneeling devotees, and a giant corner quarter medallion (from a molding) with an inset carved panel depicting a male on a horse, right hand uplifted, holding a fly whisk (?) in his left hand. Finally, there is a very small but elaborately carved chlorite pillar. At its foot is a projection with the broken feet of what was probably a yali.
  Artifacts: Moderate density ceramic scatter in area around sculptures, mostly visible in irrigation channels. No collections made.
  Temporal Affiliation: Vijayanagara.
  Illustrations: Plate 5.60.

SITE: VMS-233   Block: S   **Transect:** 14
  Primary Site Use: Unknown: wall and sculpture.
  Site Dimensions: 50 × 2 m
  Setting: Level irrigated fields.
  Present Land Use/Disturbances: Heavily disturbed. The original layout is indeterminable as features have been displaced by irrigated fields supplied by wells and pumps.
  Site Description: Sculpture and structure. This heavily disturbed site contains traces of architectural features, including a long wide north-south wall or platform, which is constructed of small cobbles and rubble and is double faced with earthen infill. Thickly plastered patches occur sporadically along both faces. Other wall stubs, some plastered, occur throughout the area. Atop this wall, at the present north end, is a broken

Plate 5.60. VMS-232, northern portion of sculpture group.

slab with Nandi and lingam on an inset panel. Below these, in a separate panel, are two round features just above the broken edge of the slab. These seem to be the hair knots of the two figures carved into this panel. East of the sculpture is a fragment of a faceted pillar, as well as a large (c. 0.3 × 0.3 m) flat section of cement with smooth plastered surface. On the west side of the wall is a large quarried and dressed slab.

Artifacts: No collections made. Heavy disturbance and water transport has probably affected the assemblage. Some ceramics are visible on surface.

Temporal Affiliation: Unknown. Sculpted elements are of Vijayanagara date; dating of the walls is unknown.

SITE: VMS-234   Block: S   **Transect:** 14
   Primary Site Use: Residential/agricultural: well.
   Site Dimensions: 12 × 7.5 m
   Setting: Level irrigated fields.
   Present Land Use/Disturbances: Half of the well is modern; it is fitted out with a pump and pump house. A power line runs overhead. Soil movement in this area has been massive.
   Site Description: Well. The extant pre-modern half of this well (south, and south half of the west side) is constructed of medium to large rectangular quarried blocks. Coursing is regular, though the stones are only loosely fit with occasional chinking. There are at least seven original courses. The highest, on the south, is composed of two long slabs, rather than of blocks. There are no steps. The well is located within a residential area, possibly along the course of a road leading to the east gopuram of the Pattabhirama temple.
   Artifacts: No collection made. The well is located in an area characterized by a localized moderate density scatter of highly fragmented ceramics.
   Temporal Affiliation: Vijayanagara.

SITE: VMS-235   Block: S   **Transect:** 14
   Primary Site Use: Residential/fortification?: platform.
   Site Dimensions: 35 × 70 m
   Setting: Level irrigated fields.
   Present Land Use/Disturbances: Site is heavily disturbed by irrigated fields to the north and south and by Hampi Power Camp on the east. Only remnant structural remains are visible in the ditches to the north and south of the modern road to Hampi Power Camp.
   Site Description: Wall and displaced structural elements. This site consists of an extensive area of poorly preserved structural remains and displaced elements. To the south of the modern road is a fragment of Vijayanagara-type concrete with a flat plastered surface. Nearby are several low unaligned rubble mounds. To the east, a large (c. 9 m wide, 2 m high) platform can be seen in the profile of the road cut. The base is buried, but loosely coursed rubble fill is visible as is an upper plastered section. A second smaller, similarly constructed platform lies 3 m to the east, also visible only in section. This smaller platform (at least 1.2 m wide) lacks the upper plastered coursing. Circa 0.8 m east of the small platform is a short rubble wall extending north-south out into the road.

Circa 30 m east of the above is a series of five closely spaced platforms. These are constructed of solid rubble, with flat cemented and plastered upper surfaces. Numerous chunks of cement and plaster have been incorporated into bordering farmers' walls. Opposite the platform area, a large dressed block has been placed on end atop a horizontal block. Nearby, several small rectangular blocks form what may be a doorway; 0.65 m wide double-faced walls extend 10 m away from the possible entrance, oriented roughly northeast-southwest. Approximately 20 m to the east of the end of the walls are two large quarried blocks aligned roughly north-south. Displaced quarried blocks occur in the vicinity.

The dissected nature of this site makes interpretation difficult. Quarry marks, construction details, and cement/plaster composition indicate

Plate 5.61. VMS-236, pavilion in temple tank.

Vijayanagara occupation. The long south wall and its associated doorway appear to divide and/or enclose an area within this zone, perhaps an elite residential zone or area of public buildings. An ornate temple (VMS-254) is located to the northeast.

Artifacts: Low density scatter of earthenware ceramics, with artifact densities somewhat higher north of the road. No collections made.

Temporal Affiliation: Vijayanagara.

SITE: VMS-236   Block: S   Transect: 6
  Primary Site Use: Religious: temple tank.
  Setting: Level irrigated fields.
  Present Land Use/Disturbances: Amid modern agriculture fields, sediment has filled much of the tank bed, and water is present only during the monsoon period.
  Site Description: Large rectangular stepped tank and surrounding portico with interior pavilions. Associated with Pattabhirama temple complex. Not documented by VMS team.
  Artifacts: Low density scatter of earthenware ceramics. No collections made.
  Temporal Affiliation: Late Vijayanagara.
  Illustrations: Plate 5.61.

SITE: VMS-237   Block: S   Transect: 6
  Primary Site Use: Religious: Pattabhirama temple complex.
  Site Dimensions: 160 × 95 m
  Setting: Level irrigated fields.
  Present Land Use/Disturbances: The temple complex is currently an ASI protected monument. Some conservation work occurred in the early twentieth century; in the 1990s, the ASI engaged in additional conservation efforts, including adding new granite paving in the enclosure interior.
  Site Description: Late Vijayanagara temple complex. The Vaishnava Pattabhirama temple complex is one of five major "royal" temple complexes at Vijayanagara (including also Virupaksha, Krishna, Vitthala, and Tiruvengalanatha complexes, all in the "Sacred Center" of the Vijayanagara urban core). The complex has been the focus of an unpublished Masters thesis by Brigitte Pascher of Norwich University (1987); this description draws heavily on her work.

The sixteenth-century temple complex is the largest of the major Vijayanagara temple complexes; its massive walls enclose an area of 160 m east-west by 95 m north-south. A massive gopuram is located in the center of the eastern wall. A columned cloister or gallery runs along the north, west, and south interior faces of the enclosure walls. Within the compound are three mandapas, the main temple, and a subsidiary shrine. These features are briefly described below.

Enclosure Walls (prakara): The enclosure walls of the compound are well-constructed double-faced walls, built of closely fitted trapezoidal blocks with brick and rubble fill. The wall stands c. 4 m high, above which is a low brick/plaster wall, ending in a rounded top. The outer face of the wall is generally plain, though here and there are blocks sculpted with fish and tortoises. Along the inner face of the enclosure walls on the north, west and south, is an attached columned porch or gallery. These consist of two rows of simple unsculpted columns (square with octagonal insets) resting on low stone platforms. The porch is roofed with long granite slabs, which project in toward the complex, tapering slightly at their ends.

Monumental Entry (gopuram): A massive monumental gateway in the eastern enclosure wall formed the main entry into the temple complex. Subsidiary entries are found in the center of the southern wall, and just west of center in the northern wall of the compound. The massive gate (16 m north-south by 8 m east-west) has a granite lower portion, surmounted by a massive brick and plaster superstructure. The gate exterior is elaborately carved, with miniature pilasters and columns, niches, and lion and yali images. The inner central passage is flanked by a two-storied chamber, reaching the full height of the doorway. The stone beams that support the upper chamber are elaborately sculpted with lotus and *kirtimukha* motifs. The doorways and passage are elaborately sculpted, with Vaishnava door guardians flanking the entry to the complex.

Above the granite gate rises an elaborate stepped brick and plaster superstructure, stepped in five stories. Many of the stucco figures that once adorned the gopuram are badly damaged.

Mandapas: In the northeast corner of the compound is a square pillared hall, 5 × 5 columns, constructed similarly to the gallery described above and abutting the compound walls. The four central pillars are raised on a low basement.

A second mandapa is located in the southeast corner of the complex. This also is built against the compound walls and is 5 × 5 columns. It is fully walled and was entered through a door on its west side. Pascher interprets this structure as a kitchen.

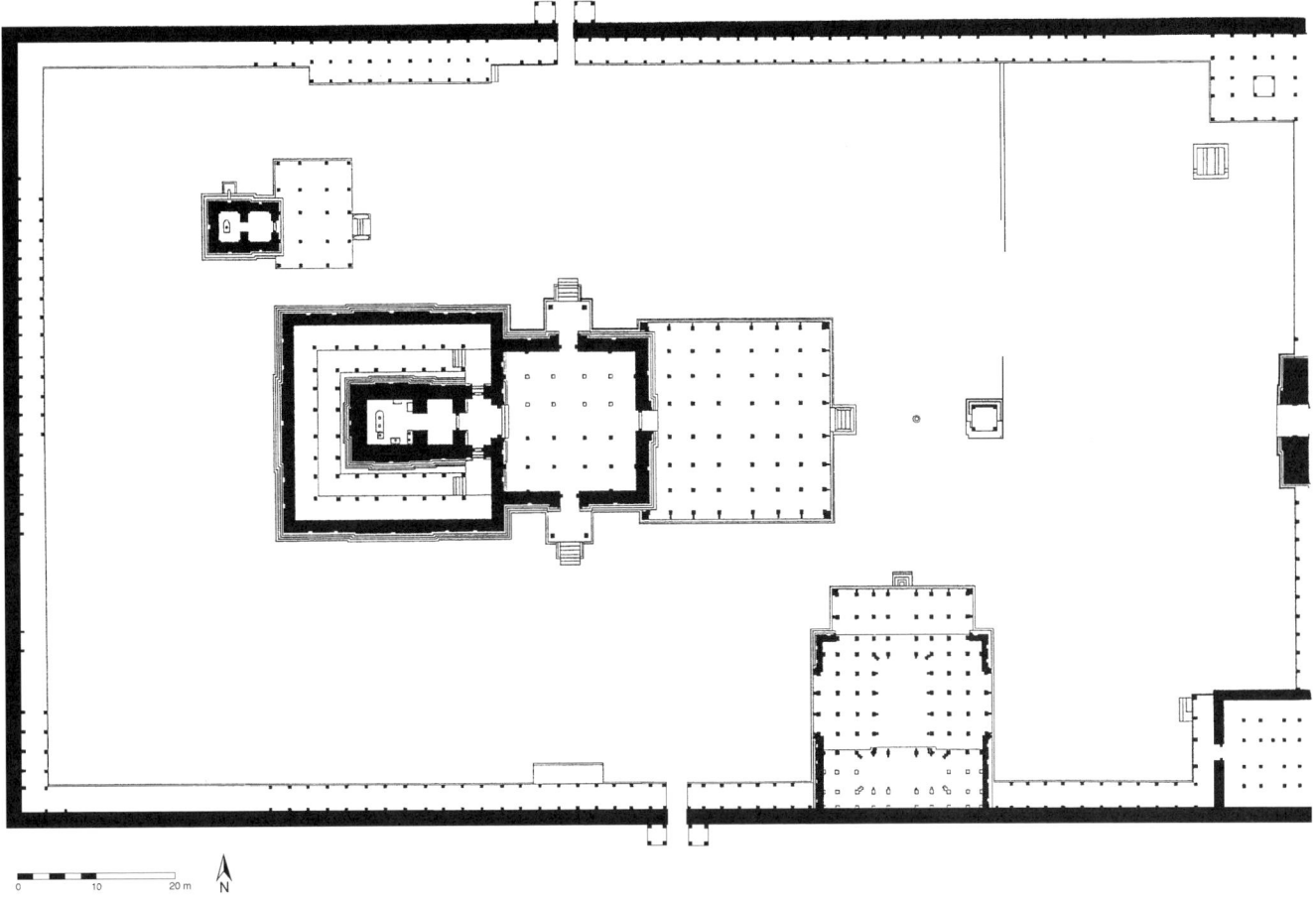

Figure 5.76. VMS-237, Pattabhirama temple complex, plan (illustration courtesy of Vijayanagara Research Project).

A third small (2 × 2 column) mandapa is located in front of the main entrance to the temple. This may have originally contained an image of Garuda, the eagle-winged sacred vehicle of Vishnu.

The largest mandapa in the complex is located along the southern wall of the enclosure. This is the *kalyana mandapa* or marriage pavilion, which was used in the annual marriage ritual of the deity. This elaborate raised structure has a square central platform (20 m on a side), with an 8 × 2 column veranda on its north (front) side. The hall was open to the north, and enclosed by walls on the east and west; it backed into the enclosure walls on the south. Its northern columns are of the elaborate late Vijayanagara composite form, with rearing sculpted horsemen projecting outward from them. Interior columns are elaborately sculpted, and several different styles of columns are present. The basement and walls of the structure are also elaborately sculpted, with dancing figures and animals. At the southern end of the hall, the floor is raised on a low platform; this area of the structure is heavily damaged.

Subsidiary Shrine (amman): Located northwest of the principal temple. It consists of a small open columned hall (5 columns north-south by 4 columns east-west), which fronts a two-chambered structure, with small walled antechamber and sanctuary. Vaishnava door guardians flank the entry to the antechamber.

Main Temple (Figure 5.77): This elaborate east-facing temple consists of five chambers, which become progressively smaller and more restricted from east to west. The easternmost chamber is an unwalled large square roofed open mandapa of 8 × 8 columns (the *mahamandapa*). This raised platform is entered from the east via a platform flanked by yali balustrades. Columns in this hall are standard Vijayanagara columns with three square panels separated by octagonal insets, and are sculpted with a variety of images.

The second chamber is walled and 6 × 6 columns (the *ardhamandapa*). It is entered from the eastern chamber as well as from stairways on the north and south. The inner walls of this structure are of long unsculpted granite slabs, and columns are of the same form as in the outer chamber.

From this chamber, one enters the heart of the temple (the *vimana*), a small three-chambered structure—two small antechambers and the sanctuary. These are enclosed by a walled circumambulatory path (*pradakshina patha*).

Artifacts: No collections made.
Temporal Affiliation: Late Vijayanagara.
Illustrations: Figures 5.76, 5.77; Plates 5.62-5.64.

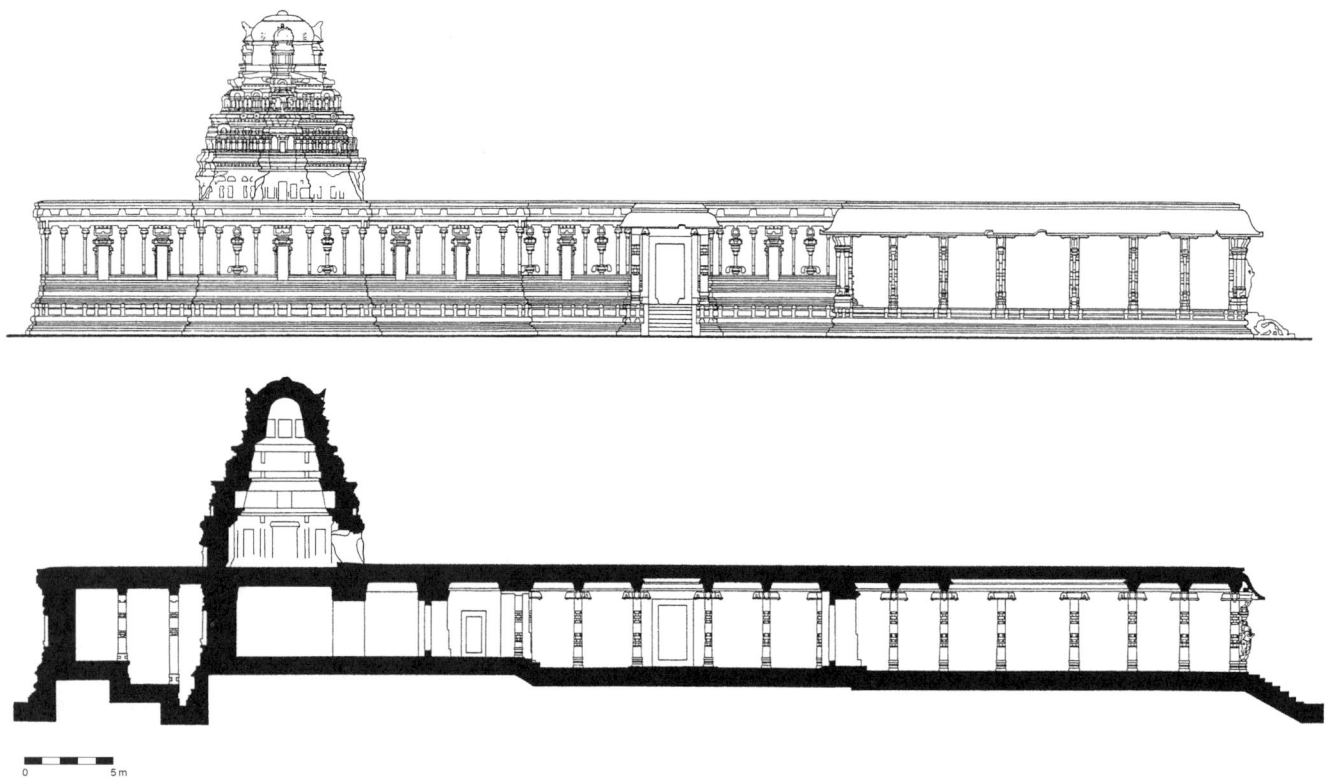
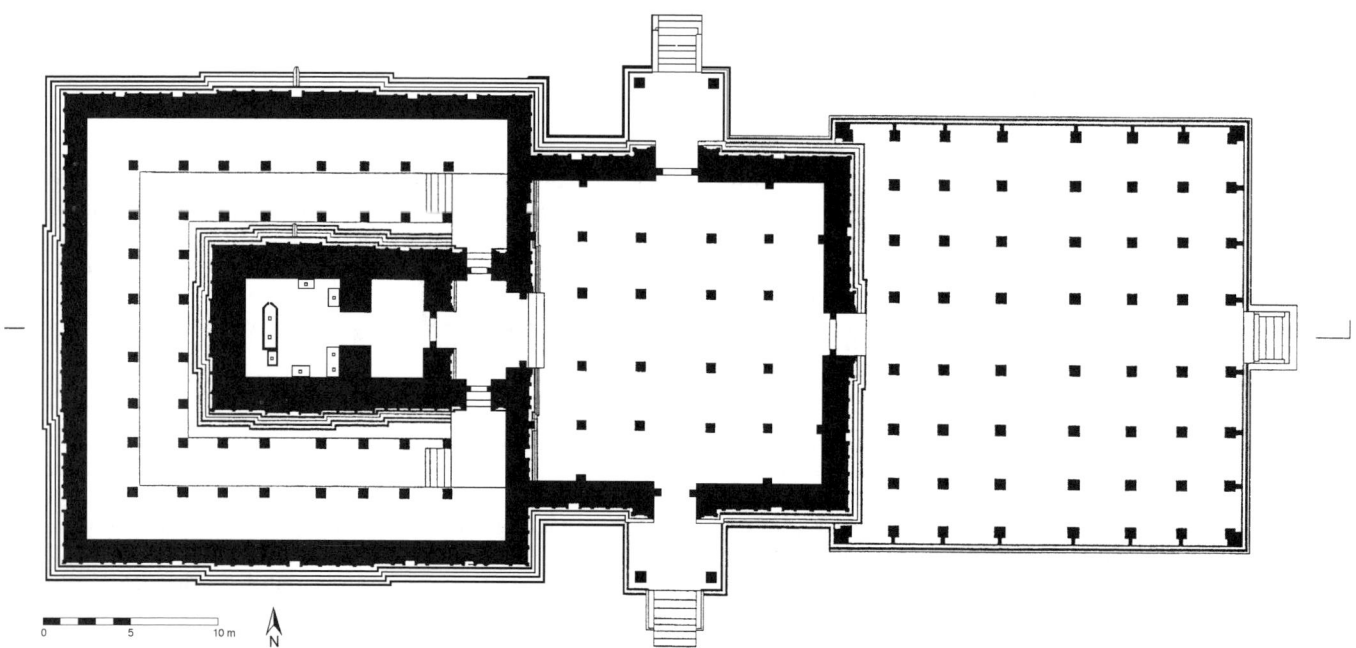

Figure 5.77. VMS-237, Pattabhirama complex, main temple—plan and sections (illustration courtesy of Vijayanagara Research Project).

Plate 5.62. VMS-237, Pattabhirama temple complex; overview from south showing major gateways and structures within compound.

Plate 5.63. VMS-237, Pattabhirama temple complex; view of eastern gateway from VMS-236.

Plate 5.64. VMS-237, Pattabhirama temple complex, main temple.

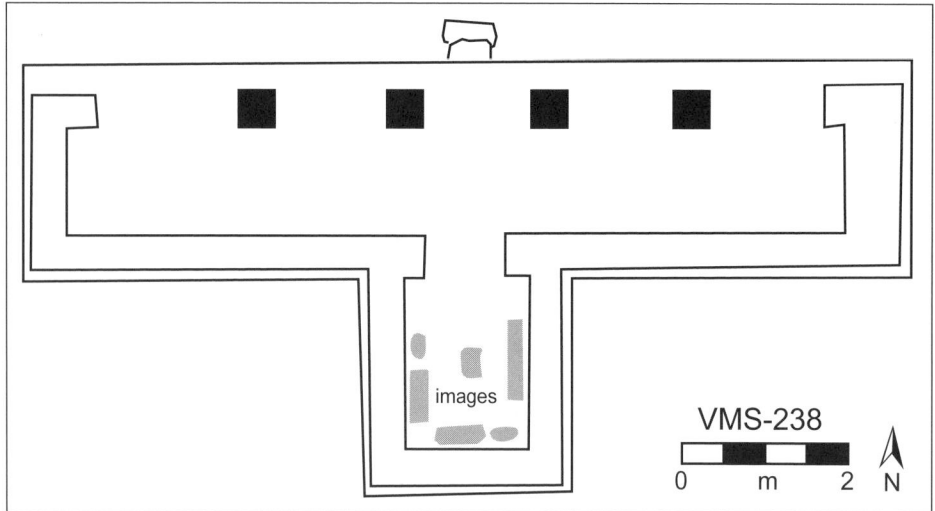

Figure 5.78. VMS-238, plan.

SITE: VMS-238 Block: S Transect: 6
  Primary Site Use: Religious: temple.
  Site Dimensions: 5 × 10.5 m
  Setting: Level irrigated fields below Kamalapuram reservoir, VMS-231.
  Present Land Use/Disturbances: The temple is currently in worship and is heavily whitewashed. Three sides have been rebuilt and/or repaired.
  Site Description: Small north-facing Vaishnava temple. VMS-238 consists of a sanctuary and a 6 × 2 column mandapa. This shrine is located in a linear arrangement with VMS-255, VMS-239, and VMS-240, defining a possible transportation route through the irrigated zone below the Kamalapuram reservoir into the city.
  The mandapa was originally 6 × 2 columns but only four of the north columns remain freestanding; the others are incorporated into modern walls. Column bases are carved into the rectangular pillars, which have double octagonal insets. The square faces of the columns have carved figures including Narasimha, geese, turtles, wrestlers, lotus, chakra, conch, bidents, nagas, half moon, and other anthropomorphic and geometric designs. Capitals are cruciform with beveled scrolls and two rectangular steps. Each side of the capital bears a teardrop-shaped carving on the beveled surface rising to the scroll. Above the capitals, rectangular beams support a slab ceiling. Eave supports project over the front columns. The roof is recent. However, a merlon carved with chakra, conch, and bident, probably from the original roof, lies in the sanctuary.
  The 2 × 2 columned sanctuary is heavily rebuilt and has a recent floor and walls. The doorway is inset from the two center columns (of the back row) of the mandapa. A lotus is carved on the threshold. The door is simply decorated with geometric designs; door sockets are present. Columns within the sanctuary are simple with half-cruciform capitals. The ceiling is composed of two rotated squares with a carved lotus in the center.
  Within the sanctuary are five sculpted images. These include: (1) a large (1.5 m × 0.75 m × 0.35 m) Hanuman; (2) a smaller Lakshmi Narasimha; (3) carved devotee feet; (4) a small Hanuman facing another broken panel; and (5) a large panel with a carved Garuda, a seated male (Rama?), and Hanuman. The original provenience of these remnants is unknown.
  Artifacts: 100% collection. 100 g ceramics; wares: 15 black plain ware, 6 brown plain ware.
  Temporal Affiliation: Vijayanagara.
  References: Morrison 1995:78.
  Illustrations: Figure 5.78; Plate 5.65.

Plate 5.65. VMS-238, Hanuman image, currently in worship.

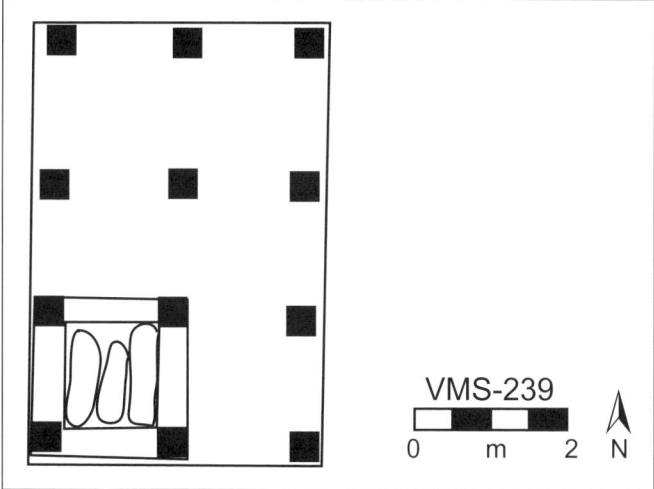

Figure 5.79. VMS-239, plan.

Plate 5.66. VMS-239, detail of column and capital.

SITE: VMS-239   Block: S   Transect: 6
Primary Site Use: Religious: shrine.
Site Dimensions: 6 × 4 m
Setting: Level irrigated fields below Kamalapuram reservoir, VMS-231.
Present Land Use/Disturbances: A recent canal running along the west side of the structure is connected to it by a slab and cement step. Several roof slabs are missing.
Site Description: 3 × 4 column mandapa with a slab floor and roof. This small mandapa lies below the Kamalapuram reservoir and may have been on a road connecting VMS-255, 238, 239, and 240, leading to the city.

The columns in this structure are highly variable in form and capital type. Column forms include: square with two inset octagonal sections; square with flat panels inscribed with lotuses; and plain square-sectioned columns. Capitals are disc-shaped, cruciform, rectangular, or square. Carved column decorations include lotuses, a coiled naga, and a Narasimha. A solidly constructed raised platform is located in the southwest corner of the structure. Traces of plaster, cement, and brick are still visible.

The mandapa presents its most elaborate facade to the west, with two ornate capitals and one ornate column; the north side of the structure also presents a facade of matched columns.
Artifacts: A sparse, localized ceramic scatter is visible amid dense vegetation. No collections made.
Temporal Affiliation: Vijayanagara.
References: Morrison 1995:77-78.
Illustrations: Figure 5.79; Plate 5.66.

SITE: VMS-240   Block: S   Transect: 6
Primary Site Use: Agricultural/transport: well.
Site Dimensions: 3 × 3 m
Setting: Level irrigated fields and aquatic vegetation.
Present Land Use/Disturbances: A recent irrigation canal bisects the well, destroying all but the west side.
Site Description: Well. This damaged well is located between the urban core wall and the Kamalapuram reservoir in an area of intensive cultivation. This site is located c. 45 m from VMS-239, and is aligned with VMS-239 and VMS-255 along the route of a probable road into the city. The well is built of up to five courses of well-dressed quarried blocks. Two slabs protrude from the west two courses above the top of the east-west wall. At the top of the wall is a large slab, fixed on its side. The layout of this well is obscured by recent construction.
Artifacts: 100% collection; no artifacts recovered.
Temporal Affiliation: Vijayanagara.
References: Morrison 1995:78.

SITE: VMS-241   Block: S   Transect: 2
Primary Site Use: Agricultural: reservoir embankment.
Site Dimensions: 240 × 10 m
Setting: Gently sloping valley between outcrops amid irrigated fields.
Present Land Use/Disturbances: This reservoir embankment lies between two recent canals: the High Level and Right Bank Main Canals. Although these recent constructions and the earlier Basavana Canal have altered the local drainage, the embankment continues to function, though solely to feed water into the Basavana Canal. An irrigation ditch runs parallel to the embankment and cuts into its east side. Sections of a cement structure are located near the midpoint of the embankment. A path truncates the embankment on the north side; the east side is dug out in several places.
Site Description: Reservoir embankment. This reservoir embankment blocks a narrow valley south of VMS-231. It is constructed of earth faced with masonry on the west side. There are three sluices. The stepped masonry face is composed of fourteen courses of rectangular blocks and cobbles, some fairly irregular but all laid horizontally. Cut blocks cluster near the sluices. The embankment is highest near the middle. An occasional rectangular slab is placed to protrude from the masonry face.

Silting has been minimal, and the base of sluice 1 is still visible. The latter consists of two uprights (c. 3 m high), square in section, connected by a lower crossbeam still *in situ*. Atop the uprights is a plain dressed rectangular slab that supports a slightly larger slab with moldings (two stepped with convex bevel and half medallions). There are traces of some brick construction between the embankment and the

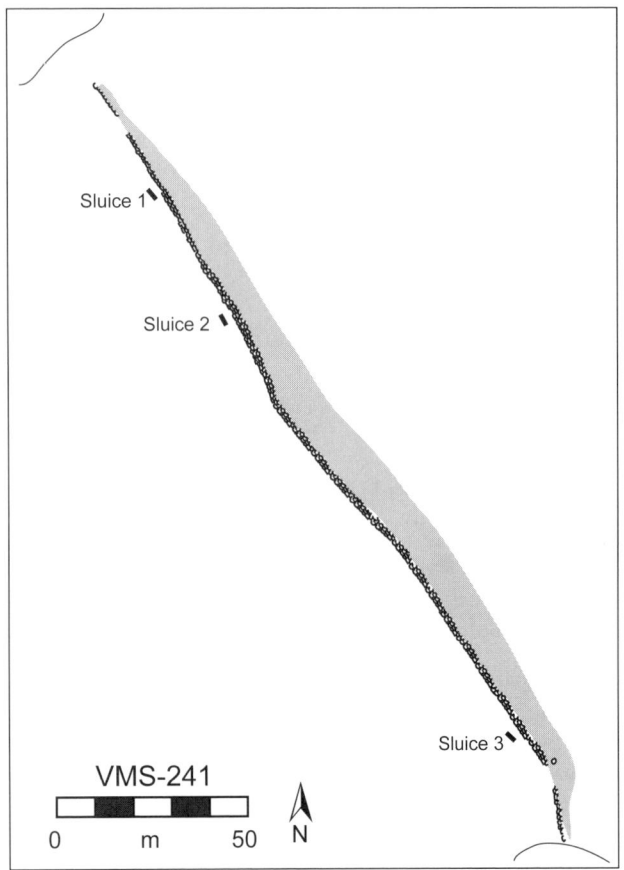

Figure 5.80. VMS-241, plan, including locations of sluices S1-S3.

Plate 5.67. VMS-241, sluice 3.

sluice. A long slab defines the beginning of the tunnel leading to the channel under the sluice.

Sluice 2 is still functioning. It is only c. 1.5 m high and plainly constructed with no dressing or molding. The end of the sluice channel (stone slabs covered by a brick and cement cap) is partly exposed where it feeds water into the Basavana Canal. A recessed staircase of nine steps is set into the embankment opposite the sluice.

Sluice 3, near the south end of the embankment, is similar to sluice 1. Although remnants of a tunnel are visible, it does not appear to be in use.

Artifacts: Scatter is sparse, localized, and variable. 100% collection on the embankment and in a 5 m circumference around its base. <50 g ceramics; wares: 4 black plain ware, 1 brown plain ware. Diagnostics: 1 bowl.

Temporal Affiliation: Vijayanagara.
References: Morrison 1995:91.
Illustrations: Figure 5.80; Plate 5.67.

SITE: VMS-242   Block: S   Transect: 8-11
Primary Site Use: Agricultural: reservoir embankment.
Site Dimensions: 650 × 230 m
Setting: Gently sloping outcrop and valley.
Present Land Use/Disturbances: Cut by the Right Bank High Level Canal. Associated debris obscures much of the surrounding area. Several cart roads cross the irrigated bed.
Site Description: Reservoir embankment. This massive mounded earthen embankment is faced with masonry on the south side. This facility would have irrigated the level plain to the north, eventually draining into the Kamalapuram reservoir (VMS-231). The embankment is remarkably high, up to 4 m above the present bed. It has been seriously disturbed by canal construction and does not now hold any water. The canal not only cut deeply into the landscape, but huge piles of debris are piled on either side of it. Near the largest breach in the embankment, the amount of backdirt is greatly increased by the fill of the embankment, which had to be moved aside to make way for the canal.

The preserved masonry consists of up to seventeen irregular courses of unshaped or split boulders of pinkish granite. A few protruding slabs form steps, but there are no visible staircases. Masonry similar to that found on the south also faces the northern downstream face of the embankment.

On both ends, outcrops form natural extensions of the embankment; two wing walls run north from these outcrops. The west wall is more massively constructed, consisting of up to seven masonry courses. The ground level is higher west of this west side wall. The east side wall closes off a small gap in the outcrop and is constructed of up to four courses.

A reservoir of this size probably originally had more than the one sluice that remains today. The sluice consists of two roughly dressed, square uprights joined by a middle cross bar with a center hole. Lintel elements are roughly dressed but have a single step angled bevel upper and lower molding. Between the embankment and the sluice is a rectangular arrangement of piled boulders. These must overlie the sluice tunnel.

Artifacts: Artifact scatter sparse, localized, and variable. No collections made. Two worked lithics were observed, a milky white vein quartz flake (possibly bipolar) with minimal modification and a gray quartz bipolar core.

Temporal Affiliation: Vijayanagara.
References: Morrison 1995:91, 102.
Illustrations: Plate 5.68.

SITE: VMS-243   Block: S   Transect: 2
Primary Site Use: Residential: rock shelter.
Site Dimensions: 4 × 10 m
Setting: Side of steeply sloping outcrop.
Present Land Use/Disturbances: Modern artifacts are found within the shelter; there is evidence for recent animal burrowing and erosion.

Plate 5.68. VMS-242, reservoir embankment, cut by recent canal construction; note stone facing on west (left) of image.

Site Description: Small (2 × 3 m), northwest-facing rock shelter situated on the north slope of a steep outcrop. The associated artifact scatter contains a high density of ceramics, charcoal, ash, and recent artifacts including a horseshoe, bottle cap, and fragments of plastic. Traces of burned earth occur in one part of the shelter, a possible hearth. This shelter appears to be a locus of repeated short-term occupations as an agricultural, pastoral, and/or transient camp. A limited range of domestic activities exceeding those associated with day-use rock shelters appear to have occurred here.

Artifacts: Very dense ceramic scatter, mostly recently broken modern ceramics. Two 2 × 2 m judgment units were collected. J1 is located 3 m north (downslope) of shelter area; J2 encompasses most of shelter interior.

J1: 700 g ceramics; wares: 151 black plain ware, 2 red plain ware, 12 brown plain ware.

J2: 700 g ceramics; wares: 24 black plain ware, 10 red plain ware, 11 brown plain ware. Diagnostics: 1 bowl, 6 jars.

Temporal Affiliation: Recent.

SITE: VMS-244 Block: S Transect: 2
   Primary Site Use: Transport: road.
   Site Dimensions: 115 × 3 m
   Setting: Along the edge of a steep outcrop.
   Present Land Use/Disturbances: No recent cultural features. Both ends of the road are eroded.
   Site Description: North-south oriented road. This site consists of an elevated (0.2-0.3 m) packed earth and gravel surface lined on either side with coursed masonry, of up to four courses of large cobbles and small boulders. In a few places, the walls have two faces, but most have only a single, exterior face. The road surface is only 2-2.5 m wide, tracking a relatively level bench on a high granitic outcrop. The south end of the road runs into a very steep hill slope and is badly broken by a drainage channel. It may be that this road was meant to facilitate movement around the outcrop by leading traffic to this drainage channel. The north end of the road also abuts a drainage. There are no indications of paths or roads on the lower part of the outcrop; the most accessible route is through the drainage.
   Artifacts: Two separate modern pot breaks occur on high outcrop to the south of the site; no collections made.
   Temporal Affiliation: Unknown, probably Vijayanagara.
   Illustrations: Figure 5.81; Plate 5.69.

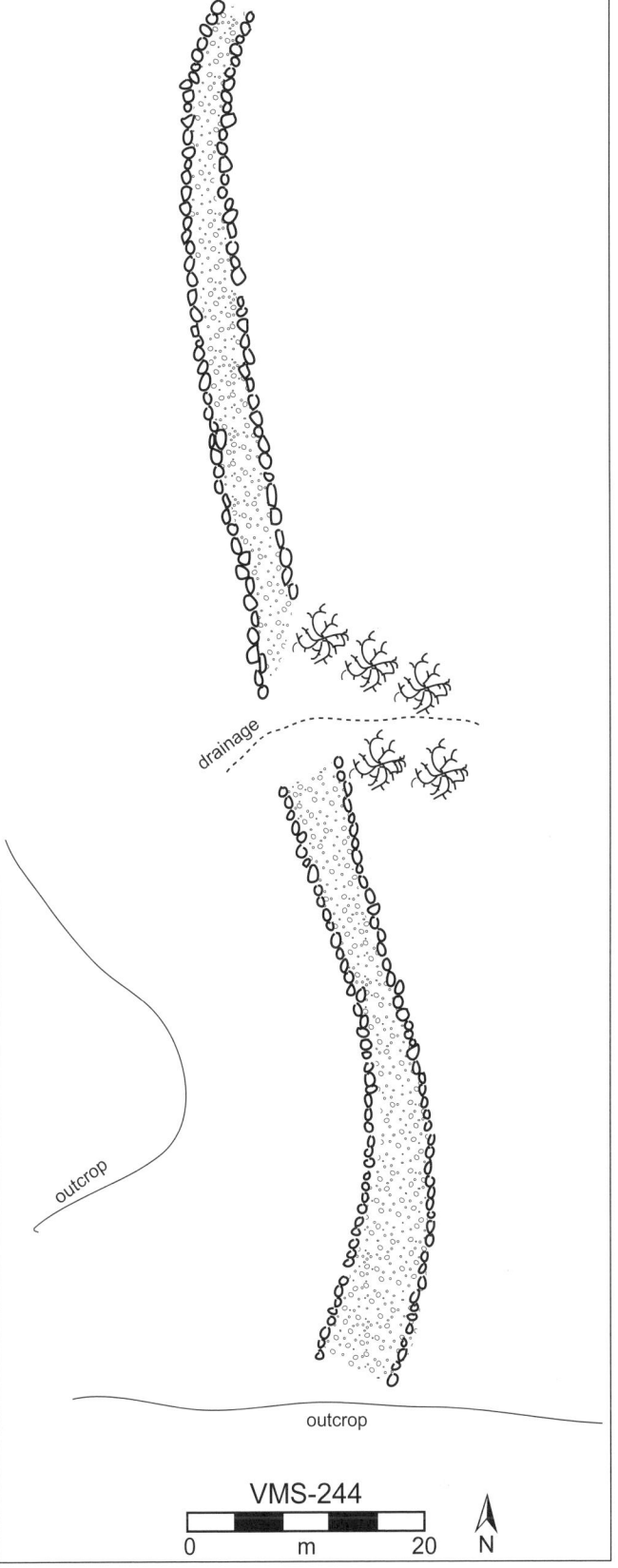

Figure 5.81. VMS-244, plan.

Plate 5.69. VMS-244, road bed and boundary walls.

Plate 5.70. VMS-245, soil control wall.

SITE: VMS-245   Block: S   Transect: 2
Primary Site Use: Agricultural: isolated wall.
Site Dimensions: 26 × 1 m
Setting: Gently sloping area.
Present Land Use/Disturbances: Minimal. A bullock cart road runs along the wall.
Site Description: Single-course retaining wall situated at the base of an outcrop. Large unmodified cobbles are placed end to end to form the wall face. The wall is in good condition except at its south end where several elements are missing. This wall checks soil erosion; a well-developed terrace is located behind the wall.
Artifacts: 100% collection. <50 g ceramics; wares: 2 brown plain ware.
Temporal Affiliation: Unknown.
Illustrations: Plate 5.70.

SITE: VMS-246   Block: S   Transect: 2
Primary Site Use: Residential/unknown: artifact scatter.
Site Dimensions: 40 × 30 m
Setting: Level irrigated field.
Present Land Use/Disturbances: Massive soil movement and excavation resulting from irrigation and plowing.
Site Description: Artifact scatter located in a broad, level area south of the Kamalapuram reservoir embankment (VMS-231). The scatter includes both Vijayanagara period and recent artifacts. Site function is unclear; the scatter could be the remains of manuring activities or debris from habitation.
Artifacts: Sparse, even scatter of earthenware ceramics, with occasional modern artifacts. One piece of slag was also noted. Some of the sherds are highly worn and eroded; others are in good condition. Systematic collections were not possible since the field was planted in sugar cane when documented. A diagnostic sweep was conducted.
Temporal Affiliation: Vijayanagara, recent.

SITE: VMS-247   Block: S   Transect: 3
Primary Site Use: Defensive: circular bastion.
Site Dimensions: 10 m diameter
Setting: In an area of level irrigated fields.
Present Land Use/Disturbances: Partially dismantled for use in a recent wall that abuts the bastion. A dirt road runs past the west edge of the site.
Site Description: Circular bastion. The c. 10 m diameter bastion is built of up to eight courses of square, quarried blocks (some dressed) and unmodified cobbles. Larger stones form the lower courses. Coursing is loose and irregular with many chinking stones. There is no clear entrance.
Artifacts: Very poor visibility; no artifacts observed; no collections made.
Temporal Affiliation: Vijayanagara or post-Vijayanagara.
References: Morrison 1995:64.

SITE: VMS-248   Block: S   Transect: 7
Primary Site Use: Agricultural: wall.
Site Dimensions: 24 × 0.5 m
Setting: In a gently sloping area on an outcrop.
Present Land Use/Disturbances: A modern path truncates the west edge of the site and an erosion channel runs along the east and west edges of the wall.
Site Description: Retaining wall. This retaining wall extends along the top of an outcrop, in a northeast-southwest orientation. It is composed of a single course of unmodified medium to large cobbles, and is only one element wide. The wall serves to limit soil erosion into the large natural water drainage to its south. The feature may have served as an agricultural terrace; there is no evidence of recent use.
Artifacts: None observed; no collections made.
Temporal Affiliation: Unknown.

SITE: VMS-249   Block: S   **Transect:** 7
Primary Site Use: Unknown/residential: lithic scatter.
Site Dimensions: 102 × 50 m
Setting: Gently sloping colluvium.
Present Land Use/Disturbances: Minimal disturbance. The area is currently used for grazing.
Site Description: Lithic scatter. The site is situated on an east-facing, gentle slope running between a large, north-south oriented drainage and low outcrops to the west. Raw materials present include: translucent white, milky white, light and dark gray vein quartz; green quartzite; volcanics; and chert. Lithics predominate, although two sherds were found in T6/2. Temporal and functional affiliation is unknown. Formal tools appear to be absent, with the scatter consisting of flakes, angular debris, bipolar debris, and cores. Remnants of several modern hearths are located in the northwest quarter of the site, probably a result of day use by shepherds. However, no remains of transient camps are visible. This site lies just to the southwest of the bed of VMS-242, a large Vijayanagara period reservoir embankment, which is now in use for grazing. A judgmental sample (J2) was taken to include the entire range of raw material variation present at the site. An extensive, diffuse scatter occurs throughout the drainage; the area designated as VMS-249 was in the most continuous and densest part of this distribution.

Artifacts: Moderate, evenly distributed lithic scatter. Vegetation inhibits visibility. Seven east-west oriented transects were laid out, at intervals of 20 m. Three 2 × 2 m units were surface collected along each transect (also at 20 m intervals). A 2 × 2 m judgment unit (J1) was placed along transect 3, at 29-31 m from its eastern edge. A similar unit was placed at 28-30 m on transect 5 (J3). In addition, crew members walked over the entire site to collect additional diagnostic artifacts (J2).

The following units contained artifacts:

Transect 1 Unit 1: Lithics: 13 flakes, 10 fragments angular debris, 1 core, 6 bipolar cores (all of quartz).

Transect 1 Unit 2: Lithics: 2 flakes, 2 fragments angular debris, 1 bipolar core (all of quartz).

Transect 1 Unit 3: Lithics: 2 flakes, 8 fragments angular debris, 2 bipolar cores (all of quartz).

Transect 2 Unit 1: Lithics: 1 flake, 3 fragments angular debris, 1 bipolar core (all of quartz).

Transect 2 Unit 2: Lithics: 3 flakes, 28 fragments angular debris, 2 bipolar cores (all of quartz).

Transect 2 Unit 3: Lithics: 5 flakes, 33 fragments angular debris, 4 bipolar cores (all of quartz).

Transect 3 Unit 1: Lithics: 1 fragment angular debris (quartz).

Transect 3 Unit 2: Lithics: 8 flakes, 16 fragments angular debris, 4 bipolar cores (all of quartz).

Transect 4 Unit 1: Lithics: 2 flakes, 4 fragments angular debris (all of quartz).

Transect 4 Unit 2: Lithics: 1 flake (quartz).

Transect 5 Unit 1: Lithics: utilized flake (black and gray banded chert), 3 fragments angular debris (quartz).

Transect 5 Unit 2: Lithics: 2 flakes, 8 fragments angular debris (all of quartz).

Transect 5 Unit 3: Lithics: 1 fragment angular debris, 2 bipolar cores (all of quartz).

Transect 6 Unit 0: Lithics: 2 flakes (1 quartz, 1 volcanic), 3 fragments angular debris (quartz), 1 biopolar core (quartz).

Transect 6 Unit 1: Lithics: 1 flake, 12 fragments angular debris, 2 bipolar cores (all of quartz).

Transect 6 Unit 2: Ceramics: <50 g; wares: 3 black plain ware. Lithics: 22 flakes (4 volcanic, 18 quartz), 36 fragments angular debris (1 volcanic, 35 quartz), 4 bipolar cores (quartz).

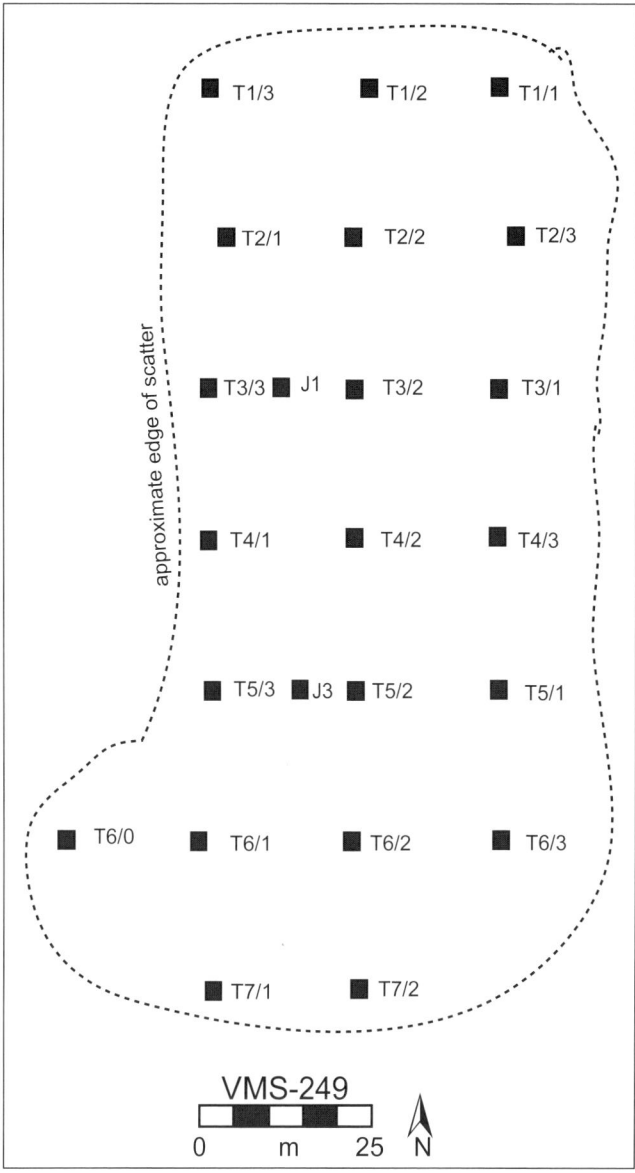

Figure 5.82. VMS-249, plan, showing approximate site boundaries and collection units.

Transect 7 Unit 1: Lithics: 2 flakes, 6 fragments angular debris, 1 bipolar core (all of quartz).

Transect 7 Unit 2: 8 flakes (6 quartz, 2 volcanic), 34 fragments angular debris (33 quartz, 1 volcanic), 2 cores (quartz), 2 bipolar cores (quartz).

Judgment Unit 1: Lithics: 28 flakes (27 quartz, 1 cryptocrystalline stone), 1 utilized flake (quartz), 27 fragments angular debris, 2 cores, 13 bipolar cores (all of quartz).

Judgment Unit 2: Lithics: 11 utilized flakes (3 chert, 3 cryptocrystalline stone, 2 volcanic, 3 quartz), 1 scraper (quartz), 1 core (chert).

Judgment Unit 3: Lithics: 7 flakes (quartz), 1 utilized flake (cryptocrystalline stone), 31 fragments angular debris (quartz), 1 core (quartz), 6 bipolar cores (quartz).

Temporal Affiliation: Unknown.
Illustrations: Figure 5.82.

SITE: VMS-250 Block: S Transect: 7
  Primary Site Use: Agricultural: erosion control wall.
  Site Dimensions: 33 × 0.4 m
  Setting: Gently sloping valley amid outcrops.
  Present Land Use/Disturbances: Uncultivated but heavily grazed.
  Site Description: Low retaining wall. This feature is constructed of three to four irregular courses of unshaped small cobbles; coursing is slightly stepped. The wall prevents soil from eroding into a seasonal drainage to the east; sediment is built up behind the wall. The stones are all stained white with calcium carbonate.
  Artifacts: 100% collection. <50 g ceramics; wares: 2 black plain ware.
  Temporal Affiliation: Unknown.

SITE: VMS-251 Block: S Transect: 7
  Primary Site Use: Residential/unknown: artifact scatter.
  Site Dimensions: 2 × 2 m
  Setting: Gently sloping terrace on outcrop.
  Present Land Use/Disturbances: Area is uncultivated and used for grazing. A footpath runs south of the site.
  Site Description: Localized, high density ceramic scatter. This small scatter, which includes some lithics, is situated in a small, relatively flat area ringed by boulders near the peak of an outcrop overlooking the small valley containing VMS-248, VMS-249, and VMS-250. The site is situated in a landscape characterized by a generalized, low density ceramic scatter. Lithic scatter VMS-249 is located to the southeast. The large boulders surrounding this scatter may define a windbreak or day-use shelter. The ceramics in the scatter are highly fragmented, suggesting repeated trampling.
  Artifacts: High density localized ceramic scatter. Very low density beyond the site area. A 2 × 2 m judgment unit was collected, covering almost the entire site area. 850 g ceramics; wares: 193 black plain ware. Diagnostics: 1 bowl, 6 jars. Lithics: 1 flake (quartz).
  Temporal Affiliation: Unknown.

SITE: VMS-252 Block: S Transect: 14
  Primary Site Use: Religious: temple.
  Site Dimensions: 8 × 8 m
  Setting: Level area inside the city wall.
  Present Land Use/Disturbances: A modern shrine with ancient sculptural elements is located 2 m to the east of the temple. This area has been used as a dump for field clearing and trash. The structure is located near the modern Hampi Camp road.
  Site Description: Small southwest-facing temple. This two-chamber temple is located c. 80 m north of the Pattabhirama temple (VMS-237). It may have faced onto a road leading to the domed gateway in the urban core wall. The shrine consists of a porch and a sanctuary. The porch was 4 × 4 columns but now only the four center columns (rectangular with octagonal insets) are standing. Other elements, including blocks, ceiling elements and cruciform capitals, are scattered throughout the area. Basement slabs set on edge define the exterior edges of the structure. Slabs also define the small sanctuary.
  A short, single-course, double-faced wall composed of small cobbles is located southeast of the shrine. No sculptures are presently associated with the temple; however, several displaced sculptural elements are located in the nearby modern shrine, including naga stones, devotee feet, and an anthropomorphic figure. Near the shrine are broken molding fragments. A 3 × 3 × 2.5 m deep rock-cut well lies 50 m northeast of

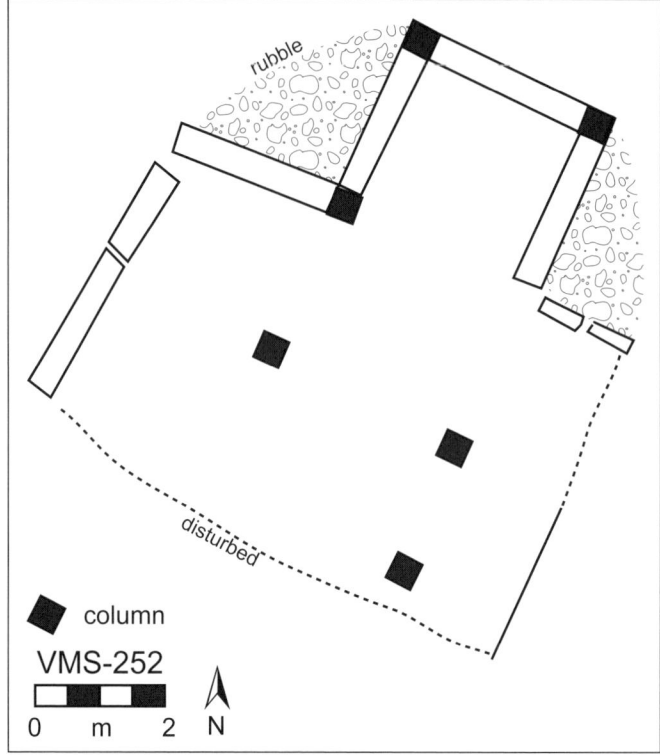

Figure 5.83. VMS-252, plan.

the temple. A ramp into the well begins on the east side and continues down the north face to the bottom.
  Artifacts: Recent trash obscures any older artifact scatter. No collections made.
  Temporal Affiliation: Vijayanagara.
  Illustrations: Figure 5.83.

SITE: VMS-253 Block: S Transect: 14
  Primary Site Use: Religious: shrine.
  Site Dimensions: 3 × 3 m
  Setting: Level colluvium inside city wall.
  Present Land Use/Disturbances: A row of abandoned and fallen structures runs the length of transect 14. Modern concrete surfaces, artifacts (tile, plastics, etc.) and earthenware ceramics are scattered around the site. The north and west sides of the shrine have been recently walled. Numerous small hearths are found within the structure.
  Site Description: Shrine. This small 2 × 2 columned south-facing structure has plain columns, which are square in section. Only the southwest column has a single cutout section in the middle. Capitals are rough rectangular blocks. On the south side, two large upright slabs abut the interior edge of the columns, forming the sides of a 0.95 m wide door. The door slabs display Shaivite door guardians, and Ganesha is carved on the lintel. The three other sides may have been originally open, although modern walls now enclose the north and west. The roof consists of a single rotated triangle covered by long rectangular slabs. The entire structure is set on a plain basement slab, most of which is buried in rubble. East of the shrine is a rubble mound. It is not clear if the mound forms a structure or if it is a waste pile.

(*Above*) Plate 5.71. VMS-253, shrine.

(*Right*) Figure 5.84. VMS-254, plan and location of collection units.

Artifacts: Sparse to moderate, localized scatter of earthenware ceramics and modern artifacts. No collections made because of prevalence of recent debris.
Temporal Affiliation: Vijayanagara.
Illustrations: Plate 5.71.

SITE: VMS-254   Block: S   **Transect:** 14
   Primary Site Use: Religious: temple complex.
   Site Dimensions: 23 × 21 m estimated; 10 × 9 cm extant
   Setting: Level irrigated fields inside city wall.
   Present Land Use/Disturbances: Soil deposition has obscured all but 0.6-0.9 m of the upper basement molding. The structure is partially dismantled and only portions of the enclosure, basement, and brick cores of the antechamber walls remain.
   Site Description: North-facing Vijayanagara temple. The sectarian affiliation of this heavily disturbed temple is unknown. Its construction and workmanship are comparable with many elaborate temples in the city core, suggesting that this was once a fairly prominent structure. It consists of two parts: an antechamber and a sanctuary. The antechamber is 9 m east-west by 6 m north-south and when documented, was piled with palm fronds, chunks of brick, and rubble. It is constructed on a basement with an upper molding of the two stepped with convex bevel type set over a plain, inset vertical face. The sanctuary is 3 × 3 m and is undecorated. Both rooms are walled; walls have brick and plaster cores faced with large, well-dressed rectangular blocks that are closely fit and evenly coursed.

The temple is capped by a brick and plaster superstructure (shikara) with ornate stucco designs including human figures, geometric designs, and miniature temples. There are four plaster tiers leading to a round, domelike top. Just north and west of the sanctuary is a north-south oriented wall segment of large rectangular, well-dressed blocks. Some brick is present on the east (outer) side.

In the surrounding fields are several displaced elements including two elaborate chlorite moldings (two steps with convex bevel and lower wavy outline), and a possible balustrade (central lotus flanked by two pilasters).
   Artifacts: Dense earthenware ceramic scatter in structure and surrounding fields. The site is located in an area of high background artifact density. Brick debris is scattered 20-30 m from the structure.

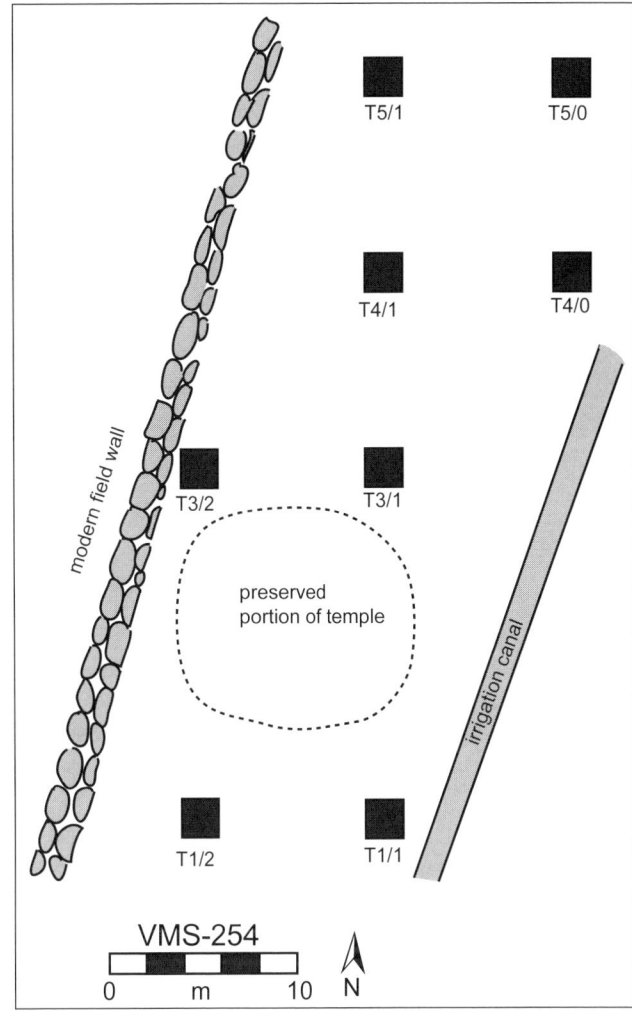

Five east-west oriented collection transects were laid out in the fields surrounding the structure, at 20 m intervals. Two 2 × 2 m units were collected along each transect (see site plan). A diagnostic collection of rim sherds was made across the entire site area, but yielded only one sherd. The following units contained artifacts:

Transect 1 Unit 1: 500 g ceramics; wares: 36 black plain ware, 1 red plain ware, 6 brown plain ware, 4 black decorated plain ware. Diagnostics: 7 bowls, 1 jar, 1 ceramic water pipe.

Transect 1 Unit 2: 100 g ceramics; wares: 9 black plain ware, 1 red plain ware, 1 red burnished ware. Diagnostics: 1 bowl, 2 jars.

Transect 3 Unit 1: 50 g ceramics; wares: 3 black plain ware. Diagnostics: 1 bowl, 1 jar.

Transect 3 Unit 2: 300 g ceramics; wares: 22 black plain ware, 2 red plain ware, 1 brown plain ware. Diagnostics: 1 bowl, 5 jars, 1 ceramic water pipe.

Transect 4 Unit 0: 200 g ceramics; wares: 23 black plain ware, 1 red plain ware. Diagnostics: 3 jars.

Transect 4 Unit 1: 200 g ceramics; wares: 17 black plain ware, 4 black burnished ware, 1 black decorated plain ware. Diagnostics: 2 jars.

Transect 5 Unit 0: 450 g ceramics; wares: 30 black plain ware, 1 brown plain ware, 7 coarse ware. Diagnostics: 2 bowls, 3 jars.

Transect 5 Unit 1: 150 g ceramics; wares: 15 black plain ware, 1 brown plain ware, 1 red burnished ware. Diagnostics: 2 jars.
   Temporal Affiliation: Vijayanagara.
   Illustrations: Figure 5.84; Plate 5.72.

Plate 5.72. VMS-254, shikara.

SITE: VMS-255 Block: S Transect: 6
Primary Site Use: Unknown: platform.
Site Dimensions: 3 × 2.75 m
Setting: Level irrigated fields immediately below Kamalapuram reservoir, VMS-231.
Present Land Use/Disturbances: In worship. The structure is whitewashed, and green flags tied to poles indicate its current Islamic affiliation.
Site Description: Rectangular platform. This may have been a 3 × 2 column mandapa, but no trace of a superstructure remains. The platform is built on a pavement of roughly dressed rectangular slabs. The slabs extend 0.5-0.6 m out from all sides of the platform, forming a walkway around the east, south, and west sides. Some of the south and west slabs are missing. Atop the basement, the side of the platform consists of alternate inset rectangles and protruding narrow piers (all formed of rectangular blocks, which are now plastered and painted). The north face is formed of a single large block. This structure lies c. 70 m north of the embankment of VMS-231 and was probably located on a road leading north from the road that runs over the embankment. Scattered elements (a dressed slab, a molding) lie to the west of the structure.
Artifacts: Scatter is sparse, localized, and variable. No collections made.
Temporal Affiliation: Vijayanagara.
References: Morrison 1995:78.

SITE: VMS-256 Block: S Transect: 7-8
Primary Site Use: Defensive/transport: Kamalapuram fort gate complex.
Site Dimensions: 50 × 26 m
Setting: Level area inside Kamalapuram village.
Present Land Use/Disturbances: Recent additions and repairs have modified some structures; this area appears to have been in continuous use since its construction. Feature 1 is in worship and the mandapas on either side of the gate have been partly enclosed. Feature 3 is now an occupied house.

Site Description: Gate complex. This complex apparently formed the main access route into the Vijayanagara-era Kamalapuram fort. The construction of the present gate is clearly of the late Vijayanagara period, based on the columns in the passage. Feature 3 and VMS-257 may date to an earlier part of the Vijayanagara period. Feature 1 is more ambiguous; it may be middle Vijayanagara in date.

Flanking the gateway are two sections of massively built fortification wall, now incorporated into the recent wall enclosing the complex. These walls and associated features ensure that movement through the gate was highly constrained for at least 40 m. This gate passage leads directly to the large round tower, VMS-258 (c. 90 m south of the gate). A Hanuman temple (VMS-257) is located c. 20 m north of the gate. Other sections of the Kamalapuram fort wall (see VMS-259) are fragmentary; this feature provides the best evidence for the boundary of "old Kamalapur."

Feature 1 is an east-facing temple just inside the gate on the west side of the passage, known locally as the Nagareshwara temple. Feature 2 consists of two small shrines located along the east side of the passage inside the gate. Feature 3 is a mandapa located just south of Feature 1. It is now an occupied house and residents denied access to the interior. The exterior has been totally modified.

The gateway itself is monumental in scale, set in a section of east-west fortification wall. The wall is considerably different in construction than the gate and is built of quarried rectangular blocks with some chinking stones and brick. Blocks become longer, narrower and more finely dressed as one moves from the bottom to the top of the wall. The penultimate course of horizontally placed slabs protrudes outward slightly (c. 0.10 m), forming a narrow ledge. Sculpted panels are located at various places in the wall on its north (exterior) face. These are rather haphazardly placed and give the impression that the wall is constructed of reused elements. Square bastions flank the north side of the gate. The bastions are bonded to the wall segment described above, but are of different construction (see VMS-259).

The gate is heavily sculpted. Sculpted panels include horses and riders; stick dancers; a panel with Rama, Sita, and Lakshmana (enclosed in a recent shrine); and several elephants. On large rectangular blocks set on either side of the gateway are double-headed geese, each head holding an elephant in its beak and in each foot. On the east side of the gate is a panel with women drummers and a Lakshmi with elephants. There is a small elaborately carved door (with Shaivite door guardians) on this side, an alternate entrance to the larger gateway. A roof supported by simple curved brackets with pendant lotus buds extends out over the gate.

The gate passage is paved with well-worn rectangular slabs. Just inside the gate, on the north side, are massive door sockets. On either side of the passage are columned, raised plinths. On the east, the small exterior doorway leads to a narrow L-shaped passage and then into the main gate passage. Along the passage are ornate late Vijayanagara columns; on the north is a rearing yali; on the south are semidetached pilasters. This mandapa is enclosed in a modern wall. Capital types vary, some simple rectangles, others with more ornate curved designs. The basement of the plinth is constructed of a footing course and a lower molding (two stepped with convex bevel, with occasional square sections) followed by an inset vertical face. This is followed by a second vertical course with carvings of women playing drums and dancing. The upper molding matches the lower.

The west side of the passage is similar, though here the plinth extends the entire length of the passage and the mandapa is much deeper, extending four to six columns back to define a space now heavily subdivided. Panels here depict stick dancers, men and women dancing, and scenes of courtly life. Another panel shows the goddess Saraswati riding a large peacock and figures riding elephants. The mandapa on this side has also been walled. One can discern thickly plastered and painted figures carved on interior columns, including Nandi and lingam.

A subsidiary shrine is located behind (northwest of) Feature 1. It now abuts the west gate mandapa, but may have been built as a separate structure. This is not clear, given the extent of modern additions. This little shrine is raised on a plinth with an upper molding (two stepped with convex bevel and corner quarter medallions). The ground level here is 0.3 m higher than that in the gate passage; basement courses are not visible. Columns here are much simpler than those in the gate passage (square in section with two inset octagonal sections). Capitals are elaborate cruciforms with pendant lotus buds. The door is carved with Lakshmi and elephants above and Shaivite door guardians on either side. Three steps up to the shrine are flanked by elephant balustrades. The image is a recent goddess sitting under a ceiling of rotated squares.

Feature 1: Small and elaborate east-facing temple located just inside the gate on the west side of the passage. The entrance faces the southern shrine of Feature 2 (below). The subsidiary shrine described above appears to be associated with Feature 1; both are Shaivite and of similar style. Worshipers now visit both shrines. The temple is located within a walled enclosure, enclosed with large blocks on all sides except the east (which is enclosed by an ornately carved wooden screen). Wall exteriors are carved with several figures including a snake, two stylized fishes, two elephants with locked trunks (each backed up by another elephant), four turtles on a raised band, and a lion facing a boar with concentric circles and lotuses.

The two-chambered temple consists of a north-south oriented 4 × 3 column antechamber and a 2 × 2 column sanctuary. The antechamber is reached by a four step staircase flanked by yali balustrades. Against the staircase and the plinth is a recently constructed lower porch with four columns, obscuring the lower part of the basement. The lower and upper moldings are two stepped with convex bevel, the upper with half medallions. Moldings on the east and south facades are more elaborate and are separated by an inset vertical course with carved female musicians, dancers, and an elephant.

The exterior columns of the antechamber on the east side are square in section with inset octagonal sections and ornate cruciform capitals with pendant lotus buds. These columns are ornately carved with linga and unidentified (heavily plastered) anthropomorphic figures. The columns flanking the door are unusual. Of quite small proportions, the shaft is octagonal, carved all of a piece with the capital and base. Atop the column is a second capital, an elaborate cruciform with pendant lotus buds. The interior columns of the antechamber include plain columns as well as ones that are square with two octagonal insets. The lower parts of the latter columns are carved with Nandi and linga (together and separately), Ganesha, Narasimha, lotus, and other zoomorphs and anthropomorphs. These columns have T-shaped lotus bud capitals. Bases are incorporated into the columns. Other columns are plain. The interior door is recent. The ceiling is composed of east-west oriented slabs resting on rectangular beams. A molding/shelf lines the interior wall, halfway up (two stepped with convex bevels, half medallions and corner quarter medallions). A large sculpted Nandi sits inside the antechamber facing the sanctuary.

The floor and walls of the largely intact sanctuary are newly tiled; it also has an interior shelf. The ceiling is constructed of rotated squares with a central lotus bud. The door is elaborately carved with floral and geometric motifs and flanked by Shaivite door guardians. A Shiva lingam is in worship within the sanctuary; a small (displaced) Ganesha image sits near the sanctuary door. A carved spout extends out from the sanctuary. On its north wall are two small windows.

The roof of the structure is delineated by triangular brackets that support simple angled eaves that are capped by a band of carved friezes depicting women dancers and musicians. Friezes occur on the mandapa's south and north sides, and on the north side of the sanctuary. On the east (facing the road) there is simply a flat face broken in the center by an ornate niche surrounding a lingam. Above the sculpted course are merlons, the latter most ornate on the east side.

Feature 2: Two small shrines located along the east side of the interior gate passage. The south shrine is located opposite the entrance to Feature 1 and contains the lamppost of that temple and a well-carved chlorite image base. The north shrine is miniature in scale, consisting of four columns set on a plastered and painted platform, each with a single, long inset octagonal section and topped by a small rectangular capital. These are joined by long slabs, on which is set a ceiling of rotated squares. A block with carved feet sits in front of the structure, and a lingam in the center. There is a recent, raised plinth joining the two shrines. It is edged by a displaced lamp pillar.

The south shrine is larger and is set on an original basement consisting of a foundation course followed by a lower molding (two stepped with convex bevel and corner quarter medallions). A matching upper molding follows an inset vertical course. This structure has evidently been altered as some corner elements now occur in the middle of the north face. The platform extends into a modern compound wall. It supports a small four-columned mandapa, similar to that on the north. The two east pillars are elaborately carved with pots, small inset sections, and carved attached pillar bases. These are topped by simple square capitals. The two pillars on the west are simpler, with only inset octagonal sections. There is a ceiling of rotated squares covered by a domed roof (probably recent). The whole thing is plastered and painted. A Vijayanagara-era Ganesha sits inside the structure. A high lamp column is located to the east of this structure. It has a square base, octagonal section and curved design near the top and is capped with a disc-shaped element, followed by a larger square element, which curves on its underside. Three naga stones lie nearby.

Feature 3: Small columned structure (3 columns east-west by 2 columns north-south) along the west side of the road inside the gate. This structure is completely enclosed within modern walls. The occupant refused access and no details of construction are available. The door of the house opens to the east; it is enclosed by an elaborately carved doorway with female donors or devotees carved on either side. The columns are ornate; round sections alternate with octagonal and square bands. Capitals are cruciform. There is no trace of the original basement. It is not clear that the door and columns were part of the same original structure. Column form suggests that Feature 3 may date to the early Vijayanagara period.

Artifacts: This area is currently in use and maintained; however, some Vijayanagara earthenware is present in the wall fill. One small piece of blue-on-white Chinese porcelain found c. 10 m north of the gateway. No collections made.

Temporal Affiliation: Vijayanagara, including both early and late construction.

References: Morrison 1995:69.

Illustrations: Figure 5.85; Plates 5.73-5.76.

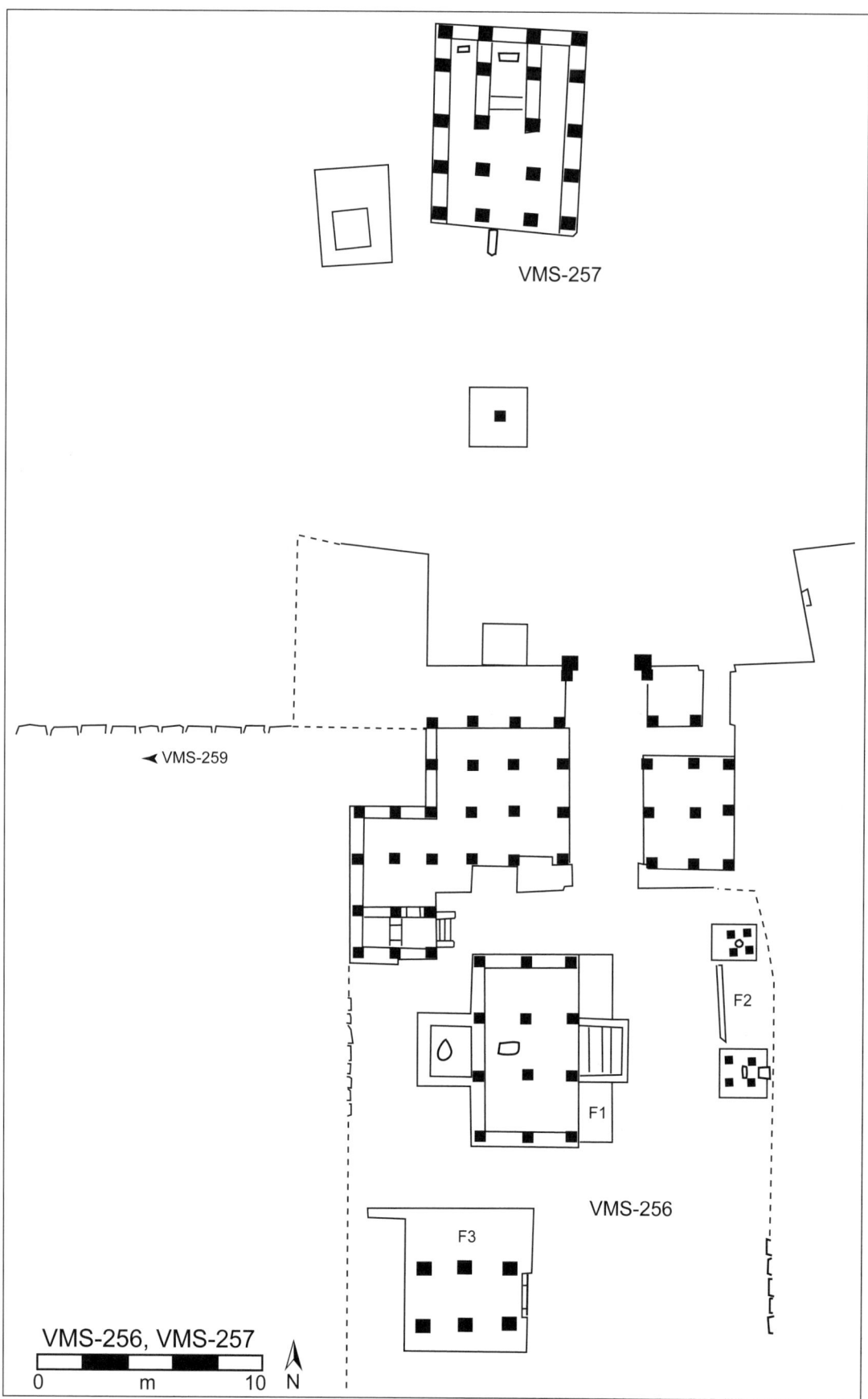

Figure 5.85. VMS-256, VMS-257, and portions of VMS-259, plan.

Plate 5.73. VMS-256, Kamalapuram gate complex; double-headed goose image on east side of gate.

Plate 5.75. VMS-256, carving on Feature 1 depicting seated royal figure and female and male supplicants.

Plate 5.74. VMS-256, Kamalapuram gate complex; interior passage showing complex columns and sculpted panels, and recent construction.

Plate 5.76. VMS-256, Kamalapuram gate complex; yali balustrade on Feature 1.

Plate 5.77. VMS-257, temple overview.

Plate 5.78. VMS-257, detail of partially buried elephant balustrade in courtyard in front of temple.

SITE: VMS-257   Block: S   Transect: 8
Primary Site Use: Religious: temple.
Site Dimensions: 14 × 14 m
Setting: In walled compound inside Kamalapuram village, near Vijayanagara period gate complex, VMS-256.
Present Land Use/Disturbances: In worship. The structure has recently undergone substantial repair and reconstruction. The plinth of the temple is now at ground level, buried in c. 0.6 m of sediment, and the exterior of the temple is obscured by a modern wall.
Site Description: Temple. This south-facing Vijayanagara temple lies just outside of and facing VMS-256, the entrance to Kamalapuram fort. It consists of a 4 × 5 column chamber, which incorporates a sanctuary and a possible circumambulation passage (now walled in). The basement is colluviated and the moldings are visible only in a freshly dug pit near the northeast corner of the structure. Upper and lower moldings (two stepped with convex bevel and half medallions) are separated by panels carved with musicians and dancers. A single partly buried elephant balustrade marks the entrance to the temple on the south. A second balustrade fragment lies with other displaced elements east of the temple.

The floor of the structure is constructed of long, well-dressed slabs and is covered with more than twenty grinding slicks, several games, and a shallow mortar. Columns are placed directly on the floor, with "bases" carved into them. The two interior columns on the south are elaborately carved. These entryway columns, like the rest of the temple, are heavily plastered and whitewashed; the upper elements are disc-shaped and capitals are cruciform. Other interior columns are similar but less elaborate and contain a fourth element between the disc and the capital: a square molding with quarter corner medallions and beveled step. Exterior columns are one-piece with simple octagonal insets. Column morphology is consistent with an early Vijayanagara date.

The sanctuary is incorporated within the mandapa rather than being a separate room. It may have been 2 × 2 columns in size, perhaps originally surrounded by a circumambulation path (*pradakshina patha*); however, recent reconstruction has obscured this. This area is entirely rebuilt, with an older door incorporated into a recent wall. The door frame is simply carved with linear and floral motifs and a lotus above the door. At present, the sanctuary contains a large striding Hanuman (Anajaneya) set into the floor. To the west of the sanctuary is a small Anjaneya carved onto a slab. These are likely not the original images in the temple. The eaves on the south side of the temple are intact but the original roof is obscured by subsequent modification.

A small stone platform (2.5 × 2.5 m) containing an intact lamp column is located to the south of the temple entrance. The platform is constructed of shaped and well-dressed slabs. A wide and shallow mortar is located next to the lamp column. Modern shrines in the compound incorporate older elements including slabs, moldings, and images. Most of the images are naga stones; devotee feet and a fragmentary chlorite Nandi are also represented. An elaborate stone doorway is incorporated into the modern compound wall. It is covered with floral, geometric, and (female) anthropomorphic motifs. Shaivite door guardians flank the door, suggesting an original Shaivite affiliation for the temple.

Feature 1: Small well located 2 m west of the temple, against the wall bordering the Kamalapuram market. The interior is built entirely of modern elements but the exterior platform (c. 3 × 3 m) is constructed of older slabs and large rectangular blocks, some with Vijayanagara-style quarry marks. It is of the same construction style as the lamp platform. The well is now silted in and is full of trash. It may be an older well with recent repairs or a recent well that incorporates older elements.

Artifacts: None observed, modern overlay. No collections made.
Temporal Affiliation: Early Vijayanagara.
References: Morrison 1995:69, 77, 99; Sinopoli and Morrison 2006.
Illustrations: Figure 5.85; Plates 5.77, 5.78.

SITE: VMS- 258   Block: S   Transect: 8
Primary Site Use: Defensive: bastion.
Site Dimensions: c. 30 m diameter, 8-9 m high
GPS Location: 15°18'39" N, 76°28'31.3" E
Setting: Located within modern Kamalapuram village, inside the old fort walls.
Present Land Use/Disturbances: In the 1990s, the structure was surrounded by modern structures, which abut it; original structure is in good condition.
Site Description: Circular bastion. This large circular masonry tower is located in the center of the Kamalapuram fort. It is freestanding and approximately 30 m in diameter by 8-9 m high. The structure is solid except for an internal staircase that leads to the flat top of the tower. The lowest ten courses of the building form the widest part of the structure. The next twenty-five or so courses are stepped in slightly. The structure is capped with horizontal rectangular slabs set all around the top of the tower. These slabs protrude over the edge of the tower by 5-10 cm. Curved brackets with pendant lotus bud motifs extend out beyond

Plate 5.79. VMS-258, bastion.

the capping course. The brackets are long slabs laid on the flat top of the tower and extend some 30-40 cm beyond its edge. Only three on the western side are visible; however, there are fragments of additional bracket slabs scattered on the roof.

The tower masonry consists of square, rectangular, and a few irregularly-shaped quarried blocks. Some chinking stones are used and courses are reasonably continuous but blocks are loosely fit. A few stones are worked across all or part of their faces.

The entrance to the stairway is now inaccessible, although it was open in 1990. The staircase is walled by masonry similar to that of the rest of the structure. It winds around the interior of the structure and emerges out on to the flat top. There is a large window or door partway up the stair.

Some naga stones and sculptural elements are piled up against the tower on the west, forming a small modern shrine. This includes a Nandi boundary stone with several characters.

Artifacts: In inhabited village; no evidence of non-recent artifacts. No collections made.

Temporal Affiliation: Vijayanagara or post-Vijayanagara (seventeenth century).

References: Morrison 1995:69-70, 77; Sinopoli and Morrison 2006.

Illustrations: Plate 5.79.

SITE: VMS-259   Block: S   Transect: 7-8
  Primary Site Use: Defensive: Kamalapuram fort walls.
  Site Dimensions: c. 80 × 80 m
  Setting: Level area engulfed by Kamalapuram village.
  Present Land Use/Disturbances: Densely settled area that has been continuously occupied for c. 600 years. Of particular interest is the fact that the ground level inside the fort walls (or their presumed location) is 1-1.5 m higher than that outside. The walls are very badly disturbed and traces of bastions and openings may have been obliterated in several places.
  Site Description: Kamalapuram fort walls. The Kamalapuram fort is an enclosed square area, some 80 m on a side and surrounded on all sides by fortification walls. There is only one known opening, VMS-256. The walls are now mostly broken down and have been preserved only where incorporated into a newer wall or structure. The walls are similar to massive fortification walls elsewhere in the Vijayanagara area and are constructed of quarried rectangular and square blocks, most of which are not dressed. Blocks vary widely in size. There are some wedge-shaped blocks, but none are currently *in situ*. Where the walls are preserved, courses are loosely fit but continuous with chinking stones used.

The walls adjacent to and west of the gate VMS-256 are the best preserved. Here there is a 45 m long and eight-course high segment that now makes up one side of the village marketplace. The south (interior) face of the wall is not finished; the ground level is higher on this side. Just inside the wall is a rock-cut well. There are two bastions—one round, one square—associated with this segment. On the west is a solidly built round bastion constructed of massive rectangular blocks fit closely together with no chinking. The lower three courses extend further out from the face of the wall than do the upper eight. Blocks get progressively smaller toward the top, and the structure tapers slightly upwards. This bastion is bonded to the wall, and contains a niche that was originally bricked and plastered. It appears to be solid. The square bastion on the east (c. 15 × 15 m) consists of eleven courses of rectangular roughly dressed blocks. It is in poor condition and is overgrown with vegetation obscuring bonding and abutting patterns. It, too, appears to be solid.

The walls of VMS-259 enclose and define the old walled settlement of Kamalapuram. It evidently contained both round and square bastions. Or, perhaps the square bastions on either side of the gate VMS-256 (with late Vijayanagara columns) could have been added with the construction/renovation of the gate complex. The area within the walls is still densely settled, with perhaps the most labyrinthine streets of the village. Portions of the walls are traceable within the village, but except in the gate area, no more than one course is ever visible.

Within the wall are numerous wells of unknown age, some of which may date to the Vijayanagara period. In addition to wells, water would have been obtained from the canal-fed Kamalapuram reservoir, VMS-231, on the southwest edge of the settlement.

It is likely that Vijayanagara period settlement was contained within the fort walls and also extended beyond them, as evident from the presence of numerous Vijayanagara period remains outside the walls. What is not clear, however, is whether or not these areas were differently incorporated into the imperial captial and how exactly the city wall (VMS-123) related to VMS-259. Based on documentary sources, the temporal affiliation of the Kamalapuram fort belongs to the early Vijayanagara period; archaeological remains show a more complex occupational history.

  Artifacts: Scatter contains unknown mixture of Vijayanagara to recent material. No collections made.
  Temporal Affiliation: Early Vijayanagara period to present.
  References: Morrison 1995:64, 69, 77.
  Illustrations: Figure 5.85.

SITE: VMS-260   Block: S   Transect: 10
  Primary Site Use: Religious: temple.
  Site Dimensions: 19 × 8 m
  Setting: In Kamalapuram village, outside the fort wall but within the outer city walls of Vijayanagara.
  Present Land Use/Disturbances: In worship. A dung floor has been spread over portions of the stone pavement. The structure is whitewashed and painted. The most significant alteration is the conversion of this Vaishnavite structure into a Shaivite temple—it now houses images of a lingam, Nandi, Ganesha, and Parvati. A recent wall incorporates two image bases.
  Site Description: Temple. This ornate east-facing temple consists of a large open mandapa, a walled antechamber, and a sanctuary. Built up against the structure on the east is a later covered porch. The basement of

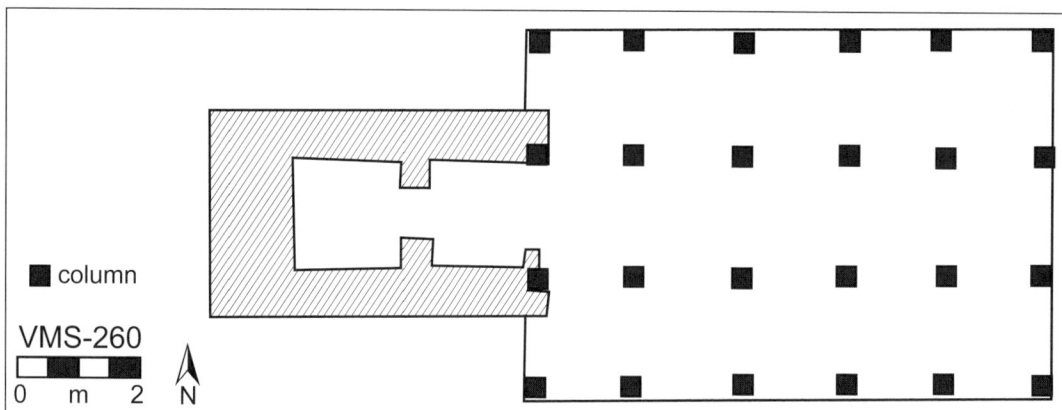

Figure 5.86. VMS-260, plan.

Plate 5.80. VMS-260, temple overview.

Plate 5.81. VMS-260, temple antechamber, view toward sanctuary.

the mandapa is ornate. Two stepped foundation courses are capped with ornate lower and upper moldings (two stepped with convex bevel and various embellishments including yali heads and wavy bands) separated by an inset vertical face with widely spaced, upright rectangular piers carved with a vine and leaf motif. This sequence is followed only on the mandapa. The basement supporting the rest of the structure is simpler (two stepped basement courses, lower and upper moldings with only an angled bevel, separated by inset plain vertical face). The severity of this foundation is broken only by corner quarter medallions. Above the plinth, the walls of the sanctuary and antechamber rest on a course of long horizontal slabs followed by a long slab beveled on three sides, then a ledge. The walls themselves contain simple "miniature temple" niches, and scattered small sculptures including the ten avatars of Vishnu, hamsa, Hanuman, and an interesting figure of two people on an elephant facing a third person holding a gun or a lance.

The later porch (2 columns east-west × 4 north-south) abutting the original structure is built of very tall square columns, each with two octagonal cutouts. One column has a donor figure carved on it. The columns are capped by simple cruciform capitals; bases are buried beneath the contemporary floor. This porch is covered by a beam and slab roof that extends over the simple angled eaves of the roof of the mandapa. The porch does not appear to be set on a plinth; perhaps it is covered, as the ground surface is elevated here.

The exterior columns of the 4 × 4 column mandapa are square with octagonal insets and plain rectangular capitals. The six interior columns are more elaborate, with attached bases and a single elaborately carved octagonal inset. The tops taper to a rounded portion. A separate disc-shaped element sits atop the column, followed by a square element. The whole is capped with a cruciform capital. The columns are carved with various figures, including both Vaishnavite and Shaivite images. This roof is also of slabs and beams; there is a roof section of rotated squares with central lotus design in the center of the mandapa. The door to the antechamber is elaborately carved, with Lakshmi and elephants over the door and Vaishnavite door guardians. Carved panels flank the door. On the south, Hanuman (Anjaneya) strides above three male devotees (donors?) wearing dhotis, with their hair in buns and hands folded. The north panel is similar, with Garuda above two well-muscled devotees or donors.

The temple has an elaborate plastered brickwork superstructure with numerous plasterwork figures. The shikara is square, and there is a facade of plastered brickwork decoration all around the roof of the mandapa. This has both large "miniature temple" niches, one on each side (north, south, and east), and small plaster figures. There is no superstructure on the porch.

To the east of the later porch is a recent platform containing naga sculptures and what appears to be a painted, plastered, broken, and upside-down lamp column. A large chlorite Vishnu and smaller chlorite Lakshmi image lean against a large boulder nearby. It seems likely that this large and well-executed Vishnu was the original inhabitant of the temple. Modern settlement in this area tends to obscure the relationship of this structure to other Vijayanagara period remains around it.

Artifacts: Very dense scatter of earthenware sherds and modern trash. No collections made.

Temporal Affiliation: Vijayanagara.

References: Filliozat and Filliozat 1988:13; Morrison 1995:77.

Illustrations: Figure 5.86; Plates 5.80, 5.81.

slabs. A roughly carved spout emerges from these blocks on the north side of the structure. The ceiling of the mandapa is constructed of stone slabs and beams; the ceiling in the sanctuary consists of two courses of rotated squares with a central lotus bud motif. The door of the shrine opens to the east. It is flanked by Shaivite door guardians, with Ganesha carved above the door. The shrine has an elaborate shikara constructed of brick, c. 2.5 m high.
Artifacts: 100% collections; no artifacts recovered.
Temporal Affiliation: Vijayanagara.
Illustrations: Plate 5.82.

SITE: VMS-262   Block: S   **Transect:** 10
Primary Site Use: Unknown: structural foundation.
Site Dimensions: 6.5 × 2 m
Setting: On gently sloping outcrop in Kamalapuram village, outside the fort wall but within the outer city walls. The structure sits atop a large granitic boulder.
Present Land Use/Disturbances: The structure has been dismantled and there is evidence of recent quarrying on the outcrop.
Site Description: Base of a small rectangular structure. Remnants of the structure include peg holes, cement patches, and rock-cut wall trenches. Footing trenches (c. 0.5 m wide × 0.08 m deep) pecked out of the rock define the north and west sides of the structure. No trace of the south side remains. Three peg holes are located in the approximate location of the southeast corner of the structure. Two small patches of cement adhere to the boulder at the approximate line of the structure's west wall. The cement is highly weathered and consistent with that found in structures dating to the Vijayanagara period.

Small wall fragments (up to 0.28 m high) remain in their foundation trenches on the north and east sides. They are constructed of small, angular cobbles fixed in cement. A column footing is located 0.9 m from the northeast corner of the north trench. Three additional peg holes are located near the northwest corner of the structure.

This small, rectangular structure is of unknown function. The boulder on which it sits directly overlooks VMS-260. Construction is consistent with Vijayanagara period materials and techniques. The structure does not appear to have had a domestic function, except possibly for storage.
Artifacts: 100% collection; no artifacts recovered.
Temporal Affiliation: Probably Vijayanagara.
References: Morrison 1995:77.

Plate 5.82. VMS-261, temple.

SITE: VMS-261   Block: S   **Transect:** 10
Primary Site Use: Religious: temple.
Site Dimensions: 5 × 3 m
Setting: Sheet rock outcrop in Kamalapuram village, outside the fort wall but within the outer city walls.
Present Land Use/Disturbances: Currently in use as a storage room for firewood. The temple is in fair condition, although it does not appear to be maintained.
Site Description: Small enclosed shrine. This Vijayanagara period Shaivite shrine is located in the northeast part of the modern village of Kamalapuram. It is situated on an extensive outcrop of sheet rock, south of VMS-260, a larger Vijayanagara period temple complex. Both of these structures may have been situated along a north-south road.

The entire structure is 3 (east-west) × 2 columns (north-south) though the enclosed sanctuary is only 2 × 2 columns. It has no formal basement, but is placed on a foundation of roughly shaped and randomly oriented blocks sitting on sheet rock. The floor, which is in poor repair, consists of slabs and small blocks. Columns are placed directly on the floor. The columns that form the entryway are well finished, with an incorporated base and two octagonal insets. Other columns are roughly finished; their capitals include both cruciform and roughly finished rectangular blocks. The walls of the sanctuary are constructed of four courses of vertical

SITE: VMS-263   Block: S   **Transect:** 18
Primary Site Use: Agricultural: terraces and gravel-mulched fields.
Setting: Dry, gently sloping area with outcrops.
Present Land Use/Disturbances: The site area is uncultivated but intensively grazed. The Tungabhadra High Level Canal has blasted through the landscape c. 25 m south of the south end of the site. A bullock cart road bordered by rubble walls lies 50 m to the west.
Site Description: Terraced gravel-mulched fields. This small area of terraced gravel-mulched fields is constructed on a hillside sloping down to the south from an east-west trending ridge. Most walls in this system are oriented perpendicular to the slope. The latter is rocky, with outcrops and spits of sheet rock that tend to be narrow and oriented east-west, acting as terraces themselves. Several walls are linear alignments of piled, rather than coursed, elements. Outcropping boulders are incorporated into terraces.

Most striking are the fields themselves, which are covered with a solid surface of quartzite pebbles. These occur in much higher concentrations inside the terrace walls than they do outside. Larger cobbles are piled atop outcrops and sheet rock to the sides of the field. Pebbles appear to derive from the many quartzite veins outcropping nearby.

Artifacts: 100% collection; no artifacts recovered.
Temporal Affiliation: Unknown.
References: Morrison 1995:92, 102.

SITE: VMS-264   Block: S   Transect: 17
Primary Site Use: Agricultural: terraces.
Setting: Dry, gently sloping grassy area.
Present Land Use/Disturbances: This area is uncultivated but intensively grazed. A bullock cart road runs east of the site; another runs through the site. Three abandoned structures (mid-twentieth century), probably related to the construction of the Right Bank High Level Canal that runs south of the site, occur in this area.
Site Description: Terraces. This broad, gently sloping hillside slopes down to the south and west and is separated from VMS-263 on the east by a narrow drainage. Terraces are widely spaced, and almost all are oriented perpendicular to the direction of runoff. There is no gravel mulch but small size-segregated piles of cobbles and boulders dot the hillside. None of the terraces has more than about 0.35 m of sediment built up behind it. Walls are simply constructed, many consisting of single-course alignments of large, unmodified cobbles. A few are linear piles of cobbles; others are simply outcrops with the gaps filled in.
Artifacts: Low density scatter of earthenware sherds and modern trash, densest near the modern structures. No collections made.
Temporal Affiliation: Unknown.
References: Morrison 1995:92-93, 102.

SITE: VMS-265   Block: S   Transect: 8
Primary Site Use: Religious: shrine.
Site Dimensions: 2 × 2 m
Setting: In Kamalapuram village, outside the fort walls on the main paved road through the village.
Present Land Use/Disturbances: In use. The structure is plastered and painted with a modern door and recent flagstone pavement.
Site Description: Small square shrine. The walls and basement appear to be recent. The superstructure is built of reused Vijayanagara period elements, including an upside-down capital. The shrine contains a large slab with an image depicting Hanuman praying to Rama. Set above this in a separate small panel are two seated figures flanked by praying figures (one on the left and two on the right). Around a tree adjacent to the shrine are numerous naga stones. Circa 25 m east, along the road, is a lintel carved with Lakshmi and elephants.
Artifacts: Recent artifact scatter in village. No collections made.
Temporal Affiliation: Unknown. Vijayanagara period elements in later structure.
Illustrations: Plate 5.83.

SITE: VMS-266   Block: S   Transect: 8
Primary Site Use: Religious: temple.
Site Dimensions: 12 × 8 m
Setting: In Kamalapuram village, outside and north of the fort walls.
Present Land Use/Disturbances: The temple has been so extensively rebuilt and renovated that it is now completely enclosed within a recent structure.
Site Description: Temple. This Vijayanagara period Shaivite temple is located in the village of Kamalapuram on an east-west oriented street

Plate 5.83. VMS-265, naga stones associated with small modern shrine.

with numerous Vijayanagara period temples. The temple appears to have three episodes of construction: the oldest elements are found in the central mandapa; the outer mandapa or porch was appended later; and recent renovation has been extensive. The outer porch and two (later?) columns of the central mandapa contain Vaishnavite motifs in an otherwise Shaivite temple. Several displaced Vijayanagara period sculpted elements, including a Lakshmi and elephant panel, a large Nandi, a slab with linga, and an image base, are incorporated into the modern courtyard. Interior images include Ganesha, Parvati, and a modern Virabhadra.

The outer mandapa consists of a single east-west row of elaborately carved columns appended to the north side of the original structure. Column bases are not visible, but the columns themselves are square in plan, each with ornately carved octagonal insets. Images carved on the columns include: Ganesha, Narasimha, Balakrishna, goose, turtle, Garuda, rishis, Vishnu, bident, conch, chakra, Hanuman, Rama, lotus, and other anthropomorphs. The north column is finished only on the exterior and capitals (cruciform with detached lotus bud motifs) are finished only on sides facing the entrance. Stone beams supporting the eaves rest directly on the capitals. Above the eaves is a molding (a simple angled bevel with half medallions) and a recent superstructure.

The central mandapa, although largely obscured by modern construction, is 3 (north-south) × 4 (east-west) columns. The basement molding is two stepped with convex bevel and half medallions. The columns have integral bases and are square in section with octagonal insets. Sitting on each column is a disc-shaped element with concave bevel, followed by a capital made out of a square molding with convex bevel and corner quarter medallions. A second capital, cruciform with inset corners, is placed atop the first. Both the ceiling beams and ceiling may be recent; however, two elaborately carved original ceiling panels are exposed. One has three concentric rings of sculpture: dancers (female), geese, and lotus. The other is square with a central lotus. Below it is a Nandi, fixed in the floor. Mandapa columns have images only on their outer faces. These include Nandi, lotus, Narasimha, hamsa, bident, and a (later) Garuda. Simple angled eaves support a recent superstructure. The sanctuary is entirely recent. However, the door appears to be original. It is carved with elaborate geometric motifs, Shaivite door guardians, Lakshmi (above), and a lotus (on the threshold).

Artifacts: Temple is heavily modified; no collections made.
Temporal Affiliation: Vijayanagara period and later.
References: Morrison 1995:77.
Illustrations: Plate 5.84.

Plate 5.84. VMS-266, columns in temple antechamber.

Plate 5.85. VMS-267, flooded temple, view of antechamber and sanctuary entrance.

SITE: VMS-267   Block: S   **Transect:** 8
  Primary Site Use: Religious: temple.
  Site Dimensions: 8 × 10 m
  Setting: In Kamalapuram village, outside and north of the fort walls.
  Present Land Use/Disturbances: The temple is whitewashed and is set off from the street by a recent wall in which is set a temple door frame and two yali balustrades. The mandapa was flooded at the time of documentation.
  Site Description: Temple. This south-facing Vijayanagara period temple was located along an east-west road that joined VMS-265, 266 and 267. It consists of only a sanctuary and a 4 × 4 columned antechamber. This temple is popular with local women and is presently dedicated to Hanuman, though the temple was originally Shaivite.
  The columns of the mandapa are square in section with octagonal insets. The exterior columns are unadorned except for the occasional carved lotus. Interior columns have ornate insets and carved depictions of Krishna, Ganesha, Narasimha, Nandi, lingam, Rama, and a three-headed figure (Brahma?). South-facing columns have ornate capitals; the remaining columns have simple cruciform capitals. The roof is intact; it supports simple angled eaves topped by a low facade with semicircular merlons. There is no superstructure. The sanctuary does not appear to be original. The door now set into the wall near the road probably once framed the sanctuary entrance. It has Shaivite door guardians.
  Artifacts: In contemporary settlement; no collections made.
  Temporal Affiliation: Vijayanagara period.
  References: Morrison 1995:77.
  Illustrations: Plate 5.85.

SITE: VMS-268   Block: S   **Transect:** 9
  Primary Site Use: Religious: temple.
  Site Dimensions: 12 × 7 m
  Setting: In Kamalapuram village, outside and north of the fort walls.
  Present Land Use/Disturbances: Site is located within modern Kamalapuram. The floor and wall are modern. The structure was flooded when visited, but generally in good condition.
  Site Description: Temple. This north-facing Vijayanagara period temple was located along an east-west road that also joined VMS-265, 266 and 267. This Vaishnava temple has some Shaivite images on its exterior columns.
  The temple is located within a small compound, the gate of which consists of two simple columns with attached lotus bud capitals supporting a block and brick roof and superstructure. The roof has a brick and plaster molding (two stepped with angled bevel) that supports a brick superstructure (c. 1 m high) containing a representation of a temple flanked by rearing yalis. The door has carved geometric designs, Vaishnavite door guardians, and a carved Lakshmi with elephants. Lying near the door are two elephant balustrades.
  The temple consists of a 3 × 4 column antechamber, with an internal sanctuary. Its basement is not visible. Although the floor is largely recent, it incorporates older slabs and at least seven mortars. Columns are square in plan with ornate octagonal insets. Above these are cruciform capitals with beveled corners. Carvings on the columns include: Ganesha, Narasimha, Nandi and linga, sages, star, lotus, hamsa, Hanuman, and several avatars of Vishnu. Only the two north rows of columns are decorated. The roof of plastered brick is supported by a ceiling of stone slabs and beams.

Plate 5.86. VMS-268, temple exterior.

Plate 5.87. VMS-269, view of lamp column looking toward temple.

The sanctuary is located between the innermost columns of the mandapa. The door to the sanctuary is carved with linear and leaf-shaped motifs with coconut pots on either side of the door and lotuses above the door and on the threshold. Enclosing this door frame is a second, exterior door. Outside the door are two granite posts, 0.7 m high, fixed in the floor. The sanctuary itself is locked, but can be seen to contain a Krishna image in a horseshoe-shaped, yali-headed niche. The sanctuary is surrounded by an enclosed circumambulation passage. A recent wall encloses the whole structure.

Artifacts: Within contemporary settlement and still in worship; no collections made.
Temporal Affiliation: Vijayanagara.
References: Morrison 1995:77.
Illustrations: Plate 5.86.

SITE: VMS-269   Block: S   Transect: 9
Primary Site Use: Religious: temple.
Site Dimensions: Unknown.
Setting: In Kamalapuram village, outside and north of the fort walls.
Present Land Use/Disturbances: A modern house compound is located within the temple. Access to the interior was denied.
Site Description: Temple. This Vijayanagara period temple is now used as a house and is inaccessible. It was located along an east-west road that also joined VMS-265, 266, 267, and 268. The original entrance to this temple was through a south-facing stone door with an elaborate stone and brick superstructure. A sculpted corner merlon with a carved bident (displaced from VMS-269?) is located on the house roof to the west. Outside the structure are a 1.5 m high lamp column set on a basement with ornate moldings and a north-south oriented mandapa. The 4 × 2 mandapa has simple columns with octagonal insets and rectangular, bevel-edged capitals.
Artifacts: Structure is occupied; no collections made.
Temporal Affiliation: Vijayanagara period and later.
References: Morrison 1995:77.
Illustrations: Plate 5.87.

SITE: VMS-270   Block: S   Transect: 9
Primary Site Use: Religious: temple.
Site Dimensions: 7 × 9 m
Setting: In Kamalapuram village, outside and north of the fort walls.
Present Land Use/Disturbances: In worship; painted and plastered with metal door on sanctuary entrance.
Site Description: Temple. This east-facing Vijayanagara period Vaishnava temple is approximately aligned with temples VMS-269, 268, 267, 266, and 265 to its west. However, unlike all of these, it faces east and not north or south. Either there was an intersection or courtyard in the road here, or perhaps this was the end of the road. The structure is reached by three steps of plain dressed granite blocks; a small lamp column is set into the steps. The temple is well constructed and surrounded by flagstone paving.

The temple consists of a 4 × 3 column antechamber and a walled sanctuary. These are set on a basement consisting of lower and upper moldings (two stepped with convex bevel and corner quarter medallions) separated by a plain inset vertical course. The most elaborate columns of the mandapa are on the east. These have attached bases and elaborate inset polygonal sections with central bands and lanceolate motifs. Carved on the columns are numerous figures including hamsa, Narasimha, Krishna, conch, Vishnu, Nandi, lingam, Ganesha, two possible donor figures (one male, one female), rishis, monkey, Balakrishna, chakra, and so on. Capitals are simple cruciforms with corner bevels.

The sanctuary is walled with large dressed granite blocks and is entered through a door capped by a carved lotus and flanked by Vaishnavite door guardians, a sun, and a moon. The main images—Rama, Lakshmana, and Sita—are recent. The beam and slab roof is original, however, and supports a stub of the original superstructure. The latter is capped by a recent shikara.

Artifacts: Artifact scatter with recent and Vijayanagara period artifacts. No collections made.
Temporal Affiliation: Vijayanagara period and later.
References: Morrison 1995:77.

SITE: VMS-271   Block: S   Transect: 10
  Primary Site Use: Religious: temple complex.
  Site Dimensions: 50 × 9 m
  Setting: Just south of city walls VMS-123, in irrigated area on outskirts of Kamalapuram village.
  Present Land Use/Disturbances: In worship; painted and plastered. A metal grill covers the sanctuary door. The Right Bank Main Canal runs c. 50 m to the east. Feature 1 has been significantly modified.
  Site Description: Temple complex. This site includes a central temple and associated features. The north-facing main shrine consists of an antechamber and sanctuary to which a later mandapa has been appended. An image of Hanuman is in worship in the sanctuary. In addition to the temple are two features. Feature 1 is a small shrine. Feature 2 is a temple tank. A short north-south wall segment 10 m west of Feature 2 may be part of an original enclosure wall. VMS-271 lies c. 80 m south of the Vijayanagara city wall (VMS-123). Given the association of Hanuman with roads and gates, it is possible that this temple complex was located just outside a gate in the wall. However, there is no trace of such an entrance now and the city wall is fragmentary in this area.

The basement of the original structure is very simple and has no moldings. Joined to the small square sanctuary is the 6 × 2 columned antechamber. Columns are square in section with octagonal insets. The north row has rectangular capitals with curved ends and pendant lotus buds; others have simpler rectangular capitals. An extra column has been stuck in to shore up a ceiling beam. The slab and beam ceiling carries simple angled eaves. There is no trace of a superstructure. The original paving of rectangular slabs is *in situ*. The sanctuary has Vaishnavite door guardians and an unsculpted lintel. A Vijayanagara period Anjaneya Hanuman is located within the sanctuary and a small Ganesha image is outside and to the west of the sanctuary door.

Built up against the temple is a second mandapa, c. 0.15 m lower than the original building. The ceiling slabs of this mandapa extend over the eaves of the antechamber. It also has a simple basement. It is the size of a 2 × 6 column mandapa, but only some of the columns are present, creating a large open area inside the structure; most of the ceiling slabs are extra long. Columns match those of the earlier structure except that the capitals are partial cruciforms with beveled edges. There is no trace of a superstructure.

Near the main shrine are remnants of a freestanding 2 × 2 columned mandapa. The columns are more elaborate, smaller, and probably earlier than those in the shrine. The mandapa, partially incorporated into the recent enclosure wall, is built on a plain basement. The square columns have ornate integral carved bases and a complex inset octagonal section. Above the inset was a disk-shaped element followed by a cruciform capital with beveled edges. A small carved element with a channel may have been a spout.

To the north of the temple is a large recently built platform that contains several Vijayanagara period sculptures including an ornate Ganesha, a tiny headless chlorite Nandi, naga stones, a block with feet encircled by a naga, a chlorite trident fragment, a chlorite Vishnu head, and a portion of a lintel slab with Lakshmi and elephants. Old slabs are used in the construction of the platform. Outside the recent enclosure wall (on the north side) is a large slab with a lingam and long inscription. East of the main shrine is a large rectangular stone trough. Two other stone basins lie outside the enclosure wall to the west. One is sub-rectangular, broken in half and partly buried. The other is circular, set in a square block.

Feature 1: A 3 (east-west) × 2 (north-south) column east-facing Vijayanagara period shrine consisting of an enclosed sanctuary and a two-column porch. The basement lacks decoration except for the sanctuary where inset vertical slabs with carved panels depict dancers and a hunting scene. Columns are simple and rectangular in plan. The plastered porch columns each have two octagonal insets. Capitals are crudely made, either rectangular or cruciform. The porch is enclosed by a recent wall.

The door to the slab-walled sanctuary has Vaishnava door guardians and a carved lotus on both the lintel and threshold. An image of a devotee is carved on the sanctuary's west interior wall. A spout exits the building to the north. The roof is constructed of bricks and stone piled into a mound and capped with cement. This shrine is awkwardly placed relative to the main shrine and probably predates it. The partially dismantled mandapa lies 2 m north of Feature 1. Both of these may have faced a road that was later displaced by the construction of the main shrine.

Feature 2: A large, north-south oriented step well (15 × 20 m). It is entered from the northeast corner via a stairway that extends to the northwest corner, then turns south. Two column footings are cut into the first step. The well is constructed of stepped courses of roughly shaped square and rectangular undressed blocks. Two carved blocks (Shiva and Anjaneya) are incorporated into the wall near the landing in the staircase. Around the top of the staircase are low benches with angled brackets. It is not clear if these originally encircled the entire feature. Four upright slabs, each with two large holes and a pointed top, now restrict access to the steps. Bars placed in the holes would have limited access to this well. The south end of Feature 2 is cut by a recent wall.

The two small shrines (Feature 1 and the disassembled one) appear to be earlier than the main temple. Both are oriented along the same axis (11° west of north), and may have once faced a road. The main shrine and Feature 2 were added later, in the roadway. A second mandapa was added to the main shrine at some point.

  Artifacts: Earthenware ceramics are embedded in the courtyard surface and outside the maintained compound of the temple. There is also a great deal of recent trash. No collections made.
  Temporal Affiliation: Vijayanagara.
  References: Morrison 1995:77.
  Illustrations: Plates 5.88-5.91.

Plate 5.88. VMS-271, temple complex, Feature 1, shrine.

Plate 5.89. VMS-271, temple complex, Feature 2, step well.

Plate 5.90. VMS-271, temple complex, detail of carving on temple basement.

Plate 5.91. VMS-271, overview.

SITE: VMS-272   **Block:** S   **Transect:** 8
Primary Site Use: Religious: shrine.
Site Dimensions: 2 × 2 m
Setting: Flat-gently sloping area.
Present Land Use/Disturbances: Irrigated fields surround this recently painted structure, which is located on the edge of Kamalapur village.
Site Description: Shrine. This small square Vijayanagara period shrine faces south. It is informally constructed of long rectangular slabs set upright to form rough columns atop a simple slab basement and is roofed with flat slabs that support a small pyramidal plastered superstructure. The shrine is situated at the visible west end of the road containing temples designated as VMS-265 to VMS-269. This road may have been connected to the north-south road located in transect 6. However, this area is now irrigated and no junction is visible.
Artifacts: 100% collection; no artifacts recovered.
Temporal Affiliation: Vijayanagara.
References: Morrison 1995:77.

SITE: VMS-273   **Block:** S   **Transect:** 8
Primary Site Use: Religious: temple.
Site Dimensions: 13 × 8 m
Setting: Near the northeast interior corner of the Kamalapuram fort (VMS-259) and within the modern village.
Present Land Use/Disturbances: In worship. The temple is plastered and painted with recent metal grills and a door.
Site Description: Harihara temple. This ornate north-facing temple consists of a lower columned porch, a mandapa raised on a stone basement, an antechamber, and a sanctuary. The temple lay near the northeast edge of the Kamalapuram fort (VMS-259). This part of the village is elevated (1 to 1.5 m) relative to parts of town to the north and east. Numerous worked stone blocks are found in the blacksmith square to the north of the temple, perhaps from the fort wall. Remains of a short wall alignment are visible in the square.

The temple's porch consists of a single row of four columns, oriented east-west. These are set on a simple basement consisting of a footing course of flat slabs above which is a slightly inset course of well-dressed rectangular slabs. The columns are tall and square in section with attached carved bases and two inset polygonal sections. The latter have many facets and a central band. Carvings on the flat portions of the columns include rishis, bidents, Narasimha, chakras, conches, lotuses, a dancer, Nandi and lingam, Krishna, and hamsa. The columns are capped by ornate capitals, generally cruciform with curved elements and attached lotus buds. Brackets atop the capitals support simple angled eaves. Above the beam and slab ceiling, a low and simple brick and plaster superstructural facade extends all around the temple.

Three stone steps flanked by yali balustrades lead up from the porch to the higher mandapa. The mandapa consists of 4 × 3 columns and is walled with large stone slabs on its south, east, and west. The plinth has an ornate molding sequence set atop two footing courses. Columns consist of a square shaft with a single ornate polygonal inset and two upper disclike segments, suggesting an early Vijayanagara date. These sit on separate carved bases and are capped with a discus-shaped and then a square element, rounded below. Capitals are simple cruciforms with beveled edges. The columns set into the outer walls are simpler. A protruding slab ledge (0.1 m) runs at about waist level inside the mandapa; niches are set at intervals above the ledge.

The basement of the antechamber differs from that of the mandapa. The lower molding is of the same type, but of squatter proportions. The inset vertical face is lower and is followed by a protruding, stepped horizontal band capped by a very ornate upper molding with yali medallions. The door to the antechamber has a small Lakshmi over it, with a Shaivite door guardian on the left (east) and a Vaishnavite one on the right (west). There is a second, larger Lakshmi above the door to the sanctuary and the same pattern of door guardians. The ceiling consists of rotated squares with a central lotus. An ornate spout protrudes from the west side of the sanctuary. Although the central image of this temple is recent, it is probable that it was dedicated to Harihara, a god who combines aspects of both Shiva and Vishnu.

Several isolated sculptural elements are present in front of the temple. These include a stone box that resembles a miniature temple with Nandis at the corners and a round apse, two fragments of what may be pointed merlons with carved female figures, a Nandi, a small octagonal column, and a molding segment.

Artifacts: Temple is in worship; no collections made.
Temporal Affiliation: Vijayanagara.
References: Filliozat and Filliozat 1988.
Illustrations: Plate 5.92.

Plate 5.92. VMS-273, temple overview.

SITE: VMS-274   Block: S   Transect: 7
  Primary Site Use: Unknown: isolated wall.
  Site Dimensions: 2 × 0.4 m
  Setting: Gently sloping hill, amid agricultural fields.
  Present Land Use/Disturbances: Area of dry farming.
  Site Description: Wall. This wall fragment is constructed of unmodified boulders with some chinking. The wall is approximately 2 m in length and one element wide. Only one course is preserved.
  Artifacts: Light ceramic scatter. 100% collection. 100 g ceramics; wares: 13 black plain ware. Diagnostics: 1 bowl, 2 jars.
  Temporal Affiliation: Unknown.
  References: Sinopoli and Morrison 2006:438.
  Illustrations: Figure 5.87.

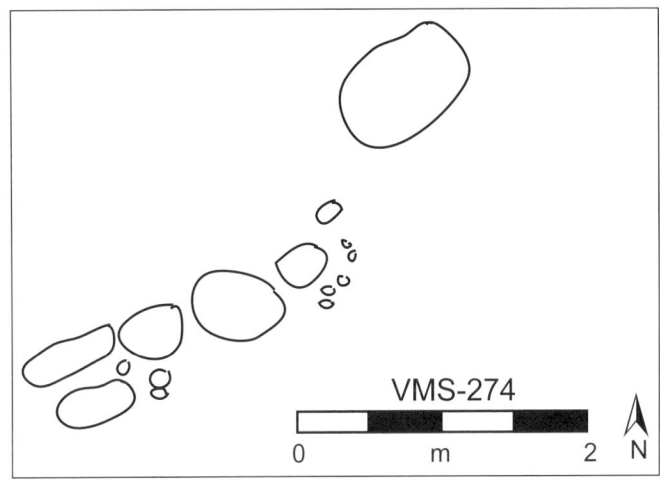

Figure 5.87. VMS-274, plan.

SITE: VMS-275   Block: S   Transect: 7
  Primary Site Use: Religious: shrine.
  Site Dimensions: 8 × 1.5 m
  Setting: On an outcropping boulder located in low-lying agricultural fields southeast of the Kamalapuram reservoir, VMS-231.
  Present Land Use/Disturbances: In use and maintained. The shrine has recently been painted.
  Site Description: Shrine on boulder. This shrine consists of four rounded areas pecked into the south end of a large boulder. These areas as well as some nearby trees are painted. South of the round features are two pecked figures, one male, and the other female. The male figure holds an umbrella in his left hand and is extending his right arm toward the female figure. To the right of the male are a sun and crescent moon. The female figure is less distinct, but her arm is also extended. A crescent moon is carved above her head.
  Artifacts: Very sparse, localized, artifact scatter, mostly earthenware and including modern ceramics. No collections made.
  Temporal Affiliation: Unknown; probably Vijayanagara based on sculpting style.
  References: Sinopoli and Morrison 2006:438.
  Illustrations: Plate 5.93.

Plate 5.93. VMS-275, overview.

SITE: VMS-276 **Block:** S **Transect:** 7
Primary Site Use: Agricultural: gravel-mulched fields and terraces.
Site Dimensions: 600 × 330 m
Setting: Slopes and tops of a moderately steep hill, amid dry fields.
Present Land Use/Disturbances: Dry farmed. A recent dirt road defines the south boundary. A footpath runs through the site.
Site Description: Agricultural terraces. This large terrace and field system is located on the slopes and top of an elevated knoll. The knoll slopes up steeply from the south and west where the terracing is most pronounced. Plot sizes and walls are somewhat larger to the north and east. The southwest edge of the site consists of a well-defined 15 m wide channel bisected by three 1-1.5 m high crosswalls. Terrace walls are oriented perpendicular to the line of the slope and are constructed of piled gravel c. 3.5 m wide, 0.5 m high. Near the top of the knoll the walls define square/rectangular enclosures (field boundaries?), ranging from c. 20 × 60 m to 30 × 200 m. On the east side of the site are several piles of gravel, some of which are sorted by size, and some of the fields are gravel mulched.
Artifacts: Light-moderate scatter of earthenware and isolated lithics. No collections made.
Temporal Affiliation: Unknown.
References: Morrison 1995:92-93, 102; Sinopoli and Morrison 2006:438.

SITE: VMS-277 **Block:** S **Transect:** 7
Primary Site Use: Agricultural: water cistern.
Site Dimensions: 7 × 4 m
Setting: Feature is carved in exposed bedrock that is surrounded by a level uncultivated area with trees and thorny scrub.
Present Land Use/Disturbances: Modern quarrying of outcrop.
Site Description: Cistern. This cistern consists of a modified natural depression. The inlet is from the north and water could have flowed out to the south. On the north end of the wall is a stone-lined channel with a capping stone. The south end had two water outlets cut into bedrock. The west side of the depression is a 1.1 m high vertical face. It is not clear if this has been deliberately modified. A low stone wall of medium blocks lines the upper area of the west face. It bears traces of plaster. Another low wall is found on the north. On the east area of the cistern the slope is more gradual. Quarry marks are visible in the area, some recent and some earlier.
Artifacts: 100% collection; no artifacts recovered.
Temporal Affiliation: Unknown: pre-twentieth century.
References: Sinopoli and Morrison 2006:438.
Illustrations: Figure 5.88.

SITE: VMS-278 **Block:** S **Transect:** 7
Primary Site Use: Residential: ceramic scatter.
Site Dimensions: 50 × 54 m
Setting: Gently sloping, dry farmed field, surrounded by irrigated fields.
Present Land Use/Disturbances: Irrigated fields to the north, east, and west have disturbed the edges of the site. Vegetation obscures visibility on the south.
Site Description: Large moderately dense artifact scatter, consisting primarily of ceramics. Many of the sherds in the slightly higher area may come from field excavations. Possible settlement area.
Artifacts: Predominantly earthenware with some tiles and possible worked basalt. Diagnostic collection only (see Chapter 6), total site coverage.
Temporal Affiliation: Vijayanagara.
References: Sinopoli and Morrison 2006:438.

SITE: VMS-279 **Block:** S **Transect:** 11
Primary Site Use: Military/fortification: wall.
Site Dimensions: 220 × 190 m
Setting: On the crest of a large U-shaped outcrop, which opens toward the east.
Present Land Use/Disturbances: Modern quarrying in area.
Site Description: Very long but discontinuous stone wall. In some areas, outcropping boulders are incorporated into the wall, which runs along the ridge of an outcrop. The double-faced, irregularly coursed wall averages 1 m in height and is 0.6-0.8 m wide. Construction is of loosely fit unmodified cobbles and boulders. There is an excellent view to the north from this site and the large Vijayanagara platform (VMS-7) is readily visible.
Artifacts: Three small, dense scatters of ceramics are visible in low-lying areas enclosed by outcropping ridges. The largest scatter is c. 20 m in diameter; the smaller is 5 m in diameter and consists of a single broken vessel (probably recent). A small piece of iron was also recovered. A judgment sample was collected from each of the scatters; ceramics are all recent in date.
Temporal Affiliation: Unknown. The ceramics are modern, but the wall appears to date to the Vijayanagara period.
References: Morrison 1995:65; Sinopoli and Morrison 2006:438.
Illustrations: Figure 5.89.

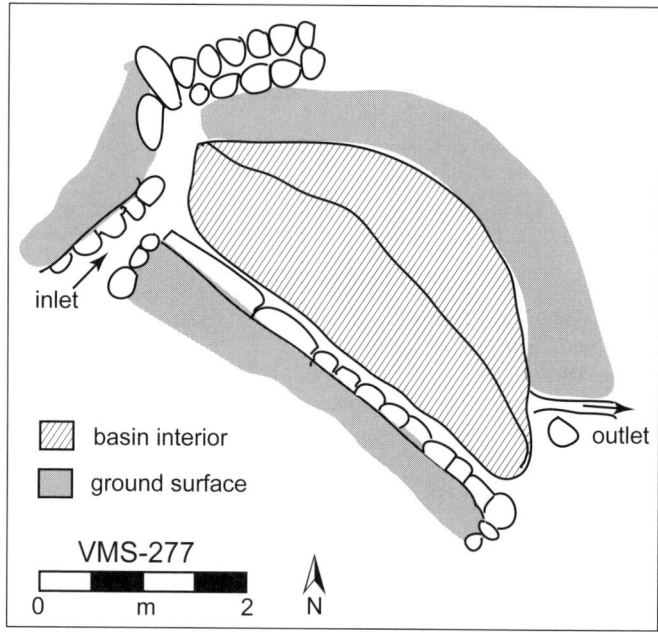

Figure 5.88. VMS-277, plan.

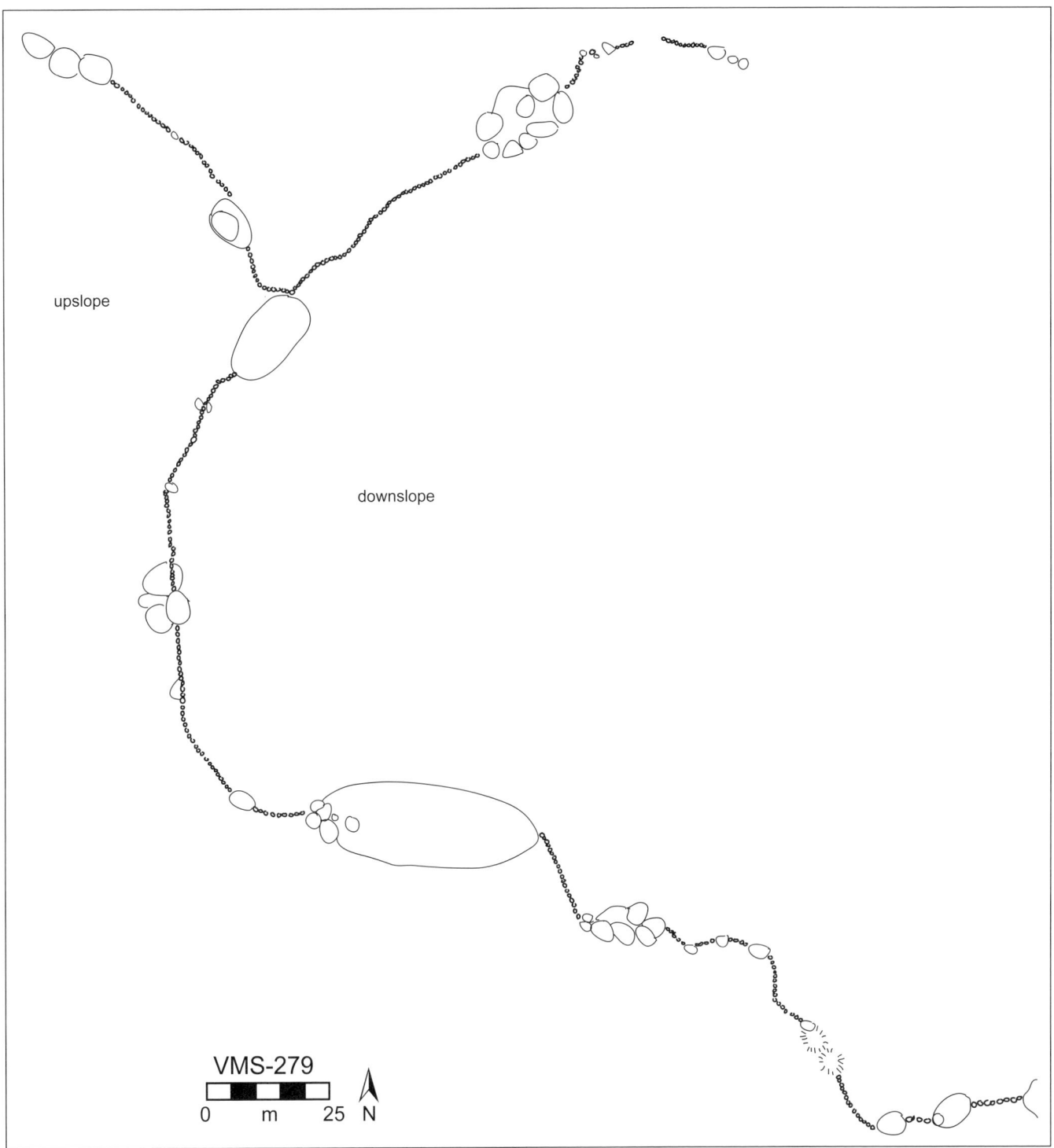

Figure 5.89. VMS-279, plan.

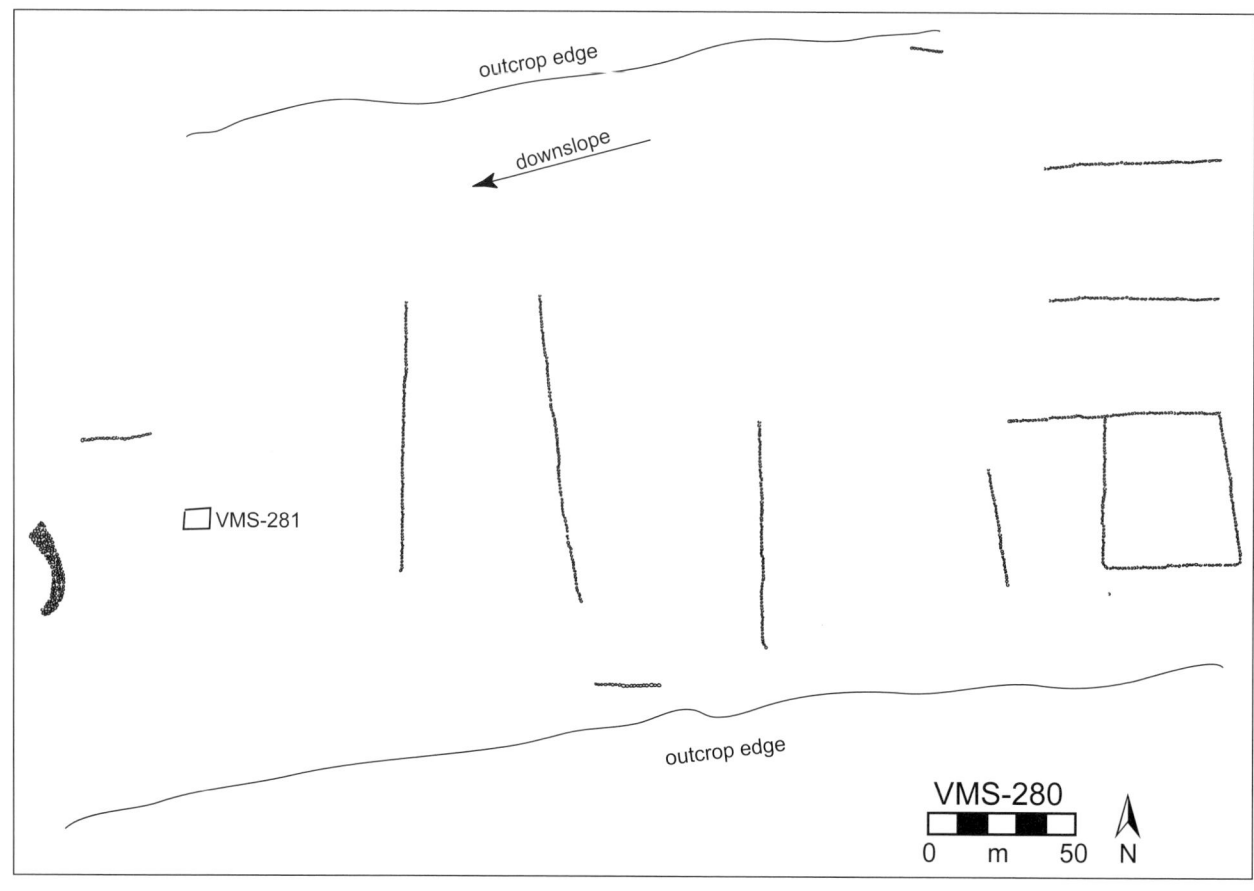

Figure 5.90. VMS-280, plan.

SITE: VMS-280   Block: S   Transect: 10-11
   Primary Site Use: Agricultural: terrace system.
   Site Dimensions: 400 × 170 m
   Setting: Small, gently sloping valley bordered by low outcrops.
   Present Land Use/Disturbances: Dry farming.
   Site Description: Large terrace system. Terrace walls consist of linear alignments built with medium to large unmodified cobbles. The terraces appear to define modern field boundaries in some cases, although not all walls are currently maintained. A low stone embankment on the southwest edge of the site is of similar construction. A well (VMS-281) is located on the west edge of this terrace system.
   Artifacts: Very sparse scatter of ceramics, lithics (worked basalt), and iron slag. Slag continues in low densities as far north as VMS-121. No collections made.
   Temporal Affiliation: Unknown. Several stones near the west edge of site (near VMS-281) have Vijayanagara style quarry marks and there is evidence for Vijayanagara period quarrying in outcropping boulders south of the site.
   References: Morrison 1995:92, 102; Sinopoli and Morrison 2006:438.
   Illustrations: Figure 5.90.

SITE: VMS-281   Block: S   Transect: 10
   Primary Site Use: Agricultural: well.
   Site Dimensions: 6 × 12 m
   Setting: Flat area.
   Present Land Use/Disturbances: Recent plastering on the west wall is evidence that the well is being maintained. Well steps may have been removed.
   Site Description: Rock-cut well. The well is enclosed on the west by a plastered masonry wall consisting of fourteen courses of medium-sized rectangular blocks. There was evidently a staircase from this wall down into the well. The staircase is represented by four remaining steps and a trench. Additional steps likely existed, and were removed in the trench's excavation. A mounded area southeast of the well may be a result of this excavation. Numerous stones with Vijayanagara style quarry marks lie scattered nearby.
   Artifacts: 100% collection; no artifacts recovered.
   Temporal Affiliation: Vijayanagara.
   References: Sinopoli and Morrison 2006:438.
   Illustrations: Figures 5.90, 5.91; Plate 5.94.

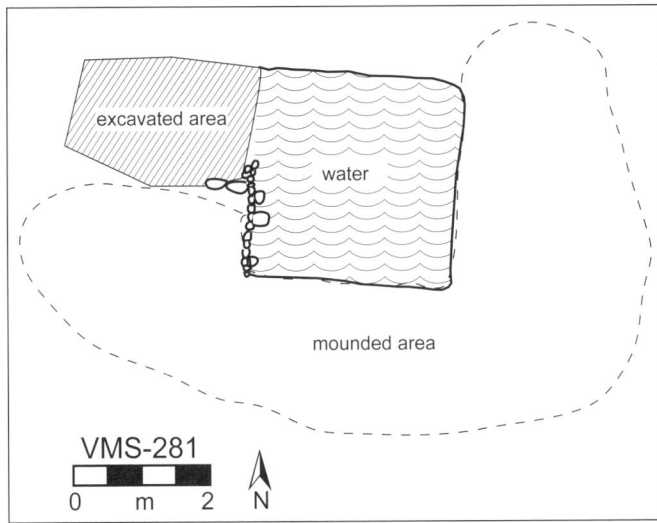

Figure 5.91. VMS-281, plan.

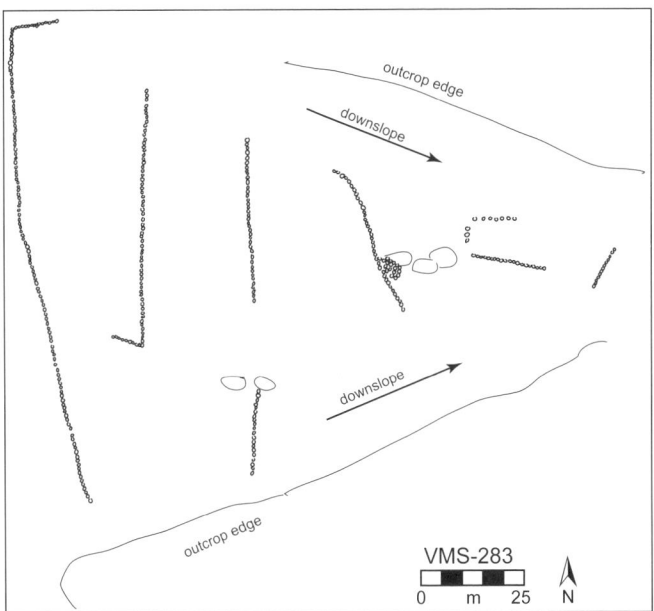

Figure 5.92. VMS-283, plan.

Plate 5.94. VMS-281, well overview.

SITE: VMS-282   Block: S   Transect: 11
  Primary Site Use: Unknown: isolated wall.
  Site Dimensions: 65 × 0.6 m
  Setting: Located along slope at the edge of an outcrop.
  Present Land Use/Disturbances: Directly south of the Tungabhadra Right Bank High Level Canal.
  Site Description: Wall. This north-south oriented wall is built up against a rocky outcrop, partway up the slope. The north end is constructed of two to six courses of large, unmodified boulders with occasional chinking stones. The south end of the wall loses height and definition as it veers west, becoming an overgrown earth and rubble mound. The wall may have had defensive and/or erosion control functions and may be associated with VMS-279.
  Artifacts: 100% collection; no artifacts recovered.
  Temporal Affiliation: Unknown.
  References: Sinopoli and Morrison 2006:438.

SITE: VMS-283   Block: S   Transect: 10
  Primary Site Use: Agricultural: terraces.
  Site Dimensions: 150 × 120 m
  Setting: An area of gently sloping fallow dry farmed fields spanning a narrow valley between two low outcrops.
  Present Land Use/Disturbances: Directly north of the Tungabhadra Right Bank High Level Canal.
  Site Description: Agricultural terraces. This facility lies in a small valley sloping down from west to east, and consists of a series of north-south walls. The west wall sits at the crest of a linear basalt outcrop and is simply built of aligned cobbles and boulders. Other walls are similarly constructed (c. 0.5 m high, 0.5-1 m wide), with basalt used in the area near the basalt outcrop and granite elsewhere. Some stones have also been piled against the north outcrop to minimize erosion. Fragmentary terrace walls are also found south of this valley, but these have been heavily disturbed by the canal, and their original alignments are impossible to discern.
  Artifacts: 100% collection; no artifacts recovered.
  Temporal Affiliation: Unknown.
  References: Morrison 1995:92, 102; Sinopoli and Morrison 2006:438.
  Illustrations: Figure 5.92.

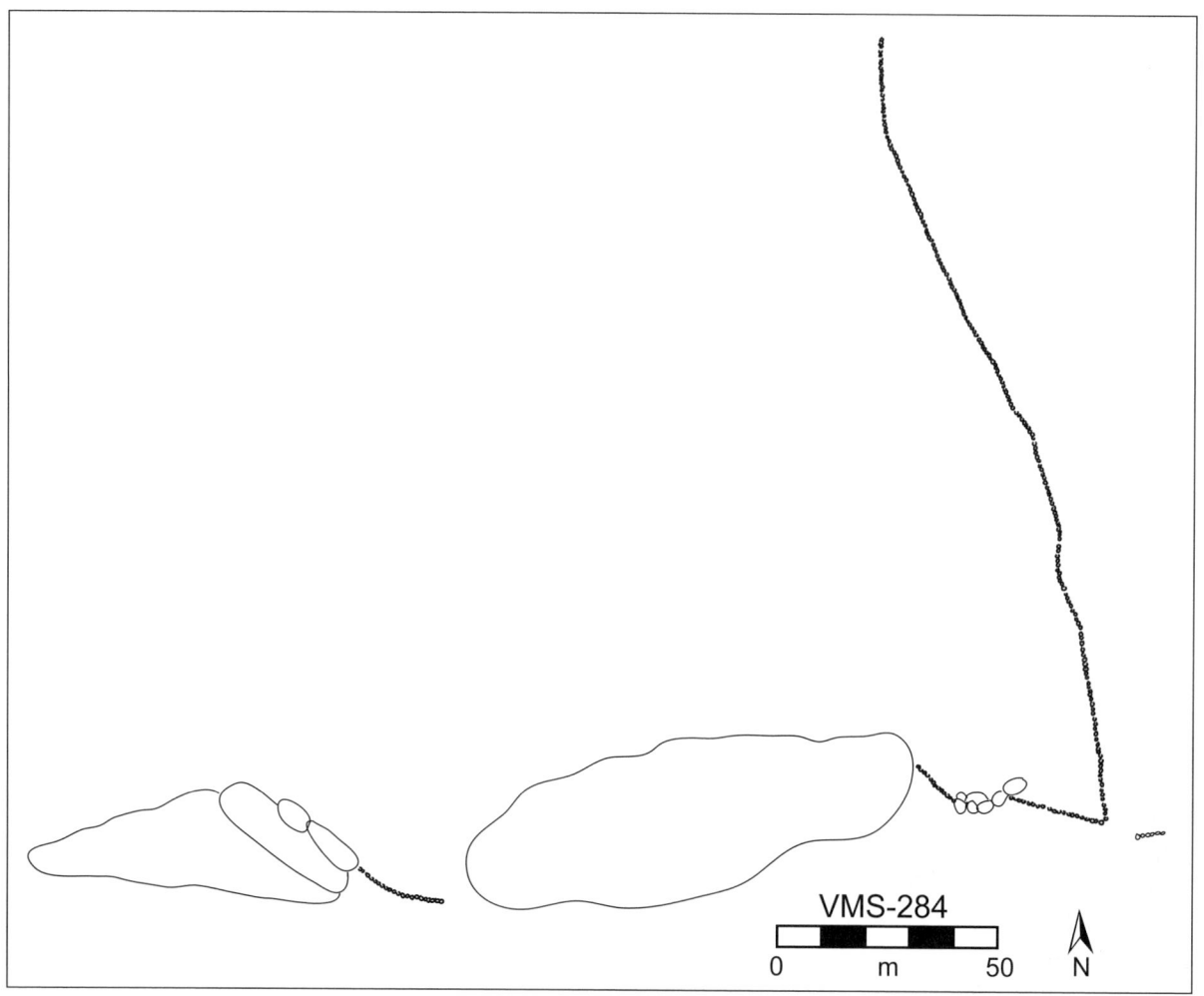

Figure 5.93. VMS-284, plan.

SITE: VMS-284   Block: S   Transect: 10
  Primary Site Use: Defensive: wall.
  Site Dimensions: 180 × 1 m
  Setting: On top of basalt ridge on outcrop.
  Present Land Use/Disturbances: Recent quarrying c. 100 m to the east of the site.
  Site Description: Walls. This site consists of several long walls. The main wall is oriented approximately north-south and runs along the top of a basalt ridge. It is constructed of four to six courses of large unmodified boulders. The wall has two faces with a cobble core and averages 1 m wide. At the south corner, the wall turns west for c. 40 m before it runs into a large outcrop. The wall picks up again on the other side of the outcrop, c. 100 m away. It then ends only a few meters from the northwest corner of VMS-283. The nature of the association, if any, between this wall and the extensive dryland terrace systems to the south and west is unclear.
  Artifacts: 100% collection 5 m on either side of the wall. No artifacts recovered.
  Temporal Affiliation: Unknown.
  References: Morrison 1995:65; Sinopoli and Morrison 2006:438.
  Illustrations: Figure 5.93.

SITE: VMS-285   Block: S   Transect: 10
  Primary Site Use: Unknown/residential?: ceramic scatter.
  Site Dimensions: 20 m diameter
  Setting: Grassy area amid outcrops.
  Present Land Use/Disturbances: Slope wash from surrounding outcrops may have influenced sherd distributions.
  Site Description: Ceramic scatter. This scatter is situated on the north edge of a low outcrop immediately north of terrace system VMS-283. Dense scatters of ceramics cluster in grassy areas amid outcropping boulders. Artifacts appear to derive from a small number of predominantly recent vessels.
  Artifacts: Variable dense ceramic scatter. Collections of three 2 × 2 m units spaced 10 m apart along a central north-south axis through site.
  Unit 1 (north): <50 g ceramics; wares: 2 black plain ware.
  Unit 2 (central): 4400 g ceramics; wares: 1069 black plain ware, 224 red plain ware. Diagnostics: 29 jars; the majority of sherds derive from a small number of broken vessels.
  Unit 3 (south): 900 g ceramics; wares: 159 black plain ware, 18 red plain ware. Diagnostics: 3 jars.
  Temporal Affiliation: Twentieth century.
  References: Sinopoli and Morrison 2006:438.
  Illustrations: Figure 5.94.

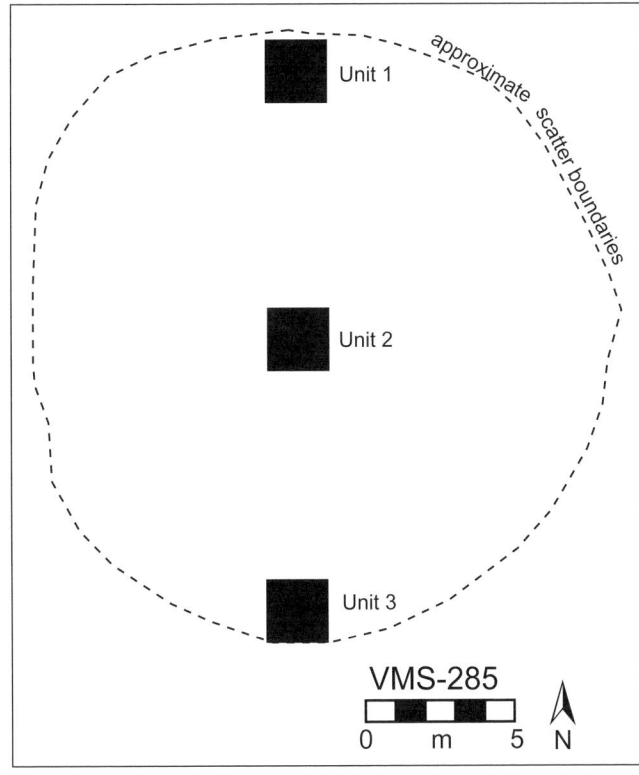

Figure 5.94. VMS-285, plan.

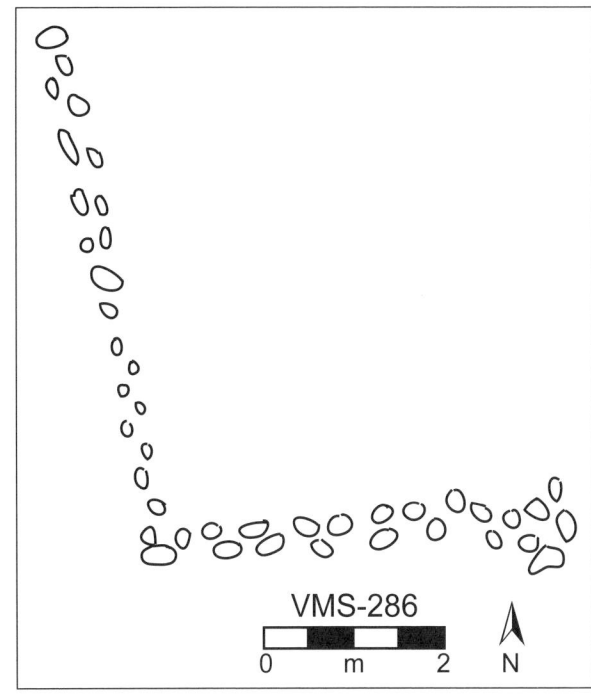

Figure 5.95. VMS-286, plan.

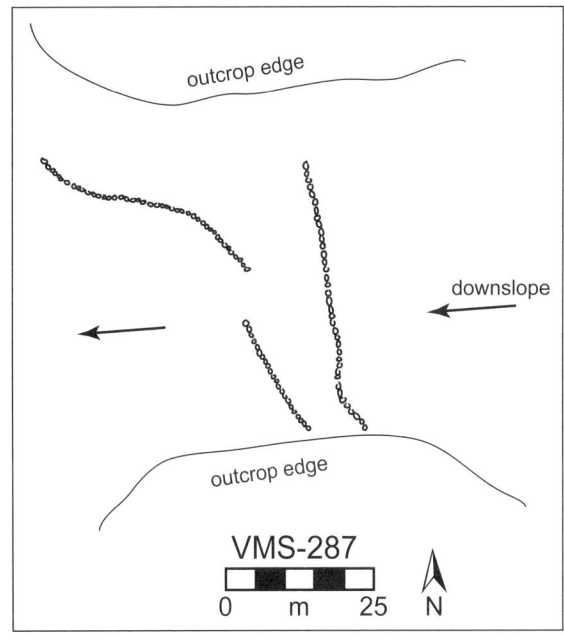

Figure 5.96. VMS-287, plan.

SITE: VMS-286   Block: S   Transect: 10
Primary Site Use: Agricultural: walls.
Site Dimensions: 11 × 9 m
Setting: Gentle slopes amid dry farmed fields.
Present Land Use/Disturbances: Dry farming. No disturbance evident.
Site Description: Walls. Two single-course roughly perpendicular walls incorporate naturally outcropping boulders and may be remnant field walls. The east-west wall is more solidly constructed.
Artifacts: A very sparse ceramic scatter was observed in nearby fields. 100% collection; no artifacts recovered.
Temporal Affiliation: Unknown.
References: Sinopoli and Morrison 2006:438.
Illustrations: Figure 5.95.

SITE: VMS-287   Block: S   Transect: 10
Primary Site Use: Agricultural: check dams.
Site Dimensions: 55 × 46 m
Setting: Moderately steeply sloping valley between two outcrops.
Present Land Use/Disturbances: Recent quarrying, dense vegetation growth, and slope wash have worked to both bury and expose the site. This area is not under cultivation.
Site Description: Check dams. This facility lies in a small valley sloping down from east to west and consists of three north-south walls as well as several natural outcropping ridges. The walls are built of unmodified irregularly coursed granite and basalt boulders of variable sizes (0.6 m wide and 0.4-0.8 m high).
Artifacts: 100% collection; no artifacts recovered.
Temporal Affiliation: Unknown.
References: Morrison 1995:92, 102; Sinopoli and Morrison 2006:438.
Illustrations: Figure 5.96.

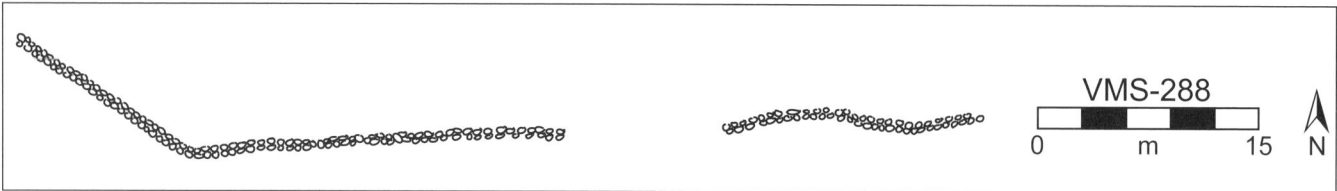

Figure 5.97. VMS-288, plan.

SITE: VMS-288   Block: S   Transect: 10
Primary Site Use: Agricultural: erosion control wall.
Site Dimensions: 70 × 0.7 m
Setting: Gentle slopes near base of outcrop, amid thorny scrub and grasses.
Present Land Use/Disturbances: A recent field wall indicates occasional dry farming in this area. A footpath runs over the wall.
Site Description: Erosion control wall. This east-west oriented wall is located along the south edge of VMS-280, a dry land terrace system. The one to two course high double-faced wall is c. 0.7 m wide and is constructed of large unmodified boulders with cobble infill. The wall incorporates several outcropping boulders. It may be associated with VMS-280 or it may be a separate erosion control feature at the edge of the valley.
Artifacts: 100% collection; no artifacts recovered.
Temporal Affiliation: Unknown.
References: Morrison 1995:102; Sinopoli and Morrison 2006:438.
Illustrations: Figure 5.97.

SITE: VMS-289   Block: S   Transect: 11
Primary Site Use: Unknown: standing columns.
Site Dimensions: 7.5 × 0.5 m
Setting: In level dry farmed fields.
Present Land Use/Disturbances: Reworked and displaced stone slabs.
Site Description: Upright stone slabs. These two standing columns are spaced 7.5 m apart. Although they have Vijayanagara style quarry marks, they are not associated with any structure and are probably reworked. The columns are rectangular in section (0.24 × 0.54 and 0.35 × 0.38 m) and c. 2.5 m tall with triangular tops. Three holes, averaging 0.18 m in diameter, have been bored through each column. Some do not go all the way through and holes are not well aligned. These are probably the roof supports for a seasonally occupied structure; such stone supports are commonly left in place throughout the year. They appear to have been modified from older quarried slabs.
Artifacts: Low density of sherds found in surrounding fields. 100% collection. <50 g ceramics; wares: 3 black plain ware, 1 red plain ware. Diagnostics: 1 jar.
Temporal Affiliation: Vijayanagara and post-Vijayanagara.
References: Sinopoli and Morrison 2006:438.
Illustrations: Plate 5.95.

SITE: VMS-290   Block: S   Transect: 11
Primary Site Use: Unknown: petroglyph.
Site Dimensions: 10 × 3 m
Setting: On low boulders outcropping in a level, uncultivated area of thorny scrub.
Present Land Use/Disturbances: Just south of small modern shrine.

Plate 5.95. VMS-289, standing columns.

Site Description: Petroglyphs and script located across three small boulder faces. Two figures appear to be checked squares but the others are less clear. A section of Kannada or Telugu script is located below a snake figure. These images appear to be recent.
Artifacts: A very sparse ceramic scatter. 100% collection. <50 g ceramics; wares: 4 black plain ware.
Temporal Affiliation: Recent.
References: Morrison 1995:75; Sinopoli and Morrison 2006:438.

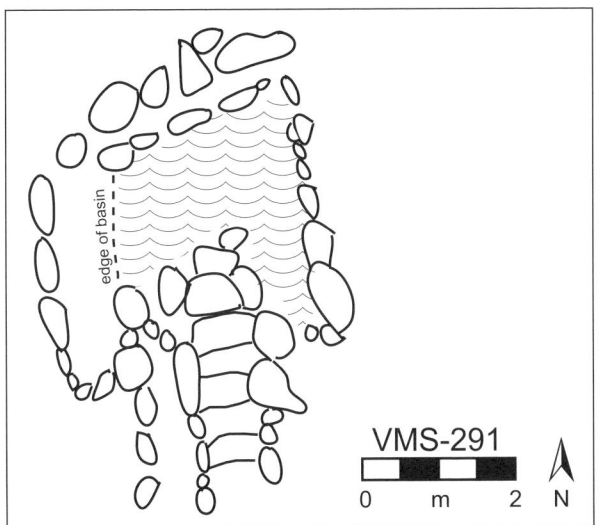

(*Above*) Figure 5.98. VMS-291, plan.
(*Above Right*) Plate 5.96. VMS-651, gate, overview from west.

SITE: VMS-291   Block: S   Transect: 11
Primary Site Use: Agricultural/transportation: step well.
Site Dimensions: 6 × 5 m
Setting: Gently sloping, dry farmed fields.
Present Land Use/Disturbances: Heavily overgrown, c. 40 m west of the Kamalapuram-Papinayakanahalli road.
Site Description: Step well. This small square well is built of seven courses of large unmodified basalt boulders. Coursing is roughly horizontal with some chinking. The west side of the well is pitted and some stones have been removed. There are seven narrow steps on the south side of the well. An outer ledge of boulders c. 1 m extends all around the well. This well may have been located on or near a road approximating the course of the present Kamalapuram-Papinayakanahalli road.
Artifacts: Very sparse ceramic scatter and one piece of slag. 100% collection. <50 g ceramics; wares: 7 black plain ware.
Temporal Affiliation: Unknown.
References: Morrison 1995:75; Sinopoli and Morrison 2006:438.
Illustrations: Figure 5.98.

SITE: VMS-651   Block: S   Transect: 18
Primary Site Use: Transport/defensive: gate.
Site Dimensions: 30 × 30 m
GPS Location: 15°18'17.0" N, 76°29'56.6" E
Setting: A flat area with gentle slopes amid agricultural fields.
Resources: None noted.
Present Land Use/Disturbances: The area is currently 20% cultivated, 20% fallow, and 60% uncultivated (sugar cane fields to the east of gate, fallow millet field to the west; area inside the gate is overgrown). A large termite mound on the southeast gate platform contains a huge black snake. The north and south sides of the gate are collapsed, and part of the roof has fallen. The layout of the structure is, however, clear. Thorns and brush are piled in the entry.
Site Description: Gate in city wall. VMS-651 is a monumental gateway set into the outer city wall VMS-123. The gate's exterior faces east. The structure is well built, of dressed blocks and slabs, and originally stood c. 8 m high. On the east, as one approaches the gate from outside the wall, two large (10 × 15 m) platforms faced with dressed horizontal slabs flank a 30 m north-south × 15 m east-west passageway. On the south wall of this entry (i.e., the north wall of the south platform) is a carved panel showing Nandi and an elite devotee worshipping a lingam.

The rectangular entry then narrows as one enters the roofed gateway. Here the passage is 4.5 m wide and, as noted, c. 8 m high. The gate is constructed of long dressed slabs; every third course consists of very long slabs that protrude slightly, creating a tiered effect. The long slabs of the roof are supported by carved brackets (each actually constructed of four courses of sculpted elements). The brackets end just below the roof in pendant bud motifs. Under each of these is a carved Yaksha (dwarf) figure holding his hands over his head and thus appearing to support the beams with the pendant buds. Under each Yaksha is a sitting yali with a fierce expression.

Two tall upright pillars define the west side of the covered passage. These once reached as high as the roof and are only dressed on their exterior (east) face. They protrude into the gate passage slightly (c. 0.4 m each), constricting the opening. If there had been a doorway in the gate it would probably have fit into the lintel (now gone) spanning these uprights. This is supported by a broken fragment lying in the gate passage that has a door socket carved into it. These uprights each have a "guardian" figure carved onto them at ground level, flanking the entrance and facing east. Both are holding a long staff or spear; the one on the north has a tall pointed hat, the one on the south a turban. Inside the gate passage on the north side is a door opening into a small room built into the gate itself. This room also has a door opening out to the west entryway.

The west entryway, inside the gate, is smaller and less imposing than the east one. The gate is also flanked by platforms on this side, but they are smaller, c. 8 m east-west × 6 m north-south. Although they are now in poor condition, they were once faced with dressed moldings (two step with angled bevel and half medallions).

The west entryway opens out onto a road, indicated in part by fragmentary road walls that extend c. 35 m to the west of the gate. The gate is aligned with the east entrance of the large temple complex VMS-142 and the road thus appears to have led directly to that temple.
Artifacts: A moderate scatter of earthenware ceramics and some slag are found all around the gate and in the surrounding fields. This is part of the more extensive scatter that occurs all across the north part of Block S. No collections made.
Temporal Affiliation: Vijayanagara.
Illustrations: Plates 5.96-5.100.

Plate 5.97. VMS-651, door guardian on north side of gate exterior.

Plate 5.99. VMS-651, royal devotee worshipping Nandi and lingam on carved panel on gate entry.

Plate 5.98. VMS-651, door guardian on south side of gate exterior.

Plate 5.100. VMS-651, gate interior, detail of corbelled roof slabs and supports, with carved Yaksha and yali figures.

– 6 –

Artifact Distributions and Analysis

As discussed in Chapter 2, an important component of site documentation in the VMS is the study of artifact distribution and forms. The presence and nature of a range of artifact materials—including earthenware and imported ceramics, lithics, iron implements and production waste, figurines, coins, and so on—provide important information on site function, chronology, and internal variability. Artifact collection strategies were reviewed in Chapter 2, while Chapters 3-5 contain summary information on collection strategies and artifacts recovered by site. In this chapter, we address general patterns of artifact distributions in surveyed areas in Blocks O, S, and T, and consider their larger implications for understanding the Vijayanagara metropolitan region.

Contexts of Artifact Recovery

The vast majority of artifacts recovered in the Vijayanagara Metropolitan Survey are derived from systematic surface collections at individual sites. The highest artifact densities, mostly of ceramics and lithics, are found in settlement sites, including nucleated settlements, isolated structures, rock shelters, and areas of dense surface scatters. Other artifact-rich sites include production locales. Prominent among the latter are iron production sites, characterized by dense scatters of slag and ceramic furnace fixtures (Lycett 1994; Sinopoli 1994, 2003). Areas of stone quarrying and construction and stone peg production (see below) also produce discrete scatters of lithic waste.

Within sites, surface artifact densities and distributions are affected by a range of factors, both cultural and natural. Cultural factors include past use of the landscape and depositional practices, as well as more modern practices of land use, disturbance, and deposition. Thus, in sites such as VMS-16, pit digging has uncovered previously buried deposits of archaeological materials, while remains of settlement VMS-101 have been almost completely obliterated by the recent construction of rice fields. Depositional and erosional processes also play a significant role in patterns of artifact distribution and visibility, with materials buried under recent colluviation or displaced as a result of soil and water movement. The latter process is especially evident in small depositional pockets in upland outcrop and sheet rock areas. In such areas, slope wash and erosion have led to the accumulation of sediments in small depressions in open areas or in rock shelters, often leading to high and highly localized densities of extremely fragmented sherds and other artifacts.

In addition to site-specific artifact collections, a smaller percentage of materials recovered in the survey consists of isolated artifacts found in non-site locations within sample transects. Such finds occur as part of the low density artifact scatter that characterizes the entire metropolitan region. We did not, as a general rule, collect the earthenware sherds that are the most common category of artifacts in this scatter, although information was recorded on their overall distribution patterns. Isolated finds that were collected include imported porcelain or celadon sherds; steatite pencil fragments (possibly diagnostic of the Vijayanagara period); beads, bangles, and other ornaments; figurines; and historic and prehistoric lithics. The location of these objects is recorded as precisely as possible in field books, but these finds are not given site designations. The presence of isolated sculptural fragments and bedrock or boulder mortars is similarly noted.

Artifact frequency in the broad, low density scatter of cultural materials in the survey area is positively correlated with the intensity of ancient land use. Proximity to constructed features—such as roads, settlements, and ancient agricultural fields—is the major cultural factor affecting density; soil erosion and deposition, watercourses and runoff patterns, and contemporary land use, construction, and agricultural activities also affect artifact preservation and visibility. In the less intensively utilized upland areas of the metropolitan region, such as the southeastern part of Block T and some canal-irrigated areas, sherds and other artifacts are quite rare, on the order of ten or fewer per hectare. In more intensively utilized areas, ceramic frequencies in the low density scatter are significantly higher, up to several dozen sherds per hectare. Areas characterized by densities of one or more sherds per square meter are defined as artifact scatters and given site designations.

The variable artifact density that occurs across the metropolitan region is likely a product of a range of cultural behaviors as well as depositional and erosional processes. The use of household waste as field manure is probably the most important source of many of these materials (Lycett 1994; Sinopoli 1994, 1999; Wilkinson 1982). This practice is important in the region today and distributional patterns suggest that it was similarly important during the Vijayanagara period. Contemporary farmers in the survey area transport household waste, including food residues, ash, and animal dung, to agricultural fields. The waste is heaped into small mounds (c. 1 m across × 0.50 m high) evenly spread across the field areas, and is eventually ploughed into the soil. A range of artifacts is included in the modern waste piles, including ceramic sherds, and bits of cloth, plastic, glass, and so on. Plowing distributes these materials across the fields, forming an extensive low density scatter. We suggest that similar practices in historic times have contributed to the distributions of archaeological materials observed today.

Low density distributions of industrial byproducts have also been observed in the survey. Prominent among these is iron slag (see below; Lycett 1994; Sinopoli 1994, 2003), light scatters of which extend a kilometer or more from known Vijayanagara period production sites. This pattern suggests that industrial waste, and in particular ash, was also used in manuring activities. Such behaviors appear to have been highly destructive of pyro-technological sites and may account for the low densities of such sites in the metropolitan region.

Other cultural behaviors no doubt also contributed to the low density artifact scatter in the metropolitan region. These include the use, breakage, and deposition of ceramics by agricultural laborers, travelers, or inhabitants of short-term encampments in the urban hinterland. Examples of these kinds of practices are abundantly evident in contemporary land use, including short-term occupations by sheep-goat pastoralists who graze their herds on field stubble (in exchange for farmers' rights to manure). Such patterns of movement and short-term occupation no doubt have a long history in the metropolitan region.

In our discussion of VMS artifact patterns, we proceed by first considering each category of materials recovered, and then by discussing general patterns in artifact distribution and inter- and intra-site patterning in artifact distributions in the greater metropolitan region. We will not consider architectural or sculptural remains in this chapter as they have already been discussed in some detail in site descriptions in Chapters 3-5. In examining overall patterns of ceramic distributions, we include data from all systematic collection units. Information from "diagnostic sweeps" (collections that focused on acquiring samples of measurable diagnostic sherds) is incorporated into discussions of specific vessel forms and comparison of vessel-use class distributions, but is not included in discussion of overall densities, since these were typically not controlled collections and the degree to which they are representative of overall site distributions can therefore not be assessed. Nonetheless, it is important to note that even in diagnostic collections, attempts were made to collect the full range of diagnostic ceramic forms present at a site in order to obtain as unbiased a sample as possible.

Earthenware Ceramics

Locally produced earthenware ceramics are the most common artifacts observed in the survey region, in both site and off-site contexts. This discussion will focus on earthenware ceramics collected from locations designated as archaeological sites. Two levels of information are recorded on ceramics and other artifact data. An initial sorting of artifacts from surface collection units (whether 100% of a site or smaller units) was conducted in the field and broad ceramic ware and form categories were recorded on standardized forms. Total ceramic weight was recorded, per collection unit, to the nearest 50 g. The presence of other artifact classes, worked sherds, and decorated ceramics was also noted on site forms along with information on surface conditions and visibility.

All sherds were sorted according to ware. Three ware categories have been defined for Vijayanagara ceramics on the basis of surface treatment and wall thickness: plain ware (red, black or brown), burnished ware (red or black), and coarse ware. Rim sherds were further subdivided into two broad vessel form classes: bowls (unrestricted vessels) or jars (restricted or necked vessels). The three major restricted vessel rim forms were also recorded (flange, straight or round rims; see Sinopoli 1986, 1993b for a discussion of these ceramic categories). This classification derives from work conducted by Sinopoli (1986, 1993b) on ceramics from three areas of the Vijayanagara urban core: the East Valley, the Islamic Quarter, and the Nobleman's Quarter. We draw on these earlier analyses as a comparative baseline from which to evaluate ceramic distributions in the metropolitan region in order to consider similarities and differences in ceramic use, forms, and distributions.

Surface finds of ceramics pose several challenges to analysis and interpretation. First, except in cases where they have been recently exposed by plowing or construction activities, the sherds tend to be highly fragmented and measurable diagnostics are therefore scarce. Second, surface materials are often heavily patinated or eroded, with features such as color, ware, and decoration difficult to identify. This is especially problematic for distinguishing brown from black plain ware sherds, a distinction that in any case appears to be of little analytical significance since both colors result when vessels are fired in reducing atmospheres, and vessel color can grade from brown to black on a single sherd. When the distinction cannot be clearly made, vessels were coded as black and for analytical purposes these wares are grouped together.

Third, the absence of clear-cut chronological indicators for Vijayanagara ceramics means that it is often difficult to date surface finds. While there are a few forms (for example, shallow bowls, round rim restricted storage vessels) that seem to be restricted to the Vijayanagara period, and other forms that are clearly recent (for example, triple flange rims; see discussion of individual vessel and rim forms below), many forms exhibit a great deal of continuity between Vijayanagara and subsequent times. Ware density and consistency, breakage, and surface treatment (for example, the contemporary use of a talc or graphite-like coating to give vessels a metallic sheen) can also be used to distinguish recent from older ceramics. As the project proceeded, our ability to identify both pre- and post-Vijayanagara ceramics has improved and our collection strategies have correspondingly become more targeted (that is, we stopped collecting definitively recent ceramic scatters). Nonetheless, precise chronological assignment of ceramics remains an unresolved problem for Vijayanagara archaeology, as it is for most South Indian archaeological periods.

Ceramic Counts and Wares

Systematic collections yielded ceramics from less than a third of the sites documented in Blocks O, S, and T ($n = 113$, Table 6.1). Measurable diagnostics were recovered from 68 sites. Not surprisingly, artifacts were least common in agricultural features such as terrace systems, check dams, and reservoir embankments, and were most common in settlements and inhabited rock shelters, artifact scatters, and craft production sites. Overall, artifact densities in the metropolitan region are significantly lower than in the urban core (see Sinopoli 1993b), though given the much broader diversity of site types and activities in the survey area, such broad comparisons mean little.

Sherd densities, calculated as the number of sherds per square meter of site or collection area, varied widely across sites and types of sites (Table 6.2). At many sites, density values are extremely low, for example, 0.0014 sherds per square meter along road segment VMS-81, or 0.002 sherds per square meter at reservoir embankment VMS-136. Low densities typically occur at extensive agricultural or fortification sites where only one or two sherds were observed on the surface of long linear sites. Such sherds are most likely part of the "background" scatter of the region, and were not necessarily directly associated with activities or behaviors carried out at the specific sites where they were found. Highest ceramic densities occurred in ceramic scatter VMS-285, where a single 2 × 2 meter collection unit yielded nearly 1300 sherds, and overall densities were 122.67 sherds per square meter. Ceramic densities at settlement sites range from approximately 2 to more than 20 sherds per square meter.

A total of 16,123 sherds were sorted and counted from the 113 sites yielding systematic collections. Of these, more than 99%, or 15,981 sherds, were plain wares, the vast majority being black or dark brown in color (compared to 91% plain wares in the urban core). Red plain ware sherds comprised approximately 7.0% of the plain ware sample (1117 sherds). This is roughly comparable to plain ware distributions within the Vijayanagara urban core, where red sherds constitute 5.5% of total plain ware sherds (Sinopoli 1993b:166).

Seventy-seven sherds were classified as coarse wares (0.005% of the total). As defined by Sinopoli (1986, 1993b:43), coarse wares range in thickness from one to three centimeters and have a distinctive red or light brown paste with high percentages of coarse sand and organic inclusions. Coarse ware vessel types include braziers, water pipes, ring well linings, and tuyeres[1] used in metal working. They are thus mostly closely associated with settlements and craft production locales. This is seen in the survey data (Table 6.1), with 21 coarse ware sherds recovered from settlement VMS-2, 21 sherds from settlement VMS-35, and 5 sherds from collection units of iron workshop VMS-7 (with many more coarse ware tuyere fragments noted on the site's surface and in the fill of nearby site VMS-121).

Burnished ware sherds are quite rare in the ceramic collections, with only 67 sherds (0.004%) documented. This is a much lower density than recorded in the urban core, where burnished sherds comprise 0.06% of the total sherds analyzed by Sinopoli (1993b:141). It is likely that the low density of burnished ware in the metropolitan region is at least in part a result of the eroded or patinated conditions of many sherds, and that counts are therefore underestimates of actual frequency of use.

Vessel Forms

As noted above, a classification of Vijayanagara vessel and rim forms has been developed by Sinopoli (1986, 1993b) in analyses of ceramics of the urban core. Vessels were grouped into two broad morphological classes—unrestricted and restricted vessels—with each category subdivided on the basis of overall shape and size. This classification system was used in the analysis of ceramics from the metropolitan region in both the sorting and counting of surface finds and in more detailed analyses of measurable diagnostics collected from sample units and diagnostic sweeps. In the discussion that follows, we consider general distributions of specific vessel forms and the information this provides on site function and chronology.

---

[1]The pipe or nozzle through which air is forced into a forge or furnace, usually with the use of a bellows.

Table 6.1. Sherd counts by site.

Site	Weight (g)*	Plain Ware: Black	Plain Ware: Brown	Plain Ware: Red	Plain Ware: Totals	Coarse Ware	Burnish Ware: Black	Burnish Ware: Red	Burnish Ware: Totals	Total Counts	Bowls	Jars
VMS-2	8500	749	0	40	789	21	3	1	4	813	10	120
VMS-7	1400	210	0	12	222	5	1	1	2	229	6	24
VMS-8	25	9	2	1	12	0	0	0	0	12	1	2
VMS-9	450	53	0	6	59	0	0	0	0	59	0	7
VMS-13	150	41	0	6	47	0	0	0	0	47	0	4
VMS-14	50	20	0	3	23	0	0	0	0	23	0	0
VMS-15	450	111	0	6	117	0	0	0	0	117	0	8
VMS-16	1050	170	0	11	181	1	0	4	4	186	0	13
VMS-18	25	4	0	0	4	0	0	0	0	4	1	0
VMS-21	600	85	0	16	101	0	0	1	1	102	0	5
VMS-24	900	517	0	48	565	0	0	0	0	565	1	15
VMS-33	1050	357	2	6	365	0	0	0	0	365	6	23
VMS-35	4300	843	0	90	933	21	11	27	38	992	2	50
VMS-37	150	27	2	5	34	0	0	0	0	34	0	1
VMS-38	250	30	0	40	70	0	0	0	0	70	0	1
VMS-39	150	10	0	0	10	0	0	0	0	10	1	0
VMS-41	250	21	0	1	22	0	0	0	0	22	1	2
VMS-43	450	149	0	8	157	0	0	0	0	157	1	7
VMS-45	800	114	0	21	135	0	0	1	1	136	1	6
VMS-53	25	4	0	0	4	0	0	0	0	4	0	0
VMS-55	25	13	0	1	14	0	0	0	0	14	0	0
VMS-57	25	8	0	0	8	0	0	0	0	8	0	0
VMS-64	50	22	0	4	26	0	0	0	0	26	0	0
VMS-65	25	4	0	0	4	0	0	0	0	4	0	0
VMS-66	500	52	0	12	64	3	0	0	0	67	3	7
VMS-67	2000	270	0	1	271	1	0	0	0	272	0	8
VMS-76	400	226	0	25	251	0	0	0	0	251	0	3
VMS-78	1675	434	4	28	466	1	0	0	0	467	2	20
VMS-79	900	392	0	1	393	0	0	1	1	394	5	11
VMS-81	25	1	0	0	1	0	0	0	0	1	0	0
VMS-83	425	168	0	30	198	1	1	0	1	200	2	6
VMS-84	25	3	0	1	4	0	0	0	0	4	0	0
VMS-88	825	208	0	62	270	2	0	0	0	272	1	1
VMS-91	300	93	0	4	97	2	0	0	0	99	2	1
VMS-94	50	1	0	0	1	0	0	0	0	1	1	0
VMS-95	25	1	0	0	1	0	0	0	0	1	1	0
VMS-101	1675	467	3	55	525	1	0	1	1	527	5	15
VMS-102	3100	1092	0	103	1195	0	4	0	4	1199	1	15
VMS-108	25	3	0	0	3	0	0	0	0	3	0	0
VMS-124	200	15	0	0	15	0	0	0	0	15	0	2
VMS-125	100	8	2	0	10	0	0	0	0	10	0	1
VMS-127	25	4	7	0	11	0	0	0	0	11	0	0
VMS-128	25	5	0	0	5	0	0	0	0	5	0	0
VMS-132	150	30	0	3	33	0	0	0	0	33	0	7
VMS-135	125	4	0	0	4	1	0	0	0	5	0	0
VMS-136	25	2	0	0	2	0	0	0	0	2	0	1
VMS-139	50	9	0	0	9	0	0	0	0	9	0	0
VMS-140	400	34	11	3	48	0	0	0	0	48	0	2
VMS-142	700	78	19	0	97	0	0	0	0	97	3	11
VMS-144	1750	380	131	14	525	2	0	0	0	527	6	25
VMS-145	1600	235	127	0	362	0	0	0	0	362	0	4
VMS-146	400	171	161	0	332	0	0	0	0	332	0	4
VMS-147	1150	252	112	0	364	0	0	0	0	364	2	6
VMS-149	750	53	26	0	79	0	0	0	0	79	2	9
VMS-150	1150	193	6	0	199	0	0	0	0	199	0	4
VMS-151	650	112	0	0	112	0	0	0	0	112	0	7
VMS-153	350	36	6	0	42	1	0	0	0	43	0	1
VMS-158	250	22	11	1	34	0	0	0	0	34	0	5

Table 6.1 cont.

Site	Weight (g)*	Plain Ware: Black	Plain Ware: Brown	Plain Ware: Red	Plain Ware: Totals	Coarse Ware	Burnish Ware: Black	Burnish Ware: Red	Burnish Ware: Totals	Total Counts	Bowls	Jars
VMS-159	25	1	0	0	1	0	0	0	0	1	0	0
VMS-160	50	6	3	0	9	0	0	0	0	9	0	0
VMS-161	700	62	15	2	79	0	0	0	0	79	1	3
VMS-163	250	37	9	1	47	0	0	0	0	47	0	1
VMS-164	725	129	16	2	147	2	3	0	3	152	2	8
VMS-165	200	25	0	0	25	0	0	0	0	25	0	1
VMS-167	1100	161	13	0	174	0	0	0	0	174	0	14
VMS-168	50	0	7	0	7	0	0	0	0	7	0	0
VMS-169	975	97	26	0	123	1	0	0	0	124	1	7
VMS-172	400	43	21	0	64	0	0	0	0	64	0	1
VMS-174	150	10	23	0	33	0	0	0	0	33	2	5
VMS-175	250	43	11	0	54	0	0	0	0	54	1	7
VMS-176	525	66	5	4	75	0	0	0	0	75	0	4
VMS-178	350	61	24	0	85	1	0	0	0	86	0	5
VMS-179	400	50	41	4	95	1	0	0	0	96	1	6
VMS-180	600	120	38	3	161	1	0	0	0	161	1	15
VMS-182	175	11	3	0	14	0	0	0	0	14	0	4
VMS-183	700	91	4	0	95	0	0	0	0	95	0	0
VMS-184	75	31	6	4	41	0	0	0	0	41	0	0
VMS-186	75	8	1	0	9	0	0	0	0	9	0	1
VMS-188	25	1	0	0	1	0	0	0	0	1	0	0
VMS-192	250	0	0	69	69	0	0	0	0	69	1	0
VMS-193	250	18	11	2	31	0	0	0	0	31	4	7
VMS-195	50	0	1	0	1	0	0	0	0	1	0	1
VMS-196	550	64	82	2	148	0	0	0	0	148	0	3
VMS-197	1375	161	39	1	201	0	0	0	0	201	0	6
VMS-198	200	10	26	0	36	0	0	0	0	36	1	1
VMS-201	1075	186	35	10	231	0	0	0	0	231	1	19
VMS-202	400	44	28	6	78	1	0	0	0	79	0	9
VMS-203	300	42	9	6	57	0	0	0	0	57	1	5
VMS-204	150	15	3	0	18	0	0	0	0	18	0	2
VMS-207	100	16	7	0	23	0	0	0	0	23	1	3
VMS-218	600	59	7	0	66	2	0	0	0	68	0	2
VMS-219	50	0	0	4	4	0	0	0	0	4	0	3
VMS-238	100	15	6	0	21	0	0	0	0	21	0	0
VMS-241	50	4	1	0	5	0	0	0	0	5	1	0
VMS-243	1400	175	23	12	210	0	0	0	0	210	1	11
VMS-245	25	0	2	0	2	0	0	0	0	2	0	0
VMS-249	25	3	0	0	3	0	0	0	0	3	0	0
VMS-251	850	193	0	0	193	0	0	0	0	193	1	6
VMS-254	1900	222	12	1	235	1	0	0	0	236	8	22
VMS-274	100	13	0	0	13	0	0	0	0	13	1	2
VMS-285	5325	1230	0	242	1472	0	0	0	0	1472	0	32
VMS-289	25	3	0	1	4	0	0	0	0	4	0	1
VMS-290	25	4	0	0	4	0	0	0	0	4	0	0
VMS-291	25	7	0	0	7	0	0	0	0	7	0	0
VMS-336	5900	177	0	1	178	0	0	0	0	178	0	8
VMS-339	700	106	0	9	115	0	0	0	0	115	0	0
VMS-340	450	42	0	3	45	0	0	0	0	45	0	6
VMS-341	2150	87	49	0	136	0	0	0	0	136	0	6
VMS-344	25	1	0	0	1	0	0	0	0	1	0	0
VMS-347	25	0	1	0	1	0	0	0	0	1	0	0
VMS-361	2625	438	355	51	844	0	0	3	3	847	1	14
VMS-365	700	154	34	8	196	2	2	2	4	202	6	10
VMS-371	750	59	9	1	69	2	0	0	0	71	1	4
All Groups	79,275	13,226	1638	1117	15,981	77	25	42	67	16,123	105	729

*Weights of less than 50 g (our smallest unit of measurement) have been assigned the arbitrary value of 25 g.

Table 6.2. Sherd counts and density by site.

Site	Area (m²)	Weight (g)	Plain Ware: Total Sherds	Total Sherd Counts*	Sherds per m² (mean)
VMS-2	150	8500	789	813	5.4200
VMS-7	40	1400	222	229	5.7250
VMS-8	440	25	12	12	0.0273
VMS-9	144	450	59	59	0.4097
VMS-13	195	150	47	47	0.2410
VMS-14	108	50	23	23	0.2130
VMS-15	5.4	450	117	117	21.6667
VMS-16	16	1050	181	186	11.6250
VMS-18	0.6	25	4	4	6.3492
VMS-21	175	600	101	102	0.9862
VMS-24	34	900	565	565	16.6176
VMS-33	84	1050	365	365	4.2939
VMS-35	505.5	4300	933	992	4.3337
VMS-37	82	150	34	34	0.4190
VMS-38	10.2	250	70	70	6.8359
VMS-39	240	150	10	10	0.0417
VMS-41	6.6	250	22	22	3.3333
VMS-43	90	450	157	157	1.7444
VMS-52	200	800	135	136	0.6800
VMS-53	7	25	4	4	0.5714
VMS-55	1.3	25	14	14	11.2000
VMS-57	10	25	8	8	0.8000
VMS-64	41	50	26	26	0.6348
VMS-65	35	25	4	4	0.1143
VMS-66	64	500	64	67	1.0469
VMS-67	117	2000	271	272	3.3571
VMS-76	220	400	251	251	1.1409
VMS-78	192	1675	466	467	2.4323
VMS-79	705	900	393	394	0.6617
VMS-81	700	25	1	1	0.0014
VMS-83	894	425	198	200	0.3765
VMS-84	1500	25	4	4	0.0027
VMS-88	1467	825	270	272	0.2405
VMS-91	750	300	97	99	0.1320
VMS-94	6	50	1	1	0.1667
VMS-95	400	25	1	1	0.0025
VMS-101	112	1675	525	527	4.7054
VMS-102	96	3100	1195	1199	12.4896
VMS-108	360	25	3	3	0.0083
VMS-124	648	200	15	15	0.0231
VMS-125	8	100	10	10	1.2500
VMS 127	168	25	11	11	0.0655
VMS-128	20	25	5	5	0.2500
VMS-132	1500	150	33	33	0.0220
VMS-135	20	125	4	5	0.2500
VMS-136	1000	25	2	2	0.0020
VMS-139	3400	50	9	9	0.0026
VMS-140	32	400	48	48	1.5000
VMS-142	28	700	97	97	3.4643
VMS-144	48	1750	525	527	10.9792
VMS-145	16	1600	362	362	22.6250
VMS-146	9000	400	332	332	0.0369
VMS-147	492	1150	364	364	0.7398
VMS-149	166	775	79	79	3.1713
VMS-150	8	1150	199	199	24.8750
VMS-151	90	650	112	112	1.2444
VMS-153	32	350	42	42	1.3100
VMS-158	6400	250	34	34	0.0053

Table 6.2 cont.

Site	Area (m²)	Weight (g)	Plain Ware: Total Sherds	Total Sherd Counts*	Sherds per m² (mean)
VMS-159	2550	25	1	1	0.0004
VMS-160	480	50	9	9	0.0188
VMS-161	32	700	79	79	2.4688
VMS-163	12	250	47	47	3.9167
VMS-164	32	725	147	152	4.7500
VMS-165	4400	200	25	25	0.0057
VMS-167	4	1100	174	174	43.5000
VMS-168	11.9	50	7	7	0.5892
VMS-169	96	1025	123	124	1.2917
VMS-172	34.8	400	64	64	1.6686
VMS-174	3.8	150	33	33	8.8000
VMS-175	63	250	54	54	0.8571
VMS-176	28	525	75	75	2.6786
VMS-178	16	350	85	86	5.3750
VMS-179	24	400	95	96	4.0000
VMS-180	25	600	161	161	6.4400
VMS-182	16	175	14	14	0.8750
VMS-183	16	700	95	95	5.9380
VMS-184	12.25	75	41	41	3.3470
VMS-186	8	75	9	9	1.1250
VMS-188	7.5	25	1	1	0.1333
VMS-192	100	250	69	69	0.6900
VMS-193	58	250	31	31	0.8967
VMS-195	4	50	1	1	0.2500
VMS-196	3400	550	148	148	0.0435
VMS-197	12	1400	201	201	16.7500
VMS-198	1000	200	36	36	0.0360
VMS-201	48	1075	231	231	4.8125
VMS-202	12	400	78	79	6.5833
VMS-203	64	300	57	57	0.8906
VMS-204	60	150	18	18	0.3000
VMS-207	66,000	100	23	23	0.0003
VMS-218	160	600	66	68	0.4250
VMS-219	3384	50	4	4	0.0012
VMS-238	52.5	100	21	21	0.4000
VMS-241	3600	50	5	5	0.0014
VMS-243	8	1400	210	210	26.2500
VMS-245	52	25	2	2	0.0385
VMS-249	2	25	3	3	1.5000
VMS-251	4	850	193	193	48.2500
VMS-254	52	1900	235	236	6.3778
VMS-274	0.8	100	13	13	16.2500
VMS-285	12	5325	1472	1472	122.6667
VMS-289	75	25	4	4	0.0533
VMS-290	300	25	4	4	0.0133
VMS-291	240	25	7	7	0.0292
VMS-336	16	5900	178	178	11.1250
VMS-339	100	700	115	115	1.1500
VMS-340	828	450	45	45	0.0828
VMS-341	161	2150	136	136	0.8447
VMS-344	15	25	1	1	0.0667
VMS-347	13,300	25	1	1	0.0001
VMS-361	52	2625	844	847	16.2885
VMS-365	50	350	102	202	2.1000
VMS-371	128	750	69	71	0.5916
All Groups	134,502.2	79,025	15,981	16,123	5.1439

*Also includes burnished and coarse wares.

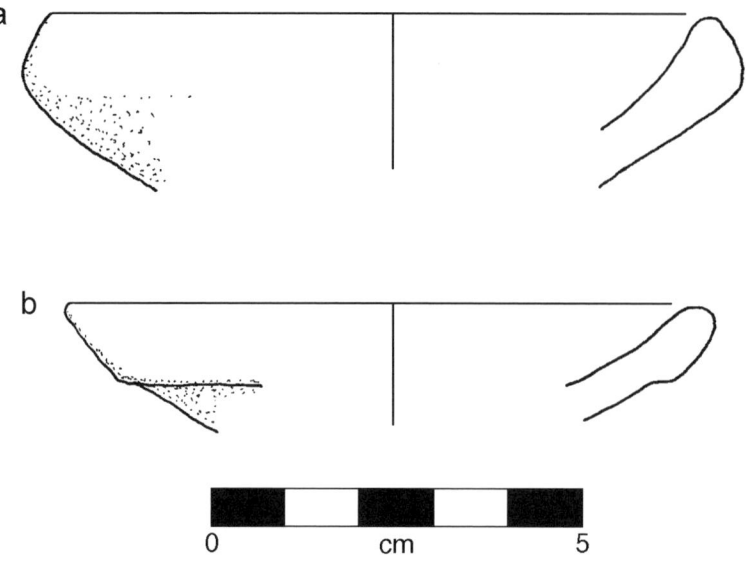

Figure 6.1. Unrestricted vessels: lamps. *a*, VMS-371/5; *b*, VMS-101/12.

In this section, we both employ the previously developed ceramic classification and evaluate its usefulness for areas outside the urban core. This evaluation entails statistical analysis of vessel attributes to examine whether categories previously defined are supported by the survey data. Given the paucity of detailed analyses on ceramics of the Vijayanagara period, and the absence of any detailed studies of ceramics of earlier *or* later periods, this is more than a formal exercise. Instead, it is an attempt to expand knowledge about ceramic forms, functions, and variability in the metropolitan region specifically, with potential relevance to early modern South India more generally.

Of the 16,123 sherds collected from controlled surface collections (that is, not including diagnostic sweeps, considered below by vessel form), 829 (5.2%) could be classed according to broad vessel form. Thus, nearly 95% of the sherds from controlled collections were body sherds or unidentifiable rim fragments. In consequence, we made targeted diagnostic collections at many sites to augment sample sizes of measurable diagnostics.

The total sample of measurable diagnostics from 68 sites in the three blocks numbered 964 sherds. A series of measurements were made on each sherd and all measurable diagnostics were drawn. Vessels were sorted by broad vessel forms (for example, unrestricted and restricted vessels, and shape or rim form variants within them); measurements differed somewhat according to vessel category. Data recorded include information on ware, percent and type of non-plastic inclusions, surface and paste color, and vessel dimensions (diameter, height, thickness) and orientations.

Unrestricted Vessels

A total of 102 diagnostic sherds or 12.3% of the identifiable diagnostics from controlled collections belong to the category of unrestricted vessel forms or bowls. These include three major vessel forms: small saucer-like vessels, or *lamps*; larger carinated vessels called *shallow bowls*; and *other bowls*, a general catch-all category for unrestricted forms that do not belong to either of the other two categories. In field sorting, unrestricted vessels were distinguished from restricted vessels, without defining finer subtypes, since such distinctions can be difficult to make without more detailed analysis. In the subsequent discussion of individual vessel forms, we employ data from measurable diagnostics derived from both systematic and diagnostic surface collections.

Measurable unrestricted vessel diagnostics include 3 lamps, 48 shallow bowls and 125 other bowl forms, a total of 176 measured vessels. Attributes recorded on each vessel form include ware; color; percent and type of non-plastic inclusions; surface treatment; and measures of diameter, thickness, height, and vessel orientation (see Sinopoli 1993b for detailed summaries of vessels by form).

Unrestricted vessels: lamps. These are small saucer-shaped vessels that range from seven to fourteen centimeters in rim diameter (Fig. 6.1). These vessels are rare in the diagnostic ceramic sample, with only three specimens measured from the three blocks. This rarity is certainly underrepresentative of their overall frequency in the metropolitan region. Two factors contribute to this underrepresentation. First, breakage patterns of these small vessels yield few measurable diagnostic sherds. Second, since modern lamps are virtually indistinguishable from Vijayanagara period lamps and are common in shrines and temples where they are used in worship, we typically did not collect such sherds unless there was supporting information that they were pre-modern (for example, if they are found in an abandoned settlement or sites where evidence of recent activity is absent). It may well be that some Vijayanagara period lamps present at sites have not been collected.

The three measured lamp sherds were recovered at: VMS-371, a small temple in Block O, and settlements VMS-101 (Block O) and VMS-361 (Block T).

Unrestricted vessels: shallow bowls. Shallow bowls are round-based bowls with pronounced exterior base carinations and vertical or everted walls and thickened rims (Fig. 6.2a-c; Sinopoli 1993b). These forms most likely served as lids and, perhaps, as serving vessels, and appear to be temporally restricted to the Vijayanagara period. That is, while bowls of various forms (the *other bowl* category, discussed below) are found in sites containing modern ceramics and are produced ethnographically, no shallow bowl forms occur in such contexts. In contrast, shallow bowls are the most common bowl forms recorded from the Vijayanagara urban core, where 923 diagnostic sherds have been documented from surface and excavated contexts (Sinopoli 1993b:45-46). Virtually all of the sites in the survey area that have yielded shallow bowls have multiple lines of evidence that date them to the Vijayanagara period. Thus, while this diagnostic vessel form cannot be precisely dated to within the Vijayanagara period, a Vijayanagara assignation is reasonably well supported by current data.

Shallow bowls are significantly more abundant in VMS sites than are the smaller lamps discussed above. A total of 48 diagnostic shallow bowl sherds, from 48 individual vessels, were measured from the three blocks (6 from block O, 18 from Block S, and 24 from Block T). Only 12 of the 107 sites that yielded ceramics contain shallow bowl forms (Table 6.3). Highest frequencies occurred in settlement VMS-361, which yielded 19 measurable diagnostics out of a total diagnostic sample of 109 sherds (17.4%). Shallow bowl sherds occur almost exclusively in settlement sites (including ceramic scatters; for instance, VMS-2, VMS-35, VMS-37, VMS-78, VMS-182, VMS-361, VMS-365), or in sites such as temples or roads located in areas of dense settlement (for example, sites VMS-140, VMS-144, VMS-201, VMS-203, VMS-254, all of which are located in the densely settled area within the outer city walls in the northeast corner of Block S). The association with settlements suggests that these were forms that were used in domestic and sedentary contexts (that is, not by mobile ceramic users or in industrial or other contexts).

All but one of the shallow bowls for which ware was recordable are of plain ware; the other is burnished ware. Of the 47 vessels for which color was recordable, 40 are black or brown and 7 are red. These distributions are generally representative of Vijayanagara ceramics overall.

Shallow bowls from the urban core were subdivided into six subtypes on the basis of size (rim diameter) and vessel orientation (rim angle), and these groupings are supported by the VMS data (though the everted rim forms are absent). The shallow bowls have a mean rim diameter of 21.17 cm, with a range of 13 to 33 cm. They fall into two size categories: small shallow bowls range from 13 to 22 cm and larger bowls range from 23 to 33 cm (Figs. 6.3a, 6.4). An examination of a histogram of diameter distributions suggests that this larger group may itself be divisible into two size categories with a break at approximately 27-28 cm, though sample sizes are small. This size distribution is virtually identical with that of the 923 vessels coded from the urban core (Sinopoli 1993b:66), indicating both that these vessels were contemporary to those recorded from urban contexts and that they derive from the same statistical and technological population.

Although sample numbers are small, there do seem to be some inter-site differences in bowl size distributions, with, for example, higher than expected frequencies of large size bowls coming from VMS-365 (Table 6.4). However, given the small numbers, the significance of this patterning is far from apparent.

Rim angle is also bimodal (missing the highly everted forms that were found rarely in the urban core; Fig. 6.3b), although this patterning is weak and interpretations therefore are tentative. The two groups suggested by this distribution are vessels with acute rims, with angles ranging from 60° to 80°, and vessels with vertical or inturning rims with rim angles ranging from 85° to 105°. Given the continuous range of angle distributions, and the lack of functional or other meaningful patterns in the distributions of vessels with different rim angles, this variable is likely a function of individual or intra- or inter-workshop motor skill differences in pottery production, perhaps with little intentionality involved. The distinction between rim orientations is worth retaining, in the hope that it may ultimately prove useful in distinguishing production centers, while the bowl size classes probably relate more directly to vessel use.

Unrestricted vessels: other bowls. The category *other bowls* was used in the analysis of ceramics from the urban core as a catch-all category to account for unrestricted vessels that were neither lamps nor shallow bowls (see Fig. 6.2d-g). In the urban core, only 470 of these varied unrestricted vessel forms were documented, about half as common as shallow bowls and approximately 3.7% of the total diagnostic ceramic sample. In the metropolitan survey, the frequency of other bowls is significantly higher; they comprise 124 of the 939 total measurable diagnostics and outnumber measured shallow bowls by more than 2.5 to 1. The higher frequency of these forms in the metropolitan region is likely a function of two factors. The first is the greater admixture of modern ceramics and a broader temporal range in the survey samples (including prehistoric ceramics as well as modern ceramics). The second and ultimately more interesting factor may relate to a broader diversity in Vijayanagara ceramic

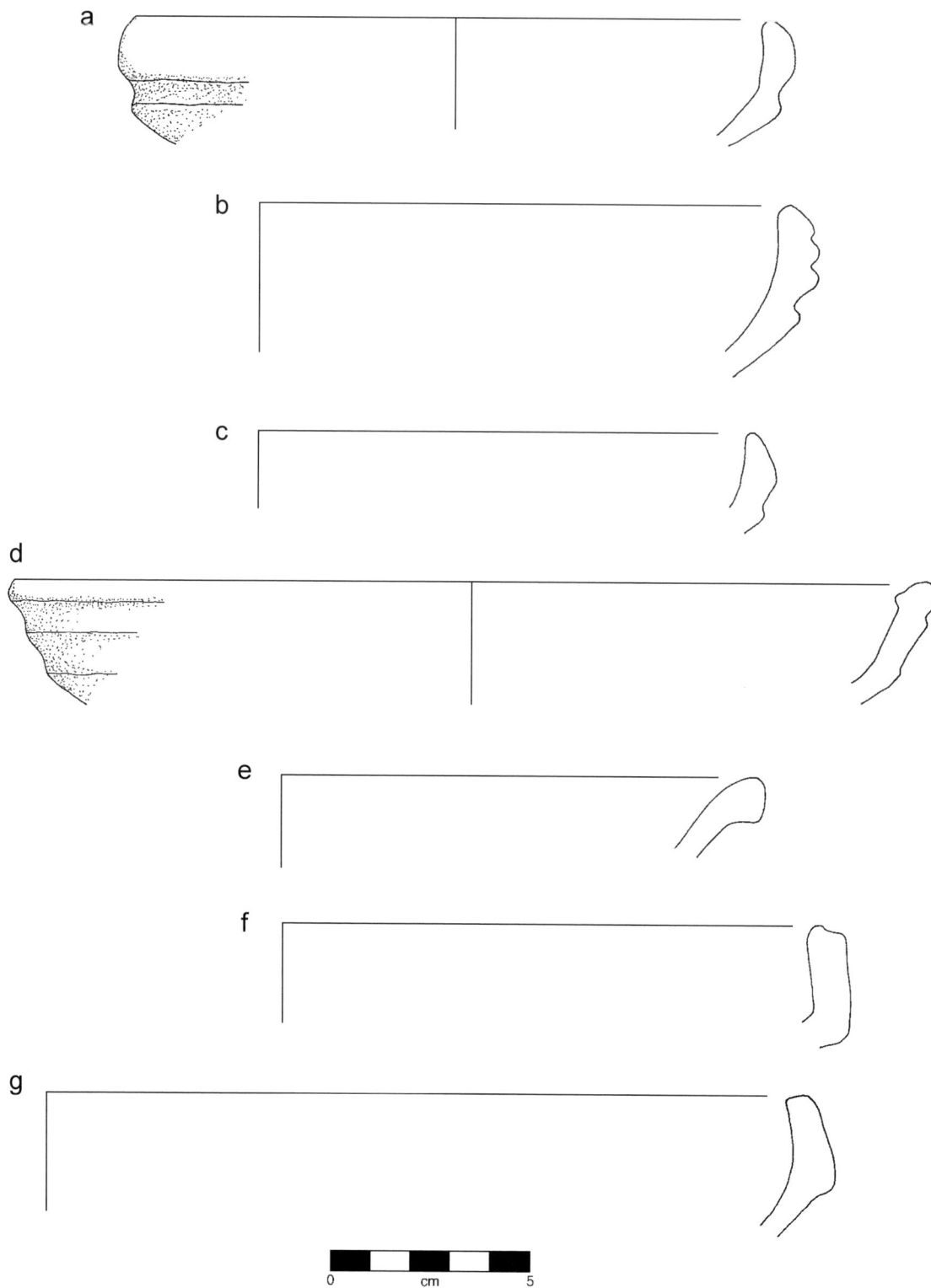

Figure 6.2. Unrestricted vessels: shallow bowls (*a-c*) and other bowls (*d-g*). All from VMS-365, Area III-D. *a*, #73; *b*, #74; *c*, #75; *d*, #76; *e*, #77; *f*, #79; *g*, #80.

Table 6.3. Shallow bowls by site.

Site	Block	Number of Measured Diagnostics	Mean Rim Diameter (cm)	Mean Carination Diameter (cm)*	Mean Rim Angle (degrees)	Mean Rim Height (cm)
VMS-2	O	1	19.00	19.00 (1)	95.00	1.03
VMS-35	O	2	22.00	21.50 (2)	85.00	1.81
VMS-37	O	1	15.00	13.00 (1)	70.00	1.56
VMS-78	O	2	20.50	16.00 (2)	100.00	1.74
VMS-140	S	7	21.71	20.86 (7)	82.86	1.51
VMS-144	S	5	19.00	18.00 (5)	92.00	1.40
VMS-182	S	1	32.00	31.00 (1)	70.00	1.24
VMS-201	S	1	16.00	16.00 (1)	100.00	1.00
VMS-203	S	1	25.00	–	100.00	1.51
VMS-254	S	3	16.33	16.33 (3)	95.00	1.46
VMS-361	T	19	21.37	21.44 (16)	88.95	1.44
VMS-365	T	5	24.40	23.80 (5)	74.00	1.70

*Number of sherds for which this variable was measurable provided in parentheses; all other variables measured on total sample.

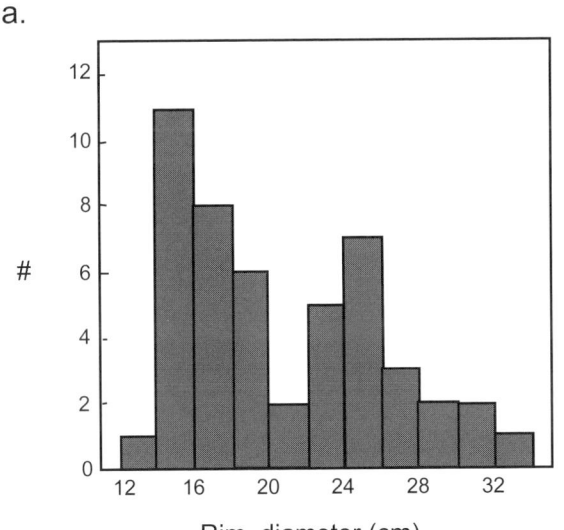
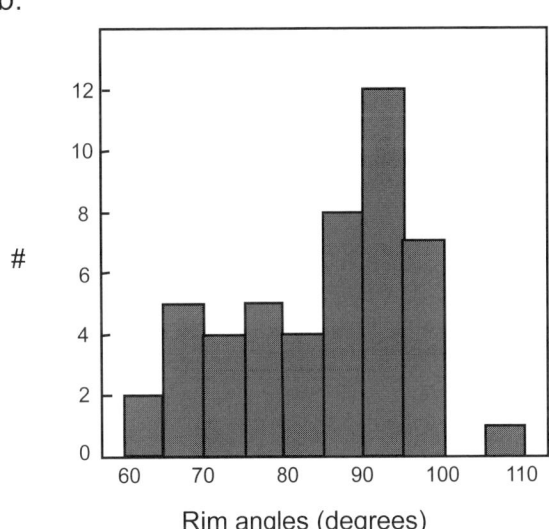

Figure 6.3. Unrestricted vessels: shallow bowls. *a*, rim diameter; *b*, rim angle.

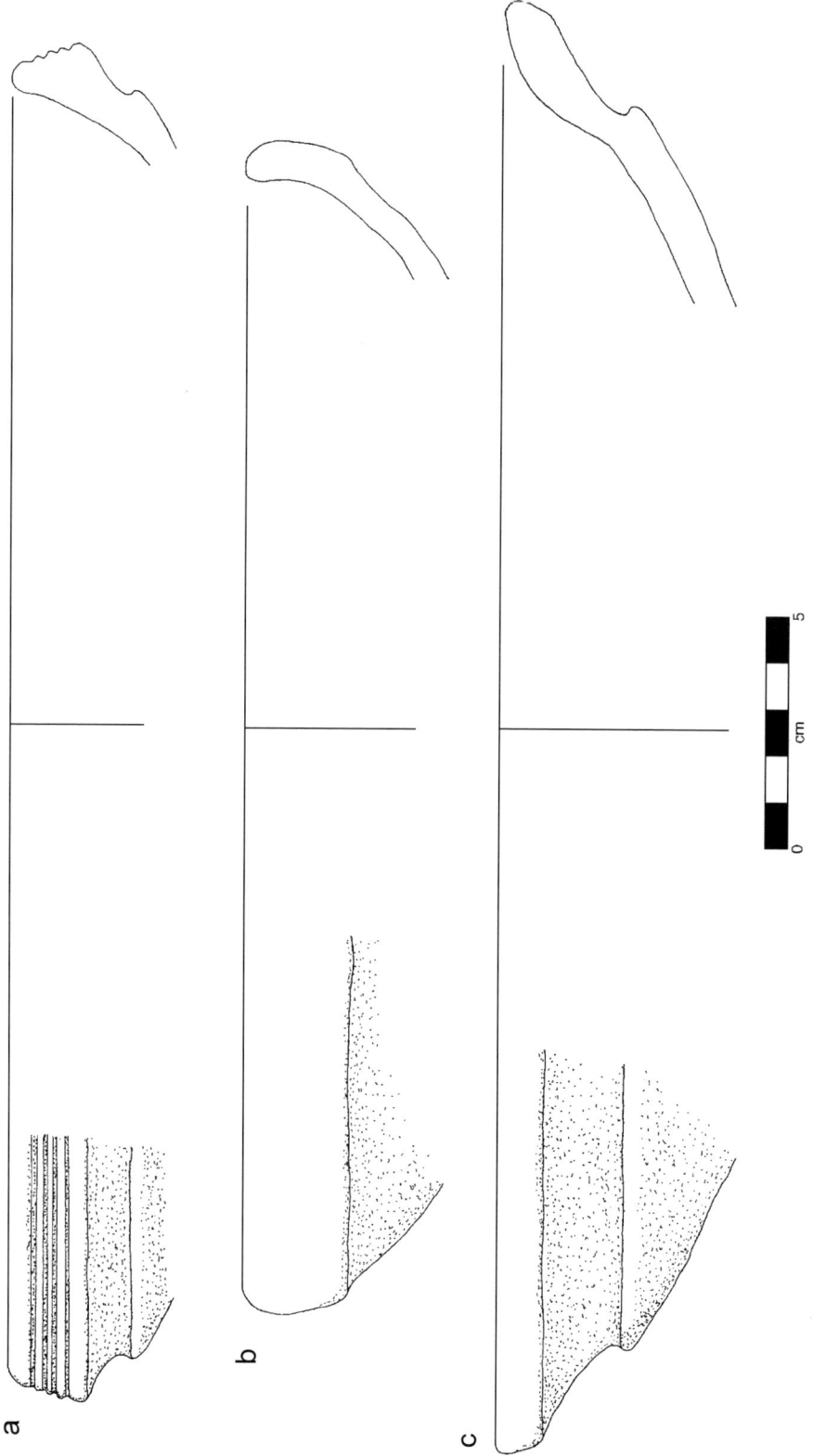

Figure 6.4. Unrestricted vessels: large shallow bowls. *a*, VMS-78/4; *b*, VMS-78/6; *c*, VMS-78/7.

Table 6.4. Shallow bowl size classes by site.

Site	Number of Small	Mean Rim Diameter (cm)	Number of Large	Mean Rim Diameter (cm)
VMS-2	1	19.00	0	–
VMS-35	1	15.00	1	29.00
VMS-37	1	15.00	0	–
VMS-78	1	17.00	1	24.00
VMS-140	4	19.25	3	25.00
VMS-144	3	16.00	2	23.50
VMS-182	0	–	1	32.00
VMS-201	1	16.00	0	–
VMS-203	0	–	1	25.00
VMS-254	3	16.33	0	–
VMS-361	12	17.50	7	28.00
VMS-365	1	16.00	4	26.50
Totals	28	17.21	20	26.70

forms beyond the urban core than within it, though with present data this is difficult to verify.

The 125 measured other bowls were derived from 35 sites (nearly three times as many as yielded shallow bowls), with numbers per site ranging from 1 to 20 (Table 6.5). Forty-one other bowls were recovered from Block O, 48 from Block S, and 36 from Block T. Highest frequencies occur at settlement sites, including VMS-2 ($n = 12$, 4 probably modern), VMS-101 ($n = 11$, 4 probably modern), and VMS-329 ($n = 20$), a settlement area located along a major east-west road and associated with VMS-361 ($n = 4$). The association with settlement areas is quite pronounced, though it is in part a function of the greater numbers of sherds overall at such sites (see below).

Nearly all of the other bowls are of plain ware (122 of 125, with one coarse ware vessel and one unidentifiable), and 119 are black or brown in color, while only 5 are red. Bowls were sorted according to broad shape categories into hemispherical ($n = 48$) or carinated bowls ($n = 26$), with a large number of small sherds for which shape was unidentifiable ($n = 51$). The vessels have a diversity of rim forms, ranging from simple straight rims to more complex thickened and everted rim forms. To a considerable extent, these rim forms grade into each other, and while some discrete forms are distinguishable, for the most part boundaries between rim forms are difficult to define. The variability in other bowl rim forms suggests that manufacture of these handmade vessels was relatively expedient and not subject to a great deal of control or concern.

These bowls likely served diverse functions, including use as lids, serving vessels, and storage vessels. They range in size from 12 to 51 cm in rim diameter, with a mean diameter of 23.66 cm (s.d. = 6.28). Three size classes are evident (Fig. 6.5): 11-22 cm ($n = 78$), 23-32 cm ($n = 39$), and 33-51 cm ($n = 8$). Given small samples from most sites, inter-site comparisons in size and form distributions could be made only in a few cases (for example, for VMS-2, 101, and 329); no significant differences existed in other bowl size, though some differences do exist in rim attributes, perhaps indicating different production sources.

Restricted or Necked Vessels

A total of 727 or 88.3% of the identifiable ceramics from controlled collections were classified as restricted vessels or jars. These vessels were further sorted by rim form into three categories: round rim, straight rim, or flange rim (Fig. 6.6; see Sinopoli 1986, 1993 for detailed descriptions). Certain rim forms are associated with vessel function (large round rim storage jars, for example); others, such as elaborate flange rims with three protruding exterior flanges (for instance, modern triple flange rims), are chronologically specific; other rim variations appear to be only minimally linked to vessel function and may indicate variations in production within and between workshops.

Of the 716 restricted vessel sherds from controlled collections for which rim type was identifiable, 117 (16.3%) were round rim, 173 straight rim (24.2%), and 426 flange rim (59.5%). The frequency of flange rims in the survey sample is virtually identical to their frequency in the urban core, where they comprise 60.6% of the restricted vessel rims. Rims recorded as round rims are significantly more common in the metropolitan region than in the urban core (16.3% versus 6.3%), while straight rims are less common (24.16% versus 33.0%). These differences are likely due in part to individual variation in coding decisions; in the urban core the round rim category was applied more conservatively to vessels that clearly could be assigned to one of a limited set of rim forms, while rims with a slightly rounded exterior profile tended to be classed as straight rims. In the more detailed analyses of measurable diagnostic sherds conducted according to the same criteria applied in the urban core (see below), straight rim forms significantly outnumber round rims, suggesting that the apparent frequency differences are a result of coding variability (many more people were involved in coding survey sherds than urban core materials, and individual variability in identification was a factor) and should not be accorded much weight.

In addition to counts from controlled collections, more detailed measurements were made on 789 diagnostic restricted vessels derived from controlled collections and diagnostic sweeps. These include 65 round rim restricted vessel rim sherds, 285 straight rim restricted vessel rim sherds, and 439 flange rim restricted vessel rim sherds. A range of measurements were made on each sherd, including diameters, orientations, thicknesses, heights, and so on, along with information on rim form variants, color, inclusions, ware, and surface treatment.

Vijayanagara restricted vessels include vessel forms ranging from shallow, relatively open low-necked vessels, probably used for cooking, to tall globular narrow-necked vessels used for transport and storage. Although some rim form variants tend to be associated with one or another morphological or functional vessel form, many vessel forms exhibit multiple rim shapes. For example, shallow low-neck cooking vessels (RV2, RV3; see

Table 6.5. Other bowls by site.

Site	Block	Number of Measured Diagnostics	Mean Rim Diameter (cm)	Mean Rim Angle (degrees)	Mean Rim Thickness (cm)	Mean Rim Height (cm)
VMS-2	O	12	23.00	55.42	1.05	1.19
VMS-16	O	1	25.00	100.00	1.31	2.06
VMS-33	O	2	15.00	105.00	0.59	1.10
VMS-35	O	3	32.67	83.33	1.06	1.78
VMS-66	O	4	19.00	65.00	0.83	0.71
VMS-78	O	5	24.80	62.00	1.11	1.35
VMS-91	O	2	25.50	27.50	1.35	1.49
VMS-101	O	11	20.64	49.09	0.88	1.14
VMS-104	O	1	20.00	100.00	0.82	2.12
VMS-7	S	5	23.00	56.00	1.11	1.50
VMS-8	S	1	18.00	45.00	0.89	1.09
VMS-135	S	3	25.00	38.33	0.88	1.00
VMS-140	S	4	24.50	90.00	0.91	1.81
VMS-144	S	1	18.00	55.00	0.79	0.90
VMS-153	S	4	22.00	66.25	1.19	1.10
VMS-164	S	7	27.86	58.57	1.33	1.53
VMS-169	S	7	22.00	48.57	0.87	1.24
VMS-175	S	3	23.00	90.00	1.01	1.36
VMS-178	S	1	23.00	60.00	1.02	1.13
VMS-179	S	2	24.50	67.50	1.03	1.37
VMS-193	S	2	20.00	50.00	0.78	0.99
VMS-199	S	1	37.00	45.00	2.26	1.17
VMS-205	S	1	20.00	45.00	0.83	1.42
VMS-207	S	1	20.00	50.00	1.08	0.77
VMS-208	S	1	22.00	55.00	1.02	1.20
VMS-212	S	2	18.00	52.50	0.70	0.96
VMS-221	S	1	22.00	60.00	1.22	1.64
VMS-254	S	1	17.00	130.00	0.86	1.01
VMS-319	T	1	16.00	40.00	0.79	0.65
VMS-327	T	2	23.50	45.00	1.33	1.37
VMS-329	T	20	25.35	39.75	1.22	1.53
VMS-335	T	2	23.00	55.00	0.83	0.82
VMS-340	T	1	23.00	70.00	0.78	1.01
VMS-361	T	4	28.00	65.00	1.03	1.26
VMS-365	T	6	27.17	75.83	0.90	1.25
Totals	–	125	23.66	58.00	1.03	1.30

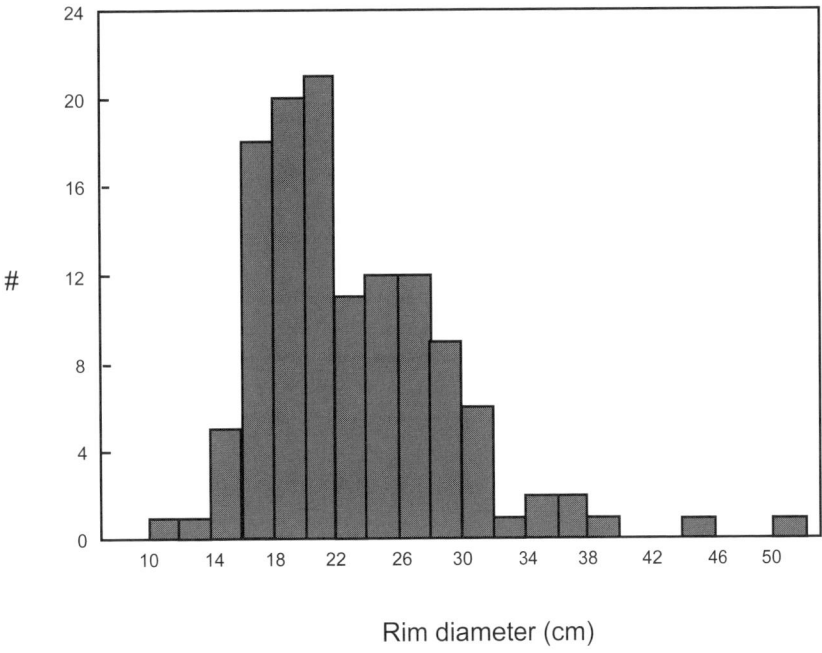

Figure 6.5. Unrestricted vessels: other bowls, size histogram.

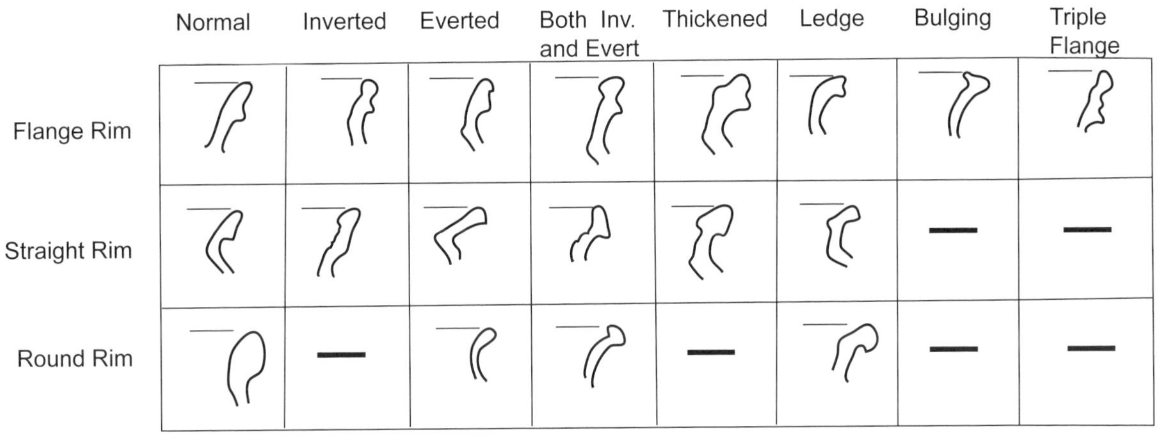

Figure 6.6. Restricted vessel rim forms.

discussion below) include a range of flange, straight, and, to a lesser extent, round rim form variants. The significance of rim form variants remains an open question in the interpretation of Vijayanagara ceramics. Ethnographic studies at contemporary ceramic workshops in the region (Sinopoli and Blurton 1986; Junker 1986) suggest that many rim forms that were common in the metropolitan region and urban core during Vijayanagara times are no longer being made, and some rim forms therefore do appear to have chronological significance, if not functional meaning. Rim form variants may also relate to variation among individual potters and within or between workshops. In this section, restricted vessels will first be examined by broad rim class, and then by general vessel form categories.

Restricted vessels: round rim forms. Round rim restricted vessels include vessel forms ranging from small serving vessels to large storage jars, with several rim shape variants (Fig. 6.7). They are relatively rare in the diagnostic sample, totaling 117 of the 716 restricted vessels from systematic controlled collections (these numbers include unmeasurable rims for which only rim form could be identified). From diagnostic collections, 65 of the total of 789 (8.2%) measurable restricted vessels were round rim vessels. Round rim restricted vessels were recovered from 25 of the 68 sites from which diagnostics were recorded, with numbers per site ranging from 1 to a maximum of 12 round rim vessels at VMS-361. Of the 57 vessels for which ware was identified, 53 (93%) are of plain ware and 4 (7%) are of burnished ware; of the 63 sherds for which color is identifiable, 50 (79%) are black or brown and 13 (21%) are red in color. Red wares are thus significantly more common among these vessel forms than in the overall survey sample or in the urban core ceramics. This is probably due to two vessel form categories: large storage vessels and small serving vessels (see below).

The large round rim storage vessels are an important form in the survey sample because like shallow bowls, they appear to be temporally restricted. They are large vessels with thick out-turned rims, low necks, and sloping shoulders (Fig. 6.7g, h). Their large size and form suggest that they were too heavy to easily move when full, nor were their wide mouths and low necks suited to water transport. They have thus been interpreted as storage vessels (see Sinopoli 1993:48). Two hundred and thirty-five (of 829) round rim storage vessels were recorded from the urban core; twenty-three of the 65 round rim jars in the survey sample belong to this category. Round rim storage vessels were recovered from 11 sites in the survey area: 9 in Block S (VMS-140, 169, 179, 180, 183, 201, 211, 254, 278) and 2 in Block T (settlements VMS-361, 365). Except for VMS-169, all of the sites in Block S containing these forms are located in the densely settled area within the outer city walls near the urban core.

A second significant class of round rim restricted vessels consists of small serving vessels with rim diameters of less than 16 cm and simple everted rims (Fig. 6.7a, c, d). Sixteen vessels belong to this category, collected from 10 sites (VMS-2, 37, 78, 101, 144, 180, 201, 335, 361, 365). These and other functional categories will be considered in more detail below in the general discussion of inter-site and intra-site distributions of vessel forms.

Restricted vessels: straight rim forms. As noted above, straight rim restricted vessel rim forms are associated with a range of vessel shape and size classes (Figs. 6.8-6.9). A total of 285 straight rim restricted vessel rim sherds were measured from the three survey blocks (Block O, $n = 84$; Block S, $n = 149$; Block T, $n = 52$). These sherds derive from 50 of the 68 sites that yielded measurable diagnostic ceramics, indicating the ubiquity of these restricted vessel rim forms.

Of the 256 straight rim restricted vessel rim sherds for which ware category was identifiable, 251 (98.05%) were of plain ware (233 black/brown, 11 red, 7 unidentifiable), and 5 (1.95%) were of burnished ware (4 black/brown, 1 red). Six categorical rim form variants have been defined for the straight rim form category (for more detailed discussion, see Sinopoli 1993:55, 63) on the basis of formal attributes and ratios, including rim height/thickness ratios, lip/rim thickness ratios, and orientations. These include: (1) normal rims ($n = 155$), (2) inverted rims ($n = 9$), (3) everted rims ($n = 16$), (4) both inturning and out-turning ($n = 10$), (5) thickened rims ($n = 41$), and (6) ledge rims ($n = 20$).

Restricted vessels: flange rim forms. A total of 439 flange rim restricted vessel rims were measured from 58 sites in the three survey blocks (Figs. 6.10-6.12; Block O, $n = 96$; Block S, $n = 208$; Block T, $n = 135$). As in the urban core, flange rim restricted vessels are the most common restricted vessel rim forms in the metropolitan region. Numbers per site ranged from 1 to 57, with highest frequencies found at VMS-361 ($n = 57$), VMS-365 ($n = 43$; Figs. 6.10-6.11), VMS-2 ($n = 40$; Fig. 6.12), VMS-329 ($n = 24$), all settlement sites, and ceramic scatter VMS-278 ($n = 28$).

Of the 382 flange rim sherds for which ware category was identifiable, 352 (92.15%) were of plain ware (323 black/brown, 23 red, 6 unidentifiable) and 30 (7.85%) were of burnished ware (17 black, 12 red, 1 unidentifiable).

Seven rim form variants had been previously defined for flange rim vessels from the urban core (Sinopoli 1993). An eighth variant has been added for the metropolitan region ceramics. This additional form, termed "triple flange rim" (Fig. 6.6), refers to rims with three exterior bulges on the outer surface. This form is a post-Vijayanagara rim shape variant; rims of this form are certainly produced today, almost none are found in well-dated contexts in the urban core, and virtually all of the examples recovered in survey seem quite recent (based on contextual data, surface wear, vessel bodies, and so on). Although we can not determine precisely when this variant first appeared, we are confident in assigning it a post-Vijayanagara, and probably twentieth-century A.D., date.

The eight flange rim shape categories are distinguished on the basis of lip/rim thickness ratios, and lip orientations. They include: (1) normal rims ($n = 146$), (2) inverted lip rims ($n = 26$),

Artifact Distributions and Analysis

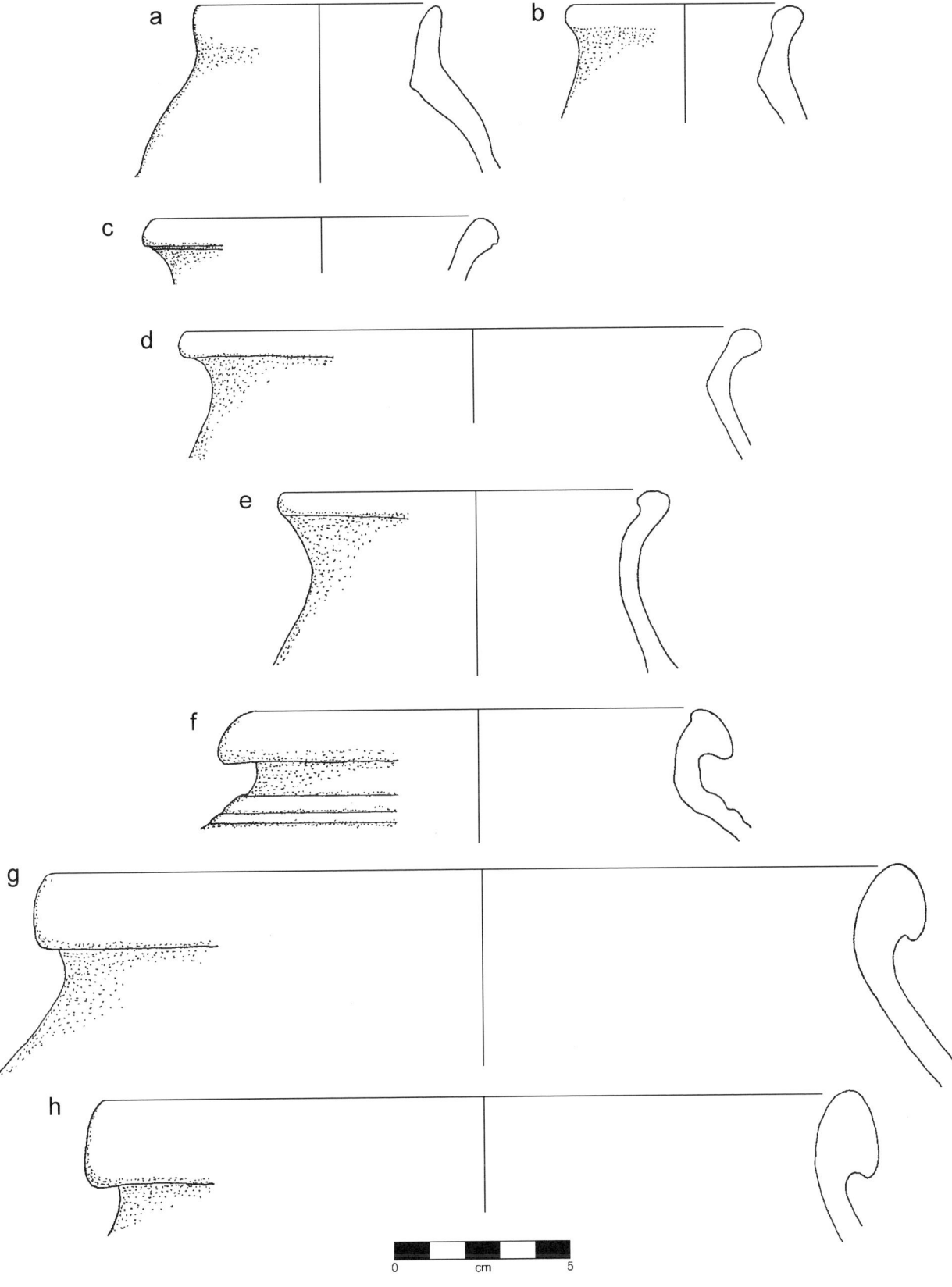

Figure 6.7. Round rim restricted vessels. *a*, VMS-78/8; *b*, VMS-78/9; *c*, VMS-78/11; *d*, VMS-66/5; *e*, VMS-35/F10N/3; *f*, VMS-35/F10S/1; *g*, VMS-16/17; *h*, VMS-16/19.

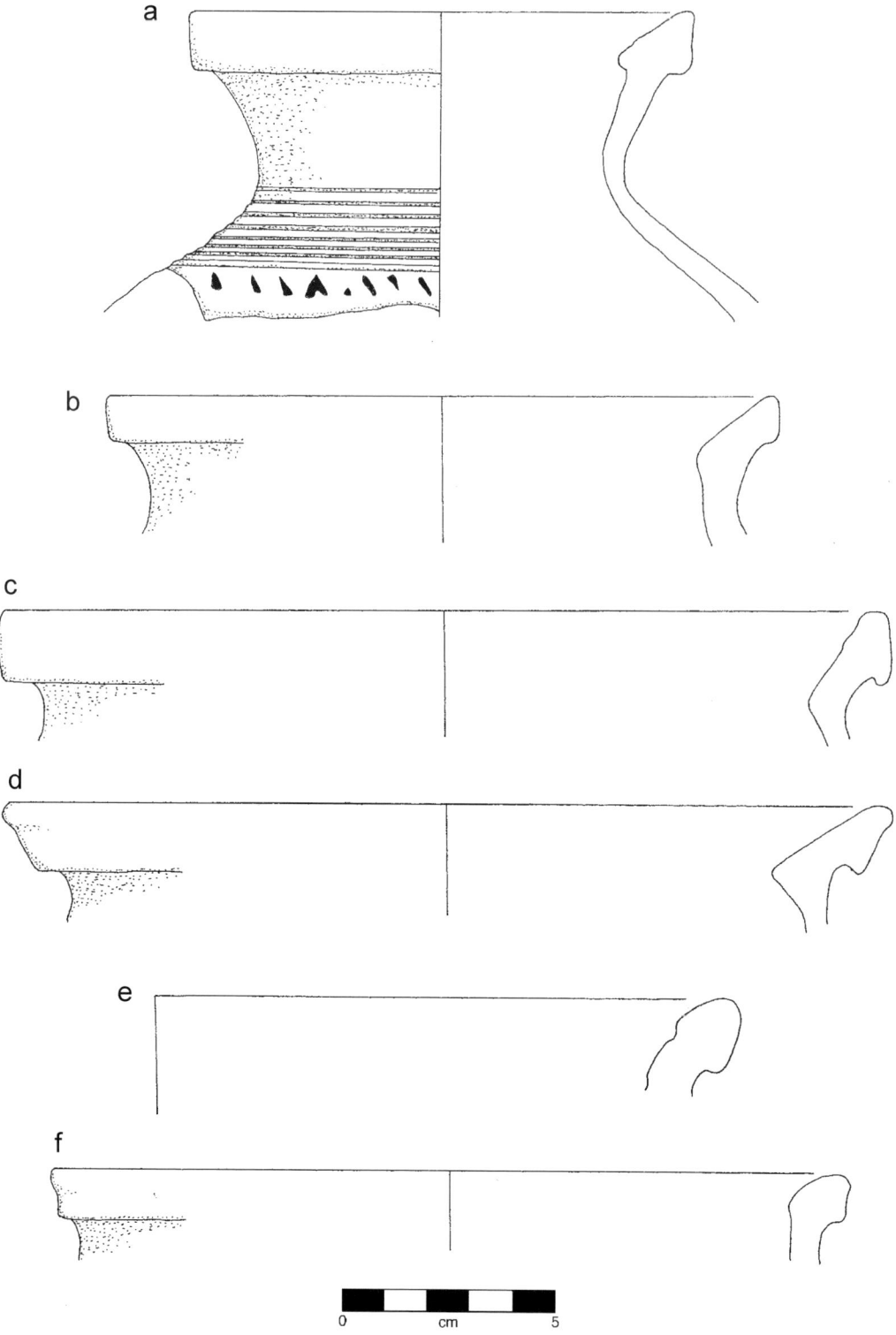

Figure 6.8. Straight rim restricted vessels. All from VMS-101, diagnostic collection. *a*, #20; *b*, #22; *c*, #23; *d*, #25; *e*, #24; *f*, #21.

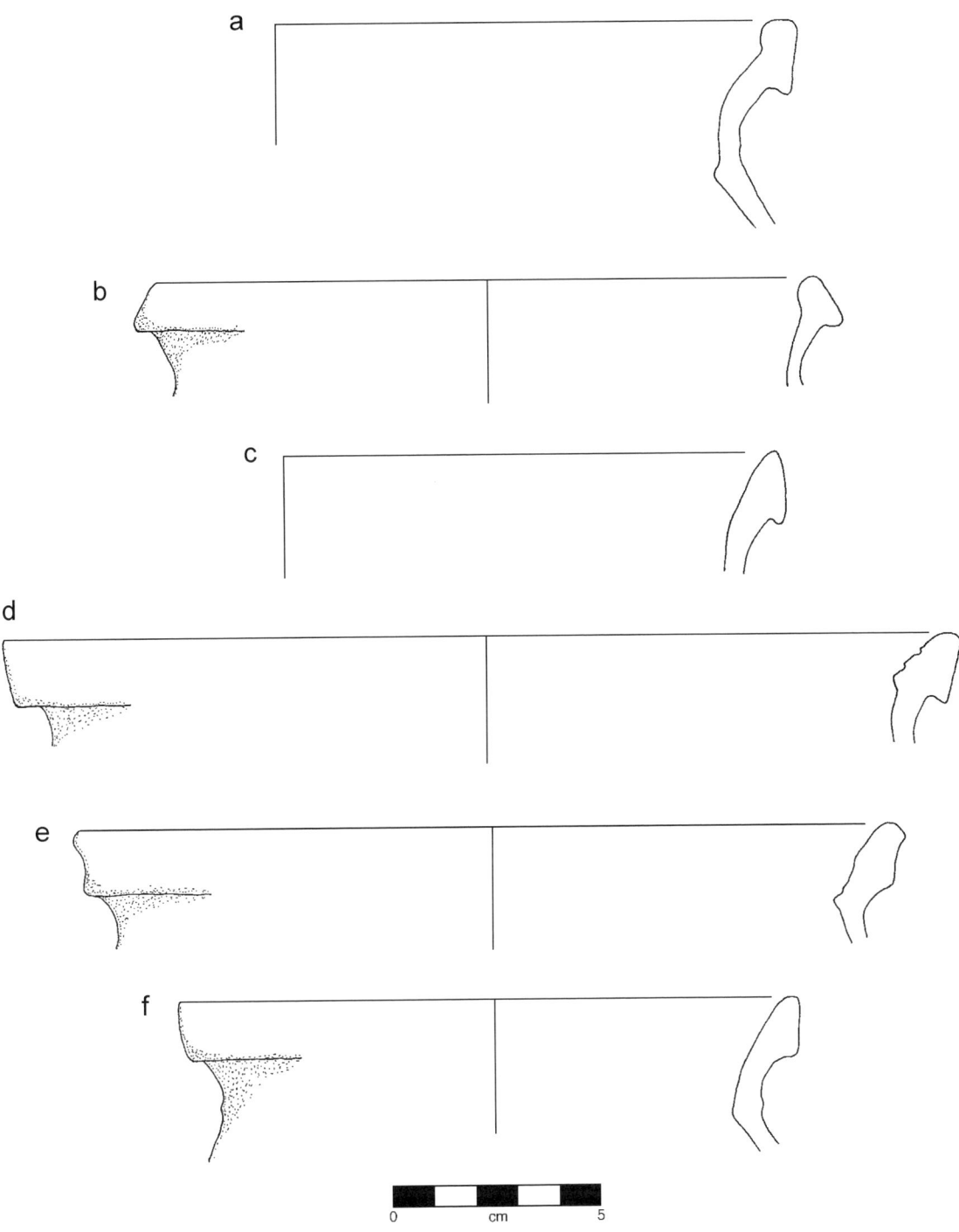

Figure 6.9. Straight rim restricted vessels. All from VMS-365, Area III-D. *a*, #55; *b*, #56; *c* #57; *d*, #58; *e*, #59; *f*, #60.

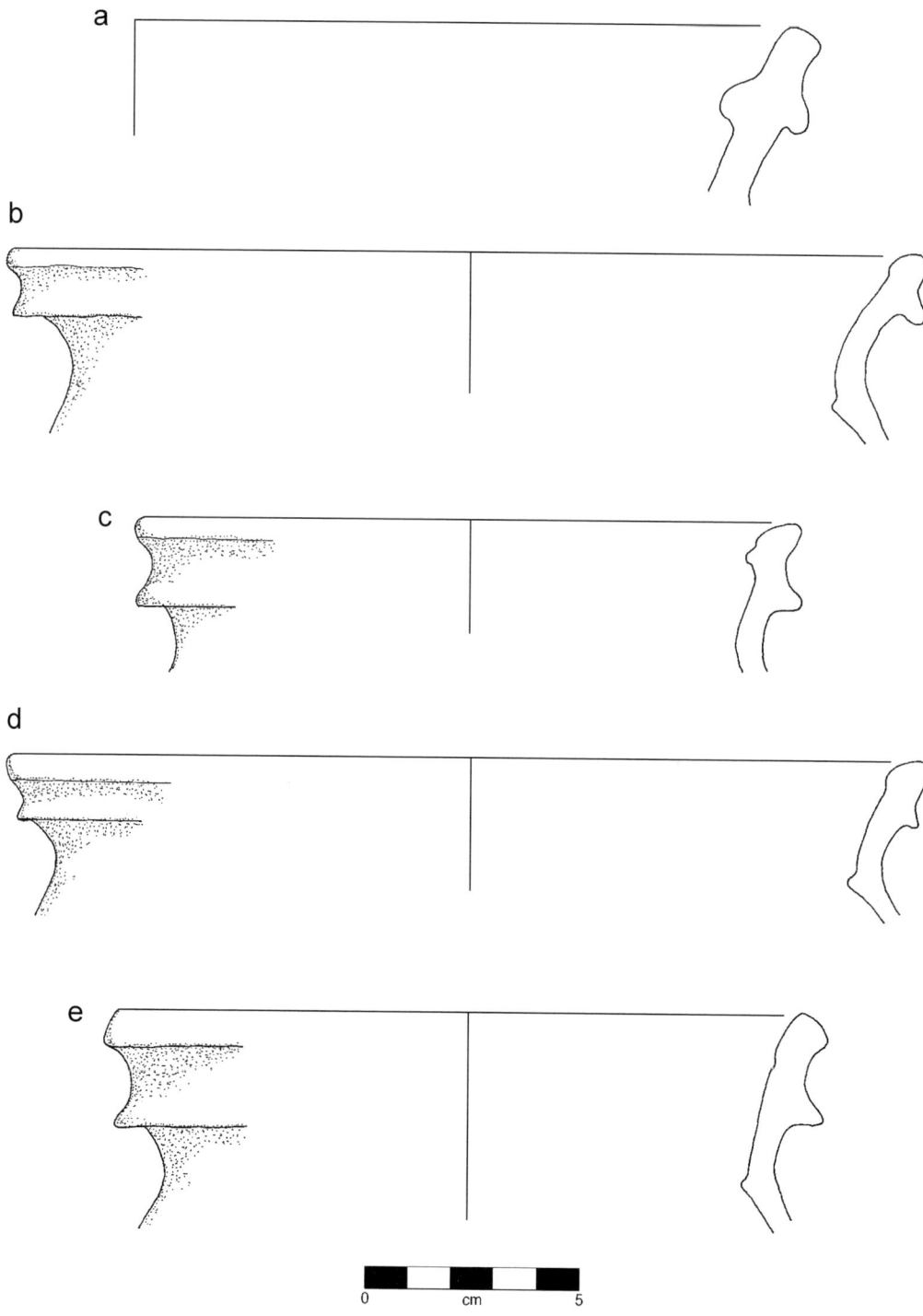

Figure 6.10. Restricted vessels: flange rims. All from VMS-365, Area III-D. *a*, #1; *b*, #2; *c*, #3; *d*, #4; *e*, #5.

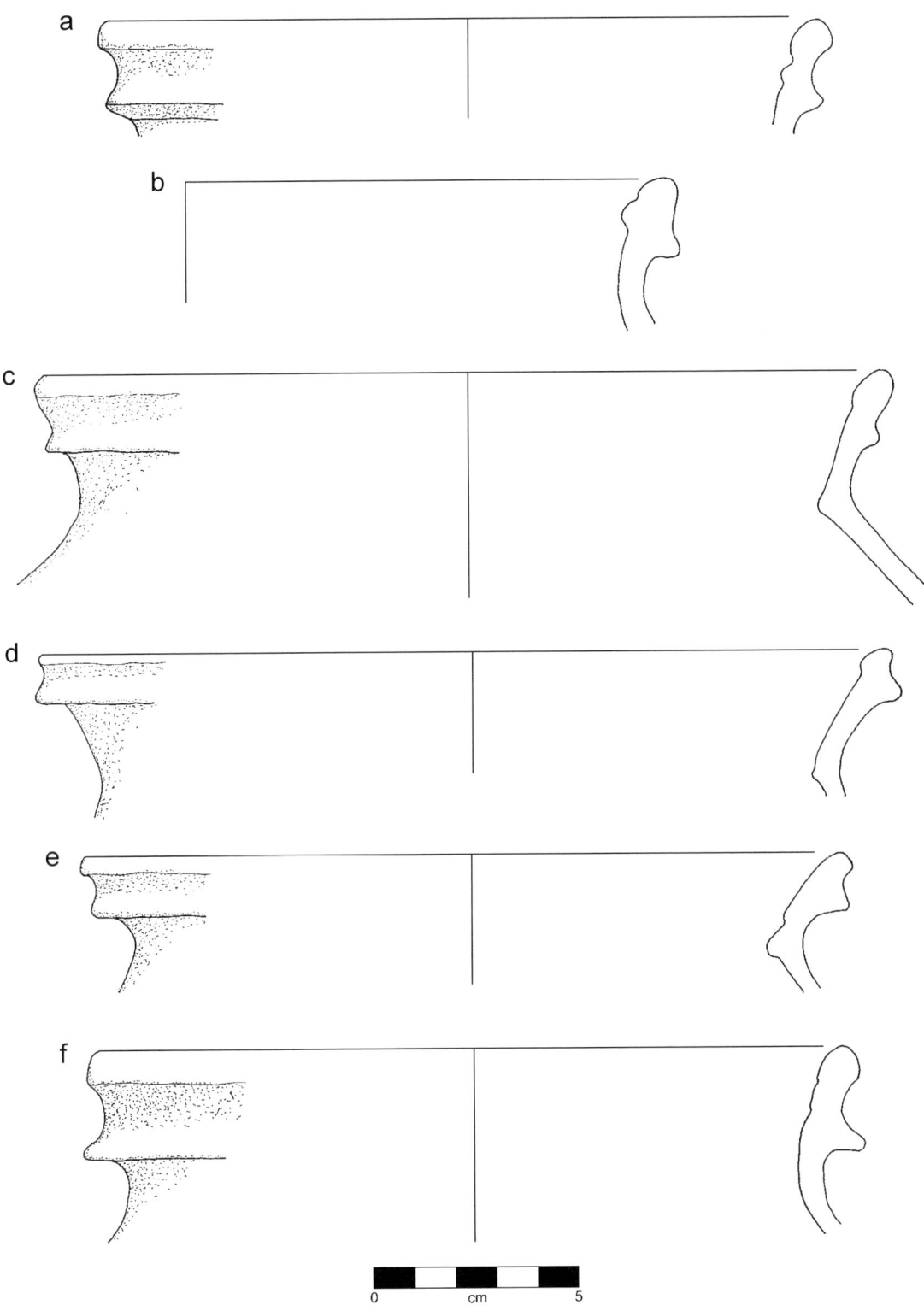

Figure 6.11. Restricted vessels: flange rims. All from VMS-365, Area III-D. *a*, #32; *b*, #33; *c*, #34; *d*, #35; *e*, #36; *f*, #37.

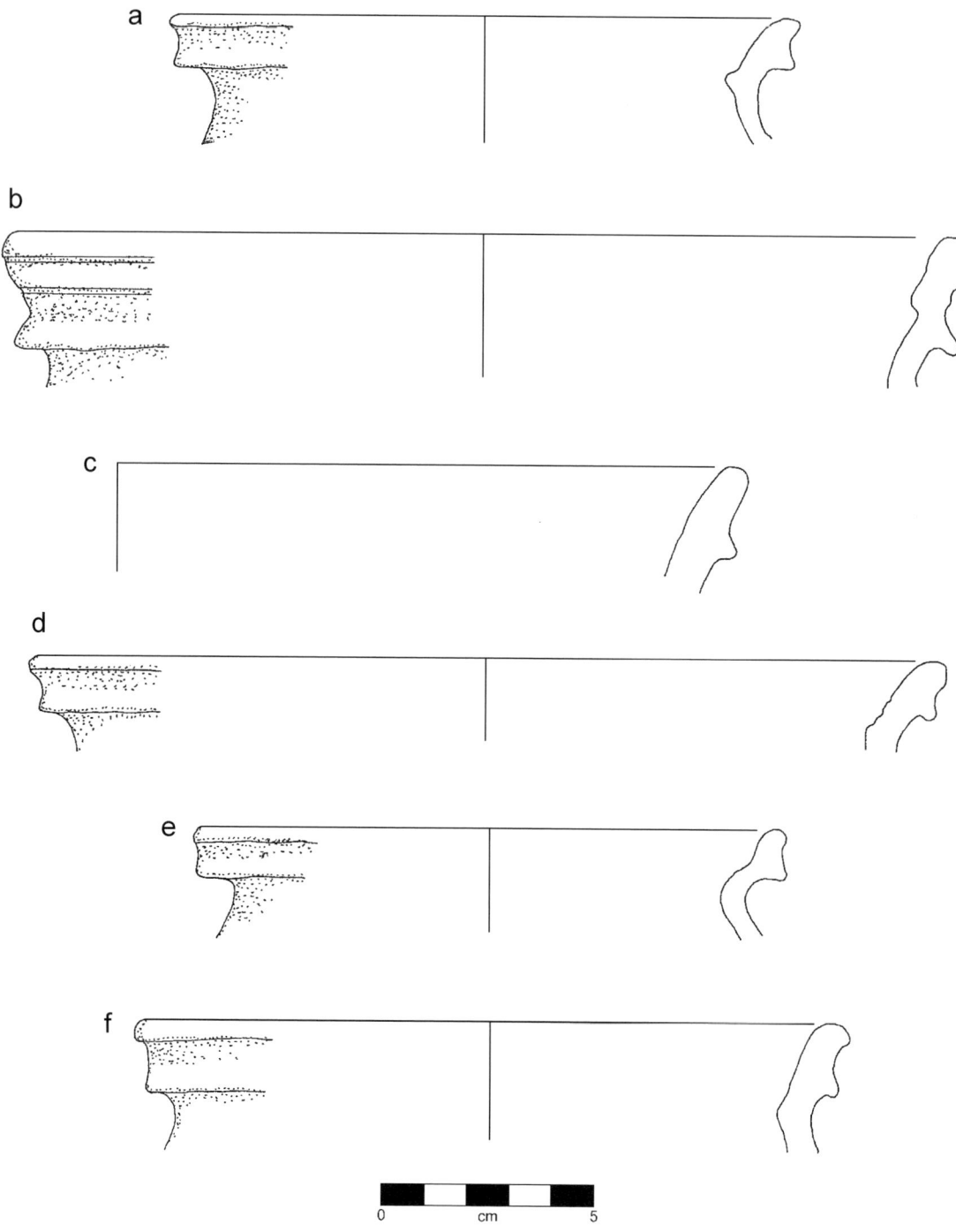

Figure 6.12. Restricted vessels: flange rims. All from VMS-2, Unit 3. *a*, #3; *b*, #4; *c*, #5; *d*, #6; *e*, #7; *f*, #8.

(3) everted lip rims ($n = 144$), (4) both inverted and everted lip rims ($n = 40$), (5) thickened rims ($n = 21$), (6) ledge rims ($n = 2$), (7) bulging rims ($n = 10$), and (8) triple flange rims ($n = 33$). Seventeen flange rims were classified as other or unidentifiable. Along with the modern triple flange rims, at least some of the variant 1 "normal" flange rims are also post-Vijayanagara in date. In some cases, these are easily identifiable on the basis of surface treatment, ware texture, or other features; there are also minor differences in form (lip to rim thickness ratios) that serve to distinguish later forms from Vijayanagara period rims, though these are evident through quantitative trends rather than through qualitative differences.

Flange rim restricted vessels, like other restricted vessel classes, include a diverse range of vessel shapes and sizes. Vessel diameters range from 11 to 47 cm, with a mean of 20.18 cm. Vessel form will be considered below in the discussion of vessel-use classifications.

Vessel-Use Class Distributions

In the above discussion, characteristics of individual ceramic classes were considered according to broad morphological category and finer subdivisions related to vessel and rim form. In this section, ceramic data are grouped according to somewhat different criteria, in an attempt to organize them according to the uses to which vessels were put. Vijayanagara vessels, like domestic ceramics throughout the world, were primarily used in activities related to the storage, preparation, and consumption of foodstuffs. Vijayanagara ceramics were also used as architectural elements (for example, roof tiles, drain pipes, and well linings), and in ritual activities (for instance, incense burners, figurines).

Interpretations of vessel function from archaeological assemblages are difficult and are especially problematic for surface ceramics, which are often highly fragmented, with whole vessels or even large vessel sections quite rare. The most secure means of identifying vessel use is through direct analyses of vessel contents, such as residue analysis using techniques such as gas chromatography. Analysis of wear traces directly related to vessel function (such as surface abrasion or erosion) is also valuable, though often of limited relevance to surface assemblages (Skibo 1992). Neither of these techniques has been possible for the study of Vijayanagara ceramic use. A less certain, but more easily applicable, approach to determining vessel use is based on the application of analogical reasoning linking vessel form to vessel use. Sources of such reasoning include the copious ceramic ethnography literature, as well as interpretation based on physical characteristics of vessel shapes. For examples, shallow vessels with broad and low necks are unlikely to be used for carrying water from a well, since spillage rates would be extremely high; such vessels would, however, function well as cooking vessels, or perhaps for storage of dry foodstuffs.

It is this last, analogical, approach to interpreting vessel function that I have taken with the ceramics of the Vijayanagara urban core and metropolitan region (Sinopoli 1986, 1991). Analogies with contemporary vessel forms produced in the region, use traces, and general form characteristics have all been used to develop broad interpretations of the primary uses to which individual vessels were most likely put. In the case of unrestricted vessels or bowls, possible vessel functions include use as: oil lamps, for ritual and home lighting; serving bowls; and lids. Restricted vessels were also likely used for diverse functions, including storage and transport of water, serving, cooking, and dry food storage. Other industrial or architectural uses of ceramics were less common in the Vijayanagara inventory and will be discussed separately below.

Given the small size of many sherds recovered in the survey, few vessels yielded sufficient information to conduct detailed quantitative analyses of vessel morphology and proposed function. Assignment of vessel-use categories thus relied on measures developed in the analysis of the much larger Vijayanagara urban core ceramic sample. Unrestricted vessels are, for present purposes, grouped only by broad vessel class. Restricted vessels have been divided into six "vessel-use" classes, RV1-RV6 (Fig. 6.13; see Sinopoli 1993:50-54). General characteristics and overall numbers of each of the six restricted vessel-use classes are presented in Table 6.6. Table 6.7 presents data on vessel-use classes by site.

Significant differences exist between the urban core and the survey data in overall frequencies of vessel-use classes (Table 6.8). In particular, in the urban core, food preparation vessels (RV2, RV3) outnumber water storage and transport vessels (RV4, RV5, RV6) by 4303 to 3862 (1.11:1), while in the survey sample, water vessels outnumber cooking vessels by 443 to 278 (1.59:1). These differences may result from demographic, occupational, and activity differences between the inhabitants of the two areas. That is, the inhabitants of the metropolitan region may have been less likely to engage in consumption activities and perhaps consumed less complex meals (involving fewer food preparation vessels) than the more affluent and elite inhabitants of the urban core. Further, large numbers of water vessels would certainly have been essential for agriculturalists and others who labored in fields and worksites such as stone quarries. An inscription associated with a well in the settlement of Malapanagudi indicates that roadside wells may have been provisioned with water vessels to serve travelers to the capital.

Table 6.8 contrasts the vessel-use class frequencies as calculated for the total urban core ceramic sample (combining data from the Noblemen's Quarter, East Valley, and Islamic Quarter) with the total sample from Blocks O, S, and T. Differences between the two areas are significant at the .001 level. Most striking, the survey ceramics included significantly higher than expected frequencies of other bowls, large water storage vessels (RV6), and large cooking vessels (RV3), and significantly lower than expected frequencies of lamps, shallow bowls, medium cooking vessels (RV2), and small water serving and transport vessels (RV4). The higher frequencies of large vessels is intriguing and may point to somewhat larger social units of consumption and food preparation in the survey area than in the urban core (for

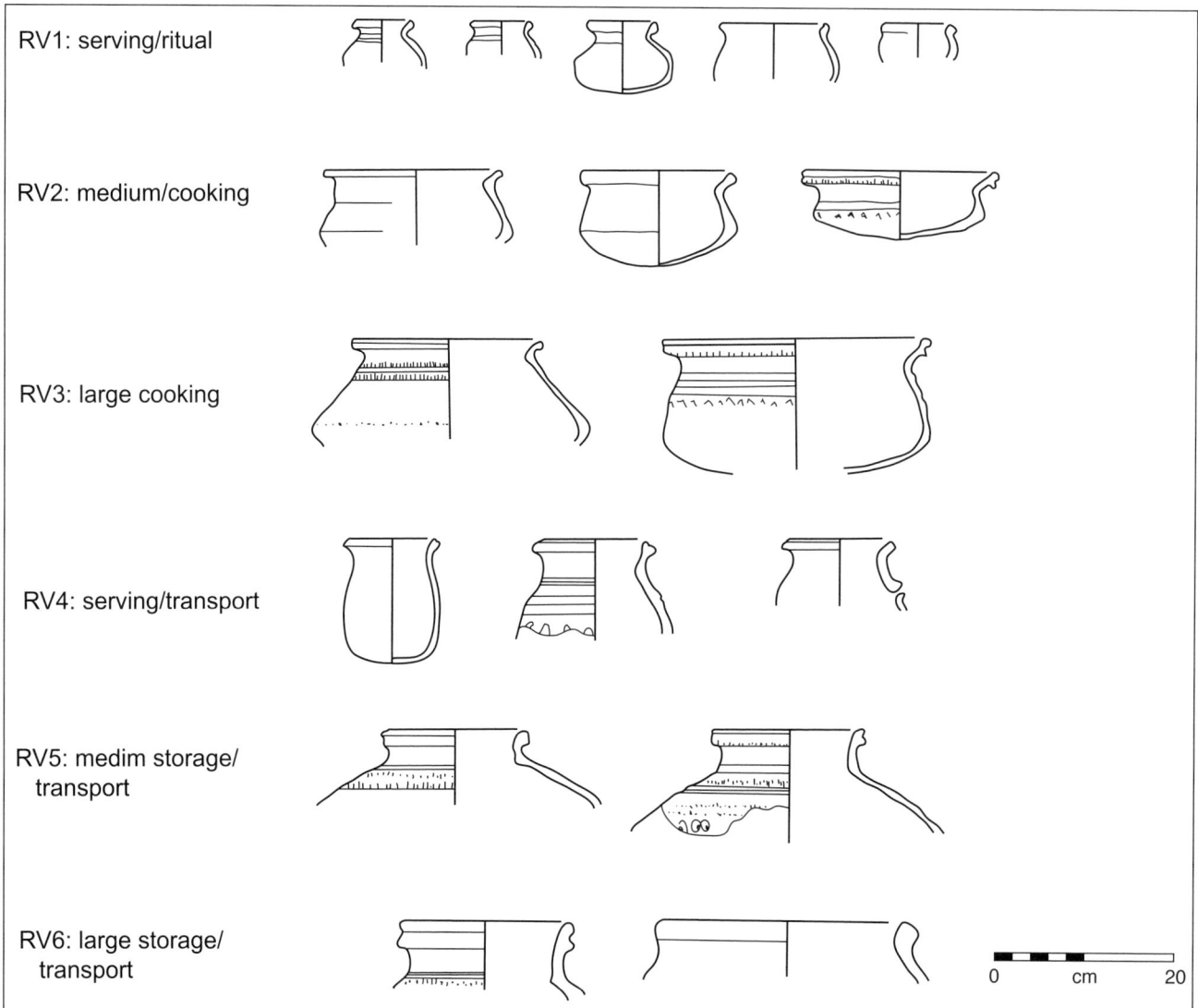

Figure 6.13. Restricted vessel categories RV1-RV6.

Table 6.6. Vessel-use classes (restricted vessels).

Vessel-Use Class	Description*	Number in Sample
RV1	Small relatively shallow vessels, 6-16 cm in rim diameter, with low outsloping necks; could have been used in serving individual portions of food or drink, or in storage of condiments, etc.	39 (5.1%)
RV2	Open relatively shallow vessels, 16-26 cm in rim diameter, with low out-turning necks and steep body angles. Vessels are typically wider than they are high. Could have been used as cooking vessels, with secondary uses in food preparation and in short-term storage of dry foods.	235 (30.9%)
RV3	Larger version of RV2, 23-45 cm in rim diameter; cooking and storage vessels.	43 (5.7%)
RV4	Small high necked vessels, with vertical necks and more or less globular bodies, 7-18 cm rim diameter; could have been used as serving vessels or for transport of liquids.	40 (5.3%)
RV5	Medium, vertical necked globular vessels, 14-26 cm in rim diameter, probably used for storage of water and/or other comestibles.	279 (36.7%)
RV6	Large, vertical necked globular vessels, 21-33 cm in rim diameter, probably used for storage.	124 (16.3%)
Totals (in Blocks O, S, and T)		760

*Assignment into vessel-use classes is based on three formal dimensions of ceramic variation: size, vessel orientations, and rim form. The overlap in rim diameter between some vessel-use classes results from the different size distributions of straight and flange rim form categories.

Table 6.7. Vessel-use classes by site.

Site	Lamps	Shallow Bowls	Other Bowls	RV1	RV2	RV3	RV4	RV5	RV6	Cannot Tell	Total
VMS-2	0	1	12	3	27	3	3	18	3	2	72
VMS-7	0	0	5	0	6	0	0	2	0	0	13
VMS-8	0	0	1	0	0	0	0	1	0	0	2
VMS-16	0	0	1	0	1	1	1	8	9	0	21
VMS-33	0	0	2	0	3	0	0	6	0	1	12
VMS-35	0	2	3	4	9	2	0	12	5	0	37
VMS-37	0	1	0	0	0	0	1	1	1	0	4
VMS-66	0	0	4	0	11	1	0	13	3	0	32
VMS-78	0	2	5	5	5	0	1	12	1	0	31
VMS-101	1	0	11	1	5	1	1	8	1	0	29
VMS-104	0	0	0	0	2	2	0	3	6	0	13
VMS-124	0	0	0	0	0	1	0	0	0	0	1
VMS-125	0	0	0	3	0	1	1	3	2	0	10
VMS-135	0	0	3	0	2	0	1	1	3	0	10
VMS-140	0	7	4	1	3	1	2	4	4	1	27
VMS-142	0	0	0	0	2	0	0	0	0	0	2
VMS-144	0	5	1	3	7	2	0	6	2	0	26
VMS-145	0	0	0	2	1	1	4	0	2	0	10
VMS-146	0	0	0	0	1	0	0	0	1	0	2
VMS-147	0	0	0	0	1	1	1	1	2	0	6
VMS-149	0	0	0	0	1	0	0	0	0	0	1
VMS-150	0	0	0	0	1	0	1	1	3	0	6
VMS-153	0	0	4	0	6	0	1	2	1	0	14
VMS-158	0	0	0	0	4	1	0	0	0	0	5
VMS-163	0	0	0	0	1	0	0	0	6	0	7
VMS-164	0	0	7	0	1	0	1	4	0	0	13
VMS-165	0	0	0	0	1	0	0	0	0	0	1
VMS-169	0	0	7	3	13	3	2	5	4	0	37
VMS-170	0	0	0	0	4	2	0	2	0	0	8
VMS-172	0	0	0	0	0	0	0	1	0	0	1
VMS-175	0	0	3	0	1	0	0	1	0	0	5
VMS-176	0	0	0	0	0	0	0	1	1	0	2
VMS-178	0	0	1	0	2	2	1	5	1	0	12
VMS-179	0	0	2	0	7	1	0	5	14	0	29
VMS-180	0	0	0	1	2	0	0	8	0	0	11
VMS-182	0	1	0	0	2	0	0	6	2	0	11
VMS-183	0	0	0	1	1	0	0	2	2	0	6
VMS-184	0	0	0	0	0	0	0	1	1	0	2
VMS-186	0	0	0	0	0	0	0	1	0	0	1
VMS-193	0	0	2	0	0	0	0	0	0	0	2
VMS-199	0	0	1	0	0	0	0	1	0	0	2
VMS-201	0	1	0	0	5	0	1	7	2	0	16
VMS-202	0	0	0	0	2	1	0	0	1	0	4
VMS-203	0	1	0	0	2	1	1	7	3	0	15
VMS-205	0	0	1	0	0	0	0	2	0	0	3
VMS-207	0	0	1	0	0	2	0	0	0	0	3
VMS-208	0	0	1	1	5	0	0	5	0	1	13
VMS-211	0	0	0	0	0	3	0	0	1	0	4
VMS-212	0	0	2	0	4	2	0	5	1	0	14

Table 6.7 cont.

Site	Lamps	Shallow Bowls	Other Bowls	RV1	RV2	RV3	RV4	RV5	RV6	Cannot Tell	Total
VMS-219	0	0	0	0	1	0	0	1	0	0	2
VMS-221	0	0	1	0	0	0	0	0	0	0	1
VMS-246	0	0	0	0	2	1	1	0	0	0	4
VMS-251	0	0	0	0	0	0	0	1	0	0	1
VMS-254	0	3	1	0	3	0	0	14	3	0	24
VMS-278	0	0	0	1	13	2	1	4	3	0	24
VMS-285	0	0	0	0	2	0	1	4	1	0	8
VMS-289	0	0	0	0	0	0	0	1	0	0	1
VMS-319	0	0	1	0	0	0	0	0	0	0	1
VMS-327	0	0	2	0	2	0	0	2	0	0	6
VMS-329	0	0	20	0	12	0	5	10	3	0	50
VMS-335	0	0	2	1	4	0	0	0	0	0	7
VMS-339	0	0	0	0	0	0	0	0	1	1	2
VMS-340	0	0	1	0	0	0	0	0	0	0	1
VMS-341	0	0	0	0	0	0	1	1	0	0	2
VMS-361	1	19	4	8	22	1	5	44	8	0	112
VMS-365	0	5	6	1	22	3	2	26	16	0	81
VMS-371	1	0	0	0	0	0	0	0	1	0	2
VMS-372	0	0	0	0	1	1	0	0	0	0	2
Totals	3	48	122	39	235	43	40	279	124	6	939

Table 6.8. Comparison of vessel-use classes between survey area and urban core.*

	Lamps	Shallow Bowls	Other Bowls	RV1	RV2	RV3	RV4	RV5	RV6	Total
VMS (Blocks O, S, T)	3 (15)	48 (82)	122 (50)	39 (34)	235 (362)	43 (35)	40 (56)	279 (259)	124 (40)	933
Urban Core	171 (159)	923 (889)	470 (542)	363 (368)	4052 (3925)	370 (378)	625 (609)	2799 (2818)	351 (435)	10,124
Totals	174	971	592	402	4287	413	665	3078	475	11,057

*Numbers in parentheses are expected values.
$\chi^2 = 389.468$, df = 8, $p < .001$

example, extended versus nuclear families), though given the limited data, this is a difficult case to make at present. The higher than expected frequencies of other bowls may, as noted above, point to the wider temporal range of VMS sites as compared to the more limited chronological span of the urban core. It may also point to functional differences between sites (for instance, perhaps the ritual constraints on eating from earthenware plates were less strictly adhered to in the metropolitan region than in the urban core).

While small sample sizes preclude consideration of intra-site variability in ceramic distributions, inter-site differences in vessel-use class frequencies are clearly evident. Table 6.9 summarizes inter-site differences in vessel-use class frequencies among the 12 survey sites that contained 25 or more identifiable diagnostics. Inter-site differences in vessel-use class frequencies likely result from multiple factors related to the range of activities that took place within sites and their social and economic composition.

Not surprisingly, sites with relatively large numbers of classifiable diagnostics include settlement sites (VMS-2, VMS-35, VMS-101, VMS-140, VMS-144, VMS-361, VMS-365) and artifact scatters (VMS-66, VMS-78), which are also likely associated with settlement locales. Other sites with comparatively large ceramic samples include iron processing sites VMS-169 (artifact scatter associated with iron slag, and with modern dumping activities) and VMS-179, and VMS-329, an area of structural foundations (basements of well-constructed temple, or administrative structure?) associated with settlement VMS-361 and step well VMS-328.

Inter-site differences in vessel-use class frequencies are suggestive (Tables 6.9a, 6.9b). High frequencies of *shallow bowls*, a form believed to be securely assignable to the Vijayanagara period, occur in sites VMS-140, VMS-144, and VMS-361. These forms are absent at the two iron smelting sites (VMS-169, VMS-179), and at VMS-66 (with at least some modern ceramics) and VMS-329. Two sites have significantly higher than expected frequencies of *other bowls*, including 37.9% at settlement VMS-101 and 40.0% at site VMS-329; shallow bowls are absent at both sites. Again, this could be a function of either or both their temporal range and differences in food consumption practices or other activities at these sites.

RV1, small serving vessels, occur in high frequencies in settlement sites VMS-35 and VMS-144, and artifact scatter/settlement VMS-78. Medium food preparation vessels, RV2, are found in higher than expected frequencies in settlement VMS-2, and in artifact scatters VMS-66 and VMS-169; large food preparation vessels, RV3, occur in higher than expected frequencies in VMS-144 and VMS-169. Forms RV4-RV6 are interpreted as associated with water serving, transport, and storage. Form RV4 occurs in higher than expected frequencies in sites VMS-140 and VMS-329; form RV5 occurs in higher than expected frequencies in VMS-66, VMS-78, and VMS-361; and form RV6 occurs in very high frequencies in VMS-179, and in high frequencies at VMS-365.

Given the small sample sizes and problems of sampling error, it is dangerous to infer too much from these differences or to inter-site variations in vessel class frequencies. Nonetheless, a few sites with striking patterns merit some (cautious) discussion. The several settlement sites yielded quite different frequencies of vessel-use classes. Ceramic frequencies at site VMS-2, a large Vijayanagara period settlement located near the edge of modern Venkatapur, are in general quite similar to those from the total urban core sample, while site VMS-361, a settlement located along a major road leading into the urban core, contains high frequencies of vessels associated with water storage and shallow bowls (lids), a pattern that may be associated with activities linked to its roadside location, and serving of travelers (a pattern weakly supported by the higher than expected frequencies of small water serving vessels, RV4, at associated site VMS-329, though here larger transport and storage vessels are, in fact, underrepresented). Cooking forms are found at settlement and non-settlement sites, including, for example, the iron processing site VMS-179 (which has very high frequencies of large water storage vessels).

Despite some suggestive patterning, however, the data also raise some serious questions concerning their representativeness. In particular, site VMS-2 is spatially and, we think, functionally associated with site VMS-78, yet their ceramic distributions are quite different. This could, of course, be related to functional differences between the two sites, but it again suggests the need for great caution in interpreting the very small samples of measurable and classified ceramics from these sites.

Other Earthenware Materials

Non-vessel categories of earthenware were quite rare in the Vijayanagara metropolitan region. Most common were secondary products of vessels—worked sherds. These are small ceramic disks, with roughly ground edges, that were formed from broken vessel fragments. Such objects may have been used as gaming pieces; it is also possible that larger ones were used as spindle whorls (though no perforated worked sherds were identified). Isolated worked sherds were documented from several sites. In Block O, they were found in VMS-2, VMS-52, and VMS-91. In Block T, a worked sherd was documented at temple site VMS-317, and in Block S at sites VMS-135, VMS-145, and VMS-169. These sherds ranged from 2.5 to 5.0 cm in diameter, and often incorporated decorative motifs from the broken bodies of restricted vessels.

A distinctive ceramic piece was found at step well site VMS-372, which is adjacent to temple VMS-371. This is a fragment from a black plain ware piece (image/figurine? vessel?) that depicted a human face (Fig. 6.14). The left eye and a portion of the nose are preserved in this $5.0 \times 2.8 \times 1.3$ cm sherd. It is not possible to determine what the larger piece looked like, though this is our only example of a fired ceramic sculpture from either the Vijayanagara metropolitan region or the urban core. Although it is likely that clay figurines were made during the Vijayanagara

Table 6.9a. Vessel-use classes (sites with more than 25 identifiable sherds).

Site	Lamps	Shallow Bowls	Other Bowls	RV1	RV2	RV3	RV4	RV5	RV6	Cannot Tell	Total
VMS-2	0	1	12	3	27	3	3	18	3	2	72
VMS-35	0	2	3	4	9	2	0	12	5	0	37
VMS-66	0	0	4	0	11	1	0	13	3	0	32
VMS-78	0	2	5	5	5	0	1	12	1	0	31
VMS-101	1	0	11	1	5	1	1	8	1	0	29
VMS-140	0	7	4	1	3	1	2	4	4	1	27
VMS-144	0	5	1	3	7	2	0	6	2	0	26
VMS-169	0	0	7	3	13	3	2	5	4	0	37
VMS-179	0	0	2	0	7	1	0	5	14	0	29
VMS-329	0	0	20	0	12	0	5	10	3	0	50
VMS-361	1	19	4	8	22	1	5	44	8	0	112
VMS-365	0	5	6	1	22	3	2	26	16	0	81
Totals	2	41	79	29	143	18	21	163	64	3	563

Table 6.9b. Frequencies of vessel-use classes by site.*

Site	Site Type	Lamps	Shallow Bowls	Other Bowls	RV1	RV2	RV3	RV4	RV5	RV6	Cannot Tell
VMS-2	settlement	0	1.4	16.7	4.2	**37.5**	4.2	4.2	25.0	4.2	2.8
VMS-35	settlement	0	5.4	8.1	**10.8**	24.3	5.4	0	32.4	13.5	0
VMS-66	artifact scatter	0	0	12.5	0	**34.4**	3.1	0	**40.6**	9.4	0
VMS-78	artifact scatter/settlement	0	6.5	16.1	**16.1**	16.1	0	3.2	**38.7**	3.2	0
VMS-101	settlement	**3.4**	0	**37.9**	3.4	17.2	3.4	3.4	27.6	3.4	0
VMS-140	settlement	0	**25.9**	14.8	3.7	11.1	3.7	**7.4**	14.8	14.8	3.7
VMS-144	temple, in settlement area	0	**19.2**	3.8	**11.5**	26.9	**7.7**	0	23.1	7.7	0
VMS-169	artifact scatter/iron processing	0	0	18.9	8.1	**35.1**	**8.1**	5.4	13.5	10.8	0
VMS-179	iron processing	0	0	6.9	0	24.1	3.4	0	17.2	**48.3**	0
VMS-329	foundations/settlement	0	0	**40.0**	0	24.0	0	**10.0**	20.0	6.0	0
VMS-361	settlement	0.9	**16.7**	3.6	7.1	19.6	0.9	4.5	**39.3**	7.1	0
VMS-365	settlement	0	6.2	7.4	1.2	27.2	3.7	2.5	32.1	**19.8**	0
Overall means		0.04	7.3	14.0	5.2	25.4	3.2	3.7	29.0	11.4	0.05

*Higher than expected frequencies denoted in bold face type.

Figure 6.14. Sculpted sherd depicting portion of a human face, VMS-372.

period, it is the case ethnographically that these are typically not fired. If this was the practice in the past, such objects would not be likely to be preserved archaeologically.

Imported Ceramics

Imported ceramics recovered in the Vijayanagara urban core include Chinese porcelains and celadon glazed stoneware and a few glazed earthenware sherds originating either in Iran or northern India. Within the urban core, such wares occur in highest frequencies in elite residential areas of the Royal Center or in the city's main Islamic residential quarter. Only four small nondiagnostic fragments of imported ceramics were found in sites in the three survey blocks. These pieces occur in settlement areas. Two porcelain fragments were recovered from sites VMS-176 and VMS-201 in the densely occupied region in the northeast quadrant of Block S, the area of the late Vijayanagara suburb of Varadadevi-ammana-pattana. A third porcelain sherd was found along Vijayanagara period road, VMS-160, in the east-central area of Block S.

A green glazed imported ceramic sherd was recovered in settlement VMS-361 in Block T. This sherd has an olive green glaze, reminiscent of celadon, but has a soft red paste, and may be a Persian or north Indian ware. Another possible imported porcelain sherd was observed on the surface of settlement VMS-2 in Block O; however, this was not collected and it could not be determined if it was recent in date or belonged to the Vijayanagara period.

Ground Stone

Ground stone mortars are widespread throughout the metropolitan region. These were primarily used for food processing and take two forms: bedrock mortars and block mortars. Bedrock mortars are circular depressions that were pecked into bedrock or the surfaces of outcropping boulders in habitation areas (see Plate 3.32). Block mortars were of similar form, but were carved on large stone blocks that could be moved. Mortars are common in habitation sites, and isolated mortars are sometimes found in outcrop areas, and are described in site descriptions in Chapters 3-5. Other *in situ* grinding features are termed "slicks"—these are grinding surfaces that occur either on boulders or on floors of structures, and again are primarily the remains of food processing activities.

Portable ground or pecked stone artifacts were found at a number of sites in the metropolitan region. These include two grinding slab fragments from Neolithic ashmound site VMS-26, and handstone or pestle fragments from four Vijayanagara period sites (VMS-2, VMS-332, VMS-365, and VMS-153). Similar fragments were noted at other settlement sites, but were not collected. Small disk-shaped granite pieces, 5-6 cm in diameter, of unknown function were found at VMS-335 ($n = 2$) and at VMS-329 ($n = 1$).

Quarrying and Peg Production

Evidence for stone quarrying is widespread throughout the extensive granitic outcrops that are so abundant in the Vijayanagara metropolitan region (Tables 6.10a, 6.10b). For the most part, this evidence takes the form of rows of small square depressions (c. 3-5 cm across), spaced c. 15-20 cm apart, that were pecked into the outcrops and defined fracture lines along which boulders were cut and shaped into blocks (most likely through placing wooden plugs in them and soaking them, causing expansion, and splitting the rock). No areas in the Vijayanagara metropolitan region have evidence for large-scale massive quarrying activities.[2] Instead, quarrying, not surprisingly, appears to have taken place near construction sites, most likely by mobile laborers who shifted from building site to building site, perhaps residing in small ephemeral structures.

Other stone workers, including artisans who shaped columns, built walls, sculpted images, and carved inscriptions, probably comprised separate groups of mobile craftspeople who traveled to construction sites throughout the metropolitan region. We do not know much about how these crafts people were recruited or compensated; Ramaswamy (1985:419) has suggested, however, that masons, carpenters and engravers experienced a rise in social and economic status during the Vijayanagara period and there must have been large numbers of such artisans in the metropolitan region to produce the vast and impressive architectural remains we see there today (see also Sinopoli 2003). We know only a small number of these individuals by name—these were the most highly skilled sculptors and architects who were acknowledged through inscriptions on their products.

One line of evidence suggests mass production of certain architectural elements. Within numerous temples throughout the urban core and metropolitan region are found columns that appear to have been constructed prior to temple construction and then modified to fit into the structure. Such modification takes the form of setting columns that are too tall for the structure and then cutting off a portion of the upper sculpted panel of the columns to decrease their length. This might indicate production of standard columns at some locale and their later modification to fit the specific requirements of individual structures following their movement to building sites. Unfortunately, we have no direct evidence of any kind for these hypothesized column manufacturing areas.

One site in the metropolitan region does contain evidence for construction debris and column shaping. VMS-79 (see Chapter 3) consists of the uncompleted remains of a small structure located along the Turtha Canal to the east of the city core. This structure, most probably a small shrine, was in the process of being built

---

[2]However, large-scale quarrying may well have obliterated large outcrops, especially within the urban core, where vast enclosure walls and massive structures were constructed.

Table 6.10a. Intensive quarrying and construction of structures.

Site	Block/Tr	Dimensions (m)	Description of Remains
VMS-79	O/10	30 × 15	Structure under construction, uncompleted structure destroyed by rockfall, partly completed columns and stone working debris, extensive quarrying, lime plaster debris, in situ manufacture of columns and elements.
VMS-341	T/9	23 × 7	Stone quarry site on sheet rock, several slabs have been partly cut and left in situ, Vijayanagara-style quarry and pick marks.

Table 6.10b. Extensive quarrying (isolated quarry marks).

Site	Block/Tr	Dimensions (m)	Description of Remains
VMS-13	O/1	15 × 13	Isolated structure, nearby is large boulder with quarry marks.
VMS-126	S/18	12 × ?	Structure on sheet rock, peg holes, quarry marks throughout area.
VMS-127	S/18	?	Isolated walls on outcrop, extensive ancient quarrying.
VMS-140	S/18	195 × 135	Settlement area, isolated quarry marks on large basalt boulders in area.
VMS-175	S/17	9 × 7	Well, extensive quarrying in area.
VMS-176	S/17	87 × 65	Residential terraces, abundant pre-modern quarrying.
VMS-181	S/16	160 × 140	Agricultural walls/embankments, pre-modern quarrying in associated outcrop.
VMS-326	T/9-14	1200 × 50	Road system, quarrying in small outcrops along road.
VMS-327	T/13	26 × 12	Watch tower on low outcrop, quarrying on boulder.
VMS-330	T/13-14	650 × 60	Reservoir embankment, quarrying on outcrop to north.
VMS-353	T/12-13	170 × 3.5	Road walls bordering high outcrop, quarrying on outcrop and boulders.
VMS-359	T/13	40 × 20	Structure on outcrop, quarry marks and quarried slabs on outcrop.
VMS-360	T/18	800 × 30	Road, quarrying among boulders abutting road.
VMS-364	T/18	190 × 45	Reservoir embankment, quarrying on outcrops bounding embankment.

Table 6.10c. Peg production.

Site	Block/Tr	Dimensions (m)	Description of Remains
VMS-2	O/9-10	390 × 100	Settlement, with basalt pegs, spheres, and debris, no sheet rock in this area of site.
VMS-35	O/2	200 × 170	Settlement area, basalt pegs, handstones, and flaked basalt scatter.
VMS-140	S/18	195 × 135	Architectural rubble, and artifact scatter, with flaked basalt scatter.
VMS-172	S/17	87 × 35	Platforms along Penukonda Road, some flaked basalt fragments.

in an area of sheet rock along the face of a large outcropping boulder when a portion of the overhanging outcrop collapsed on it. Remains at the site consist of column footings that were pecked into the sheet rock, a completed column lying beneath the fallen overhang, and several partially completed columns lying nearby. Also present were significant quantities of granite flakes and debris, indicating that the columns were being shaped at the construction site itself. This site presents a rare glimpse of construction activities in progress.

Numerous structures at Vijayanagara were built on granitic sheet rock or boulders. The walls of these structures were supported by flaked basalt pegs, which were placed into small square holes pecked into the granite rock (Plate 6.1; Fig. 6.15). Evidence for peg production in the form of completed pegs and/or flaked basalt debris has been found at four sites (Table 6.10c). Three of these were settlements: a small village (VMS-35) and a large town site in Block O (VMS-2), and the late Vijayanagara suburb associated with Achyutaraya in Block S (VMS-140). The third area of basalt flaking was also associated with this late burst of urban growth in Block S, just outside the urban core (VMS-172). Basalt working within settlements appears to have been localized to only limited neighborhoods or households, suggesting relatively small-scale workshops or localized production areas, perhaps for local use.

Artifact Distributions and Analysis 293

Plate 6.1. Basalt pegs, VMS-2.

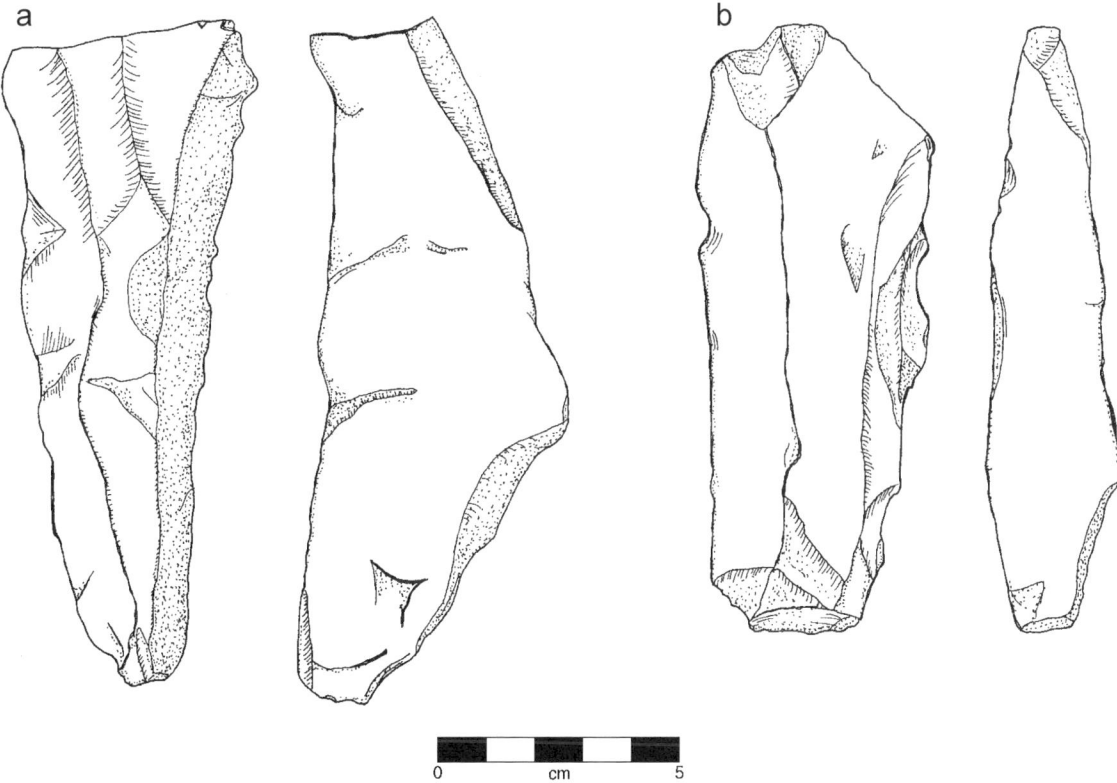

Figure 6.15. Basalt pegs (both from VMS-2, Unit 3).

Other Chipped Stone Artifacts

The basalt pegs discussed above constitute one group of flaked or chipped stone artifacts identified by the VMS—used for architectural supports. Numerous other flaked stone artifacts and chipping debris were also recovered from 27 archaeological sites in Blocks O, S, and T (see Tables 6.11-6.12; Figs. 6.16-6.18; Plate 6.2). These were analyzed by project member Mark T. Lycett (Lycett 1991) and the following description summarizes his research. A total of 1600 fragments of flaked stone (6639.4 g) were recovered in systematic surface collections and as stray finds. These span a broad temporal range from prehistory to the Vijayanagara period, and provide persuasive evidence that an ad hoc informal lithic industry persisted in the region long after metal tools became available. Thus, prehistoric site VMS-26 contained flakes, angular flaking debris, and one core tool of quartz/quartzite and volcanic stones (Fig. 6.16); Vijayanagara period settlement VMS-2 yielded flakes, a core and a tool of quartz/quartzite, as well as a glass core (Fig. 6.18). Other sites containing lithics are of uncertain date, such as rock shelter VMS-33 (Block O) and lithic scatter VMS-249 (Block S). Systematic surface collections at the latter site yielded the largest sample of lithics recovered from any site, 463 fragments (1165.7 g). Few of the artifacts were finished.

Lithic materials were sorted by material type and then grouped into one of five morphological categories. Artifacts of quartz/quartzite were the most common, comprising more than 92% of the artifacts recovered ($n = 1471$; 4682 g). White, brown, and gray quartz veins are common in the granodiorite hills throughout the survey area and quartz pebbles and cobbles are found in the gravels of the Tungabhadra River. Next in frequency are volcanic stones, most of dolerite, which occurs in intrusive dykes in the survey region. Only 63 volcanic chipped stone artifacts were recovered (40 flakes, 21 fragments angular debris, and 2 cores). These comprise less than 4% of the total number of flaked stone artifacts, but nearly 16% of the sample by weight, attesting to their large size compared to the more common quartz/quartzite artifacts. Other artifacts were of chert or other cryptocrystalline stone ($n = 26$, 893.4 g). These came in several colors including translucent white, milky white, white with red inclusions, green, gray, gray-banded, and brown. Chert deposits are exposed in the eastern Sandur Hills and in the eastern fringes of the Vijayanagara metropolitan region; cobbles of chert also occur in the alluvial gravels of the Tungabhadra River. Finally, two flaked glass cores were recovered at Vijayanagara period settlement sites VMS-2 and VMS-102 (terraces and shrine). Both of these are of dark green translucent glass, and likely derived from a large bottle or other container (Lycett 1991:191).

As noted, each item of chipped stone was sorted into one of five general morphological categories: flakes, angular debris, cores/parent material, bipolar debris, and tools or edge modified pieces. All artifacts showing evidence for edge modification were further documented. As defined by Lycett (1991:86-87), flakes are items detached from a parent material by means of a unidirectional application of force, and which exhibit ventral and dorsal surfaces, and a visible bulb of percussion on the ventral surface. Angular debris exhibits evidence of concoidal fracture but lacks discernible ventral surfaces. Cores or parent materials refer to all raw materials from which flakes or angular debris have been detached. Bipolar debris refers to fragments that have been detached from a parent material that rests on a stone anvil through the application of force, resulting in opposing striking platforms or zones of percussion on the same axis. Tools include artifacts with evidence for edge modification through retouch or through use as an informal tool.

Sixty of the 1600 (3.75%) chipped stone artifacts identified had evidence for edge modification (Table 6.12). The majority of these ($n = 48$) were utilized flakes; these lacked evidence for deliberate retouch, but had clear evidence of use as a cutting tool or for other tasks for which a sharp implement was required. Other tools included scrapers ($n = 5$), utilized core or pebble tools ($n = 4$), utilized chunks ($n = 2$), and a single denticulate.

The chipped stone data from the VMS demonstrates a largely expedient lithic industry, oriented to locally available stones and informal tools, which were likely struck off from nearby materials as needed, used for a few tasks, and then discarded (Lycett 1994:93). Chipped stone implements are relatively rare, comprising less than 4% of the total flaking debris. Nonetheless, the persistent presence of flaked stone tools well into the Vijayanagara period was an unexpected discovery of the survey, although in retrospect it is not surprising that villagers, herders, and other inhabitants of the metropolitan region would have made use of abundant raw materials as the need arose.

Table 6.11. Chipped stone artifacts.

Site	Unit	Block	Raw Material	Weight (g)	Flakes	Angular Debris	Cores	Bipolar Debris	Tools	Other/Comment
VMS-002	J	O	quartzite	40	0	0	0	0	1	
VMS-002	U1	O	glass	100	0	0	1	0	0	translucent green glass
VMS-002	U2	O	quartz	20	0	0	0	1	0	
VMS-002	U7	O	quartz	20	1	0	0	0	0	
VMS-002	U8	O	quartz	80	0	0	1	0	0	
VMS-021	T0/1	O	quartzite	20	0	0	0	0	1	green quartzite
VMS-026	0N/0E	O	chert	160	0	0	0	0	1	core tool
VMS-026	0N/12E	O	volcanic	100	1	0	0	0	0	
VMS-026	12N/0E	O	volcanic	40	0	1	0	0	0	
VMS-026	12N/12E	O	quartz	20	0	1	0	0	0	
VMS-026	12N/12E	O	volcanic	140	2	0	0	0	0	
VMS-026	12S/0E	O	volcanic	20	0	1	0	0	0	
VMS-026	12S/12E	O	quartz	20	0	1	0	0	0	
VMS-026	12S/12E	O	volcanic	280	0	0	1	0	0	tested cobble
VMS-026	mound	O	chert	280	0	0	1	0	0	
VMS-031	J	O	quartzite	60	2	3	0	0	0	green quartzite
VMS-033	Area A	O	quartz	220	1	5	4	2	0	
VMS-033	Area B	O	quartz	140	3	10	2	0	2	
VMS-033	Area D	O	quartz	60	0	8	0	0	0	bipolar
VMS-033	Area E	O	quartz	40	0	1	0	1	0	
VMS-035	F18	O	quartz	20	2	0	0	0	0	
VMS-035	F19	O	quartzite	120	0	0	1	0	0	
VMS-035	F1	O	quartz	40	0	3	0	0	0	
VMS-035	F10/13	O	quartzite	200	0	1	1	1	1	white quartzite
VMS-035	F21	O	quartz	220	1	0	2	0	0	
VMS-037	J	O	chert	0	0	0	0	0	1	green-gray chert, pebble tool
VMS-037	K	O	quartz	40	2	5	0	0	0	
VMS-037	O-2	O	chert	20	1	0	0	0	0	green-gray chert
VMS-037	P	O	quartz	20	0	2	0	0	0	
VMS-048		O	quartz	80	0	0	1	0	1	pebble core
VMS-075	J	O	quartz	100	0	2	1	1	1	
VMS-075	J	O	volcanic	120	4	2	0	0	0	large flakes
VMS-075	T1/1	O	quartz	40	8	13	3	4	0	
VMS-075	T1/2	O	quartz	20	1	5	0	2	0	
VMS-075	T1/3	O	chert	20	3	0	1	0	0	white chalcedonic chert
VMS-075	T1/3	O	quartz	100	5	19	1	4	0	
VMS-075	T1/3	O	volcanic	20	3	1	0	0	0	
VMS-075	T1/4	O	chert	20	0	0	1	0	1	white chert
VMS-075	T1/4	O	quartz	200	11	63	6	11	0	
VMS-075	T1/4	O	volcanic	120	14	14	0	0	0	
VMS-075		O	chert	20	1	1	0	0	1	white, green and gray cherts
VMS-092		O	cryptocrystalline	4.4	0	0	1	0	0	
VMS-102	J	O	glass	20	0	0	0	0	1	translucent green glass
VMS-108	J	O	chert	20	0	0	0	0	1	gray banded chert
VMS-125	T1/4	S	cryptocrystalline	5.5	1	0	0	0	0	
VMS-140	D1	S	quartz	44.9	0	0	2	0	0	
VMS-145		S	cryptocrystalline	0.7	2	0	0	0	0	
VMS-145		S	quartz	477.5	90	83	2	11	0	
VMS-145		S	volcanic	23.5	2	0	1	0	0	globular core
VMS-153	D1	S	quartz	11.0	0	0	1	0	0	

Table 6.11 cont.

Site	Unit	Block	Raw Material	Weight (g)	Flakes	Angular Debris	Cores	Bipolar Debris	Tools	Other/Comment
VMS-169	D1	S	quartz	90.0	7	0	0	5	0	
VMS-169	D1	S	volcanic	40.0	1	0	0	0	0	
VMS-169	D1	S	volcanic	15.2	1	0	0	0	0	
VMS-169		S	cryptocrystalline	11.7	0	0	0	1	0	
VMS-169		S	quartz	19.8	7	2	0	2	0	
VMS-169		S	quartz	33.3	4	2	0	1	0	
VMS-169		S	volcanic	21.5	1	0	0	0	0	
VMS-192	T1/3	S	quartz	128.2	33	72	0	8	0	
VMS-192	T2/2	S	quartz	30.1	4	20	0	3	0	
VMS-192	T2/3	S	quartz	113.3	35	128	0	11	0	
VMS-192		S	quartz	296.1	35	90	1	6	0	
VMS-195		S	cryptocrystalline	0.6	1	0	0	0	0	
VMS-195		S	quartz	59.6	2	10	1	2	0	
VMS-196		S	quartz	145.2	9	13	1	8	0	
VMS-197		S	quartz	160.6	16	50	3	4	0	
VMS-198		S	quartz	3.9	1	0	0	1	0	
VMS-199		S	quartz	16.7	1	1	1	0	0	
VMS-212	D2	S	quartz	81.0	7	0	1	2	0	
VMS-212	D2	S	volcanic	6.0	1	0	0	0	0	
VMS-212		S	quartz	88.5	3	19	0	4	0	
VMS-249	D1	S	cryptocrystalline	312.2	5	0	1	0	0	
VMS-249	D1	S	quartz	36.5	1	0	0	3	0	
VMS-249	D1	S	quartzite	39.6	1	0	0	0	0	
VMS-249	D1	S	volcanic	31.8	2	0	0	0	0	
VMS-249	J1	S	cryptocrystalline	1.2	1	0	0	0	0	
VMS-249	J1	S	quartz	148.0	27	37	2	13	0	
VMS-249	J3	S	quartz	58.4	7	31	1	6	0	
VMS-249	T1/1	S	quartz	73.4	13	10	1	6	0	
VMS-249	T1/2	S	quartz	28.5	2	2	0	1	0	
VMS-249	T1/3	S	quartz	24.8	2	8	0	2	0	
VMS-249	T2/1	S	quartz	5.0	1	3	0	1	0	
VMS-249	T2/2	S	quartz	29.1	3	28	0	2	0	
VMS-249	T2/3	S	quartz	140.8	5	33	0	4	Tools	
VMS-249	T3/1	S	quartz	0.3	0	1	0	0	0	
VMS-249	T3/2	S	quartz	19.3	8	16	0	4	0	
VMS-249	T4/1	S	quartz	3.5	2	4	0	0	0	
VMS-249	T4/2	S	quartz	1.0	1	0	0	0	0	
VMS-249	T5/1	S	quartz	1.9	0	3	0	0	0	
VMS-249	T5/2	S	quartz	5.1	2	8	0	0	0	
VMS-249	T5/3	S	quartz	20.6	0	1	0	2	0	
VMS-249	T6/0	S	quartz	6.3	1	3	0	1	0	
VMS-249	T6/0	S	volcanic	0.1	1	0	0	0	0	
VMS-249	T6/1	S	quartz	19.3	1	17	0	2	0	
VMS-249	T6/2	S	quartz	100.1	18	35	0	4	0	
VMS-249	T6/2	S	volcanic	17.6	4	1	0	0	0	
VMS-249	T7/1	S	quartz	13.1	2	6	0	1	0	
VMS-249	T7/2	S	quartz	14.6	6	34	2	4	0	
VMS-249	T7/2	S	volcanic	13.6	2	1	0	0	0	
VMS-251		S	quartz	53.1	1	0	0	0	0	
VMS-321		T	volcanic	14.7	1	0	0	0	0	
VMS-365		T	cryptocrystalline	37.1	0	0	1	0	0	

Table 6.12. Edge modified flaked stone artifacts from Blocks O, S and T.

Site	Utilized Flakes	Scrapers	Core Tools	Denticulate	Utilized Chunks	
VMS-2	1	0	1	0	0	
VMS-21	1	0	0	0	0	
VMS-26	1	0	0	0	0	
VMS-33	2	0	0	0	0	
VMS-35	1	0	0	0	0	
VMS-37	0	0	1	0	0	pebble tool
VMS-48	1	0	0	0	0	
VMS-75	2	0	0	0	0	1 unknown
VMS-102	0	1	0	0	0	
VMS-108	1	0	0	0	0	
VMS-123	1	0	0	0	0	
VMS-145	1	0	0	0	0	
VMS-150	0	1	0	0	0	
VMS-153	1	0	0	0	0	
VMS-167	0	0	1	0	0	
VMS-169	4	1	0	1	0	
VMS-192	13	1	0	0	1	
VMS-193	1	0	0	0	1	
VMS-196	1	0	0	0	0	
VMS-197	1	0	0	0	0	
VMS-221	1	0	0	0	0	
VMS-249	14	1	1	0	0	
Totals	48	5	4	1	2	

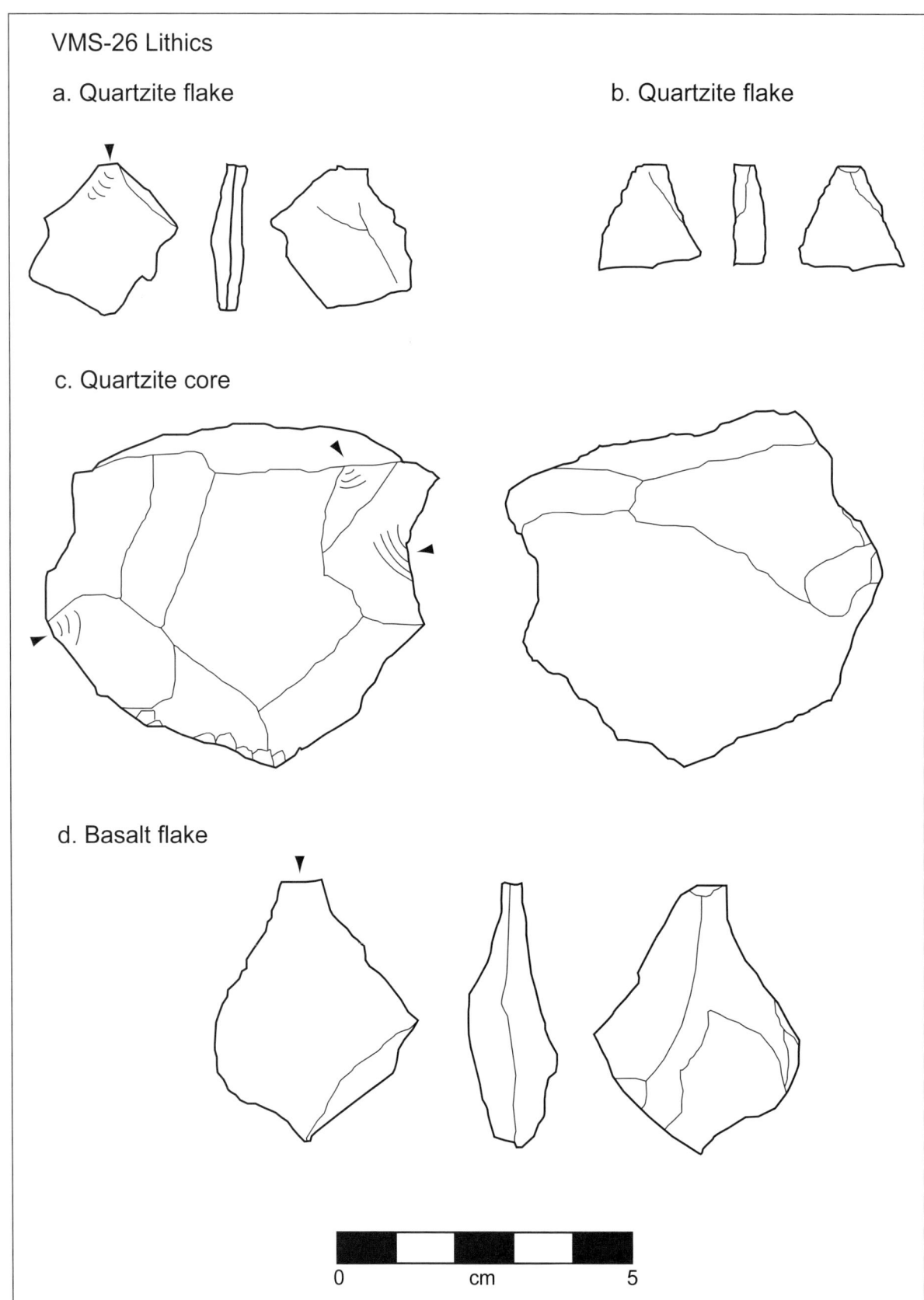

Figure 6.16. Flaked stone artifacts, VMS-26.

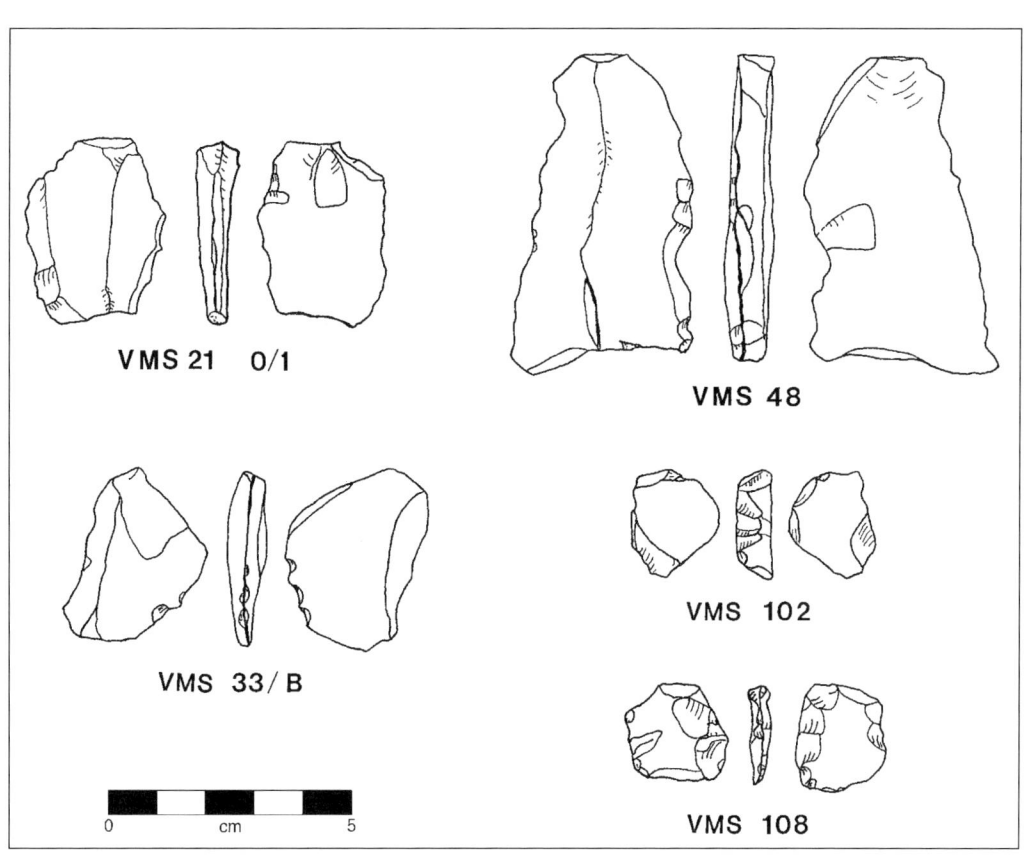

(*Left*) Figure 6.17. Flaked stone artifacts.

(*Below*) Figure 6.18. Flaked stone artifacts.

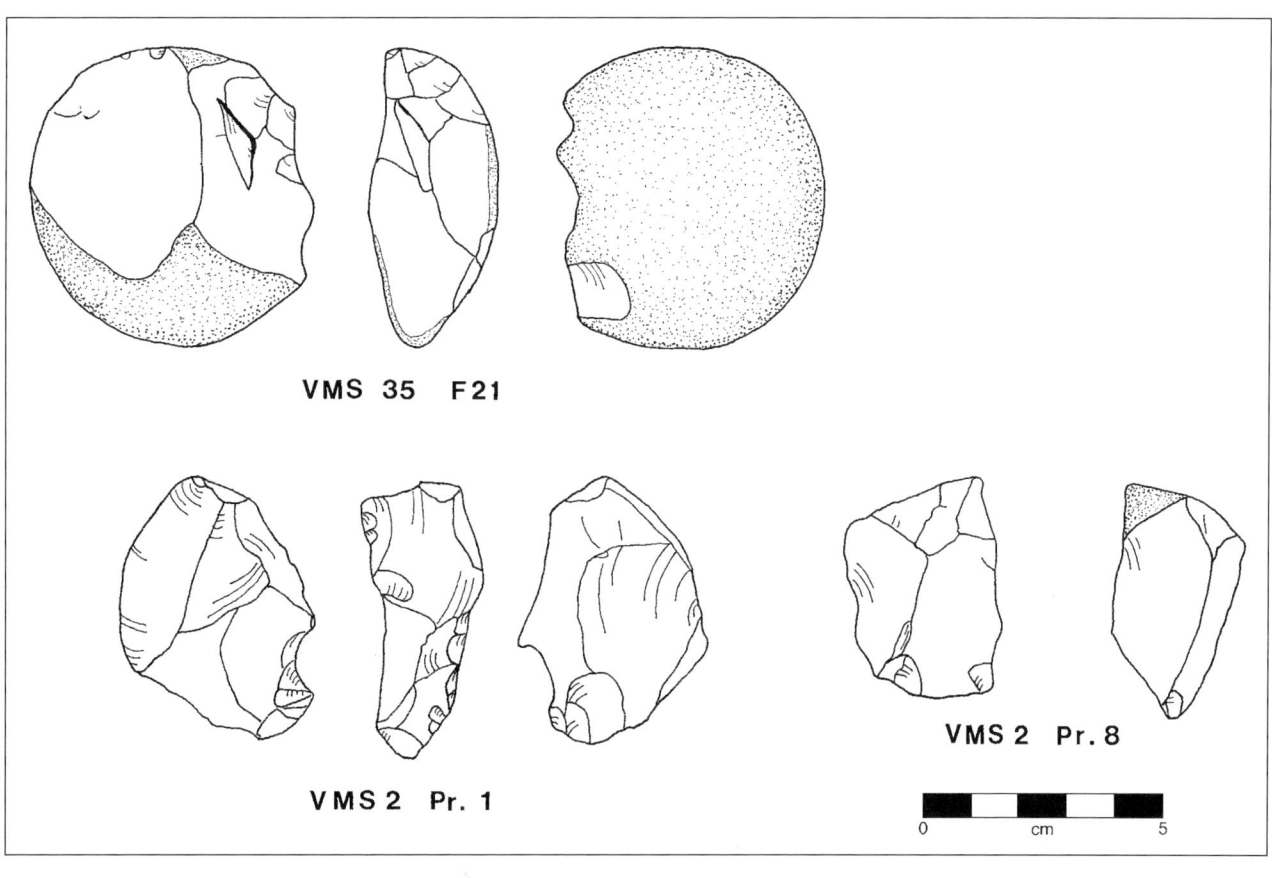

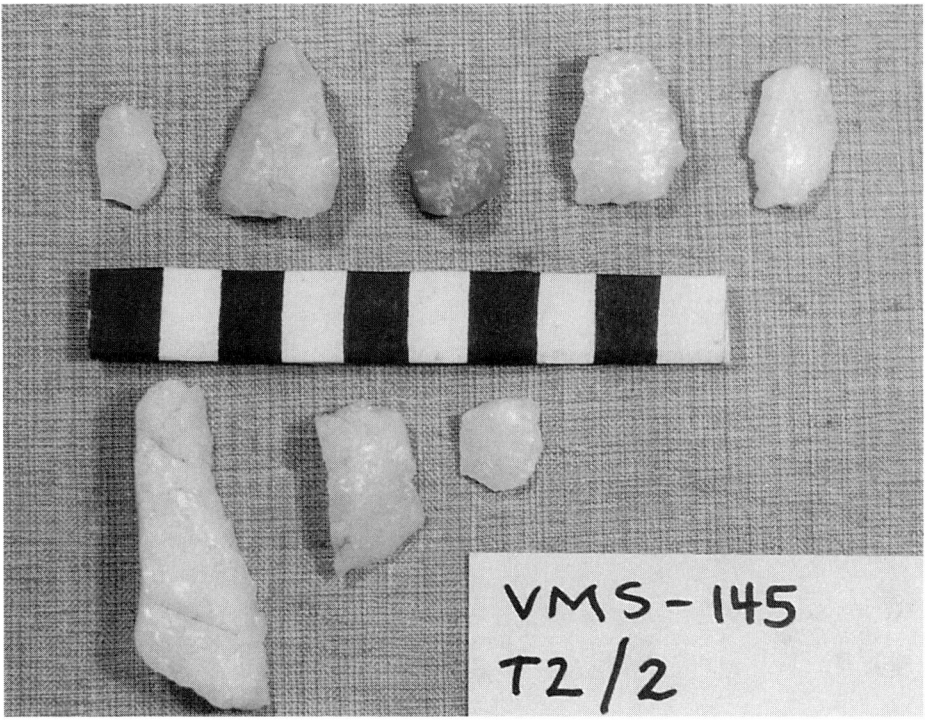

Plate 6.2. Quartz/quartzite flaked stone artifacts, VMS-145.

Metal Artifacts and Slag

Iron or other metal artifacts are rare in the survey area and are extremely difficult to date. Finds include an iron (knife?) blade from VMS-15 (see Fig. 3.10), a single-room structure documented in Block O, and a copper bangle fragment from VMS-35 (Fig. 6.19). Also from VMS-15 we recovered a small iron sphere, approximately 2.5 m in diameter, that rattles when shaken. Its function is unknown. Other unidentifiable fragments of iron implements have been recovered in small numbers, but most appear to be recent, and while noted, were typically not collected. A copper coin was recovered at VMS-37; this is described below.

Iron slag, in contrast, is more common and has been recovered from 27 sites in the three blocks (Table 6.13). Remains of iron working activities found in the Vijayanagara metropolitan region fall into two categories. The first includes locations with dense scatters of iron slag, vitrified brick or furnace fragments, often with slag adhering, and remains of ceramic pipes (tuyeres) (Plate 6.3). Three sites in Block S (VMS-121, VMS-169, VMS-179) and one in Block T (VMS-317) fall in this category (see Table 6.13a). Only one of these (VMS-121) contains clear evidence for preserved furnace features—a low rectangular platform, approximately 3 × 5 m in dimension, with stone and earthen walls and tuyere fragments projecting from the wall. No superstructure is preserved, though fired clay fragments are abundant on the surface surrounding the site.

None of the iron working locales is directly associated with residential architecture. Instead, all are located in flat open areas within a kilometer of identified settlement areas and near permanent or seasonal water sources. While some of the sites have quite extensive scatters of waste materials, the absence of architecture and permanent facilities suggests that these were not long-term permanent production sites, but instead represent the accumulation of multiple episodes of small-scale smelting or processing activities. Lycett (1994) has identified the association of many of these sites with seasonal water sources, and suggested that smelting activities occurred on a seasonal basis (see also Sinopoli 2003). The bulk of the evidence for iron working in surveyed areas of the metropolitan region thus appears to be the remains of the activities of small-scale mobile specialists, rather than large-scale permanent workshops or factories.

Dense scatters of iron working debris typically occur within much more diffuse scatters of iron slag, often extending for

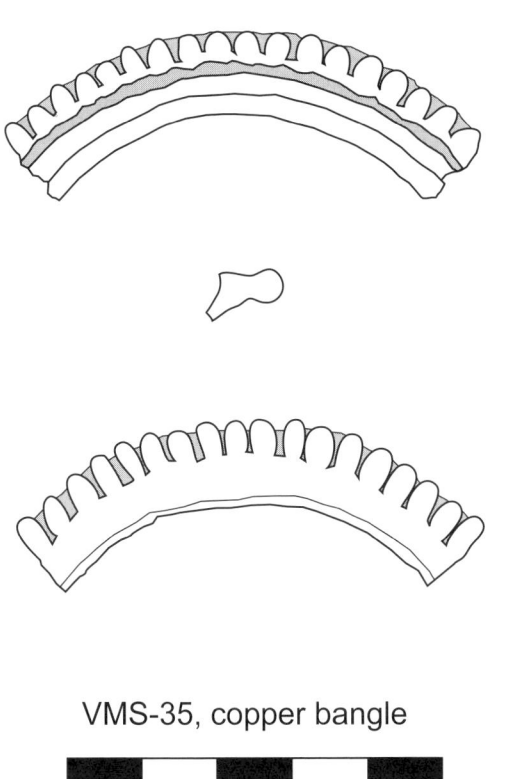

Figure 6.19. Copper bangle, VMS-35.

Plate 6.3. Ceramic tuyere, VMS-7.

several hundred meters beyond the areas of highest densities of slag and other waste. Thus, occasional pieces of slag were observed more than half a kilometer south of smelting locale VMS-121. In addition, low densities of iron slag were recorded in 23 sites in the three blocks, including many located in the densely occupied area in the northeast corner of Block S. Slag occurs as well in non-site locales as isolated finds in agricultural fields (Table 6.13b). These isolated finds consist of small slag fragments no more than a few centimeters across. Similar light slag distributions were also observed in surface collections in residential zones in Vijayanagara's urban core (Sinopoli 1986).

In some cases, slag was used as fill in structures constructed near iron working facilities. The most striking example of this is a high platform (VMS-7) located approximately 60 m from the small furnace mentioned earlier (VMS-121); the fill of the platform consists of stone rubble and numerous large pieces of iron slag and vitrified ceramics. In most cases, however, these non-production sites appear to be associated with different kinds of redepositional events, in which ash from the furnaces was deposited on agricultural fields as fertilizer.

Other Small Finds

Other categories of temporally diagnostic non-ceramic artifacts were rare in the survey region. Materials included in this category of goods are glass, steatite ornaments and objects, and a single coin. Several small cowrie shells and shell fragments were also recovered, but dating of these is highly problematic. The contemporary practice of field manuring with household waste and other land use in the region (including pastoralist camps) has resulted in the deposition of plastic, glass, and other artifacts in agricultural areas. While many of these objects are unambiguously recent in date (such as the plastic, glass bottle fragments, and so on), other materials are more problematic. This is particularly the case for objects such as glass bangles, cowrie shells, and other materials with a long history of use. Such artifacts were only documented by the VMS if they occurred in contexts with little evidence for recent disturbance.

Glass artifacts include a bangle fragment from VMS-35 and two pieces of flaked glass (see above). Artifacts of steatite include a small rectangular bead with circular motifs from VMS-15 (see Fig. 3.10), and a steatite bowl fragment (unmeasurable) from Vijayanagara period settlement VMS-365. A small figurine of a

Table 6.13a. Iron working locales.

Site	Block/Tr	Dimensions (m)	Description of Remains
VMS-121	S	3 × 5 (feature); 150+ m diam (slag scatter)	Remains of iron smelting furnace; small platform with projecting ceramic pipes or tuyere fragments, and vitrified brick. Associated with dense surface scatters of iron slag and droplets, vitrified ceramic, tuyere fragments. Slag from this site has been used as fill in VMS-7, and a light scatter extends for more than 500 m to the south.
VMS-169	S	150 × 150	Diffuse scatter of lithics, iron slag, and ceramics. Densities are highest in eastern half of the site.
VMS-179	S/16	50 × 35	High density surface scatter of iron slag and vitrified ceramics in localized area.
VMS-317	T/3	60 × 50	Moderate to high density scatter of slag associated with temple complex, feature of decaying brick and fired earth.

Table 6.13b. Sites containing light densities of iron slag.

Site	Block/Tr	Dimensions (m)	Description of Remains	Assoc with
VMS-2	O/9-10	390 × 100	Settlement, localized artifact scatter, basalt, ceramics, and small quantities of iron slag.	
VMS-37	O/3	150 × 86	Settlement, rubble wall structures, sparse scatter of small fragments of iron slag.	
VMS-7	S/11	22 × 22	Mandapa, high platform, platform fill in large part comprised of slag and vitrified ceramics.	VMS-121
VMS-122	S/11	80 × 7	Reservoir embankment, disturbed, low density of iron slag.	VMS-121
VMS-140	S/18	195 × 135	Artifact scatter, ceramics, one piece slag, flaked basalt.	
VMS-141	S/17	10 × 10	Displaced Vijayanagara slabs, and architectural elements, light ceramic and basalt scatter, sparse slag.	
VMS-142	S/16	95 × 50	Vaishnava temple complex, sparse scatter of ceramics and slag.	
VMS-144	S/16	75 × 75	Temple, sparse localized distributions of ceramics, slag and lithics.	
VMS-153	S/16	70 × 62	Artifact scatter, largely ceramics, but some large pieces of iron slag.	
VMS-161	S/17-18	53 × 25	Artifact scatter, ceramic with small isolated slag fragments.	
VMS-176	S/17	87 × 65	Walls, associated with sparse scatter of ceramics and slag.	
VMS-178	S/16	80 × 100	Artifact scatter and structural debris, ceramics, lithics, and slag.	
VMS-185	S/16	3.5 × 3.5	Mandapa, within diffuse ceramic scatter, some slag.	
VMS-212	S/14	96 × 35	Artifact scatter, ceramics, and sparse distribution of iron slag and virtrified ceramics/furnace debris.	
VMS-213	S/14	10 × 8	Water storage/cistern, single slag fragment.	
VMS-214	S/16	32 × 30	Step well and road, light ceramic scatter, single slag fragment.	
VMS-221	S/13-14	276 × 117	Settlement, rubble walls and artifact scatter, isolated slag fragments.	
VMS-225	S/11-12	16 × 10	Road segment, light ceramic scatter, a few pieces of slag observed.	
VMS-227	S/15	9 × 8	Rock-cut step well, in area of moderate artifact density, ceramics with some slag.	
VMS-246	S/2	40 × 30	Artifact scatter, one piece slag.	
VMS-280	S/10-11	400 × 170	Terrace system, sparse scatter of ceramics, worked basalt, slag.	VMS-7
VMS-291	S/11	6 × 5	Step well, light scatter of ceramics, one piece slag.	
VMS-366	T/4	16 × 11	Isolated sculptures, sparse to moderate scatter of ceramics, one piece slag.	

Nandi (seated bull; the sacred vehicle of Shiva) was recovered from VMS-24, a small settlement feature consisting of a single rectangular structure and associated bedrock mortar and artifact scatter. This figurine was crudely formed and asymmetrical, 4.5 cm in length × 2.5 cm high (Fig. 6.20). It is probably of steatite or a similar soft stone. Cylindrical steatite fragments, approximately 0.8-1.0 cm in diameter and 2-3 cm long, were recovered at VMS-14 and VMS-339. Similar kinds of artifacts are known to have been used as writing implements during the Vijayanagara period (see Sinopoli 1986).

Only one coin was found in the 380 sites recorded in the three blocks. This is a small copper coin, approximately 1.0 cm in diameter. No script is visible on the heavily eroded coin, but traces of a motif are still evident. This appears to be of a standing elephant. Comparisons with published coins of the Vijayanagara period suggest that this low denominational coin most likely dates to the reign of Devaraya II (1426-1446 A.D.).

Discussion

As noted earlier, it is not surprising that artifacts are relatively rare in the metropolitan region as compared to the more densely settled urban core of Vijayanagara. Like the urban core, the metropolitan region was an area of settlement. However, such settlement was by and large restricted to a small number of well-defined nucleated towns and villages located along major transport routes. Many of the Vijayanagara period settlements we have identified in the survey lie underneath or adjacent to contemporary settlements or have been heavily disturbed by recent activities, making interpretations of artifact distributions within them problematic.

The most common artifacts recovered in settlement contexts are, as expected, locally produced earthenware ceramics. These artifacts were used in a range of domestic activities, including food and water storage, food preparation and serving. Differences in vessel-use frequencies at diverse settlement sites suggest some functional differences among them—in the size of consuming groups and in activity distributions. However, sample sizes are small and collections were limited; a more intensive program of surface collections and test excavations would be necessary to more thoroughly examine inter-settlement variation.

The metropolitan region was also an area of intensive agricultural production, involving a variety of productive regimes (see Morrison 1995). Although artifacts are rare in agricultural sites, small quantities of artifacts were deposited in such features. Two contexts of artifact deposition can be expected in agricultural sites. These include the discard of consumed or broken materials by laborers, and the redistribution of household and industrial waste as field manure. As noted earlier, we suggest that manuring was widespread in the metropolitan region and that it accounts for much of the low density artifact distribution found throughout the survey area. Artifacts included in this low density scatter include ceramics and slag. The presence of the latter suggests that ash

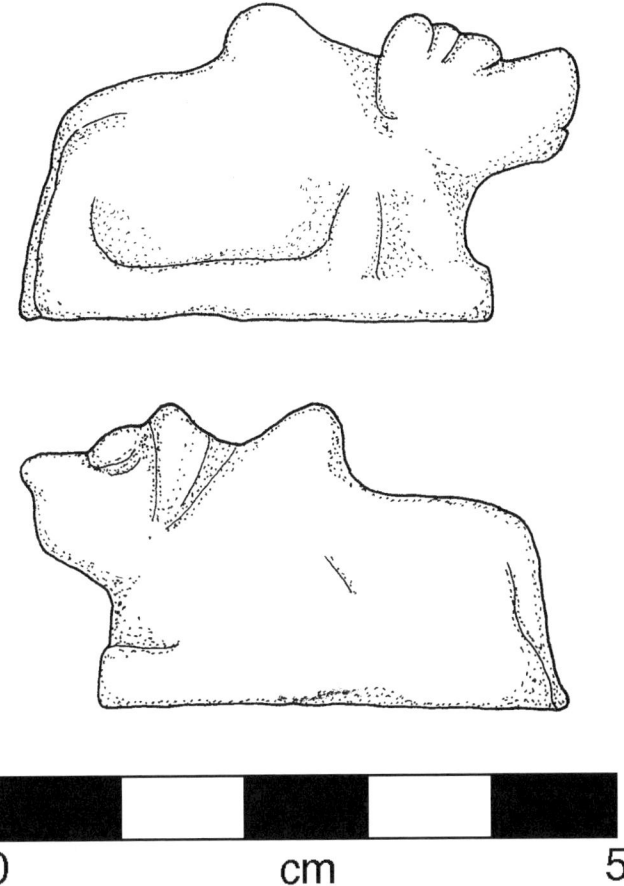

Figure 6.20. Nandi figurine, VMS-24.

from industrial sites, such as iron furnaces, and, perhaps, ceramic production sites may have been redistributed over extensive areas. Such distribution likely contributed to extensive disturbance of production sites that may in part explain their comparative paucity in the region's archaeological record.

Several industrial sites are identifiable from artifact evidence. These include the iron smelting sites of VMS-121, VMS-169, VMS-179, and VMS-317, each characterized by high densities of iron slag and furnace fragments. Twenty-three other sites in the three blocks yielded lower densities of slag, perhaps associated with smithing activities (as opposed to smelting) and/or manuring practices. The presence of iron working sites in the metropolitan region is hardly surprising, given the rich ore sources of the Sandur Hills at the southern boundary of the region, and the high demand for tools, weapons and other iron goods that must have existed. What is perhaps more surprising is the absence of any sites that could be considered to have been large-scale industrial complexes. The production sites documented by the VMS are all relatively small in spatial extent, and were likely restricted in use to only a few smelting episodes carried out over brief periods. The smelting sites documented are likely the remains of small-scale and short-lived production sites, perhaps associated with itinerant producers. Larger scale iron and steel production occurred during the Vijayanagara period, and indeed South India is known to have exported steel and ores to the Middle East during this period. Much of this production appears to have occurred to the east of the imperial capital, in Andhra Pradesh. If large-scale production did occur in the metropolitan region, it was likely in the Sandur Hills to the south of the survey area. This region is being intensively mined today and has not been surveyed. It is likely, however, that most traces of ancient mining and smelting activities have been obliterated.

Other industrial activities documented in the survey area are stone quarrying and stone working. Evidence for this includes the widespread quarry marks on boulders, and flaking debris at the uncompleted temple site VMS-79 in Block O. Given the scale and rapidity of constructions in the region, it is certainly the case that large numbers of stoneworkers were present in the area during the Vijayanagara period. Quarriers, masons, and sculptors likely moved throughout the metropolitan region, and processed the abundantly available raw materials from areas near building sites. The extent of such construction was sizeable; massive quantities of stone were used in fortification walls, temple complexes, and other constructions. We unfortunately know little about how such labor was recruited or where the laborers who produced these remains resided.

Among the more interesting and unexpected artifact categories recovered in the survey area were flaked stone and glass artifacts and debitage. It is, in retrospect, not at all surprising that flaked stone tools remained in use in South India long after metal tools became available. The Vijayanagara chipped stone inventory was an expedient one; artifacts were not finely shaped to meet specific aesthetic and functional criteria. Instead, individuals who required a sharp-edged implement for a specific task made stone (and glass) tools on an "as needed" basis, often using simple bipolar technology. While some of the sites with stone tools found in the survey area may well have prehistoric components (such as rock shelters VMS-33 and VMS-75), the presence of flaked stone and glass implements in numerous Vijayanagara period sites (for example, settlement VMS-2) indicate that this was indeed a long-lived tradition. Along with the production of expedient single-use tools, stone peg manufacture (often of basalt) was another category of chipped stone production that is documented at several sites in the metropolitan region. These artifacts were used to support constructions on bedrock or outcrops. Evidence for peg production was found in three settlements, VMS-2, VMS-35, and VMS-172. At these sites, peg production appears to have been carried out in relatively restricted areas, suggesting small specialized workgroups.

Few goods that could be classified as luxury goods were found in the metropolitan region. This is no doubt in part a function of the limitations of small-scale surface collections and of the centuries of activities that have taken place in the area between site abandonment and our field research. However, it is also likely the case that goods such as imported ceramics, glass artifacts, and some categories of ornaments were more common among the higher status residents of the urban core than in the broader and more functionally diverse metropolitan region.

The recovery and analysis of artifacts from surface contexts in archaeological surveys has several aims. Such materials can help us to date our sites. This is a particularly cogent issue for Vijayanagara, where chronological differentiation within the Vijayanagara period remains problematic. The analysis of surface ceramics from survey sites and their comparisons with distributions in the Vijayanagara urban core has helped in allowing us to clearly distinguish some forms that appear exclusive to the Vijayanagara period (for instance, shallow bowls) and some that are of recent date (for example, triple flange rims). This is of considerable value in helping us to sort out some of the chronological variation in our sites. However, much work needs to be done to refine the existing chronology and for that stratigraphic excavations in well-controlled contexts will be essential.

Analysis of surface artifacts is also important for exploring inter- and intra-site differences across the metropolitan region, and between the metropolitan region and urban core. A preliminary effort at conducting such an exploration has been presented in this chapter for sites from Blocks O, T, and S. Future studies will incorporate materials from sites in the remainder of the intensive survey area.

- 7 -
End Note

We provide no formal conclusions to this volume since it contains information on only a portion of the sites recorded by the Vijayanagara Metropolitan Survey project. Instead, we wish to look ahead to Volume 2. As discussed in Chapters 1 and 2, our survey efforts spanned ten years and ultimately extended over eight blocks in the intensive survey area (Fig. 7.1), with additional documentation of select sites in the larger 650 km^2 metropolitan region (in what we termed "the extensive survey area"). By the end of the project, we had documented a total of 750 archaeological sites (Table 7.1): 663 in the intensive survey area (Figs. 7.2-7.6) and 87 in the extensive survey area.

In this volume we have reported on 380 of those sites, located in the first three blocks that we intensively surveyed—Blocks O, T, and S. The other 4.5 km^2 blocks subject to 50% transect survey were Blocks R (Fig. 7.6), M (Fig. 7.5), and J (Fig. 7.4). The northwest quadrant of Block H (Fig. 7.3) fell outside the survey area, as did its southeast corner, which contained the Vijayanagara period settlement of Anegondi. Anegondi was both part of the Vijayanagara urban core and had already been intensively documented by Sugandha Purandare (1986) and Natalie Tolbert (2000). Only the southern portion of Block G (Fig. 7.2) was surveyed, as its rugged northern portion lay outside the boundaries we defined for Vijayanagara's metropolitan region (see Chapters 1 and 2).

Results from the additional five survey blocks, where a total of 283 sites were documented, both supported and expanded upon the general patterns identifiable in the portions of the survey area discussed in this volume. Information on the sites will be presented in detail in Volume 2 of this report. Areas south of the Tungabhadra River in Blocks M and R were dominated by relatively flat terrain and provided rich evidence for diverse agricultural activities, including both canals and large reservoirs. We also documented complex transport networks, including a major road leading from the Vijayanagara urban core through several Vijayanagara-era settlements and toward the sixteenth-century Vijayanagara suburb of Hospet, which defined the southwestern boundary of the metropolitan region. Smaller roads connected to agricultural fields and areas of settlement. As in all areas of the survey, shrines and temples were common in settlements and along roads, as well as in more isolated locales. To the north of the river, in the northern portions of Blocks M and J, and in Blocks G and J, we documented evidence for extensive fortification networks—including fortification walls, hilltop forts, and watch posts. These sites secured the northern boundary of the imperial capital and metropolitan region. Vijayanagara-era settlement, agriculture, and sacred sites were also documented.

Interestingly, as we shifted north of the river (as well as in the southeast quadrant of Block J, just south of the river), evidence for pre-Vijayanagara occupation of the region became increasingly visible. More than 30 late prehistoric sites were identified, mostly within survey Block J. These include large megalithic mortuary sites, rock art sites, and settlements—predominantly belonging to the first millennium B.C. South Indian Iron Age. Traces of such sites were found in other portions of the survey region, particularly in northern Block O and even in the Vijayanagara urban core in the hills above the Vitthala temple complex. But, not surprisingly, they are best preserved in the areas where Vijayanagara construction and landscape impact

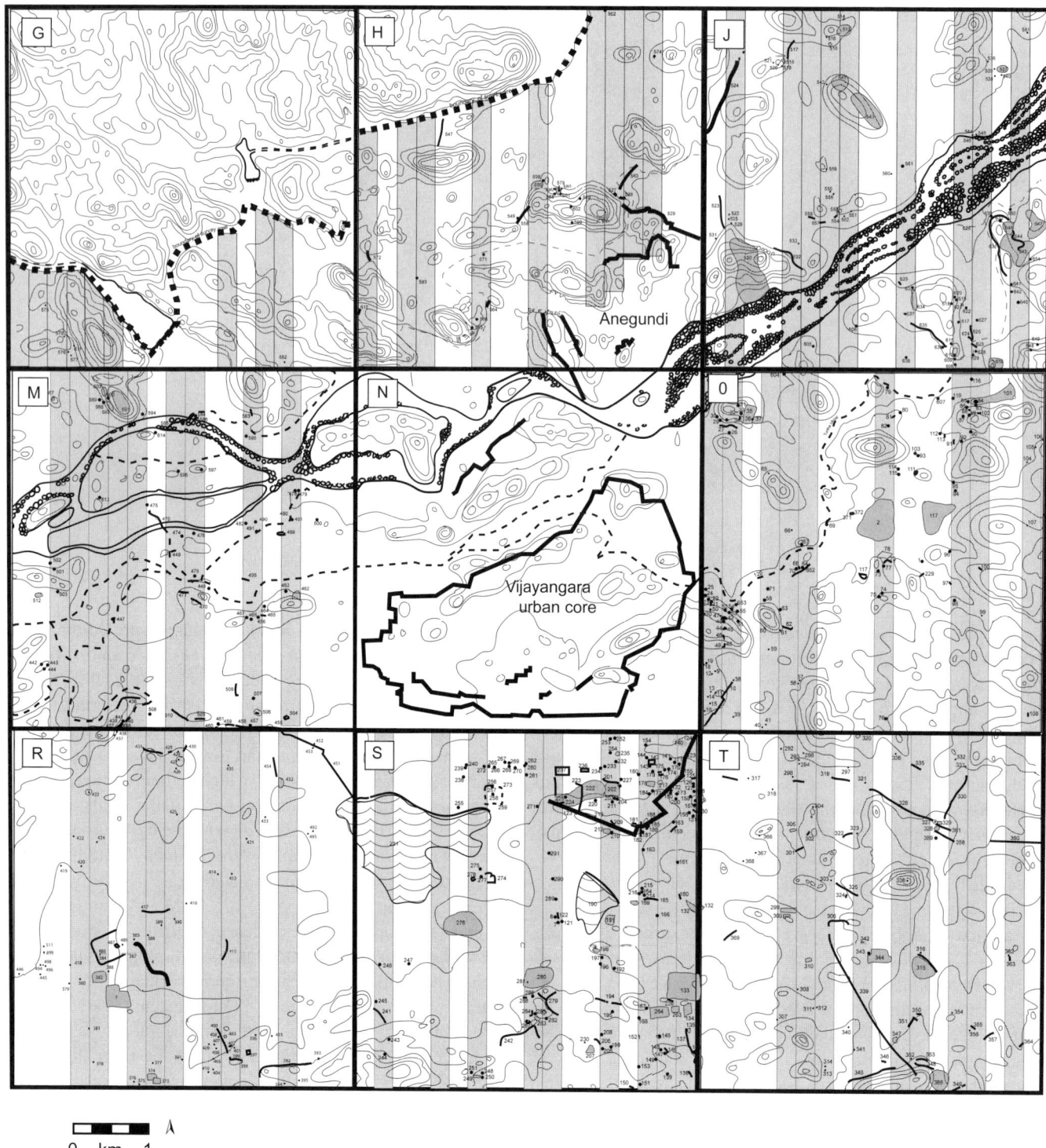

Figure 7.1. Intensive survey region: all recorded sites.

Table 7.1. Vijayanagara Metropolitan Survey: sites.

VMS #	Block	Transect(s)	Primary Function	Site Type
1	O		industrial	lime kiln
2	O	9, 10	residential	settlement
3	N		agricultural	aqueduct
4	R	7-9	agricultural	reservoir embankment
5	R	6, 7	industrial	artifact scatter
6	W		military/fortification	settlement
7	S	11	religious	temple
8	S	11	religious	step well
9	O	1	residential	rectilinear structures and artifacts
10	O	1-3	military/fortification	wall(s)
11	O	1	hydraulic	cistern
12	O	1	residential	rectilinear structures
13	O	1	residential	rectilinear structures
14	O	1	residential	rectilinear structures
15	O	1	residential	rectilinear structures
16	O	1	unknown	modified boulder/sheet rock
17	O	1	transport	gate
18	O	1	residential	rock shelter
19	O	1	military/fortification	wall(s)
20	O	1	military/fortification	wall(s)
21	O	1	agricultural	reservoir embankment
22	O	1	religious	modified boulder/sheet rock
23	O	1	hydraulic	cistern
24	O	2	residential	rectilinear structures
25	O	1	military/fortification	wall(s)
26	O	2	unknown	neolithic ashmound
27	O	1, 2	military/fortification	wall(s)
28	O	1, 2	unknown	artifact scatter
29	O	1	residential	rectilinear structures
30	O	1	residential	rectilinear structures
31	O	2	unknown	artifact scatter
32	O	2	military/fortification	mounded rubble
33	O	2	residential	rock shelter
34	O	2	military/fortification	wall(s)
35	O	3	residential	settlement
36	O	3	religious	shrine
37	O	3	residential	settlement
38	O	2	residential	rectilinear structures
39	O	2	residential	rectilinear structures
40	O	4	hydraulic	well
41	O	4	residential	rectilinear structures
42	O	2	religious	temple complex
43	O	2	religious	runoff basin
44	O	2	transport	stairs
45	O	2	military/fortification	wall/road
46	O	2	transport	stairs
47	O	2	transport	stairs
48	O	1, 2	agricultural	reservoir embankment
49	O	2	residential	wall(s)
50	O	1	transport	stairs
51	O	2	transport	stairs
52	O	2	agricultural	wall(s)
53	O	2	agricultural	wall(s)
54	O	2	industrial	lime kiln
55	O	2	unknown	wall(s)
56	O	6	unknown	wall(s)
57	O	6	unknown	wall(s)
58	O	4	agricultural	wall(s)
59	O	4	agricultural	reservoir embankment
60	O	4	agricultural	wall(s)
61	O	5	unknown	wall(s)
62	O	5	military/fortification	embankment

Table 7.1 cont.

VMS #	Block	Transect(s)	Primary Function	Site Type
63	O	5	unknown	wall(s)
64	O	6	transport	rectilinear structures
65	O	4	unknown	wall(s)
66	O	5	unknown	artifact scatter
67	O	6	residential	rectilinear structures
68	O	6	military/fortification	wall(s)
69	O	7	religious	temple
70	O	5	residential	rock shelter
71	O	4	religious	image(s)
72	O	10	agricultural	reservoir embankment
73	O	10	residential	rectilinear structures
74	O	10	unknown	wall(s)
75	O	10	residential	rock shelter
76	O	10	unknown	artifact scatter
77	O	10	unknown	wall(s)
78	O	10	unknown	artifact scatter
79	O	10	religious	rectilinear structures
80	O	11	religious	temple
81	O	10, 11	transport	road
82	O	10	unknown	wall(s)
83	O	15	religious	temple complex
84	O	15	hydraulic	well
85	O	14	military/fortification	bastion
86	O	14	military/fortification	wall(s)
87	O	14	transport	wall/road
88	O	14	unknown	wall(s)
89	O	14	military/fortification	wall(s)
90	O	15	unknown	wall(s)
91	O	14	agricultural	reservoir embankment
92	O	14	unknown	gold mine
93	O	11	transport	gate
94	O	14	religious	inscription
95	O	14	agricultural	wall(s)
96	O	14	unknown	wall transport/defensive?
97	O	14	agricultural	reservoir embankment
98	O	14	agricultural	wall(s)
99	O	15	hydraulic	runoff basin
100	O	15	agricultural	wall(s)
101	O	14-17	residential	settlement
102	O	15	residential	shrine
103	O	12	religious	image(s)
104	O	18	religious	shrine
105	O	18	hydraulic	well
106	O	18	agricultural	wall(s)
107	O	18	unknown	wall(s)
108	O	18	agricultural	reservoir embankment
109	?	–	residential	Daroji Valley: abandoned settlement
110	W	–	prehistoric settlement	Daroji Valley: prehistoric settlement
111	O	12	religious	temple complex
112	O	13	hydraulic	step well
113	O	13	agricultural	reservoir embankment
114	O	11	unknown	mounded rubble and artifacts
115	O	11	residential	rectilinear structures
116	O	15	religious	temple complex
117	O	12-14	agricultural	reservoir embankment
118			religious	temple complex
119	O	14	religious	temple
120	M, N, O, J	–	agricultural	Turtha canal
121	S	12	industrial	iron furnace
122	S	11	agricultural	reservoir embankment
123	S	9-11	military/fortification	southeast outer city wall
124	S	18	unknown	isolated wall(s)

Table 7.1 cont.

VMS #	Block	Transect(s)	Primary Function	Site Type
125	S	18	agricultural	reservoir embankment
126	S	18	unknown	games and peg/postholes
127	S	18	unknown	isolated walls, rubble, artifacts
128	S	18	residential	columned structure, grinding slicks
129	S	18	religious	temple complex
130	S	18	unknown	isolated wall(s)
131	S	18	religious	4 × 2 column shrine
132	S	18	agricultural	reservoir embankment
133	S	15-18	agricultural	terrace system
134	S	18	agricultural	terrace system
135	S	18	unknown	artifact system
136	S, T	18, 1	agricultural	runoff basin
137	S	18	transport	road
138	S	18	agricultural	reservoir embankment
139	S	17	agricultural	check dam(s)
140	S	18	residential	settlement
141	S	17	unknown	secondary use
142	S	16	religious	temple complex
143	S	16	religious	step well
144	S	16	religious	temple
145	S	17	residential	rock shelter
146	S	17	agricultural	wall(s)
147	S	17	residential	rock shelter
148	S	17	unknown	rectilinear structures
149	S	16	agricultural	artifact scatter
150	S	16	agricultural	reservoir embankment
151	S	16	agricultural	well
152	S	16	transport	road
153	S	16	unknown	artifact scatter
154	S	16	religious	image(s)
155	S	18	hydraulic	cistern
156	S	18	religious	image(s)
157	S	18	unknown	image(s)
158	S	18	military/fortification	road
159	S	17	agricultural	reservoir embankment
160	S	18	transport	road
161	S	17, 18	unknown	artifact scatter
162	S	17	religious	image(s)
163	S	16	religious	rock shelter
164	S	16	religious	temple complex
165	S	16, 17	agricultural	reservoir embankment
166	S	17	unknown	isolated wall(s)
167	S	16	unknown	isolated wall(s)
168	S	16	unknown	rectilinear structures
169	S	15, 16	unknown	artifact scatter
170	S	18	transport	rock shelter
171	S	17	religious	image(s)
172	S	17	unknown	platform(s)
173	S	17	religious	temple
174	S	17	transport	wall(s)
175	S	17	agricultural	well
176	S	17	residential	terraces
177	S	16	religious	Hanuman shrine
178	S	16	residential	habitation area
179	S	16	industrial	iron processing area
180	S	16	residential	probable step well
181	S	16	agricultural	runoff control embankments
182	S	16	religious	road with shrine
183	S	16	religious	temple and walls
184	S	16	transport	mandapa
185	S	16	agricultural	isolated walls
186	S	16	civic-ceremonial	platform(s)
187	S	16	religious	step well

Table 7.1 cont.

VMS #	Block	Transect(s)	Primary Function	Site Type
188	S	16	unknown	rectilinear structures
189	S	17	transport	step well
190	S	13-15	agricultural	reservoir; Halla kere
191	S	14	agricultural	terraces
192	S	14	unknown	isolated walls/artifact scatter
193	S	14	agricultural	terraces/check dams
194	S	13-15	agricultural	reservoir
195	S	14	unknown	lithic scatter
196	S	14	unknown	isolated walls
197	S	14	unknown	artifact scatter
198	S	14	agricultural	check dams
199	S	14	agricultural	terraces/check dams
200	S	17	religious	step well
201	S	13-15	transport	structures along road
202	S	14	residential	residential area/sculptures
203	S	14	residential	room/platform
204	S	14	residential	tank/basin
205	S	14	agricultural	terrace system
206	S	14	agricultural	tank
207	S	13	agricultural	terrace system
208	S	14	agricultural	check dams
209	S	14	transport	road
210	S	14	residential	step well
211	S	14	residential	terraces
212	S	14	residential	artifact scatter
213	S	14	residential	well/cistern
214	S	16	religious	step well and road
215	S	16	religious	mandapa
216	S	16	agricultural	well
217	S	17	military/fortification	Penukonda gate
218	S	17	religious	temple/shrine
219	S	13	agricultural	terraces/soil control
220	S	13	religious	mandapa
221	S	13, 14	residential	settlement area
222	S	13	residential	settlement area
223	S	12	military/fortification	fortification wall
224	S	11, 12	transport	road and well
225	S	11, 12	religious	road
226	S	18	agricultural	reservoir
227	S	15	residential	rock-cut well
228	S	12	residential	settlement area
229	O	12	agricultural	reservoir
230	S	13	agricultural	reservoir
231	S	3	agricultural	Kamalapuram reservoir
232	S	14	religious	displaced sculptures
233	S	14	unknown	sculpture and structure
234	S	14	residential	well
235	S	14	residential	wall and platforms
236	S	12, 13	religious	Pattabhirama tank
237	S	11, 12	religious	Pattabhirama temple
238	S	6	religious	temple
239	S	6	religious	mandapa
240	S	6	agricultural	well
241	S	2	agricultural	reservoir
242	S	8-11	agricultural	reservoir
243	S	2	agricultural	rock shelter
244	S	2	transport	road
245	S	2	agricultural	soil control wall
246	S	2	unknown	artifact scatter
247	S	3	military/fortification	bastion/fortification
248	S	7	agricultural	soil control wall
249	S	7	unknown	lithic scatter
250	S	7	agricultural	retaining wall

Table 7.1 cont.

VMS #	Block	Transect(s)	Primary Function	Site Type
251	S	7	unknown	artifact scatter
252	S	14	religious	temple
253	S	14	religious	shrine
254	S	14	religious	temple
255	S	6	unknown	platform
256	S	7, 8	military/fortification	Kamalapuram fort/gate
257	S	8	religious	Kamalapuram fort/temple
258	S	8	military/fortification	Kamalapuram end bastion
259	S	7, 8	military/fortification	Kamalapuram fort walls
260	S	10	religious	temple
261	S	10	religious	temple
262	S	10	unknown	isolated structures
263	S	18	agricultural	terraces
264	S	17	agricultural	terrace system
265	S	8	religious	shrine
266	S	8	religious	temple
267	S	8	religious	temple
268	S	9	religious	temple
269	S	9	religious	temple
270	S	9	religious	temple
271	S	10	religious	temple complex
272	S	8	religious	shrine
273	S	8	religious	temple
274	S	7	religious	isolated wall
275	S	7	religious	shrine
276	S	7	agricultural	terrace system
277	S	7	agricultural	water cistern
278	S	7	unknown	ceramic scatter
279	S	11	military/fortification	fortification wall
280	S	10, 11	agricultural	terrace system
281	S	10	agricultural	rock-cut well
282	S	11	military/fortification	wall
283	S	10	agricultural	terrace system
284	S	10	military/fortification	wall (fortification/agricultural?)
285	S	10	unknown	ceramic scatter
286	S	10	unknown	isolated walls
287	S	10	agricultural	terrace system
288	S	10	agricultural	wall (soil control)
289	S	11	transport	standing columns
290	S	11	unknown	petroglyphs
291	S	11	agricultural	step well
292	T	5	religious	shrine
293	T	6	religious	temple
294	T	6	unknown	step well
295	T	6	religious	inscription
296	T	5	religious	modified boulder/sheet rock
297	T	8	mortuary	tomb(s)
298	T	5	agricultural	step well
299	T	5, 6	agricultural	terrace system
300	T	5	agricultural	terrace system
301	T	6	agricultural	reservoir embankment
302	T	6	agricultural	reservoir embankment
303	T	7	transport	rectilinear structures
304	T	6	religious	shrine
305	T	5, 6	transport	embankment
306	T	7, 8	military/fortification	wall(s)
307	T	5	agricultural	wall(s)
308	T	6	agricultural	wall(s)
309	Y	6	agricultural	reservoir embankment
310	T	6	agricultural	terrace system
311	T	7	unknown	mounded rubble
312	T	7	agricultural	step well
313	T	7	agricultural	wall(s)

Table 7.1 cont.

VMS #	Block	Transect(s)	Primary Function	Site Type
314	T	7	agricultural	wall(s)
315	T	12, 13	agricultural	reservoir embankment
316	T	12	religious	shrine
317	T	3	religious	temple complex
318	T	4	religious	shrine
319	T	7, 8	agricultural	reservoir embankment
320	T	9	agricultural	terrace system
321	T	9	military/fortification	wall(s)
322	T	8, 9	agricultural	reservoir embankment
323	T	9	agricultural	wall(s)
324	T	8	agricultural	reservoir embankment
325	T	8	transport	wall/road
326	T	9-14	transport	road
327	T	13	military/fortification	tower
328	T	13	agricultural	step well
329	T	13, 14	religious	mounded rubble
330	T	13, 14	agricultural	reservoir embankment
331	T	14	agricultural	wall(s)
332	T	14	agricultural	wall(s)
333	T	14	other	stone cairn
334	T	12	other	stone cairn
335	T	12	agricultural	reservoir embankment
336	T	11	residential	rock shelter
337	T	11	other	stone cairn
338	T	11	religious	shrine
339	T	8-12	military/fortification	wall(s)
340	T	8	military/fortification	rectilinear structures
341	T	9	industrial	quarry
342	T	9	agricultural	reservoir embankment
343	T	9	residential	rectilinear structures
344	T	9-11	agricultural	terrace system
345	T	9	transport	wall/road
346	T	10	agricultural	reservoir embankment
347	T	11	agricultural	wall(s)
348	T	12, 13	transport	wall/road
349	T	13-15	agricultural	reservoir embankment
350	T	12	agricultural	wall(s)
351	T	12	agricultural	wall(s)
352	T	12	transport	wall(s)
353	T	12, 13	transport	wall(s)
354	T	14	transport	wall(s)
355	T	15	agricultural	reservoir embankment
356	T	15	transport	rectilinear structures
357	T	15	agricultural	reservoir embankment
358	T	14	transport	wall/road
359	T	13	transport	other
360	T	16-18	transport	wall/road
361	T	13	residential	settlement
362	T	17	agricultural	terrace system
363	T	17	agricultural	wall(s)
364	T	18	agricultural	reservoir embankment
365	T	13,14	residential	settlement
366	T	4	religious	image(s)
367	T	3	religious	shrine
368	T	3	religious	temple
369	T	2	agricultural	reservoir embankment
370	U	–	military/fortification	wall(s)
371	O	7	religious	Nandi temple
372	O	7	civic-ceremonial	step well
373	R	8	agricultural	terraces
374	R	7, 8	agricultural	terraces and platform
375	R	7	religious	temple
376	R	7	agricultural	isolated wall

Table 7.1 cont.

VMS #	Block	Transect(s)	Primary Function	Site Type
377	R	8	agricultural	isolated wall
378	R	5	agricultural	wall and artifact scatter
379	R	4	other	outcrop with game
380	R	4	other	outcrop with game
381	R	5	agricultural	isolated walls
382	R	5	industrial	artifact/lithic scatter
383	R	6, 7	military/fortification	Mallappanagudi enclosure wall
384	R	6	military/fortification	Mallappanagudi west gate
385	R	7	military/fortification	Mallappanagudi east gate
386	R	5	recreation	outcrop with game
387	R	7	religious	shrine
388	R	8	agricultural	step well
389	R	8	religious	shrine
390	R	9	agricultural	rock-cut well
391	R	9	agricultural	check dam
392	R	14-16	transport	roadway/walls
393	R	17	transport	stairway
394	R	15	residential	enclosure, single room structure
395	R	16	religious	shrine
396	R	13	transport	passageway in outcrop
397	R	13	agricultural	check dams
398	R	13	residential	rock shelter
399	R	12	military/fortification	fortification/walls
400	R	12	agricultural	reservoir
401	R	12	agricultural	isolated wall
402	R	12	agricultural	isolated wall
403	R	12	residential	artifact scatter
404	R	11	residential	square structure
405	R	11	agricultural	isolated wall
406	R	12	agricultural	well
407	R	11	transport	platform
408	R	11	residential	structure
409	R	11	agricultural	structure
410	R	11	agricultural	wall
411	R	11	recreation	isolated wall
412	R	11	agricultural	reservoir embankment
413	R	12	religious	reservoir
414	R	12	religious	shrine
415	R	11	religious	shrine
416	R	14	religious	isolated Hanuman sculpture
417	R	10	agricultural	shrine
418	R	8	religious	reservoir
419	R	4	religious	Nandi sculpture
420	R	3	civic-ceremonial	Hanuman sculpture and structure
421	R	4	religious	incised Shaivite slab
422	R	4	civic-ceremonial	incised slab
423	R	5	industrial	artifact scatter/quarrying locale
424	R	5	military/fortification	bastion/stupa
425	R	9	unknown	displaced architectural elements
426	R	9	transport	road
427	R	9	military/fortification	terrace on outcrop
428	R	9	military/fortification	fortification wall
429	R	9	transport	road
430	R	9, 10	transport	road
431	R	8, 9	transport	road
432	R	15	residential	ceramic scatter
433	R	14	religious	platform and Nandi
434	R	13	residential	single-room structure
435	R	11	transport	road wall
436	M	6	unknown	fortification wall and shrine
437	M	6	religious	structure/mandapa
438	M	6	religious	temple
439	M	6	religious	temple tank and structures

Table 7.1 cont.

VMS #	Block	Transect(s)	Primary Function	Site Type
440	M	6	religious	temple complex
441	M	6	religious	mandapa
442	M	2	religious	Hanuman temple
443	M	2	military/fortification	enclosed outcrop/walls
444	M	2	religious	Nagamma shrine
445	R	2	transport	rock-cut well
446	R	1	religious	shrine with brick shikara
447	M	6	religious	temple
448	M	11	religious	temple
449	M	9	transport	roadway
450	S	18	transport	gateway
451	R	15-18	military/fortification	outer city wall
452	R	16	transport	gateway
453	R	16	religious	Hanuman shrine
454	R	14	transport	wall
455	M	13-15	military/fortification	outer city wall (continuation)
456	M	12, 13	agricultural	embankment on city wall
457	M	13	religious	sati sculpture
458	M	12	religious	platform, Hanuman, and sculpture
459	M	11	residential	ceramic scatter
460	M	11	civic-ceremonial	inscription
461	M	11	military/fortification	wall/room
462	M	15	religious	shrine/wall alignments
463	M	15	religious	sculptured boulder/shrine
464	M	13	agricultural	wall/check dam
465	M	13	transport	walls/road segments
466	M	13	transport	wall/road segment
467	M	13	religious	temple complex on outcrop
468	M	13	civic-ceremonial	platform
469	M	14, 15	religious	mandapas
470	M	10	transport	road
471	M	9, 10	religious	road
472	M	8	agricultural	Turtha anicuts/diversion weirs
473	M	7	agricultural	Turtha anicuts/north diversion weir
474	M	9	other	footings/weir
475	M	10	other	wall
476	M	10	other	footings/weir
477	M	15	other	ceramic scatter
478	M	15	religious	shrine
479	M	15	religious	mandapa
480	M	15	transport	bridge
481	M	15	other	Nandi boundary stone
482	M	13	other	blocks and ceramic scatter
483	M, N, O, J	–	agricultural	Turtha canal; see 120
484	M		agricultural	Turtha canal, sluice feature
485	M	–	agricultural	Kalaghatta canal
486	M	–	agricultural	Raya canal
487	R	7	religious	Mallappanagudi temple
488	R	6	transport	Mallappanagudi step well
489	R	7	religious	temple
490	M	13	religious	features on sheet rock, sculpture
491	M	13	agricultural	cistern and rubble wall
492	R	16	religious	shrine
493	R	16	religious	shrine
494	R	2	military/fortification	bastion
495	M	13	transport	roadway/wall
496	M	18	religious	temple
497	R	2	transport	gateway
498	R	2	religious	temple (Vaishnava)
499	R	2	religious	Shiva temple and inscriptions
500	M	16	religious	Nandi temple
501	M	3	transport	path/road
502	M	3	transport	road/wall
503	M	3	military/fortification	walls (terrace and fortification?)

Table 7.1 cont.

VMS #	Block	Transect(s)	Primary Function	Site Type
504	M	15	mortuary	Kadirampur tombs and cemetery
505	M	10, 11	other	wall
506	M	13	agricultural	wall/erosion control
507	M	13	other	wall
508	M	8	religious	shrine
509	M	12	military/fortification	outer city wall
510	M	9, 10	agricultural	reservoir
511	R	2	religious	mandapa/shrine
512	M	2	residential	settlement
513	J	7, 8	residential	settlement
514	J	8	religious	temple complex
515	J	7	residential	artifact scatter
516	J	7	religious	cave shrine
517	J	5	agricultural	embankment/cemetery
518	J	4	residential	walled settlement
519	J	4	military/fortification	bastion on boulder
520	J	4	military/fortification	possible bastion
521	J	4	military/fortification	bastion
522	J	2	religious	temple complex
523	J	1	agricultural	reservoir embankment
524	J	1	transport	road and associated features
525	J	2	religious	mandapa
526	J	2	religious	boulder/slab images
527	H	14	military/fortification	fortification wall
528	H	14	military/fortification	fortification wall
529	H	14-18	military/fortification	Anegondi fortification wall
530	J	2, 3	prehistoric settlement	iron age settlement, Kadebakele
531	J	1	religious	mandapa with hero stone
532	J	4-6	transport	road and associated features
533	J	5	unknown	artifact scatter
534	J	7-9	agricultural	Ramasagara channel anicut
535	J	3	agricultural	reservoir embankment
536	J	15	transport	road/wall
537	J	15, 16	residential	settlement
538	J	15	religious	unfinished Hanuman slab
539	J	15	transport	road/wall
540	J	16	residential	stepped well
541	J	7, 8	residential	settlement
542	J	7	transport	road/wall
543	J	8, 9	prehistoric mortuary	prehistoric cemetery
544	J	14	religious	temple
545	J	14	residential	settlement area
546	J	14	military/fortification	fortification wall
547	H	5	agricultural	reservoir embankment
548	H	10	military/fortification	Anegondi fortification wall
549	H	9	military/fortification	Anegondi fortification gate
550	H	10	residential	settlement
551	J	8	agricultural	soil/erosion control wall
552	J	8	transport	paved road
553	J	8	military/fortification	horse stones
554	J	7	transport	road/wall
555	J	7	other	platform?
556	J	7	religious	displaced sculpture/architectural elements
557	J	6, 7	transport	road/wall and associated features
558	J	6	military/fortification	horse stones
559	J	6	other	boulder inscription
560	J	10	religious	mandapa/shrine
561	J	11	residential	structure and artifact scatter
562	H	14	religious	temple
563	H	15	agricultural	reservoir embankment
564	H	7	agricultural	reservoir embankment
565	H	7	transport	paved road
566	M		religious	temple

Table 7.1 cont.

VMS #	Block	Transect(s)	Primary Function	Site Type
567	M	3	residential	settlement
568	M	5	residential	rock shelter
569	M	5	prehistoric mortuary	megaliths
570	M	6	hydraulic	runoff basin/lithic scatter
571	J	7	unknown	artifact scatter
572	H	1	agricultural	reservoir embankment
573	H	15, 16	agricultural	reservoir embankment
574	H	16	other	boulder image
575	G	2	agricultural	agricultural terraces
576	G	3	agricultural	reservoir embankment
577	G	3	agricultural	reservoir embankment
578	G	3	unknown	rock shelter
579	H	11	prehistoric settlement	settlement
580	H	10	military/fortification	fortification wall
581	J	17	unknown	platform
582	G	15	unknown	lithic scatter
583	M	13	agricultural	reservoir embankment
584	M	10	religious	bastion along Anegondi channel
585	M	8-10	agricultural	Anegondi canal and anicut
586	M	10	agricultural	Anegondi channel outlet
587	M	9	unknown	isolated wall and artifact scatter
588	H	10	residential	structure and artifact scatter
589	H	12	unknown	rock shelter with paintings
590	H	11	agricultural	runoff basin
591	M	4-7	military/fortification	fort
592	M	6	residential	settlement area
593	H	4	agricultural	stepped well
594	M	7	religious	sculptures
595	M	2	religious	displaced sculpture and architectural elements
596	M	9	recreation	game boards and peg/postholes
597	M	10	unknown	artifact scatter
598	H	11	prehistoric mortuary	megalith
599	H	12	prehistoric mortuary	megalith
600	M	6	unknown	megalith and petroglyphs
601	H	11	prehistoric rock art	rock shelter with paintings and artifacts
602	H	12	prehistoric mortuary	megalith
603	M	5, 6	prehistoric mortuary	megalithic cemetery
604	O	5	residential	megalithic rock shelter
605	J	6	unknown	displaced architectural elements
606	J	8	residential	settlement area
607	O	13	religious	sculpture in modern shrine
608	J	14	military/fortification	fortification wall
609	J	14	transport	road and stairs
610	J	14	military/fortification	terrace/platform
611	G	3	unknown	parallel stone alignments
612	H	1	agricultural	reservoir embankment
613	M	5	religious	shrine
614	M	8	unknown	agricultural wall
615	J	14	prehistoric mortuary	megalith and associated features
616	J	13	prehistoric mortuary	rock shelter with megalith
617	J	14	prehistoric mortuary	mortuary rock shelter
618	J	13	agricultural	agricultural terrace
619	J	14	prehistoric mortuary	megalith, crack feature, petroglyph
620	J	14	prehistoric mortuary	megaliths
621	J	14	prehistoric mortuary	megaliths and associated features
622	J	14	agricultural	circular enclosure
623	J	15	agricultural	reservoir embankment
624	J	15	transport	probable road wall
625	J	15	agricultural	Turtha canal feeder
626	?		agricultural	Ramasagara canal
627	J	15	transport	road
628	J	15	religious	images on boulder
629	J	15	transport	road/wall

Table 7.1 cont.

VMS #	Block	Transect(s)	Primary Function	Site Type
630	J	15, 16	religious	temple complex
631	J	16	military/fortification	road/wall/fortification
632	J	17	religious	shrine
633	J	11	residential	rock shelter with paintings, artifacts
634	J	11	prehistoric settlement	settlement, ashmound
635	J	12, 13	transport	road/artifacts
636	J	13	agricultural	well and artifacts
637	J	11	residential	reservoir embankment
638	J	11	unknown	platform
639	J	11	military/fortification	horse stones
640	J	17	transport	paved road
641	J	17	religious	image on boulder
642	J	17	religious	image on sheet rock
643	J	16-18	prehistoric mortuary	prehistoric cemetery
644	J	16, 17	transport	road
645	J	16, 17	prehistoric mortuary	prehistoric cemetery
646	J	17	agricultural	agricultural terrace and artifacts
647	J	17, 18	prehistoric mortuary	prehistoric cemetery
648	J	18	religious	shrine
649	J	18	prehistoric mortuary	megaliths
650	J	16	transport	rubble and possible bridge
651	S	18	military/fortification	gate in fortification wall
652	O	12, 13	transport	road/wall
653	O	2	religious	images on boulder
654	J	17	transport	paved road
655	J	16	military/fortification	Bukkasagara fort
656	?		transport	road
1000	W		hydraulic	drainage channel, Daroji
1001	W		religious	shrine, Daroji Valley
1002	W		agricultural	reservoir, Daroji Valley
1003	W		agricultural	reservoir, Daroji Valley
1004	W		agricultural	reservoir, Daroji Valley
1005	X		agricultural	reservoir, Daroji Valley
1006	X		agricultural	reservoir, Daroji Valley
1007	X		agricultural	reservoir, Daroji Valley
1008	X		religious	Papinayakanahalli temple complex
1009	X		military/fortification	Papinayakanahalli fort
1010	X		agricultural	reservoir, Daroji Valley
1011	Y		agricultural	possible reservoir, Daroji Valley
1012	Y		agricultural	reservoir, Daroji Valley
1013	Y		agricultural	reservoir, Daroji Valley
1014	Y		agricultural	reservoir
1015	Y		agricultural	Dharmasagara reservoir
1016	Z		agricultural	trans-valley reservoir
1017	Z		agricultural	reservoir
1018	W		agricultural	reservoir
1019	W		agricultural	Daroji Kere/reservoir
1020	W		military/fortification	Daroji fort
1021	E		agricultural	trans-valley reservoir
1022	E		agricultural	reservoir, Daroji Valley
1023	W		agricultural	reservoir, Daroji Valley
1024	W		?	artifact scatter
1025	?		military/fortification	walls north of Sultanpur
1026	?		religious	shrine east of Papanayakanahalli
1027	?		religious	shrine, Daroji Valley
1028	?		religious	temple, Daroji Valley
1029	?		?	walls and road south of Vithalapura
1030	?		religious	Saiva Temple, Daroji Valley
1031	?		agricultural	Avinamodugu reservoir and settlement
1032	?		religious	temple, Daroji Valley
1033	?		prehistoric, uncertain	ashmounds, Daroji Valley
1034	?		agricultural	reservoir south of Toranagallu
1035	?		prehistoric, uncertain	Kudatini ashmound
1036	?		agricultural	well associated with VMS-1010

Table 7.1 cont.

VMS #	Block	Transect(s)	Primary Function	Site Type
1037	X		religious	temple south of Papinayakanahalli
1038	X		agricultural	reservoir, Daroji Valley
1039	X		religious	shrine, Daroji Valley
1040	W		military/fortification	Ingaligi settlement walls
1041	?		religious	Idgah near Sultanpur
1042	U		military/fortification	Tungabhadra Island fort
1043	K		military/fortification	hilltop mandapa
1044	K		military/fortification	horse stone field across road
1045	K		military/fortification	fortification wall south of Bukkasagara
1046	K		military/fortification	wall wnw of Kanavai Timmapura
1047	P		military/fortification	wall west of Kanavai Timmapura
1048	K		residential	settlement wnw of Kanavai Timmapura
1049	K		transport	road associated with VMS-1045
1050	K		military/fortification	cobble wall associated with VMS-1045
1051	K		military/fortification	Bukkasagara/Ramasagara
1052	K		military/fortification	fortification wall north of horse stones
1053	K		military/fortification	Ramasagara fort
1054	P		military/fortification	walls atop outcrop
1055	K		military/fortification	cobble wall associated with VMS-1045
1056	A		military/fortification	Kampli fort
1057	D		military/fortification	Hire Jantakallu fort
1058	D		religious	Hire Jantakallu shrine
1059	A		military/fortification	Chikka Jantakallu fort
1060	R		military/fortification	fort wnw of Daroji fort
1061	R		military/fortification	2 walls east of VMS-370
1062	M		military/fortification	Lingadahalli bastion and reservoir
1063	H		military/fortification	wall across pass nw of Kodalu
1064	H		military/fortification	wall across pass north of Kodalu
1065	H		military/fortification	wall across gap ne of Kodalu
1066	H		military/fortification	long "Sultanpur" wall
1067	J		military/fortification	wall east of Sultanpur wall
1068	D		military/fortification	wall across Bellary road
1069	D		military/fortification	wall across gap north of ashmound
1070	J		military/fortification	wall south of Bellary road gap wall
1072	C		military/fortification	e-w wall across gap east of Toranagallu
1073	D		military/fortification	n-s wall across gap east of Toranagallu
1074	Z		military/fortification	wall across Chitradurg gap
1075	P		military/fortification	fort north of Tungabhadra River
1076	T		military/fortification	bastion near Ningapur
1077	C		military/fortification	Toranagallu fort and shrine
1078			prehistoric, uncertain	ashmound, Daroji Valley
1079			military/fortification	fortification wall, Daroji Valley
1080			agricultural	reservoir, Daroji Valley
1081			agricultural	reservoir, Daroji Valley
1082			military/fortification	Gundlavaddigeri fort
1083			unknown	petroglyphs, Daroji Valley
1084			transport	road, Daroji Valley
1085			military/fortification	trans-valley fortification wall, Daroji
1086			agricultural	reservoir, Daroji Valley

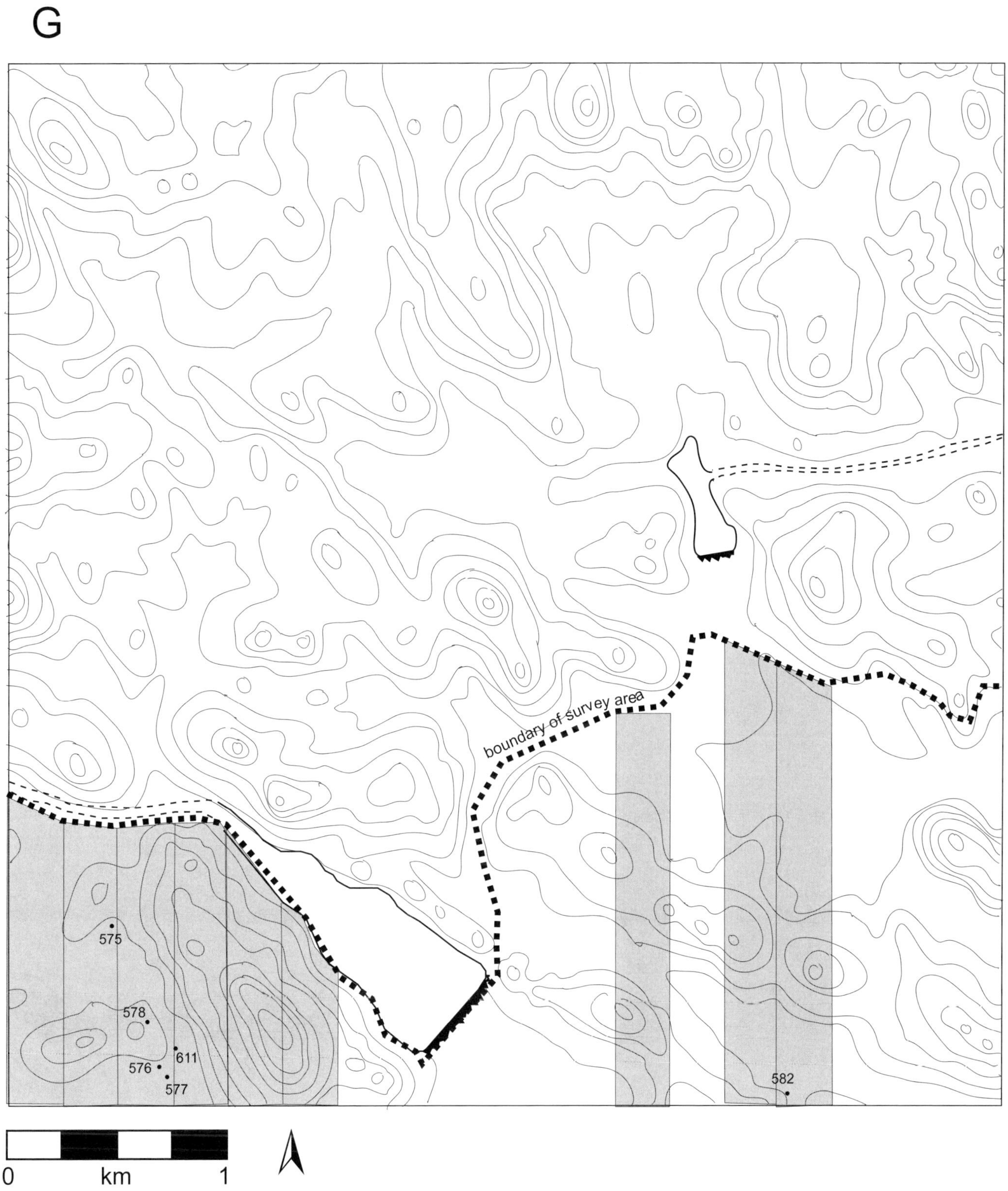

Figure 7.2. Block G: setting, sample transects, and sites (note: only areas to the south of the hatched line were surveyed).

320 *The Vijayanagara Metropolitan Survey*

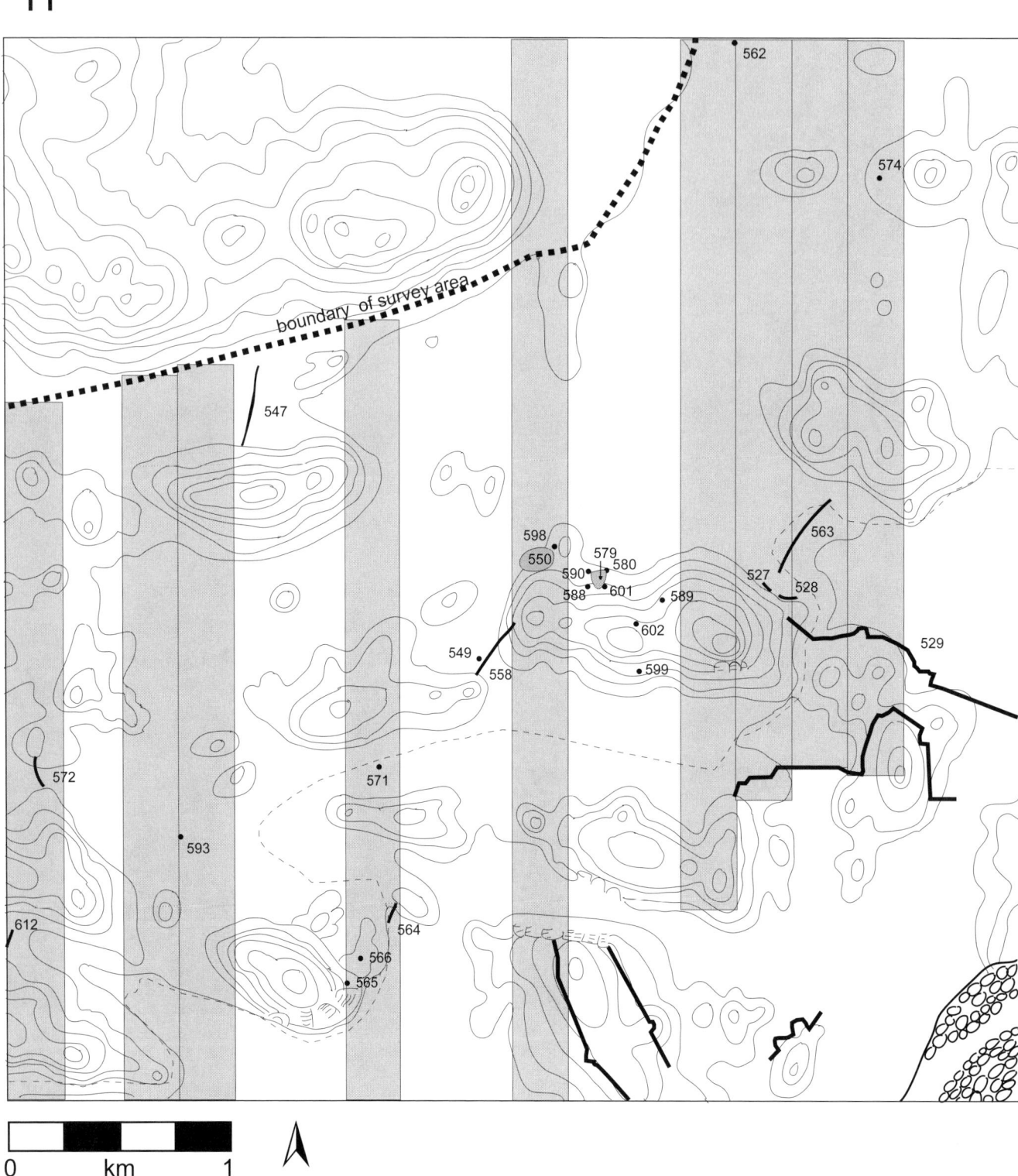

Figure 7.3. Block H: setting, sample transects, and sites (note: only areas to the south of the hatched line were surveyed).

End Note

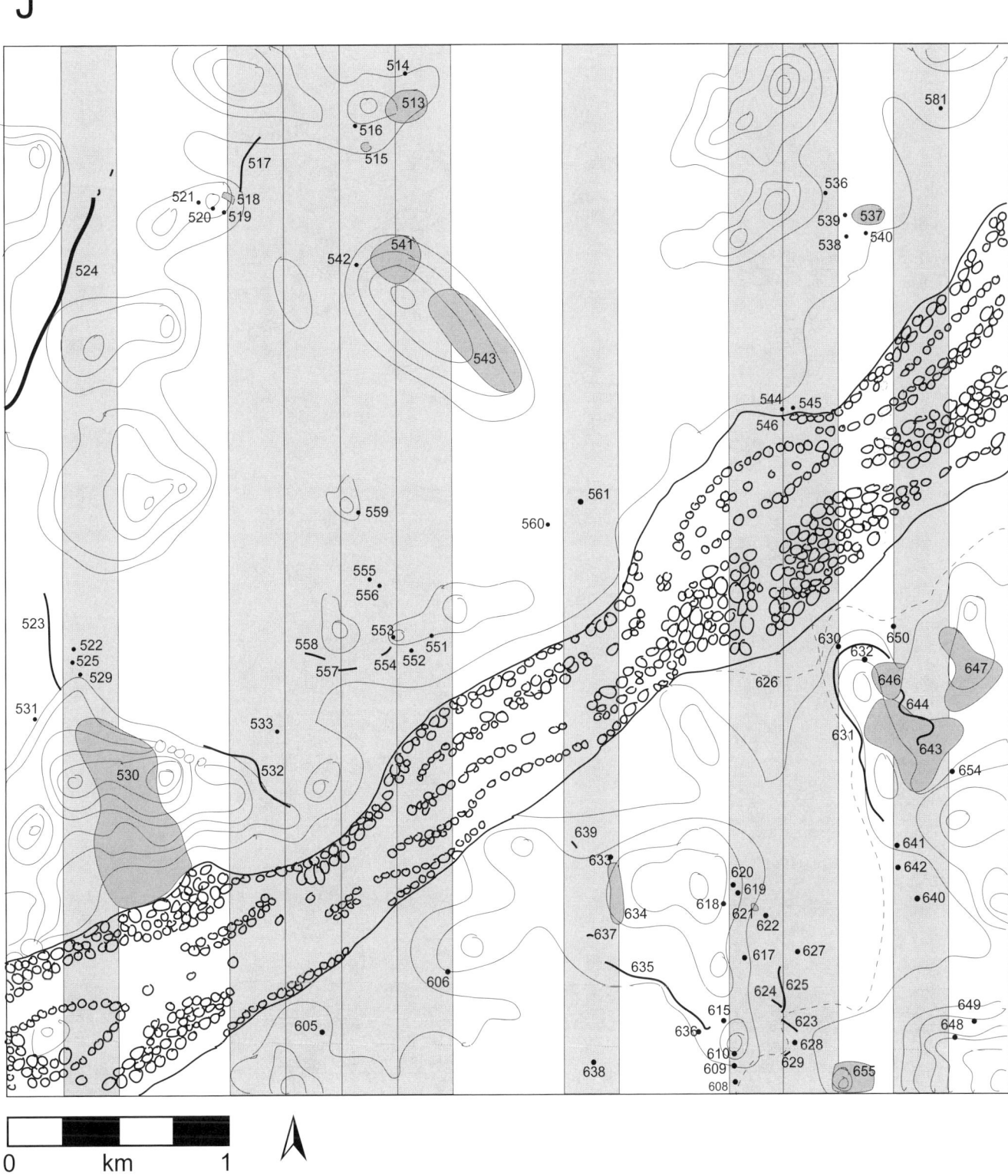

Figure 7.4. Block J: setting, sample transects, and sites.

Figure 7.5. Block M: setting, sample transects, and sites.

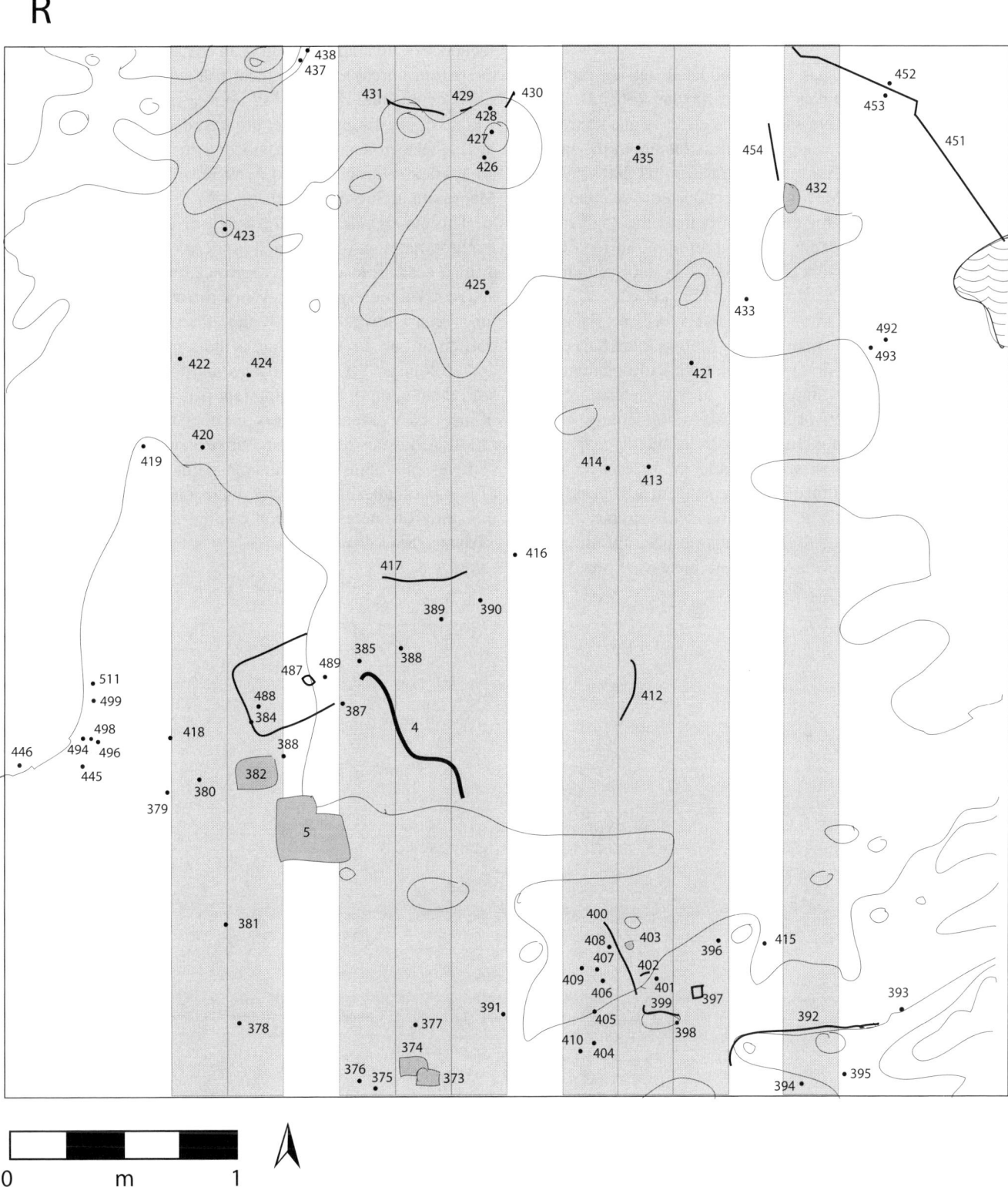

Figure 7.6. Block R: setting, sample transects, and sites.

were the least intense. The Iron Age sites documented by the Vijayanagara Metropolitan Survey project are the focus of our current research.

Additional research has been conducted outside the eight blocks of the intensive survey area. In particular, Robert Brubaker has documented defensive sites on the edges of the metropolitan region to explore the defensive infrastructure of the capital. Results of this research are summarized in his 2004 doctoral dissertation. Kathleen Morrison has conducted a detailed study of the "Daroji Valley" region, which defines the southeastern boundaries of the sixteenth-century metropolitan region and contains a complex network of irrigation reservoirs, settlements, and other sites (summarized in Morrison, in press).

As demonstrated in this volume, and as will be elaborated further in Volume 2, the Vijayanagara Metropolitan Survey has employed systematic survey methodologies to document the hinterlands of the great imperial city of Vijayanagara, one of the largest cities in the world in the sixteenth century. Unlike virtually all other pre-modern cities in India and the majority of capitals of early empires around the world, the material record on the nature and organization of the Vijayanagara urban landscape was accessible to systematic archaeological research at the time our survey was conducted. This situation has, unfortunately, changed somewhat in recent years, with increasing populations and economic growth in the region. Both irrigation agriculture and industrial activities are increasing rapidly. A negative consequence of this rapid growth is an equally rapid distribution of the region's archaeological record. A significant portion of the sites documented by the VMS no longer exist and many more will no doubt disappear over the next decade; their only record lies in the documentation provided in this volume, and the notes, photographs, drawings, and other records of the Vijayanagara Metropolitan Survey project.

This monograph reports on a wide diversity of archaeological features, ranging from isolated single-room structures and small artifact scatters to enormous fortifications, temple complexes, and reservoir embankments. While many of the larger sites have long been known, the small sites that comprise a significant portion of our survey data are seldom noticed by South Asian archaeologists. Yet, these locales and the activities associated with them comprised an important part of the urban landscape of imperial Vijayanagara. It is our hope that the documentation of all of the sites recorded in our survey allows for a far more complex and sophisticated understanding of the urban landscape of this particular imperial city, with scholarly implications for the study of ancient imperial centers that extend far beyond Vijayanagara's city walls.

Glossary of Indian Names and Architectural Terms[1]

Achyutadeva Raya. Sixteenth-century Vijayanagara ruler; reigned A.D. 1529-1542.
amman. Subsidiary shrine, typically dedicated to the goddess consort of the main deity of a temple complex.
anandanidhi. A gift.
Anjaneya. Name of Hanuman; often depicted in striding posture.
antarala. Vestibule fronting the shrine of a temple; antechamber.
ardhamandapa (also called **antarala**). Vestibule in front of shrine of a temple; antechamber.
avatara. Descent of a god; often refers to the incarnations of **Vishnu**.
ayagar. Village officers and servants.

Balakrishna. Child form of **Krishna**, the avatar of **Vishnu**. Depicted in a variety of forms—as an infant or child stealing butter, playing the flute, dancing.
basement. Course between ground and floor level, often with a series of moldings.
bastion. Rectangular or square wall projection to strengthen fortifications.
Bhairava. Terrible aspect of Shiva. Depicted with round eyes, side tusks and a flabby stomach. Wears a garland of skulls and is adorned with snakes. Carries weapons and skull (of **Brahma**). Is associated with a dog (pariah symbol in India).

Bhairavi. Consort of **Bhairava**.
bracket. Projecting element above a column, usually supporting a beam or overhang.
Brahma. The creator of the orthodox Hindu triad; the equilibrium between **Vishnu** and **Shiva**.

cairn. Pyramid of small stones functioning as a memorial.
capital. Upper part of a column or pilaster, providing a transition to the bracket.
chakra. Discus, wheel, weapon; an attribute of **Vishnu**.
chandra. Moon, one of the planetary deities.
corbel, corbelled. Projecting horizontal block or stone course that supports a vertical structure or covers an overhang.

dargarh. Funerary complex with tomb.
deva. A god.
Deva Raya. Fifteenth-century Vijayanagara ruler; reigned A.D. 1406-1422.
Devi. A goddess. Although there are many individual goddesses in Hindu mythology, they are often subsumed under one great female deity called Devi or Mahadevi—the great goddess.
Dharmashala. Rest-house for visiting pilgrims.

---

[1] Based on Dallapiccola and Verghese (1998) and Michell (1989).

dhoti. Men's attire consisting of a cloth worn around the waist, passing between the legs, and tucked in behind.

Durga. Principal goddess of Shakti cult; depicted riding on a lion or tiger and armed with the weapons of all the gods; she destroys demons, especially **Mahisha**.

Dvarapala. Door guardian; **Yaksha** who guards temple doorways; depicted with the attributes of the enshrined deity.

epigraph. Inscription incised onto stone.

finial. Ornamental top of dome or roof.

Ganesha or **Ganapati**. Eldest son of **Shiva** and **Parvati**. Deity with head of elephant and a human body, depicted dancing, standing or seated. Often depicted with his vehicle, a small rat. Remover of obstacles.

Garuda. Mythical eagle mount of **Vishnu**.

garbagriha. Sanctuary, chamber of shrine, where image of main deity is found.

gopi. Cowherd companions of **Krishna**.

gopuram. Massive towered gateway to temple complex.

half-pilaster. "Split" design with only half a capital and bracket, usually in pairs flanking a niche.

Hanuman. Monkey god, hero of the Ramayana. Very common representation at Vijayanagara, particularly at gateways and along roads; protector deity. Often depicted striding (Anjaneya), with snake, lotus, long-stemmed flower in one hand, sometimes carrying mountain.

hamsa. Goose; symbol of supreme achievement. Is the vehicle of **Brahma**.

Harihara. Composite deity, half **Vishnu**-half **Shiva**.

hero stone. Commemorative sculpted panel, memorial to deceased warrior. Sometimes depicts exploits of the hero.

jamb. Side post of a doorway.

Kala or **Kaliya**. Poisonous black serpent subdued by the Lord **Krishna**.

Kali. Black; terrifying aspect of the goddess **Durga**, recognized by her withered body and skull necklace.

kalyana mandapa. Pavilion with elevated platform in the center.

kapota. Uppermost molding of a basement or cornice.

Karkiteya (also known as **Subramanya** or **Kumara**). Second son of **Shiva**; depicted seated on a peacock.

kirtimukha. Face of glory; lionlike monster mask; often found on doorway and niches of temples.

Krishna. Eighth incarnation of **Vishnu**; popular cult deity who appears in various forms.

Krishnadeva Raya. Sixteenth-century Vijayanagara ruler; reigned A.D. 1509-1529.

Kubera. Chief of the **Yakshas**; pot-bellied keeper of the treasures of the earth.

kudu. Windowlike element, often on a **kapota**; either blocked out or decorated with foliation.

kumbha. Vase, jar, pot.

laddu. A sweet; attribute of **Ganesha**.

Lakshmana. Younger brother of **Rama**. Usually depicted standing; distinguished from Rama by having bow slung over one shoulder and hands clasped.

Lakshmi. Popular goddess, responsible for wealth and good fortune; usually associated with lotus, sometimes depicted being bathed by elephants.

linga(m). Shiva as the phallic emblem; cylindrical stone or natural stone formation. Often set on a pedestal, known as a **yoni**.

lintel. Horizontal beam over a doorway.

madapali. Kitchen area.

mahamandapa. Large pillared hall next to the **ardhamandapa** in a temple; antechamber.

Mahisha. Buffalo demon killed by **Durga**.

makara. Aquatic monster; often described as a crocodile with an elephant trunk.

mandapa. Open or closed columned structure, often built on raised basement. Precedes the sanctuary in a Jain or Hindu temple; sometimes occurs as an independent structure.

matha. Religious institutions; provided lodging, charity, schools, and so on, to ascetics or travelers.

medallion. Circular design, mostly filled with stylized lotus (as in ceilings).

merlon. Parapet element, shaped like a battlement, usually with a pointed top.

mihrab. Prayer niche in a mosque; faces Mecca.

mudra. Symbolic hand gesture.

naga. Snake deity; symbol of fertility and protection. Are worshipped in the belief that they can confer blessings and protection from disease.

Nagamma. Snake goddess.

nagi, nagini. Female snake deity; represented with human torso and snake tail.

Nandi. Bull mount of **Shiva**. Sometimes depicted as human with face of a bull; most often depicted in animal form.

Narasimha. Lion-headed fourth avatar of **Visnu**. Depicted in a variety of forms.

padma. Lotus flower.

parapet. Topmost portion of wall, extending above roof line (often sculpted in temples).

Parvati. Goddess; consort of **Shiva**; generally looked upon as a fertility and mother deity.

pilaster. Slender column, part of wall fabric.

pitha. Bench, seat, throne. Pedestal for an image.

porch. Covered entrance to a shrine or hall, generally open and with columns.

pradakshina patha. Circumambulatory route, often roofed, around sanctuary; **pradakshina** refers to circumambulation in a clockwise direction.
prakara. Courtyard.

Radha. Consort of **Krishna**.
Ragunatha. Name of **Rama**.
Rama. Seventh incarnation of **Vishnu** and hero of the Ramayana; embodiment of perfect king, husband, and son.
Ramachandra. Name of **Rama**.
ranga mandapa. Pavilion for musical performances; with four openings.
raya. King.
rishi. Sage or poet.
rotated squares. Common ceiling motif; stepped tiers of triangular pieces create a design of squares within squares, rotated at 45°.

sadhu. Ascetic.
sanctuary. Chamber housing the principal votive image or emblem of a temple deity.
sati. Wife who kills herself through immolation in the funeral pyre of her husband.
Shaivite. Pertaining to the cult of **Shiva**.
shakti. Generative force of godhead, power, energy; female principle—represented in variety of forms.
shankha. Conch shell held by **Vishnu**.
shikara. Towered roof over temple sanctuary.
Shiva. Principal deity of one of main Hindu cults; generally worshipped as a **lingam**, but also represented in a variety of forms. Usually shown with his consort **Parvati** (or **Devi**); father of **Ganesha** and **Karkiteya**.

Sita. Wife of **Rama**; personification of female devotion.
socket. Hole in pedestal to secure stone or metal image.
stambha. Free standing column, often set in front of temple.

Tiruvengalanatha. Name of **Vishnu**.
Trimurti. Composite deity; the triad constituted by the principal gods **Brahma**, **Vishnu**, and **Shiva**.
trishula. Trident held by **Shiva**.

Vaishnavite. Pertaining to the cult of **Vishnu**.
Vamana. Dwarf; fifth avatar of **Vishnu**.
Varaha. Boar; third avatar of **Vishnu**.
vimana. Includes towered sanctuary and its first antechamber.
Virabhadra. Destructive aspect of **Shiva**. Four-armed; holds sword, shield, bow and arrow. Found as main deity in shrines and temples. May be associated with a small standing figure depicted with head of ram or goat.
Vishnu. Principal cult deity in Hinduism; creator and preserver of universal order. Appears in a series of ten incarnations, as well as a variety of other forms.
Vitthala. Heroic form of **Krishna**. Wears a tall cylindrical crown and jewelry; stands erect with hands near hips; sometimes holds conch shell or bag.

Yaksha. Supernatural being or godling who inhabits the wild lands; originally associated with nature in folk religion; ruled by **Kubera**.
yali. Horned lion; mythical composite beast, with elements of horse, lion, elephant, and other animals; often depicted rearing.
Yellama. Folk goddess, worshipped in Karnataka.
yoni. Female sexual organ; pedestal on which **linga** is placed.

References Cited

Adams, Robert McC.
1965 *Land Behind Baghdad: A History of Settlement on the Diyala Plains*. Chicago: University of Chicago Press.
1981 *Heartland of Cities: Survey of Ancient Settlement and Land Use on the Central Floodplain of the Euphrates*. Chicago: University of Chicago Press.

Adams, Robert McC., and Hans Nissen
1972 *The Uruk Countryside: The Natural Setting of Urban Societies*. Chicago: University of Chicago Press.

Alcock, Susan E., and John F. Cherry (editors)
2004 *Side by Side Survey: Comparative Regional Studies in the Mediterranean World*. Oxford: Oxbow.

Allchin, F. Raymond
1963 *Neolithic Cattle Keepers of South India*. Cambridge: Cambridge University Press.

Allchin, Bridget, and F. Raymond Allchin
1982 *The Rise of Civilization in India and Pakistan*. Cambridge: Cambridge University Press.

Annual Report on South Indian Epigraphy (ARIE)
1889 *Annual Report on South Indian Epigraphy*. Government Publication, Madras.

Appadorai, A.
1990 [1936] *Economic Conditions in Southern India, 1000-1500 A.D.* 2 vols. Madras: University of Madras.

Appadurai, Arjun
1978 Kings, sects, and temples in South India, 1350-1800 AD. In *South Indian Temples: An Analytical Reconsideration*, edited by B. Stein, pp. 47-73. New Delhi: Vikas.

Archaeological Survey of India (ASI)
1923 *South Indian Inscriptions*. Vol. 4, *Miscellaneous Inscriptions in Tamil, Telugu and Kannada*. Calcutta: Archaeological Survey of India.

Begley, Vimala
1983 Arikamedu reconsidered. *American Journal of Archaeology* 87:461-68.
1986 From Iron Age to Early Historical in South Indian archaeology. In *Studies in the Archaeology of India and Pakistan*, edited by J. Jacobsen, pp. 297-319. New Delhi: Oxford and I.B.H.

Begley, Vimala, and Richard D. De Puma (editors)
1992 *Rome and India: The Ancient Sea Trade*. Delhi: Oxford University Press.

Behura, N.K.
1965 The potter servants of Jagannath at Puri. *Man in India* 45(2):127-33.

Blanton, R., L. Finsten, and Eva Fisch
1982 *The Prehispanic Settlement Patterns of the Central and Southern Parts of the Valley of Oaxaca, Mexico*. Memoirs, no. 15. Museum of Anthropology, University of Michigan. Ann Arbor.

Brubaker, R.P.
2004 *Cornerstones of Control: The Infrastructure of Imperial Security at Vijayanagara, South India*. PhD dissertation, Department of Anthropology, University of Michigan, Ann Arbor.

Chakrabarti, D.K.
1988 *A History of Indian Archaeology from the Beginning to 1947*. New Delhi: Munshiram Manoharlal.
2001 *Archaeological Geography of the Ganga Plain: The Lower and Middle Ganga*. Delhi: Permanent Black.

Champakalakshmi, R.
1981 Peasant state and society in medieval South India: a review article. *The Indian Economic and Social History Review* 18:411-26.
1996 *Trade, Ideology and Urbanization: South India 300 BC to AD 1300*. Delhi: Oxford University Press.

Chopra, P.N., T.K. Ravindran, and N. Subrahmanian
1979 *History of South India*. New Delhi: S. Chand and Company.

Chowdhury, K.A.
1989 Archaeobotany. In *An Encyclopaedia of Indian Archaeology, Volume I*, edited by A. Ghosh, pp. 6-9. Delhi: Munshiram Manoharlal.

Cowgill, George
1990 Toward refining concepts of full-coverage survey. In *The Archaeology of Regions: A Case for Full-Coverage Survey*, edited by S.K. Fish and S.A. Kowalewski, pp. 249-60. Washington, D.C.: Smithsonian Institution Press.

Dallapiccola, Anna L. (editor)
1985 *Vijayanagara City and Empire: New Currents of Research*. 2 vols. Wiesbaden: Franz Steiner Verlag.
2003 *King, Court and Capital: An Anthology of Kannada Literary Sources from the Vijayanagara Period*, translated by C.T.M. Kottraiah. New Delhi: American Institute of Indian Studies and Manohar Press.

Dallapiccola, Anna L., and Anila Verghese
1991 Ramayana panels on the gopura of the "Old Shiva" temple, Vitthalapura. In *Vijayanagara: Progress of Research 1987-88*, edited by D.V. Devaraja and C.S. Patil, pp. 143-53. Mysore: Directorate of Archaeology and Museums.
1998 *Sculpture at Vijayanagara: Iconography and Style*. New Delhi: American Institute of Indian Studies and Manohar Press.

Dallapiccola, A.L., J.M. Fritz, G. Michell, and S. Rajasekhara
1992 *The Ramachandra Temple*. New Delhi: American Institute of Indian Studies and Manohar Press.

Davison-Jenkins, Dominic J.
1988 *The Irrigation and Water Supply Systems of the City of Vijayanagara*. PhD dissertation, Department of Oriental Studies, University of Cambridge, Cambridge.
1997 *The Irrigation and Water Supply Systems of Vijayanagara*. Delhi: American Institute of Indian Studies and Manohar Press.

Deo, S.B.
1985 Historical archaeology: review and perspective. In *Archaeological Perspective of India since Independence*, edited by K.N. Dikshit, pp. 87-97. New Delhi: Books and Books.

Desai, P.B., S. Ritti, and B.R. Gopal
1981 *History of Karnataka*. Dharwad: Kannada Research Institute.

Devaraj, D.V., and C.S. Patil (editors)
1991a *Vijayanagara: Progress of Research 1984-87*. Mysore: Directorate of Archaeology and Museums.
1991b *Vijayanagara: Progress of Research 1987-88*. Mysore: Directorate of Archaeology and Museums.

Dhavalikar, M.K.
1999 *Historical Archaeology of India*. Delhi: Books and Books.

Dunnell, R., and W.S. Dancey
1983 The siteless survey: a regional scale data collection strategy. In *Advances in Archaeological Method and Theory*. Vol. 6, edited by M.B. Schiffer, pp. 267-87. Orlando: Academic Press.

Filliozat, Pierre S., and Vasundhara Filliozat
1988 *Hampi-Vijayanagar: The Temple of Vithala*. New Delhi: Sitaram Bhartia Institute of Scientific Research.

Filliozat, Vasundhara
1973 *Epigraphie de Vijayanagar de debut a 1377*. Paris: L'Ecole Francais d'Extreme-Orient.

Fish, Paul, and S. Kowalewski (editors)
1990 *The Archaeology of Regions: A Case for Full Coverage Survey*. Washington, D.C.: Smithsonian Institution Press.

Francis, W.
1904 *Madras District Gazetteers: Bellary*. Government of India, Madras.

Fritz, John M.
1986 Vijayanagara: authority and meaning of a South Indian imperial capital. *American Anthropologist* 88:44-55.
1991 The city of Vijayanagara: description, analysis, interpretation. The 1988 field season. In *Vijayanagara Progress of Research 1987-1988*, edited by D.V. Devaraj and C.S. Patil, pp. 44-54. Mysore: Directorate of Archaeology and Museums.
1996 Vijayanagara: city plan and meaning: 1990-1991 season (December-March). In *Vijayanagara Progress of Research 1988-1991*, edited by D.V. Devaraj and C.S. Patil, pp. 24-58. Mysore: Directorate of Archaeology and Museums.

Fritz, John M., Robert Brubaker, and Teresa Raczek (editors)
2006 *Vijayanagara: Archaeological Exploration, 1990-2000. Papers in Memory of Channabasappa S. Patil*. New Delhi: Manohar.

Fritz, John M., and George Michell
1985 Map series on cultural remains at Vijayanagara. In *Vijayagara Progress of Research 1983-84*, edited by M.S. Nagaraja Rao, pp. 164-98. Mysore: Directorate of Archaeology and Museums.

Fritz, John M., George Michell, and M.S. Nagaraja Rao
1985 *Where Kings and Gods Meet: The Royal Centre at Vijayanagara*. Tucson: University of Arizona Press.

Fritz, John M., and Kathleen D. Morrison
in prep a *The Royal Centre at Vijayanagara: Enclosures I-IX and the West Alley*. New Delhi: Manohar Press.
in prep b *The Royal Centre at Vijayanagara: Enclosures XI-XXXI*. New Delhi: Manohar Press.

Fuller, Dorian
2002 Fifty years of archaeobotanical study in India: laying a solid foundation. In *Indian Archaeology in Retrospect: Vol III: Archaeology and Interactive Disciplines*, edited by S. Settar and Ravi Korisettar, pp. 247-365. Delhi: ICHR and Manohar Press.

Gaussen, H., P. Legris, L. Labroue, V.M. Meher-Homji, and M. Viart
1966   *Carte Inernationale Du Tapis Vegetal, Notice de la Feuille: Mysore*. Extrait des Travaux de la Section Scientifique et Technique de L'Institut Francais de Pondicherry, Hors Serie 7.

Gopal, B.H.
1985   *Vijayanagara Inscriptions*. Vol. 1. Mysore: Directorate of Archaeology and Museums.

Inden, Robert
1990   *Imagining India*. London: Basil Blackwell.

Johansen, Peter
2004   Landscape, monumental architecture and ritual: a reconsideration of the South Indian ashmounds. *Journal of Anthropological Archaeology* 23:309-30.

Johnson, Greg
1973   *Local Change and Early State Formation in Southwestern Iran*. Anthropological Papers, no. 51. Museum of Anthropology, University of Michigan. Ann Arbor.

Junker, Laura Lee
1986   Morphology, function and style in traditional ceramics: a study of contemporary pottery from Bellary District, Karnataka. In *Vijayanagara: Progress of Research, 1983-84*, edited by M.S. Nagaraja Rao, pp. 144-51. Mysore: Directorate of Archaeology and Museums.

Kanitkar, N.V.
1960   *Dry Farming in India*, 2nd ed. New Delhi: Indian Council of Agricultural Research.

Karashima, Noburu
1992   *Toward a New Formation: South Indian Society Under Vijayanagar Rule*. Delhi: Oxford and IBH.

Kardulias, P. Nick (editor)
1994   *Beyond the Site: Regional Studies in the Aegean Area*. Lanham, Maryland: University Press of America.

Kelsall, J.
1872   *Manual of the Bellary District: Compiled Under the Orders of Government*. Madras: Lawrence Asylum Press.

Kintigh, Keith
1990   Comments on the case for full-coverage survey. In *The Archaeology of Regions: A Case for Full-Coverage Survey*, edited by S.K. Fish and S.A. Kowalewski, pp. 237-42. Washington, D.C.: Smithsonian Institution Press.

Korisettar, Ravi, P. Venkatasubbaiah, and Dorian Fuller
2002   Brahmagiri and beyond: the archaeology of the Southern Neolithic. In *Indian Archaeology in Retrospect. Vol 1: Prehistory: Archaeology of South Asia*, edited by S. Settar and R. Korisettar, pp. 151-219. New Delhi: ICHR and Manohar.

Kotraiah, C.T.M.
1959   Ancient anicuts on the River Tungabhadra. *Indian Journal of Power and River Valley Development Tungabhadra Project* 1:49-53.

1978   Boundary stones: a short study with special reference to those available in the Hampi Museum. *Journal of the Andhra Historical Society* 37:129-46.
1983   Hampi before founding of Vijayanagara. In *Shrinidhi: Perspectives in Indian Art and Archaeology*, edited by K.V. Raman, K.G. Krishnan, M.S. Ramaswami, N. Karashima, A.V. Narasimha Murty, P. Shanmugam, and S. Srinivasan, pp. 381-88. Madras: New Era Publications.

Krishnamurthy, M.
1978   *Geology and Mineral Resources of the Bellary District, Karnataka (Mysore) State*. Memoirs of the Geological Survey of India 108, New Delhi.

Krishnaswami Ayyangar, S. (editor)
1919   *Sources of Vijayanagara History*. Madras: University of Madras.

Krishnaswami Ayyangar, S.
1921   *South India and Her Muhammedan Invaders*. Madras: University of Madras.

Krishnaswami Pillai, A.
1964   *The Tamil Country Under Vijayanagara*. Annamalai Historical Series, 20. Annamalainagar: Annamalai University.

Kulke, Hans
1985   Maharajas, Mahants, and historians: reflections on the historiography of early Vijayanagara and Sringeri. In *Vijayanagara City and Empire: New Currents of Research*. Vol. 1, edited by A.L. Dallapiccola, pp. 120-43. Wiesbaden: Franz Steiner Verlag.

Kulke, Hans, and Dieter Rothermund
1986   *A History of India*. New York: Dorsett Press.

Lahiri, Nayanjot
1992   *The Archaeology of Indian Trade Routes*. Delhi: Oxford University Press.

Lewarch, Dennis, and Michael O'Brien
1981   The expanding role of surface assemblages in archaeological research. In *Advances in Archaeological Method and Theory*. Vol. 4, edited by M.B. Schiffer, pp. 297-342. Orlando: Academic Press.

Longhurst, A.H.
1917   *Hampi Ruins Described and Illustrated*. Madras: Government Press.

Lycett, Mark T.
1991   Chipped stone tools of the Vijayanagara Metropolitan Region. In *Vijayanagara: Progress of Research 1987-88*, edited by D.V. Devaraj and C.S. Patil, pp. 85-94. Mysore: Directorate of Archaeology and Museums.
1994   Searching for patterns in ambiguous categories: nonarchitectural sites of the Vijayanagara Metropolitan Region. In *South Asian Archaeology 1993*, edited by Asko Parpola and Petteri Koskikallio, pp. 413-23. Annales Academiae Scientiarum Fennicae, Series B, Vol. 271. Helsinki: Suomalainen Tiedeakatemia.

Mate, M.S.
1985 Daulatabad. In *Recent Advances in Indian Archaeology: Proceedings of a Seminar Held in Poona in 1983*, edited by S.B. Deo and K. Paddayya, pp. 110-12. Poona: Deccan College.

Means, Bernard K.
1991 A small settlement near the city of Vijayanagara. In *Vijayanagara: Progress of Research, 1987-88*, edited by D.V. Devaraj and C.S. Patil, pp. 154-64. Mysore: Directorate of Archaeology and Museums.

Michell, George A.
1985a Architecture of the Muslim quarters at Vijayanagara. In *Vijayanagara Progress of Research 1983-84*, edited by M.S. Nagaraja Rao, pp. 101-18. Mysore: Directorate of Archaeology and Museums.
1985b A never forgotten city. In *Vijayanagara City and Empire: New Currents of Research*. Vol. 1, edited by A.L. Dallapiccola, pp. 196-207. Wiesbaden: Franz Steiner Verlag.
1990 *Architectural Inventory of Vijayanagara*. 2 vols. Mysore: Directorate of Archaeology and Museums.
1991 Architectural documentation at Vijayanagara in 1987 and 1988: Hemakuta Hill and the Virupaksha temple complex at Hampi. In *Vijayanagara Progress of Research 1987-1988*, edited by D.V. Devaraj and C.S. Patil, pp. 35-43. Mysore: Directorate of Archaeology and Museums.
1992 *The Vijayanagara Courtly Style*. Delhi: American Institute of Indian Studies and Manohar Press.
1994 Revivalism as the imperial mode: religious architecture during the Vijayanagara period. In *Perspectives on South Asia's Visual Past*, edited by C.B. Asher and T.R. Metcalf, pp. 187-98. New Delhi: Oxford University Press and IBH.
1995 *Architecture and Art of Southern India: Vijayanagara and the Successor States*. Cambridge: Cambridge University Press.

Michell, George A. (editor; coordinated by U.S. Moorti)
2001 *Encyclopaedia of Indian Temple Architecture. South India: Dravidesa Later Phase c. AD 1289-1798*. New Delhi: American Institute of Indian Studies.

Michell, George A., and Vasundhara Filliozat
1981 *Splendours of the Vijayanagara Empire – Hampi*. Bombay: Marg Publications.

Michell, George A., and Philip Wagoner
2001 *Vijayanagara: Architectural Inventory of the Sacred Center*. 3 vols. New Delhi: Manohar Press.

Morrison, Kathleen D.
1990 Patterns of urban occupation: surface collections at Vijayanagara. In *South Asian Archaeology 1987*, edited by M. Taddei. Rome: Istituto Italiano per il Medio ed Estremo Oriente.
1991 The Vijayanagara Metropolitan Survey: preliminary season. In *Vijayanagara: Progress of Research 1984-1987*, edited by D.V. Devaraj and C.S. Patil, pp. 136-41. Mysore: Directorate of Archaeology and Museums.
1992 *Transforming the Agricultural Landscape: Intensification of Production at Vijayanagara, India*. PhD dissertation, Department of Anthropology, University of California at Berkeley.
1993 Supplying the city: the role of reservoir irrigation in an Indian urban landscape. *Asian Perspectives* 32:133-51.
1994a Power, *Prasad*, and the marketplace: food grains in Southern India. Paper presented in *Food as Power*, 93rd Annual Meeting of the American Anthropological Association, Atlanta, GA.
1994b Monitoring regional fire history through size-specific analysis of microscopic charcoal: the last 600 years in South India. *Journal of Archaeological Science* 21:675-85.
1995 *Fields of Victory: Vijayanagara and the Course of Intensification*. Contributions of the Archaeological Research Facility 53, Berkeley.
2006 Pollen analysis from the Kamalapuram *Kere*. In *Vijayanagara: Archaeological Explorations, 1990-2000. Papers in Memory of Channabasappa S. Patil*, edited by John M. Fritz, Robert P. Brubaker, and Teresa P. Raczek, pp. 587-98. New Delhi: Manohar and American Institute of Indian Studies.
in press *Oceans of Dharma: Landscapes, Power, and Place in Southern India*. Seattle: University of Washington Press; Delhi: Permanent Black.

Morrison, K.D., and M.T. Lycett
1994 Centralized power, centralized authority? Ideological claims and archaeological patterns. *Asian Perspectives* 32:327-50.

Morrison, K.D., and C.M. Sinopoli
1992 Economic diversity and integration in a precolonial Indian empire. *World Archaeology* 23:335-52.
1996 Archaeological survey in the Vijayanagara Metropolitan Region: 1990. In *Vijayanagara Progress of Research 1999-1991*, edited by D.V. Devaraj and C.S. Patil, pp. 59-73. Mysore: Directorate of Archaeology and Museums.
2006a Production and landscape in the Vijayanagara Metropolitan Region: contributions of the Vijayanagara Metropolitan Survey. In *Vijayanagara: Archaeological Explorations, 1990-2000. Papers in Memory of Channabasappa S. Patil*, edited by John M. Fritz, Robert P. Brubaker, and Teresa P. Raczek, pp. 423-35. New Delhi: Manohar and American Institute of Indian Studies.
2006b The Vijayanagara Metropolitan Survey: overview of the 1994 season. In *Vijayanagara: Archaeological Explorations, 1990-2000. Papers in Memory of Channabasappa S. Patil*, edited by John M. Fritz, Robert P. Brubaker, and Teresa P. Raczek, pp. 459-74. New Delhi: Manohar and American Institute of Indian Studies.

Nagaraja Rao, M.S. (editor)
1983 *Vijayanagara: Progress of Research 1979-83*. Mysore: Directorate of Archaeology and Museums.
1985 *Vijayanagara: Progress of Research 1983-84*. Mysore: Directorate of Archaeology and Museums.
1988 *Vijayanagara Through the Eyes of Alexander J. Greenlaw, 1856, and John Gollings, 1983*. Mysore: Directorate of Archaeology and Museums.

Nagaraja Rao, M.S., and C.S. Patil
1985 Epigraphical studies. In *Vijayanagara Progress of Research 1983-84*, edited by M.S. Nagaraja Rao, pp. 21-53. Mysore: Directorate of Archaeology and Museums.

Nagaraju, H.M.
1991 *Devaraya II and His Times: History of Vijayanagara*. Mysore: Prasaranga University of Mysore.

Naqvi, S.M., and J.J.W. Rogers
1987 *Precambrian Geology of India*. Oxford Monographs on Geology and Geophysics 6. New York: Clarendon Press.

Narasimaiah, B.
1992 *Metropolis Vijayanagara: Significance of Remains of Citadel.* Delhi: Book India Publishing Co.

Neely, James A., and Henry T. Wright
1994 *Early Settlement and Irrigation on the Deh Luran Plain: Village and Early State Societies in Southwestern Iran.* Technical Report 26. Museum of Anthropology, University of Michigan. Ann Arbor.

Nilakanta Sastri, K.A.
1966 *A History of South India*, 3rd ed. London: Oxford University Press.

Nilakanta Sastri, K.A., and M.A. Venkataramanayya (editors)
1946 *Further Sources of Vijayanagara History.* Madras: University of Madras.

Paddayya, K.
1973 *Investigations into the Neolithic Culture of the Shorapur Doab, South India.* Leiden: E.J. Brill.
1993 Ashmound investigations at Budihal, Gulbarga District, Karnataka. *Man and Environment* 18(1):57-88.
2002 The problem of ashmounds of Southern Deccan in the light of recent research. In *Recent Studies in Indian Archaeology*, edited by K. Paddayya, pp. 81-111. Indian Council of Historical Research, Monograph Series 6. New Delhi: Munshiram Manoharlal Publishers.

Palat, R.
1987 The Vijayanagara empire: re-integration of the agrarian order of medieval South India. In *Early State Dynamics*, edited by H.J.M. Claessen and P. van der Velde, pp. 170-86. Leiden: E.J. Brill.

Parasher-Sen, A.
1993 Culture and civilization: the beginnings. In *Social and Economic History of Early Deccan*, edited by A. Parasher-Sen, pp. 66-114. Delhi: Manohar.

Parsons, Jeffrey R.
1990 Critical reflections on a decade of full-coverage regional survey in the Valley of Mexico. In *The Archaeology of Regions: A Case for Full-Coverage Survey*, edited by S.K. Fish and S.A. Kowalewski, pp. 7-32. Washington, D.C.: Smithsonian Institution Press.

Parsons, Jeffrey R., K.W. Kintigh, and Susan A. Gregg
1983 *Archaeological Settlement Pattern Date from the Chalco, Xochimilco, Ixtapalapa, Texcoco and Zumbango Regions.* Technical Report 14. Museum of Anthropology, University of Michigan. Ann Arbor.

Pascher, B.
1987 *The Pattabhirama Temple: A Description and Iconographic Analysis.* MA thesis, Department of Art History, Vermont College of Norwich University.

Patil, C.S.
1991a Epigraphical studies. In *Vijayanagara Progress of Research 1987-88*, edited by D.V. Devaraj and C.S. Patil, pp. 15-34. Mysore: Directorate of Archaeology and Museums.
1991b Further epigraphical references to city gates and watch towers of Vijayanagara. In *Vijayanagara Progress of Research 1984-87*, edited by D.V. Devaraj and C.S. Patil, pp. 191-94. Mysore: Directorate of Archaeology and Museums.

Patil, C.S., and Balasubramanya
1991 Epigraphical studies. In *Vijayanagara Progress of Research 1984-87*, edited by D.V. Devaraj and C.S. Patil, pp. 19-70. Mysore: Directorate of Archaeology and Museums.

Patil, Channabasappa S., and Vinoda C. Patil (editors)
1995 *Inscriptions at Vijayanagara (Hampi).* Mysore: Directorate of Archaeology and Museums.

Possehl, G.L., and P.C. Rissman
1992 The chronology of prehistoric India: from earliest times to the Iron Age. In *Chronologies in Old World Archaeology*, edited by R.W. Ehrich, pp. 465-74. Chicago and London: University of Chicago Press.

Purandare, S.
1986 *The History and Archaeology of Anegondi.* PhD dissertation, Department of Archaeology, Deccan College Postgraduate and Research Institute, Pune.

Ramaswamy, V.
1985 *Textiles and Weavers in Medieval South India.* New Delhi: Oxford University Press.

Ray, Himanshu P.
1986 *Monastery and Guild: Commerce under the Satavahanas.* Delhi: Oxford University Press.
1994 *The Winds of Change: Buddhism and the Maritime Links of Early South Asia.* New Delhi: Oxford University Press.
2003 *Archaeology of Seafaring in Ancient South Asia.* Cambridge: Cambridge University Press.

Ray, Himanshu P., and Carla M. Sinopoli (editors)
2004 *Archaeology as History.* New Delhi: ICHR and Aryan Books.

Saletore, B.A.
1934 *Social and Political Life in the Vijayanagara Empire (A.D. 1346-A.D. 1646).* Madras: Paul and Company.
1982 *Vijayanagara Art.* Delhi: Sundeep.

Sanders, W., J.R. Parsons, and R.S. Santley
1979 *The Basin of Mexico: Ecological Processes in the Evolution of a Civilization.* New York: Academic Press.

Schiffer, M.
1995 *Behavioral Archaeology: First Principles.* Salt Lake City: University of Utah Press.

Sewell, R.
1900 *A Forgotten Empire (Vijayanagar): A Contribution to the History of India.* London: S. Sonnenschein and Company.

Shaw, J.
2000 Sanchi and its archaeological landscape: Buddhist monasteries, settlements, and irrigation works in Central India. *Antiquity* 74:775-76.

Singh, R.L., K.N. Singh, M.S. Vishwanath, and S.N. Singh
1971 Karnataka plateau. In *India: A Regional Geography*, edited by R.L. Singh, pp. 791-820. Varanasi: National Geographic Society of India.

Singh, N.P.
1988 *The Flora of Eastern Karnataka*. New Delhi: Mittal.

Singh, Upinder
2004 *The Discovery of Ancient India: Early Archaeologists and the Beginnings of Archaeology*. New Delhi: Permanent Black.

Sinopoli, C.M.
1985 The earthenware pottery of Vijayanagara: documentation and interpretation. In *Vijayanagara City and Empire: New Currents of Research*. Vol. 1, edited by A.L. Dallapiccola, pp. 216-28. Wiesbaden: Franz Steiner Verlag.
1986 *Material Patterning and Social Organization: A Study of Ceramics From Vijayanagara*. PhD dissertation, Department of Anthropology, University of Michigan, Ann Arbor.
1988 The organization of craft production at Vijayanagara, South India. *American Anthropologist* 90:580-97.
1989 Standardization and specialization: ceramic production at Vijayanagara, South India. In *Old Problems, New Perspectives in the Archaeology of South Asia*, edited by J.M. Kenoyer. Wisconsin Archaeological Reports 2, Madison.
1991a Vijayanagara ceramics: the 1986 field season. In *Vijayanagara: Progress of Research 1987-88*, edited by D.V. Devaraj and C.S. Patil, pp. 97-104. Mysore: Directorate of Archaeology and Museums.
1991b A Vijayanagara period road system: VMS-42, VMS-47, VMS-50. In *Vijayanagara: Progress of Research 1987-88*, edited by D.V. Devaraj and C.S. Patil, pp. 70-80. Mysore: Directorate of Archaeology and Museums.
1993a Defining a sacred landscape: temple architecture and divine images in the Vijayanagara suburbs. In *South Asian Archaeology 1991*, edited by A.J. Gail and G.J.R. Mevissen, pp. 625-36. Stuttgart: Franz Steiner Verlag.
1993b *Pots and Palaces: The Archaeological Ceramics of the Noblemen's Quarter of Vijayanagara*. Delhi: Manohar Press.
1994 *Movement and Distribution of Craft Producers and Products at the Vijayanagara Imperial Capital*. Paper presented in Trade and Contact in the Vijayanagara Empire, World Archaeology Congress, New Delhi, India.
1996 The archaeological ceramics of the Islamic quarter of Vijayanagara. In *Vijayanagara Progress of Research 1988-91*, edited by D.V. Devaraj and C.S. Patil, pp. 105-23. Mysore: Directorate of Archaeology and Museums.
1997 Nucleated settlements in the Vijayanagara Metropolitan Region. In *South Asian Archaeology 1995*, edited by B. Allchin and F.R. Allchin, pp. 475-87. New Delhi: Oxford and IBH Press.
1999 Levels of complexity: ceramic variability at Vijayanagara. In *Pottery and People: A Dynamic Interaction*, edited by J. Skibo and G.M. Feinman, pp. 115-36. Salt Lake City: University of Utah Press.
2003 *The Political Economy of Craft Production: Crafting Empire in South India, c. 1350-1650*. Cambridge: Cambridge University Press.
2006a Regional survey at Vijayanagara, South Asia: New World methodologies in Old World contexts. In *Settlement, Subsistence and Social Complexity: Essays Honoring the Legacy of Jeffrey R. Parsons*, edited by Richard E. Blanton, pp. 19-42. Los Angeles: Cotsen Institute, University of California.
2006b VMS-365: a walled settlement site. In *Vijayanagara: Archaeological Exploration, 1990-2000. Papers in Memory of Channabasappa S. Patil*, edited by John M. Fritz, Robert P. Brubaker, and Teresa P. Raczek, pp. 525-38. New Delhi: Manohar and American Institute of Indian Studies.

Sinopoli, C.M., and T.R. Blurton
1986 Modern pottery production in rural Karnataka. In *Dimensions of Indian Art: Pupul Jayakar Seventy*, edited by L. Chandra and J. Jain, pp. 439-56. New Delhi: Agam Kala Prakashan.

Sinopoli, C.M., and K.D. Morrison
1991 The Vijayanagara Metropolitan Survey: the 1988 season. In *Vijayanagara: Progress of Research 1987-88*, edited by D.V. Devaraj and C.S. Patil, pp. 55-69. Mysore: Directorate of Archaeology and Museums.
1995 Dimensions of imperial control: the Vijayanagara capital. *American Anthropologist* 97(1):83-96.
2006 The Vijayanagara Metropolitan Survey: overview of the 1992 season. In *Vijayanagara: Archaeological Exploration, 1990-2000. Papers in Memory of Channabasappa S. Patil*, edited by John M. Fritz, Robert P. Brubaker, and Teresa P. Raczek, pp. 437-58. New Delhi: Manohar and American Institute of Indian Studies.

Skibo, James
1992 *Pottery Function: A Use-Alteration Perspective*. New York: Plenum Press.

Spate, O.H.K.
1954 *India and Pakistan: A General and Regional Geography*. London: Methuen.

Stein, B.
1980 *Peasant State and Society in Medieval South India*. Delhi: Oxford University Press.
1982 South India: some general considerations of the region and its early history. In *The Cambridge Economic History of India*. Vol. 1: c. 1200–c. 1750, edited by T. Rayachaudhuri and I. Habib, pp. 14-42. New Delhi: Orient Longman.
1985 Vijayanagara and the transition to patrimonial systems. In *Vijayanagara: City and Empire*, edited by A.L. Dallapiccola, pp. 73-87. Wiesbaden: Franz Steiner Verlag.
1989 *Vijayanagara*. Vol. 1, Part 2, *The New Cambridge History of India*. Cambridge: Cambridge University Press.

Sugandhi, Namita
2004 Context, content, and composition: questions on the intended meaning of the Asokan inscriptions. *Asian Perspectives* 42(2):224-46.

Sundara, A.
1989 Brahmagiri. In *An Encyclopaedia of Indian Archaeology, Volume II*, edited by A. Ghosh, pp. 82-84. Delhi: Munshiram Manoharlal.

Sundstron, Linea
1993 A simple mathematical procedure for estimating the adequacy of site survey strategies. *Journal of Field Archaeology* 20:91-96.

Thapar, Romila
1966 *A History of India, Volume 1.* London: Penguin Books.
1984 *From Lineage to State.* Bombay: Oxford University Press.
1992 *Interpreting Early India.* Delhi: Oxford University Press.
1997 *Aśoka and The Decline of the Mauryas*, rev. ed. Delhi: Oxford University Press.

Tolbert, Natalie
2000 *Anegondi: Architectural Ethnography of a Royal Village.* New Delhi: American Institute of Indian Studies and Manohar.

Tripathi, R.C. (editor)
1987 *Indian Archaeology 1984-85 – A Review.* New Delhi: Archaeological Survey of India.

Verghese, A.
1995 *Religious Traditions at Vijayanagara as Revealed through Sculpture.* New Delhi: Manohar Press.
2000 *Archaeology, Art and Religion: New Perspectives on Vijayanagara.* Delhi: Oxford University Press.

Wagoner, P.B.
1991 Architecture and mythic space at Hemakuta Hill: a preliminary report. In *Vijayanagara Progress of Research 1984-1987*, edited by D.V. Devaraj and C.S. Patil, pp. 142-48. Mysore: Directorate of Archaeology and Museums.
1993 *Tidings of the King: A Translation and Ethnohistorical Analysis of the Rayavacakamu.* Honolulu: University of Hawaii Press.

Wandsnider, LuAnn, and Eileen Camilli
1992 The character of surface archaeological deposits and its influence on survey accuracy. *Journal of Field Archaeology* 19:169-88.

Wheeler, R.E.M.
1947 Brahmagiri and Chandravalli 1947: megalithic and other cultures in the Chitaldurg District, Mysore State. *Ancient India* 4:181-309.

Wilkinson, T.J.
1982 The definition of ancient manured zones by means of extensive sherd-sampling. *Journal of Field Archaeology* 9:323-33.

Willey, Gordon R.
1953 *Prehistoric Settlement Patterns in the Viru Valley, Peru.* Bulletin 155, Bureau of American Ethnology. Washington, D.C.: Smithsonian Institution.

Wilson, David
1988 *Prehispanic Settlement Patterns in the Lower Santa Valley, Peru: A Regional Perspective on the Origins and Development of Complex North Coast Society.* Washington, D.C.: Smithsonian Institution.

Wright, Henry T., and Greg Johnson
1975 Population, exchange, and early state formation in Southwestern Iran. *American Anthropologist* 77:267-89.